CAREER MANAGEMENT

THIRD EDITION

CAREER
MANAGEMENT

THIRD EDITION

JEFFREY H. GREENHAUS
Drexel University

GERARD A. CALLANAN
The Federal Reserve Bank of Philadelphia

VERONICA M. GODSHALK
The Pennsylvania State University, Great Valley

THOMSON
™
SOUTH-WESTERN

Career Management, 3rd Edition
Jeffrey H. Greenhaus, Gerard A. Callanan, Veronica M. Godshalk

Publisher:
Mike Roche

Acquisitions Editor:
John Weimeister

Market Strategist:
Lisé Johnson

Developmental Editor:
Bobbie Bochenko

Project Editor:
Colby Alexander

Art Director:
Van Mua

Production Manager:
Lois West

Library of Congress Control
Number: 99-067541

ISBN: 0-03-022418-7

Dedications

To Adele and Joanne Greenhaus,
and Michele and Jeff Levine

To Laura, Michael, Timothy,
and Ryan Callanan

To Robert, Timothy,
and Lauren Godshalk

For most individuals, work is a defining aspect of life. Indeed, our happiness and fulfillment can hinge on how well we are able to control the course of our work lives, and manage the effects of our work on our family and personal life. Yet many people enter their careers with a lack of insight and purpose, drifting to and from jobs, or lamenting unwise career choices. For others, the task of career management, because of the risks of not making personally correct decisions, is frightening and full of anxiety. We believe that individuals at any age need to approach career management with care and attention, and must have an appropriate decision-making framework in order to achieve personal success and satisfaction.

These beliefs are especially relevant in the 21st century. Recent changes in the world of work—mergers, acquisitions, downsizing, cost containment, and outsourcing to mention a few—have had a dramatic effect on careers. We can no longer expect to spend 20 or 30 years in one company, or even in one industry. We can no longer expect our employer to take the responsibility for managing our career. In today's world, the relationship between employer and employee has a short-term focus. Neither party seems highly committed to the well being of the other. Therefore, we will increasingly have to take the responsibility for managing our careers and managing our lives. In the third edition of *Career Management* we provide a vehicle for individuals to direct their careers successfully over the life cycle. We hope this book is integral to your successful career management and all its attendant rewards.

CONTENTS. In the third edition of *Career Management* we focus on four essential views of careers and career management. **First,** career management is a process by which individuals can guide, direct, and influence the course of their careers. The model of career management presented in this edition—an active, problem-solving approach to work and life—specifies how people can collect information, gain insight into themselves and their environment, develop appropriate goals and strategies, and obtain useful feedback regarding their efforts. The career management model is presented and examined in **Part One (Chapters 1 through 4)** of the book. Chapter 1 introduces the notion of career management as an ongoing problem-solving process. In Chapter 2, we present the model of career management that forms the foundation for the remainder of the text. Chapters 3 and 4 apply the career management model to individual career decision making, covering such career management skills as career exploration, career goal setting, and career strategy development.

Second, it is useful to view a career in developmental terms as it evolves throughout a person's life. Different career stages present unique tasks and issues, ranging from a young adult's preoccupation with choosing an initial occupation, to a middle-aged adult's concern about a devastating job loss, to an older employee's need to remain productive and to prepare for retirement. Despite these differences, the role of career management is fundamentally the same at each stage of career development: to make sound decisions based on insight and to implement the decisions effectively. **Part Two (Chapters 5 through 9)** of *Career Management* discusses the different stages of career development and emphasizes the role of active career management at each stage. Chapter 5 provides an introduction to the topic of career stages, and the next two chapters trace the process by which people choose occupations (Chapter 6) and enter organizations (Chapter 7). Chapter 8 deals with the tasks facing employees in their early career, and Chapter 9 concentrates on issues relevant to the middle and later phases of a person's career.

Third, career management efforts must take into account a number of additional demands, including dealing with job stress, the intertwining of work and personal lives, facing the challenges of a culturally diverse workforce, and the potential for embarking on an entrepreneurial career. **Part Three (Chapters 10 through 13)** of *Career Management* is devoted to these issues. In Chapter 10, we examine the effect of work stress on the individual's quality of life. Chapter 11 considers the relationship between work and family, focusing on the two-career relationship as a dominant life-style. Chapter 12 discusses career management in the context of cultural diversity, with material on the careers of women and men in contemporary organizations, the careers of minority employees, and the career challenges faced by employees and employers in culturally diverse settings. In Chapter 13, which discusses the choice of an entrepreneurial career, we profile the entrepreneur, review different forms of social, educational, and emotional support, address issues facing female and minority entrepreneurs, and describe the unique demands of entrepreneurial career management. Hopefully, this chapter will help individuals decide whether an entrepreneurial career and life-style are right for them.

Fourth, individual career management can be assisted through a number of organizationally sponsored programs. In **Part Four (Chapters 14, 15, and 16),** we discuss a variety of career management practices available to organizations and we offer specific examples of these practices as used by real companies. Chapter 14 offers an overview of the broader spectrum of human resource activities, with special emphasis on how human resource systems can support employee career management. We illustrate how human resource and career management systems must be integrated to maximize individual and organizational well being and we encourage the development of career-oriented human resource support systems. Chapter 15 is devoted to describing and illustrating career management practices in organizations. This information should be useful to human resource specialists in organizations as well as students and employees assessing employers' or prospective employers' support of career management. Moreover, an understanding of the organization's role in career management can help individuals become more effective managers of people over the course of their careers. Chapter 16 provides our closing thoughts on career management and reinforces our belief that individuals can—and must—take the initiative to manage their own careers.

Career Management is intended for several different audiences. First, it is ideal for all individuals who wish to learn more about career dynamics and how to manage their careers, whether they are students, working adults, or simply intellectually curious. *Career Management* is written to provide an understanding of career development and a framework in which career management can be pursued. Indeed, the third edition contains up-to-date information on different forms of self-assessment—the ways in which individuals can learn more about themselves, their interests, talents, aptitudes, and life-style preferences. *Career Management* can be used as a primary or supplementary text for undergraduate and graduate courses in careers, human resource management, organizational behavior, psychology, and education. And it can also be utilized in organizations as a resource for employees seeking guidance in the management of their careers.

Our second audience, human resource professionals, can certainly profit from the material in the third edition. It is impossible to develop effective career management programs in organizations without a full appreciation of the types of decisions and dilemmas individuals face in their careers. The material on the career management process, the stages of career development, job stress, work-family balance, and the management of diversity sets the stage for Chapters 14 and 15, which deal explicitly with human resource and career management initiatives.

Finally, this edition of the book was written for our peers, researchers in career development and career management. We hope it helps pull together the most recent research and theory on careers and stimulates additional research in this area.

LEARNING-ORIENTED FEATURES. To meet the needs of these audiences, the book contains the following learning-oriented features:

A balance of theory and application. The material in *Career Management* is theory- and research-based because individuals, whether they are students or working adults, must appreciate the concepts that underlie career management principles and techniques. In addition, nearly every chapter offers pragmatic applications of the concepts. It is hoped that readers of this text will emerge with a framework and a set of guidelines that can serve as a career management "map"throughout their work lives.

Mixture of individual and organizational actions. Although career management is viewed as an individual problem-solving and decision-making process, work organizations can play an integral part in stimulating and fostering effective career management. Therefore, most chapters include examples of actions or programs that organizations can provide to promote employee career management, and Chapter 15 provides a series of examples of organizational career management programs.

Learning exercises to help readers practice career management skills. The exercises offer an opportunity for the reader to engage in career exploration, career goal setting, and career strategy development, key ingredients in the career management process. Although the conceptual material can be grasped independently of the learning exercises, the experiential learning derived from the exercises can provide extremely valuable insight into one's career. There are three issues to consider regarding the use of the learning exercises. First is the question of timing. Learning Exercises I through IV are introduced in Chapter 3. It is suggested that individuals read Chapter 3 fully before beginning these exercises. Learning Exercises V and VI are introduced in Chapter 4, and Learning Exercises VII and VIII, in Chapter 6. Again, it is suggested that the relevant chapters be read before the exercises are begun.

Second is the issue of where readers should enter their responses to the learning exercises. In the third edition of *Career Management,* all of the learning exercises can be accessed and downloaded from the Internet at **http://www.swcollege.com/management/greenhaus**. We recommend that you download the learning exercises from the website and complete them using a personal computer. This approach will provide a great deal of flexibility since it permits you to add more information to a previous exercise at a later point. If you choose to complete the learning exercises using a paper-and-pencil approach, we recommend that you create a separate notebook in which to write your responses to these exercises. A separate career management notebook should provide the same flexibility to add more information to an exercise at a later point.

Third, the learning exercises can—at an instructor's discretion—be converted into group or team assignments. Although the learning exercises should initially be completed by individuals working alone, some instructors have found it helpful for groups of students to share their responses to the learning exercises so that they can provide feedback and guidance to each other in a supportive group environment.

Cases to examine individual and organizational career management. The third edition has substantially expanded the use of cases as learning tools. All four Parts of *Career Management* conclude with one or more cases, each of which is accompanied by questions in order to facilitate case analysis. The cases—like the learning exercises—can be downloaded from the Internet **http://www.swcollege.com/management/greenhaus**, and can easily be discussed in a group or team environment.

Summaries. Each chapter concludes with a summary of the material and key issues contained in the chapter. The summaries reiterate main themes and give a useful synopsis of important concepts.

Assignments and discussion questions. At the end of each chapter the reader is asked to complete an assignment that links the material in the chapter with real-life experience. Further, every chapter is supplemented with a series of relevant questions that are useful in guiding discussion of the important material presented in the chapter. These may also be downloaded from the Internet at **http://www.swcollege.com/management/greenhaus.**

ACKNOWLEDGMENTS. A number of people have provided stimulation, advice, and/or support and have directly or indirectly contributed to this edition of the book. First, we are indebted to the many other scholars whose research has influenced our thinking about careers and whose works are cited extensively in this book. We hope our interpretation of others' research does justice to their contributions.

We also thank our students for their enthusiasm in discussing their views of career management and their willingness to share many personal career experiences. Our thanks go to Professor Saroj Parasuraman of Drexel University's Department of Management, who provided critical and constructive reviews of selected chapters in the original and revised editions of the book. We are also grateful to several members of the Federal Reserve Bank of Philadelphia who offered helpful feedback and production support on the second edition, and we appreciate the help of Susan Cerwonka who provided assistance in the preparation of the third edition. From the School of Graduate Professional Studies at Penn State Great Valley, we thank Georgia Gordon-Martin for her assistance in gathering research materials, Jackie Herbst and Cheryl Holl for their assistance in preparing the manuscript, and Professor John J. Sosik for his support throughout the research and writing process.

We are also very grateful to Professors Deborah Brown, Santa Fe Community College; Joan Coll, Seton Hall University; Linda Gibson, Pacific Lutheran University; and Thomas Gutteridge, University of Connecticut for their insightful and critical assessments of the second edition of *Career Management,* all of which were very helpful in preparing the third edition. We especially appreciate the efforts of Professor Gerald Klein of Rider University, who generously met with us to provide his assessment of the book and extensive suggestions on how we might further strengthen the book.

Special thanks go to the corporate officials who shared with us the many leading-edge career management programs offered by their companies: James Brockington (Air Products and Chemicals, Inc), Marge Costello (Nabisco Foods), Deborah Davis (Johnson & Johnson), Susan Eams (American Greetings), Fran Engoron (Price Waterhouse), John Epperheimer (Career Action Center), Gregory Mayville (Dow Corning Corporation), and Rich Vintigni (DuPont).

We thank John Weimeister, Acquisitions Editor, for his assistance and support throughout the revision process. We are also grateful for the expertise, dedication, and care provided by Ellen Hostetler and Bobbie Bochenko, Developmental Editors. Our deep appreciation goes to Colby Alexander, Project Editor, for his guidance through the production process. We also appreciate the efforts of The Dryden Press production and design staff: Lois West, Production Manager; Linda Blundell, Picture and Rights Editor; Van Mua, Art Director; Lisé Johnson, Marketing Manager, and Kim Samuels, Manufacturing Manager.

On a more personal level, we are forever grateful for the love, guidance, and support of our parents—Marjorie and Sam Greenhaus, Loretta and Augustine

Callanan, and Catherine and Lawrence Brooks—whose influence extends far beyond this book. Our nuclear families deserve our deepest heartfelt thanks: Adele and Joanne Greenhaus, and Michele and Jeff Levine; Laura, Michael, Timothy, and Ryan Callanan; and Robert, Timothy, and Lauren Godshalk. Their love and support made this edition of the book possible. We are forever grateful for the love you have given and the sacrifices you have made.

Jeffrey H. Greenhaus
Gerard A. Callanan
Veronica M. Godshalk

Philadelphia, Pennsylvania
April 1999

Jeffrey H. Greenhaus holds the William A. Mackie Professorship in the Department of Management at Drexel University. He received his Ph.D. degree in Industrial/Organizational Psychology from New York University. Jeff is a member of the Academy of Management and the American Psychological Society, and his current research focuses on career dynamics, work-family linkages, and the management of diversity. His research has appeared in such journals as the *Academy of Management Journal, Academy of Management Review, Human Resource Planning, Journal of Applied Psychology, Journal of Organizational Behavior, Journal of Vocational Behavior,* and *Organizational Behavior and Human Decision Processes.* Former Associate Editor of the *Journal of Vocational Behavior,* Jeff is co-editor (with Saroj Parasuraman) of *Integrating Work and Family: Challenges and Choices for a Changing World* (Quorum Books, 1997), and co-author (with Stewart D. Friedman) of the forthcoming *Allies or Enemies? How Choices about Work and Family Affect the Quality of Men's and Women's Lives* to be published by the Oxford University Press in 2000.

Gerard A. Callanan is a Vice President with the Federal Reserve Bank of Philadelphia. He also serves as an adjunct Assistant Professor of Management at Rider University. He received his B.B.A. degree from Temple University and his M.B.A. degree from LaSalle University. Gerry's Ph.D. degree in organizational behavior is from Drexel University. He is a member of the Academy of Management and his research has appeared in the *Journal of Vocational Behavior* and in the *International Journal of Career Management.*

Veronica M. Godshalk is an Assistant Professor in the Department of Management and Organization at Penn State Great Valley's School of Graduate Professional Studies, where she teaches in the M.B.A. program. Having received her Ph. D. degree in organizational behavior from Drexel University, Ronnie's research focuses on career management issues, mentoring, stress, and the intersection of work and non-work domains. She has published articles in the *Journal of Vocational Behavior, Journal of Organizational Behavior, Group and Organizational Management,* and the *Journal of Management Systems.* Ronnie is an active member of professional associations, such as the Academy of Management, the Eastern Academy of Management, and the Society for Industrial and Organizational Psychology. She had worked in the computer industry in sales and sales management prior to entering academia, and has been a consultant for several Fortune 500 companies.

CONTENTS

I

CAREER MANAGEMENT PROCESS: THEORY AND APPLICATION

INTRODUCTION TO THE STUDY OF CAREERS

Why was Richard's decision to leave his employer of 14 years such a shock? Maybe it was the outstanding reputation of the company he had decided to leave—a company known for innovative computer technology and progressive human resource practices. Perhaps it was his steady advancement in title, responsibilities, and salary or his obvious enthusiasm for his work and for the company that had treated him so well.

Richard had made a significant career decision that, in retrospect, should not have been so surprising. At 38 he yearned for more—more money and a more prestigious title—but most significantly, he wanted more responsibility and an opportunity to make a meaningful contribution to the destiny of his employer. This opportunity may have come eventually with his current company, but it would have taken a while, and Richard was growing impatient. In Daniel Levinson's terms, Richard was in the midst of the BOOM ("Becoming One's Own Man") phase of his career, a period in which the need to have a greater degree of authority and independence, to be listened to seriously, and to come into one's own, so to speak, becomes paramount. Aware of his needs and the opportunities in his company, Richard decided to risk security in a known environment and pursue his goals. This decision shaped the course of his career and life in profound ways.

Richard left his former employer with good will and enormous optimism. Having accepted a position of Director of Information Systems at a brokerage firm, he approached his new job with the enthusiasm and energy that had produced success in earlier years. He upgraded his employer's back office information system and built a management structure within his division that was sorely needed. His accomplishments were substantial and were recognized by his superiors, peers, and subordinates alike. His decision had undoubtedly paid off!

But Richard did not count on the corporate changes and the internal politics. Not that he was particularly naive, but who could have anticipated the management shakeup that was to overrun his firm? Facing intense competition and resultant pressures to cut costs, a new senior management team was appointed. Richard's boss and major ally was replaced by a new executive who was given carte blanche to "clean house." After months of uncertainty, Richard got the not-so-subtle message; it would be best for his career if he started looking for employment elsewhere. Sure, his performance was excellent, and yes, he had instituted changes his predecessors had not even contemplated. But management believed it was time for a change. It is one thing to know intellectually that politics can outweigh job performance in the real world; it is quite another to be the victim of major political maneuvering for the first time at age 40, with two children to eventually put through college and heavy mortgage obligations to fulfill.

Richard found himself unemployed for the first time since junior high school. Finding a new position became a full-time job, and he approached this task with enthusiasm and extensive planning. After all, he still had his dreams! After what must have seemed like an eternity, he found a higher-level position with another brokerage firm heading up its information systems group. Burned once, he comforted himself that this company was on firmer financial ground than his previous employer. After 2 years of outstanding contributions, however, this firm is now undergoing a major reorganization and reshuffling of personnel. Richard's future? He is not so sure anymore, although he was recently promoted to vice president. Still, when asked whether he had any regrets about his decision to leave his initial employer, Richard gives an emphatic "no."

We begin Chapter 1 with this short career vignette to highlight a fundamental quality about career management: Career decisions have their roots not only in past experiences but also in a vision of the future. Encounters with the world can teach people about themselves—what they enjoy doing, what they are good at, and what really matters in work and in life.[1]

In most cases, career decisions are based on the belief that the future in a particular occupation, job, or organization can provide experiences, opportunities, and rewards that are meaningful and satisfying. Richard's experiences also illustrate the unpredictability of careers—especially in today's world. Richard could not have foreseen the organizational and political turmoil that awaited him. How Richard and the rest of us cope with these twists and turns in our careers is what distinguishes effective from ineffective career management.

The aim of this book is to help the reader understand the principles of effective career management and to provide opportunities to develop and practice skills in career management. The book devotes a great deal of attention to the issues faced by people at different stages of their careers, so that individuals can manage their careers effectively throughout their lives. This book is also designed to help managers and future managers respond constructively to their subordinates' career needs and to help human resource specialists develop effective career management systems within their organizations.

A major premise of *Career Management* is that individuals can exert considerable—although not total—control over their careers. Effective career management requires not only keen insight into oneself and the world of work but also sound decision-making skills that can be developed and improved. As we see in Chapter 2, career management is essentially a problem-solving process in which information is gathered, insight is acquired, goals are set, and strategies are developed to attain the goals.

The study of careers is becoming increasingly popular. Witness the number of career planning and other self-help books in local bookstores and the growing number of career-planning activities provided by companies, social or professional organizations, and adult education programs. Research on careers has also gained prominence in recent years. The Academy of Management, one of the most prestigious professional organizations for management scholars, now includes a division devoted to the study of the career, and professional journals have published more and more articles on career-related issues.

The primary reason for this popularity lies in the belief that the concept of career, like no other, can help one to understand the fundamental relationship between people and work, a relationship that has plagued scholars, mystified organizations, and frustrated people in all sorts of occupations. Consider the following situations:

- An engineer, 20 years out of college, has recently been laid off in a corporate downsizing move and is beginning to question her competence and drive to succeed.

- A young physician realizes that he chose a career in medicine to please his parents and dreads spending the next 40 years pursuing someone else's dream.

- A regional sales manager in Denver refuses a promotion to corporate headquarters in New York. He enjoys the outdoor life, and his wife is committed to her successful career. He wonders about his future in the company.

- A 35-year-old financial analyst whose employer has just been acquired by an international conglomerate watches nervously as her colleagues get terminated one after another. Will she be next?

- A recent college graduate has been unable to find employment in his chosen field and has no idea about what career options to pursue.

- A harried dual-career mother is frustrated in her career because she receives little support from her husband, children, or company.

- A 39-year-old manager is frustrated by a stalled career with no promotions in sight.

All these situations require an individual to actively manage his or her career. They provide an opportunity for a person to make an effective career decision or, by default, to allow someone else to make the decision. This book provides a framework for individuals to manage their careers more effectively and for organizations to develop policies and practices to help their employees with the task of career management.

Before we provide a more formal definition of a career, we need to set the stage by describing changes in the world of work that have occurred over the past several decades. After all, it is in this new economic reality—amidst a great deal of uncertainty and turbulence—that our careers will unfold and our efforts to manage our careers will take place.

CHANGING LANDSCAPE OF WORK

The world is changing rapidly and dramatically, and these changes—economic, political, technological, and cultural—are having profound effects on the world of work. Accompanying these changes is a level of uncertainty that is playing havoc with people's careers and lives. Intense competition in the corporate world has been fueled by increased productivity of foreign competitors and an uncertain world economy. Many companies in the United States are fighting for a larger share of their market, if not for their very survival. This fierce competition has produced numerous acquisitions, internal reorganizations, and attempts at "downsizing" to contain costs.

JOB LOSS

Reading the financial pages can be frightening. It is estimated that 43 million jobs had been lost in the United States from 1979 to 1995, and the pace of job loss has accelerated in the 1990s.[2] During the 1980s the average annual job loss was 2.3 million, whereas the 1990s saw the number of jobs lost each year climb to 3.2 million, an increase of 39 percent. Nor are these uncertainties limited to the private sector, as local, state, and federal governments are also under severe financial strains. In addition, these streamlining activities are hitting many of us closer to home, as white collar, professional, and managerial employees are becoming increasingly vulnerable to reductions in force. Clearly, the prospect of a secure, continuous, lifetime career with one employer (or even within one industry) is fading rapidly.

INTERNATIONALIZATION

The global economy reflects another major change in the world of work, and organizations will need to adopt a global perspective to survive and flourish.[3] The presence of a global perspective will radically change the face of business and, as a result, how careers develop within these organizations.

The appearance of new world markets, foreign competition, and political realignments have forced many companies to adopt more global strategies. International exports throughout the world are projected at $5.3 trillion in 1997, an increase of nearly 10 percent since 1995.[4] By the beginning of the 1990s, 2,167 parent companies (excluding banks) had operated 17,835 affiliates employing 6.6 million workers.

The emergence of the multinational corporation, with extensive sales revenues coming from operations outside the company's home country, has transformed managerial careers immensely. In many such firms, the route to the top now includes significant exposure to the management of international operations. Moreover, all managers, whether or not they are executive-bound, must learn to understand foreign politics, markets, cultures, employees, and new management styles if they are to be effective in today's multinational corporation. The complete integration of the European Community, "Europe 92," will require many multinational corporations to relocate significant facilities to areas of greater opportunity.[5] Job assignments and career paths in these corporations may never be the same!

TECHNOLOGY

Technological advances have affected every phase of business from operations to sales to financial management. Computer technology has upgraded the skill requirements of many jobs and eliminated the existence of others. Rapidly changing technologies have created new career paths for employees with the proper mix of skills, while their less adaptable colleagues have often found themselves out of tune with their employers' future plans. In addition, technology, in combination with shifting demands for products and services, will continue to create new occupations. One list of occupations that might appear in a future occupational handbook included artificial intelligence technician, divorce mediator, issues manager, and robot salesperson.[6]

Because technological changes produce new—but unpredictable—options, career management will become even more crucial in the years ahead.[7] What is required, as we will see, is a career management style that is flexible and attuned to the many changes that lie ahead in the world of work.

CHANGING STRUCTURE OF ORGANIZATIONS

To meet the challenges of a highly competitive, global marketplace, many organizations have experienced dramatic changes in their structure, and this trend is expected to escalate into the 21st century. For example, the customer-driven "horizontal" organizational structure contains fewer levels of management and uses cross-functional autonomous work teams to manage virtually every process from manufacturing to marketing.[8] Organizations of the future will be flatter and more decentralized than the bureaucracies with which most of us are familiar.[9] They may employ a relatively small number of "core" employees and handle much of their work through outsourcing and a large cadre of temporary or contingent workers. In fact, it has been estimated that 20 percent of the new jobs created during the period between 1991 and 1993 were temporary positions.[10]

Organizations with this new "network" structure will form many partnerships or networks with other organizations and individuals outside their formal boundaries. Not unlike a computer network, network organizations link a variety of firms together to provide the expertise and resources necessary to complete particular projects or manufacture specific products.[11] Some scholars have used the term *boundaryless* to describe the characteristics of these organizations because the organization typically accomplishes its goals through collaboration with many resource providers that lie outside its boundaries.[12]

In sum, although bureaucratic organizations—with their emphasis on stability and predictability—will undoubtedly continue into the future, more and more organizations in the 21st century are likely to take on the following characteristics:

- A small permanent work force with an extensive reliance on contingent, part-time, and contract workers
- A flat hierarchy with self-managed groups taking responsibility for most important activities
- An extensive set of alliances with internal and external partners
- A rapid introduction and utilization of advanced technology into work processes

These changes in organizational structure have often been accompanied by a revision in the basic "psychological contract" between employer and employee. A psychological contract is an implicit, unwritten understanding that specifies the contributions an employee is expected to make to the organization and the rewards the employee receives from the organization in exchange for his or her contributions.[13] In the traditional "relational" contract that has prevailed for years, the employee received job security in exchange for satisfactory performance and loyalty to the organization.[14]

Because of their need for flexibility in a highly competitive environment, many organizations have adopted a more short-term "transactional" psychological contract that involves lower levels of commitment by both parties. Instead of exchanging performance and loyalty for job security, employees are now expected to be flexible in accepting new work assignments and be willing to develop new skills in response to the organization's needs. In return, the organization does not offer promises of future employment but rather "employability" (with the current employer or some other organization) by providing opportunities for continued professional growth and development.[15] This shift in the psychological contract from relational to transactional—from employment to employability—has major implications for employees' careers.

CHANGING NATURE OF WORK

As we have seen, many organizations have or will become leaner, flatter, and more flexible. These organizational changes have significant implications for the type of work performed by managers and professionals. It will be difficult for managers in flat organizations to supervise their people in a traditional manner and closely monitor their performance. Indeed, there will be fewer managers in the organization to supervise anyone. And the managers who do remain will derive their power from their expertise and the respect they have earned rather than from their position in the organizational hierarchy.[16] All employees will need to become skilled in self-management as the locus of responsibility shifts downward in the organization.

Managers and nonmanagers will be required to become effective members and leaders of cross-functional and cross-organizational teams and will attain power and influence as they gain greater information and visibility through their participation in these groups. All these factors will require the flexibility to move skillfully from one project to another, the ability to interact with people from a variety of different functional areas, and a more collaborative and participative interpersonal style.

CULTURALLY DIVERSE WORK FORCE

A more culturally diverse work force will produce changes in the way organizations function. These changes will be every bit as significant as changes arising from economic competition and technological change. The findings of the well-known Workforce 2000 project indicate that the future labor force will be older, more female, and more disadvantaged.[17] It is estimated that only 15 percent of the net new entrants into the U.S. work force by the year 2000 will be native-born white men. The vast majority of the new workers will either be women (64 percent), native-born nonwhite men (7 percent), or immigrant men (13 percent).

The increasing proportion of women, racial minorities, and immigrants in the work force will put pressures on organizations to manage this sexual, racial, and ethnic diversity effectively. But it will also challenge employees to understand different cultures and to work cooperatively with others who may hold different values and perspectives. Career success in many organizations may well depend on an employee's ability to thrive in a multicultural environment.

WORK AND FAMILY LIFE

The management of work and family lives will also pose a substantial challenge to employer and employee alike. The neat separation of work and family, where neither role interferes with the other, now seems like a distant memory. In 1996, 61 percent of all married women aged 16 and older were in the work force compared with just 30 percent in 1960. In addition, nearly 63 percent of all married women with children younger than 6 were in the work force, compared with only 19 percent in 1960. The employment rate for married women with children aged 6 to 17 was 76.7 percent in 1996, nearly twice the rate (39 percent) of 1960.[18]

The burgeoning employment of women has created new challenges of juggling work and family commitments. Moreover, the soaring divorce rate has substantially increased the number of single-parent households—the vast majority headed by women—with particularly intense work and family pressures.[19] Dual-career couples and single parents must learn to balance their careers with extensive family responsibilities, often including the care of elderly parents or in-laws. Indeed, with the passage of the federal Family and Medical Leave Act in 1993, the 1990s will probably be remembered as the decade in which the management of "work-family conflict" and the achievement of a "balanced life-style" became issues of national priority. The 21st century will provide even more challenges to women and men pursuing demanding careers and active family and personal lives.

Work and family roles have also been altered by technological advances, which have blurred the demarcation between these two spheres of life.[20] Personal computers have moved work activities from the office to the dining room or study, and fax machines and portable telephones have enabled even the most remote location to function as an office. These changes provide opportunities for achieving work-family balance but also require considerable support from spouses, children, and employers.

DEFINITIONS OF CAREER CONCEPTS

Now that we have painted the changing landscape of work, we discuss what constitutes a career, first presenting its historical meaning and then presenting a definition of a career that more closely fits today's world. We also introduce the career management process and examine the concept of career development.

WHAT IS A CAREER?

In broad terms, there are two ways of viewing a career. One approach views a career as a structural property of an *occupation* or an *organization*.[21] For example, one could think of a career in law as a sequence of positions held by a typical or "ideal" practitioner of the occupation: law student, law clerk, junior member of a law firm, senior member of a law firm, judge, and ultimately retirement. A career could also be seen as a mobility path within a single organization, as the following path in a marketing function illustrates: sales representative, product manager, district marketing manager, regional marketing manager, and divisional vice president of marketing, with several staff assignments interspersed among these positions.

The other approach views a career as a property of an *individual* rather than an occupation or an organization. Because almost everyone accumulates a unique series of jobs, positions, and experiences, this view acknowledges that each person, in effect, pursues a unique career. Even within this individual perspective, however, several different definitions of career have appeared over the years, each reflecting a certain theme embodied in the meaning of a career.[22]

For example, an *advancement* theme has been present in many definitions of a career. Such definitions imply that a person is pursuing a career only if he or she exhibits steady or rapid advancement in status, money, and the like. This definition severely limits the meaning of a career because it implies that people who have not experienced advancement or other substantial achievements do not really have a career.

A second theme places an emphasis on the career as a *profession*. For example, physicians and lawyers are thought to have careers, whereas clerks and machinists are not. This emphasis, too, appears to be rather limiting, because it suggests that one must achieve a certain occupational or social status for one's work activities to constitute a career.

A third theme revolves around the career as a source of *stability* within a single occupational field or closely connected fields. In this context, we often hear of the "career soldier" or "career police officer." Similarly, a person's pursuit of closely connected jobs (teacher, guidance counselor, private tutor) is thought to represent a career, whereas a sequence of apparently unrelated jobs (novelist, politician, advertising copywriter) violates a neat consistency of job content and would not constitute a career.

Because these three themes (advancement, professional status, stability) put severe limitations on the meaning of a career, less restrictive definitions have recently emerged. Michael Arthur, Douglas Hall, and Barbara Lawrence consider the career to be an evolving sequence of a person's work experience over time.[23] This definition is unencumbered by the requirements of advancement, professional status, or occupational stability. In *Career Management,*

> A career is defined as the pattern of work-related experiences that span the course of a person's life.

In our definition, work-related experiences are broadly construed to include (1) objective events or situations such as job positions, job duties or activities, and work-related decisions; and (2) subjective interpretations of work-related events such as work aspirations, expectations, values, needs, and feelings about particular work experiences. Exhibit 1.1 portrays some significant elements of a person's hypothetical career. Notice that an examination of the objective events by themselves would not provide a full, rich understanding of a person's career. Similarly, an exclusive focus on subjective feelings or values would not do justice to the complexity of a career. Both objective and subjective components are necessary. As we see in subsequent chapters, one can manage a career by changing the objective environment (e.g., switching jobs) or by modifying one's subjective perception of a situation (e.g., changing expectations). Similarly, the unfolding or development of a career frequently involves systematic changes in objective events (as when a person's opportunity for future promotions becomes limited) as well as changes in subjective reactions to events (e.g., changes in values or goals).

Our definition of a career does not require that a person's work roles be professional in nature, be stable within a single occupation, or be characterized by upward mobility. Indeed, anyone engaging in work-related activities is, in effect, pursuing a career. This broad definition fits nicely with the changes in the work world discussed earlier in the chapter. For example, the definition's omission of advancement in the corporate hierarchy as a defining characteristic of a career meshes well with the limited vertical mobility opportunities within today's flat organization. Similarly, to require that a career provide stability within one organization—or even one career path—is unrealistic in today's world of downsizing, contingent workers, and constantly changing jobs.

In this sense, our definition is consistent with the notion of a "boundaryless career" developed by Michael Arthur.[24] A boundaryless career aptly captures life

· EXHIBIT 1-1

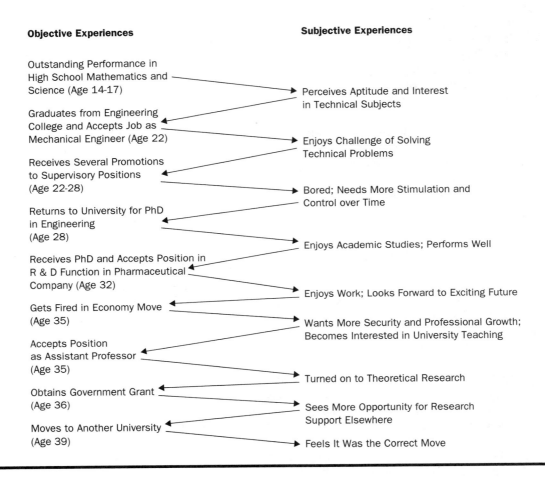

Objective Experiences

Outstanding Performance in
High School Mathematics and
Science (Age 14-17)

Graduates from Engineering
College and Accepts Job as
Mechanical Engineer (Age 22)

Receives Several Promotions
to Supervisory Positions
(Age 22-28)

Returns to University for PhD
in Engineering
(Age 28)

Receives PhD and Accepts Position in
R & D Function in Pharmaceutical
Company (Age 32)

Gets Fired in Economy Move
(Age 35)

Accepts Position
as Assistant Professor
(Age 35)

Obtains Government Grant
(Age 36)

Moves to Another University
(Age 39)

Subjective Experiences

Perceives Aptitude and Interest
in Technical Subjects

Enjoys Challenge of Solving
Technical Problems

Bored; Needs More Stimulation and
Control over Time

Enjoys Academic Studies; Performs Well

Enjoys Work; Looks Forward to Exciting Future

Wants More Security and Professional Growth;
Becomes Interested in University Teaching

Turned on to Theoretical Research

Sees More Opportunity for Research
Support Elsewhere

Feels It Was the Correct Move

in emerging organizations that deemphasize internal boundaries (e.g., hierarchical levels and functional partitions) and that require the repeated passage across boundaries between the organization and the myriad of networks it establishes with other organizations and individuals. The essence of a boundaryless career—as with our definition—is its independence from a particular organization and its existing career paths.

Another emerging view that is consistent with our approach and is well suited to the realities of work is the "Protean" career.[25] Named for Proteus, the Greek god who could change shape at will, the Protean career is not tied to a particular organization or occupation. In a Protean career, an individual pursues his or her personal conception of what is important in work and life.

OBJECTIVE AND SUBJECTIVE ELEMENTS OF A HYPOTHETICAL CAREER

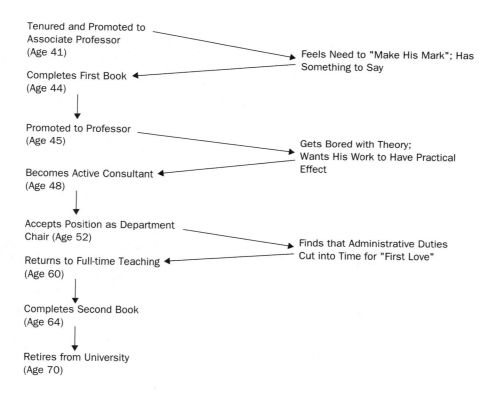

Tenured and Promoted to Associate Professor (Age 41)

Feels Need to "Make His Mark"; Has Something to Say

Completes First Book (Age 44)

Promoted to Professor (Age 45)

Gets Bored with Theory; Wants His Work to Have Practical Effect

Becomes Active Consultant (Age 48)

Accepts Position as Department Chair (Age 52)

Finds that Administrative Duties Cut into Time for "First Love"

Returns to Full-time Teaching (Age 60)

Completes Second Book (Age 64)

Retires from University (Age 70)

These newer conceptions of a career recognize that individuals' careers can unfold in many different ways. Recently, researchers have advocated a "multiple career concept" that distinguishes four different career patterns: (1) a traditional *linear career* that emphasizes upward mobility; (2) an *expert* career that focuses on stability in a specialty area (e.g., financial analysis) with little advancement; (3) a *spiral* career in which major career shifts occur periodically, perhaps every 7 to 10 years; and (4) a *transitory* career, which is characterized by changes in career field as frequently as every 3 to 5 years.[26] As we see throughout this book, individuals need to take responsibility for understanding the type of career they wish to pursue and making career decisions that are consistent with these preferences.

CAREER MANAGEMENT

Like the concept of the career itself, career management has been defined in a number of ways.

> We view career management as a process by which individuals develop, implement, and monitor career goals and strategies.[27]

Because the process of career management is central to this book, Chapters 2, 3, and 4 are devoted to the explanation and application of our model of career management. For the time being, career management can be briefly described as an ongoing process in which an individual

1. gathers relevant information about himself/herself and the world of work.
2. develops an accurate picture of his/her talents, interest, values, and preferred life-style as well as alternative occupations, jobs, and organizations.
3. develops realistic career goals based on this information.
4. develops and implements a strategy designed to achieve the goals.
5. obtains feedback on the effectiveness of the strategy and the relevance of the goals.

Notice that career management is an individual—not an organizational—activity. Indeed, as we show in Chapter 2, it is the individual's responsibility to manage his or her career. More and more organizations are relinquishing an activist role in their employees' careers and are laying the responsibility for career management squarely on the shoulders of the individual.[28] Douglas Hall has observed that "the new career contract is not a pact with the organization; it is an agreement with one's self and one's work."[29]

Moreover, individuals will need to develop a set of career competencies that enable them to develop insight into themselves and their environment so they can navigate their increasingly unpredictable and "chaotic" careers.[30] The specific steps in the career management process—and the qualities necessary to carry them out—are discussed extensively in the next chapter.

CAREER DEVELOPMENT

As we see in Chapter 5, people go through relatively predictable phases or stages in their careers. Moreover, each career stage is characterized by a somewhat distinctive set of themes or tasks that need to be confronted. For example, a 23-year-old trainee is likely to be preoccupied with gaining competence, acceptance, and credibility in his or her early career. The same person at midcareer (e.g., age 45) might be wrestling with gnawing self-doubts about the sacrifices his or her career has required. At age 55 or 60, that person might be faced with the task of remaining productive in later career years or even switching career fields entirely. The concept of career development also plays a significant role in this book and is treated in detail in Part II. We define career development as

An ongoing process by which individuals progress through a series of stages, each of which is characterized by a relatively unique set of issues, themes, and tasks.

One primary goal of this book is to demonstrate the interplay between career management and career development. If individuals understand the developmental tasks associated with each career stage, they can develop goals and strategies that are most appropriate for their particular career phase. Moreover, organizations attuned to the unfolding of careers can design developmental programs and experiences most relevant to an employee's career stage.

NEED TO UNDERSTAND CAREER MANAGEMENT

An understanding of career management is important in two respects. First, it can help individuals manage their careers more effectively. Second, organizations can profit from understanding the career decisions and dilemmas that confront their employees. In this section, we consider the importance of career management both from an individual employee's perspective and from an organization's viewpoint.

INDIVIDUAL PERSPECTIVE

From an individual's point of view, effective career management is particularly important in the light of the turbulent economic, technological, and cultural environment discussed in previous sections of the chapter. In rapidly changing and uncertain times, career success and satisfaction will most likely be achieved by individuals who understand themselves, know how to detect changes in the environment, create opportunities for themselves, and learn from their mistakes—all elements of effective career management. In an era of downsizing, outsourcing, and corporate reorganization, individuals who have insights into themselves and their options should be more able to overcome obstacles to their career growth.

Moreover, careers will become less structured, less automatic, and more unpredictable. Established career paths may be replaced by more innovative, idiosyncratic routes to success. As organizations become more responsive to rapidly changing business priorities, greater flexibility will be required on the part of the employee.[31] Flexibility and adaptability are hallmarks of effective career management.

Another pressure for effective career management is the very nature of contemporary employees—active and assertive—who demand a high degree of control over their careers and their lives. Behavioral scientists have observed the following significant changes in the work force in recent years:

HIGH EXPECTATIONS. The desire for interesting and meaningful work has been matched by the belief that the attainment of these desires is likely. To want something from life is one thing; to expect it is another matter. Research suggests that new employees tend to hold inflated, unrealistic expectations about work.[32] High expectations can produce anger, disappointment, and dissatisfaction if work experiences do not live up to values and expectations. Effective career management can play a particularly significant role in the attempt to secure a match between expectations and experiences.

AUTONOMY. One of the most significant values held by the contemporary employee is the achievement of freedom and autonomy in the workplace.[33] Having substantial freedom to select work projects, to decide how a job gets accomplished, and to set work schedules is crucial to a large number of employees in today's world. Indeed, attaining high-quality job performance on challenging, autonomous projects may be more important to many employees than receiving a promotion.

WEAKENING OF SEX-ROLE BOUNDARIES. The arbitrary divisions of labor between men's and women's participation in work roles have become far less rigid in recent years. Women are entering the legal, medical, and business professions at increasing rates and have also made progress in gaining access to some male-dominated blue-collar occupations.[34] As occupational sex-typing continues to weaken, women and men will perceive a much wider range of career options and will need to choose from these options wisely, therefore increasing the need for effective career management.

A CONCERN FOR TOTAL LIFE-STYLE. The quest for meaningful and challenging work has been accompanied by an intense concern for a satisfying personal life. The pursuit of "career success" has potential costs—less time or energy for family, recreation, and self-development.[35] Refused promotions or relocations and an unwillingness to work 14-hour days and 7-day weeks reflect a belief among many employees that the trade-offs associated with the pursuit of career success are excessive.

In a survey conducted by Robert Half International, 92 percent of the executives polled believed that employees were more concerned with balancing work and family than they had been 5 years earlier. Moreover, 49 percent reported that the number of executives willing to work long hours had declined over the same 5-year period. And the Gallup Organization posed the following question to employees: "If you were offered a job with significantly more money and prestige—but it would require significant time away from your family—would you take it?" Nearly 60 percent of those polled said they would refuse the job, and an additional 32 percent said they would accept it with some reservations!

This desire for a balanced life-style can produce ambivalent feelings in many employees. On one hand, money, advancement, challenge, responsibility, and interesting work are sought and valued. On the other hand, leisure, family, and self-development are also seen as legitimate and important activities that, at times, take precedence over work. In a sense, then, many employees seem to be seeking a bounded involvement with work. That is, they are placing boundaries around their work involvement so that work does not incessantly intrude into other parts of their lives. As we see in later chapters, career decisions must take into account the satisfaction of work, family, and personal needs. Whether the blurring of work and family lives has positive or negative consequences (and it probably has elements of both), career management in the 21st century will require new insights and strategies to manage not only one's career but one's overall life as well.

Moreover, as noted earlier, women are entering (or reentering) the work force in record numbers. The increasing prevalence of single-parent households and dual-career couples puts immense pressures on women and men to balance their own work, family, and personal responsibilities. The interaction between work and family is considered in detail in Chapter 11. At this point, however, one must note that the added complexity of a nontraditional family structure requires effective career management on the part of women and men.

DIVERSITY OF CAREER ORIENTATIONS. Our discussion of the contemporary work force does not imply that all employees hold the same values and pursue the same type of careers. In fact, there is considerable diversity among employees' career orientations.[36] Although some of us value advancement or freedom above all else, others primarily value the intrinsic excitement of work, and still others place the most significance on security and balance in their lives.[37] Although we examine career orientations more extensively in later chapters of the book, we should realize at this point that active career management is essential if we are to satisfy our unique career values, whatever they might be.

ORGANIZATIONAL PERSPECTIVE

As indicated in the preceding section, individuals who define career success in broad terms and who feel the need to combine different parts of their lives into a satisfying life-style have a real need to understand the nature of careers and to manage their careers actively. Organizations also have incentives for understanding careers. In fact, an organization's ability to manage its human resources effectively depends on how well it understands its employees' career needs and helps them engage in effective career management.

SELECTION OF HUMAN RESOURCES. Successful human resource management begins with the effective recruitment, selection, and socialization of new employees. An organization needs to be concerned with identifying a pool of talented applicants, selecting those applicants with the greatest likelihood of success, and bringing the new recruits on board in a way that increases their contribution to the organization. To accomplish these tasks, an organization must understand the type of careers it provides and the career values that it believes are most conducive to success and satisfaction in the organization.

Moreover, an organization must understand the way applicants approach the job search process so it can present itself to these applicants in the most favorable way. Yet an organization must also avoid overselling itself to the point at which new recruits hold unrealistic and unattainable expectations.[38] Finally, an organization must help its new employees understand their jobs, appreciate the organization's culture, and begin to "learn the ropes."[39] An organization is more likely to succeed in these activities if it understands the career needs experienced by job applicants and new employees, a topic we treat in depth in Chapter 7.

DEVELOPMENT AND UTILIZATION OF HUMAN RESOURCES. Many organizations contend that their employees are their most valued assets. However, employees who are placed in inappropriate jobs and who are frustrated with their opportunities for growth and development can ultimately turn into liabilities, either through poor performance or voluntary termination. Therefore, it is in the best interest of the organization to help its employees plan and manage their careers. Career planning workshops, job posting, supportive performance appraisal systems, career counseling, and job redesign are but a few of the career-related programs that organizations have used to facilitate effective career management.

Furthermore, to enhance the performance and development of its employees, an organization should understand the critical tasks faced by people in different stages of their careers.[40] Programs designed to help employees in their early careers, such as a challenging initial job assignment, are likely to be different to some extent than developmental activities most relevant to someone in midcareer (e.g., learning to become a mentor) or in late career (preretirement counseling).

Moreover, to ensure a steady movement of human resources to key positions, an organization needs to understand the basis on which employees make their career decisions. It is no longer practical for an organization to assume that employees will automatically accept promotions or other job assignments offered to them. Personal career interests, family considerations, and life-style choices often upset a company's best-laid plans. Therefore, the organization needs to understand the dynamics of career decision making and be aware of its employees' career concerns to avoid miscalculation of its human resource needs.

MANAGEMENT OF THE CAREER PLATEAU. There is an additional problem experienced by companies that are either not expanding rapidly or are contracting in size. In these firms, there are fewer advancement opportunities for managers and other employees because the number of employees ready for a position may greatly exceed the number of openings. This problem is exacerbated by the "baby boom" generation that is now approaching middle age in large numbers.[41]

Therefore, employees may become plateaued relatively early in their careers, stuck in jobs with little likelihood of promotion or with few opportunities for increased responsibility.[42] Many of these employees may experience a diminished level of work motivation or, as seen in Chapter 13, may leave their employers to establish an entrepreneurial career. Organizations need to keep plateaued employees performing effectively. To a considerable extent, success in meeting this challenge depends on an understanding of the principles of career management.

MANAGEMENT OF CULTURAL DIVERSITY. The movement toward equal employment opportunity—fueled by the passage of the Civil Rights Act of 1964 and reinforced by judicial decisions and the Civil Rights Act of 1992—has had a profound effect on organizations' management of their human resources. The focus on equitable career opportunities within organizations will require companies to develop fair assessment techniques so candidates for promotions or other job assignments will be judged on their competence, not on their sex, race, ethnicity, or age. Beyond that, however, employers will need to leverage the perspectives of different cultural groups to create a more effective work force.[43] As Chapter 12 demonstrates, an understanding of career management is essential to accomplish this goal.

FAMILY RESPONSIVENESS. Organizations stand to lose the services of valuable human resources—women and men—if they fail to help their employees resolve difficulties in achieving balance between work and family responsibilities. Family-responsive organizations will increasingly provide more flexible work schedules, part-time employment, opportunities for job sharing, and child care arrangements in an attempt to retain employees who are experiencing extensive work-family conflicts.[44] Moreover, employers may well need to reconsider the level of commitment and involvement they can reasonably expect from employees who are juggling work and family pressures. As we see in Chapter 11, an understanding of the work and family demands facing employees at different stages of their career development will be required to attract, motivate, and retain an effective work force.

SUMMARY OF THE CONTEMPORARY WORKPLACE

Organizations will be staffed by an increasingly diverse group of employees. In general, employees will want to derive more meaning from work than simply money and security and will pay considerable attention to balancing their work, family, and personal lives. As part of a more general trend, employees are likely to be more assertive and vocal about their needs and will be willing to leave organizations that fail to provide opportunities to meet these needs.

In addition, work organizations will face pressures from other sources. International competition, technological advances, and the constant focus on efficiency will present a variety of human resource problems. Lean and mean may be a corporate rallying cry, but it can violate employees' expectations for rapid advancement and thereby frustrate the attainment of previously reasonable goals. Changing technologies may eliminate jobs and career paths in favor of other career routes. Work and family lives are increasingly intertwined as individuals and families attempt to achieve balance in their lives. The adoption of a global perspective and increasing prevalence of a multicultural work environment will require new insights into the cultural underpinnings of behavior.

This turbulence will exist in an era of employee rights and insistence on social justice on one hand and the need for greater organizational efficiency on the other. Although an understanding of careers will not by itself solve these problems, a failure to understand and apply principles of career management could have unfortunate consequences for employees and their employers.

SUMMARY

A career is defined as the pattern of work-related experiences that span the course of a person's life. All careers have objective and subjective elements that together form the basis of an individual's career.

Career management is seen as an ongoing problem-solving process in which information is gathered, awareness of oneself and the environment is increased, career goals and strategies are developed, and feedback is obtained. This process can help individuals deal with the tasks and issues they face in various stages of their careers.

It is essential that individual employees and organizations develop an understanding of career management in today's turbulent world. Contemporary employees tend to be assertive and vocal about their needs, and they desire control over their professional and private lives. Organizations concerned with the productive utilization of their human resources can also benefit from understanding the many dilemmas and challenges faced by employees as they attempt to help them plan and manage their careers.

ASSIGNMENT

Interview a friend, family member, or co-worker to review the key events in his or her career. Remember to examine objective and subjective factors. Sketch a diagram of the person's career as in Exhibit 1.1.

DISCUSSION QUESTIONS

1. What is the impact of recent changes in the business environment on individuals' careers? Consider the consequences of intense competition, internationalization, technology, changes in organizational structure and managerial work, work-family issues, and cultural diversity on career management.
2. Does the characterization of the contemporary work force described in this chapter (high expectations, autonomy, weakening sex-role stereotypes, and concern for total life-style) fit your picture of yourself, your friends, or your family members? Could there be age, social class, cultural, or gender differences in how people view work and life?
3. Why should people be concerned about managing their careers? What can happen if people do not actively plan and manage their careers?
4. What is the incentive for an organization to help its employees manage their careers? How can the organization stand to gain from this venture? Are there any risks?

ENDNOTES

1. M. W. McCall, "Developing Executives through Work Experiences," *Human Resource Planning* 11 (1988): 1–11.

2. L. Uchitelle and N. R. Kleinfield, "On the Battlefields of Business, Millions of Casualties," *The New York Times,* March 3, 1996, p. 1.

3. P. R. Harris and R. T. Moran, *Managing Cultural Differences,* 3d ed. (Houston, TX: Gulf Publishing Company, 1991).

4. *International Financial Statistics* (Washington, DC: International Monetary Fund, December 1997).

5. C. Lee, "EC's Business Centers May Be Shifting," *The Wall Street Journal,* September 16, 1991, p. 490.

6. S. N. Finegold, "Emerging Careers: Occupations for Post-Industrial Society," in *Careers Tomorrow: The Outlook for Work in a Changing World,* ed. E. Cornish (Bethesda, MD: World Future Society, 1988), 17–24.

7. D. C. Borchard, "New Choices: Career Planning in a Changing World," in *Careers Tomorrow,* ed. Cornish, 25–33.

8. J. A. Byrne, "The Horizontal Corporation," *Business Week,* December 20, 1993, pp. 76–81.

9. N. Nicholson, "Career Systems in Crisis: Change and Opportunity in the Information Age," *Academy of Management Executive* 10, no. 4 (1996): 40–51.

10. C. von Hippel, S. L. Mangum, D. B. Greenberger, R. L. Heneman, and J. D. Skoglind, "Temporary Employment: Can Organizations and Employees Both Win?" *Academy of Management Executive* ,11, no. 1 (1997): 93–104.

11. B. B. Allred, C. C. Snow, and R. E. Miles, "Characteristics of Managerial Careers in the 21st Century," *Academy of Management Executive* 10, no. 4 (1996): 17–27; quote is on p. 20.

12. A. Bird, "Careers as Repositories of Knowledge: A New Perspective on Boundaryless Careers," *Journal of Organizational Behavior* 15 (1994): 325–344.

13. S. L. Robinson, M. S. Kraatz, and D. M. Rousseau, "Changing Obligations and the Psychological Contract: A Longitudinal Study," *Academy of Management Journal* 37 (1994): 137–152.

14. Ibid.; G. A. Callanan and J. H. Greenhaus, "Personal and Career Development: The Best and Worst of Times," in *Evolving Practices in Human Resources Management: Responses to a Changing World of Work,* ed. A. K. Korman and A. I. Kraut (San Francisco, CA: Jossey-Bass, 1999), 146–171; D. M. Rousseau and K. A. Wade-Benzoni, "Changing Individual-Organization Attachments: A Two-Way Street," in *The Changing Nature of Work,* ed. A. Howard (San Francisco, CA: Jossey-Bass, 1995), 290–322.

15. R. H. Waterman, J. A. Waterman, and B. A. Collard, "Toward a Career Resilient Workforce," *Harvard Business Review* July–August (1994): 87–95.

16. R. M. Kanter, "The New Managerial Work," *Harvard Business Review* November–December (1989): 85–92.

17. W. B. Johnston and A. H. Packer, *Workforce 2000: Work and Workers for the 21st Century* (Indianapolis, IN: Hudson Institute, 1987).

18. U. S. Bureau of the Census. *Statistical Abstract of the United States: 1997,* 117th ed. (Washington, DC, 1997), 404.

19. J. Singer, "Women's Work," *Report from the Institute for Philosophy and Public Policy* (College Park, MD: School of Public Affairs, University of Maryland, 1991), 1–5.

20. C. Dressler, "Home, Office Merging," *Philadelphia Inquirer,* December 29, 1991, pp. 1, 3.

21. S. R. Barley, "Careers, Identities, and Institutions: The Legacy of the Chicago School of Sociology," in *Handbook of Career Theory,* ed. M. B. Arthur, D. T. Hall, and B. S. Lawrence (Cambridge, UK: Cambridge University Press, 1989), 41–65.

22. D. T. Hall, *Careers in Organizations* (Glenview, IL: Scott Foresman, 1976); J. Van Maanen and E. H. Schein, "Career Development," in *Improving Life at Work: Behavioral Science Approaches to Organizational Change,* ed. J. R. Hackman and J. L. Suttle (Santa Monica, CA: Goodyear, 1977), 30–95.

23. M. B. Arthur, D. T. Hall, and B. S. Lawrence, "Generating New Directions in Career Theory: The Case for a Transdisciplinary Approach," in *Handbook of Career Theory,* ed. Arthur, Hall, and Lawrence.

24. M. B. Arthur, "The Boundaryless Career: A New Perspective for Organizational Inquiry," *Journal of Organizational Behavior* 15 (1994): 295–306.

25. P. H. Mirvis and D. T. Hall, "Psychological Success and the Boundaryless Career," *Journal of Organizational Behavior* 15 (1994): 365–380; D. T. Hall, "Protean Careers of the 21st Century," *Academy of Management Executive* 10, no. 4 (1996): 8–16.

26. K. R. Brousseau, M. J. Driver, K. Eneroth, and R. Larsson, "Career Pandemonium: Realigning Organizations and Individuals," *Academy of Management Executive* 10, no. 4 (1996): 52–66.

27. Our definition of career management is similar to that provided by T. G. Gutteridge, "Organizational Career Development Systems: The State of the Practice," in *Career Development in Organizations,* ed. D. T. Hall et al. (San Francisco, CA: Jossey-Bass, 1986), 50–94.

28. Callanan and Greenhaus, "Personal and Career Development."

29. Hall, "Protean Careers of the 21st Century"; quote is on p. 10.

30. R. J. DeFillippo and M. B. Arthur, "The Boundaryless Career: A Competency-Based Perspective," *Journal of Organizational Behavior* 15 (1994): 307–324; Hall, "Protean Careers of the 21st Century."

31. Kanter, "The New Managerial Work."

32. J. P. Wanous, *Recruitment, Selection, Orientation, and Socialization of Newcomers* (Reading, MA: Addison-Wesley, 1992).

33. D. T. Hall and J. Richter, "Career Gridlock: Baby Boomers Hit the Wall," *Academy of Management Executive* 4 (1990): 7–22.

34. K. Deaux and J. C. Ullman, *Women of Steel* (New York: Praeger, 1983); S. Parasuraman and J. H. Greenhaus, "Personal Portrait: The Life-Style of the Woman Manager," in *Women in Management: Trends, Issues, and Challenges in Managerial Diversity,* vol. 4, ed. E. A. Fagenson (Newbury Park, CA: Sage, 1993), 186–211.

35. J. H. Greenhaus, "The Intersection of Work and Family Roles: Individual, Interpersonal, and Organizational Issues," in *Work and Family: Theory, Research, and Applications,* ed. E. B. Goldsmith (Newbury Park, CA: Sage, 1989), 23–44; J. H. Greenhaus and N. J. Beutell, "Sources of Conflict between Work and Family Roles," *Academy of Management Review* 10 (1985): 76–88.

36. M. Igbaria, J. H. Greenhaus, and S. Parasuraman, "Career Orientations of MIS Employees: An Empirical Analysis," *MIS Quarterly* June (1991): 151–169; Brousseau *et al.,* 52–66.

37. E. H. Schein, "Career Anchors Revisited: Implications for Career Development in the 21st Century," *Academy of Management Executive* 10, no. 4 (1996): 80–88.

38. Wanous, *Recruitment, Selection, Orientation, and Socialization of Newcomers.*

39. D. C. Feldman, "Careers in Organizations: Recent Trends and Future Directions," *Journal of Management* 15 (1989), 135–156.

40. H. Levinson, "How Adult Growth Stages Affect Management Development," *Training, HRD* 14 May (1977): 42–47.

41. V. M. Godshalk, *The Effects of Career Plateauing on Work and Nonwork Outcomes,* unpublished doctoral dissertation, Drexel University, 1997.

42. J. M. Bardwick, *The Plateauing Trap* (Toronto, Canada: Bantam Books, 1986); E. K. Warren, T. P. Ference, and J. A. F. Stoner, "Case of the Plateaued Performer," *Harvard Business Review* 53, no. 1 (1975): 30–38, 146–148.

43. T. Cox, *Cultural Diversity in Organizations: Theory, Research, and Practice* (San Francisco, CA: Berrett-Koehler Publishers, 1993).

44. D. E. Friedman, and A. A. Johnson, "Moving from Programs to Culture Change: The Next Stage for the Corporate Work-Family Agenda," in *Integrating Work and Family: Challenges and Choices for a Changing World,* ed. S. Parasuraman and J. H. Greenhaus (Westport, CT: Quorum Books, 1997), 192–208.

2

MODEL OF CAREER MANAGEMENT

To manage a career is to make a decision or—more accurately—a series of decisions. Should you pursue a career in computer science, marketing, or accounting work? Should you accept a position with Intel or Microsoft or obtain a graduate degree instead? Should you move into general management or stay in a staff position? Should you change employers at the present time? How might a job change affect your spouse or significant other's career? How can you obtain employment after an unexpected job loss? Will a transition into a new career at midlife be a lifesaver or a disaster? If you pursue "early retirement," will you do volunteer work or start your own company?

Although these illustrations are all unique in some respect, they do possess a basic similarity: They all require active career management and decision making. As indicated in Chapter 1, if we do not actively manage the direction of our career, then we leave our career up to chance or whim. In today's less certain business environment, we need to be proactive and responsible for our careers. Career management is the process by which individuals can make reasoned, appropriate decisions about their work life. It is also an approach to problem solving that can be used to address a wide variety of career decisions.

In this chapter, we discuss a model of career management. First, an overview of the model and the research that forms the basis of the model are presented. Next, the value of using the career management process in a continual manner is articulated. Finally, four indicators of effective career management are outlined.

In Chapters 3 and 4, we delve more deeply into the career management process and emphasize the pragmatic application of the model to career decision making. These chapters include specific guidelines to apply the career management model as well as learning exercises to practice the skills required by the model.

———————————————————■———————————————————

OVERVIEW OF THE CAREER MANAGEMENT MODEL

In the social sciences, a model is a picture or representation of reality.[1] A model contains a set of variables that are related to each other in a specified manner so that we can better understand some piece of the world. The model of career management considered in this book describes how people should manage their careers. Not everybody manages a career in this fashion, but the activities represented in the model can lead to desirable outcomes for the individual. The reasons for this assumption will become clear as the model unfolds.

The career management model is portrayed in Exhibit 2.1. Before defining the key components in a formal sense, the career management cycle is introduced with a brief example.

A young chemical engineer is pondering her future in her company. Although she enjoys her position as a staff engineer, a career in plant management has

· **EXHIBIT 2-1**

MODEL OF CAREER MANAGEMENT

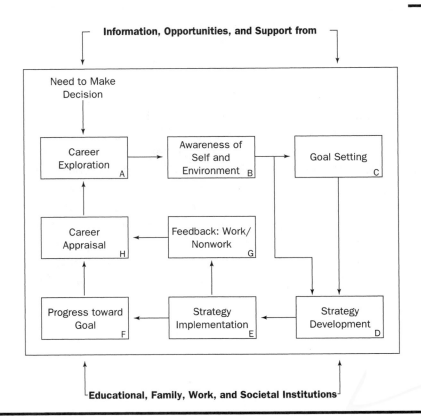

Information, Opportunities, and Support from

Need to Make Decision

Career Exploration — A
Awareness of Self and Environment — B
Goal Setting — C
Career Appraisal — H
Feedback: Work/Nonwork — G
Progress toward Goal — F
Strategy Implementation — E
Strategy Development — D

Educational, Family, Work, and Societal Institutions

intrigued her for a while. She could lay low and follow the company's "plan" for her. However, she decides to take a more active role in the management of her career. She has some decisions to make.

The first step in the career management model indicates that the engineer should engage in career exploration (Box A in Exhibit 2.1). That is, she should begin gathering information. She might collect information about herself (what she enjoys doing, where her talents lie, the importance of work in her total life), about alternative jobs inside or outside the organization (What does a plant manager really do, anyway? What are the salaries of veteran chemical engineers?), and about her organization (or other organizations) as a total system (Is it possible to move from staff to line in this company? How do you get promoted around here?).

Career exploration, if conducted properly, should enable the engineer to become more fully aware of herself and her environment (Box B). She ought to gain insight, for example, into her values, interests, and talents in both her work and nonwork lives. She should become more aware of job options and their requirements and of opportunities and obstacles in the environment.

A greater awareness of herself and her environment can help the engineer choose a career goal to pursue (Box C). The goal, in this case, may be to attain the position of assistant plant manager in a specified period of time, to move into a project engineering position, or even remain in her current position for the foreseeable future.

The establishment of a realistic goal or set of goals can facilitate the development (Box D) and implementation (Box E) of a career strategy (i.e., a plan of activities designed to attain the desired career goal). For example, if the engineer's goal is to become assistant plant manager, she may enroll in one or more management development seminars sponsored by the company, encourage her boss to assign her more managerial tasks in her present position, and learn more about the operation of the entire plant.

The implementation of a reasonable career strategy can produce progress toward the stated career goal (Box F). If the engineer chose a wise plan of action, she is more likely to attain her goal than if she did not pursue a strategy or developed an inappropriate strategy.

The implementation of a career strategy can provide useful feedback to the person. This feedback, in conjunction with feedback from other work and nonwork sources (Box G), can enable the engineer to appraise her career (Box H). The additional information derived from career appraisal becomes another vehicle for career exploration (see the arrow from Box H to Box A) that continues the career management cycle. For example, the engineer may discover that she has performed poorly on the newly acquired managerial portions of her job. This appraisal might lead the engineer to consider changing her goal; she may no longer wish to enter management. Or she may retain the goal but revise the strategy (see the arrow from B to D). For example, she might choose to pursue a graduate degree in management.

In sum, the career management cycle is a problem-solving, decision-making process. Information is gathered so individuals can become more aware of themselves and the world around them. Goals are established, plans or strategies are developed and implemented, and feedback is obtained to provide more information for ongoing career management.

Individuals who follow this approach to career management do not live in a vacuum. As indicated by the border around Exhibit 2.1, the usefulness of exploration, goal setting, strategies, and feedback often depends on the support received from various people and organizations. For example, internship and counseling programs provided by colleges; performance appraisals, self-assessment workshops, and mentoring and training programs offered by work organizations; and advice, love, and support from families can all contribute to effective career management.

The successful application of this career management model depends both on the individual and the organization. It involves an exchange of information between employees, current and potential employers, co-workers, friends, and families. Individuals must be willing to take on the task of being proactive and responsible for their careers. It takes effort to gather the information needed to make appropriate career decisions. Studies have shown that individuals who receive social support from family and friends feel more secure and are better able to progress in their career development.[2]

Organizations must also be willing and able to share information with employees, to make the necessary resources available, and to support employees in their attempts to manage their careers. Subsequent chapters consider what individuals and organizations can do to stimulate career growth and effective career management.

THEORY AND RESEARCH ON THE CAREER MANAGEMENT PROCESS

In this section, we examine the theory and research that form the conceptual base for the model of career management.[3] We discuss, in turn, career exploration through career appraisal, defining key terms, offering a rationale for each component of the model, and summarizing relevant research.

This model is based on the assumption that people will be more fulfilled and more productive when their work and life experiences are compatible with their own desires and aspirations. People are more satisfied with their career choices and jobs when their work experiences are consistent with their needs, values, interests, and life-style preferences. Performance in a career is enhanced when the job requires the application of skills and abilities that the individual possesses.[4] For these reasons, the career management model attempts to optimize the compatibility or "fit" between individuals and their work environments.

CAREER EXPLORATION

Career exploration is the collection and analysis of information regarding career-related issues.

Most people need to gather information so they can become more keenly aware of their own values, interests, and talents, as well as the opportunities and obstacles in their environment. It is assumed that the more extensive and more appropriate the career exploration, the more likely people will become aware of different facets of both themselves and the world of work.

Why does career exploration promote awareness? First, people may not know themselves nearly as well as they think they do. For example, they may not have a clear understanding of what they really want from a job or from life. Perhaps they have not given it much thought, or possibly past decisions were guided more by what others wanted for them than what they wanted. People often need to collect the necessary data to increase awareness in these areas.

Moreover, people's insights into their talents may be incomplete. They may never have thought, for example, that success as the advertising manager of the high school yearbook was a reflection of their persuasive and interpersonal skills or that accomplishments on a special task force at work reveal substantial leadership qualities. Oftentimes, individuals hold rigid ideas about appropriate work roles based on their gender. Ideas about what are appropriate work roles for men are more rigidly held than those for women.[5] Therefore, we may allow biases, rather than factual data, to determine what we think our abilities are.

In addition, individuals may on occasion overestimate strengths in certain areas and judge themselves to be more talented than they really are.[6] Conversely, some people may persistently underestimate their competence. For these reasons, career exploration can provide an individual with a more complete and accurate picture of him- or herself. The ability to be self-aware, that is, one's ability to reflect on and accurately assess one's demonstrated behaviors and skills in the workplace, has been linked to effective job performance.[7]

In a similar vein, knowledge of different occupations, organizations, and career opportunities can also benefit from an active exploration of the environment. It is known, for example, that people can develop expectations about jobs and organizations that are not realistic. Again, a thorough exploration of the world can help clarify alternatives and options and aid adaptability.[8]

TYPES OF CAREER EXPLORATION

It is helpful to think of career exploration in terms of the type of information that is sought (see Table 2.1). For example, self-exploration can provide a greater awareness of personal qualities. People may come to possess a deeper understanding of the activities they like and dislike (interests). They may examine how much challenge (or security, money, or travel) they want from a job (work values). As noted earlier, self-exploration can also provide substantial information about strengths, weaknesses, talents, and limitations. Finally, self-exploration can provide a better understanding of the balance of work, family, and leisure activities that best suit a preferred life-style.

Environmental exploration, as the name implies, helps one learn more about some aspect of the environment. For a student (or someone considering a career change), environmental exploration is likely to be occupationally focused. What does a systems analyst really do? What skills are required for a career in electrical engineering? What is the difference between a career in private and public accounting?

For employed people, environmental exploration may be oriented more toward alternative jobs within a particular organization. In this context, exploration can provide information on one's current job or alternative future jobs. For what jobs would I qualify in 2 to 3 years? What experiences are needed to move from my current line position to a particular staff assignment? Is my current career path likely to come to a dead-end within a few years?

Environmental exploration can also help a person learn more about alternative organizations or about one particular organization in more depth. For someone in the job market, either by choice or by necessity, such exploration may provide information about the relative merit of working in the chemical industry versus the fashion industry or about the likelihood of career advancement in one company versus another. Environmental exploration can also provide employees with information about their current organization. Who in the organization is willing and able to be my sponsor? Who really gets rewarded in the organization? What training and development opportunities are available to me?

Another important aspect of the environment for many employees is their family. For example, knowing your spouse's willingness to relocate might help you to make a decision to pursue career opportunities 2,000 miles away. There-

· TABLE 2-1

TYPES OF CAREER EXPLORATION

Self-Exploration	Environmental Exploration
• Interests	• Types of occupations
• Talents	• Types of industries
Strengths	• Necessary job skills
Weaknesses	• Job alternatives
• Work Values	• Company alternatives
Job challenge	• Impact of family on career decisions
Job autonomy	
Security	
Work/life balance	
Money	
Working conditions	
Helping others	
Power or influence	

fore, environmental exploration can also provide useful information about a family's needs and aspirations, a spouse's career values, and about the relationship between one's work life and family life.

EFFECT OF CAREER EXPLORATION ON CAREER MANAGEMENT

Research suggests that career exploration has a beneficial effect on career management. The most immediate consequence of career exploration is an enhanced awareness of self and environment. A number of studies demonstrate that as individuals engage in more career exploration, they become more aware of themselves and their chosen career.[9] In a similar vein, certain forms of career exploration can increase the amount of information people acquire during the job-search process.[10]

Research also indicates that career exploration can help people develop occupational goals, although it is likely that the focus and the quality of the exploration, rather than its mere quantity, facilitate goal setting.[11] Moreover, individuals' occupational decisions tend to be more appropriate or satisfying when their decisions are preceded by extensive career exploration.[12]

In an extensive series of studies on the exploration process, Stephen Stumpf and his colleagues demonstrated the usefulness of career exploration to people pursuing job prospects. It was found that students who engaged in extensive exploration could generate more job interviews and offers, obtain higher salary offers, and develop more realistic job expectations.[13] Career exploration can also help people develop more extensive career strategies and perform more effectively in job-interview situations.[14]

In short, career exploration can help people become more aware of themselves and the world of work. They are "ready" to handle the formidable task of formulating career goals and decisions and are able to develop strategies necessary to accomplish significant goals. Indeed, the more exploration that is conducted, the more useful are such activities perceived to be.[15] This does not mean that career exploration is either easy or guaranteed to provide profound and useful information. It does suggest, however, that career management can be more effectively conducted if it is based on a solid foundation of accurate information.

The purpose of this section is to examine the meaning and relevance of career exploration. Specific career exploration techniques are presented in Chapter 3.

AWARENESS

Awareness is a relatively complete and accurate perception of one's own qualities and the characteristics of one's relevant environment.

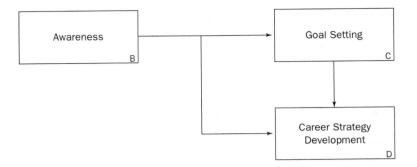

In our model of career management, a thorough awareness of self and environment enables a person to set appropriate career goals and to develop appropriate career strategies. Awareness is a central concept in career development.

Indeed, it would be difficult to set realistic goals in the absence of an accurate view of self and work. How can one set a realistic goal to become an actuary, for example, without a clear picture of the duties, requirements, and rewards of actuarial positions as well as an accurate assessment of one's talents and interests in those relevant areas? To extend this illustration further, how can a person reasonably decide whether to remain an actuary or move into a general management track without clearly understanding his or her motives and abilities that might help or hinder a career in management?

This does not mean that people are always aware of themselves and their options when they set a goal or make a decision. In fact, we can all think of many career decisions that were based on stereotyped, biased, or distorted information. The point is that goals are likely to be more appropriate and more realistic when they are based on an accurate picture of self and environment.

Support for this notion comes from several sources. Researchers have found that students who reported extensive awareness of their values and their chosen field tended to establish more satisfying occupational goals than those who were relatively unaware of self and career field. Information and awareness are likely to enhance the presence and clarity of career plans.[16] Furthermore, information acquired about oneself or one's environment can help people develop realistic job expectations and attain higher levels of job satisfaction.[17] Thus, research evidence suggests that awareness can have a positive effect on career management.

CAREER GOAL

A career goal is a desired career-related outcome that a person intends to attain.

One of the most consistent research findings in the organizational behavior literature is that employees who are committed to specific, challenging task goals outperform those who do not have goals or have a weak commitment to established goals.[18] The advantage of establishing a career goal is that a person can direct his or her efforts in a relatively focused manner. Once goals are in place, complementary behaviors and attitudes that reinforce these goals occur.[19] For example, a sales representative who sets a goal to become the regional marketing manager can begin to plan a strategy around attainment of the goal. Without an explicit goal, a plan of action is difficult to develop.

In our view, a career goal need not imply a promotion. Certainly, an appropriate career goal may be a lateral move within the same or a different organization. In fact, a career goal does not have to involve a job change at all. A staff engineer's goal may be to remain in the same position while increasing technical skills and job responsibilities.

Up to a point, the more specific the career goal, the greater the likelihood of developing an effective strategy to achieve the goal. For instance, a financial analyst whose goal is to become a department manager within 3 years can ask what training or educational experiences, job assignments, and visibility will help to attain that position. Another analyst whose goal is to be wealthy or enjoy life may flounder because of the inexact nature of the goal.

Although many writers on career management discuss the virtues of goal setting, there is little research in the area of career goals. One study found that managers who set specific 1- to 2-year career goals were more optimistic about their careers than managers who had not set a specific goal. Furthermore, the more committed the managers were toward their goals, the more likely they were to develop an extensive career strategy.[20] Indeed, clear career goals and plans have been associated with increasing levels of career effectiveness, career resilience, job involvement, and successful job search.[21] Edwin Locke and his associates have extensively investigated why certain individuals perform better than others. These researchers have found that individuals are motivated to perform better when they set challenging but achievable goals.[22] In Chapter 4, we examine in more detail the characteristics of effective career goals and specific techniques for developing realistic goals.

CAREER STRATEGY

A career strategy is a sequence of activities designed to help an individual attain a career goal.

Many organizations develop explicit strategic plans that enable them to pursue their goals successfully. The same principle of strategic planning is applicable to individual career management. Much of the research on career strategies can be traced to Melville Dalton's seminal observation that managers' advancement within a manufacturing plant seemed less influenced by their formal education or years of service than by such "strategic" behaviors as joining a prestigious social or political organization. Eugene Jennings' classic analysis revealed that highly mobile managers developed rather conscious strategies to move into the "executive suite," and successful managers took an active part in managing their careers and did not rely on the "loyalty ethic" of dutiful hard work, uncritical subordination to superiors, and undying respect for the corporate community.[23] As Jennings pointed out, this loyalty-based approach may have worked in the past; however, today's companies require employees with the right experiences and career competencies, not merely longevity in the company. Organizations are beginning to view employees as assets or intellectual capital, and "for the first time in centuries workers will own the means for production . . . knowledge and information."[24]

Research has sought to identify the kinds of strategies employees use (or think they should use) to improve their chances of career success. These studies suggest that there are seven broad types of career strategies:

- Competence in the present job
- Extended work involvement (working long and hard)
- Development of skills (through training and job experiences)
- Opportunity development (through self-nomination, visible assignments, and networking)
- Development of supportive relationships (mentors, sponsors, peers)
- Image building (to convey an appearance of success)
- Organizational politics

A more detailed discussion of these specific strategies along with guidelines for development of career strategies is provided in Chapter 4.

CAREER APPRAISAL

Career appraisal is the process by which people acquire and use career-related feedback. The career-appraisal process is portrayed in Exhibit 2.2. In work, as in all of life, people need to know how they are doing.

Constructive feedback enables people to determine whether their goals and strategies still make sense. Career appraisal, which enables a person to "monitor" the course of a career, represents the adaptive, feedback function of career management.[25]

Feedback can come from a number of different sources. The very act of implementing a career strategy can provide feedback regarding work and nonwork

· EXHIBIT 2-2

CARRER APPRAISAL PROCESS

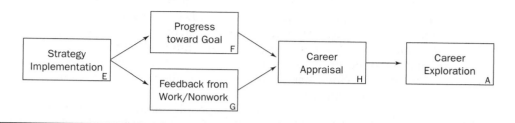

lives. For example, spending weekends in the office (extended work involvement) can provoke praise from a boss and hostility from a family. Participating in a training session or developing a close mentor relationship can teach people valuable lessons about themselves as well as about jobs and organizations. In addition, feedback about progress toward specific goals can be obtained from a superior in a coaching or performance-appraisal session, from peers, or from other significant persons. The information derived from career appraisal closes the career management cycle by becoming another piece of exploratory information that can enhance one's awareness of self and environment.

As noted earlier, the career-appraisal process may lead to a reexamination of career goals. The feedback one obtains from work or nonwork sources can reinforce or lead to modification of a goal. An enthusiastic response to a training seminar or an outstanding performance review on a new project, for example, may convince an employee that his or her goal to reach the next management level remains desirable and feasible. Disappointments in the outcome of such activities, however, could propel a person to shift goals.

Career appraisal can also affect strategic behavior. For example, in the course of a performance feedback session, an employee and his or her superior may conclude that additional formal training is unnecessary but that greater exposure to key managers through a new work assignment is essential. In this case, the goal remains intact, but the strategy is revised. One's ability to self-monitor and revise career strategies has been found to lead to greater career mobility— including more cross-company promotions and more within-company promotions.[26]

In short, career appraisal provides a feedback loop that perpetuates career exploration and the entire career management cycle. The usefulness of feedback for learning and performing tasks has been repeatedly demonstrated in the literature. Feedback's function as a self-corrective mechanism is equally applicable to the management of careers.

CAREER MANAGEMENT AS AN ONGOING PROCESS

There are a number of reasons why career management should be a regular, ongoing process. First, because work is such a central part of life, a satisfying career can promote feelings of fulfillment, whereas a string of poor career decisions can have a devastating effect on a person's sense of well-being. In addition, it is not easy to develop a deep understanding of our place in the world of work. Goals are often unrealistic, and strategies are frequently ill conceived. Without continual, conscious, active career management, past errors might very well be prolonged and repeated.

Complicating the matter further, people often continue their commitment to a prior decision—even as they face repeated failure and frustration—to prove to themselves and others that their initial decisions were correct.[27] Such people may fool themselves into believing their past failures will be reversed and their prior efforts will therefore be justified. These individuals may actually create alternative explanations, or further self-justifications, as to why their initial decisions were correct.[28] Active career management on an ongoing basis, including feedback from many sources, is necessary to avoid digging deeper holes from which one may never emerge.

Furthermore, changing environments demand ongoing career management. In developing new business strategies, organizations substitute new missions for old, wiping out old career paths in favor of new mobility channels. Technological changes, reorganizations, downsizings, mergers, and acquisitions can all affect a person's career within a particular organization. Employees who are not sensitive to the implications of such changes in the environment may find themselves unaware of their options.

People change as well. Goals that were so important during one time of life may require reexamination in later stages. Parts of jobs that were exhilarating at age 30 may be tedious or even aversive at 50. New talents and values can emerge with age, maturity, and experience. Changing family situations can provide constraints and opportunities to careers. Again, those who are insensitive to changes in themselves will be missing a chance to make career decisions that are more compatible with current values and life-style preferences.

For these reasons, career management should be a continual, problem-solving process. This is not to say that people must constantly be conducting self-assessment activities or revising their goals or strategies every week or every month. However, people should generally be attuned to changes in themselves and the environment. As will be seen in subsequent chapters, there are periods when active career management is particularly critical. The choice of a college major and an initial career field, the job-search process, the decision to remain specialized or broaden one's experiences, the reaction to a job loss, and the decision to reevaluate involvements in work and family roles all require accurate information, realistic goals and plans, and an openness to feedback from the environment.

INDICATORS OF EFFECTIVE CAREER MANAGEMENT

How can people tell whether they are managing their careers effectively? Because career management is a problem-solving, decision-making process, it is tempting to examine the outcomes of career decisions at a particular point in time to assess the effectiveness of career management practices. One could, for example, look at advancement in title or responsibility or level of job performance to gauge the effectiveness of career management.

These temptations should be avoided because, at least in the short run, career advancement and job performance are merely outcomes (although important ones) that do not necessarily reflect the process by which the outcomes were reached. They do not address the dynamics of career decision making.

Because career management is an ongoing, adaptive process, a snapshot view of a person's performance, status, or mobility does not reveal the manner in which the career has been managed. Following are four indicators of effective career management, which can serve as a review of the career management model itself.

1. Effective career management requires a deep knowledge of oneself and an accurate picture of the environment. Some people have little insight into themselves and alternatives in the work environment. Without such knowledge, one may be fortunate enough to fall into a job that meets one's needs and permits the use of valued abilities. Over the long run, however, one cannot count on luck alone. A career is composed of many decisions during the course of a person's life. Accurate knowledge about self and environment enables a person to take an active role in making appropriate career decisions.

2. Effective career management requires the development of realistic goals that are compatible with one's values, interests, abilities, and desired lifestyle. Accurate knowledge about self and environment is a necessary but insufficient condition for effective career management. This knowledge has to be translated into a decision to pursue a particular goal. That is, the goal, if accomplished, should have a reasonable chance of meeting the person's needs. There is a tendency for some people to choose career goals that others (parents, spouses, professors, supervisors) think are appropriate, regardless of whether the goals meet their own needs.[29] It is the compatibility or fit of goals and accomplishments with personal needs and values that characterizes effective career management.

3. Effective career management requires the development and implementation of appropriate career strategies. It is one thing to develop a valid career goal; it is another to attempt to accomplish the goal according to a plan. Again, some people may, on occasion, achieve goals without any conscious strategic plan, but such good fortune is not likely to recur regularly. Because careers require many diverse types of decisions to be made over the long haul, skills in the development and implementation of career strategies are essential to effective career management.

4. Perhaps most important, effective career management requires a continual feedback process that permits adaptation in the face of changing circumstances. No one possesses totally accurate information about oneself or the environment, especially when people and the world are in a state of change. Moreover, goals and strategies may need fine-tuning or even a major overhaul. At different points, we all feel "stuck" in our careers or feel as if we have hit a career plateau or "roadblock."[30] This situation may help us to realize that our career plans are inappropriate in the light of the dynamically changing work environment. It is not incomplete awareness or even inappropriate goals or strategies per se that signal ineffective career management. The real problem is a person's inability to recognize these difficulties and do something constructive about them. Effective career management, therefore, is a striving process in which imperfect information and decisions are replaced by better (yet still imperfect) information and decisions.

For these reasons, it is not easy to assess the effectiveness of a person's career management practices. Certainly, the external trappings of "success" tell us little about the accuracy of a person's information or the appropriateness of his or her goals and strategies. Nor does a person's apparent satisfaction with his or her work tell the whole story, because people can become "satisfied" by meeting other people's needs. Rather, effective career management represents a process of using information and insight to attain outcomes capable of satisfying personally meaningful values and aspirations.

At this juncture, the reader may wonder whether we are advocating a purely "rational" approach to career management. In a very real sense, our career management model is based on rational thinking and actions. We recommend that individuals explore themselves and their environment in a systematic manner, select career goals and strategies in a conscious way, and pay close attention to changes in themselves and the world around them. Indeed, research indicates that a rational approach to career decision making can be very useful and that a proactive, self-confident orientation to career management can reap benefits for the individual.[31]

Nevertheless, to say that career management should be rational and systematic does not mean that it is mechanical, unemotional, or clear-cut. Career management is, by its very nature, a "messy" endeavor. Information is never complete, awareness is difficult and can come in fits and spurts, and goals and strategies may have to be revised many times before they make sense. Individuals should not become robots when managing their careers, and "gut" feelings should, at times, take precedence over techniques and procedures.

Please keep these thoughts in mind when you examine the specific guidelines for applying the career management model in Chapters 3 and 4 and when you work on the learning exercises throughout the book. View the guidelines as just that—guidelines—rather than as unbending rules. Look for incremental advances in awareness, not instant insight. Accept the fact that you will make mistakes and will occasionally have to take two steps backward before progress is experienced. And most important, remember that career management is, at its core, a learning experience. Learning is occasionally rapid but is more often sporadic. It is often exciting but is frequently frustrating, and it is usually hard work. So relax, be patient with yourself, ask for support from those around you, and enjoy the process.

Summary

This chapter presents a model of career management and developed a rationale for each component in the model. Career exploration, the driving force of the model, involves the collection and analysis of career-related information. This information can increase awareness of personal qualities (interests, values, talents, and life-style preferences) as well as the environment (the world of occupations, jobs, organizations, and family).

Awareness of self and environment enables people to set realistic career goals. The development of specific career goals can help individuals choose and implement appropriate career strategies designed to help them attain these goals. However, no particular strategy is likely to be effective in every situation, hence the need for ongoing career appraisal in which career-related feedback is acquired and used. Such feedback can help people reexamine the effectiveness of their strategies and the appropriateness of their goals.

Because people and environments can change over time, career management should be an ongoing process. Four indicators of effective career management were identified: knowledge of self and the environment; the development of career goals that are consistent with values, interest, talents, and desired life-style; the development and implementation of appropriate career strategies; and a continual feedback loop that permits adaptation in the face of changing circumstances.

Assignment

Interview a friend (perhaps a classmate or a co-worker) about his or her career management activities. Has your friend engaged in career exploration? What is his or her level of awareness of self and environment? Has your friend set a career goal? Developed a career strategy? Why or why not? What should he or she be doing next?

Discussion Questions

1. Why is career exploration such a critical component of career management? How, if at all, can people develop insights into themselves and their environment in the absence of deliberate attempts to seek information? What career exploration activities have you undertaken in the past year? In the past 3 years? How successful have they been?

2. Should career management be primarily a rational, systematic process? What are the advantages and disadvantages of adopting a highly rational approach to career management?

3. Why is it important to monitor and appraise your career? Why should career appraisal be conducted periodically? How frequently should you conduct a career appraisal? How do individuals and environments change in ways that can influence a person's career? What role does family play in career appraisal?

ENDNOTES

1. R. Dubin, "Theory Building in Applied Areas," in *Handbook of Industrial and Organizational Psychology*, ed. M. D. Dunnette (New York: Wiley, 1983), 17–39.

2. D. L. Blustein, M. S. Prezioso, and D. P. Schultheiss, "Attachment Theory and Career Development: Current Status and Future Directions," *The Counseling Psychologist* 23, no. 3 (1995): 416–432.

3. See the following sources for early similar approaches to career decision making: T. G. Gutteridge and F. L. Otte, "Organizational Career Development: What's Going on out There?" *Training and Development Journal* 37, no. 2 (1983): 22–26; W. L. Mihal, P. A. Sorce, and T. E. Comte, "A Process Model of Individual Career Decision Making," *Academy of Management Review* 9 (1984): 95–103.

4. R. D. Gatewood and H. S. Feild, *Human Resource Selection*, 3d ed. (Fort Worth, TX: The Dryden Press, 1994); D. M. Muchinsky and C. J. Monahan, "What Is Person–Environment Congruence? Supplementary versus Complementary Models of Fit," *Journal of Vocational Behavior* 31 (1987): 268–277.

5. S. D. Phillips and A. R. Imhoff, "Women and Career Development: A Decade of Research," *Annual Review of Psychology* 48 (1997): 31–59.

6. W. L. Mihal and J. L. Graumenz, "An Assessment of the Accuracy of Self-Assessment for Career Decision Making," *presented at the Annual Meeting of the Academy of Management*, Dallas, TX, 1983.

7. L. E. Atwater and F. J. Yammarino, "Does Self-Other Agreement on Leadership Perceptions Moderate the Validity of Leadership and Performance Predictions?" *Personnel Psychology* 45 (1992): 141–164; A. Church, "Managerial Self-Awareness in High-Performing Individuals in Organizations," *Journal of Applied Psychology* 82, no. 2 (1997): 281–292; V. M. Godshalk and J. J. Sosik, "Does Mentor-Protégé Agreement on Mentor Leadership Style Influence the Quality of Mentoring Relationships?" *Group and Organization Management* (in press); E. Van Velsor, S. Taylor, and J. B. Leslie, "An Examination of the Relationships among Self-Perception Accuracy, Self-Awareness, Gender, and Leader Effectiveness," *Human Resource Management* 32, nos. 2–3 (1993): 249–263.

8. D. L. Blustein, "A Context-Rich Perspective of Career Exploration across the Life Roles," *Career Development Quarterly* 45, no. 3 (1997): 260–274; J. P. Wanous, *Recruitment, Selection, Orientation, and Socialization of Newcomers* (Reading, MA: Addison-Wesley, 1992).

9. D. L. Blustein, "The Relationship between Motivational Processes and Career Exploration," *Journal of Vocational Behavior* 32 (1988): 345–357; J. H. Greenhaus, B. L. Hawkins, and O. C. Brenner, "The Impact of Career Exploration on the Career Decision-Making Process," *Journal of College Student Personnel* 24 (1983): 495–502; H. D. Grotevant, C. R. Cooper, and K. Kramer, "Exploration as a Predictor in Adolescents' Career Choices," *Journal of Vocational Behavior* 29 (1986): 201–215.

10. S. A. Stumpf and K. Hartman, "Individual Exploration to Organizational Commitment or Withdrawal," *Academy of Management Journal* 27 (1984): 308–329.

11. J. H. Greenhaus and T. F. Connolly, "An Investigation of Career Exploration among Undergraduate Business Students," *Journal of College Student Personnel* 23 (1982): 314–319; R. A. Noe and B. Steffy, "The Influence of Individual Characteristics and Assessment Center Evaluation on Career Exploration Behavior and Job Involvement," *Journal of Vocational Behavior* 30 (1987): 187–202; T. Sugalski and J. H. Greenhaus, "Career Exploration and Goal Setting among Managerial Employees," *Journal of Vocational Behavior* 29 (1986): 102–114.

12. Greenhaus, Hawkins, and Brenner, "The Impact of Career Exploration on the Career Decision-Making Process."

13. S. A. Stumpf, E. J. Austin, and K. Hartman, "The Impact of Career Exploration and Interview Readiness on Interview Performance and Outcomes," *Journal of Vocational Behavior* 24 (1984): 222–235; Stumpf and Hartman, "Individual Exploration to Organizational Commitment or Withdrawal."

14. Sugalski and Greenhaus, "Career Exploration and Goal Setting among Managerial Employees"; Stumpf et al., "Impact of Career Exploration and Interview Readiness."

15. S. D. Phillips, "Readiness for Career Choices: Planning, Exploring, and Deciding," *Career Development Quarterly* 43, no. 1 (1994): 63–73; S. A. Stumpf and M. C. Lockhart, "Career Exploration: Work Role Salience, Work Preference, Beliefs, and Behavior," *Journal of Vocational Behavior* 30 (1987): 258–269.

16. Greenhaus, Hawkins, and Brenner, "The Impact of Career Exploration on the Career Decision-Making Process"; S. Gould, "Characteristics of Career Planners in Upwardly Mobile Occupations," *Academy of Management Journal* 22 (1979): 539–550; R. A. Noe and B. Steffy, "The Influence of Individual Characteristics and Assessment Center Evaluation on Career Exploration Behavior and Job Involvement," *Journal of Vocational Behavior* 30 (1987): 187–202.

17. Stumpf and Hartman, "Individual Exploration to Organizational Commitment or Withdrawal"; J. H. Greenhaus and H. K. Springob, "Managerial Perceptions of Career Planning Information," *Journal of Management* 6, no. 1 (1980): 79–88.

18. E. A. Locke, G. P. Latham, and M. Erez, "The Determinants of Goal Commitment," *Academy of Management Review* 13 (1988): 23–39.

19. S. Aryee, "A Cross-Cultural Application of a Career Planning Model," *Journal of Organizational Behavior* 14, no. 2 (1993): 119–127; G. Audia, K. G. Brown, A. Kristof-Brown, and E. A. Locke. "Relationship of Goals and Microlevel Work Processes to Performance on a Multipath Manual Task," Journal of Applied Psychology 81, no. 5 (1996): 483–497.

20. T. Sugalski, "Some Tests of a Model of Career Management," Ph.D. dissertation, Stevens Institute of Technology, Hoboken, NJ, 1985; Sugalski and Greenhaus, "Career Exploration and Goal Setting among Managerial Employees."

21. R. A. Noe, A. W. Noe, and J. Bachhuber, "An Investigation of the Correlates of Career Motivation," *Journal of Vocational Behavior* 37 (1990): 340–356; R. A. Noe and B. Steffy, "The Influence of Individual Characteristics and Assessment Center Evaluation on Career Exploration Behavior and Job Involvement," *Journal of Vocational Behavior* 30 (1987): 187–202; A. Pazy, "The Relationships between Organizational and Individual Career Management and the Effectiveness of Careers," *Group and Organization Studies* 13 (1988): 311–331; N. D. Stevens, "Job-Seeking Behavior: A Segment of Vocational Development," *Journal of Vocational Behavior* 3 (1973): 209–216.

22. G. P. Latham and E. A. Locke, "Self-Regulation through Goal Setting," *Organizational Behavior and Human Decision Processes* 50, no. 2 (1991): 212–247; E. A. Locke and G. P. Latham, "Goal Setting Theory," in *Motivation: Theory and Research,* ed. H. F. O'Neal, Jr., and M. Drillings. Hillsdale, NJ: L. Erlbaum Associates (1994), 13–29.

23. M. Dalton, "Informal Factors in Career Advancement," *American Journal of Sociology* 56 (1951): 407–415; E. E. Jennings, *Routes to the Executive Suite* (New York: Macmillan, 1971).

24. M. O'Hara-Devereaux and R. Johansen, *Global Work* (San Francisco, CA: Jossey-Bass, 1994); quote is on p. 28.

25. T. G. Gutteridge and F. L. Otte, "Organizational Career Development: What's Going on out There?" *Training and Development Journal* 37, no. 2 (1983) 22–26.

26. M. Kildiff and D. V. Day, "Do Chameleons Get Ahead? The Effects of Self-Monitoring on Managerial Careers," *Academy of Management Journal* 37, no. 4 (1994): 1047–1060.

27. B. M. Staw and J. Ross, "Knowing When to Pull the Plug," *Harvard Business Review* March–April (1987): 68–74.

28. J. Brockner, "The Escalation of Commitment to a Failing Course of Action: Toward Theoretical Progress," *Academy of Management Review* 17, no. 1 (1992): 39–61.

29. J. D. Werbel and A. G. Roberg, "A Role Theory Perspective on Career Decision Making," *Research in Personnel and Human Resources Management* 7 (1989): 227–258.

30. F. L. Otte and W. M. Kahnweiler, "Long-Range Career Planning during Turbulent Times," *Business Horizons* 38, no. 1 (1995): 2–7.

31. D. L. Blustein, "Decision-Making Styles and Vocational Maturity: An Alternative Perspective," *Journal of Vocational Behavior* 30 (1987): 61–71; D. L. Blustein and S. D. Phillips, "Individual and Contextual Factors in Career Exploration," *Journal of Vocational Behavior* 33 (1988): 203–216; Pazy, "The Relationships between Organizational and Individual Career Management and the Effectiveness of Careers" ; K. M. Taylor and J. Popma, "An Examination of the Relationships among Career Decision-Making Self-Efficacy, Career Salience, Locus of Control, and Vocational Indecision," *Journal of Vocational Behavior* 37 (1990) 17–31.

3

Applications of the Career Management Model: A Guide to Career Exploration

Chapter 2 presented a model of career management and provided a theoretical rationale for each component of the model. This chapter takes a pragmatic look at career exploration, the driving force of the model. In particular, we identify the underlying principles of career exploration, discuss exploration activities used in organizations, provide the reader with opportunities to participate in career exploration activities, and offer guidelines for successful career exploration. Chapter 4 examines the remaining components of the career management model—goal setting, strategy development, and career appraisal.

NOTE TO THE READER ON LEARNING EXERCISES

Chapter 3 contains references to a number of learning exercises that appear at the end of the book and can be downloaded from the Internet at **http://www.dry-den.com/management/humresources.html.** Each learning exercise involves a different aspect of career exploration. By investing time in these exercises, you can develop and practice critical career exploration skills. We recommend that you read Chapter 3 in its entirety before beginning the exercises. Moreover, although it may be possible to complete all exercises in one sitting, it is less tiring and more effective to allow some time for reflection in between them. Downloading the learning exercises from the Internet allows you to keep a record of your thoughts and reactions and provides a great deal of flexibility, because it permits you to add information to a previous exercise at a later time.

TYPES OF CAREER EXPLORATION

Career exploration refers to the collection and analysis of information on career-related issues. As noted in Chapter 2, it can provide information about one's own qualities as well as information about the environment: occupations, jobs, organizations, and families. The purpose of career exploration is to help the individual develop a greater awareness of self and the environment so that realistic goals can be established and appropriate strategies developed. Exploration activities have become more critical in recent years as reengineering and downsizing have continued to play havoc with the standard approaches to career management. Knowing yourself and understanding the work environment can help you set reasonable and meaningful goals and can prepare you for career changes, regardless of whether these alterations are planned or not. The ability to be prepared for career change and disruptions is the essence of managing the "boundaryless" career as we discussed in Chapter 1.

SELF-EXPLORATION

When one engages in self-exploration, information is sought about a variety of personal qualities and attitudes that are relevant to career decision making. These qualities can include values, interests, personality factors, talents or abilities, life-style preferences, and any weaknesses or shortcomings. To develop an accurate career identity and set meaningful career goals, it is essential to understand what one wants from work and nonwork roles and what skills and abilities can be brought to (or developed in) the work environment. Let us examine values, interests, personality, talents, and life-style preferences in more detail.

Values are abstract outcomes that a person wants to attain. They highlight individual differences in preferences for the rewards, payoffs, or other aspects of a job or a career.[1] It has been proposed that there are six primary life values: theoretical, economic, aesthetic, religious, social, and political.[2] Although some people may place a high value on helping others (social) or gaining power (political), others are more concerned with creating beauty in the world (aesthetics) or discovering knowledge (theoretical). Each person probably has a unique combination of values that are personally significant. Understanding one's value structure can provide considerable insight into career aspirations. To take an extreme example, a person with strong material and political values is unlikely to be happy in an occupation that pays poorly and provides little opportunity to exercise leadership qualities.

As shown in Table 3.1, Donald Super proposed a set of values that are more specifically related to work.[3] People may differ substantially in the importance they place on different values such as creativity, independence, and job security. Moreover, occupations and specific jobs vary in the extent to which they satisfy these values. In general, people tend to be satisfied with jobs in which they have an opportunity to attain their significant work values.

It should not be surprising that most career planning programs encourage individuals to examine their values carefully. People can learn about their values by analyzing their life history, identifying the kinds of career decisions they have made, and examining the reasons behind these decisions. Often, such informal analyses are supplemented by more structured value inventories.[4]

▪ TABLE 3-1

ILLUSTRATIONS OF WORK VALUES,
INTERESTS, AND TALENTS

Work Values[a]	Interests[b]	Talents[c]
Altruism	Realistic	General Intelligence
Esthetics	Agriculture	Manual Dexterity
Creativity	Nature	Verbal Reasoning
Intellectual Stimulation	Athletics	Numerical Ability
Independence	Military Activities	Spatial Ability
Achievement	Mechanical Activities	Logical Reasoning Skills
Prestige	Investigative	Interpersonal Skills
Management	Science	Precision of Movement
Economic Returns	Mathematics	Writing Skills
Security	Medical Science	Creativity
Surroundings	Artistic	Memory
Supervisory Relations	Music/Dramatics	Clerical Skills
Associates	Art	Speed of Response
Variety	Applied Arts	Perceptual Ability
Way of Life	Culinary Arts	Finger Dexterity
	Writing	Athleticism
	Social	
	Teaching	
	Social Service	
	Medical Service	
	Religious Activities	
	Enterprising	
	Public Speaking	
	Law/Politics	
	Merchandising	
	Sales	
	Organizational Management	
	Conventional	
	Data Management	
	Computer Activities	
	Office Services	

[a]Scales derived from Donald E. Super, *Work Values Inventory* (New York: Houghton Miffin, 1970).

[b]The 25 Basic Interest Scales included in the Strong Interest Inventory arranged by the six Holland Interest Types. (F. Borgen and J. Grutter, *Where Do I Go Next? Using Your Strong Results to Manage Your Career,* Consulting Psychologists Press, 1995.)

[c]Compilation from different models of talents.

Interests refer to likes and dislikes attached to specific activities or objects. Interests, therefore, are expressions of what a person likes to do. Interests are derived from such factors as values, family life, social class, culture, and the physical environment.[5] Although they are reflective of values, interests are attached to particular tasks or activities. For example, two people may each value creativity in their work. Although one person may have strong scientific interests and the other may be interested in literary activities, both sets of interests can serve the broader creative value for each person. Understandably, people who choose career fields that are compatible with their interests tend to be more satisfied than those whose chosen career is incompatible with their interests. Indeed, congruence between interests and career choice is related to subsequent satisfaction and tenure in the job.[6]

John Holland identified six general interest orientations that reflect one's personality, values, and preferred life-style.[7] Holland's theory assumes that vocational interests are an important expression of personality and that the six orientations correspond with specific personality factors.[8] The six orientations, which are similar to the primary life values described earlier, include realistic, investigative, social, conventional, enterprising, and artistic. Individuals who have a realistic orientation tend to be more practical and task-oriented, whereas investigative types are more scientific, scholarly, and research-oriented. Individuals in the social category are more humanistic, personal, and value-oriented and show skill in interpersonal relations. The conventional style reflects an orientation toward structure, tradition, and detail, whereas artistic people prefer unstructured situations, in which creativity and self-expression are possible. Finally, an enterprising designation indicates a preference for entrepreneurial, managerial, and goal-centered activities.

In the 1920s, Edward Strong of Stanford University developed an inventory of interests that reflected specific occupational preferences. Strong believed that interests supply something that is not disclosed by ability or achievement.[9] They point to what the individual wants to do and what they consider satisfying. Today's version of the Strong Interest Inventory (SII) includes descriptions of a person's interests in 25 basic areas.[10] The 25 basic interests can be grouped according to Holland's six occupational orientations described above.[11] Table 3.1 lists the interests according to occupational orientation. The SII provides information on the similarity of one's interests to those of members of more than 200 different occupational types. Use of the SII and other assessment instruments as tools for individual self-exploration is discussed later in this chapter.

One's basic **personality** is another area of self-exploration that can influence career choices. Research has shown, with some disagreement over exact elements and appropriate labels, that there are five basic personality factors.[12] The five factors are typically classified as extraversion, agreeableness, conscientiousness, emotional stability, and openness to experience. In general, these dimensions serve as the basis for personality questionnaires (e.g., the Myers-Briggs Type Indicator and the 16-PF, both of which are profiled later in this chapter) used widely in organizations for personnel selection, employee development, and individual self-assessment.

A person's **talents** should also be a significant component in career management. Talents refer to aptitudes or capacities and currently developed skills or proficiencies (Table 3.1) and reflect what a person can do or could do with proper training. Accordingly, they can set constraints on our potential accomplishments, and it is clearly necessary to consider our talents and abilities when making career decisions. Unfortunately, many people choose occupations or jobs that either require abilities they do not possess or do not take advantage of the talents they do possess. Therefore, many career-planning programs provide the opportunity for participants to assess their own strengths and weaknesses. Talents can be appreciated by reviewing accomplishments in school, work, and other parts of our lives.

Interests, values, personality, and talents are interrelated in several respects. First, as indicated above, interests are rooted in deeper values. But it is also true that interests are related to abilities.[13] People come to enjoy activities at which they excel. Through practice, they may also become more proficient at those activities they enjoy. Therefore, although it may be convenient to separate values, interests, personality, and talents, at some point they must be appreciated as a coherent whole. Edgar Schein's concept of a career anchor probably comes closest to capturing this notion.[14] Schein introduced the concept of the career anchor to recognize different forms of orientation toward work. A career anchor is a cluster of self-perceived talents, motives, and values that forms the nucleus of a person's occupational self-concept. An anchor also can provide the basis for career choices, because a person is likely to make job and organizational selections that are consistent with his or her own self-image. It is only through a number of years of work experience and many reality tests that one can fully clarify and understand his or her career anchor. Using his long-term research on Sloan School of Management (MIT) alumni, Schein identified the following eight career anchors:

Technical/Functional Competence anchor, in which the primary concern is the actual content of the work. Employees who hold this anchor typically want to remain within their technical/functional area (e.g., finance, human resources, marketing).

Managerial Competence anchor, in which the major goal is general line management rather than a particular functional area within the organization. For individuals who possess this anchor, the dominant concerns are the integration of the efforts of others, accountability for total results, and the tying together of different functions in the organization.

Autonomy/Independence anchor, in which the primary concern is with freeing oneself from organizational rules and restrictions in favor of a career in which you can decide when to work, on what to work, and how hard to work. People with this anchor would be willing to turn down a promotion to retain autonomy.

Security-Stability anchor, in which long-term career stability is the underlying drive. The need for security may be satisfied by remaining in the same organization, the same industry, or the same geographic location. People with this anchor generally prefer stable and predictable work.

Service/Dedication anchor, in which the primary concern is to achieve some valued outcome, such as improving the lives of others, perhaps by working in a "helping" occupation.

Pure Challenge anchor, in which the primary work demands involve solving seemingly unsolvable problems or surmounting difficult obstacles. Individuals with this anchor primarily seek novelty, variety, and challenge in their work.

Life-Style Integration anchor, in which the dominant theme is achieving balance in all the major sectors of one's life. Specifically, individuals with this anchor would want harmonious integration of family and career activities.

Entrepreneurship anchor, in which the major goal is to create something new, involving such demands as overcoming obstacles, running risks, and the achievement of personal prominence. People with this anchor want the freedom to build and operate their own organization in their own way.

As important as work is to many people, it is only one of many significant roles in life. What type of family life do you want? In what way can you express your spiritual needs? How can community or leisure activities satisfy your basic values? How important is career success in your total life? In short, what type of life-style is most desirable?

A thorough analysis of nonwork involvements is critical for a number of reasons. First, it is likely that some basic values may be difficult or impossible to satisfy in work. Second, some career fields or jobs can take so much time or emotion that little is left for private lives. To make appropriate career decisions, the importance and variety of nonwork interests and values need to be examined. For example, a parent strongly devoted to coaching his or her child's Little League team would find a job requiring extensive travel frustrating. Third, there is evidence that the importance of nonwork and leisure activities may fluctuate over the course of a person's life.[15] People must be sensitive to such changes to make career decisions that are consistent with as many parts of their lives as possible.

The relationship between work and nonwork lives is treated in detail in Chapter 11. For now, it is important to recognize that an accurate picture of work and nonwork aspirations should produce an awareness of a **desired life-style,** that is, a satisfying pattern of work and nonwork involvements. An understanding of a desired life-style requires answers to the following questions:

1. What are my significant life values?
2. What kinds of activities do I like/dislike?
3. What are my talents, and which ones are significant and personally meaningful?
4. Which of my values, interests, and talents are best met in the world of work?
5. Which of my values, interests, and talents are best met outside of work?
6. How can I achieve a balance of work and nonwork involvements to find expression for my most significant values, interests, and talents?

TECHNIQUES FOR EFFECTIVE SELF-EXPLORATION

Let us now examine specific techniques designed to enhance self-awareness. Self-assessment requires the collection of data or information about ourselves, the organization of that data into meaningful and understandable themes, and the interpretation of these themes in the light of their implications for career decision making.[16]

COLLECTION OF DATA

The first step in self-assessment is to gather data on one's values, interests, personality, talents, and life-style preferences. Techniques for gathering information and the sources of data are both quite varied. Overall, the techniques and sources can be broken down into four general categories: individual assessment instruments, integrated career planning systems, organizational programs, and informal means of assessment.

INDIVIDUAL ASSESSMENT INSTRUMENTS. There are, literally, hundreds of assessment instruments available to assist individuals in gaining a better understanding of themselves. A few of the more prominent and most widely used for self-exploration purposes are discussed below. Note that nearly all assessment instruments must be administered and interpreted by professional counselors.

The *Strong Interest Inventory* is perhaps the most well known of the tools available to isolate interests and related occupations. The SII consists of 317 questions that measure various dimensions related to one's vocational interest pattern. Output from the Strong consists of three related sections—General Occupational Themes, Basic Interest Scales, and Occupational Scales. The General Occupational Themes are based on the six basic vocational interest orientations of Holland, as discussed earlier in this chapter. The 25 Basic Interest Scales (see Table 3.1) measure the strength and consistency of the individual's interests in specific areas, such as mechanical or artistic activities. The Occupational Scales reflect the degree of similarity between the individual's interests and those of women and men employed in 211 different occupations. Thus, the SII attempts to link an individual's fairly broad interest orientation (one of the six occupational themes) with the somewhat more specific interests (one or more of the basic interest scales) and with specific occupational titles (the 211 occupational scales, representing 109 occupations).

The *Vocational Preference Inventory* (VPI) Scale and the *Self Directed Search* (SDS) are two other occupational assessment instruments, developed by John Holland, that are used extensively.[17] Both of these instruments are conceptually similar to the Strong in that they are based in part on the notion that well-adjusted and satisfied individuals within specific occupational fields possess common psychological characteristics, interests, and preferences. All three instruments—the SII, the VPI, and the SDS—attempt to measure one's pattern of interests and then link it to specific occupations that are satisfying to individuals with the same interest pattern. Also, like the SII, the VPI and the SDS use Holland's six major interest orientations as the link between individual characteristics and specific occupations.

The *General Aptitude Test Battery* (GATB) was developed for employment service counseling and placement by various agencies of the U.S. Department of Labor. The GATB is designed to measure nine cognitive, perceptual, and psychomotor skills.[18] It is one of the most frequently used tests and is unequaled in the size of its occupational data base.[19] The basic aptitudes and capabilities measured by the GATB can be compared with occupational aptitude patterns that have been established for more than 460 different occupations.

The *Myers–Briggs Type Indicator* (MBTI) was developed by a mother and daughter team, Katherine Briggs and Isabel Myers. Based on the work of Carl Jung, a Swiss psychiatrist, the MBTI provides a useful measure of personality by looking at eight separate personality preferences that all people use at different times.[20] The eight types are organized into four bipolar scales. The four preferences that are identified as most like you (one from each scale) are combined into what is called a type. Included among the four personality dimensions are how a person energizes, how one perceives information, how one makes decisions, and the individual's life-style preference. For the energizing scale, the two categories are extraversion and introversion. Extroverts have an affinity for drawing energy from the outside world of people, activities, or things. Introverts draw energy from their own internal world of ideas, emotions, or impressions. The two perception categories are designated as sensing and intuition. Sensing individuals prefer to gather information through the five senses by noticing what is actual. Intuitive individuals gather information through a "sixth" sense and notice what possibilities are available. The decision-making dimension includes thinking and feeling orientations. Thinking types prefer organizing and structuring information to make decisions in a logical fashion. Feeling types prefer to make decisions in a personal and value-oriented way. For the life-style preference, the two types are judgment and perception. The judgment type prefers living a planned and organized life, whereas the perception type prefers spontaneity and flexibility. The four bipolar scales result in 16 possible personality types. Like the SII, the MBTI can be a useful mechanism for the assessment of personal characteristics and the determination of one's preferred work environment. Used in conjunction with the SII, the individual is provided with information on personality type, interests, and possible work environments and occupations.[21]

The *Sixteen Personality Questionnaire* (16 PF) was originally developed by Raymond Cattell in 1949. Now in its fifth edition, the 16 PF measures 16 personality dimensions as follows: level of warmth, reasoning ability, emotional stability, dominance, liveliness, rule consciousness, boldness, sensitivity, distrust, abstractedness, privateness, worrying, openness to change, self-reliance, perfectionism, and tension. The 16 factors can be further grouped into five global personality categories: extraversion, anxiety, tough-mindedness, independence, and self-control. The full 16 PF questionnaire consists of 185 items, with the average testing time ranging from 35 to 50 minutes for pencil administration and 25 minutes for computer administration. In terms of career planning, the 16 PF can be used to create a Personal Career Development Profile.[22] This profile allows individuals to gain greater insight into personality as it relates to personal and career interests. The profile consists of six sections detailing one's patterns for problem solving, coping with stressful conditions, interpersonal interactions, organizational role and work patterns, career activity interests, and life-style considerations. As with the MBTI, the 16 PF is used extensively in organizations as a tool to help employees understand themselves and manage their careers.

The *Fundamental Interpersonal Relations Orientation-Behavior* (FIRO-B) is an assessment tool that looks at how an individual's needs affect his or her behavior toward other people. The FIRO-B, which consists of 54 items and takes about 15 minutes to complete, offers insights into a person's compatibility with other people, as well as related individual characteristics. In essence, the FIRO-B measures three interpersonal needs as follows:

- inclusion, or the extent of contact and prominence an individual seeks and wishes from others

- control, or the extent of power or dominance that a person seeks or wishes from others

- affection, or the amount of closeness that a person seeks and wishes from others

The *Life-Styles Inventory—Level I* provides individuals with a profile of their self-concept and thinking approaches.[23] Individuals are rated on 12 scales depicting different thinking patterns or life-styles. The 12 scales are humanistic, affiliative, approval, conventional, dependent, avoidance, oppositional, power, competitive, competence, achievement, and self-actualizing. The Life-Styles Inventory consists of 240 items and is self-administered and self-scored. It can be interpreted independently by the individual or with the help of a counselor.

The *Rokeach Value Survey* consists of two lists of values (18 in each list).[24] Individuals rank the values on each list on the basis of how important each one is as a guiding principle in their life. The first list covers "terminal" values, or those values that relate to what one wants out of life, whereas the second list consists of "instrumental" values that relate to ways of behaving in the world. A significant aspect of the survey is the relative ordering of the values, in that individuals must rely on their own internal value system to guide them in the choices they make.

In summary, interest inventories, personality measures, and other assessment tools can be particularly helpful for career counseling, both with young people making an initial career choice and with adults dissatisfied with their present work and/or considering a career change.[25] Nonetheless, psychological tests and assessment instruments have limitations. Accordingly, the results of these tests should be used as discussion guides and as a reference for theme identification and future decision making.[26] They are not intended to be, nor should they be used as, the conclusive answer to one's career direction.

INTEGRATED CAREER PLANNING SYSTEMS

Career planning systems (CPS) are defined as sophisticated vocational assessment methods designed to further individual growth with regard to career planning and decision-making issues and thereby facilitate the individual's career development.[27] Many of these systems have as a central focus one or more of the primary assessment instruments such as the SII, the SDS, or the MBTI. Indeed, one of the primary objectives of CPSs is to help individuals discover important career-related information about themselves, such as interests and values.[28] CPSs can be offered through different venues, including a classroom, a counselor's office, a career resource center/placement office, or the human resources department of an organization. The CPSs can be grouped into three categories based on form of delivery and methodology: **paper and pencil-based, computer-assisted, and curricular.**[29]

Karen Taylor lists and reviews 15 different paper and pencil-based programs that are available commercially.[30] Her review of the programs includes content and specific instruments used, the publishing company, the author(s), targeted user population, and the rationale for the program. Computer-assisted planning and guidance systems allow efficient and personalized access to self-exploration information.[31] Taylor reviews 13 different computer-assisted programs that are also available commercially, using the same evaluation criteria as those used for the pencil and paper programs. In addition, Lee E. Isaacson and Duane Brown in their recent text provide a detailed description and assessment of 10 of the most widely used computer-assisted career guidance systems.[32] They note that the widespread availability of personal computers, the expansion in computer power, and the related reduction in cost make computer-assisted career guidance a practical and available tool for counselors and others involved in helping individuals in the career development process.

Curricular-based CPSs incorporate many aspects of career planning, including self-assessment, in a classroom setting. Taylor states that most curricular programs are designed for a career course that is taught over an entire academic term. Many schools and universities offer a career course for academic credit, but these programs are not available commercially.

Taylor cautions that users of CPSs should be careful not to prematurely choose a career direction based solely on the results of a CPS. As with individual assessment instruments, CPSs should be used as one of several aids in gaining a better understanding of one's personal preferences and needs. They certainly should not be used as the definitive guide to career selection.

ORGANIZATION-SPONSORED SELF-EXPLORATION PROGRAMS

For working adults, one of the most effective methods for gaining a better understanding of abilities, interests, and talents is through career management assistance programs offered at work. In an ideal sense, organization-sponsored programs should have benefits both for the individual employee and for the company.

Various researchers have noted a number of organizational career development tools that can enhance the self-knowledge of the working adult.[33] These programs include individual self-assessment through such activities as career-planning workshops, career workbooks, and organizational assessment centers. A description of each technique is offered below.[34]

Career planning workshops use a structured, interactive group format in which participants formulate, share, and discuss with each other personal data concerning such factors as strengths, weaknesses, values, and other personal information. One of the goals of the workshops is to encourage a systematic approach to self-analysis.

Career workbooks are intended to fulfill the same basic objectives as a group career workshop but do so in an individual, self-directed fashion rather than on a participative, interactive basis. The workbooks use a series of exercises and reference materials to guide employees through the individual assessment process. Also, the workbooks are designed to be completed by the individual alone and are self-paced.

Assessment centers were traditionally used to assess employee career potential, wherein the focus was primarily on quantifying the promotability of selected employees. More recent evidence suggests the growing tendency for companies and individuals to use the centers for career and job development purposes.[35] Employees use the assessment center to gain feedback on their personality styles, proficiencies, and weaknesses.

In addition to the above programs, working adults have other options for obtaining self-information through the organization. For example, periodic performance appraisals and supervisory feedback can offer insight into personal strengths and weaknesses and can add to employed adults' exploration process. Many of the more prominent executive development programs use the 360-degree evaluation technique, which provides feedback to the individual from a wider perspective. This fuller perspective, which includes assessments from superiors, subordinates, and peers, can give more extensive information on personal strengths and weaknesses, especially in the work role.

The self-exploration programs offered by organizations will often use, as part of the total package, one or more of the commercial assessment instruments and career planning systems described earlier in this chapter. Similarly, individual assessment instruments have become more widely used in organizations. There are manuals that discuss the application of the SII, the MBTI, and the 16 PF in organizations.[36] Indeed, the MBTI has been used by major corporations such as Allied-Signal, Apple, AT&T, Citicorp, Exxon, General Electric, Honeywell, and 3M.[37]

INFORMAL SELF-EXPLORATION

A variety of informal techniques is open to individuals in their self-exploration journey. For example, one popular approach includes the following data-gathering devices:[38]

1. Written Interview: a personal life story including educational experiences, hobbies, work experiences, significant people in one's life, changes and turning points in life, key decisions, and projections into the future.
2. 24-Hour Diary: a blow-by-blow account of two 24-hour periods, one on a weekday and the other on a weekend.
3. Life-Style Representation: a narrative and pictorial portrayal of one's life.

Other informal self-assessment programs have included such activities as:

1. Ranking significant work values.
2. Analyzing "peak" (high and low) experiences in life.
3. Developing a present and future obituary notice.
4. Analyzing one's current job satisfactions and dissatisfactions.
5. Describing an ideal job.
6. Fantasizing about one's future life.

There are also several self-help books, CD-ROMs, and audio/video tapes that are available commercially that are designed to assist individuals in better understanding themselves. One of the most well known is Richard N. Bolles book *What Color Is Your Parachute?*[39] This book, which has been published annually since 1970, helps individuals in their job search efforts by having them focus on such factors as one's preferred work setting, favorite skills, favorite types of people and things, favorite kinds of information, and preferred rewards/outcomes.

It is also important to informally share the results of one's exploration activities with other trusted individuals as another means of gaining additional personal insight. These other individuals might include parents, spouse or significant other, other family members, close friends, co-workers, and manager.[40]

THEME IDENTIFICATION

Information is most useful when it is organized into coherent, understandable units. Therefore, it is necessary to make sense out of the data supplied by various inventories, exercises, and essays. You need to ask what you have learned about yourself and whether there are consistencies that cut across the different data-gathering devices. You need to discover, in other words, what themes have emerged from the data.

A significant theme (e.g., "I want to get my own way" or "I need to work cooperatively with other people") can combine values, interests, and talents into meaningful wholes. The identification of themes is an inductive process. Much like a detective, the individual scrutinizes the specific data for clues about what it is saying, draws preliminary hypotheses about the presence of certain themes, and tests the data further to confirm or reject the hypotheses.

The following steps may be helpful in identifying themes:[41]

1. Thoroughly examine each data-generating device for the presence of themes. Underlining key words or phrases is a helpful technique.

2. Look for data across different data-generating devices that support or refute the presence of a theme. The more consistently the theme emerges from the data, the more likely the theme is important.

3. Label the themes in as specific a fashion as possible.

4. Assess the accuracy and importance of the themes. How much data support the theme? In how many different devices has the theme been identified? How much, if any, contradictory evidence has been found? (The fewer the contradictions, the more accurate the theme.)

Theme identification is clearly an active process, but it is rarely simple and straightforward. This is understandable, because the results of self-exploration activities may prove insufficient, inconclusive, or contradictory. Further, self-assessment, as a process of uncovering personality and psychological attributes, could produce feelings of anxiety and doubt. Nonetheless, the results of exploration activities are important and necessary in the setting of career goals and in the management of one's career. Thus, self-exploration must be conducted, even though the process may at times be uncomfortable.

Learning Exercise I is available at the end of this text and on the Internet at **http://www.dryden.com/management/humresources.html**. It includes several activities designed to help you collect self-related data. Although you may examine Exercise I at this stage, it is recommended that you finish reading Chapter 3 before you begin the exercise.

ENVIRONMENTAL EXPLORATION

Self-exploration is an essential ingredient in effective career management because it provides the information that is needed to answer a number of related questions: What do I find interesting? What are my strengths and weaknesses? What rewards are important to me? What do I want from my work and nonwork lives?

However, self-assessment represents only half of the equation. Careers are embedded in occupations, jobs, and organizations. It is through interaction with the work environment that values are met, talents are used, and interests are stimulated. Moreover, work environments differ in the extent to which they are compatible with a person's particular pattern of values, interests, and talents. Compatibility between the person (e.g., interests, abilities, preferences) and the work environment has a strong influence on such outcomes as job satisfaction, tenure, and career success.[42] In addition, research supports the "gravitational"

Learning Exercise II is available at the end of this text and on the Internet at **http://www.dryden.com/management/humresources.html**. It provides an opportunity for you to identify themes that emerged from the data collected in Exercise I. Although you may examine Exercise II at this time, it is recommended that you finish reading Chapter 3 before you begin the exercise.

view of employment, which states that individuals will, over the course of their labor market experiences, try to seek out jobs that are compatible with their interests, values, and abilities.[43] That is, individuals seek positions for which there is good person-work environment fit. Accordingly, self-awareness needs to be accompanied by an active exploration of one's environment.

Although there are many facets to an environment, four are particularly important in career management: **occupations, jobs, organizations, and families**. The aim of environmental exploration is to learn enough about these facets to make decisions about occupational fields, career paths, and different organizations. Effective environmental exploration should enable a person to identify the setting in which he or she is most likely to meet significant values and to find expression for interests, talents, and a preferred life-style.

The most relevant facet of the environment depends on the type of decision that is required in a particular situation. A student who is floundering about a major or a person in midcareer who is dissatisfied with his or her career may need to focus on exploring alternative occupational fields. An imminent college graduate, however, is probably going to need to know about entry-level jobs in different organizations.

Regardless of the particular decision to be made, individuals need to explore the potential of a match between a particular environment and desired work/life-style. To accomplish that task, environments need to be understood in the light of the information derived from self-exploration. A bridge should be built between self-exploration and alternative environments. This section of the chapter considers how such a bridge can be constructed. Specific applications of these principles to the choice of an occupation, organization, and career path are discussed in subsequent chapters.

Table 3.2 summarizes the types of information relevant to the environment. First of all, occupations differ in the particular tasks that need to be performed. Physicists and social workers, for example, engage in different activities. These activities have implications for a person's interests, values, and abilities. Someone who has interests in scientific activities, values intellectual stimulation, creativity, and independence and has conceptual skills may be drawn to a research career in theoretical physics. Someone who strongly values social welfare, enjoys working closely with other people, desires variety in work, and has strong interpersonal skills may find a career in social work more attractive. A knowledge of occupationally related tasks is basic to linking self-assessment to career decisions.

In addition to task differences, occupations frequently differ in context or environment. Economic rewards, such as income and job security, are not equally distributed across all occupations. Similarly, the physical setting of the work, the degree and type of interaction with other people, and even the dress code can vary substantially from one occupational field to another.

Because occupational fields require different tasks, provide different rewards, and permit different physical and social settings, they often have implications for different life-styles. Two particular life-style considerations that should be examined are an occupation's time demands and its associated stresses and strains. Extensive time commitment to a job and/or exposure to extremely stressful work environments can produce conflicts between one's work life and other life roles. Therefore, occupations that require an extraordinary time involvement (e.g., extensive travel, 7-day work week) and are highly stressful may be incompatible with a life-style that attempts to achieve a balance between work and family or leisure activities.

Table 3.2 also summarizes the type of information relevant to jobs and organizations. Notice first the similarity between occupational information and job information. Because a job (e.g., market research analyst) is merely a vehicle for

---

▪ TABLE 3-2

ILLUSTRATIVE INFORMATION RELEVANT TO ENVIRONMENTAL EXPLORATION

Occupations	Jobs
Task Activities	Task Variety
Ability/Training Requirements	Task Significance
Financial Rewards	Ability/Training Requirements
Security	Financial Rewards
Social Relationships	Security
Physical Setting	Social Relationships
Life-Style Considerations	Physical Setting
Time Commitment to Work	Life-Style Considerations
Work Stress	Time Commitment to Work
	Work Stress
	Amount of Independence/Autonomy
	Relation of Jobs to Other Jobs

Organizations	Families
Industry Outlook	Spouse's Career Aspirations
Financial Health of Organization	Spouse's Emotional Needs
Business Strategies	Child(ren)'s Emotional Needs
Career Path Flexibility	Other Family Members' Needs
Career Management Practices/Policies	Family's Financial Needs
Size and Structure	Family's Desired Life-Style
Reward System	Family Stage
	Self and Spouse Career Stage

pursuing an occupation (e.g., market research), the similarity in information needs is understandable. However, a thorough occupational exploration does not preclude the need for additional job exploration. To illustrate, design engineers in one company do not necessarily perform the same activities with the same rewards as those in another company. Therefore, exploration focused on jobs and positions within particular organizations is essential.

In addition, notice that several additional pieces of information are relevant to job exploration. First, job autonomy can vary substantially between organizations or even between two units of the same organization. Sales representatives in two different companies may have essentially the same duties, but more autonomy in decision making may be granted in one company than in the other. This is particularly important to identify because autonomy can satisfy one's values for intellectually stimulating, independent, and creative work.

Second, it is critical to examine the relationship between a particular job and other jobs in the same or different organizations. Some jobs, in effect, are "dead end" in that movement to other jobs is extremely limited. Some jobs, in other words, provide more options than others. Job families and career paths are examined in more detail in Chapter 8.

It should be clear by now that nearly all jobs are inextricably connected to organizations. Therefore, whether one is entering a first full-time job or is currently employed, it is important to realize that:

1. The outlook of the industry or industries served by an organization can affect career possibilities.
2. The financial health of the organization can place limits on career opportunities.
3. The company's business strategy affects the type of human resources required and, therefore, the nature of career opportunities.
4. An organization's size and structure can affect mobility opportunities.
5. Organizations differ in the extent to which they support career management through such practices as training and development programs, performance appraisal systems, job posting, and career seminars.
6. Organizations differ in the degree to which they provide flexible career paths that enable employees to move in a number of different career directions.
7. Organizations differ in the importance they place on various financial, social, and intrinsic rewards. Some companies, for example, may pay high salaries but offer few opportunities for challenging work.

In short, the culture, outlook, and financial health of an organization affect the nature of specific career opportunities. Business plans and strategies, assumptions about people, and reward systems all have significant consequences for career management. In reality, the exploration of jobs and organizations is naturally intertwined in career decision making. For example, a graduating MBA normally examines alternative jobs and organizations at the same time. A student interviewing for a sales position in company A and one in company B needs to examine the two jobs in detail as well as the characteristics of the two companies. Similarly, a manager considering his or her future in an organization needs to consider alternative jobs within that organization as well as in different organizations.

TECHNIQUES FOR EFFECTIVE WORK EXPLORATION

Essentially, the exploration of the work environment can be broken down into two categories—the external and the internal.[44] Exploration of the external work environment involves the gathering of information on specific occupations, jobs, organizations, and industries. Students just entering the work force and employed adults interested in locating a job with another organization would engage in exploration of the external work environment. A few of the key sources of information would include:

- industry profiles and summaries, such as Standard Industrial Classification (SIC) guides,
- a company's 10K and annual report,
- family, friends, and former co-workers employed in different companies and industries,
- reference materials describing specific jobs and occupations,
- outplacement and career-counseling firms,
- Department of Labor's *Occupational Outlook Handbook,*
- *Dictionary of Occupational Titles.*

In addition to those sources listed above, public libraries in several states have Career Information Centers that were funded by grants from the W. K. Kellogg Foundation. The centers offer extensive client-centered activities that include the provision of occupational information and advisement/counseling. Informational tools used include a materials collection, interactive software packages, and other related services. At some of the centers, there are career counselors working on-site, whereas at others the librarians refer clients to services of professional career counselors. Overall, the centers have been successful in allowing increased awareness of career options and in the provision of information on different occupations and businesses.[45]

External environmental exploration has been helped immensely in recent years by the Internet. Substantial amounts of industry, organizational, and occupational information now resides on the worldwide web. This information can range from listings of open jobs to specific descriptions of various occupations. As one example, the *Occupational Outlook Handbook* as listed above is available on the worldwide web.

Internal work exploration involves the gathering of career-related information within one's own firm. Several organizational career development tools could be used to gather data on jobs and opportunities within one's organization.[46] These

Learning Exercise III is available at the end of this text and on the Internet at **http://www.dryden.com/management/humresources.html.** It provides an opportunity to practice environmental exploration. Although you may examine Exercise III at this time, it is recommended that you finish reading Chapter 3 before you begin the exercise.

include job-posting programs, career ladders/career path planning, career resource centers, and in-house seminars and workshops. Other employees can also provide information on jobs and opportunities within other departments and subsidiaries owned by the company.

Whether the primary focus is on gathering information about occupations, jobs, or organizations, it is essential to understand the needs and feelings of family members. Understanding the family's emotional and financial needs, career aspirations, and desired life-style is necessary if one wants to integrate work and nonwork lives. As Chapter 11 shows, the most significant source of information about the family's needs is the family itself—people need to talk and listen to the important people in their lives.

UNDERSTANDING ONE'S PREFERRED WORK ENVIRONMENT

Once a set of themes is identified and confirmed and related environmental exploration has been conducted, it is necessary to address the significance of the findings for career management. An effective self-assessment should help people become more aware of the kinds of work experiences that will be personally meaningful and interesting, will meet their significant values, and will allow them to use those talents that are important to them. In addition, exploration of the work environment should lead to an understanding of occupations, industries, and geographic regions that hold promise. In short, self-assessment and environmental exploration should enable one to develop a portrait, however tentative, of a preferred work environment.

A statement on a preferred work environment is a summary of what you have learned from the exploration process. Based on the analyses of the themes that emerged from your self-assessment, you should try to identify the type of work environment that seems most compatible with your own qualities. The preferred work environment summary should touch on the following issues:

1. What type of tasks or activities are most interesting to you? For example, do you enjoy analytical activities, mechanical tasks, helping others, or scientific projects?
2. What talents do you wish to use in your work? Interpersonal? Quantitative? Creative? Writing skills?
3. How much freedom and independence do you want in your work?

Learning Exercise IV is available at the end of this text and on the Internet at **http://www.dryden.com/management/humresources.html**. It provides an opportunity to develop a statement on your preferred work environment. Although you may examine Exercise IV at this time, it is recommended that you finish reading Chapter 3 before you begin the exercise.

4. What type of working relationship with other people do you prefer? Do you prefer working alone or with other people? How do you feel about exerting power or influence over other people?

5. What type of physical work setting is desirable (e.g., factory, office, outdoors)?

6. What is the role of money and security in your life?

7. How important is work in your total life, and what relationship do you desire between your work and other parts of your life?

8. What types of occupations and industries best fit your interests, talents, values, and preferred life-style?

OVERCOMING OBSTACLES TO CAREER EXPLORATION: A SET OF GUIDELINES

Despite the logical role of career exploration in the career management process, it should not be assumed that exploration is always effective. That is, it does not always produce an enhanced awareness of self and/or the environment. Following is a list of potential obstacles to effective career exploration and guidelines for overcoming the obstacles.

1. *Incomplete Exploration*. Career exploration sometimes does not provide a sufficient amount of information to be useful. In other cases, a person may participate in little or no exploration, despite a recognized need for information. There are at least three reasons for inadequate exploration: complacency, hopelessness, and fear.

First, people may complacently accept the status quo. If they uncritically accept their course in life, there is no need to collect additional information. One explanation for this complacency is that people do not see the significance of career decisions. They often do not understand that a decision does have consequences in terms of future rewards and enjoyment. Furthermore, some people attach such little importance to the work role that career exploration and career decisions are not going to make much difference in their lives. An uncritical complacency with things as they are or as they might be is unfortunate because decisions have to be made regardless of participation in career exploration. Students still have to choose majors, graduates still have to choose jobs, and even the most indifferent employees have to make decisions about their work lives.

Even if employees are not complacent, they may forego career exploration if they perceive it to be useless. For example, research has found that managers who perceive few mobility opportunities in their organizations participate infrequently in career exploration.[47] In addition, people who believe that they have little control over their lives may engage in inadequate exploration. Unfortunately, this aversion to career exploration creates a vicious cycle in which decisions made by others (by default) reinforce the view that control over one's fate is impossible.

Finally, fear may block an active approach to career exploration. People who fear that their exploration will fail to provide useful information may avoid risking such failure and simply not pursue exploration activities. Those with low self-esteem may fear confronting their own weaknesses and thereby reduce their participation in exploratory activities.

Even among those who initiate career exploration, it may be tempting to bring exploration to a premature halt to gain a sense of security.[48] This may be a false sense of security, however, because exploration may raise issues that take time to understand or resolve. Therefore, one key ingredient to successful career exploration is the ability to tolerate a certain amount of ambiguity and frustration. Sometimes it is important to be persistent in career exploration.

Career planning workshops, as described earlier, can often provide information and support to overcome these forms of resistance to career exploration. Interactions with other more experienced career planners can help participants:

- Realize that many career-related decisions can have a significant effect on the course of their lives; decisions do matter.

- Recognize that they can exert sufficient control over their careers to make career exploration worthwhile.

- Understand that fear of the unknown is natural but should not stifle their attempts to understand themselves and their environment.

2. *Coerced Exploration.* Despite the need to acquire additional information, coercion is not a useful stimulant to successful exploration. Pressure from a superior, relative, or friend may be sufficient to initiate participation in a career exploration program. However, people learn and change when the motivation comes from within and when there is a personal commitment to the learning process.[49] A potential career explorer needs to assess his or her readiness to profit from such an experience.

3. *Random and Diffuse Exploration.* This is exploration that is unfocused and does not build on the results of prior exploration activities. Effective exploration requires skill and practice. Therefore, some instruction in these skills, through classes, workshops, and/or workbooks, would help many people develop a more systematic approach to career exploration. This does not mean that career exploration, or career management in general, requires constant participation in formal programs, but rather that some initial,

structured experience would be helpful in developing the appropriate skills.

4. *Ineffective Forms of Career Exploration.* As this chapter has shown, people committed to career exploration have choices to make about the manner in which they will seek information. Should they see a counselor, speak to family members, attend a career day seminar, seek part-time employment, contact professional organizations, or pursue some of these activities in combination?

There is not sufficient evidence at this point to indicate which of these (or other) exploratory activities are most effective for a particular person in a specific situation. Research does suggest, however, that the most potentially useful exploratory activities are not necessarily the ones that are engaged in the most frequently.[50] It is likely that some people pursue the most easily accessible or the most comfortable exploratory activities and shy away from those that are more difficult to pursue or are more threatening. Although this is a natural, understandable tendency, it may result in a sense of false security.

Perhaps the most critical task is to estimate the likelihood that a particular activity will meet your informational needs. Although there is no easy solution to this problem, it is important not to equate ease with quality. Again, a structured experience can help provide guidance on the most useful, constructive forms of exploration.

5. *Defensive Self—Exploration.* In self-exploration, people need to obtain information from an activity and process it accurately and constructively. Some people are better able to accomplish this task than others.

In particular, highly anxious people may not profit extensively from self-exploration.[51] It has been suggested that such people, when facing career decisions, focus on their own anxious feelings rather than on the information at hand. Therefore, people who are anxious about themselves or their careers may react defensively to threatening self-related information, may ignore, distort, or misinterpret the information, and may generally not use career exploration effectively. In terms of career decision making, highly anxious people may feel compelled to reach a premature or hastily contrived decision or may avoid the decision entirely.[52]

The solution to this problem would seem to involve reducing feelings of anxiety to the point at which they do not interfere with productive exploration. Fortunately, stress management programs have been found to stimulate exploratory behavior. It is also possible that group-oriented career-planning workshops can help people become less anxious in career decision-making situations.

6. *Exclusion of Nonwork Considerations.* Effective career exploration requires attention to all segments of life. The time and emotion spent at work can affect the quality of one's family or personal life. Too many people fail to examine the implications of work-related decisions for other parts of their

lives. Occupations are chosen, jobs are sought, and promotions are accepted without consideration of the consequences. Work, family, community, leisure, and religion all need to be examined and incorporated into career-planning programs. Fortunately, these life-style issues are increasingly being included in structured career-planning programs. The career exploration exercises included in this chapter periodically remind you to consider the impact of work experiences on other significant parts of your life.

SELF- AND ENVIRONMENTAL EXPLORATION: A RECIPROCAL RELATIONSHIP

Career exploration provides an awareness of self and environment that enables a person to set valid, realistic career goals. Although the discussion has separated self-exploration and environmental exploration, in practice they are connected in several respects.

First, a particular exploratory activity may provide useful information about both self and environment. For example, a student who accepts a part-time or summer position as an accounting intern may not only learn about the work life of an accountant but may also test the compatibility of his/her abilities and interests with the field of accounting. A performance-appraisal review with a superior cannot only provide information about one's performance and progress in the organization but can also suggest alternative opportunities for future mobility in the organization. Therefore, individuals need to be sensitive to the full range of information that can be acquired through a particular activity.

Second, there is a reciprocal relationship between self-exploration and environmental exploration; each can and should influence the direction of the other. For example, it is reasonable to engage in a certain amount of self-exploration before extensively exploring the environment. Self-awareness of interests, values, abilities, and life-style preferences can guide one's search for information regarding an occupation, job, or organization. Self-awareness also provides a framework for environmental exploration. Extensive environmental exploration without sufficient understanding of self is likely to be aimless and random.

However, because gaining self-awareness is often a fragmented process, it is impractical to try and complete the task of self-insight before beginning an assessment of the environment. Moreover, environmental exploration may highlight the need to engage in additional self-exploration. For example, a job search might reveal that a job in one organization requires much more extensive travel than a similar job in a different organization. This piece of information might stimulate the person to consider the impact of travel (positive or negative) on his or her desired life-style.

In reality, people need to use self-exploration to direct environmental exploration and vice versa. The more one learns about oneself, the more likely that certain questions about the environment become relevant. In a similar fashion, the more information that is acquired about an occupation, a job, or an organization, the more one has to think about the relevance of that information for one's own values and aspirations.

SUMMARY

Career exploration can be directed toward learning more about oneself and/or learning more about the environment. Self-exploration requires that we collect information about our interests, values, talents, and desired life-style, organize the information into meaningful themes, and identify the implications of these themes in terms of the kind of work environment that is most likely to provide interesting tasks, use our talents, satisfy important values, and provide a desired life-style.

Environmental exploration can help us learn more about different occupations, jobs, and organizations as well as our family's needs and desires. The two forms of exploration, self and environmental, can reinforce each other by suggesting different areas in which we need to collect additional information. Learning exercises were included to provide the opportunity to practice career exploration.

Several obstacles to effective career exploration were discussed: incomplete exploration, coerced exploration, random and diffuse exploration, ineffective forms of exploration, excessive defensiveness, and exclusion of nonwork considerations. Suggestions were made for overcoming each obstacle.

ASSIGNMENT

Take a few moments and reflect on the things you like to do, the things you believe are important, your preferences, your competencies, and your weaknesses. On a separate sheet of paper, prepare a list of what you see as your interests, values, talents, and weaknesses. You can use the information provided in Table 3.1 to help guide you in the preparation of the list. Ask a friend, family member, or colleague to review your list and give you feedback on whether they see it as an accurate reflection of you. Ask them to explain any differences they see. How do you think the list you prepared and the feedback you received could help you in your career management process?

DISCUSSION QUESTIONS

1. What are the differences among values, interests, personality, and talents? How does understanding these factors help us manage our careers effectively?

2. How important is work in your total life? What makes you feel that way? Has the importance of work in your life changed in recent years? Do you think it will remain the same in the future? In what ways could your desire for a specific type of life-style affect your career decisions?

3. Is career exploration worth the effort? Because the world can change so rapidly, is the information collected through career exploration going to be irrelevant and/or outdated?

4. Reexamine the six obstacles to effective career exploration. Which of them have you experienced in the past? How can you overcome these obstacles in the future?

Now that you have finished reading Chapter 3, it is time to complete Learning Exercises I, II, III, and IV that are included at the end of this text and on the Internet at **http://www.dryden.com/management/humresources.html**. Be thoughtful and patient in the completion of these exercises. You will refer to them as you complete later chapters in this book.

ENDNOTES

1. D. E. Super and M. J. Bohn, Jr., *Occupational Psychology* (Belmont, CA: Wadsworth, 1970); N. E. Betz, L. F. Fitzgerald, and R. E. Hill, "Trait-Factor Theory: Traditional Cornerstone of Career Theory," in *Handbook of Career Theory*, ed. M. B. Arthur, D. T. Hall, and B. S. Lawrence (Cambridge, UK: Cambridge University Press, 1989), 26–40.

2. G. W. Allport, P. E. Vernon, and G. Lindzey, *Study of Values: A Scale for Measuring Dominant Interests in Personality* (Boston, MA: Houghton Mifflin, 1960).

3. D. E. Super, *Work Values Inventory* (New York: Houghton Mifflin, 1970).

4. Ibid.; Allport, Vernon, and Lindzey, *Study of Values*; M. Rokeach, *Nature of Human Values* (Palo Alto, CA: Consulting Psychologists Press, 1973).

5. M. Downes and K. G. Kroeck, "Discrepancies between Existing Jobs and Individual Interests: An Empirical Application of Holland's Model," *Journal of Vocational Behavior* 48 (1996): 107–117.

6. Betz, Fitzgerald, and Hill, "Trait-Factor Theory"; D. Oleski and L. M. Subich, "Congruence and Career Change in Employed Adults," *Journal of Vocational Behavior* 49 (1996): 221–229.

7. J. L. Holland, *Making Vocational Choices: A Theory of Vocational Personalities and Work Environments* (Englewood Cliffs, NJ: Prentice-Hall, 1985).

8. S. Strack, "Relating Millon's Basic Personality Styles and Holland's Occupational Types," *Journal of Vocational Behavior* 45 (1995): 41–54; D. M. Tokar and J. L. Swanson, "Evaluation of the Correspondence between Holland's Vocational Personality Typology and the Five-Factor Model of Personality," *Journal of Vocational Behavior* 46 (1995): 89–108.

9. E. K. Strong, *Vocational Interests of Men and Women* (Stanford, CA: Stanford University Press, 1943).

10. J. C. Hansen and D. P. Campbell, *The Strong Manual* (Palo Alto, CA: Consulting Psychologists Press, 1985).

11. S. K. Hirsch and T. Vessey, *Introduction to the Strong in Organizational Settings* (Palo Alto, CA: Consulting Psychologists Press, 1987); F. Borgen and J. Grutter, *Where Do I Go Next? Using Your Strong Results to Manage Your Career* (Palo Alto, CA: Consulting Psychologists Press, 1995).

12. M. R. Schmit and A. M. Ryan, "The Big Five in Personnel Selection: Factor Structure in Applicant and Non-Applicant Populations," *Journal of Applied Psychology* 78 (1993): 966–974.

13. G. J. Randahl, "A Typological Analysis of the Relations between Measured Vocational Interests and Abilities," *Journal of Vocational Behavior* 38 (1991): 333–350; J. L. Swanson, "Integrated Assessment of Vocational Interests and Self-Rated Skills and Abilities," *Journal of Career Assessment* 1 (1993): 50–65.

14. E. H. Schein, *Career Anchors: Discovering Your Real Values* (San Diego, CA: University Associates, 1985).

15. F. Bartolome and P. Evans, "Professional Lives versus Private Lives: Shifting Patterns of Man-

agerial Commitment," *Organizational Dynamics* 7 (1979): 3–29; D. J. Levinson, C. N. Darrow, E. B. Klein, M. H. Levinson, and B. McKee, *Seasons of a Man's Life* (New York: Knopf, 1978); D. E. Super, "Life Career Roles: Self-Realization in Work and Leisure," in *Career Development in Organizations*, ed. D. T. Hall et al., (San Francisco, CA: Jossey-Bass, 1986), 95–119.

16. J. G. Clawson, J. P. Kotter, V. A. Faux, and C. C. McArthur, *Self-Assessment and Career Development*, 3rd ed. (Englewood Cliffs, NJ: Prentice-Hall, 1992).

17. J. L. Holland, *Manual for the Vocational Preference Inventory* (Odessa, FL: Psychological Assessment Resources, 1985); J. L. Holland, *Self-Directed Search* (Odessa, FL: Psychological Assessment Resources, 1985); J. L. Holland, *Supplement Manual for the Self-Directed Search* (Odessa, FL: Psychological Assessment Resources, 1987).

18. J. L. Vevea, N. C. Clements, and L. V. Hedges, "Assessing the Effects of Selection Bias on Validity Data for the General Aptitude Test Battery," *Journal of Applied Psychology* 78 (1993): 981–987.

19. D. G. Zytowski and F. H. Borgen, "Assessment," in *Handbook of Vocational Psychology*, vol. 2, ed. W. B. Walsh and S. H. Osipow (Hillsdale, NJ: Lawrence Erlbaum Associates, 1983), 5–40.

20. S. K. Hirsch and J. M. Kummerow, *Introduction to Type in Organizations* (Palo Alto, CA: Consulting Psychologists Press, 1990).

21. J. E. Kummerow, "Using the Strong Interest Inventory and the Myers-Briggs Type Indicator Together in Career Counseling," in *New Directions in Career Planning and the Workplace*, ed. J. E. Kummerow (Palo Alto, CA: Consulting Psychologists Press, 1991), 61–93.

22. *The 16 PF Manual*, 5th ed. (Champaign, IL: Institute for Personality and Ability Testing, 1993).

23. *Life Styles Inventory-Level I, Self-Development Guide* (Plymouth, MI: Human Synergistics, 1989).

24. Rokeach, *Nature of Human Values*.

25. Betz, Fitzgerald, and Hill, "Trait-Factor Theory."

26. J. A. Waterman, "Career and Life Planning: A Personal Gyroscope in Times of Change," in *New Directions in Career Planning and the Workplace*, ed. J. M. Kummerow (Palo Alto, CA: Consulting Psychologists Press, 1991), 1–32.

27. K. M. Taylor, "Advances in Career-Planning Systems," in *Career Decision Making*, ed. W. B. Walsh and S. H. Osipow (Hillsdale, NJ: Lawrence Erlbaum Associates, 1988), 137–211.

28. Ibid.

29. Ibid.

30. Ibid.

31. F. J. Minor, "Computer Applications in Career Development Planning," in *Career Development in Organizations*, ed. Hall et al. , 202–235.

32. L. E. Isaacson and D. Brown, *Career Information, Career Counseling, and Career Development* (Needham Heights, MA: Allyn & Bacon, 1997).

33. T. G. Gutteridge, "Organizational Career Development Systems: The State of the Practice," in *Career Development in Organizations*, ed. Hall et al. , 50–94; J. E. Russell, "Career Development Interventions in Organizations," *Journal of Vocational Behavior* 38 (1991): 237–287.

34. Gutteridge, "Organizational Career Development Systems."

35. G. C. Thornton, *Assessment Centers in Human Resource Management* (Reading, MA: Addison-Wesley, 1992).

36. Hirsch and Kummerow, *Introduction to Type in Organizations*; Hirsch and Vessey, *Introduction to the Strong in Organizational Settings*.

37. T. Moore, "Personality Tests Are Back," *Fortune,* March 30, 1987, pp. 74–82.

38. Clawson et al., *Self Assessment and Career Development.*

39. R. N. Bolles, *What Color Is Your Parachute?* (Berkeley, CA: Ten Speed Press, 1996).

40. D. T. Jaffe and C. D. Scott, "Career Development for Empowerment in a Changing Work World," in *New Directions in Career Planning and the Workplace,* ed. J. M. Kummerow (Palo Alto, CA: Consulting Psychologists Press, 1991), 33–59.

41. Clawson et al., *Self-Assessment and Career Development.*

42. R. D. Bretz and T. A. Judge, "Person-Organization Fit and the Theory of Work Adjustment: Implications for Satisfaction, Tenure, and Career Success," *Journal of Vocational Behavior* 44 (1994): 32–54.

43. S. L. Wilk, L. B. Desmaris, and P. R. Sackett, "Gravitation to Jobs Commensurate with Ability: Longitudinal and Cross-Sectional Tests," *Journal of Applied Psychology* 80 (1995): 79–85.

44. G. A. Callanan and J. H. Greenhaus, "The Career Indecision of Managers and Professionals: Development of a Scale and Test of a Model," *Journal of Vocational Behavior* 37 (1990): 79–103.

45. J. C. Durrance, "Kellogg Funded Education and Career Information Centers in Public Libraries," *Journal of Career Development* 18 (1991): 11–18; K. E. Tice and S. J. Gill, "Education Information Centers: An Evaluation," *Journal of Career Development* 18 (1991): 37–50.

46. Gutteridge, "Organizational Career Development Systems."

47. T. Sugalski and J. H. Greenhaus, "Career Exploration and Goal Setting among Managerial Employees," *Journal of Vocational Behavior* 29 (1986): 102–114.

48. G. A. Callanan and J. H. Greenhaus, "The Career Indecision of Managers and Professionals: An Examination of Multiple Subtypes," *Journal of Vocational Behavior* 41 (1992): 212–231.

49. A. H. Souerwine, *Career Strategies: Planning for Personal Achievement* (New York: AMACOM, 1978).

50. J. H. Greenhaus, B. L. Hawkins, and O. C. Brenner, "The Impact of Career Exploration on the Career Decision-Making Process," *Journal of College Student Personnel* 24 (1983): 495–502.

51. J. H. Greenhaus and N. D. Sklarew, "Some Sources and Consequences of Career Exploration," *Journal of Vocational Behavior* 18 (1981): 1–12.

52. Callanan and Greenhaus, "The Career Indecision of Managers and Professionals" (1992).

APPLICATIONS OF THE
CAREER MANAGEMENT MODEL:
GOALS, STRATEGIES, AND APPRAISAL

Chapter 4 focuses on career goal setting, career strategy development, and career appraisal. As in the previous chapter, we stress the pragmatic application of the career management model. Additional learning exercises are provided at the end of this text as well as on the Internet at **http://www.dryden.com/management/humresources.html** to help the reader develop and practice key career management skills. We also offer guidelines for effective goal setting, strategy development, and career appraisal.

CAREER GOAL SETTING

We all know or have heard stories of individuals who declared that they were going to be a millionaire by the time they were 30. Or perhaps we know someone who expressed a strong desire to become a CEO, or a top trial lawyer, or a surgeon. Most children begin projecting careers for themselves at young ages—"I'm going to be a police officer" or "I'm going to be a ballet star." Even older individuals on the verge of retirement will often set plans to open their own business or perhaps get involved with some type of volunteer work.

The common theme in these examples is the setting, however tentative or ill defined, of career goals. A goal has been defined as the object or aim of one's actions.[1] The usefulness of goal setting is based on the belief that goals regulate human action. Goals can affect behavior and performance in a number of ways. First, they can spur high levels of effort. Second, they can give focus or direction to effort because a specific goal provides a particular target toward which to strive. Third, goals may produce high levels of persistence on a task. Fourth, a specific goal can help one develop a useful strategy for accomplishing the task. Finally, because of their concrete nature, goals provide opportunities for feedback on task performance. **We define a career goal as a desired career-related outcome that a person intends to attain.**

Even with the acknowledged positive attributes, one can question, especially in this era of downsizings and economic uncertainty, whether career goal setting is still a relevant exercise. Some researchers have argued that with the current environment, goal setting is futile at best and harmful at worst. Under this view, the work world is seen as so uncertain that setting any kind of goal is useless, with the person setting the goal subject to bitterness and disappointment. Further, it has been stated that career goals promote rigidity in terms of actions and strategies, when what is really needed is flexibility in being able to pursue other options or career directions.

In our view, career goal setting is, in most cases, a useful and productive process. As we noted, goals provide direction, and they serve as a benchmark against which progress can be measured. In addition, the presence of a career goal, in and of itself, should not cause inflexibility in the management of one's career. The career goal is simply a descriptive target toward which one aims; it does not specify how one gets to the desired end state. Further, goals can, and should, change as conditions dictate.

Although recognizing the beneficial aspects of career goals, there are times when the setting of goals can be counterproductive. Later in this chapter we discuss how **not** setting career goals is an appropriate response when one does not have sufficient knowledge to make an informed decision.

With the preceding introduction as background, this section examines several components of career goals, discusses the career goal-setting process, and provides a set of guidelines for effective goal setting.

COMPONENTS OF CAREER GOALS

A career goal can be viewed in three different ways: by its conceptual and operational components, by its expressive and instrumental functions, and by its time dimension.

CONCEPTUAL GOAL VERSUS OPERATIONAL GOAL. A conceptual career goal summarizes the nature of the work experiences one intends to attain without specifying a particular job or position. It should reflect the person's significant values, interests, talents, and life-style preferences. For example, an individual's conceptual goal may be to hold a marketing job that involves extensive research and analysis, offers a great deal of responsibility, is broad and varied in pace, requires interaction with a variety of clients, does not chronically interfere with family responsibilities, and is situated in a small, growth-oriented company in a warm weather climate. This conceptual goal addresses the nature of the task, interpersonal and physical settings, and total life-style concerns.

However, an operational career goal is the translation of a conceptual goal into a specific job or position. In the example described above, the operational goal may be to attain the position of marketing research manager at company X. For another individual, it may be to remain in his or her current position for the foreseeable future. It is important to realize that an operational goal is simply a vehicle for meeting an underlying conceptual goal. It is helpful for career goals to be stated in both conceptual and operational terms.

EXPRESSIVE VERSUS INSTRUMENTAL FUNCTIONS OF A CAREER GOAL. The expressive function of a career goal refers to the intrinsic enjoyment derived from goal-related experiences. Goals are expressively appropriate to the extent to

· **TABLE 4-1**

**SHORT-TERM AND LONG-TERM GOALS FOR
AN ASSISTANT MANAGER OF HUMAN RESOURCES**

	Short-Term Goal	Long-Term Goal
Conceptual	More responsibility for administering human resources operation Broad exposure to all facets of human resources More interaction with line management	Involvement in human resource planning activities Involvement in corporate long-range planning Involvement in policy development and implementation
Operational	Manager of Human Resources within 2–3 years	Director of Corporate Human Resources within 6–8 years

which their accomplishment permits a person to engage in enjoyable, fulfilling, and satisfying work activities, use his or her valued talents at work, and experience a satisfying life-style.

However, a career goal can also have an instrumental function. This instrumental element means that an accomplished goal can lead to (or is instrumental in) the attainment of a subsequent goal. For example, attaining the goal of marketing manager may enable a person to achieve his or her next goal of vice president of marketing. Again, the usefulness of a career goal depends on both its expressive and instrumental qualities.

SHORT-TERM VERSUS LONG-TERM CAREER GOAL. Career goals have a time dimension. We will adopt the convention of distinguishing short-term and long-term goals. Of course, what is considered short versus long is rather arbitrary and is likely to vary. Here, a long-term goal is generally considered to have a time frame of 5 to 7 years; a short-term goal is one that has a more immediate focus, perhaps 1 to 3 years. Table 4.1 illustrates hypothetical short-term and long-term goals for an assistant manager of human resources.

DEVELOPMENT OF LONG-TERM AND SHORT-TERM CONCEPTUAL GOALS

Ideally, the first step in setting a career goal is to identify a long-term conceptual goal. As an outgrowth of the self-exploration and assessment process, the long-term conceptual goal takes into account one's needs, values, interests, talents, and expectations. It should, therefore, touch on job duties, degree of autonomy, type and frequency of interaction with other people, the physical environment, and life-style concerns. A long-term conceptual goal is, in effect, a projection of one's preferred work environment into a specific 5- to 7-year time frame. Ask yourself what type of job duties, activities, rewards, and responsibilities you would like to experience in the long-term future.

Next, consider a short-term conceptual goal. In an instrumental sense, the short-term conceptual goal needs to support the long-term one. To derive a short-term goal from a long-term goal, one should ask the following kinds of questions: What type of work experiences will prepare you to attain the long-term goal? What talents need to be developed or refined? What type of visibility is useful to reach a subsequent goal? These questions raise strategic issues. That is, the decision to pursue a particular short-term goal for its instrumental value is an illustration of a career strategy.

But a short-term goal should have an expressive quality as well. Quite apart from its value as a stopping point, it must be viewed in terms of its capacity to provide important personal rewards, interesting and meaningful tasks, and the possibility of a desired life-style. As with the long-term goal, a short-term objective should be consistent with the significant elements of one's preferred work environment.

DEVELOPMENT OF LONG-TERM AND SHORT-TERM OPERATIONAL GOALS

An operational goal is the translation of a conceptual goal into a specific job or position. Environmental exploration is required to convert conceptual goals into operational ones: What specific occupation (or job or organization) will provide an opportunity to meet your significant values, interests, talents, and life-style requirements (i.e., your conceptual goal)?

There is no automatic formula that can (or should) dictate the selection of an operational goal. Your judgment (with input from trusted others) about the desirability and realism of each operational goal should be your guide. You should, however, attempt to estimate the likelihood that a particular operational goal will enable you to satisfy the significant elements of your conceptual goal. By examining these estimates for one or more operational goals, you can begin to assess the appropriateness of each operational goal.

The conversion of a goal from conceptual to operational terms clearly cannot be conducted in a vacuum. Instead, extensive information is required to assess the activities and rewards associated with each operational goal. This information cannot simply come from introspection. The individual needs data, much of which can be provided by the employer or potential employer. The role of the employer in providing such assistance is treated in subsequent chapters. Through the career appraisal process (discussed later in this chapter), the accomplishment or nonaccomplishment of a goal can serve as an additional piece of career-related information.

ARE LONG-TERM CAREER GOALS NECESSARY?

The goal-setting process assumes it is possible to develop long-term conceptual and operational goals. However, it is not always feasible to project 5 to 7 years in the future with any sense of accuracy or confidence. In such cases, the person should attempt to formulate at least a partial conceptual goal, even if it is

Learning Exercise V is available at the end of this text and on the Internet at **http://www.dryden.com/manage-ment/humresources.html.** It provides an opportunity to practice developing career goals. Although you may examine Exercise V at this time, it is recommended that you finish reading Chapter 4 before beginning the exercise.

somewhat vague and even if it cannot be associated with a specific operational goal at the present time.

For example, Jose, who is 28 years old, hopes to work in an environment in which he can help others, work with clients as individuals and groups, and develop educational programs for the community, all in a setting in which weekend and evening work could be kept to a minimum. This constitutes his long-term conceptual goal.

Extensive environmental exploration indicates that a position in social work will likely enable Jose to achieve his conceptual goal. This long-term operational goal (to become a social worker) is admittedly vague, but the vagueness is appropriate at the present time. What type of social work position is most suitable for him? Should he work with children, adults, or a wide range of age groups? Should he work in a hospital, a school, a mental health clinic, or industry? At this time, these factors are unknowns.

As vague as his long-term goal is, it can enable Jose to develop an appropriate short-term conceptual goal: to acquire the relevant education, experiences, and credentials to become a qualified social worker. His short-term operational goal is equally relevant: to obtain a master's degree in social work within 2 to 3 years.

Jose's experiences illustrate that one does not always have to develop a highly specific and elaborate long-term goal to develop a sensible short-term goal. It is important to think through the long-term future, develop a sense (however tentative) of what combination of work and life-style seems appropriate, and develop a short-term goal that is most consistent with this future, however hazy.

One can think of many situations in which a long-term goal is vague or uncertain. A mechanical engineer does not know whether she would like to remain in an engineering position or move into general management within 5 years. An accountant does not know whether he should remain at the firm in which he currently works or start his own small CPA practice. An upper-level manager is still uncertain whether the rewards of being a company president outweigh the costs. The engineer, the accountant, and the manager may not have formulated clear, certain long-term goals at this point, but they will be better able to identify short-term goals and appropriate strategies if they examine the long-term future and alternative options than if they have not given any serious thought to such issues.

OVERCOMING OBSTACLES TO GOAL SETTING: A SET OF GUIDELINES

Like career exploration, the goal-setting process is not without obstacles. Ultimately, the quality of a career goal depends on whether the achievement of the goal is compatible with the individual's preferred work environment and whether the goal can be realistically achieved. Listed below are a number of obstacles to effective goal setting and suggestions for overcoming them.

GOALS THAT BELONG TO SOMEONE ELSE. The achievement of a career goal is meaningless if the goal does not meet your needs and values, if the tasks are not interesting to you, and if the talents needed to be successful are not possessed and valued by you. It is your work, your career, and your life.

Yet some people seem to base career decisions on pleasing someone else—a parent, a professor, a spouse, or a boss. They place little value on meeting their own needs and rely on others to decide what is appropriate for them. In what is probably an unconscious process, such people, in effect, say, "I'm not important, I don't know what's best for me," or "I don't really deserve to get my own needs met." Ultimately, such people may choose occupations or jobs that do not take advantage of their own abilities and that are not personally interesting or rewarding. In the long run, such goals, even if accomplished, will produce frustration and alienation rather than fulfillment and growth.

The solution to this problem is twofold. First, people must be in touch with their own values, interests, talents, and life-style preferences. Second, they must recognize the importance of meeting goals that are compatible with these qualities. Regarding the first point, virtually all self-assessment procedures provide opportunities for awareness of personal characteristics. Autobiographical statements, value clarification exercises, and analyses of life experiences hopefully enable the individual to separate personal abilities and desires from others' wishes and values and from society's expectations.

The more difficult task is acting constructively on this awareness. Career-planning programs can only go so far. Perhaps the ultimate answer is feeling good enough about yourself to pursue goals that are relevant to your own personal aspirations and values. Discussions with family, friends, and colleagues about the importance of meeting personal needs would be a significant first step.

GOALS THAT EXCLUDE TOTAL LIFE-STYLE CONCERNS. Many people pursue a career goal without regard for its impact on other parts of their lives. It is only after marital difficulties or a personal tragedy that some people recognize the relationship between work life and private life. Many people in midcareer become particularly aware of the trade-offs between work responsibilities and family or leisure activities. Nevertheless, work and nonwork roles interact at all phases of a person's life.

The effective career manager anticipates the interrelationships between work and nonwork and sets career goals consistent with a desired total life-style. As noted earlier, many career planning programs include considerations of life-style. But it is still easy to focus so narrowly on job challenges, rewards, and prestige that family, religious, leisure, and community roles are virtually ignored. It takes a conscious effort to retain a total life-style perspective in career goal setting.

GOALS THAT FAIL TO TAKE INTO ACCOUNT ONE'S CURRENT JOB. A career goal (either short-term or long-term) need not involve job mobility. Any particular job is merely a vehicle for the satisfaction of more basic values (i.e., the conceptual goal). If goals are first stated in conceptual terms, then the current job's capacity to meet these values can be thoroughly examined. Often, successful career management is based on understanding the conceptual goal and the ability to use the current job to achieve that goal.

On too many occasions, however, individuals focus so narrowly on pursuing other jobs that they ignore their current job as a source of career growth and satisfaction. This myopic preoccupation with mobility could be a serious problem in today's work environment, in which promotions or lateral moves are in short supply or in which such moves, if attained, have serious negative consequences for family or leisure activities (e.g., when another job requires relocation or extensive travel). A number of approaches to career planning include an examination of the ways in which one's current job can be improved, perhaps through increased responsibility or a greater variety of projects. This requires a constructive interaction between the career planner and his or her supervisor. This is a healthy focus that can be usefully incorporated into many career management activities.

GOALS THAT ARE OVERLY VAGUE.   It is well understood that specific goals are generally more useful than vague goals. Because they present a particular target toward which to strive, specific goals can direct one's efforts more efficiently than vague goals. In addition, a specific goal offers a greater opportunity for feedback because progress toward the goal is easier to detect.

Consider the vague conceptual goal "to do things that are interesting to me." It would probably be more useful to specify what kinds of activities are considered personally interesting (e.g., working with detailed statistics, writing reports, or meeting frequently with colleagues and clients). A set of specific conceptual goal elements can be more easily translated into an operational goal than a vaguely stated conceptual goal. Moreover, stating a conceptual goal in specific terms forces a person away from generalizations and toward a deeper understanding of his or her aspirations.

There are also advantages to setting a specific operational goal. It is difficult to compare a vague operational goal with one's conceptual goal. To "move into marketing" is probably too vague to be helpful because different marketing jobs may match one's conceptual goal to varying degrees. An operational goal "to become a market research analyst" is more specific and more useful because its connection to the underlying conceptual goal is more explicit and the path to the goal is more easily determined. As noted earlier, however, it may not be possible or desirable to develop a highly specific long-term goal in many circumstances. Perhaps the litmus test to determine whether a goal is specific enough is to examine whether it provides enough information to guide your behavior in a useful way.

PREOCCUPATION WITH INSTRUMENTAL GOAL ELEMENTS.   Despite its many advantages, a specific goal can create tunnel vision. In the quest to accomplish a specific goal, people may forget why they wanted to reach the goal in the first place. They may also become so committed to a course of action that they resist new information that runs counter to the value of the goal. Perhaps most important, striving for a sequence of goals, each of which is designed to accomplish a subsequent goal, can rob people of the enjoyment of the here-and-now. In effect, people can be driven and tyrannized by the desire to reach some end state. Preoccupation with the destination, in other words, can make the voyage joyless.

This possibility presents a dilemma. On the one hand, the presence of a career goal may enhance future career growth and satisfaction. However, a specific goal can, in some circumstances, detract from the intrinsic satisfaction of the present. Perhaps the solution is to maintain a balanced concern for the expressive and instrumental qualities of a goal—a concern for the present and the future.

Consider the case of an engineering school graduate who, early in his career, set his sights on the presidency of a large manufacturing organization. Every job assignment, every promotion, every transfer was chosen for its instrumental value. His commitment to this goal was so strong, he could not allow himself the luxury of reexamining its importance. Nor could he stop and ask whether all the intermediate goals and accomplishments were enjoyable, satisfying, and fulfilling and whether they played havoc with the rest of his life. Mortgaging the present for the future is a risky business.

A healthy concern for the expressive, intrinsic quality of a goal is therefore an essential part of career management. This requires an ongoing focus on conceptual goals. There is nothing inherently satisfying about a company presidency or any other operational goal. The tasks, activities, opportunities, and rewards associated with an operational goal, however, can be intrinsically satisfying. A simultaneous concern for present satisfaction and future direction is critical. This can only come from an ongoing assessment of oneself and the environment.

GOALS THAT ARE TOO EASY OR TOO DIFFICULT. It has been argued that feelings of psychological success are essential for individual development and satisfaction.[2] Feelings of psychological success are experienced by accomplishing tasks that are challenging and meaningful. Therefore, career goals that are too easy are unlikely to provide a real sense of accomplishment and success. Whether a goal is directed toward one's current job (e.g., to improve in certain areas) or attaining a different job, it must be challenging enough so that the achievement of the goal produces feelings of real success.

Goals that are too difficult, on the other hand, are unlikely to be accomplished. The inability to reach a desired goal can bring a deep sense of frustration and failure. There is a fine line between a goal that is challenging and one that is virtually impossible. Detecting the fine line requires insight into one's own talents, the ability to develop new talents, and an accurate perception of opportunities and obstacles in the work environment. Therefore, if one selects an extremely difficult goal, he or she should understand the risks involved and be willing to assume those risks.

INFLEXIBLE CAREER GOALS. Although goal setting is intended to be a flexible process, flexibility is often lost in practice. For one thing, people can become highly committed to a course of action to which they have devoted significant time and energy.[3] Second, the analytical, rational orientation toward the future built into the goal-setting process tends to emphasize the end goal and render it an objective reality that is difficult to question.[4] Moreover, because change is a difficult process for most people, a thorough reexamination of career goals and a possible change in career direction are particularly threatening.

Yet as we have stressed previously, flexible goals are essential to effective career management. Because the work milieu and people inevitably change over time, goals that have been appropriate in the past may no longer be valid at present or in the future. In today's turbulent economic world, the setting of a concrete long-term career goal is probably not advisable. Indeed, because of employment uncertainty in nearly all companies, individuals may find flexibility in the setting and changing of career goals to be a more appropriate action. For example, jobs and career paths may disappear or change as organizations restructure or develop new strategic plans, thereby leaving inflexible employees out in the cold. Similarly, technological and structural changes can give birth to new career routes that may require revisions in an individual's career goals. In the broadest sense, people need to learn from their work and life experiences so that career goals can remain relevant and realistic. Career appraisal, discussed in a later section of this chapter, is the process by which learning and feedback provide flexibility to career management.

INABILITY TO SET CAREER GOALS: CAREER INDECISION

Although we have suggested that career goal setting is a critical part of the career management process, for many people, both students and working adults, the selection of a career goal is a difficult (or even impossible) task. **Individuals are considered career undecided if they have either not established a career goal or if they have set a career goal over which they experience significant uncertainty or discomfort.**[5] Because the selection of a career goal is viewed as a paramount task in the career management process, one would presume that the presence of career indecision would be both unsettling and detrimental to career success. As this section shows, however, career indecision should not be viewed as necessarily inappropriate, just as career decidedness (i.e., the selection of a career goal) should not be viewed as necessarily appropriate.

Given the importance of understanding career indecision, this section discusses three related topics: the underlying causes and sources of career indecision, the existence of different types of career indecision, and the possible actions that could be taken to allow individuals to become career decided.

CAUSES AND SOURCES OF CAREER INDECISION. Prior research on the career indecision of high school and college students found a variety of underlying reasons why individuals could not select a specific occupation or career goal. In general, this research identified four sources of career indecision: lack of information about oneself, lack of information about the work environment, lack of self-confidence in decision making, and the presence of psychological conflicts.

Our research, which studied a large sample of working adults, identified seven sources of indecision that were somewhat more refined than those listed above:[6]

1. **Lack of Self-Information** reflects the individual's insufficient understanding of his or her interests, strengths, values, and life-style preferences.
2. **Lack of Internal Work Information** reflects insufficient knowledge of career opportunities and job possibilities within one's own organization.
3. **Lack of External Work Information** reflects insufficient knowledge of opportunities outside of one's organization, including other occupations, companies, and industries.
4. **Lack of Decision-Making Self-Confidence** reflects insufficient self-assurance in making career-related decisions.
5. **Decision-Making Fear and Anxiety** reflects decisional paralysis resulting from fear and anxiety over making a career decision.
6. **Nonwork Demands** reflect individual conflicts between personal career desires and nonwork (e.g., family) pressures.
7. **Situational Constraints** reflect individual career constraints produced by financial strain, age, and years invested in a given career direction.

In general, the first three sources—lack of self-information and the lack of information on the internal and external work environments—reinforce the discussion in Chapter 3, which stated that an awareness of self and the work environment is an essential requirement in career decision making. In contrast to the information-related sources that could be resolved with increased exploration activities, the lack of self-confidence and decision-making fear and anxiety may reflect more deep-seated personality dispositions and psychological conditions. Finally, nonwork demands and situational constraints could place limitations on personal career choices and desires and may either impair the setting of a career goal or cause substantial uncertainty/discomfort over a selected goal. Exhibit 4.1 contains a series of items, adapted from a more extensive instrument we developed, that can help you assess where you stand on the seven career indecision sources.[7]

TYPES OF CAREER INDECISION. Past research on the career decision making of students indicated two forms of career indecision. "Being undecided" was viewed as stemming from limited experience and knowledge, whereas "being indecisive" was seen as reflecting a more permanent inability to make a career decision.[8] The "being undecided" type was later termed developmental indecision, whereas the "being indecisive" type was termed chronic indecision. In our study of managers and professionals, we also found support for the existence of developmental and chronic indecision.[9] Developmentally undecided employees were younger, had limited knowledge about the internal and external work environments, and experienced extensive nonwork demands. The chronically undecided group was comparatively older than their developmentally undecided

■ EXHIBIT 4-1

SELECTED ITEMS FOR THE SEVEN SOURCES OF CAREER INDECISION

Source of Career Indecision[a]	Illustrative Item[b]
Lack of Self-Information	"I know exactly what I want most from a job (e.g., a lot of money, a great deal of responsibility, travel)."[c]
Lack of Internal Work Information	"I have a good understanding of where my organization is heading in the next 5 to 10 years."[c]
Lack of External Work Information	"I have a good grasp of what career opportunities might exist for me with a different employer."[c]
Lack of Self-Confidence	"I am confident that I can make career decisions that are right for me."[c]
Decision-Making Fear and Anxiety	"The idea of making a career-related decision frightens me."
Nonwork Demands	"Family pressures conflict with the direction that I would like my career to follow."
Situational Constraints	"The number of years I have invested in my current career prevents me from considering other careers that hold more appeal."

[a] Sources identified in G.A. Callaman, and J.H. Greenhaus, "The Career Indecision of Managers and Professionals: Development of a Scale and Test of a Model," *Journal of Vocational Behavior* 37 (1990): 79–103.
[b] Items scored on a scale of 1 (Strongly Disagree) to 5 (Strongly Agree).
[c] Item is reverse scored.

counterparts. In addition, they lacked sufficient self-information, had lower self-confidence, displayed more extensive decision-making fear and anxiety, and experienced extensive situational constraints.

Our research also isolated two other types in which managers had selected a career goal.[10] Borrowing from the typology developed by Irving Janis and Leon Mann,[11] we were able to isolate a hypervigilant type and a vigilant type of career decidedness. The hypervigilant group had selected a career goal, but their profiles indicated that the decision may have been made with insufficient information and/or was hastily contrived due to pressure and anxiety. The vigilant group had likewise selected a career goal, but their profile showed that the decision was made in a well-informed manner with low levels of stress and anxiety.

Brief examples might help clarify the differences among the four types:

■ Annie is a 35-year-old internal audit manager for a consumer products company located in New York. After nearly 12 years with the firm, she is dissatisfied with her present responsibilities and believes her chances for further advancement within the organization are limited. Moreover, the "rat race" of the big city has started to wear on her and her family. Consequently, Annie is not really sure what she wants to do with her career. Annie has taken the Myers-Briggs Type Indicator and other assessment instruments that show she has an entrepreneurial personality. In fact, managing her own business has quite an appeal for Annie. She has also begun to look at a couple of interesting business ventures back in her native Mississippi.

- Jay is a 27-year-old sales representative for a paper products company. He has held four different jobs in the 6 years since he graduated from college with a degree in business administration. Jay cannot seem to set goals for himself, and he still is not sure about what type of career he should pursue. Making decisions has always been difficult for Jay because he becomes anxious and "tenses up" whenever the need to make a commitment arises. Right now, Jay is unsure on how to go about selecting a longer-term career goal, but he is certain that his current sales position is not for him.

- Jennifer is 26 and has just completed law school. Her whole family is excited about her future career as a lawyer. Her father, who is an attorney himself, is especially pleased that his daughter has decided to follow in his footsteps. Unfortunately, amid the euphoria and hoopla over her graduation, Jennifer is beginning to think that she may have been prematurely "pushed" into selecting the legal profession as a career. Jennifer's parents put undue pressure on her to enter law school. They were visibly upset when her two older brothers decided not to pursue legal careers, and Jennifer did not wish to disappoint her parents again. Because of her quick selection of law as her vocation, Jennifer never really explored her own interests and values and did not look at other possible occupations. At present, her life is full of stress because she is concerned about her future happiness as a lawyer.

- At age 48, Dan is as happy as he has ever been. As a high school math teacher, Dan enjoys the chance to work with young people, and he really does like teaching such subjects as algebra and geometry. Although Dan has only been teaching for 4 years, he is pleased that he made the "tough" decision to get out of his former career as a systems analyst. Dan is certain that his satisfaction with teaching is a function of the painstaking and thorough job he did of selecting it as his career goal. Dan took the time to reexamine his interests and values. He knew he loved to work with numbers and apply logical thinking, but he also liked working with young people. With some exploration, he learned that the local school district had a shortage of qualified math teachers. After discussing his thoughts with his wife and receiving her encouragement, Dan decided to try to become a teacher. Once he received his teaching certificate, Dan was set. He has not regretted the move.

It should be clear that these four scenarios represent the different types. In the first case, Annie could be described as developmentally undecided because she does not have a career goal but is actively exploring her interests and opportunities. However, Jay could be considered chronically undecided given his ongoing inability to set career goals and his associated high level of anxiety. In the third case, Jennifer is representative of the hypervigilant type. Her decision to pursue a law career was made prematurely, and she did not consider her own interests, abilities, and talents. She chose to pursue the career that would please her parents but not herself. Dan represents the vigilant type. His decision to pursue the teaching of math as his career goal was the product of a thorough assessment of his interests and life-style preferences, as well as the work environment.

As these examples show, the usefulness and appropriateness of setting a career goal depends on the circumstances. There are times when the selection of a career goal is beneficial (as with Dan), and there are times when it is useless or even harmful. For an individual such as Annie who lacks sufficient information, being developmentally undecided is an appropriate state and, as reflected in the case of Jennifer, being prematurely decided is an inappropriate state. Career goals should not be set until the individual is sufficiently aware of self and the environment and is confident that the goal is capable of providing compatibility with personal qualities.

POSSIBLE STEPS TO BECOME CAREER DECIDED.   As stated in Chapter 3, the key activity that precedes the setting of a career goal is exploration. Individuals should engage in various forms of career exploration to enhance awareness of themselves and their environment. This heightened awareness of self and environment should enable individuals to set realistic career goals that are compatible with their personal qualities and preferred work environment. Certainly, being developmentally undecided is appropriate, as long as you are in the process of learning more about yourself and your environment. For those who tend to be chronically undecided, the accumulation of additional information may be helpful, but it might not be enough to allow the selection of a career goal. In the chronic case, individuals must find ways to break the "paralysis" brought on by the high degrees of unproductive fear and anxiety and situational constraints. Career counseling programs and other activities that reduce debilitating stress and anxiety and improve self-confidence could prove useful in overcoming chronic indecision. Other career planning activities as described in Chapter 3, such as career workshops and the informal sharing of personal feelings and beliefs, could serve to reduce stress and promote exploration behavior and career goal setting. It should be noted that the complete elimination of decision-making anxiety and stress may not be advisable. Indeed, research has shown that some degree of stress and anxiety may, in fact, facilitate, and provide the incentive for, needed career exploration behavior.[12]

For those who are decided on a career goal, the key consideration is whether the selection was made in a well-informed fashion (the vigilant type) or was conducted in a tense and hasty manner (the hypervigilant type). The premature selection of, and commitment to, an inappropriate career goal could have unfavorable consequences. Our research found that those managers who made a premature selection of a career goal held less favorable work attitudes and experienced more extensive life stress than managers whose career goal selection was more vigilant in nature.[13] Hypervigilant individuals should be encouraged to reexamine their career decisions to assess whether their choices are truly consistent with their talents, interests, and aspirations.

In summary, the important lesson to be learned from the discussion on career indecision is that the selection of a career goal is not positive or negative per se but is dependent on the circumstances. Being undecided about one's career because of a lack of sufficient information (i.e., developmentally undecided) is appropriate. By contrast, being career decided but ignoring one's true interests and talents could prove to be a source of dissatisfaction for the individual and could cause unfavorable work outcomes for the employing organization. In an ideal sense, all career decision making should be performed in a "vigilant" fashion, wherein the career goal is selected with substantial knowledge and awareness. Schools and organizations should strive to offer programs that encourage vigilant career decision making.

IMPLICATIONS OF GOAL SETTING FOR ORGANIZATIONS AND THEIR EMPLOYEES

Employees who set career goals in a vigilant manner—based on insights into themselves and their alternatives as well as a balanced concern for their present and future—should have the greatest likelihood for productive and satisfying careers.[14] Organizations can promote a vigilant approach to career goal setting in a number of ways.

FACILITATE SELF-AWARENESS

Reasonable and appropriate career goals are unlikely to be developed without a foundation of accurate information regarding one's talents, values, interests, and life-style preferences. Organizations can promote self-awareness by providing career counseling and sponsoring career-planning activities. However, considerable self-insight can also be derived from everyday work experiences within organizations. Effective performance appraisal and feedback systems, education and training activities, temporary assignments, job changes, and an expansion of the current job can all serve as potential learning experiences. Employees can learn from these activities most effectively when they have an opportunity to discuss the insights they have acquired with other knowledgeable people, especially their own manager.

FACILITATE AN AWARENESS OF THE ENVIRONMENT

Extensive information about the environment is necessary to set realistic and appropriate career goals. What rewards are associated with a market research position? How much travel is required for a product manager in this company? What skill areas are most critical for success as a sales manager? What is this company going to look like in 1 to 2 years or in 5 to 10 years?

An organization can promote an awareness of the environment by providing employees with access to key information about alternative jobs in the organization, such as duties, responsibilities, required skills, travel, and time commitment pressures. This requires that the organization itself understand the *behavioral* requirements of different jobs and career fields so that this information can be provided to employees. Additionally, the organization should communicate its mission, structure, and culture to employees who are trying to determine the presence of a fit between the organization's needs and their needs.

In today's decentralized environment, it is likely that many employees will move outside their functional areas for their next jobs. Networking—either through formal or informal corporate sponsorship—encourages employees to broaden their horizons with regard to setting future career goals. An alternative is to provide exposure through ad hoc groups or task forces as well as temporary positions and/or lateral moves. These opportunities provide a flexible approach for employees to learn about other areas and functions of the organization. Such activities can be particularly helpful for women and minorities who may be less likely than white males to have had effective sponsorship.

ENCOURAGE EXPERIMENTATION

Much learning about oneself and the environment comes from active experimentation. People can learn a great deal from trying on new roles. A financial analyst or a salesperson contemplating a move into management should be encouraged to incorporate managerial responsibilities into his or her current job, perhaps through a special assignment or project. Experimentation can also take the form of seeking information from previously unfamiliar sources. Speaking with a counselor about a career dilemma, joining a support group for newly transferred employees, attending a seminar on marketing in the financial services industry, or enrolling in a graduate course or program can all stimulate an employee to think about his or her future from a different perspective.

RESPOND TO CHRONIC INDECISION

Our prior suggestions are based on one rather critical assumption: that the undecided employee simply needs to learn more about him- or herself, the environment, or alternative courses of action (i.e., the employee is "developmentally" undecided). Perhaps recent changes in an employee's work situation, family pressures, or career interests triggered a reevaluation of his or her future. Or changes in one's personal life (aging and feelings of mortality), work environment (merger or acquisition, change in corporate strategy), or family environment (empty nest, a spouse's career aspirations) have produced major uncertainties regarding career aims. Career indecision in the face of such changes suggests that an adaptive, developmental process is helpful in achieving career decidedness.

However, as noted earlier, some employees may be indecisive about making a career decision because of an extraordinarily high level of anxiety and stress surrounding the decision-making process. Managers should learn to recognize when indecision about a career goal represents a kind of chronic indecisiveness and paralysis. Observations about prior career moves might be helpful in this respect. In addition, discussions with the employee about his or her career attitudes might reveal a considerable degree of stress about making a career decision. The employee may be reluctant to make any career decision for fear of making a poor one. The employee may claim that more information is needed to make a decision (more testing, more counseling, more course work), when in reality no amount of additional information is likely to move the employee closer to a decision.

We are not suggesting that managers become therapists but rather that they probe the basis for employees' indecision and recommend appropriate courses of action. For example, because chronically undecided employees tend to be anxious and lack confidence in their decision making, they might benefit from career counseling on a one-to-one basis as a supplement to company-sponsored workshops. Because chronically undecided individuals may also manifest high levels of life stress, a critical aspect of counseling is to determine whether part of the problem involves a need for a more comprehensive form of support, such as financial management skills or stress reduction before undertaking any career goal setting. In short, simply providing more information to chronically undecided employees may not be enough.

DISCOURAGE CAREER HYPERVIGILANCE

Hypervigilant employees tend to make career decisions in a reactive mode without adequate time for reflection, preparation, and thinking through their options and alternatives. Often, this results in a decision that is not compatible with the employee's values, talents, and interests, thereby setting up a cycle of dissatisfaction or failure. For such individuals, getting away from everyday pressures and concerns to have proper time to reflect is critical. Effective career management programs that enable these employees to distinguish between the different dimensions of career goals can be particularly helpful. As they reflect on what may be truly fitting choices and goals, some combination of seminars, workshops, computer-based programs, and individual counseling may be especially useful.

BENEFITS TO THE ORGANIZATION

Although it may be desirable for employees to set realistic career goals, there has to be some tangible benefit for the organization to promote such activities. One major incentive for an organization to encourage career goal setting is that its employees learn to take responsibility for their careers. A second advantage is that when employees become involved in career goal setting they are likely to become more highly skilled and more useful to the organization.

Moreover, many career goal-setting programs include analyses of employees' skills not only by the individuals themselves but by their superiors and/or peers as well. Understanding how others view their strengths and weaknesses further encourages employees to improve, particularly when these views do not threaten their self-concept. Taking stock of one's plans can aid in determining what types of training and development activities are needed. Such activities should be viewed in a positive light as they frequently result in more highly skilled employees. And in the event of a downsizing, the employee has a "skills portfolio" to take along to another job or another organization.

For these reasons, career goal setting is often in the best interest of the employee and the organization. Although there are certainly risks to the individual (e.g., disappointment) and the organization (the potential loss of talented individuals), we would argue that the advantages justify the risks. As with any development program, support from the organization's top management is necessary for success. Of particular importance is the creation of a work climate in which individuals feel safe enough to engage in career goal setting. All too often in today's business environment, employees are not willing to openly voice an interest in career goal setting. Many believe that an interest in future career plans calls into question their loyalty to their present position and boss. In other cases, senior executives make positive statements about career issues while their managers ignore them in practice.

In our view, it is important for companies and their managers to show a strong commitment to continued employee development through career planning. Even under turbulent conditions, employees should be expected to consider options and alternatives. Often, however, managers believe that while they are encouraged to develop their employees, they themselves are forgotten. Therefore, it is important for organizations to promote career management across the various hierarchical levels of the organization. The best way to ensure this is to incorporate subordinate career growth into each manager's reward system. In the light of our previous discussion, the most appropriate criterion to apply is *not* whether the subordinate has set a career goal or is ready for a promotion but whether the subordinate is being encouraged to explore him- or herself and the environment and is being provided with useful feedback, guidance, and support.

Finally, it is important for organizational managers to recognize the need for consistency between the strategic needs of the company on the one hand and the career management practices used by the firm on the other. More precisely, an organization's business strategies and other competitive factors normally will dictate the type and level of individuals who are employed. The career management practices described in this chapter can help fulfill these human resource needs by linking individual aspirations with organizational staffing responsibilities.

Knowledge of individual career goals can also aid senior organizational managers in the critical task of succession planning. Individuals with career goals that fit the demands of top management positions can be targeted and groomed for these posts. Thus, a company can take advantage of the embedded knowledge of its existing personnel by deploying them in areas and in jobs that mesh with individual aspirations in the form of career goals. Without knowing individual differences, organizations are apt to make unwarranted or haphazard job assignments.

In summary, we believe that organizations and their employees can benefit from well-designed and maintained career management programs. We have shown how career goals that are the product of a thorough assessment of one's own interests, talents, and life-style preferences, as well as an examination of the work environment, can produce positive work attitudes. We also stated that career goals that are set without benefit of this thorough assessment can be counterproductive. Organizations that implement career management programs to help individuals explore themselves and their work environment can reap rewards in the form of potentially more productive employees and a more efficient matching of employee desires with corporate human resource requirements.

CAREER STRATEGIES

The concept of the boundaryless career is, in large part, based on the idea that individuals must be adaptable and flexible in the actions they pursue and the changes they make in the management of their careers. It also reflects the notion that the "single" organizational career, with job security taken for granted, is no longer viable.[15] Indeed, research has shown that careers are increasingly dominated by interfirm as opposed to intrafirm mobility. Employees in the United States experience 10 employers over their work lives,[16] whereas Japanese male employees work for six employers, on average, during their lifetimes.[17] These results are not surprising, given that traditional job ladders and career paths are being dismantled at an accelerating pace. With this environment, it becomes even more critical for individuals to be proactive in their career management. Specifically, individuals must set career goals and pursue career strategies that give them the greatest chances of personal and professional success. Career strategies are activities designed to help a person meet career goals. They involve conscious individual choices as to which human capital investments to make and which to avoid.[18]

TYPES OF CAREER STRATEGIES

As mentioned in Chapter 2, research suggests that there are seven broad types of career strategies that individuals can use to enhance their chances of career success and fulfillment. Table 4.2 presents a brief summary of the career strategies.

Competence in the present job is probably a necessary but insufficient condition for attaining most career goals. Certainly, organizations make promotion decisions based, in part, on the employee's current level of performance. Thus, to ignore one's current job performance in pursuit of other positions is unwise. Furthermore, the skills developed in one job may be helpful or even essential for successful performance in other jobs (both within and outside of one's current employer). As with other career strategies, the new work world that has evolved over the past several years dictates that employees have "task relevant" skills at the specific times when they are needed by employing organizations. Therefore, it is important to focus on developing abilities in a current job that can improve one's chances for employability in the future.

Extended work involvement has several potential virtues. First, up to a point, working beyond normal hours, either at home or at the work site, can enhance performance in one's current job. Second, extended work involvement can demonstrate to the organization that one is committed to the job and capable of taking on large volumes of work.

· TABLE 4-2

MAJOR CAREER STRATEGIES

I. Competence in Current Job
Meaning: The attempt to perform effectively in one's current job.

II. Extended Work Involvement
Meaning: The decision to devote considerable amounts of time, energy, and emotion to one's work role. It is often considered a contributor to competence in the present job. It might also interfere with family and personal life.

III. Skill Development
Meaning: The attempt to acquire or enhance work-related skills and abilities through education, training, and/or job experience. It is intended to help one's performance on one's current job or could be used on a future job.

IV. Opportunity Development
Meaning: Actions designed to have one's interests and aspirations known to others and to become aware of opportunities that are consistent with those aspirations.

V. Development of Mentor and Other Supportive Alliances
Meaning: Actions designed to seek, establish and use relationships with a significant other to receive or provide information, guidance, support, and opportunities. Although a major function of the mentoring process is to receive (or give) information, the mentoring relationship goes beyond the mere exchange of information and has a deeper emotional meaning.

VI. Image Building
Meaning: The attempt to communicate the appearance of acceptability, success, and/or potential for success. It also can include the acceptance and completion of high-profile assignments that build one's reputation within the organization.

VII. Organizational Politics
Meaning: The attempt to use flattery, conformity, coalition, and trading of favors and influence as a means for attaining desired outcomes. It can include overt and covert actions, such as sabotage and other self-serving behaviors, that raise one's standing in the organization possibly at the expense of others.

This is not to suggest that extended work involvement is always necessary or even useful. We all know of organizations in which many employees are present evenings and weekends because it is expected, not necessarily because any real work gets accomplished. In addition, as we discuss in Chapter 11, extended work involvement may cut drastically into the time a person can spend on family or personal activities. The point, for the time being, is that extended work involvement is often used as a career strategy and can be successful in some circumstances.

Skill development refers to the acquisition (or enhancement) of skills that either help performance on one's current job or will be required on subsequent jobs. Michael Arthur, Priscilla Claman, and Robert DeFillippi refer to this strategy as "knowing how."[19] They note that skill development or "knowing how" draws on formal occupational training as well as experiential learning. Indeed, skill development can take the form of participation in training seminars (e.g., first-line supervision, financial planning) or degree or nondegree university programs. Frequently, however, employees can develop skills by seeking out and acquiring additional responsibilities on their current job (e.g., serving on a task force) or by working closely with a more experienced colleague. In addition, employees can develop a broader array of skills by joining occupational associations that sponsor continuing education for members.[20] In essence, a commitment to skill development and lifelong learning helps ensure that a person's work abilities and knowledge are kept relevant with present work demands (and thereby transferable to other organizations).

Another skill-enhancing activity that has gained prominence more recently is "moonlighting," or the use of a second job to develop a broader portfolio of proficiencies.[21] Moonlighting not only allows development of additional skills, but it can also be used to make contacts and build self-confidence. Statistics indicate that moonlighting is at historically high levels. Indeed, as of 1996, 7.8 million Americans, or 6.2 percent of all employed people, were working at more than one job.[22]

Opportunity development is composed of a number of more specific strategies, all of which are designed to increase one's career options. In their typology, Arthur, Claman, and DeFillippi refer to this career strategy as "knowing whom."[23] For example, self-nomination, a frequently observed strategy, refers to the willingness to inform superiors of accomplishments, aspirations, and desired assignments.[24] Visiposure combines two strategies, visibility (being able to view the top of the organization) and exposure (being seen by the top of the organization).[25] Visibility enables one to understand and model those who are higher in the hierarchy, and exposure can bring recognition, special assignments, and sponsorship. Networking, the identification of and communication with a group of relevant acquaintances and friends, can provide information, advice, and support. Another strategy that allows opportunity development is "temping," or the acceptance of a temporary or interim assignment. Interim assignments can be used to gain additional skills and to "audition" for a permanent job.[26] Many large organizations are using temporary assignments as a way to fill critical needs and to gain specific expertise for brief periods of time. Use of temporary staff is also at historically high levels, with 2.1 million U.S. workers classified as such in mid-1995.[27]

Opportunity development has traditionally been seen in terms of progress within a specific organization (i.e., in terms of intraorganizational mobility). However, in today's environment, with the virtual elimination of the relational psychological contract between employer and employee, this strategy should be viewed in a broader sense. More precisely, individuals should work on cultivating opportunities both in the internal and in the external labor markets. Depending on one's career stage, actively seeking out opportunities in the external labor market can prove beneficial, especially in terms of compensation.[28]

The **development of mentor and other supportive alliances** has received considerable attention in recent years. Mentoring can be defined generally as relationships between junior and senior colleagues, or between peers, who provide a variety of developmental functions.[29] The mentoring role can be filled by a variety of individuals, not by just one person. A mentor can provide coaching, friendship, sponsorship, and role modeling to the younger, less experienced protege.[30] In the process, the mentor can satisfy his or her need to have a lasting influence on another person's life. Frequently recommended as a career strategy for both mentor and protege,[31] the mentoring relationship is examined more closely in Chapter 8.

Image and reputation building is a strategy designed to convey an appearance of success and suitability. For example, being married, participating in community activities, and dressing properly can provide a positive public image that can bring career rewards.[32] It is not suggested that this type of strategy is necessarily important in all or most situations, although it has been stated that significant numbers of employees make the investment in image building because of the perceived high value to the individual's career.[33] Building one's work reputation is an important strategy because it is naturally assumed that people's past experiences and accomplishments bode well for future performance and assignments. Therefore, an individual focus on building a strong work reputation can improve employability regardless of the changing fortunes of an individual employer.[34] One can build a positive reputation by accomplishing such tasks as engineering a turnaround of an unfavorable work situation or by showing leadership on a particular assignment.

Organizational politics encompasses such diverse strategies as agreeing with or flattering your boss, advocating company practices, not complaining about rules or regulations, and forming alliances or coalitions with others in the organization. Organizational politics is somewhat similar to the "knowing why" strategy as described by Arthur, Claman, and DeFillippi.[35] It is not suggested here that organizational politics is either necessary or personally acceptable, but that it is one of several career strategies that could be used.

Research examining the effectiveness of specific career strategies is beginning to emerge. For example, research from the Center for Creative Leadership found that skill development and diversity of experience promoted a high level of career success.[36] In addition, other research has found that employees' use of four strategies—self-nomination, other enhancement, creating opportunities, and networking—contributed to their career success.[37] It is more likely, however, that the usefulness of a particular career strategy will depend on many factors: the type of job, the nature of the industry, and the practices and norms of the organization.[38] What works in one situation or economic environment may not work in another. Career strategists recommend that individuals choose strategies that provide the greatest increase in chances for a desired success over the probability of random success.[39]

GUIDELINES FOR THE DEVELOPMENT OF CAREER STRATEGIES

Overall, the research on career strategies seems to suggest the following:

1. There is no "one best" strategy that is equally effective in all situations.
2. The effectiveness of a particular strategy depends on the nature of the career goal. A person striving to reach the presidency of an organization, for example, is likely to benefit from a different strategy than one whose goal is to become an engineering project manager.

3. The effectiveness of a particular strategy depends on the organization's norms and values. For example, some organizations may encourage secrecy and political machinations, whereas others may reward openness and collaboration.

4. Individuals should not limit themselves to one single strategy but should engage in a variety of strategic behaviors.

5. Strategies should be used not only to reach a career goal but also to test one's interest and commitment to a goal. Planning is best viewed as a process of learning more about ourselves and the environment.

6. Career strategies should reflect steps to be taken, as well as areas to be avoided. Findings from research at the Center for Creative Leadership not only identified positive career strategies that lead to career success (or arrival), but also pointed out a number of inappropriate actions that can cause career failure (or derailment) and thus should be avoided.[40]

It is impossible (and undesirable) to specify in advance each and every component of a career strategy. An essential part of the career management process is "learning by doing." As a person begins to develop and implement a strategy, additional strategic behaviors may be more obvious than they were before the process began. In this section, we propose a five-step process for developing a set of career strategies.

1. **Reexamine your long-term goal. Make sure you understand what the goal represents in terms of desired activities, rewards, and life-style (conceptual goal) and why the particular occupation or job (operational goal) is appropriate for meeting the conceptual goal.**

2. **Identify behaviors, activities, and experiences that will help you reach the long-term goal. Two questions need to be raised regarding each element of a career strategy: Will it help you attain your goal? Regardless of its usefulness, do you want to engage in that behavior?**

One first needs to estimate the potential usefulness of a set of activities. The most useful sources of information are discussion and observation. Conversations with others in the organization, for example, may provide helpful information and dispel myths about certain strategies (e.g., that everyone must follow the same career path to a particular job).

Usually, one can profit the most from conversations with others who have more experience in the organization than you, such as a superior or a more established colleague. Because there can be an element of rivalry between superior and subordinate that prevents information sharing in some circumstances, a mentor is sometimes the more appropriate source of information about the potential usefulness of certain career strategies. In fact, the establishment of a mentor relationship is itself part of a career strategy. Nonetheless, formal feedback from superiors through such activities as performance appraisal and participative goal setting can serve to identify career strategies and developmental activities.

Consider as an example the case of Beth, a 28-year-old manager in the accounting department of a medium-sized insurance company. At the age of 22, Beth received a bachelor's degree in accounting from a large state university. After working 2 years in the billing department of a hospital, Beth accepted an accounting analyst position with the insurance company. In her 4 years there, she advanced quickly, assuming the position of manager at a comparatively young age. She enjoys working at the insurance company, and her longer-term goal is to be a vice president by age 35. During her annual performance review Beth asked her supervisor, the officer-in-charge of the department, what actions she could take to facilitate further advancement. Her supervisor willingly offered several ideas. First, he told her that the company normally filled officer positions with employees who had earned an MBA. In addition, the supervisor stated that officers generally would have to show competence in a variety of skills and should have a fairly broad range of experience in other departments within the organization. Finally, he stated that working on assignments that would give her exposure to the firm's senior management would help her chances for promotion. With this information in hand, Beth set about to develop specific career strategies, including enrollment in an MBA program, monitoring the company's job postings to increase awareness of opportunities in other departments, and requesting high-profile assignments that would give her a chance to work with senior management.

The second issue involves a person's decision to engage in a strategic behavior regardless of its apparent usefulness. Some behaviors may help attain one element of a career goal but interfere with the attainment of other elements. For example, frequent job changes and accompanying relocations may enable a person to acquire useful experiences and skills but may interfere substantially with family life. Therefore, the effectiveness of a particular career strategy must be judged in a holistic sense.

Moreover, certain strategies may be useful but personally distasteful. Forming political alliances, making oneself look good at the expense of a colleague, and loyally supporting an organization's questionable practices may violate ethical and/or religious values. A career strategy cannot simply be viewed in utilitarian terms.

One should emerge from this process with a relatively small list of critical and acceptable strategic plans, with statements of purpose and approximate time frames if possible. Table 4.3 presents a statement of hypothetical career strategies.

3. **Examine the short-term goal. In particular, examine the fit between the short-term goal and the long-term goal. In the light of long-term career strategies, does your short-term goal still appear instrumental to the attainment of your long-term goal? If not, you may want to revise the short-term goal to improve the fit.**

4. **Identify behaviors, activities, and experiences that will help you attain the short-term goal. As with step 2, potential usefulness and personal acceptability should be twin criteria by which a strategy is evaluated. Develop a small list of critical and acceptable strategic plans for accomplishing the short-term goal.**

· TABLE 4-3

STATEMENT OF CAREER STRATEGIES FOR AN ASSISTANT MANAGER OF HUMAN RESOURCES

Strategies to Achieve Long-Term Goal of Director of Corporate Human Resources

Activity	Purpose	Time Frame
Perform effectively on current job	To remain productive, grow on job	Ongoing
Receive promotion to manager of human resources	To gain competence, experience, and visibility in company	2–3 years
Receive MBA degree with specialization in human resources	To gain specialized knowledge and credibility	3–4 years

Strategies to Achieve Short-Term Goal of Manager of Human Resources

Activity	Purpose	Time Frame
Perform effectively on current job	To remain promotable, grow on job	Ongoing
Take beginning courses in MBA program	To gain greater knowledge of labor relations	0–6 months
Discuss career goals with supervisor	To make supervisor aware of career aspirations, obtain feedback and suggestions	0–6 months
Obtain information on possible human resources manager opening	To assess likelihood of achieving short-term goal in company	0–6 months
Contact search firm	To assess likelihood of achieving short-term goal in another company	6–12 months
Attempt to initiate quality of work-life program in conjunction with current personnel manager and operations	To enhance productivity, develop relationships with line management, gain experience in quality of work life	1–2 years

5. Combine the lists of strategies for short-term and long-term goals. It is likely that strategies designed to attain both types of goals are particularly critical and should remain at the top of the combined list. Keep the list manageable by ordering the strategic activities in a logical time sequence.

The planning and implementation of a career strategy is not nearly so mechanical as this five-step process may suggest. First, the five steps overlap somewhat in time. It is artificial to separate discussions about goals, long-term strategies, and short-term strategies. Second, strategies cannot always be specified in advance. One may have to implement one part of a strategy to determine the next step. The important outcome of this process is an appreciation of how different strategies relate back to your significant goals. The essential ingredient in this process is openness to information and willingness to reexamine and possibly revise goals and/or strategies, in short, to monitor and appraise your career.

Learning Exercise VI is available at the end of this text and on the Internet at **http://www.dryden.com/management/humresources.html**. It provides an opportunity to practice developing a career strategy. Although you may examine Exercise VI at this time, it is recommended that you finish reading Chapter 4 before beginning the exercise.

CAREER APPRAISAL

If career management is to be a flexible, adaptive process, there must be some way for people to adjust to new information about themselves and/or the environment. Career appraisal, the process by which career-related feedback is gathered and used, serves this function.

The feedback obtained through career appraisal has two specific functions. First, it can test the appropriateness of a particular career strategy. Is the strategy effectively moving a person closer to his or her goal? Second, feedback can test the appropriateness of the goal itself. Is the career goal still relevant and attainable?

Consider the situation of a 36-year-old high school history teacher who has become increasingly bored with his job. After extensive self-assessment, he has concluded that he should seek work in an educational setting that is more varied than his current position, that offers the opportunity for greater financial rewards, and that takes advantage of his skills at working with people on an individual basis (the conceptual goal). After reading materials on careers in education and talking with a number of people in the field, his conceptual goal is translated into a specific operational goal; he intends to move into secondary school administration within the next 3 years.

The teacher's strategy was two pronged. First, he applied for admission to a part-time master's program in educational administration at the local university. Completion of the graduate program would enable him to be certified in administration and eligible for future openings in administrative positions. Second, he obtained permission to represent his school at local and state conferences and PTA activities. The latter strategy was designed to give him a broader perspective on his school's operations. Actually, his strategy was developed as much to test his interests and talents in administration as to prepare him for his future career shift.

The teacher's graduate school experiences were enlightening. After one semester, he realized he was less interested in administering a school (he hated the courses in budgeting, personnel, and curriculum development) than in helping kids on an intensive one-on-one basis. Several psychology electives in the second semester reinforced his recent discovery. As a result of these revelations, he has applied to a doctoral program in school psychology.

As the teacher's experiences indicate, career appraisal reflects the problem-solving nature of career management. With an effective appraisal process, career management becomes a learning experience in which one looks for signs that either confirm or disconfirm prior decisions. These signs are pieces of information that close the career management cycle by reinstigating career exploration. The teacher's disillusionment with his initial master's program was the result of a strategic experience that heightened his awareness of his own interests as well as the day-by-day duties of a school administrator. It was this awareness, gained through strategy-based exploration, that enabled him to revise his goal in a more suitable direction.

Types and Sources of Information Derived from Career Appraisal

An individual open to his or her environment can acquire a great deal of information relevant to goals and strategies. Although information cannot be pigeon-holed so neatly, career-related feedback can conveniently be classified in terms of the following:

1. **The Conceptual Goal** What has the individual learned about values, interests, talents, and desired life-style? Is this information consistent or inconsistent with the person's conceptual goal? For example, the history teacher's strategic experiences essentially reinforced his conceptual goal of greater variety, opportunities for more money, and more individualized work with other people.

2. **The Operational Goal** What has the individual learned about the appropriateness of the operational goal? Is a match still possible between the conceptual goal and the operational goal? Put another way, is it still believed that the targeted job is compatible with the conceptual goal? Note that the history teacher's most significant conclusion was that a career in school administration would not necessarily meet his values and interests.

3. **Strategy** What has the individual learned about the appropriateness of the strategy? Is it working? Does the individual experience a sense of progress toward the goal? If the goal involves gaining additional competencies in the current job, has it been reflected in favorable performance appraisals? If the career goal involves a different job, does the organization still view the person as a viable candidate for the job? In the teacher's case, he realized that although his strategy was appropriate for his initial goal, it would have to be revised if he were to pursue a career in psychology. His application to a doctoral program in psychology was the first step of this revised strategy.

Feedback regarding goals and strategies can come from a variety of sources. At least three sources of feedback have previously been identified in the organizational behavior literature.[41] One source consists of social interactions with other people who have either observed the person's behavior or undergone similar experiences themselves. Supervisors, subordinates, mentors, clients, family members, friends, or acquaintances would fall in this category.

A second source of feedback resides in observing the work and nonwork environments. A salesperson losing three consecutive sales may gain insights into his or her job performance. Production rates, quotas reached, and patents established can all provide useful information. So can the observation that five of your colleagues (but not you) have received recent promotions. The observation of an improved or deteriorated family life can also be a significant environmental cue.

People can also serve as their own source of feedback. Judgments about one's own performance can be independent of what other people in the environment can communicate.

GUIDELINES FOR EFFECTIVE CAREER APPRAISAL

Successful career appraisal requires what has been called an "early warning" control system that serves to detect when a strategy is or is not working as expected.[42] This early warning orientation is likely to be more helpful than simply carrying a strategy to completion before examining its usefulness. The ongoing feedback effort suggested in the career management model requires a more or less consistent monitoring of activities and their consequences.

Ongoing career appraisal can be aided by considering the following guidelines:

1. The most basic principle, and perhaps the most difficult to follow, is the willingness to see the world clearly and to make revisions in goals and strategies when appropriate. As noted earlier, an "escalation effect" has been observed in which people persist in a course of action despite its lack of success.[43] Research suggests that some people continue their commitment to a "losing cause" to justify to themselves and others that their prior decision was sound. This practice is inconsistent with effective career management, which requires people to incorporate new data and revise prior decisions when necessary. Therefore, we suggest the following:

   ■ Be honest with yourself. If things are not working well, seriously consider the possibility that either your prior decisions were faulty or circumstances have changed.

   ■ Be less concerned with having to justify your prior decisions to others.

   ■ Be willing to appear and perhaps be inconsistent at times. Although persistence and consistency of action are generally valued in our society, they can be dysfunctional if carried to the extreme.

2. Use your career strategy to provide benchmarks of accomplishments. Statements of strategies should include purposes and desired outcomes. Test the usefulness of the strategies against these specific benchmarks. Usually, strategies are neither completely appropriate nor totally useless. The establishment of benchmarks can help identify specific strengths and weaknesses of a strategy.

3. Strategies are as much learning opportunities as they are vehicles for accomplishment. Periodically review the appropriateness of your conceptual and operational goals in the light of any new information you have

acquired. In a study of nearly 200 executives, researchers from the Center for Creative Leadership documented how successful managers are able to learn from experiences and make necessary adjustments in career goals and strategies.[44]

4. If you are employed, structure your interactions with your supervisor to acquire desired information. Come into a performance appraisal meeting with your own agenda to supplement (not replace) your supervisor's. What can you learn from your manager about your current performance, your strengths and weaknesses, and the organization's needs that will help you appraise your goals and strategies? What should your manager know about your aspirations that will help him or her provide useful feedback?

5. Share experiences and feelings with trustworthy people. Frank discussions among peers can be beneficial to all parties. First, others may see parts of you that are hidden to yourself. Second, verbally articulating goals, desires, reservations, and strategies may help clarify your own feelings. Third, others may be willing to share their own successes, failures, and revelations that bear on your circumstances.

In effect, try to form a network that provides mutual feedback, guidance, support, and stimulation. In doing this, choose colleagues with whom you can communicate freely. Since it is often difficult to reveal sensitive career matters, the members of the network need to build trust and openness, a climate that takes time and patience to develop. Whether such a network is offered and sanctioned by the organization or whether it takes place informally is less important than the members' willingness to share and help each other.

6. Seek feedback from nonwork sources. Work and nonwork lives, as we have repeatedly argued, affect each other. Not only do work decisions affect family lives, but family situations (e.g., spouse's career needs) can affect work lives. For example, one part of a person's career strategy may be to demonstrate competence and loyalty by working extraordinarily long hours. It may have initially been assumed that these work hours would not adversely affect family relationships. After some time, however, it is necessary to examine the accuracy of that assumption. Because a person can easily misperceive a family's feelings and attitudes, candid sharing of information is often necessary to balance work and nonwork activities.

CAREER MANAGEMENT: A BLEND OF FORMAL AND INFORMAL ACTIVITIES

It may appear that the career management process is highly structured and formal. There are meetings to attend, autobiographies to write, goals to list, and exploratory interviews to conduct. Must it require an endless stream of seminars and forms? Career management does have its structured side. Formal programs

· **TABLE 4-4**

PERIODIC CAREER MANAGEMENT ACTIVITIES

Activity	Intensity	Frequency	Sources of Input and Help
General evaluation of year's performance and of satisfaction with various aspects of life. Any problems?	1–2 day's worth of work	Once a year	Organization-initiated formal performance appraisal
Analysis of changes in you and your opportunities. Are changes needed?	Up to one week's worth of work, at one time or spread out over a few months.	Every 3–4 years	Conversations with important people in your life 3- to 7-day career planning seminars
Major reassessment of self and opportunities.	Of the magnitude described in this book.	Once every 7–10 years	Assessment centers Career counselors Three- to four-month university programs

SOURCE: From James G. Clawson, John P. Kotter, Victor A. Faux, and Charles C. McArthur, *Self-Assessment and Career Development* (Englewood Cliffs, NJ: Prentice-Hall, Inc., 1992), 425.

include vocational counseling and/or testing, career planning seminars or workshops, and self-administered career-planning workbooks. Of course, many programs combine these activities in various ways.

Career management activities, however, need not always be formally organized, structured programs. Indeed, any activity that is pursued to develop or act on career-related information is a form of career management. For example, one can learn about one's interests and strengths through course work (How many pre-med students switch majors after the first course in organic chemistry?), part-time or full-time work experiences, conversations with colleagues, family members and friends, or conscious introspection and reflection.

Because career management is an ongoing process, informal activities are probably more potent in the long run. It is not feasible (or even desirable) to buy another workbook or join another seminar every time you face a significant career decision. What you need to learn are the skills for translating your daily experiences into learning opportunities. A formal program can frequently provide these analytical skills.

As shown in Table 4.4, career theorists suggest three types of reassessment activities that vary in formality and intensity. Perhaps it is easy to see the usefulness of a year-end assessment of accomplished and unaccomplished goals and satisfying and dissatisfying experiences. It may be less obvious, but periodic reassessments can also be useful, because they roughly coincide with the time frames for short-term and long-term goals, respectively.

But the real importance of career management lies in a way of thinking. The core of effective career management is a mental set, an awareness of one's own concerns as well as environmental opportunities and constraints, an alertness to changes in self and environment, and a willingness to make conscious decisions and plans to revise them accordingly. This philosophy of active career management should serve as a foundation for lifelong participation in formal and informal activities.

SUMMARY

Career exploration paves the way for the establishment of career goals. A career goal should not focus exclusively on a specific job or position but should be conceived more broadly in terms of desired work experiences. A career goal should also (1) focus on the intrinsic enjoyment derived from work experiences, (2) include total life-style concerns, (3) take into account one's current job as a source of satisfaction and growth, (4) be sufficiently challenging and flexible, and (5) be capable of meeting one's own needs and values, not other people's expectations. A general procedure was outlined for establishing career goals, and learning exercises were provided to practice this procedure.

Career indecision was defined as the inability to select a career goal or to subsequently experience significant uncertainty or discomfort over a selected goal. A variety of factors can cause career indecision, including insufficient self-awareness, a lack of information on the internal and external work environments, low self-confidence, decisional fear and anxiety, nonwork demands, and situational constraints. Different types of career indecision and decidedness have been observed indicating that the appropriateness of being undecided or decided depends on the underlying circumstances. Individuals should strive to achieve vigilance in their career decision making, such that their career goals are selected confidently and patiently, and are based on sufficient knowledge of self and the work environment.

Career strategies are actions designed to help you attain your career goals. The development of a career strategy is itself a learning experience that encourages you to reexamine your career goal and identify key behaviors, activities, and experiences that can help you reach your goal. It is helpful to specify the purpose of each part of a career strategy and an approximate time frame for accomplishment. Observation as well as conversation with peers, managers, and other knowledgeable people can help you devise a reasonable plan. A learning exercise was provided to practice career strategy development.

However reasonable a career strategy may appear, it is essential to monitor and appraise its effectiveness. As a strategy is implemented, ask yourself whether your initial goal still makes sense and whether the strategy still appears capable of helping you achieve the goal. You need to be willing to revise your goals and strategies when necessary.

Career management is a blend of formal and informal activities that should be pursued throughout one's working life. Periodic reappraisals of career accomplishments and aspirations are useful. The heart of active career management is a

Now that you have completed reading Chapter 4, it is time to begin Learning Exercises V and VI, which can be found at the end of this text and on the Internet at **http://www.dryden.com/management/humresources.html.**

willingness to assume responsibility for one's career, take the necessary steps to influence the course of one's career, and make revisions in plans and strategies when appropriate.

ASSIGNMENT

Think about whether you have a career goal or goals. If you have a goal, do you think you set it based on self-insight, or did you feel pressured into setting a career goal? Why? If you have not set a career goal, do you believe it is because you are "developmentally" or "chronically" undecided? Why? What steps should you take next and why?

DISCUSSION QUESTIONS

1. Why is it dangerous to focus primarily on the operational and instrumental qualities of a career goal?

2. Career goal setting as described in this chapter emphasizes rational analysis of conceptual and operational goals. Should emotions and "gut-level feelings" also play a role in goal setting? Why do you feel that way?

3. Have your career decisions and aspirations been based primarily on your own needs and values, or have you been heavily influenced by other people's hopes and expectations for you? What can you do to ensure that future career decisions are guided by goals that are personally meaningful to you?

4. Why can career goals easily become rigid and inflexible? Have you ever continued to pursue a goal that no longer makes sense? Why? Why are inflexible goals inconsistent with the model of career management presented in this book?

5. Do you think that you are presently experiencing career indecision? If you are, what do you see as the primary cause(s)? If you are career decided, do you consider yourself vigilant or hypervigilant? Why?

6. Although some strategies may help you achieve your career goals, they may be unacceptable to you on other grounds. What factors should be taken into account when judging the personal acceptability of a career strategy? Have you (or someone you know or have read about) pursued, avoided, or abandoned a career strategy that was personally unacceptable? What were the consequences of this decision?

ENDNOTES

1. E. A. Locke, K. N. Shaw, L. M. Saari, and G. P. Latham, "Goal Setting and Task Performance: 1969-1980," *Psychological Bulletin* 90 (1981): 125–152.

2. P. H. Mirvis and D. T. Hall, "Psychological Success and the Boundaryless Career," *Journal of Organizational Behavior* 15 (1994): 365–380.

3. B. M. Staw and J. Ross, "Knowing When to Pull the Plug," Harvard Business Review March–April (1987): 68–74.

4. M. B. McCaskey, "Goals and Direction in Personal Planning," *Academy of Management Review* 2 (1977): 454–462.

5. G. A. Callanan and J. H. Greenhaus, "The Career Indecision of Managers and Professionals: Development of a Scale and Test of a Model," *Journal of Vocational Behavior* 37 (1990): 79–103.

6. Ibid.

7. Ibid.

8. J. O. Crites, *Vocational Psychology* (New York: McGraw-Hill, 1969); L. D. Goodstein, "Behavioral View of Counseling," in *Theories of Counseling*, ed. B. Stefflre (New York: McGraw-Hill, 1965), 140–192.

9. G. A. Callanan and J. H. Greenhaus, "The Career Indecision of Managers and Professionals: An Examination of Multiple Subtypes," *Journal of Vocational Behavior* 41 (1992): 212–231.

10. Ibid.

11. I. L. Janis and L. Mann, "Coping with Decisional Conflict," *American Scientist* 64 (1976): 657–667.

12. D. L. Blustein and S. D. Phillips, "Individual and Contextual Factors in Career Exploration," *Journal of Vocational Behavior* 33 (1988): 203–216.

13. Callanan and Greenhaus, "The Career Indecision of Managers and Professionals," (1992).

14. J. H. Greenhaus, G. A. Callanan, and E. Kaplan, "The Role of Goal Setting in Career Management," *The International Journal of Career Management* 7 (1995): 3–12.

15. G. A. Callanan and J. H. Greenhaus, "Personal and Career Development: The Best and Worst of Times," in *New Concepts and Practices for Human Resources Management: Contributions from Industrial-Organizational Psychology*, ed. A. I. Kraut and A. K. Korman (San Francisco, CA: Jossey-Bass, 1999), pp. 146–171.

16. R. H. Topel and M. P. Ward, "Job Mobility and the Careers of Young Men," *The Quarterly Journal of Economics* May (1992): 439–479.

17. M. T. Cheng, "The Japanese Permanent Employment System," *Work and Occupations* 18 (1991): 148–171.

18. J. B. Barney and B. S. Lawrence, "Pin Stripes, Power Ties and Personal Relationships: The Economics of Career Strategy," in *Handbook of Career Theory*, ed. M. B. Arthur, D. T. Hall, and B. S. Lawrence (Cambridge, UK: Cambridge University Press, 1989), 417–436.

19. M. B. Arthur, P. H. Claman, and R. J. DeFillippi, "Intelligent Enterprise, Intelligent Careers," *Academy of Management Executive* 9 (1995): 7–20.

20. R. J. DeFillippi and M. B. Arthur, "The Boundaryless Career: A Competency-Based Perspective," *Journal of Organizational Behavior* 15 (1994): 307–324.

21. B. Nussbaum, "I'm Worried about My Job" and "A Career Survival Kit," *Business Week*, October 7, 1991, pp. 94–104; P. T. Kilborn, "In New Work World, Employers Call All the Shots," *The New York Times*, July 3, 1995, pp. 1, 7.

22. *Statistical Abstract of the United States,* 117th ed. (U.S. Department of Commerce, Economic and Statistics Administration, Bureau of the Census, 1997).

23. Arthur, Claman, and DeFillippi, "Intelligent Enterprise, Intelligent Careers."

24. D. C. Feldman, "Careers in Organizations: Recent Trends and Future Directions," *Journal of Management* 15 (1989): 135–156; S. Gould and L. E. Penley, "Career Strategies and Salary Progression: A Study of Their Relationships in a Municipal Bureaucracy," *Organizational Behavior and Human Performance* 34 (1984): 244–265.

25. E. E. Jennings, *Routes to the Executive Suite* (New York: Macmillan, 1971).

26. Nussbaum, "I'm Worried about My Job" and "A Career Survival Kit."

27. Kilborn, "In New Work World, Employers Call All the Shots."

28. J. M. Brett and L. K. Stroh, "Jumping Ship: Who Benefits from an External Labor Market Career Strategy?" *Journal of Applied Psychology* 82 (1997): 331–341.

29. K. E. Kram, *Mentoring at Work: Developmental Relationships in Organizational Life* (Lanham, MD: University Press of America, 1988).

30. J. G. Clawson, "Mentoring in Managerial Careers," in *Work, Family, and the Career,* ed. C. B. Derr (New York: Praeger, 1980), 144–165.

31. C. D. McCauley, *Developmental Experiences in Managerial Work: A Literature Review* (Greensboro, NC: Center for Creative Leadership, 1986).

32. W. J. Heissler and G. R. Gemmill, "Executive and MBA Student Views of Corporate Promotion Practices: A Structural Comparison," *Academy of Management Journal* 21 (1978): 731–737; L. Larwood and U. E. Gattiker, "Career Strategies and Success in Fourteen Corporations," paper presented at the Annual Meeting of the Academy of Management, Dallas, TX, 1983; J. A. Schneer and F. Reitman, "Effects of Alternate Family Structures on Managerial Career Paths," *Academy of Management Journal* 36 (1993): 830–843.

33. Barney and Lawrence, "Pin Stripes, Power Ties and Personal Relationships."

34. M. B. Arthur, "The Boundaryless Career: A New Perspective for Organizational Inquiry," *Journal of Organizational Behavior* 15 (1994): 295–306.

35. Arthur, Claman, and DeFillippi, "Intelligent Enterprise, Intelligent Careers."

36. M. W. McCall, M. M. Lombardo, and A. M. Morrison, *The Lessons of Experience: How Successful Executives Develop on the Job* (Lexington, MA: Lexington Books, 1988).

37. Gould and Penley, "Career Strategies and Salary Progression."

38. Ibid.; Larwood and Gattiker, "Career Strategies and Success in Fourteen Corporations"; J. Van Maanen, "Career Games: Organizational Rules of Play," in *Work, Family, and the Career,* ed. C. B. Derr (New York: Praeger, 1980), 111–143.

39. Barney and Lawrence, "Pin Stripes, Power Ties and Personal Relationships."

40. McCall, Lombardo, and Morrison, *The Lessons of Experience.*

41. D. R. Ilgen, C. D. Fisher, and M. S. Taylor, "Consequences of Individual Feedback on Behavior in Organizations," *Journal of Applied Psychology* 64 (1979): 349–371.

42. A. H. Souerwine, *Career Strategies: Planning for Personal Achievement* (New York: AMACOM, 1978).

43. Staw and Ross, "Knowing When to Pull the Plug."

44. McCall, Lombardo, and Morrison, *The Lessons of Experience.*

Careers of Michele Terry and Joe Francis

The principles of effective career management discussed in Part I of *Career Management* can be reinforced by examining the hypothetical but realistic career portraits of two managers, Michele Terry and Joe Francis. First, read the descriptions of Michele and Joe. Then answer the questions that follow the case.

MICHELE TERRY

Michele Terry is a 45-year-old manager of marketing services at Federal Bank (fictitious name), a medium-sized financial institution. The fact that some of the staff she once hired have been promoted above her in recent years is a daily reminder that Michele's longtime ambition to become president of Federal Bank is not likely to be fulfilled. Her recent performance appraisal meetings with her 40-year-old superior, an assistant vice president, left no doubt in Michele's mind about Federal's plans: She will most likely retire at her current level.

In fact, the handwriting had been on the wall for more than 5 years. During this time, Michele reexamined her original goal. How important was it for her to become president of the bank? Her conclusion was that it was still a personally important goal. As a result, Michele had at least 15 interviews during the past 5 years with other banks. In each case, she got a polite but negative response. All the institutions were hiring MBAs, and Michele had only a bachelor's degree. More important, Michele was competent enough but did not have sufficiently varied experiences in the financial services industry and did not seem to project the image of an officer, let alone a president. In a state of dismay, she also spoke with officers of other institutions in the financial services industry. The reactions to these inquiries were all similarly negative.

Last year, several conversations with Federal's officers and her husband convinced Michele to give up her dream of becoming president of the bank. It was simply out of the question. Although there was a chance of further advancement, Michele concluded that it was slim.

In the meantime, Michele reexamined why she always wanted to become president of the bank. In addition to money and status, she wanted the opportunity to affect broad policies to make inroads in the services that banks could provide to the community. Therefore, she concentrated on broadening the scope of her current position by looking for ways to influence the bank's approach to community reinvestment. Michele enrolled in several training seminars on community reinvestment and convinced her boss that she should chair a task force on new market development. She also began to serve as a mentor to several of Federal's younger managers, helping them get their careers established and perhaps avoid some of the mistakes she may have made earlier in her career.

On the home front, Michele seems more relaxed than she has been in some time, and she is better able to enjoy her family. She has encouraged her husband to switch to a more personally satisfying career field, has freely given him advice and support, and seems to enjoy the success her husband is beginning to experience in his rejuvenated career. Michele is also spending more time with her children and her infant grandchild and has rekindled her interest in the local political scene.

Michele's most recent performance appraisal was outstanding. Although she does not put in nearly so many weekends and evenings as she had in the past, her job performance has not suffered. To the contrary, her marketing group is working on several innovative projects, the task force she heads is making real progress, and she is deriving great pleasure from her relationships with several of the bank's younger managers. Although Michele is periodically frustrated with her lack of advancement, she is a respected contributor at the bank and, little by little, is coming to terms with her disappointment.

JOE FRANCIS

At age 39, Joe Francis should have been pleased. In fact, he has been proud of his rapid rise to the position of vice president of sales at Infotek (fictitious name), an established computer software development firm. Having started as a sales representative at Infotek on graduation from college, Joe's sales performance at the district and regional levels was legendary. However, his promotion to the vice presidency came as a surprise. He did not seek the position, always preferring sales to pencil-pushing and administration. But it was hard to turn down the promotion with its hefty salary increase and the other executive perks.

Although he has not complained to anyone, Joe has had gnawing doubts about his work. For one thing, he has had strong reservations about the quality of Infotek's products. He has found it increasingly difficult to get enthusiastic about software systems that fall short of personal and industry standards. Joe's comments to the research and marketing departments have fallen on deaf ears. In fact, he has offered suggestions in a number of areas that the company seems unwilling to consider seriously. In addition, his fears about getting drowned in paperwork and administration have been realized. Joe has been bored for a while. Moreover, although the travel was fun initially, the seemingly constant business trips of the past few years have left him tired and irritable and with little time for his family.

Joe has had to suppress many of these feelings. After all, his salary and bonus reach well into six figures. His family has expensive consumption habits, two of his children are nearing college age, and his family wants a larger summer house at the lake. He does not dare even discuss his feelings with his family, who have become pretty accustomed to "the good life."

Joe dreads going to work but believes that he must do it for the sake of his family. He is unhappy much of the time but has been pleased with his status in the company. Anyway, Joe has found that the traveling is not so bad after four stiff drinks on the flight. For the sake of his wife and kids, Joe had decided he would stay put for the next 15 or 20 years until early retirement.

But Joe never saw it coming. His monthly meeting with the senior vice president was anything but regular. Joe was fired! As part of a restructuring move, Joe's position was eliminated in favor of self-managed sales teams reporting to the senior vice president. Although Joe could have been kept on as a sales representative, Infotek thought that a clean break would be better for both parties. Apparently, Joe's lack of enthusiasm for his work and his employer affected his job performance, and the sales force had been complaining about Joe's lack of attention to detail for some time.

Joe left the meeting in a state of shock. Although relieved that his frustrating experiences at Infotek were coming to an end, Joe was scared to death. How will he tell his wife? And what will he do next? He hadn't the slightest idea.

CASE ANALYSIS QUESTIONS

1. Career Exploration

   a. What specific career exploration activities have Michele and Joe undertaken to gather information about themselves (their values, needs, abilities, interests, and desired life-style) and their environment (different jobs, employers, industries, their families)? What could each of them have done to acquire more information?

   b. How much insight do Michele and Joe currently have about themselves and their environment?

2. Career Goals

   a. Does Michele currently have a career goal? If so, what is it and is it different from the goal she had earlier in her career? Has it helped her achieve her Preferred Work Environment? If not, explain why you believe that Michele does not currently have a career goal.

   b. Is Michele currently decided or undecided about her future career? If decided, does she appear to be vigilant or hypervigilant? If undecided, does she appear to be developmentally or chronically undecided?

   c. Did Joe have a career goal throughout his career with Infotek? If so, what is it and how did he arrive at it? Has it helped him achieve his Preferred Work Environment? If not, explain why you believe that Joe does not have a career goal.

    d. Is Joe currently decided or undecided about his future career? If decided, does he appear to be vigilant or hypervigilant? If undecided, does he appear to be developmentally or chronically undecided?

3. Career Strategies

    a. What specific career strategies has Michele implemented? Were they effective? Why or why not?

    b. What specific career strategies has Joe implemented? Were they effective? Why or why not?

4. Career Appraisal

    a. To what extent has Michele received useful feedback regarding her career? Why? What has she done or not done to receive feedback?

    b. To what extent has Joe received useful feedback regarding his career? Why? What has he done or not done to receive feedback?

5. Overall Effectiveness of Career Management:

    a. Who is more effective in career management, Michele or Joe? Why do you believe that?

    b. What personality characteristics enable individuals to manage their careers effectively, and what characteristics prevent individuals from managing their careers effectively? What personality characteristics did you observe for Michele and Joe, and how have they helped or hampered them in managing their careers?

6. What Is Next?

    a. What should Michele be doing now to manage her career effectively? Why?

    b. What should Joe being doing now to manage his career effectively? Why?

STAGES OF CAREER DEVELOPMENT

5

CAREER DEVELOPMENT: AN OVERVIEW

William Shakespeare recognized a long time ago that people change in significant ways as they make their voyage through life. In his famous "all the world's a stage" passage from As You Like It, Shakespeare vividly describes his view of the seven ages of man: from infancy ("mewling and puking in the nurse's arms") through middle age ("in fair round belly . . . full of wise saws and modern instances") to near-helpless old age ("second childishness and mere oblivion, sans teeth, sans eyes, sans taste, sans everything").

It has long been recognized that children pass through a series of rather predictable periods or stages that shape their personality, intelligence, and sense of morality.[1] More recently, scientists have come to believe that adulthood may also unfold or develop in a predictable manner. It is increasingly recognized that each phase of adulthood has its own particular developmental tasks and concerns that need to be addressed, and an understanding of career dynamics requires an awareness of development throughout adulthood.[2]

Do careers also unfold in orderly stages of development? The answer seems to be yes, although there is still disagreement about the exact nature and timing of the career stages. Changes in the business world over the past two decades have also affected the orderliness of the ideal progression through career stages. Downsizings may cause job loss. Women in the work force may wish to halt their careers to bear children. Many employees are returning to school to gain new skills. When individuals step out of the work force, either voluntarily or involuntarily, gaps are created in their employment histories. Research indicates that discontinuous employment histories have a negative impact on future income beyond that attributable to diminished work experience for both men and women.[3] Clearly, the evolving worldwide economy is having immediate and long-term effects on many individuals' progression through the career stages.

Despite these occurrences in the workplace, it is useful to view a career as a series of stages or phases. Surely, the career needs and concerns of a 25-year-old management trainee are bound to be somewhat different from those of a 45-year-old manager or a 65-year-old executive. Even people of the same age may experience different career concerns. Consider a stay-at-home mother re-entering the work force at age 45, or a 65-year-old retiree taking on part-time employment. Individuals face a variety of career tasks and developmental issues at different life stages. Moreover, changes in the nature of career motivation are likely to occur over the course of an employee's life.[4] An understanding of the tasks and developmental implications of different career stages can help individuals manage their careers more effectively and can help organizations manage and develop their human resources.

Chapter 5 introduces the concept of adult life development and examines the stages of career development within the larger context of adult life development. The aim is to provide an overview of life and career development so we can move to more detailed discussions of specific career stages in subsequent chapters. This chapter first considers several views of adult life development, placing special emphasis on the pioneering work of Daniel Levinson and his colleagues. It then discusses briefly our view of career development and previews subsequent chapters on the specific stages of career development.

ADULT LIFE DEVELOPMENT

There is a commonly held stereotype that adulthood, especially old age, is synonymous with decline. In our youth-oriented culture, it is not surprising that adulthood is often viewed (and feared) as a period of deterioration of physical, intellectual, and emotional functioning. Several findings question many aspects of this stereotype. For example, although various aspects of biologic functioning undoubtedly decline during adulthood, the decline is generally gradual until very late adulthood. Similar observations may be made about intellectual functioning. Although some forms of cognitive ability (such as short-term memory and speed-related tasks) do decline in many older adults, other forms of intelligence—those based on accumulated knowledge, experience, and wisdom—may continue to increase during adulthood.[5]

But there is more to the study of adulthood than simply cataloging physical, intellectual, and psychological functions. There is a much broader question of concern: "Is there an underlying order in the progression of our lives over the adult years, as there is in childhood and adolescence?"[6] A number of researchers believe that adulthood does progress in a systematic, orderly fashion.

ERIKSON'S APPROACH TO LIFE DEVELOPMENT

One of the earliest, most influential writers on life development, Erik Erikson, proposed that people progress through eight stages of psychosocial development (Table 5.1). Each stage poses a crisis of sorts and, depending on the outcome of the stage, provides the setting for either growth or arrested development. For example, at the first stage of development, the helpless infant is totally dependent

· TABLE 5-1

ERIKSON'S EIGHT STAGES OF DEVELOPMENT

Stage of Development	Age
1. Basic trust versus mistrust	Infancy
2. Autonomy versus shame and doubt	Ages 1 to 3
3. Initiative versus guilt	Ages 4 to 5
4. Industry versus inferiority	Ages 6 to 11
5. Identity versus role confusion	Puberty and adolescence
6. Intimacy versus isolation	Young adulthood
7. Generativity versus stagnation	Middle adulthood
8. Ego integrity versus despair	Maturity (late adulthood)

NOTE: Based on material from the following: E. H. Erikson, *Chilhood and Society* (New York: W. W. Norton & Company, Inc., 1963); G. J. Craig, Human Development, 3rd ed. (Englewood Cliffs, NJ: Prentice-Hall, 1983); L. J. Bischof, *Adult Psychology* (New York: Harper & Row, 1976).

on others for its nurturance and survival. Under favorable circumstances, the infant will develop a sense of trust in parents and other people. Under unfavorable conditions, the child will emerge with a basic mistrust of the world that may be difficult to reverse throughout life. At each stage of development, the ratio of positive and negative experiences determines the nature of the outcome.

The last three stages of Erikson's model are most relevant to adulthood and careers. The major task of early adulthood is the development of intimacy, a deep commitment to other people and groups. Failure to develop and maintain intimate relationships can bring a sense of isolation to the young adult and impair one's ability to love. As a person approaches middle adulthood, the development of generativity (literally guiding the next generation) becomes particularly important and can be accomplished through parenting and/or serving as a mentor to a younger colleague. Failure in this task can bring a feeling of stagnation in which no contribution or legacy is left to future generations. During late adulthood, people need to understand and accept the ultimate meaningfulness and limitations of their lives or risk ending life with despair.

Erik Erikson's major contributions to the study of life and career development are twofold. First, he proposed an underlying order in which certain key issues present themselves at critical parts of our lives. Although "success" at each stage does not guarantee permanent resolution of a conflict, "failure at an early stage jeopardizes full development at a later stage."[7] Second, he identified three key developmental tasks of adulthood—intimacy, generativity, and ego integrity— that, as we will see, are particularly relevant to an understanding of careers.

LEVINSON'S APPROACH TO ADULT LIFE DEVELOPMENT

Several researchers have made valuable contributions to our understanding of life development.[8] However, the work of Daniel Levinson and his colleagues plays a particularly significant role in our approach to career development and therefore warrants more extensive treatment. Levinson's research team conducted interviews with 40 American-born men between the ages of 35 and 45. Each man in the sample (10 business executives, 10 university biologists, 10 novelists, and 10 industrial workers) was seen between five and 10 times, and the interview transcripts generated an average of 300 pages of text per man.[9] These biographic interviews attempted to reconstruct the story of each man's life from childhood to the present.

After this initial study, Levinson conducted interviews with 45 women, also ranging in age from 35 to 45.[10] Fifteen women were homemakers, 15 were pursuing corporate careers in finance, and 15 were pursuing academic careers. Levinson and his associates conducted interviews similar to that of the male sample, generating biologic reconstructions of the stages of the women's lives.

Levinson proposed that there are four eras of the human life cycle: pre-adulthood, early adulthood, middle adulthood, and late adulthood (Table 5.2). Each era is composed of alternating stable and transitional periods. In stable periods, which usually last 6 or 7 years, people pursue goals to accomplish their significant life values. Stable periods are not necessarily tranquil, but they are stable in the sense that people attempt to create a desired life structure or lifestyle. Because no life structure remains appropriate forever, transitional periods, normally of 4 or 5 years' duration, are necessary to question and reappraise the established life structure and to consider making changes in various parts of one's life. Let us now examine the periods of adulthood and see how stable and transitional periods combine to foster personal development.

EARLY ADULTHOOD. Early adulthood normally begins at age 17 (with the early adult transition) and ends at age 45 with the termination of the midlife transition. In the early adult transition (ages 17–22), people emerge from adolescence and try to create a niche for themselves in adult society. Young adults need to begin the process of separation from their parents, often leaving home and becoming less financially and emotionally dependent on their parents. They also need to take some tentative steps into early adulthood by imagining or even trying out an adult role in some manner.

The entry life structure for early adulthood (ages 22–28) is a stable period in which the young person enters into the adult world but faces two potentially conflicting tasks: (1) to explore adulthood by trying out different roles (e.g., jobs, relationships) while keeping one's options open, and (2) to settle down and create a stable life structure. Whereas some people emphasize the exploratory task and form no real commitments to people or organizations, others form relationships that are expected to endure well into the future. Whatever decisions are made in this period, there are bound to be flaws. People who emphasized options and exploration may begin to wonder whether they are capable of developing and maintaining meaningful relationships. (Recall Erik Erikson's need for intimacy during early adulthood.) People who emphasize stability and commitments to an occupation, a company, or another person may wonder whether these commitments were premature and overly constraining.

· TABLE 5-2

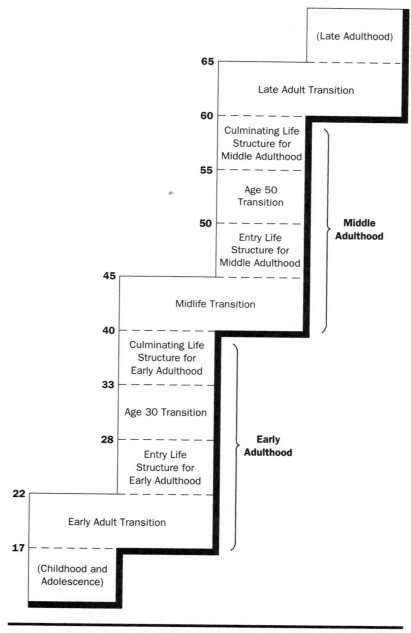

SOURCE: Based on a diagram originally included in *The Seasons of a Man's Life*, by Daniel J. Levinson et al. (1978). Updated to be consistent with terminology in Levinson's "A Conception of Adult Development," *American Psychologist* 41 (1986: 3–13).

In either case, the age-30 transition (ages 28–33) stimulates a reappraisal of one's current life structure. "A voice from deep within the self says: 'If I want to change my life—if there are things in it I want to modify or exclude, or things missing I want to add—I must now make a start for soon it will be too late.'" [11] In this sense, the age-30 transition, like all transitional periods, provides the opportunity for reflection, growth, and a redirection of one's life.

These first three periods comprise the novice phase of early adulthood in which one is struggling to become a "real" adult. A major task of this novice phase is to form, refine, and pursue a "Dream," a powerful view of how one wants to live his or her life. The Dream frequently has occupational goals (e.g., becoming a rich and famous financier), but it can extend beyond work to one's role in family, community, or the larger society.

The age-30 transition is followed by the second stable period in early adulthood. In this culminating life structure for early adulthood (ages 33–40), a person has two major tasks: (1) to establish a niche in adult society in areas of life (work, family, leisure) that are central to the person, and (2) to "make it"—that is, to advance along some timetable in an effort to build a better life. Traditionally, men in American society have been preoccupied with making it occupationally, and the mid- and late 30s are typically productive times in which to establish career success. The culminating life structure is devoted largely to pursuing the Dream. Daniel Levinson evokes the imagery of a ladder, which includes all dimensions of achievement such as rank, income, power, fame, and quality of family life, to characterize this period. The aim is to climb the ladder whatever the dimensions and become a full-fledged adult. Levinson believes that this period culminates in a BOOM/BOOP phase (becoming one's own man, or the gender neutral, becoming one's own person) between ages 36 and 40, in which the need to attain one's Dream becomes more powerful and intense.

Levinson states that women go through similar developmental stages in early adulthood. The main issue that plagues women at this stage (and throughout their lives) is the clash between the internal traditional homemaker figure and the antitraditional career woman figure. The traditional homemaker figure is best characterized by June Cleaver, the stay-at-home mother in the 1950's television show "Leave it to Beaver." All the homemakers in Levinson's sample exemplified and fulfilled this traditional female role model throughout the early adulthood period.

In the 1990's television show "Mad about You," Jamie Buchman epitomizes the antitraditional career woman figure. This character tries to balance her aspiring career with her family life. In Levinson's study, the women pursuing corporate and academic careers had similar tasks to accomplish during this period as the men, yet their tasks were made more complex by the presence of the traditional homemaker/antitraditional career woman conflict. The early adult career woman knew "what she wanted *not* to do but found it more difficult to determine what to do in a more positive [goal related] sense, and there were few alternative models available to her."[12] Many of the career women developed antitraditional Dreams. These Dreams were not only occupationally focused but also included hopes of "greater equality with men, in work as well as family."[13] Even as these dreams were developed and the goals associated with them identified, many career women "renounced it [the dream], temporarily or permanently, in order to pursue other, more pragmatic goals favored by . . . family [or society]." [14]

It is important to realize that data from Levinson's sample of women were gathered throughout the early 1980s, and attitudes of contemporary working women may be changing. Today's anti-traditional career women may not be renouncing their Dreams but are establishing traditional Dreams of career success (like their male counterparts) while at the same time managing family needs.[15] These early adult women are attempting to become "supermoms" and are not acknowledging their own needs for personal time because the needs of career and family take precedence. The most significant issues for these women are the logistics concerning child care and the parallel issue of establishing themselves as achievement-oriented, valuable employees.[16]

It appears that a significant difference between men and women at this early stage of adulthood is that men are free to ask and answer the question "What do I really want for myself?" Women, however, are constrained by many complexities and interrelationships and have difficulty answering this question. They, therefore, have a more vague sense of "self-in-world" and greater problems identifying the goals and associated tasks to become one's own person and pursue the Dream.[17]

MIDDLE ADULTHOOD. Middle adulthood is greeted by the midlife transition period (ages 40–45). The very life structure that was pursued so intensely during the prior period is reappraised, often with a great deal of turmoil and agony. "What have I done with my life? What do I really get from and give to my wife [or husband], children, friends, work, community, and self? What is it I truly want for myself and others?"[18] Daniel Levinson and his associates concluded that 80 percent of the men and 85 percent of the women in their samples experienced a moderate or severe crisis during the midlife transition.

Why do some people begin such a painful reevaluation during the early or mid-40s? Levinson points to the significance of three related factors. First, even modest decline in bodily functioning around age 40 may be interpreted as a loss of youthful vigor and may stimulate an increasing awareness of one's mortality. The opportunity to make a lasting contribution to the world (Erik Erikson's "generativity") can be threatened by the realization that one's life is more than half over.

Second, a generational shift normally occurs in the 40s. People in their 20s and 30s are apt to view someone in his or her forties as a member of the "older" generation. With the possibility of teenage children at this point and the likelihood of ailing or deceased parents, the person in his or her 40s feels pushed into senior status in the adult world and fears that youth (and all that it stands for) is largely completed.

Also, by the 40s, a person has experienced enough of life to assess progress toward the youthful Dream. A person who has failed to accomplish this Dream must deal with the failure and make some choices for the future. The person who has successfully climbed the ladder may begin to doubt whether the quest was worth it. The choices made in the 30s may have emphasized certain aspects of the self (e.g., success, achievement, power, competition) over others (e.g., friendships, nurturance, spiritual development). Business-related deadlines, travel, and a competitive life-style may have nourished a part of one's self at the expense of other parts. During the midlife transition, "these neglected parts of the self urgently seek expression and stimulate a man to reappraise his life."[19]

For many women, the midlife transition is a time for assessing the "supermom" syndrome. This is the realization that although an antitraditional career woman may "want it all," she may not be able to "have it all," or a series of trade-offs will have to be made. In Levinson's study, the appraisals women make during this transition regard three components: full-time career, marriage, and motherhood. Only two women (4 percent) really "had it all"—married while managing a full-time career and motherhood.[20] Most only had one or two components—career and marriage but no children; single divorced mothers with careers; or full-time mothers who had left their careers for their families. The midlife transition period allowed the women in Levinson's study to recognize that "efforts to combine love/marriage, motherhood, and full-time career had not given her as much satisfaction as she had hoped and that she would have to find a new basis for living in middle adulthood."[21] A recent study has noted that midcareer women were focused on preparing for the different family, career, and personal challenges of the next decade, as well as revising their definitions of success to include both personal and professional accomplishments.[22] In many cases, midcareer women have recognized the need to balance all their concerns, have acknowledged their need for more personal time, and have resolved the logistical issues of child care.[23]

It appears that today's antitraditional career woman has learned from her predecessors. The efforts of the early antitraditional career women have created support networks on which women and men rely heavily. These support networks not only include help and assistance from family members but also include support from organizations and the government. Chapter 11 discusses the intersection of work and family lives, and describes programs that provide support for career women and men.

Daniel Levinson speculates that the midlife transition is followed by a stable period (entry life structure for middle adulthood, ages 45–50) in which a person must try to fashion a satisfactory life structure for the middle years. Douglas Hall and Philip Mirvis suggest that midlife adults need to pursue a "protean career" (initially discussed in Chapter 1) that can be best exemplified by a free agent in the sporting world.[24] Flexibility and autonomy allow the midlife adult to tailor a career and pursue more options when compared with his or her younger peer. The protean career "involves more horizontal growth, expanding one's range of competencies and ways of connecting to work and other people . . . the protean form can embrace both mastery and relational growth—i.e., both 'male' and 'female' ways of developing."[25]

This period, in turn, is followed by the age-50 transition (ages 50–55), the purpose of which is to work further on the issues raised and the new goals developed during the midlife transition. Again, a stable period follows (culminating life structure for middle adulthood, ages 55–60), in which one attempts to build a life structure suitable for the remainder of middle adulthood.

LATE ADULTHOOD. The late adult transition (ages 60–65) terminates middle adulthood and begins late adulthood. Bodily decline may appear more devastating; illness and death may begin to take away one's family and friends. Retirement, with the attendant loss of status and power, seems closer and closer. Consistent with Erik Erikson's views of late adulthood, Levinson speaks of the developmental work that must be accomplished during this era: "to gain a sense of the integrity of his life—not simply of his virtue or achievement, but of his life as a whole. If he succeeds in this, he can live without bitterness or despair during late adulthood. Finding meaning and value in his life, however imperfect, he can come to terms with death."[26]

Although it is true that individuals in late adulthood (and Levinson's late, late adulthood period) may be preparing for the end of their lives, many also are preparing for a new life-style that may or may not include work-related activities. In *The Ageless Self,* Sharon Kaufman notes that older people do not see themselves as "old" and are not treated as "old" by their family and friends as long as they remain active and productive in some meaningful sense.[27] Continued productive activity may be a key to following the path of successful aging. When compared with low or moderately productive older adults, highly productive older adults were found to be engaged in three times more housework, twice as much yard work, more than three times more paid work, and nearly four times as much volunteer work.[28] These research findings contribute to a growing realization that older adults can and do remain highly productive well after retirement from formal work roles.

Adults entering late adulthood had previously represented a shrinking minority of the population. Today, there are many active septuagenarians, octogenarians, and nonagenarians, and predictions suggest that as the large number of baby boomers mature, many will lead long, healthy lives. An analysis estimated the maximum individual longevity potential is more than 130 years for those born in the early 1990s. This is consistent with the highest documented age of 121.5 years and multiple reports of U.S. survivors to later ages.[29] Daniel Levinson's model may one day need to be extended to incorporate the life stages subsequent to late adulthood!

EVALUATION OF LEVINSON'S MODEL. Levinson proposed the existence of four eras of the human life cycle in which a number of stable and transitional periods enable the individual to work on the major developmental tasks of each era. Despite the plausibility of the model, a number of questions become evident. How closely are the eras and the transitional periods linked to age? Is the sequence of periods fixed or can people "skip" periods? How universal are the periods? Are these periods applicable to both men and women in American society? To his credit, Levinson has not ducked these questions.

First, Levinson does believe that the periods are closely related to age. Although the participants in his samples showed some variation in the onset or termination of a period, the range was rather small, perhaps 2 years on either side of the average. Thus, Levinson believes that there is a close, but by no means perfect, correspondence between chronologic age and period of life development for both men and women.

Daniel Levinson also believes that each person goes through each period in a fixed sequence. Levinson's replication of his model with the female sample provides additional evidence for the orderly sequence of tasks and events. This does not mean that a person actively or successfully deals with each developmental task in each period—only that the developmental tasks present themselves in a fixed order. Failure to address the tasks of a certain period may well come back to haunt one in later life.

The generalizability of Levinson's model to all people in all societies has also been questioned. Although Levinson acknowledges that the answer to this question is unknown, he tentatively argues in favor of universal applicability. He cites literature from ancient Chinese, Greek, and Hebrew civilizations to support his view that "individuals go through the periods in infinitely varied ways, but the periods themselves are universal. These eras and periods have governed human development for the past five or ten thousand years."[30]

Perhaps most intriguing is the role of gender in adult life development. The above-noted research findings from Daniel Levinson and his colleagues indicate that women go through the same developmental periods as men. However, although Levinson notes that some of the specific issues may differ, other researchers have identified the salient issues as those that regard the balance of career progression with wife/motherhood.[31] Because of this delicate "balancing act," Joan Gallos and others claim that the very nature of life development is different for men and women. The Dream to achieve career success is tempered in many women by an early and enduring concern for significant relationships with other people. Therefore, the meaning of a career and of career success appears to be more complex for women than for men. According to Gallos, women pursue a "split dream," which provides a balance between career and relationships.[32]

It is also possible that the sequence of developmental issues is reversed for women and men. Although many men in early adulthood are preoccupied with achieving career success, Judith Bardwick similarly believes that women's early adult transition is dominated by a concern for balancing career, family, and dual-career issues. This may be due to society's pressure on women toward marriage at a relatively young age and because of women's definition of themselves in terms of their interpersonal relationships.[33] Even the pursuit of career success for women in their 30s is coupled with concerns about balancing multiple life roles (if they are a parent) or about the ticking away of the "biological clock" (if they are childless). However, middle adulthood, when many men are reducing their involvement in work, can be a period of professional involvement and accomplishment for women as they become more independent and somewhat freer of family demands.[34]

Adding to these complexities is the great variety of career patterns pursued by women.[35] Whereas some women pursue sequential career patterns (employment-then motherhood; employment-motherhood-employment; motherhood-then employment), other women simultaneously pursue employment and mother-hood, and still others choose not to have children. For these reasons, it is possible that the adult lives of women unfold in a less predictable manner than the lives of men.

It is our opinion that Daniel Levinson's model of life development is intuitive and impressive. Although research has produced intriguing results in the area of gender differences,[36] considerably more research needs to be conducted before we can fully understand the specific gender-related career stage issues. Although the career progression of women may be more complex than men, the careers of both genders are now so complex that it is unclear to what we should attribute these differences. However, the notion of period-related developmental tasks seems applicable to adulthood, and the alternating stable and transitional peri-ods seems to permit continued growth and development throughout adulthood. Finally, the three eras of adulthood—early, middle, and late—offer a useful structure for examining career-related issues during one's lifetime.

STAGES OF CAREER DEVELOPMENT

In Chapter 1, we defined career development as an ongoing process by which individuals progress through a series of stages, each of which is characterized by a relatively unique set of issues, themes, or tasks. Although the concepts of life development and career development are compatible, there is a greater emphasis on work-related issues in career development models.

Table 5.3 summarizes four of the more frequently cited approaches to career development. Despite some differences, the approaches share a number of common elements. First, they all propose that people progress through an orderly sequence of stages, each of which poses a set of tasks or challenges. Moreover, each stage is associated with an approximate age range, although variations in ages are generally acknowledged. In addition, each model tends to view the per-son in his or her total life, with work, family, and self-development concerns all interrelated. The emphasis may focus on career issues, but it is generally recog-nized that a person's work or career cannot be divorced from other aspects of his or her life. There also is considerable overlap in the content of the career stages.

This book views the development of a career in terms of five stages. This view is based in part on the literature in career development and in part on Levinson's view of adult life development. The five stages of this model are summarized in Table 5.4 and are discussed below.

STAGE 1: OCCUPATIONAL CHOICE: PREPARATION FOR WORK

From a career perspective, the major tasks of this stage are to form and refine an occupational self-image, explore the qualities of alternative occupations, develop at least a tentative occupational choice, and pursue the type of education or training required to implement the choice. The accomplishment of these tasks

· TABLE 5-3

FOUR MODELS OF CAREER DEVELOPMENT

Miller and Form				Super		
Age	Stage			Age	Stage	
0–15	Preparatory Work Period			0–14	Growth	
15–18	Initial Work Period			15–24	Exploration	
18–34	Trial			25–44	Establishment	
35–65	Stable			45–64	Maintenance	
65+	Retirement			65+	Decline	

Hall and Nougaim				Schein		
Age	Stage			Age	Stage	
0–25	Pre-Work			0–21	Growth, Fantasy, Exploration	
25–30	Establishment			16–25	Entry into World of Work	
30–45	Advancement			16–25	Basic Trainig	
45–65	Maintenance			17–30	Full Membership in Early Career	
65+	Decline			25+	Full Membership in Midcareer	
				35–45	Midcareer Crisis	
				40+	Late Career	
				40+	Decline and Disengagement	
				?	Retirement	

NOTE: Based on research by D. C. Miller and W. H. Form, *Industrial Sociology* (New York: Harper & Row, 1951); D. T. Hall and K. Nougaim "An Examination of Maslow's Need Hierarchy in an Organizational Setting," *Organizational Behavior and Human Performance* 3 (1968): 12–35; E. H. Schein, *Career Dynamics Matching Individual and Organizational Needs* (Reading, MA: Addison-Wesley, 1978); D. E. Super "A Life-span, Life-space Approach to Career Development," *Journal of Vocational Behavior* 16 (1980): 282–298.

requires considerable insight into one's own talents, interests, values, and desired life-style, as well as the requirements, opportunities, and rewards associated with alternative occupational fields.

The initial time frame for this stage, birth to 25, signifies that the formation of an image of oneself and the world of work takes place throughout childhood, adolescence, and early adulthood. However, the model of career management adopted here is based on continual exploration and discovery, and many people develop second or third occupational choices in the course of their work lives. Because occupational choices can occur at other stages, the tasks associated with occupational choice can reappear throughout one's lifetime. Chapter 6 focuses extensively on the occupational choice process.

STAGE 2: ORGANIZATIONAL ENTRY

The main task at this stage is to select a job and an organization in one's chosen career field. A positive outcome at this stage is the choice of a job that can satisfy one's career values and use one's talents. Unfortunately, many individuals' job

· TABLE 5-4

FIVE STAGES OF CAREER DEVELOPMENT

1. Occupational Choice: Preparation for Work
Typical Age Range: Initially 0–25; then variable
Major Tasks: Develop occupational self-image, assess alternative occupations, develop initial occupational choice, pursue necessary education.

2. Organizational Entry
Typical Age Range: Initially 18–25; then variable
Major Tasks: Obtain job offer(s) from desired organization(s), select appropriate job based on accurate information.

3. Early Career: Establishment and Achievement
Typical Age Range: 25–40
Major Tasks: Learn job, learn organizational rules and norms, fit into chosen occupation and organization, increase competence, pursue dream.

4. Midcareer
Typical Age Range: 40–55
Major Tasks: Reappraise early career and early adulthood, reaffirm or modify dream, make choices appropriate to middle adult years, remain productive in work.

5. Late Career
Typical Age Range: 55–Retirement
Major Tasks: Remain productive in work, maintain self-esteem, prepare for effective retirement.

selections are based on incomplete or unrealistic information. Such people may experience considerable disillusionment and dissatisfaction when the reality of the work environment does not live up to their inflated expectations. The organizational entry stage is identical to Edgar Schein's entry into the work world and is consistent with portions of stages in the other models.[37]

The organizational entry stage, which may take several months of job search to complete, initially takes place between the ages of 18 and 25, often depending on the number of years of education one has pursued. Although this stage is experienced initially by persons who are moving directly from school to their first career-related work assignment, one can enter a new organization at any age; therefore, the age range can be variable. Chapter 7 elaborates on the tasks associated with the organizational entry process. It reviews how individuals choose jobs and organizations, considers several obstacles to a match between the individual and the organization, and suggests ways to manage the organizational entry process more effectively.

The next three career stages are largely organized around Daniel Levinson's view of adult development. That is, stage 3, the early career, coincides with the vast portion of early adulthood; stage 4, midcareer, coincides with middle adulthood; and stage 5, late career, roughly coincides with late adulthood. The organization of these career stages around Levinson's view of adulthood is based on the belief that the three eras of adulthood have somewhat distinct themes that are reflected in specific career-related issues.

STAGE 3: THE EARLY CAREER

Stage 3, which really encompasses two periods, reflects the dominant issue of early adulthood: finding a niche for oneself in the adult world and striving to "make it" along the chosen path.

Having already selected an occupation and an initial job, a critical first task of the early career is to become established in one's career and organization. The new employee must not only master the technical aspects of his or her job but must also learn the norms, values, and expectations of the organization. In this establishment period of the early career, the individual's major task is to learn about the job and the organization and to become accepted as a competent contributor to the organization, in other words, to make a place for oneself in the occupation and the organization. Note that in Table 5.3 several of the career development models refer to an establishment stage.

In the achievement period of the early career, the individual "is not so concerned with fitting into the organization (moving inside) as he is with moving upward and mastering it."[38] It should not be surprising that this success-oriented period of the early career coincides with Levinson's culminating life structure of early adulthood and the BOOP period. Note that in Table 5.3 one of the career development models refers to an advancement stage.

It may seem odd that the early career can extend all the way up to age 40. In fact, the achievement period in this stage coincides with what Edgar Schein called full membership in midcareer. But the entire stage, in our view, does reflect the early career in that the individual typically continues to pursue youthful aspirations—Daniel Levinson's Dream—as yet unencumbered by the sometimes painful reappraisal of the midlife transition. Thus it is suggested that the dominant theme of the early career, becoming established and making it (however defined), can maintain itself in one form or another for a full 15 years. Chapter 8 examines issues pertaining to the early career in considerable depth.

STAGE 4: THE MIDCAREER

An individual's midcareer (ages 40–55) is initiated by the midlife transition, which serves as a bridge between early and middle adulthood. A number of tasks and concerns characterize the midcareer years. First, the individual is likely to reappraise the life structure that dominated his or her early career. Next, it is necessary to begin to form a life structure (with its career implications) to move oneself fully into middle adulthood. Whether the new life structure is consistent with the prior one or constitutes a minor or radical departure, a number of specific work-related issues confront the individual in midcareer.

The midcareer stage is consistent with portions of the maintenance stage and the stable period referred to in Table 5.3 and also with portions of Schein's late career. Again, one may think it strange that midcareer can extend all the way to age 55. We would argue, however, that midcareer, like middle adulthood, raises qualitatively different concerns than do the later years, when, to a considerable extent, the "die is cast" and one has to deal with retirement and the anxiety that disengagement from the work role may evoke.

Chapter 9 is devoted to an examination of midcareer issues. Among the major concerns treated are the distinctive requirements of the midlife transition, the dynamics of midcareer change, the dangers of obsolescence, and the possibilities of midcareer plateauing. As with the other career stages, we consider individual and organizational actions that can contribute to effective functioning during midcareer.

STAGE 5: LATE CAREER

Although there has not been a great deal of research on the late career, it appears that two major tasks dominate this stage. First, the individual must continue to be a productive contributor to the organization and maintain his or her sense of self-worth and dignity. However, the maintenance of productivity and self-esteem is often hindered by changes within the individual and by society's bias against older people. Second, the individual in late career must anticipate and plan for an effective retirement, so that disengagement from work is not devastating to the individual and that the postretirement years are meaningful and satisfying.

The late career extends roughly from the mid-50s to retirement. Although Levinson indicated that late adulthood begins at age 60, late career issues, especially the need to think seriously about retirement, can become significant at a somewhat earlier age. Rapid technologic changes, age-related stereotypes, and pressures toward early retirement can all combine to stimulate late career concerns in one's 50s. The issues that dominate the late career are examined more thoroughly in Chapter 9.

DIFFICULTIES IN APPLYING A CAREER-STAGE PERSPECTIVE

We have traced five career stages that provide the developmental context for the next four chapters. There is no claim that this is the only or the best way to view career development, but it does seem to structure our knowledge about careers in a meaningful manner.

We have purposefully chosen to organize career stages around typical—although approximate—age ranges. Some approaches to career development, most notably that of Gene Dalton and Paul Thompson,[39] define career stages on the basis of work activities, relationships, and psychological issues rather than on the basis of age. Despite the many valuable contributions of that approach, we take the position that age, or more generally life experience, strongly shapes career aspirations, experiences, and concerns and therefore plays a critical role in the identification of career stages.

However, there are several factors that complicate all attempts to link career stages to age. First, all age ranges are approximations. The onset and termination of stages can vary. Thus, a high school graduate may accept a first full-time job at age 18, whereas a PhD graduate may take a first academic post at 27 or 28.

More complicating, however, is the assumption that the stages of a career cycle depict development in a "normal" career, that is, a career in which a person chooses an occupation at an early age and remains continually in the same career field (or in the same organization) for the duration of one's work life. Perhaps Edgar Schein is most explicit in this regard when he says, "I am specifying more of an 'ideal state,' or a model of what a career would look like if pursued fully and successfully."[40]

What are the complications that arise from deviations from this "normal" or "ideal" career cycle? Consider the following illustrations:

■ A 42-year-old woman accepts paid employment for the first time in nearly 20 years. Is she beginning her midcareer years or is she entering the establishment period of her early career?

■ A 38-year-old banker pursues a promotion to senior vice president with a different bank. Is he deeply entrenched in the achievement period of his early career or is he beginning another organizational entry stage?

■ A 55-year-old computer executive leaves Silicon Valley to become a novelist. Is he entering his late career or is he struggling to establish himself in the early career stage of his new literary pursuits?

These kinds of classification problems are inherent in all age-related theories of career development. But they may not be problems after all. Our aim is not merely to classify an individual into a particular stage but to understand how careers unfold and how people relate to work at different stages of their careers and lives. The newly employed woman primarily has to deal with the early career issues of socialization and establishment, but from the perspective of a 42-year-old. The 38-year-old banker does have to deal with the problems of organizational entry but with the experience and concerns of a person who is advanced in his early career and is "on the move." The 55-year-old former computer executive does, in most respects, have to establish himself in his new career field but from the vantage point of a man nearing late adulthood.

We should not bemoan these deviations from a neat classification system, because they reflect the rich diversity of careers and lives. In Table 5.5, we attempt to portray this diversity by linking the tasks of career development with the three eras of adulthood. Notice that the selection of an occupation, the entrance into an organization, the establishment of oneself in a new setting, and the striving for achievement in that setting occur most prominently in early adulthood. However, the selection of a different occupation or organization can occur during middle adulthood or late adulthood, necessitating renewed establishment and achievement concerns in the different career field or organization. Conversely, the tasks most closely aligned with midcareer and late career (reappraisal, remaining productive, preparation for retirement) may also occur to some extent during early adulthood. Perhaps our aim should be to understand the typical issues that people generally experience at each career stage and then consider the possible variations that can occur at each stage. This approach is followed in subsequent chapters when we delve more deeply into the different career stages.

▪ TABLE 5-5

RELATIONSHIP BETWEEN CAREER DEVELOPMENT TASKS AND STAGES OF ADULTHOOD

Career Development Tasks	Stages of Adulthood		
	Early Adulthood	Middle Adulthood	Late Adulthood
Occupational Choice	XXX	XX	X
Organizational Entry	XXX	XX	X
Early Career			
Establishment	XXX	XX	X
Achievement	XXX	XX	X
Midcareer			
Reappraisal	X	XXX	XX
Remain Productive	X	XXX	XXX
Late Career			
Remain Productive	X	XXX	XXX
Prepare for Retirement	X	XX	XXX

XXX Very Frequently

XX Frequently

X Occasionally

SUMMARY

The basic theme of this chapter is that adult lives and careers develop in a relatively orderly manner. The research of Erik Erikson and Daniel Levinson suggests that the early, middle, and late stages of adulthood present somewhat different tasks and challenges that need to be addressed. Early adulthood is characterized by a preoccupation with establishing oneself as an adult and "making it" in the adult world. Middle adulthood often involves a reappraisal of one's life situation and a concern with making a lasting contribution to the world. In late adulthood, one needs to come to terms with the meaning and value of one's life. Possible gender differences in stages of life development were also considered.

Five stages of career development were identified: (1) occupational choice, in which one develops an occupational self-image, explores alternative occupations, and forms an occupational decision; (2) organizational entry, during which one selects a job and an organization in one's chosen career field; (3) early career, in which one is concerned with establishing him- or herself in a career field and achieving competence and recognition; (4) midcareer, during which time a person may need to reexamine the course of his or her career and life and perhaps make adjustments for the future; and (5) late career, in which one needs to maintain a satisfactory level of productivity and self-esteem and plan for an effective retirement. These five career stages provide the structure for the next four chapters of the book.

ASSIGNMENTS

1. Interview a friend, acquaintance, co-worker, or relative who is in a different career stage than you are. What career-related tasks and activities is this person currently undertaking? What are the issues and concerns that are uppermost in his or her mind? In what ways are these issues and concerns consistent or inconsistent with the approach to life development and career development proposed in this chapter?

2. Chart the career histories of a male and female friend, acquaintance, co-worker, or relative. Are the two career histories parallel and similar to each other? Are they similar to Levinson's model? Do employment gaps exist in either career history? If so, ask whether these employment gaps have had any effect on the individual's career.

DISCUSSION QUESTIONS

1. Using Levinson's model as a framework, in what stage of adult life development do you see yourself? What concerns are uppermost in your mind at this time? Are these concerns consistent with Levinson's model?

2. Some people experience a crisis during their early or middle 40s. What factors are responsible for a midlife crisis? Does everybody experience a midlife crisis? Why or why not?

3. Do you think everybody follows the same developmental path through adulthood? Is Levinson's model applicable to women as well as men? To single people as well as married people? To working-class adults as well as upper-middle-class adults? Why do you feel that way?

ENDNOTES

1. E. H. Erikson, *Childhood and Society* (New York: W. W. Norton & Company, Inc., 1963); S. Freud, *Collected Papers* (New York: Basic Books, 1959); L. Kohlberg, "Development of Moral Character and Moral Ideology," in *Review of Child Development Research,* vol. 1, ed. M. L. Hoffman and L. W. Hoffman (New York: Russell Sage Foundation, 1964), 383–431; J. Piaget, *The Child's Conception of Number* (London: Routledge & Kegan Paul, 1952).

2. S. Cytrynbaum and J. O. Crites, "The Utility of Adult Development Theory in Understanding Career Adjustment Process," in *Handbook of Career Theory,* ed. M. B. Arthur, D. T. Hall, and B. S. Lawrence (Cambridge, UK: Cambridge University Press, 1989), 66–88.

3. J. A. Schneer and F. Reitman, "Effects of Employment Gaps on the Careers of M.B.A.'s: More Damaging for Men than for Women?" *Academy of Management Journal* 33, no. 2 (1990): 391–406.

4. A. Howard and D. W. Bray, *Managerial Lives in Transition* (New York: Guilford Press, 1988).

5. G. J. Craig, *Human Development,* 3rd ed. (Englewood Cliffs, NJ: Prentice-Hall, 1983).

6. D. J. Levinson, C. N. Darrow, E. B. Klein, M. H. Levinson, and B. McKee, *Seasons of a Man's Life* (New York: Knopf, 1978); quote on p. ix.

7. L. J. Bischof, *Adult Psychology* (New York: Harper & Row, 1976); quote is on p. 32.

8. R. L. Gould, "The Phases of Adult Life: A Study in Developmental Psychology," *The American Journal of Psychiatry* 129, no. 5 (1972): 33–43; B. L. Neugarten, "Adult Personality: Toward a Psychology of the Life Cycle," in *Middle Age and Aging*, ed. B. L. Neugarten (Chicago: University of Chicago Press, 1968), 137–147.

9. D. J. Levinson, "A Conception of Adult Development," *American Psychologist* 41 (1986): 3–13; Levinson et al., *Seasons of a Man's Life.*

10. D. J. Levinson and J. D. Levinson, *Seasons of a Woman's Life* (New York: A. A. Knopf, 1996).

11. D. J. Levinson, "The Mid-Life Transition: A Period in Adult Psychosocial Development," *Psychiatry* 40 (1977): 99–112; quote is on p. 104.

12. Levinson and Levinson, *Seasons of a Woman's Life*; quote is on p. 231.

13. Ibid.; quote is on p. 232.

14. Ibid.; quote is on p. 239.

15. P. Amos-Wilson, "Accomplishing Career Development Tasks: Are There Gender-Related Differences?" *The International Journal of Career Management* 5, no. 5 (1993): 11–16; L. F. Fitzgerald and L. M. Weitzman, "Women's Career Development: Theory and Practice from a Feminist Perspective," in *Adult Career Development: Concepts, Issues and Practices*, ed. H. D. Lea and Z. B. Leibowitz (Alexandria, VA: The National Career Development Association, 1992), 124–160; J. R. Gordon and K. S. Whelan, "Successful Professional Women in Midlife: How Organizations Can More Effectively Understand and Respond to the Challenges," *Academy of Management Executive* 12, no. 1 (1998): 8–24.

16. Fitzgerald and Weitzman, "Women's Career Development"; Gordon and Whelan, "Successful Professional Women in Midlife."

17. Levinson and Levinson, *Seasons of a Woman's Life*; K. L. Spenner and R. A. Rosenfeld, "Women, Work and Identities," *Social Science Research* 19 (1990): 266–299.

18. Levinson, "The Mid-Life Transition"; quote is on p. 107.

19. Ibid.; quote is on p. 108.

20. Levinson and Levinson, *Seasons of a Woman's Life.*

21. Ibid.; quote is on p. 372.

22. Gordon and Whelan, "Successful Professional Women in Midlife."

23. Ibid.

24. D. T. Hall and P. H. Mirvis, "The New Career Contract: Developing the Whole Person at Midlife and Beyond," *Journal of Vocational Behavior* 47 (1995): 269–289.

25. Ibid.; quote is on p. 278.

26. Levinson et al., *Seasons of a Man's Life*; quote is on p. 37.

27. S. R. Kaufman, *The Ageless Self: Sources of Meaning in Late Life* (Madison, WI: The University of Wisconsin Press, 1986).

28. T. A. Glass, T. E. Seeman, A. R. Herzog, R. Kahn, and L. F. Berkman, "Change in Productive Activity in Late Adulthood: MacArthur Studies of Successful Aging," *Journal of Gerontology* 50, no. 2 (1995): 65–80.

29. K. G. Manton and E. Stallard, "Longevity in the United States: Age and Sex-Specific Evidence on Life Span Limits from Mortality Patterns 1960–1990," *Journal of Gerontology* 51, no. 5 (1996): 362–389.

30. Levinson et al., *Seasons of a Man's Life*; quote is on p. 322.

31. Amos-Wilson, "Accomplishing Career Development Tasks"; R. Caffarella, S. Olson, "Pscho-social Development of Women," *Adult Education Quarterly* 43, no. 3 (1993): 125–151; Fitzgerald and Weitzman, "Women's Career Development"; B. White, "The Career Development of Successful Women," *Women in Management Review* 10, no. 3 (1995): 4–15.

32. J. V. Gallos, "Exploring Women's Development: Implications for Career Theory, Practice, and Research," in *Handbook of Career Theory,* ed. Arthur, Hall, and Lawrence, 110–132.

33. J. M. Bardwick, "The Seasons of a Woman's Life," in *Women's Lives: New Theory, Research, and Policy,* ed. D. McGuigan (Ann Arbor, MI: University of Michigan Center for Continuing Education of Women, 1980) pp. 35–58; Gallos, "Exploring Women's Development."

34. Bardwick, "The Seasons of a Woman's Life."

35. Ibid.; J. Marshall, "Re-visioning Career Concepts: A Feminist Invitation," in *Handbook of Career Theory,* ed. Arthur, Hall, and Lawrence, 275–291; U. Sekaran and D. T. Hall, "Asynchronism in Dual–Career Couples," in *Handbook of Career Theory,* ed. Arthur, Hall, and Lawrence, 159–180.

36. Amos-Wilson, "Accomplishing Career Development Tasks"; P. J. Ohlott, M. N. Ruderman, and C. D. McCauley, "Gender Differences in Managers' Developmental Job Experiences," *Academy of Management Journal* 37, no. 1 (1994): 46–67; S. Ornstein, W. L. Cron, and J. W. Slocum, "Life Stage versus Career Stage: A Comparative Test of the Theories of Levinson and Super," *Journal of Organizational Behavior* 10 (1989): 117–133; P. Tharenou, S. Latimer, and D. Conroy, "How Do You Make It to the Top? An Examination of Influences on Women's and Men's Managerial Advancement," *Academy of Management Journal* 37, no. 4 (1994): 899–931; White, "The Career Development of Successful Women."

37. E. H. Schein, *Career Dynamics: Matching Individual and Organizational Needs* (Reading, MA: Addison-Wesley, 1978).

38. D. T. Hall, *Careers in Organizations* (Glenview, IL: Scott Foresman, 1976); quote is on p. 54.

39. G. W. Dalton and P. H. Thompson, *Novations: Strategies for Career Development* (Glenview, IL: Scott Foresman, 1986).

40. Schein, *Career Dynamics*; quote is on p. 37.

OCCUPATIONAL CHOICE:
PREPARATION FOR WORK

Take a moment and consider the following four scenarios:

- Jessica is a 22-year-old woman who has just accepted her first full-time position on graduation from college. As a newly hired junior accountant at an industrial products company, Jessica is finally about to embark on her career. She is hopeful that her college degree in accounting and her summer bookkeeping jobs have prepared her well for this new job.

- Tom is a 34-year-old commercial lending officer for a large bank and has just tendered his resignation after 11 years with the firm. Tom determined that his career in banking, although thus far financially rewarding, was not turning out the way he expected. In Tom's view, the bureaucracy of the bank imposed needless constraints and restrictions, and its overly cautious approach to lending went against his entrepreneurial spirit. Moreover, with the spate of mergers in the banking industry, Tom was not sure about his prospects for keeping his job in the future. Consequently, Tom adjusted his career goals and has accepted a new job as a sales representative for a small pharmaceutical company.

- Wilma is a 46-year-old woman whose youngest child just started high school. After some hesitation, Wilma has decided to reenter the work force full time. Although she was not sure what job she should pursue, Wilma was certain she wanted to work in an environment in which she could demonstrate her computer skills. After taking Internet certification classes, she began her job search. Two months later, Wilma landed a position as a webmaster for a small company.

- Antonio is a 58-year-old man who was told 3 months ago that his job as a production supervisor at a specialty chemical company was being eliminated in a cost-cutting move. Working with the outplacement firm that his former company provided, Antonio assessed what he wanted to do with the rest of his career until he would retire in 10 years or so. After considering all his options, Antonio accepted a position as head of the maintenance staff at a local hospital.

What these cases represent are four distinct examples of occupational choice. Although it is generally accepted that occupational choice is a key activity in the growth and exploration stages of development, these examples show that the dynamics of occupational selection can be relevant at each career stage. The experiences of Jessica, Tom, Wilma, and Antonio illustrate that the choice of an appropriate occupation (either initially or as a career change) is a pivotal task in the career management process, one that can take place really at any point in one's life.

Are you in the process of selecting an occupation? If you are, are you confident that you will make the right decision, or do frequent doubts enter your mind? Do you know where to turn for information and insight? Have you thought about how to select an occupation from among competing alternatives?

This chapter examines the ways in which people go about the task of choosing occupations. After reviewing the theory and research on occupational choice, we examine several obstacles to the occupational choice process, and we offer recommendations for improving the process.

THEORIES OF OCCUPATIONAL CHOICE

An occupation is a group of similar jobs found in several establishments.[1] This definition distinguishes a specific job in a particular organization (e.g., a marketing research analyst at Procter & Gamble) from the broader notion of an occupation (marketing research). Therefore, we can think of such diverse occupations as accounting, pharmacy, computer engineering, and the ministry, each of which has a somewhat unique set of requirements and rewards.

A comprehensive review of the theories of occupational choice is beyond the scope of this book. Such a detailed review is available elsewhere[2] and is not necessary to appreciate the variety of psychological, social, economic, and cultural factors that enter into occupational decisions. Instead, there are six significant themes that can help us understand the manner in which people make occupational choices:

1. occupational choice as a matching process
2. occupational choice as a developmental process
3. occupational choice as a decision-making task
4. occupational choice as a function of social and cultural influences
5. occupational choices of women
6. occupational choices of minorities

For each theme, we review the relevant research, highlight important findings, and illustrate its significance to our model of career management.

• TABLE 6-1

ILLUSTRATIONS OF HOLLAND'S TYPOLOGY OF PERSONALITY AND OCCUPATIONS

I. Realistic
Personal Characteristics: Shy, genuine, materialistic, persistent, stable
Sample Occupations: Mechanical engineer, drill press operator, aircraft mechanic, dry cleaner, waitress

II. Investigative
Personal Characteristics: Analytical, cautious, curious, independent, introverted
Sample Occupations: Economist, physicist, actuary, surgeon, electrical engineer

III. Artistic
Personal Characteristics: Disorderly, emotional, idealistic, imaginative, impulsive
Sample Occupations: Journalist, drama teacher, advertising manager, interior decorator, architect

IV. Social
Personal Characteristics: Cooperative, generous, helpful, sociable, understanding
Sample Occupations: Interviewer, history teacher, counselor, social worker, clergy

V. Enterprising
Personal Characteristics: Adventurous, ambitious, energetic, domineering, self-confident
Sample Occupations: Purchasing agent, real estate salesperson, market analyst, attorney, personnel manager

VI. Conventional
Personal Characteristics: Efficient, obedient, practical, calm, conscientious
Sample Occupations: File clerk, CPA, typist, teller

NOTE: The entries are selected illustrations. For complete classification, see J. L. Holland, *Making Vocational Choices: A Theory of Vocational Personalities and Work Environments* (Englewood Cliffs, NJ: Prentice-Hall, 1985).

OCCUPATIONAL CHOICE AS A MATCHING PROCESS

Most theories of occupational choice contend that a person, consciously or unconsciously, chooses an occupation that "matches" his or her unique set of needs, motives, values, and talents. One of the earliest approaches to occupational choice, the so-called trait and factor theory, is perhaps most explicit in this regard. "According to this viewpoint, confronted with the necessity of choosing an occupation, an individual consciously proceeds to make an analysis of his vocational assets and liabilities, accumulates information about occupations, and arrives at a decision."[3] Consistent with this view, a person would be expected to identify his or her abilities, needs, and values, select appropriate career goals, and then choose an occupation thought to be most compatible with these goals.

The work of John Holland also views occupational choice as a process of matching occupations and people.[4] In particular, he believes that people express their personalities in making an occupational choice. Holland's theory classifies people in terms of their similarity to the six personality types that were described previously in Chapter 3. Recall that these types included realistic, investigative, artistic, social, enterprising, and conventional. Each personality type is characterized by a common set of activity preferences, interests, and values. For example, as Table 6.1 indicates, enterprising personality types perceive themselves as adventurous, ambitious, and energetic, whereas conventional types see themselves as efficient, obedient, practical, and calm.

Holland proposes that occupational environments can also be classified into these six categories. Each environment is dominated by a particular personality type and reinforces those qualities possessed by that type as noted above. Moreover, Holland classified specific occupations into the same six environments as he had classified the personality types. For example, realistic occupations include engineering and construction work, investigative occupations include the physical and biologic sciences, artistic occupations include music and art, social occupations include teaching and the ministry, enterprising occupations include public relations and advertising, and conventional occupations include administrative work.

One of John Holland's major assumptions is that "people search for environments that will let them exercise their skills and abilities, express their attitudes and values, and take on agreeable problems and roles."[5] In addition, it is expected that people's stability in an occupational area will depend on the fit or match between personality type and occupational environment. For instance, social personality types who find themselves in electrical engineering could become dissatisfied with the occupation and might choose another occupation more consistent with their social orientation. Research has found that congruence between personality and occupational environment can lead to such favorable outcomes as higher job satisfaction, improved job stability, and increased job involvement.[6] In addition, a mismatch between one's personality and occupational choice could be a reason for an individual to pursue a career change.

In general, traditional or classic views on the matching of individuals with occupations are based on the notion of "supplementary" congruence, or the matching of individuals with environments in which they are similar to people already in those environments.[7] However, some researchers have noted the possibility of a "complementary" congruence wherein personality characteristics and abilities of the individual can serve to complement personal characteristics and abilities already present in the work environment.[8] In this sense, the strengths of the individual may fill a void in a given work environment and thereby improve overall group performance.

Donald Super's extensive work is also based on the notion of a match between individuals and occupations. The key concept in his model is the person's self-concept, "the individual's picture of himself, the perceived self with accrued meanings."[9] Our self-concept, in other words, consists of attributes we think we possess: our abilities, personality traits, needs, interests, and values.

Super believes that an occupational choice enables a person to play a role appropriate to the self-concept. A person "implements" his or her self-concept in developing an occupational choice; that is, he or she selects an occupation that is compatible with significant parts of the self-concept. In effect, people develop a self-concept, develop images or beliefs about a series of occupations, and take steps to enter the occupation that is most compatible with their self-concept. As an example of Super's view, a college student might see herself as analytical, persuasive, and extroverted and have a deep interest in individual rights and social justice. After some exploration of different occupations, she might conclude that a career in civil rights law would take advantage of her analytical and inter-personal skills and would enable her to contribute to society in a significant way. The student's chosen occupation, civil rights law, represents the expression or im-plementation of her self-concept. A great deal of evidence supports the notion that people prefer and choose occupations that are compatible with their self-concept.[10]

OCCUPATIONAL CHOICE AS A DEVELOPMENTAL PROCESS

Although evidence indicates that people match or implement their self-concept in choosing an occupation, one's selection of an occupation does not take place at a single point in time. The decision to become a pharmacist, for example, does not begin and end when a high school junior or senior decides to attend a pharmacy college.

The choice of an occupation can be considered a developmental process that evolves over time. For one thing, the decision to pursue a particular occupation is really a series of decisions that span a significant portion of one's life. The pharmacist-to-be may have decided to participate in the fifth grade science fair, to take an accelerated mathematics program in junior high school, to join the chemistry club in high school, and to seek summer employment at a local pharmacy. A number of educational and vocational decisions and activities culminate in an occupational choice.

Second, as Donald Super and others have indicated, one's self-concept is formed, clarified, and modified over an extended period of time. It takes time and experience for talents to emerge and for interests and values to crystallize. Time is also required for people to learn about the world of work. Misinforma-tion is hopefully replaced by more accurate perceptions as we learn about different occupations and jobs. Potential occupations are pursued or discarded as new information becomes available to the child, adolescent, young adult, and mature employee.

For these reasons, it is proper to view occupational choice as an unfolding, gradual, evolving process. Although a number of researchers have contributed to our understanding of the developmental nature of occupational choice, we focus on the research of Donald Super and his colleagues. Super proposed that individ-uals progress through a series of developmental stages that enable a person's self-concept to be formed, translated into occupational terms, and implemented as an occupational decision.[11]

As seen in Chapter 5, Super suggested that people move through five stages relevant to career development: growth, exploration, establishment, mainte-nance, and decline.[12] As we indicated earlier in this chapter with the examples of Jessica, Tom, Wilma, and Antonio, the need to make occupational choices can oc-cur throughout the life cycle. Likewise, the gathering of information and the gaining of personal insights relevant to one's occupational choice can occur through the various career stages.

People learn about themselves and the work world through exploratory behavior. Super pointed out that a child's exploration takes place in the home, at school, and through part-time work experiences.[13] At home, children learn by observing and interacting with parents, siblings, and other relatives and friends. Children develop role models and identify with significant persons. They see what others do, and as they perform their own tasks at home, they learn what they like, what they excel at, and who they are. "The self-concept begins to take shape, the kind of role one may play in life begins to emerge, even in childhood, even within the shelter of the home."[14]

People also learn about themselves through educational experiences. Inside and outside the classroom, they have opportunities to gain insights into themselves. Performance in course work, participation in extracurricular activities, and discussions with fellow students or teachers can all shape the self-concept and a view of the world. For example, in successfully running for treasurer of her junior high school, a young girl learned, to her surprise, that she enjoyed the competitiveness of the campaign and the power and status her elected office brought her. At the conclusion of the election, she decided she wanted to be an attorney. The stability of her occupational preference may be brief (tomorrow she may want to be a manufacturer's sales representative), but what is important is that she began to translate her daily experiences to the world of work.

Part-time and summer employment also provide substantial opportunities for reality testing—a firsthand look at ourselves. By waiting tables, clerking, selling, or repairing, we can not only test our talents and interests, but we also can learn what it is like to work outside the home.

Thus, childhood and adolescence provide time for maturation. Our self-concept becomes more stable, more clear, and more realistic. This approach is similar to Erik Erikson's model of life development, in which the child and adolescent are confronted with the tasks of developing competencies, testing reality, and developing a more certain sense of self-identity. In our earlier example, Jessica's selection of accounting as an occupation was a product of her developing as a person, learning from earlier job-related experiences, and knowing her likes, dislikes and special competencies.

Life-long learning and personal development have become the mantras of the workplace. Adults continue to gain personal insights over the later stages of the life cycle. We constantly reassess ourselves and our achievements in relation to our career goals. Incongruities between expectations and reality can lead to changes in career goals and alterations in occupational preferences. From our earlier examples, Tom's decision to make a midcareer change by leaving the banking profession and making another occupational choice reflected his dissatisfaction with his work environment and his desire to express his entrepreneurial personality.

Transitions and changes in life roles can also necessitate the making of occupational choices. Our example of Wilma, who returned to work after the demands of caring for younger children had diminished, is representative of an occupational choice that resulted from a change in a life role. Finally, organizational actions can force a change in one's occupational field. Downsizings, mergers and acquisitions, and business failures can serve to make new career goals and an associated occupational choice a necessity. Loss of one's job, as given in the example of Antonio at the beginning of the chapter, is a powerful if not overwhelming inducement to seek a new occupation.

Donald Super's portrait of vocational development is one of progressive insight into strengths and weaknesses, enhanced awareness of occupations, adequate planning, and confidence in career-related decisions. This does not imply that these accomplishments are automatic. Some people seem to clarify and implement occupational preferences in a more timely, realistic, or confident fashion than others. Undoubtedly, people differ considerably in their ability and willingness to gather information, develop insight, and plan and implement decisions, the very activities so critical to our model of career management. Vocational tasks may appear in an orderly and progressive fashion, but nobody said that their accomplishment was easy!

OCCUPATIONAL CHOICE AS A DECISION-MAKING TASK

We have seen how occupational choice can be viewed essentially as a developmental process in which experiences and increasing maturity enable a person to develop, modify, and clarify the self-concept, gain further insights into the world of work, and attain a match between a chosen occupation and one's self-perceived interests, abilities, needs, and values.

Given a set of alternative occupations, how does one choose which occupation to pursue? According to the career management model presented in Chapter 2, a person should engage in career exploration, acquire a greater awareness of self and alternative occupations, and develop a career goal. In the context of occupational choice, the career goal is to enter a particular occupation. But this does not explain *how* individuals select a particular occupational field. How, for example, does one determine whether finance or marketing will provide a better match? What psychological process guides one in the selection of a particular occupational field?

A number of models of vocational decision making have been developed to address this very issue. Although there are several differences among them, most are based on some form of psychological decision theory. As David Osborn has noted, research on occupational decision making has generally assumed that individuals use compensatory or "trade-off" approaches in which unfavorable aspects of a given job are offset by the favorable elements of the job.[15] Osborn states that the most widely used compensatory choice model is expectancy theory as based on the work of Victor Vroom.[16] Expectancy theory is essentially a rational, calculative, goal-directed model of human decision making in which people choose courses of action that are expected to produce desirable consequences.

First, expectancy theory assumes that people approach an occupational choice situation with a fairly well-established set of desired outcomes or rewards. In expectancy theory terminology, we are aware of the *value* of a wide range of job outcomes (e.g., advancement opportunities, salary, or interesting work). In fact, we rate (mentally at least) the value of each outcome on some scale before we consider different occupations.

Next, expectancy theory assumes that we examine a number of occupations and determine the likelihood that each occupation will provide us with the job outcomes. These beliefs are called instrumentality perceptions because they refer to our perception of how instrumental an occupation will be in attaining each job outcome. As with the value of outcomes, our instrumentality perceptions are assumed to be mentally rated on a scale. Expectancy theory assumes that individuals will mentally multiply the value of each outcome by the instrumentality for that outcome to obtain a total attraction score. A person is predicted to be most attracted to the occupation with the highest score. However, finding an occupation attractive is not the same as choosing to enter an occupation. There may be many attractive occupations (e.g., professional athlete, politician, brain surgeon) that we ultimately reject for one reason or another. Perhaps we believe we do not have the right mix of talents for a particular occupation or that our financial resources (or our patience) are not adequate for the extensive training required.

According to expectancy theory, people develop expectancies regarding the likelihood that they could successfully enter a particular occupation if they put forth sufficient effort. Expectancy theory assumes that people mentally multiply the attractiveness of an occupation by their expectancy of being able to enter the occupation. They then choose the occupation with the highest expected attractiveness. In other words, we are most likely to pursue an occupation that we not only find attractive but also have a decent chance of entering.

Do people really choose occupations in such a rational, calculative manner? Do people compare occupations on a long list of job outcomes, multiply the value of each outcome by its perceived instrumentality, and choose occupations that maximize the likelihood that they will obtain desirable outcomes and avoid undesirable outcomes?

Research studies would seem to answer "yes" to these questions.[17] Our occupational preferences and decisions do seem to be guided by our desire to seek maximum rewards from work. However, competing theories of decision making suggest that occupational choice is neither as rational nor as systematic as expectancy theory implies. Individuals "facing a real organizational choice situation may use non-compensatory strategies to simplify the decision-making process."[18] Decision makers may use strategies wherein the first option that fulfills the individual's minimally acceptable standards on specific occupational attributes is chosen.[19] Research on "unprogrammed" (i.e., nonroutine) decision making has drawn several conclusions that are inconsistent with expectancy theory predictions.[20]

First, people do not initially assess a job on a long list of outcomes but rather focus on one or two significant outcomes. Jobs that fail to reach an acceptable level on these significant outcomes are rejected from further consideration, even if they would provide many other desirable outcomes. The jobs that survive this cut would not be compared with one another (as expectancy theory would suggest), but rather are placed on an "active roster" of acceptable alternatives. From this active roster, the person often makes an "implicit" decision (unknown even to oneself) to favor one alternative over the others, based on just one or two outcomes.

After having made this implicit choice, one attempts to justify the decision by comparing the (implicitly) chosen job with the rejected alternatives on a wide range of outcomes. It is at this point, after the decision is made (but before it is fully recognized), one identifies the instrumentalities of each job, multiplies each instrumentality by the value of each outcome, and compares the jobs in a calcula-tive manner. But the purpose of these calculations is not to make a decision but rather to confirm a decision that has already been implicitly made. During this confirmation stage, "a great deal of perceptual and interpretational distortion takes place in favor of the choice candidate" (i.e., chosen job).[21]

There has not been sufficient research to draw sound conclusions about the relative usefulness of the compensatory and the noncompensatory decision-making approaches to occupational choice behavior. As noted earlier, extensive research has supported an expectancy theory view, yet the "unprogrammed" view has been supported as well.[22] Although the jury is still out, both approaches share one important principle, namely, that choices are based on perceptions of different occupations or jobs. Whether the choice is based on one or two critical outcomes or on a longer list of outcomes weighted by value and instrumentality, beliefs about an occupation's ability to provide these outcomes determine occu-pational preferences. If beliefs and perceptions are unrealistic, occupational deci-sions are likely to be faulty. If a person is mistaken in his or her view that a cer-tain occupation will provide interesting work activities, that person will be disappointed and disillusioned in the job. The implications of these unmet expectations are treated in considerable detail in the next chapter.

SOCIAL AND CULTURAL INFLUENCES ON OCCUPATIONAL CHOICE

Behavior is a function of the person and the environment. The choices we make are reflections of our personal characteristics and the environment in which we live. The occupational choice process is no exception to this general rule. Career decisions are not made in a vacuum.

Most of the research on occupational choice seems to focus on the person as an active agent in the formulation of occupational plans and decisions. Certainly, our model of career management emphasizes what one can or should do to plan, manage, and appraise a career. Much of the psychologically oriented theory and research discussed so far consider personal goals and intentions, awareness, information seeking, and strategy development as key influences on occupa-tional decision making.

However, there are other approaches to the study of occupational choice and decision making. In particular, the sociologic approach to careers "is fundamen-tally based on the notion that elements beyond the individual's control exert a major influence on the course of life, including educational and vocational deci-sions."[23] Undoubtedly, the environment—both past and present—plays a major role in occupational decision making. A person's past environment includes family of origin, social class, income, and place of residence. The present environment includes the economic, political, and cultural climate in which a person lives.

First, consider the ways in which a child's social background can influence his or her orientation to the work world. Although the United States may be less class conscious than other cultures, there can be distinctive life-styles associated with membership in different socioeconomic classes. Social class not only affects the availability of resources for one's career choice, but also affects the network of attitudes, customs, and expectations one may experience.[24]

Several studies have shown that differences in values and attitudes, especially occupational and educational aspirations, can be attributed to one's social class.[25] Accordingly, a parent's occupation can determine the kind of people met and admired during childhood. Growing up as a child of a physician is likely to expose one to different role models than growing up as a child of a firefighter—not better or worse, but different. Selective exposure to different adults can stimulate widely different occupational aspirations.

Moreover, social class can affect the values we hope to attain at work. A father or mother who has lived through some unstable time (a strike or extended layoff, lapses in continued employment caused by downsizings, or the Great Depression) may encourage a child to value security in a job above all else. A college professor or scientist may encourage a life of study and research, a social worker or physician a life of service, and an entrepreneur a life of competition. This is not to say that a child automatically adopts a parent's work values, but that the opportunity to identify with parents and internalize their values is certainly present.

Parents' occupations can influence the development of their children's interests and skills in certain areas, particularly regarding the choice of white- or blue-collar jobs.[26] An automobile mechanic's son or daughter is likely to get an early introduction to the world of "things" and mechanical operations. A physician's daughter may accompany her mother or father to the office or hospital and develop an interest and ability in working with people in emergency situations. It appears that close relationships between a father and his children strongly influences the children's (both boys' and girls') choice of nontraditional occupations.[27] This may be due to the strong emotional ties between the father and his sons or daughters, as well as the father's participation in child rearing, typically a maternal function.

In addition, parents' occupations affect family income. A wealthy family can provide the resources to pursue special hobbies and perhaps develop some latent interests and skills. Financial resources also make it easier for the child to attend college and perhaps graduate or professional school. In a study on the "inheritance" of a career, it was found that a father's occupational level ultimately affected his son's occupational aspirations.[28] In that study, fathers who had themselves attained high occupational accomplishments "passed on" these values by encouraging their sons to attend college. Also, second-generation college students have been found to perceive more support from their parents (who also attended college) than did first-generation college students.[29]

Parents' occupations and income can also influence the type of neighborhood in which a family lives. A place of residence is influential because it determines whom we meet and interact with in our daily lives. Because of their residents' background and values, neighborhoods differ in their emphasis on athletic achievements, academic attainments, and occupational success. Peer pressure among children can work to encourage or discourage educational accomplishments and aspirations.

In addition to the cultural norms of a particular social class or neighborhood, the geographic location of one's residence can affect occupational decisions.[30] Young people growing up in a city may have little knowledge of the life of a forest ranger, and Floridians may not seriously consider a career in ski resort management. These geographic considerations do not pose insurmountable barriers (a Miami-bred college student at a New England university could develop an interest in and proficiency at skiing), but they do restrict a view of what constitutes a feasible career.

In addition to the influences of family, social class, and geography, career decisions are always made in the context of the larger society. Economic conditions and consumer preferences promote certain industries and occupations over others. The growth in many service industries is a result of increased consumer buying power and preference for a more leisurely life-style. Technological changes create positions that were unheard of just a few years before. Political events can also affect career plans. To site a historical example, the launching of the Russian satellite Sputnik I in 1957 led to a reemphasis on the science curriculum in American schools. It almost seemed patriotic at that time to pursue a career in science or aerospace technology. Edgar Schein's analysis highlights the significance of a society's culture in shaping the meaning of a career and the legitimacy of different career values.[31]

The role of "accidents" in career decision making must not be forgotten. If you did not attend that political rally, you never would have met your fiancé, who could not have introduced you to his cousin, who would not have asked you to go to the conference in social planning, which ultimately stimulated your interest in public administration. These kinds of "random" accidental events occur all the time and can easily influence the course of our lives.

In summary, one's social background can stimulate or suppress certain skills, values, and abilities. Social class has been found to be related to beliefs about one's ability and control over a situation, as well as the importance of work to one's identity.[32] One's social background provides or withholds financial resources and, to a large extent, determines the people who will play a major role in one's early life. Moreover, the cultural environment reinforces certain values, legitimizes certain career aspirations, and places occupational decisions in a larger economic, political, and technological milieu. In short, the environment can influence how people view themselves, their future, and the world of work.

It is important to recognize the influence of the environment, past and present, on vocational plans because it gives additional insight into one's motives and aspirations. *However, people still have the opportunity to manage their own careers.* Social learning theory posits that career choice is a function of the unique learning experiences of the individual.[33] Specifically, one's career choice is seen as a product of the interaction between one's environment (home, school, work, social, and cultural milieu) and the learned experiences from the environment. The value and impact of relationships outside of work also may affect the employee during self-assessment and occupational selection processes and should not be underestimated.[34] Social learning reflects "different reinforcement histories, interacting with differences in biology and environment, [that] produce distinctive sets of response skills and attitudes in individuals."[35] Thus, the individual can act on the environment, just as the environment simultaneously has a distinct influence on the individual. In summary, there is a large element of truth to the popular phrase that "today is the beginning of the rest of our lives." Information still needs to be gathered, goals and strategies are still useful vehicles for focusing and accomplishing desired outcomes, and appraisal is required to maintain adaptability and flexibility. In other words, career management is still a critical process.

OCCUPATIONAL CHOICES OF WOMEN

We have discussed several views of the occupational choice process: as a development of clear concepts of self and work, as a matching of personal qualities to a compatible work environment, and as a decision-making task in which one searches for information about alternative occupations. These three approaches are consistent with one another in that they all view the decision maker as one who is motivated to enter an occupation that can fulfill a wide range of work values and can enable the utilization of various talents.

Does this picture describe the occupational choice process of women as well as men? Put another way, are the theories developed to understand occupational choice equally applicable to women and men? Although the answers to these questions are still not settled, there has been a burgeoning interest in the study of women's career development.[36] Indeed, this topic of study is a prime illustration of the significance of social and cultural influences on occupational decision making.

There are differences of opinion regarding whether the existing theories of career development are completely applicable to women. For example, Barbara Gutek and Laurie Larwood argue that the current theories on men's careers do not fit the experiences of women due to the fact that women face a different range of opportunities and problems than those experienced by most men. By contrast, Louise Fitzgerald and John Crites state that the career development process for women is essentially the same as that for men.[37] Fitzgerald and Crites' view supports the studies of Daniel Levinson.

Perhaps the most fundamental differences between the way men and women approach occupational decisions are reflected in the following observations:

Many occupations are sex stereotyped. Some (e.g., engineering) are thought to be more appropriate for men, and others (e.g., nursing) are thought to be more appropriate for women. Children learn occupational sex stereotypes very early in life, perhaps as early as 2 1/2 years of age.[38] And one study of 5- and 6-year-olds found that gender stereotypes held by young children were strongly influenced by the traditional [female-dominated] occupations pursued by their mothers.[39] Nevertheless, gender stereotyping of occupations among college students seems to have declined in recent years.[40]

Stereotypically female jobs are frequently characterized by low pay and modest training requirements. Moreover, they are thought to require traits that are stereotypically feminine (e.g., nurturance, warmth) and require less career continuity than male-dominated occupations.[41]

Women tend to select an occupation from a much narrower range of alternatives than men.[42] Although women may more often choose careers from fewer alternatives, the reason may not be due to stereotypes alone. Female students in male-dominated fields of study (e.g., engineering, physics, computer science, medicine, and law) reported that they would be more likely to pursue a career in medicine and law because these careers play a useful social role and allow a higher level of social contact than the more technical fields.[43] The study concluded that women choose occupations with high levels of social involvement, which is consistent with other findings regarding women's preferences for strong social relationships.[44]

In the past, women have aspired to lower-level and less prestigious occupations and positions than men.[45] However, research has indicated that "historical change has caused some young women to prepare for greater work involvement and more non-traditional jobs which are associated with better pay and better potential for advancement than the jobs traditionally held by women."[46] Women who pursue nontraditional jobs have been found to be more risk taking, were less certain about marriage plans, desired fewer children, and were more likely to hold an androgynous gender role orientation. However, negative consequences have also been noted by women who pursue nontraditional occupations.[47] These consequences include more job stress, more adverse working conditions, less job satisfaction, high levels of sexual harassment, sexual discrimination, and racial discrimination.

Most important, because of their selection of restricted and stereotyped occupational alternatives, women tend not to use fully their talents and skills in their chosen occupation. It is claimed that "women's career aspirations and choices are frequently far lower in level than are the aspirations of males with comparable levels of ability."[48]

Why do many women consider such a small set of alternative occupations? Why do so many women still choose to enter traditional, female-dominated, female-stereotyped occupations? We examine three possible explanations: the relationship between work and family life, women's self-perceived competence in the occupational arena, and the absence of strong social support.

RELATIONSHIP BETWEEN WORK AND FAMILY. First, and perhaps most significant, women generally consider the implications of their occupational choice for their present or future family lives. When a young man chooses to enter engineering, he rarely asks, "If I become an engineer, will I still be able to get married and raise a family?" It has always been taken for granted that a man can pursue a career without having to consider family matters.

Many women, however, perceive that they have to choose between working and marriage/parenthood. If a woman holds a demanding, high-level position, who will watch the children during the day? Is day care the answer? What about weekend meetings and business trips? Who will stay home when a child is sick? Will my husband share the home and child-rearing responsibilities?

Research indicates that female college students are more likely than male students to anticipate the presence of work-family conflict and that the anticipation (or presence) of such conflict can dampen a woman's career interests and motivation.[49] It has been pointed out that many women first make a choice about life-style.[50] Will they marry? What type of marriage will it be? Will they follow the traditional homemaker model or will they follow the antitraditional career woman model? Do they want children? Will they interrupt their work during the child-rearing years? How important is work? Only after these basic questions are answered will a woman be ready to select an occupation that is compatible with the anticipated life-style. The decision about when and where to become employed is often made in the light of the woman's family demands and needs. As discussed by Joan Gallos, marriage and relationships, not careers, are of primary importance in the dreams and self-identities of many women.[51] Perhaps because of these greater complexities, women making decisions regarding occupational choices report less certainty in articulating their life goals than men.[52]

Thus, women tend to place their occupational plans in the larger context of family and life aspirations. Frequently, the anticipation of conflicts channels women into lower-level, less prestigious, female-dominated occupations that could, if necessary, be pursued on a part-time, interrupted, or low-involvement basis. Under these conditions, it is unlikely that a woman's real interests and talents will find expression in her occupational world.

SELF-PERCEIVED COMPETENCE. A second reason for the restricted occupational choices of many women may involve their self-perceived competence in a variety of occupations. There is evidence that women are generally less confident of their abilities than men and that people who lack self-confidence aspire to less prestigious occupations than those with high self-esteem.[53]

The issue of self-perceived competence has been addressed by using a social learning perspective and emphasizing the role of "self-efficacy expectations" in vocational behavior.[54] Self-efficacy expectations are personal beliefs of competence in a particular area and are thought to be a major determinant of goals and activities. That is, people are more likely to engage in behaviors in which they believe they are competent and are drawn to occupations for which they hold high self-efficacy expectations. Several studies have found that women hold significantly lower mathematics self-efficacy expectations than do men. Because proficiency in mathematics is seen as a "critical filter" for so many technical and professional occupations, relatively lower levels of self-efficacy expectations in this area among women can severely restrict their choice of occupations.[55]

In addition to mathematics, women have been reported to hold lower self-efficacy expectations for other male-dominated occupations than do men. Moreover, the weaker the self-efficacy expectations for nontraditional occupations, the less likely a student will express a strong interest in entering a nontraditional occupation.[56] Conversely, women who pursue nontraditional jobs have been found to demonstrate strong self-concepts and high levels of self-efficacy.[57]

These findings all point to the significant role of self-efficacy expectations in occupational decision making. How do people develop (or change) self-efficacy expectations in a particular area? Albert Bandura considered four sources of high self-efficacy expectations: (1) successful past performance on a particular behavior, (2) vicarious learning experiences in which we observe others perform the behavior successfully, (3) verbal persuasion and encouragement, and (4) reduced levels of anxiety regarding the behavior.[58]

All four sources have implications for the career development of women. If, in general, women perform poorly or are anxious in mathematics and other "masculine" activities or if they are discounting their true performance accomplishments, they will tend to develop low self-efficacy expectations in these areas and avoid certain nontraditional occupations.[59] Moreover, up until recently, the shortage of female role models in nontraditional occupations has made it difficult for many women to observe success vicariously, thereby thwarting self-efficacy expectations for nontraditional occupations. In addition, as the next section shows, the lack of encouragement and support to enter nontraditional occupations has undoubtedly played a major role in many women's occupational decisions. Nancy Betz and Louise Fitzgerald offer a number of recommendations to strengthen the self-efficacy expectations of women. These recommendations include "facilitating performance accomplishments, providing exposure to female role models, assisting girls and women to manage, if not conquer, anxiety with respect to nontraditional domains, and providing active support of girls' and women's efforts to increase the extent and range of their feelings of competency."[60]

SOCIAL SUPPORT.   Most people require some encouragement, praise, and support before navigating untested waters. Indeed, women who have entered nontraditional occupations report encouragement and support of their efforts from a wide range of sources, both female and male.[61] Parents, spouses, siblings, friends, and instructors are all potential sources of encouragement (or discouragement) to pursue different occupational roles.

It is interesting to see how parents can influence the occupational choices of their daughters. Studies have described how fathers who have achieved success in their careers served as role models and sources of occupational identification for their daughters. Perhaps it is not surprising that fathers of women in nontraditional occupations are more highly educated than fathers of women in traditional occupations.[62] But such influence is not limited to the father. Women in nontraditional occupations frequently grew up with mothers who were employed and highly educated. Indeed, the hopes, expectations, encouragement, and support of both parents play a role in women's career development. In support of these views, studies have found that parental support has a significant influence on women's selection of highly nontraditional careers.[63]

Is there any evidence that such support has been absent for many women? Early research found that faculty members held relatively low expectations for their female students' careers.[64] In addition, female managers have reported receiving less career counseling from professors than did male managers. It has also been suggested that many school counselors provide little support and encouragement for women to consider nontraditional occupations, may be misinformed about opportunities for women, may hold their own biases against women who combine family and career responsibilities, and should be careful not to offer biased career placement testing services.[65]

It should be recognized that these three factors—anticipated conflict between career and family, low self-efficacy expectations, and lack of support—reinforce each other in several ways. Women who favor a traditional, female-typed occupation to ward off extensive work-family conflict may send signals to parents and teachers that they are not interested in nontraditional career fields, thereby receiving little encouragement from these people. Such lack of encouragement may then reinforce already shaky self-efficacy expectations in certain areas.

Also, these three factors may be changing. Certainly, more women are entering male-dominated occupations than in previous years. Does this indicate a greater willingness on the part of women to combine career and family activities? Are women reducing the salience of the family role (e.g., by not having children) so that a high-level career can take precedence? Or have women been receiving more support for their nontraditional choices in recent years and developed higher self-efficacy expectations for a wider range of skills and occupations? Perhaps the answer is "yes" to all these questions, more or less. Women's lives now and in the future will provide the ultimate answer.

OCCUPATIONAL CHOICES OF AMERICAN MINORITIES

Because culture and environment play a significant role in the occupational choice process, it has been suggested that members of American minority groups may exhibit different patterns of career behavior than nonminorities. Undoubtedly minorities, which include African-Americans, Asians, Hispanics, and Native Americans, have faced considerable prejudice and discrimination in employment situations. The following issues have been observed.[66]

- There are substantial differences in jobless rates between minorities and nonminorities.
- Differences in income between minorities and nonminorities are substantial, even when controlling for level of education.
- Minorities tend to be concentrated in a more restricted range of occupations than nonminorities.
- Minorities are often blocked from learning the skills necessary to break the cycle of poverty and discrimination.

- Minorities many times come from low- and middle-class families and may not have the resources to attend college.

- Minorities who do attend college may be concerned about assimilating into campus life and becoming estranged from their family and community bonds.

- Minorities often have high aspirations that are not realized in occupational attainment.

- Minorities, especially minority women, tend to enter less prestigious occupations than nonminorities.

It is beyond the scope of this book to attempt to explain these conclusions. Certainly, vicious cycles of racism, discrimination, poverty, and hopelessness have left their mark on the careers and lives of many members of America's minorities. However, we are still left with a central question: Do minorities approach the task of forming an occupational choice in a substantially different way than other individuals? It has been suggested, for example, that existing theories of occupational choice cannot fully explain minorities' occupational choices. Based primarily on research of white populations, current theories of occupational choice seem to assume an open labor market and sufficient individual resources to implement one's self-concept. However, the following has been observed, "External constraints, limited economic resources, and racial discrimination make the concept of life-stage development for racial minorities more of a dream than a reality for all but the most persistent, the most fortunate, and the group or mixture of individuals perceived as most socially desirable within a given racial group."[67]

According to this view, minority group members may not generally seek and find expression for their self-concept in work because of the overwhelming obstacles, financial and societal, that lie in their paths. If this is true, then the matching premise and the career management model may not accurately describe the process pursued by many minorities because they assume that people believe they have real choices, that occupations and organizations are open and available to those who have the talents and the values to pursue them. If historical patterns of discrimination have closed doors to occupational opportunities, then many minorities may believe that they have few viable options to express their talents and values in the work world.

Despite these very real concerns, it is premature to dismiss the relevance of occupational choice theories for minorities. More and better research needs to be conducted to understand the nature and roots of minorities' occupational choices. For one thing, it is inappropriate to lump together minority groups as diverse as African-Americans, Asians, Hispanics, and Native Americans.[68] Moreover, there are likely to be substantial individual differences in occupational choice behavior within a particular minority group, perhaps due to differences in social class and subcultural background.

Ideally, there should be no major differences in the occupational choice process of majority and minority Americans. That is, self-insight and knowledge of occupational alternatives should enable all people to pursue occupational goals consistent with their talents, values, interests, and life-style preferences. Obstacles, in the form of societal discrimination and a sense of personal powerlessness, are inimical to the American ideal. It would be presumptuous to suggest that obstacles as pervasive as poverty, prejudice, and discrimination can be easily overcome by individual members of minority groups. However, if one believes that recent progress in reducing discrimination has been significant and durable, then active career management (exploration, goal setting, and strategy development) can become increasingly relevant to all individuals, regardless of race or ethnic background. Members of all cultural groups in any society should be able to choose occupations that use talents, satisfy aspirations, and contribute to society.

GUIDELINES FOR EFFECTIVE OCCUPATIONAL DECISION MAKING

Despite our position that occupational choice is a matching process, observation and common experience tell us that many people do not necessarily choose occupations that are compatible with their talents, values, and interests. Some choose occupations that fail to use their talents, that provide for little satisfaction of their needs and values, and that involve job duties in which they have little or no interest. In this section, we apply the career management model by examining several factors that can contribute to the choice of an appropriate occupation.

DEVELOPMENT OF SELF-AWARENESS

Self-awareness is the cornerstone of effective career management. In the absence of a deep understanding of one's talents, interests, values, and preferred lifestyle, one would require considerable luck to fall into a compatible occupation. The major obstacles to the development of self-awareness were discussed in Chapter 3. At this time, it is appropriate to consider your degree of self-awareness. Review your responses to Learning Exercises I (data collection), II (theme identification), and III (preferred work environment). Do the themes still make sense to you? Is your preferred work environment summary consistent with these themes? Does your summary touch on all eight of the elements listed in Exercise III? If not, ask yourself why certain elements are missing.

Learning Exercise VII provides an opportunity for you to revise or complete your preferred work environment statement. If you believe you need more information in certain areas, indicate how you can go about obtaining the information. Consider the possibility of seeing a vocational counselor, taking tests, reading materials on self-assessment, and speaking to friends, relatives, spouse, colleagues, co-workers, or professors. Remember that self-exploration is a process; it is never really completed. Therefore, a periodic appraisal of your preferred work environment can be helpful.

DEVELOPMENT OF ACCURATE OCCUPATIONAL INFORMATION

Self-awareness needs to be combined with a satisfactory understanding of alternative occupations. However, lack of relevant work experience, stereotypes of occupations, and unfamiliarity with certain occupational fields all detract from development of a solid base of occupational information.

Actually, there are two related steps in occupational exploration. The first is to identify a number of occupations that may be potentially compatible and satisfying. Then, collect more in-depth information on each occupation. Obviously, one can go back and forth between the two steps, but some form of screening is necessary, if for no other reason than time and information overload. We cannot explore hundreds of occupations in depth.

Effective screening can be accomplished by consulting sources that provide information on a wide range of occupations. For example, the *Occupational Outlook Handbook,* published by the U.S. Department of Labor and available in many libraries and counseling centers, provides information on job duties, working conditions, employment statistics, education and other job requirements, job outlook, earnings, related occupations, and sources of additional information for more than 200 occupations. Similar information, although perhaps less detailed, can be obtained from such sources as the *Dictionary of Occupational Titles.* Regardless of the sources consulted, a person should seek occupational information that is relevant to his or her preferred work environment.

Once some initial screening has been conducted, it is possible to collect more extensive information on a smaller number of occupational alternatives. Again, an understanding of one's preferred work environment can help focus a person's information search. A partial list of information sources includes:

- Books on specific occupations and industries, which are frequently available in public and academic libraries and counseling centers.

- Web sites.[69]

- Pamphlet files on occupations, also generally available in libraries and counseling centers. In addition, the *Occupational Outlook Handbook* provides names and addresses of organizations that publish information on specific occupations. One can also contact trade or professional associations (e.g., the American Psychological Association) for literature on occupational opportunities in the field.

- Other people, such as counselors, professors, friends, relatives, and work associates who can provide information on specific occupations. In addition, personal or family contacts can frequently identify individuals who are currently employed in a particular occupation and are willing to share their experiences and opinions.

- Seminars on specific occupations (e.g., "Careers in Advertising"), which can also provide useful information and possible contacts. Seminars are often sponsored by student groups (e.g., the Society for the Advancement of Management), counseling offices, and professional associations.

■ Work experience, which has frequently been mentioned as a source of information about oneself and the world of work, is also helpful. For students, cooperative work assignments or internships and special part-time or summer job programs should be explored for potential employment possibilities.

EFFECTIVE GOAL SETTING

One of the most significant components of the career management process is the development of a realistic, appropriate career goal. In the context of occupational choice, the goal is to enter a specific occupational field. Assuming that a person has conducted sufficient self and occupational exploration, how should he or she decide from among alternative occupations?

Learning Exercise V provides an opportunity for you to develop long-term and short-term conceptual goals and to compare the appropriateness of operational goals. If you examined specific occupations in Exercise V, this would be a good time to reexamine the advantages and disadvantages you listed for each occupation. If you did not examine occupations in Exercise V, you should do so at the present time. List the elements of your conceptual goal (long-term or short-term), identify two occupations in which you have some interest, and list the advantages and disadvantages of each occupation.

The choice of an occupation is, at the end, a subjective, emotional experience. And no absolute criteria are available to determine what represents a "good" career choice. No easy, automatic formulas exist (or should exist) to eliminate the subjective element. However, a systematic collection and analysis of relevant information can provide a realistic data base in making such decisions.

DEVELOPMENT OF CAREER STRATEGIES

Once a career goal is selected, we need to identify strategic behavior, activities, and experiences that facilitate goal accomplishment. The twin criteria by which strategies should be chosen are their potential usefulness and their personal acceptability. Moreover, one important function of a strategy is to enable a person to test the viability of his or her career goals. In this case, strategies can help to confirm or disconfirm the wisdom of an occupational choice. Among the strategies described in Chapter 4, several seem particularly relevant to the occupational choice process:

SKILL DEVELOPMENT. Because each occupational field has a somewhat unique set of job duties, the necessary skills and abilities can vary significantly from one occupation to the next. Therefore, one component of an effective career strategy is to acquire or develop occupationally related skills. Such skills can be developed by exposure to appropriate educational environments. The selection of a college major, the choice of electives, and attendance at a graduate or professional school can provide the opportunity for enhancing one's proficiencies and knowledge base. For students about to enter the work force, participation in selected extracurricular activities (e.g., the student newspaper), nonacademic programs (e.g., assertiveness training), and work experiences (e.g., internships) can be valuable supplements to one's formal education.

For working adults, skill development can be pursued in a number of ways. Many organizations use structured job posting programs to announce open positions in other departments and functions within the firm. Movement into other areas within the company on a regular basis can enhance the depth of one's knowledge and skills, which can help prepare the individual for other occupational fields. Organizations also sponsor a variety of training and devel-opment programs (e.g., workshops on presentation skills, sales skills, and supervisory training) that employees can use to supplement existing job skills. As discussed in Chapter 4, working adults can take on additional assignments or "moonlight" as a way to build specific competencies and test out other occupations.

COMPETENCE IN CURRENT ACTIVITIES. Although it may seem obvious, mere participation in academic, extracurricular, and work activities is not sufficient. For skills to be developed, real learning needs to take place. For most people, this demands some combination of natural talent, hard work, and effective work or study skills. Any activity that can help one to become more proficient is worth doing well.

OPPORTUNITY DEVELOPMENT. Opportunity development refers to activities designed to convey one's interests and aspirations to others and to become aware of opportunities consistent with these aspirations. Self-nomination is an important career strategy in many different situations. Informing professors, friends, and colleagues of career plans can lead to part-time employment, graduate school recommendations, or job leads on graduation. The rationale is simple; people cannot advise and help you unless they know your interests.

In a similar fashion, networking can provide valuable information and support. Participation in formal organizations and professional associations, as well as informal discussions, can help develop useful contacts as well as compatible acquaintances and friendships. Closely related to self-nomination and networking, seeking guidance from others can provide information on oneself, specific occupational requirements and opportunities, and leads for jobs or skill development opportunities.

Regardless of which combinations of strategies are chosen, it is important to understand the purpose of each activity, sequence the activities, and establish timetables for completion.

If a strategy to enter an occupation (or change occupations) is relevant to you at the present time, use Learning Exercise VIII to formulate the strategy.

Again, it is necessary to be flexible in developing and implementing a career strategy. No list of strategies should ever be considered final. Even if goals remain the same, specific strategic behaviors should be added or deleted as necessary. Most important, take advantage of the feedback and appraisal functions of strategies. Periodically ask yourself whether your chosen occupation still makes sense to you. If the evidence is consistently and convincingly negative, be prepared to change your course of action—or pay the price somewhere along the line.

SUMMARY

Six themes capture much of the thinking and research on the occupational choice process: (1) occupational choice is a matching process in which individuals seek an occupation that is consistent with their talents, values, interests, and desired life-style; (2) occupational decisions evolve over time as people develop and refine their knowledge of themselves and the work world; (3) occupational choice is a decision-making task in which people evaluate the likelihood that alternative occupations will provide desirable outcomes; (4) individuals' occupational decisions are influenced by their social background and the current economic, political, and technological environment; (5) many women choose occupations that do not fully use their talents; and (6) many members of minority groups, faced with external barriers to occupational aspirations, may perceive few options to express their talents and values in the work world.

Self-awareness, the cornerstone of career management, is a necessary ingredient in effective occupational decision making. In addition, people need to develop a solid base of information to screen alternative occupations for potential appropriateness. The choice of an occupation from a set of alternatives should maximize the compatibility of the chosen occupation with one's conceptual goal. Career strategies particularly relevant to occupational choice include competence in current activities, self-nomination, networking, and seeking guidance.

ASSIGNMENTS

1. Interview your parents and/or other relatives to understand how your family background can influence (or has already influenced) your career choices. Think back to when you were growing up—your parents' ideas and aspirations, other relatives and friends, family income, neighborhood, sports, and religious training. Try to trace the significance of these factors to your current career plans. What influence (if any) has your spouse or others from your peer group (siblings, friends, or colleagues) had on your career choices?

2. Use expectancy theory to compare two or more occupations in which you might be interested. List five job outcomes that are of at least some importance to you. How important is each outcome? How instrumental

will each occupation be in attaining each job outcome? What is the probability that you could enter each occupation if you wanted to?

DISCUSSION QUESTIONS

1. Do most people choose occupations that match their talents, values, interests, and desired life-style? What are some obstacles to establishing such a match?

2. Do you believe that the occupational choices of women and minorities are severely constrained by external barriers? Do women face similar issues or different issues in choosing an occupation than people of color?

ENDNOTES

1. J. O. Crites, *Vocational Psychology* (New York: McGraw-Hill, 1969).

2. D. Brown, L. Brooks, and Associates. eds. *Career Choice and Development* (San Francisco, CA: Jossey–Bass, 1990); S. H. Osipow, "Convergence in Theories of Career Choice and Development: Review and Prospect," *Journal of Vocational Behavior* 36 (1990): 122–131.

3. Crites, *Vocational Psychology;* quote is on p. 119.

4. J. L. Holland, *The Psychology of Vocational Choice* (Waltham, MA: Blaisdell, 1966); J. L. Holland, *Making Vocational Choices: A Theory of Vocational Personalities and Work Environments* (Englewood Cliffs, NJ: Prentice-Hall, 1985); J. L. Holland, "Some Speculations about the Investigation of Person–Environment Transactions," *Journal of Vocational Behavior* 31 (1987): 337–340.

5. Holland, *Making Vocational Choices;* quote is on p. 4.

6. G. J. Blau, "Using a Person–Environment Fit Model to Predict Job Involvement and Organizational Commitment," *Journal of Vocational Behavior* 30 (1987): 240–257; J. C. Smart, C. F. Elton, and G. W. McLaughlin, "Person–Environment Congruence and Job Satisfaction," *Journal of Vocational Behavior* 29 (1986): 216–225; A. R. Spokane, "A Review of Research on Person–Environment Congruence in Holland's Theory of Careers," *Journal of Vocational Behavior* 26 (1985): 306–343.

7. N. E. Betz, L. F. Fitzgerald, and R. E. Hill, "Trait–Factor Theory: Traditional Cornerstone of Career Theory," in *Handbook of Career Theory,* ed. M. B. Arthur, D. T. Hall, and B. S. Lawrence (Cambridge, UK: Cambridge University Press, 1989), 26–40.

8. D. M. Muchinsky and C. J. Monahan, "What Is Person-Environment Congruence? Supplementary versus Complementary Models of Fit," *Journal of Vocational Behavior* 31 (1987): 268–277.

9. D. E. Super, "Toward Making Self-Concept Theory Operational," in *Career Development: Self–Concept Theory,* ed. D. E. Super, R. Starishevsky, N. Matlin, and J. P. Jordaan (New York: College Entrance Examination Board, 1963), 17–32; quote is on p. 18.

10. N. Fouad, "Annual Review 1991–1993: Vocational Choice, Decision Making, Assessment and Intervention," *Journal of Vocational Behavior* 45 (1994): 125–176.

11. Super, "Toward Making Self-Concept Theory Operational."

12. D. E. Super, *The Psychology of Careers* (New York: Harper & Row, 1957); D. E. Super, "A Life-Span, Life-Space Approach to Career Development," in *Career Choice and Development,* ed. Brown et al., 197–261.

13. Super, *The Psychology of Careers*.

14. Ibid.; quote is on p. 84.

15. D. P. Osborn, "A Reexamination of the Organizational Choice Process," *Journal of Vocational Behavior* 36 (1990): 45–60.

16. V. H. Vroom, *Work and Motivation* (New York: Wiley, 1964).

17. D. D. Baker, R. Ravichandran, and D. M. Randall, "Exploring Contrasting Formulations of Expectancy Theory," *Decision Sciences* 20 (1989): 1–13; J. P. Wanous, T. L. Keon, and J. C. Latack, "Expectancy Theory and Occupational/Organizational Choices: A Review and Test," *Organizational Behavior and Human Performance* 32 (1983): 66–86.

18. Osborn, "A Reexamination of the Organizational Choice Process"; quote is on p. 47

19. Ibid.

20. P. O. Soelberg, "Unprogrammed Decision Making," *Industrial Management Review* 8 (1967): 19–29.

21. Ibid.; quote is on p. 23.

22. Osborn, "A Reexamination of the Organizational Choice Process"; J. E. Sheridan, J. W. Slocum, and M. D. Richards, "Expectancy Theory as a Leading Indicator of Job Behavior," *Decision Sciences* 5 (1974): 507–522.

23. S. H. Osipow, *Theories of Career Development* (Englewood Cliffs, NJ: Prentice-Hall, 1983); quote is on p. 225.

24. S. H. Osipow and L. F. Fitzgerald, *Theories of Career Development* (Needham Heights, MA: Allyn & Bacon, 1996).

25. M. T. Brown, C. Fukunaga, D. Umemoto, and L. Wicker, "Annual Review, 1990–1996: Social Class, Work, and Retirement Behavior," *Journal of Vocational Behavior* 49 (1996): 159–189; V. D. Kimbrough and P. R. Salomone, "African Americans: Diverse People, Diverse Career Needs," *Journal of Career Development* 19 (1993): 265–279; K. Marjoribanks, "Adolescents' Learning Environments and Aspirations: Ethnic, Gender, and Socio-Status Group Differences," *Perceptual and Motor Skills* 72 (1991): 823–830; D. G. Solorzano, "An Exploratory Analysis of the Effects of Race, Class, and Gender on Student and Parent Mobility Aspirations," *Journal of Negro Education* 61 (1992): 30–44.

26. J. A. Jacobs, D. Karen, and K. McClelland, "The Dynamics of Young Men's Career Aspirations," *Sociological Forum* 6 (1991): 609–639.

27. J. J. Hoffman, C. Hofacker, and E. B. Goldsmith, "How Closeness Affects Parental Influence on Business College Students' Career Choices," *Journal of Career Development* 19 (1992): 65–73; E. Williams, N. Radin, and T. Allegro, "Sex Role Attitudes of Adolescents Reared Primarily by Their Fathers: An 11 Year Follow-Up," *Merrill Palmer Quarterly* 38 (1992): 457–476.

28. J. G. Goodale and D. T. Hall, "On Inheriting a Career: The Influence of Sex, Values, and Parents," *Journal of Vocational Behavior* 8 (1976): 19–30.

29. D. C. York-Anderson and S. L. Bowman, "Assessing the College Knowledge of First-Generation and Second-Generation College Students," *Journal of College Student Development* 32 (1991): 116–122.

30. Osipow and Fitzgerald, *Theories of Career Development*.

31. E. H. Schein, "Culture as an Environmental Context for Careers," *Journal of Occupational Behavior* 5 (1984): 71–81.

32. Brown et al. "Annual Review, 1990–1996."

33. L. K. Mitchell and J. D. Krumboltz, "Social Learning Approach to Career Decision Making: Krumboltz's Theory," in *Career Choice and Development*, ed. Brown et al., 145–196.

34. V. A. Parker, "Growth-Enhancing Relationships outside Work (GROWs)," in *The Career Is Dead — Long Live the Career: A Relational Approach to Careers*, ed. D. T. Hall et al. (San Francisco, CA: Jossey-Bass, 1996), 180–222.

35. Osipow, "Convergence in Theories of Career Choice and Development"; quote is on p. 125.

36. N. E. Betz and L. F. Fitzgerald, *The Career Psychology of Women* (Orlando, FL: Academic Press, 1987); L. F. Fitzgerald and L. M. Weitzman, "Women's Career Development: Theory and Practice from a Feminist Perspective," in *Adult Career Development: Concepts, Issues and Practices*, ed. H. D. Lea and Z. B. Leibowitz (Alexandria, VA: The National Career Development Association, 1992), 124–160; J. V. Gallos, "Exploring Women's Development: Implications for Career Theory, Practice, and Research," in *Handbook of Career Theory*, ed. Arthur, Hall, and Lawrence, 110–132; B. A. Gutek and L. Larwood, "Introduction: Women's Careers Are Different and Important," in *Women's Career Development*, ed. B. A. Gutek and L. Larwood (Newbury Park, CA: Sage, 1987), 7–14.

37. L. F. Fitzgerald and J. O. Crites, "Toward a Career Psychology of Women: What Do We Know? What Do We Need to Know?" *Journal of Counseling Psychology* 27 (1980): 44–62.

38. D. Alpert and D. T. Breen, "Liberality in Children and Adolescents," *Journal of Vocational Behavior* 34 (1989): 154–160; J. Stockard and J. McGee, "Children's Occupational Preferences: The Influence of Sex and Perceptions of Occupational Characteristics," *Journal of Vocational Behavior* 36 (1990): 287–303.

39. A. Barak, S. Feldman, and A. Noy, "Traditionality of Children's Interests as Related to Their Parents' Gender Stereotypes and Traditionality of Occupations," *Sex Roles* 26 (1991): 511–524.

40. M. J. White, T. A. Kruczek, M. T. Brown, and G. B. White, "Occupational Sex Stereotypes among College Students," *Journal of Vocational Behavior* 34 (1989): 289–298.

41. Betz and Fitzgerald, *The Career Psychology of Women*; S. Hess-Biber, "Male and Female Students' Perceptions of Their Academic Environment and Future Career Plans," *Human Relations* 38 (1985): 91–105; V. F. Nieva and B. A. Gutek, *Women and Work: A Psychological Perspective* (New York: Praeger, 1981).

42. Betz and Fitzgerald, *The Career Psychology of Women*.

43. P. Lightbody, G. Siann, L. Tait, and D. Walsh, "A Fulfilling Career? Factors Which Influence Women's Choice of Profession," *Educational Studies* 23, no. 1 (1997): 25–37.

44. Betz and Fitzgerald, *The Career Psychology of Women*; Gallos, "Exploring Women's Development."

45. G. F. Epstein and A. L. Bronzaft, "Female Modesty in Aspiration Level," *Journal of Counseling Psychology* 21 (1974): 57–60; A. Harlan and C. L. Weiss, "Career Opportunities for Women Managers," in *Work, Family, and the Career*, ed. C. B. Derr (New York: Praeger, 1980), 188–199.

46. L. W. Harmon, "Longitudinal Changes in Women's Career Aspirations: Developmental or Historical," *Journal of Vocational Behavior* 35 (1989): 46–63; quote is on p. 62.

47. L. A. Douce and J. C. Hansen, "Willingness to Take Risks and College Women's Career Choice," *Journal of Vocational Behavior* 36 (1990): 258–273; P. K. Mansfield, P. B. Koch, J. Henderson, J. R. Vicary, M. Cohn, and E. W. Young, "The Job Climate for Women in Traditionally Male Blue-Collar Occupations," *Sex Roles* 25 (1991): 63–79; K. S. Pfost and M. Fiore, "Pursuit of Nontraditional Occupations: Fear of Success or Fear of Not Being Chosen? *Sex Roles* 23 (1990): 15–24.

48. Betz and Fitzgerald, *The Career Psychology of Women*; quote is on p. 8.

49. S. Karpicke, "Perceived and Real Sex Differences in College Students' Career Planning," *Journal of Counseling Psychology* 27 (1980): 240–245; R. A. Valdez and B. A. Gutek, "Family Roles: A Help or Hindrance for Working Women?" in *Women's Career Development*, ed. Gutek and Larwood, 157–169.

50. Nieva and Gutek, *Women and Work;* D. J. Levinson and J. D. Levinson, *Seasons of a Woman's Life* (New York: A. A. Knopf, 1996).

51. Gallos, "Exploring Women's Development."

52. J. H. Larson, M. Butler, S. Wilson, and N. Medora, "The Effects of Gender on Career Decision Problems in Young Adults," *Journal of Counseling and Development* 73, no. 1 (1994): 79–84.

53. Betz and Fitzgerald, *The Career Psychology of Women;* A. P. Brief, M. Van Sell, and R. J. Aldag, "Vocational Decision Making among Women: Implications for Organizational Behavior," *Academy of Management Review* 4 (1979): 521–530; A. G. Bedeian, "The Roles of Self-Esteem and Achievement in Aspiring to Prestigious Vocations," *Journal of Vocational Behavior* 11 (1977): 109–119.

54. A. Bandura, "Self-Efficacy: Toward a Unifying Theory of Behavioral Change," *Psychological Review* 84 (1977): 191–215; N. E. Betz and G. Hackett, "The Relationship of Mathematics Self-Efficacy Expectations to the Selection of Science-Based College Majors," *Journal of Vocational Behavior* 23 (1983): 329–345; G. Hackett and N. K. Campbell, "Task Self–Efficacy and Task Interest as a Function of Performance on a Gender Neutral Task," *Journal of Vocational Behavior* 30 (1987): 203–215.

55. Betz and Hackett, "The Relationship of Mathematics Self-Efficacy Expectations to the Selection of Science-Based College Majors"; N. K. Campbell and G. Hackett, "The Effects of Mathematics Task Performance on Math Self–Efficacy and Task Interest," *Journal of Vocational Behavior* 28 (1986): 149–162; S. F. Chipman, D. H. Krantz, and R. Silver, "Mathematics Anxiety and Science Careers among Able College Women," *Psychological Science* 3 (1992): 292–295; R. T. Lapan, K. R. Boggs, and W. H. Morrill, "Self–Efficacy as a Mediator of Investigative and Realistic General Occupational Themes on the Strong–Campbell Interest Inventory," *Journal of Counseling Psychology* 36 (1989): 176–182; T. Matsui, K. Matsui, and R. Ohnishi, "Mechanisms Underlying Math Self–Efficacy Learning of College Students," *Journal of Vocational Behavior* 37 (1990): 225–238.

56. T. Matsui, H. Ikeda, and R. Ohnishi, "Relations of Sex-Typed Socializations to Career Self–Efficacy Expectations of College Students," *Journal of Vocational Behavior* 35 (1989): 1–16; N. E. Betz and G. Hackett, "The Relationship of Career-Related Self-Efficacy Expectations to Perceived Career Options in College Women and Men," *Journal of Counseling Psychology* 28 (1981): 399–410.

57. C. K. Greene and W. L. Stitt-Gohdes, "Factors That Influence Women's Choices to Work in the Trades," *Journal of Career Development* 23, no. 4 (1997): 265–278.

58. A. Bandura, "Self-Efficacy: Toward a Unifying Theory of Behavioral Change," *Psychological Review* 84 (1977): 191–215.

59. S. T. Meier, "Vocational Behavior, 1988–1990: Vocational Choice, Decision-Making, Career Development Interventions, and Assessment," *Journal of Vocational Behavior* 39 (1991): 131–181.

60. Betz and Fitzgerald, *The Career Psychology of Women;* quote is on p. 253.

61. B. B. Houser and C. Garvey, "The Impact of Family, Peers, and Educational Personnel upon Career Decision Making," *Journal of Vocational Behavior* 23 (1983): 35–44; P. W. Lunneborg, "Role Model Influences of Nontraditional Professional Women," *Journal of Vocational Behavior* 20 (1982): 276–281.

62. C. J. Auster and D. Auster, "Factors Influencing Women's Choice of Nontraditional Careers: The Role of Family, Peers, and Counselors," *Vocational Guidance Quarterly* 29 (1981): 253–263; S. Greenfeld, L. Greiner, and M. M. Wood, "The 'Feminine Mystique' in Male-Dominated Jobs: A Comparison of Attitudes and Background Factors in Male-Dominated Versus Female-Dominated Jobs," *Journal of Vocational Behavior* 17 (1980): 291–309.

63. Auster and Auster, "Factors Influencing Women's Choice of Nontraditional Careers"; Betz and Fitzgerald, *The Career Psychology of Women;* J. L. Fitzpatrick and T. Silverman, "Women's

Selection of Careers in Engineering: Do Traditional–Nontraditional Differences Still Exist?" *Journal of Vocational Behavior* 34 (1989): 266–278.

64. Research by Dickinson cited by Nieva and Gutek, *Women and Work.*

65. Betz and Fitzgerald, *The Career Psychology of Women;* F. E. Gordon and M. H. Strober, "Initial Observations on a Pioneer Cohort: 1974 Women MBAs," *Sloan Management Review* 19, no. 2 1978: 15–23; D. L. Keierleber and L. S. Hansen, "A Coming of Age: Addressing the Career Development Needs of Adult Students in University Settings," in *Adult Career Development: Concept, Issues and Practices,* ed. H. D. Lea and Z. B. Leibowitz (Alexandria, VA: The National Career Development Association, 1992), 312–339.

66. C. Arbona, "Career Counseling Research with Hispanics: A Review of the Literature," *The Counseling Psychologist* 18 (1990): 300–323; D. Brown, C. W. Minor, and D. A. Jepson, "The Opinions of Minorities about Preparing for Work: Report of the Second NCDA National Survey," *Career Development Quarterly* 40 (1991): 5–19; L. Hotchkiss and H. Borow, "Sociological Perspectives on Work and Career Development," in *Career Choice and Development,* ed. Brown, Brooks, and Associates 262–307; L. K. Mitchell and J. D. Krumboltz, "Social Learning Approach to Career Decision Making: Krumboltz's Theory," in *Career Choice and Development,* ed. Brown, Brooks, and Associates 145–196.

67. E. J. Smith, "Issues in Racial Minorities' Career Behavior," in *Handbook of Vocational Psychology,* vol. 1 edited by W.B. Walsh and S.H. Osipow. Hillsdale, NJ: Lawrence Erlbaum Associates, 161–222; quote on p. 186.

68. K. M. Evans and E. L. Herr, "The Influence of Racism and Sexism in the Career Development of African American Women," *Journal of Multicultural Counseling and Development* 19 (1991): 130–135; J. Yang, "Career Counseling of Chinese American Women: Are They in Limbo?" *Career Development Quarterly* 39 (1991): 350–359.

69. A new book offers many web sites to consider. G. Crispin and M. Mehler, *CareerXRoads* (career cross roads) (Kendall Park, NJ: MMC Group, 1998).

7

ORGANIZATIONAL ENTRY

Chapter 6 discussed several different views on the occupational choice process. Once an occupational field is selected, the next step is finding a job. A discussion of organizational entry explains the manner in which job seekers assess and choose prospective employers.

Organizational entry is the process by which individuals cross the boundary from outside to inside an organization; it reflects the movement into such entities as businesses, schools, or the armed forces.[1] The organizational entry process consists of two simultaneous activities. On one hand, individuals assess organizations to determine which one is most likely to meet their career needs and values. On the other hand, organizations assess candidates' talents so they can select those with the highest likelihood of succeeding in the firm. Just as candidates make decisions about organizations, organizations make decisions about job candidates.

Research has identified four phases in the organizational entry process, with each phase having different but related tasks for the job candidate and the hiring organization.[2] The four stages are **recruitment, selection, orientation,** and **socialization. Recruitment** is defined as the process of mutual attraction between the individual and the organization. At this stage, the individual locates information on job sources and firms, whereas the organization is concerned with finding and attracting job candidates. **Selection** involves the process of mutual choice. Individuals in this phase must deal with job interviews, assessments, and making choices among job offers. For the hiring organization, the key task is an assessment of candidates for future job performance and retention. **Orientation** is defined as the period of initial adjustment. For the individual, this means coping with the stress of entry, whereas the organization must attend to the emotional and information needs of newcomers. The last stage, or **socialization,** is termed the process of mutual adjustment. During this phase, the individual moves through typical work stages and experiences various successes. The organization uses socialization techniques and tactics to influence newcomers' behavior and ensure their assimilation into the organization. This chapter covers the recruitment and selection processes, and Chapter 8 discusses orientation and socialization.

The ultimate objective of organizational entry is to attain a match between the individual and the organization. The candidate's capabilities and the job's requirements must match, as should the individual's needs and the organization's

· EXHIBIT 7-1

MATCHING INDIVIDUAL
AND ORGANIZATION

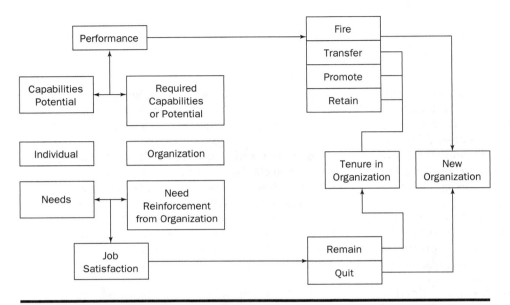

SOURCE: J. P. Wanous, "Realistic Job Previews: Can a Procedure to Reduce Turnover Also Influence the Relationship between Abilities and Performance?" *Personnel Psychology*, 1978, vol. 31, 250. Reprinted with permission.

rewards or reinforcements. A model presented by John Wanous in his text *Organizational Entry* illustrates these two components of an individual-organizational match.[3] As Exhibit 7.1 indicates, the capability-job requirement match can affect the level of job performance an employee attains, whereas the need-reinforcement match can influence the level of job satisfaction an employee experiences. Both matches affect the contribution a new employee makes to his or her organization.

Consequences of a mismatch can be severe. From the employee's perspective, a mismatch can produce dissatisfaction and disappointment, can be a threat to self-esteem, and might result in a decision to pursue another job in a different organization. From the organization's point of view, poor performance can detract from the organization's effectiveness, and extensive turnover can be costly because replacements need to be recruited, selected, trained, and developed into productive employees. For these reasons, it is important to understand the dynamics of organizational entry. This chapter examines how individuals choose jobs in organizations and explores the role of expectations in the organizational entry process. We also discuss what individuals and organizations can do to increase the likelihood of successful organizational entry.

THEORIES OF ORGANIZATIONAL CHOICE

Chapter 6 applied two psychological models—expectancy theory and unprogrammed decision making—to the occupational choice process. These models have also been used to understand how people choose a specific job in an organization.

According to **expectancy theory,** job candidates are attracted to the organization that is most likely to provide desirable outcomes and avoid undesirable outcomes. In this sense, individuals would gather relevant information during the recruiting process and would then use this information to estimate the likelihood that alternative employers will provide the desired set of outcomes. The individual then (consciously or unconsciously) multiplies the value of each outcome by these estimates and sums the products across all possible outcomes. Thus an individual would be expected to accept a job offer from the firm that is most compatible with one's values (i.e., the one most likely to provide such positive outcomes as interesting work, pleasant working conditions, advancement opportunities, and others). A rival theory, **unprogrammed decision making,** portrays job candidates as considerably less thorough and rational than does expectancy theory. According to this view, candidates initially become attracted to organizations that are acceptable according to just one or two critical outcomes (not a long set of outcomes), develop an implicit (often unconscious) choice of an organization, and then engage in perceptual distortion in favor of the organization they have already implicitly chosen.[4] Organizational choice, in this view, is based on the subjective perception that an organization can provide a satisfactory opportunity to attain just a few highly significant outcomes. Further, research has shown that an organization's "corporate image" has a strong influence on an individual's choice to pursue employment with that organization.[5]

Which approach more accurately describes the organizational choice process? Several researchers have provided considerable evidence supporting expectancy theory.[6] On the opposite side, other researchers have offered support for the unprogrammed style in organizational choice.[7] Perhaps the most relevant question is not which type of job search is more typical, but which type is more beneficial for the individual and the organization. Although there is not a great deal of research in this area, one can argue that the more thorough the search and the greater the number of outcomes and organizations considered, the greater the likelihood of a favorable match.

Consistent with this view, there is research evidence that candidates whose job search parallels the assumptions of expectancy theory express satisfaction with their decision process and chosen organization.[8] Moreover, this same research found that two-thirds of the candidates whose job search resembled unprogrammed decision making were uncertain about the appropriateness of their decision process and expressed reservations about their eventual choice.[9] Ultimately, it seems that a thorough search for extensive information enables a candidate to be more confident and satisfied with the organizational entry process.

ROLE OF EXPECTATIONS IN ORGANIZATIONAL ENTRY

Both models of organizational choice—expectancy theory and unprogrammed decision making—reflect a matching process in that people choose jobs that will satisfy significant values. In effect, both models suggest that candidates develop expectations about an organization's capacity to provide valued outcomes. These expectations (instrumentalities in expectancy theory terminology) guide us toward or away from various job opportunities. A person's attraction to a certain job is based on the expectations that the job will provide such desirable outcomes as interesting work and autonomy on the job. Whether accurate or not, these expectations strongly influence one's choice of jobs in organizations. Yet job expectations—for interesting work, advancement opportunities, financial security, and the like—may not be realized when a candidate actually enters the organization as a new employee. There is convincing evidence that job candidates' expectations tend to be unrealistically inflated. For example, research has demonstrated how the expectations of applicants to MBA programs were severely inflated, compared with the experiences of the students already enrolled in the programs.[10] Moreover, the more abstract the topic (e.g., opportunity for personal growth), the more unrealistic were the applicants' expectations. Similarly, in a study of American Telephone and Telegraph (AT&T) employees, researchers found that new recruits (both college educated and non–college educated) held unrealistically inflated expectations concerning their jobs on organizational entry.[11] Often times, new employees experience "reality shock," a sense of disillusionment, disappointment, and dissatisfaction on realization that the reality of the job and the organization do not match their preconceived expectations.

Several typical expectations held by job seekers as they embark on their job search are identified in Table 7.1, along with the true realities of being a new employee. It is not suggested that all candidates hold these expectations or that all new employees experience the same realities. However, there is certainly an opportunity for a gap between naive expectations and day-to-day job experiences.

DEVELOPMENT OF UNREALISTIC EXPECTATIONS

What happens when expectations prove to be unrealistic? It has been argued that candidates who hold such expectations become dissatisfied when faced with the realities of a job and, ultimately, may choose to leave the organization.[12] The reasons for this devastating effect of unrealistic expectations are examined in a later section. For now, assume that recruits who hold unrealistic expectations

· TABLE 7-1

COMPARISONS OF EXPECTATIONS
AND EXPERIENCES

A Recruit May Expect That:	A New Employee May Experience That:
1. "I will have a great deal of freedom in deciding how my job gets done."	1. "My boss pretty much determines what I do and how I do it."
2. "Most of my projects will be interesting and meaningful."	2. "It seems like I have an endless stream of trivial, mundane tasks."
3. "I will receive helpful, constructive feedback from my boss."	3. "I really don't know how I am doing on the job."
4. "Promotions and salary increases will be based on how well I do my job."	4. "Promotions and money are tight, and they appear to be based on factors other than my performance."
5. "I will be able to apply the latest techniques and technologies to help the organization."	5. "People resist adopting my suggestions, even though the old ways are antiquated and inefficient."
6. "I will be able to balance my work and family responsibilities without much difficulty."	6. "My job and family responsibilities often interfere with one another."

about a job and organization will, at the very least, be surprised when they confront a reality on the job that does not confirm their expectations, and this surprise may be accompanied by dissatisfaction and disillusionment if the job experiences are generally undesirable.[13]

If we assume for the moment that unrealistic expectations can have a negative effect on new employees, we need to pose certain questions: **Why do people develop unrealistic expectations? Where do these expectations come from? Why do they end up being unrealistic?** We attempt to answer these questions by identifying a number of factors that can lead to unrealistic expectations.

CAREER TRANSITIONS. Perhaps the most fundamental explanation for unrealistic expectations is that the path from the job seeker role to the employee role represents a career transition. A **career transition** is a period in which a person either changes career roles (interrole transition) or changes orientation to a current role (intrarole transition). For example, when a person leaves school and enters a work organization (an interrole transition), there are many differences between the old and the new settings: differences in tasks, required behaviors, norms, and expectations. Indeed, the lives of students and employees are vastly different. Even a job change within the same organization or from one organization to another represents a career transition, although the differences in settings may not be as severe as those between student and employee roles.

There are a number of interesting differences between the role of the college student and the role of the new employee.[14] For one thing, college students operate on a short-time cycle of 3 months (a quarter) or 4 months (a semester).

Because projects (i.e., courses) are completed within this brief time period, the student quickly gets a sense of closure and accomplishment. By contrast, work projects are not nearly as brief or clear-cut. Many projects may extend beyond a year or two, and some may never really be completed. Contributing to their sense of accomplishment, students normally get "promoted" every year. In the work world, promotions are not nearly so regular or frequent and are usually based on outstanding, not merely acceptable, levels of performance.

There are also noted differences between students' and new employees' relationships with superiors. In fact, students really do not have a boss. They can often choose (or avoid) certain professors by a judicious selection of courses. Moreover, if they decide they do not like their professor, students can drop a course or change a major. For the new employee, the selection and avoidance of a superior is virtually impossible. Therefore, the employee needs to deal with a potentially influential superior, whether the employee likes the person or not. Students also get accustomed to frequent feedback on their performance. Two or more exams or papers may be completed in one course, and the feedback (the grade received) is rapid and explicit. Feedback from a superior at work is apt to be less frequent and less explicit.

In short, many new employees, whether coming directly from school or from another organization, have to face a set of demands with which they may be unfamiliar. New employees must confront such experiences as reliance on other people (bosses, peers, customers), low levels of freedom and autonomy, extensive resistance to changes they might suggest, too much or too little job structure, and the politics of organizational life.[15] The organization is not typically going to change to accommodate a new employee. Often times, close supervision, mundane tasks, little responsibility, and tight controls are an organization's way of ensuring the satisfactory performance of new, untested employees.

Organizations' policies and practices may explain the nature of the job experiences a new employee must confront. But what about the expectations? Why do so many people expect to have considerable freedom in a job, to get promoted in a short time, to be appraised and counseled by a supportive, caring boss, and to obtain challenging, meaningful, and rewarding assignments? Where do people get such ideas in the first place? To answer these questions, several other critical influences on unrealistic expectations must be explored.

RECRUITMENT PROCESS. Even though organizations commit significant resources to recruiting (on average 16 percent of the total personnel department budget according to one survey),[16] the recruitment process has often been viewed as the most significant source of unrealistic expectations. In essence, it is claimed that organizations often portray jobs in overly optimistic terms, thus inducing unrealistic expectations on the part of the job candidate.

To understand why this occurs, one must appreciate that the organization's goal is to attract qualified candidates. To keep qualified candidates interested in the organization, recruitment often focuses on "selling" the organization. This is done by presenting incomplete or overly flattering accounts of what it is like to work in the organization.

For instance, even a cursory examination of recruiting brochures illustrates how companies emphasize the positive: challenging and exciting work, rewards based on job performance, good opportunities for promotion, and timely, constructive feedback from your boss. Of course, there is the question of whether organizations can deliver on these promises. Even if they could, these descriptions omit some of the less flattering qualities that characterize almost any job in any organization. One study found that companies rely most heavily on brochures to communicate with prospective applicants.[17] The dependence on the use of brochures and their overly positive message is a key source of unrealistic expectations.

This is not to say that organizations deliberately lie, but in their effort to put their best foot forward, they can easily slant their presentations in favor of positive information. Moreover, employees responsible for recruitment often times have little direct line experience in the organization.[18] Accordingly, they might also believe these glowing accounts of the organization and, in the process, pass on these unrealistic expectations to job candidates.

Of course, individual candidates have their own goal during recruiting: to keep the organizations interested in them so they may select the most appropriate organization for which to work. To keep an organization interested, candidates are likely to emphasize their strengths and omit potential weaknesses or reservations. This all amounts to a "mutual sell" in which each party (the candidate and the organization) may be reluctant to reveal less desirable qualities.

These goal conflicts are hardly conducive to an open, complete sharing of information during recruitment and selection. As a later section of this chapter shows, organizations can choose to modify their recruitment practices to offer candidates a "realistic job preview" that is intended to convey a more complete, accurate picture of the organization than traditional recruitment normally permits.

ORGANIZATIONAL STEREOTYPES. Many candidates hold images and stereotypes of certain companies or industries even before they have had extensive contact with an organization. For example, research has found that job candidates hold specific stereotypes of small companies that differ substantially from those of big firms.[19] In addition, candidates can hold highly specific images of particular companies. Job candidates perceive a company's image in terms of its job opportunities, products, labor relations posture, administrative practices, geographic location, pay practices, and financial performance. Moreover, the image of a company is an important factor in a candidate's decision to pursue a job with that company.[20]

In a sense, then, stereotypes of images breed expectations. Because stereotypes are, by definition, partially incomplete or inaccurate, the resulting expectations may not be particularly realistic. A candidate who holds a stereotype about company X ("Great reputation. People are promoted quickly. Good money and lots of challenge.") may not bother to test out these assumptions during recruiting or may not believe any piece of discrepant information a company may provide.

EDUCATIONAL PROCESS. Some of the major distinctions between the student role and the role of the new employee have been considered. Also to be considered is the extent to which specific courses at the college or graduate level prepare students for the reality of the work world. For example, technically oriented courses in engineering or business rarely dwell on the problems inherent in working within an organizational structure as a new employee. Moreover, many colleges try to instill in their students a sense of pride in themselves and an ardent enthusiasm for their chosen career field. Under these conditions, it is not surprising that many graduates emerge with an unrealistic picture of what they will face in their first job. Such disillusionment may be particularly severe for graduates of highly prestigious colleges and in situations in which employers deliberately hire overqualified job candidates.[21] It is almost inevitable that such employees will see themselves as underused.

LACK OF PRIOR WORK EXPERIENCE. Job candidates without extensive prior work experiences may be particularly susceptible to the development of unrealistic expectations. Indeed, job candidates with a variety of prior work experiences seem to engage in a more thorough information search during recruiting than candidates without such experience.[22] Presumably, varied work experiences teach people that all organizations are not the same; hence the need for obtaining more information about each potential employer.

SELF-DELUSION. So far we have considered the effects of the environment (recruiting, education, work experience) on the development of unrealistic job expectations. We also must consider the possibility that some people fool themselves into believing what they want to believe. Several studies have demonstrated a strong positive relationship between a person's values and his or her expectations.[23] In other words, people come to expect job characteristics they want to experience.

Why the tendency to fool ourselves during a job search? First, candidates who are initially attracted to a job may distort or ignore negative information because they do not want to be confronted with anything unfavorable about a job they have already decided they prefer. Also, candidates with few alternative opportunities may only hear the positives of a job that they believe they might ultimately be forced to take.

Distortions also may be due to the feelings of dissonance or tension people experience after having reached an important decision. Whenever individuals make a choice, they normally reject one alternative in favor of another. They may then engage in distortion or selective attention to convince themselves of the wisdom of their decision. After students accept a job, they upgrade the attractiveness of the chosen organization and downplay the attractiveness of the rejected organization.[24] In this way, they convince themselves that they made the correct decision. In the process, however, they set themselves up for disillusionment because the overly glowing picture of the chosen organization could not be matched by the realities of the first year of employment.

Thus, one source of unrealistic expectations is our own natural tendency to see the world through rose-colored glasses (i.e., to see it as we would like it to be).

This tendency may be exacerbated by unrealistic recruitment, the severity of the transition between job seeking and employee roles, and prior educational and work experiences. Nevertheless, when it comes to the development of unrealistic job expectations, we may be our own worst enemy.

ORGANIZATIONAL ENTRY IN LATER ADULTHOOD

In Chapter 5 we discussed the view that specific age ranges can demarcate career stages. The organizational entry stage, and the challenges associated with it, normally would be experienced in the earliest period of adulthood or in the time frame of 18 to 25 years old. Of course, the need to make career changes or job switches, either by choice or by circumstance, makes the issues surrounding organizational entry relevant at any age. Thus, although an individual may be in the middle or late adulthood stages in a chronologic sense, he or she could be looking for a new job or accepting a new position, thereby facing the demands of recruitment, selection, orientation, and socialization that come with organizational entry. The important distinction is that older adults confront these demands from a different, more experienced perspective. In other words, recruitment, establishment, and socialization are still important tasks for older adults, but they are addressed in a hopefully wiser and more mature fashion. Consider the following example:

> Sharon never thought she would have to prove herself again. After all, in the first 22 years of her career, she had built a record of significant accomplishment—several promotions, ultimately to the level of vice president for planning and development; a salary of $110,000; an executive MBA degree from a top school; a recognized leadership position in the organization, with admiration from her peers and subordinates alike; and the opportunity to help map her company's future. In the twenty-third year, Sharon's fast track rise came to an abrupt end. Her company was purchased in a hostile takeover, and the new company saw Sharon's position as expendable. At the age of 46 Sharon found herself out of a job. Working with an executive search firm, Sharon put together a new résumé and pursued several promising leads. With few white-collar and executive-level jobs available, Sharon found the competition to be intense for the open positions that fit her background and experience. Sharon made sure she was well prepared for each interview by researching each prospective company extensively. After several months of job search, Sharon accepted the position of business planning and forecasting manager for a small automotive products retailer. The salary and status were comparatively much lower than her previous job, but Sharon was convinced that her new employer was a good match for her.

Even though Sharon is in the middle adulthood stage she was forced to "cycle back," by confronting the variety of tasks associated with finding a new employer and gaining entry. In this sense she was like a graduating college student looking for a first professional position. She had résumés to prepare, companies to research, questions to ask, and offers to assess. But Sharon approached these tasks from a more mature perspective. Her 23 years of corporate experience had provided extensive knowledge of her own talents and interests, as well as an understanding of the inner workings of business organizations. Accordingly, she was clear on the type of work situation she wanted, and she also knew which conditions to avoid. Because of her experience Sharon was not prone to the development of unrealistic expectations about her new job. Thus, although Sharon was forced to endure the rigors of organizational entry, she was able to manage the process as a mature adult.

ORGANIZATIONAL ACTIONS DURING THE ENTRY PROCESS

Organizations have three major tasks to accomplish during the organizational entry process. First, they need to attract talented and qualified candidates into the applicant pool and keep them interested in the organization. Second, they need to attract candidates in such a way as to minimize the development of unrealistic job expectations on the part of the candidates. Third, they must assess candidates accurately and extend offers to those who are likely to succeed in the organization. This section focuses on techniques and approaches that organizations can use to attract and select candidates in an effective, realistic manner.

ATTRACTION OF JOB CANDIDATES

Certainly, organizations will not be able to staff themselves properly unless they can induce talented candidates to enter and remain in the recruitment process. Extensive research on candidates' reactions to recruitment has only recently begun. Nevertheless, several issues have been identified that have significant implications for organizations.

IMPACT OF THE RECRUITER. For many candidates for managerial, professional, and technical positions, the first formal contact with the organization is with the recruiter, and the first activity is the screening interview. Researchers are beginning to accumulate information on the desirable qualities of this initial interaction between the candidate and the organization.[25]

For one thing, candidates' reactions to interviews are most positive when the recruiter is perceived as knowledgeable. Recruiters who are familiar with the candidate's background and understand the organization and job qualifications in detail are viewed favorably.[26] Given the straightforward nature of these findings, it would seem surprising that recruiters are often perceived as unprepared and/or unknowledgeable. However, the lack of interview preparation and knowledge may be a function of the way organizations train and prepare their recruiters. One study found that only 41 percent of the Fortune 1000 respondent companies replied that they offered standardized recruiter training programs, and of those, only about half (48 percent) required that the recruiters be trained prior to beginning their assignments.[27]

In addition to adequate knowledge and preparation, recruiters' behavior during the interview affects candidates' attitudes.[28] Recruiters who ask relevant questions, answer candidates' questions accurately, and discuss career paths and job qualifications produce positive responses from candidates.[29] Finally, the perceived qualities of the recruiter play a prominent role in the interview setting.

A warm, enthusiastic, perceptive, and thoughtful recruiter understandably affects the recruit's reactions affirmatively.[30]

Although there is no direct evidence on the frequency of poorly conducted interviews, it is clear that interviews can cause negative reactions among job candidates. One possible explanation for this phenomenon is recruiters' apparent lack of awareness of job candidates' values, needs, and aspirations. For example, there may be substantial differences between an individual's work values and recruiters' perceptions of that person's values.[31] Recruiters often overestimate or underestimate the significance that individuals attach to specific aspects of the job and the organization. It seems unlikely that they can present favorable information on topics of special significance to candidates if they misjudge the importance of these topics.

The implications of these findings are clear. Organizations need to pay sufficient attention to the initial interview process to ensure that proper information about the organization is presented to candidates. To present this information satisfactorily, recruiters need to better understand candidates' concerns, develop a deeper knowledge of the organization, and project a positive, concerned image. Careful selection and training of recruiters is certainly one place for an organization to begin.

FOLLOW-UP ACTIVITIES. On completion of the initial screening interview with a candidate, organizations decide whether to carry the process to the next step (normally a site visit) or to terminate the relationship with the candidate. A study that examined the time lag between the initial contact and the go/no-go decision found that candidates believed that a time lag of 1 to 3 weeks was acceptable. However, the study also found that more than 26 percent of the candidates reported a time lag that exceeded 3 weeks. The researchers concluded that many companies may profit from shortening this lag whenever feasible and, at the very least, should indicate during the initial interview what the time lag is likely to be.[32]

The organization should also pay close attention to the site visits for candidates who survive the initial screening. Positive attitudes regarding the visit have been associated with the opportunity to meet with supervisors and peers, to ask questions and to have them answered frankly, and to receive sufficient information about the job and the company. Candidates should also be informed about the specifics of the on-site activities in advance of the visit. Recent research has found that positive evaluations by job candidates of the site visit and the "likableness" of the host increased the probability that a candidate would accept a job offer.[33]

Organizations must also be mindful of how they handle the job offer. Candidates hold more positive attitudes toward offers when the organization contacts them after the offer to provide additional information, is open to candidates' questions, and is willing to discuss specific terms of employment.[34]

In summary, organizations can take steps to attract candidates during the recruitment process. The importance of the recruiter and the initial interview cannot be overemphasized. The manner in which the site visit is planned and implemented and in which the job offer is extended also influence candidates' attitudes. All these activities contribute to the image an organization projects to the public. The fact that an organization's image and reputation can attract or repel potential candidates is a reminder of the importance of the recruitment process.

REALISTIC RECRUITMENT

The preceding section examined ways for organizations to project an attractive image to job candidates. However, as previously discussed, an organization's image can be "too positive" if it is not based on reality. Because the recruitment process is one source of candidates' unrealistic job expectations, it is a prime target for reexamination and possible revision.

Realistic recruitment means presenting candidates with relevant and undistorted information about the job and the organization.[35] It is often contrasted with traditional job previews (TJP), in which organizations paint overly optimistic (and hence unrealistic) pictures of their jobs and practices. The vehicle through which realistic information is conveyed to candidates has been called the realistic job preview (RJP). As the term indicates, an RJP presents job candidates with a balanced, realistic picture of the job and the organization and with a preview of the positive and negative aspects of the job. An RJP may be presented through films, booklets, lectures, or one-on-one discussions.

The presentation of realistic information to job candidates should reduce the level of voluntary turnover among candidates who ultimately join the organization. Several arguments have been advanced to support such a position. **First,** realistic previews lower candidates' expectations to more appropriate levels—expectations that are more likely to be met on the job. Employees whose expectations have been met tend to be satisfied with their jobs, and satisfied employees are less likely to quit than are dissatisfied employees. According to this "met expectations" view, RJPs function by deflating initial expectations so that new employees experience little disappointment, disillusionment, and dissatisfaction when they confront reality.

A **second** explanation views a realistic preview as a vaccination against the reality of the job.[36] In medical terms, a vaccination is an injection of a small dosage of a disease-producing organism that helps the body form antibodies to ward off a full-blown form of the disease. In recruitment, an RJP vaccinates the candidate by presenting a dosage of reality about the job. The antibodies formed by the RJP are coping strategies that can help the candidate deal with the potentially disappointing and dissatisfying aspects of the job. For example, candidates who learn during recruitment that a job requires a great deal of close supervision may prepare themselves by rehearsing how they would deal with close supervision or perhaps by convincing themselves that close supervision may not be so terrible after all. In either case, RJPs should help new employees develop successful coping activities.

A **third** explanation is that RJPs convey an air of honesty to job candidates. This can have two effects. First, candidates may admire and respect an organization that is candid enough to "tell it like it is."[37] This attitude can bond a new employee to the organization and reduce the likelihood of turnover. In addition, candidates who accept a job after receiving an honest disclosure of its negative qualities will become committed to the job and organization because they believe they made their decision with full knowledge of the facts and without coercion or distortion on the part of the organization.

Fourth, it has been suggested that realistic previews offer candidates a basis to self-select out of the recruitment process.[38] In other words, they should enable candidates to determine whether a job will meet their significant values. Faced with an accurate, balanced portrayal of a prospective job, some candidates might choose to reject a job offer because they do not perceive a match between their needs and values and the organization's rewards and opportunities.

Do Realistic Job Previews Work?

The major objective of realistic recruitment is to reduce voluntary turnover among new employees. Therefore, a fair test of an RJP's effectiveness is to compare the turnover rates of new employees who received an RJP during recruitment with a comparable group who did not. Several reviews have evaluated the overall effectiveness of RJPs.[39] Such studies suggest that RJPs can reduce turnover. For example, a research effort that combined the results of 11 RJP studies, observed that the turnover rates for new employees who had received a realistic preview (19.8 percent) was lower than that for employees who had not received one (25.5 percent).[40] This nearly 6 percentage point differential can provide considerable savings to organizations that have to recruit, select, and train fewer new employees to replace those who terminate.

However, there are two caveats. First, RJPs do not significantly reduce turnover in every case. Thus, the impact of RJPs on turnover can vary from setting to setting. Second, there is little evidence to support any of the four mechanisms (met expectations, coping, air of honesty, self-selection) that presumably explain the effectiveness of RJPs. Taken together, these two problems indicate that it is not fully understood when and why RJPs are effective. In addition, research has shown that when job candidates face a choice between an RJP-based job or a TJP-based job prospect, a significantly larger proportion will choose the TJP-based job assuming all other factors are equal.[41] However, a more recent study found that an RJP-based job with higher compensation than a comparable TJP-based job resulted in the RJP-based job being viewed as attractive as the traditionally previewed job.[42] Thus, compensation can be used as a mechanism to mitigate the potential negative effect on job attractiveness that results from an RJP.

Based on the findings of past research, shown below are the circumstances in which RJPs are likely to be most effective:[43]

1. **When job candidates can be selective about accepting a job offer.** The self-selection mechanism is based on the assumption that candidates have alternative job choices. If candidates feel compelled to accept a job because alternative employment is unavailable, then the self-selection function of RJPs would not have an opportunity to operate. Moreover, people who see

few alternative opportunities may distort or discount negative information during recruitment.

2. **When job candidates would have held unrealistic expectations in the absence of an RJP.** Although outsiders may typically hold unrealistic expectations not all candidates are equally naive or unrealistic. Further, candidates for more visible jobs may know quite well what the jobs are all about even before recruitment begins. In such cases, expectations prior to recruitment may be sufficiently realistic to make RJPs unnecessary.

3. **When job candidates would have had difficulty coping with job demands in the absence of a realistic preview.** Again, if some candidates enter recruitment with a well-established repertoire of coping mechanisms, RJPs may not improve these skills and hence may not reduce turnover.

4. **When information presented during an RJP is understandable, credible, and consistent.** If candidates obtain information that is ambiguous or contradictory, they may not receive the intended message or they may receive mixed messages. This can lead to confusion, may cause lower acceptance rates by job candidates, and may increase subsequent turnover.

5. **When information presented during an RJP touches on topics that are significant or relevant to the candidates.** An RJP may include information that is irrelevant to some candidates and may omit discussions of topics that are particularly significant. If RJPs are to foster self-selection and effective coping behavior, they must include topics that are relevant to a wide variety of job candidates.

6. **When an optimal amount of realism is presented to the candidate.** Although most recruiting efforts provide too little realism, it is possible that RJPs may occasionally include so much negative information that candidates will be frightened off. Although RJPs do not seem to reduce an organization's ability to attract qualified candidates, they have the potential to do so if the information is too negative.

CONCLUSION. RJPs are potentially valuable ingredients in an organization's recruitment program. Not only may they reduce turnover among new employees, they can present an image of the organization as an honest, caring employer. Moreover, the concept of the RJP is not limited to new hires. It can be extended to situations in which employees are faced with a promotion, job transfer, and/or geographic relocation. In each of these situations, a realistic forewarning of future circumstances may help the individual and the organization.

Nevertheless, considerably more research is needed to better understand realistic recruitment. Certainly, the six circumstances just described need to be examined to see if they affect the success of realistic recruitment. In addition, there are unresolved issues regarding the timing of the preview (e.g., before or after an offer is extended and accepted) and the appropriateness of different media such as films, books, lectures, and one-on-one discussions.[44]

In addition, realistic recruitment is no substitute for making needed changes in the organization. If a job has a number of dissatisfying elements (e.g., close supervision, little challenge), merely telling candidates in advance about these elements is not going to solve the problem in the long run. The jobs themselves may need to be changed. There is nothing contradictory about these two positions. Organizations can and should strive to provide jobs that are potentially satisfying and motivating. At the same time, they can forewarn candidates about the (hopefully few) elements of the job that may be frustrating and dissatisfying. Realistic recruitment, in other words, does not preclude job redesign. They are complementary approaches to human resource management.

Regardless of an organization's recruitment practices, some reality shock is inevitable. There are many sources of unrealistic expectations other than organizational recruitment. Organizational entry is a career transition, and there are going to be some unpleasant surprises and required adjustments. The first 6 to 12 months on a new job challenge the new employee and the organization. These challenges are examined in more detail in Chapter 8.

ASSESSMENT AND SELECTION

Once prospective job candidates have been attracted and realistically recruited, the next step for the organization is final assessment and selection. This section discusses briefly the process by which organizations assess and select their employees. More extensive treatments of this topic are available in other texts.[45]

In the selection of individuals for employment, organizations first attempt to achieve a match or fit between the knowledge, skills, and abilities of the individual and the specific requirements of the job. In addition, some recruiters are also assessing the fit between the job candidate and such broader organizational factors as strategy, culture, and corporate values.[46] Simultaneously, organizations also look to align individual desires for a preferred work environment with the different cultures and climates within the firm.[47] Ideally, organizations should use selection techniques (and make actual selections) that are based on the accomplishment of both match-ups. In this sense the "total" person is selected, one who is hired not only to meet the challenges of a particular job, but also to "fit" with the work and cultural environment of the organization.

In contrast to the "total" person view of hiring, some prominent organizations have begun to challenge the precise matching approach in selecting individuals for employment. Some firms are making hiring decisions by using a single criterion (or a limited number of criteria). Orlando Behling has noted in a recent article that Bill Gates of Microsoft values intelligence as the primary factor in offering a position to a job candidate.[48] Behling reports that other companies, such as Southwest Airlines, Nucor Steel, and Silicon Graphics, have emphasized employee character or "conscientiousness" as the primary factor in making employment selections.[49] Although Behling makes a compelling argument for using a limited number of criteria in making hiring decisions, we continue to believe that the total person strategy of matching individual to organization is the most appropriate approach to ensure longer-term satisfaction for the individual and the hiring organization. Nonetheless, it is obvious that individual intelligence and character do play a critical role in most, if not all, hiring decisions.

David Bowen, Gerald Ledford, and Barry Nathan offer a four-step approach for organizations to achieve total person-organization fit in the selection and hiring of employees.[50] In the **first** step, the organization should assess the overall work environment to identify specific organizational characteristics and components that are important in determining job success. In the **second** step, the organization infers the type of person required to fill a specific job. More precisely, the company determines the knowledge, skills, abilities, and personal characteristics that should match both the "content and context" of the job.

The **third** step involves the use of programs that allow the organization and the individual to assess fit. For the organization, assessment of fit can take many different forms, including: simulations of work, structured job interviews, previous work experience, cognitive ability tests, reference checks, education, and personality tests. Although somewhat controversial, the use of tests of cognitive ability and personality are becoming more prevalent in employee selection.[51] Given the costs associated with selecting and employing a person who is mismatched with either the job or the work environment, organizations are using all available means, including personality tests, as a way to better guarantee a proper "fit."

For the individual, assessment of fit with the organization also can be accomplished in a variety of ways, including simulations, job interviews, on-site visitations, and informal contacts. As was discussed previously, the most important tool for individuals to assess prospective work positions is a realistic job preview.

The **fourth** step in selection of employees to achieve person-organization fit is reinforcement once the individual is hired. Specifically, organizations should provide such programs as orientation, training, mentoring, and other supportive alliances that emphasize the symbiotic nature of the relationship between individual and organization. In this way, the individual feels like an accepted and valued member of the firm.

Overall, the selection of individuals whose abilities and personal characteristics match the job and the work environment can have positive consequences for the organization in terms of lower turnover and a more involved and productive work force. Thus, it is in the organization's (and the individual's) best interests to use selection methods that serve to ensure a proper person-environment fit. Chapter 14 provides a more extensive discussion of the contemporary selection techniques used by organizations.

INDIVIDUAL ACTIONS DURING THE ENTRY PROCESS

From an individual's perspective, the primary aim of organizational entry is to obtain a job that is reasonably consistent with one's preferred work environment. As with other stages of the career life cycle, the individual can take certain steps to improve the likelihood of a positive outcome. This section considers five major tasks people need to confront during organizational entry. In each task area, there are guidelines that can effectively influence the organizational entry process.

DEVELOPMENT OF SELF-AWARENESS

It should be clear by now that effective career management decisions rest on a foundation of self-awareness. It is impossible to evaluate jobs and organizations without understanding one's personal values, interests, and talents. Perhaps most important, it is essential to expose oneself to opportunities for feedback, to use daily experiences as sources of information about oneself. These suggestions are consistent with earlier observations on the importance of self-awareness to career management (Chapter 3).

At the organizational entry stage, candidates will be exposed to information about different organizations. This information can be used to assess alternative organizations and to help a candidate clarify his or her own preferred work environment. For example, a particular company may emphasize its "fast track" development program for high-potential managers. The candidate may not have thought too much about the potential for rapid advancement and all that it implies. This piece of recruiting information should stimulate the candidate's appraisal of the preferred work environment. With appropriate questions ("What types of jobs do these fast-track managers obtain?" "How many relocations are typically required?"), this information can be a valuable source of self-exploration.

IDENTIFICATION OF PROSPECTIVE EMPLOYERS

Research has identified five major sources of job leads.[52] In order of prevalence, the five sources are college placement offices, unsolicited direct application, personal contacts, advertisements in newspapers and journals, and personnel agencies and search firms. We also add to this list corporate and professional Web sites as significant sources of information about job opportunities.

Although college placement offices are the most widely used sources of job leads for college students, the importance of personal contacts cannot be over estimated. Research has shown that for professional, managerial, and technical employees who recently changed jobs, personal contacts provided the most useful information about potential employers. Furthermore, jobs obtained through personal contacts produced the highest levels of satisfaction.[53]

There exist two broad types of personal contacts: (1) family members, friends, and social acquaintances and (2) work contacts such as present or past bosses, colleagues, and teachers. People who use personal contacts typically hold a position in a "social network" that enables them to draw on these resources when necessary. That is, they know many people who are either aware of job openings or know others who are.

· TABLE 7-2

SOURCES OF INFORMATION
AND REFERRALS

Friends and Family

- Who work in industry or company of interest
- Who know people in industry or company of interest
- Who know people with contacts

Written Sources

- Career libraries
- Placement offices
- Department of Labor's *Occupational Outlook Handbook*
- Corporate annual reports
- Investment analyst reports
- Trade publications and directories
- Journal articles about companies
- Recruiting brochures
- Advertisements
- Newspaper articles
- Industry/company case studies

People in Industry and Professions

- Alumni
- Trade associations
- Professional societies
- Visiting speakers
- Chamber of commerce

Social, Religious, and Political Organizations

- Kiwanis, etc.
- Rotary Club
- Church groups
- Political parties

People with Contacts

- Bankers
- Doctors, dentists
- Lawyers
- Accountants
- Insurance agents

SOURCE: M. London and S. Stumpf, *Managing Careers,* (Reading, MA: Addison-Wesley, 1982). Reprinted with permission of the publisher.

Normally it is more difficult for younger people to use personal contacts because their social networks are not as extensive as older, more experienced people. Nevertheless, it is never too early to begin to establish networks. Part of the challenge is identifying potential sources of information. Faculty members, fellow students, relatives, and friends of the family may all possess useful information. Participation in campus clubs and student professional organizations (e.g., Society for the Advancement of Management) also may provide job leads and future contacts. However, meeting people is not enough. A person also has to communicate his or her needs, values, and aspirations so others are aware of one's desires. This requires an assertive posture that is essential to all aspects of career management.

EFFECTIVE JOB INTERVIEW BEHAVIOR

Just like an organization, a job candidate has multiple goals during recruitment. Candidates need to make a favorable impression to receive a job offer, and they must gather useful information about companies so they can assess alternatives. Sometimes, these goals can conflict with one another. This section examines impression management, and the next turns to accurate assessment of jobs and organizations.

Although companies may scrutinize candidates' educational and work experiences and may, on occasion, administer psychological tests or use more elaborate assessment techniques, the most widely used procedure is the personal interview. Therefore, job candidates should be aware of the factors that contribute to a successful interview. Interviews were judged most effective when the interviewee knew about the company, had specific career goals, asked good questions, was socially adept, and was articulate.[54] These five factors seem to reflect two underlying dimensions of interviewee behavior: preparation/knowledge and effective interpersonal communication skills.

The first dimension underscores the need for candidates to conduct thorough research on the organization. Table 7.2 identifies a number of possible information sources. In addition to commonly available documentation (e.g., newspaper articles, annual reports, and corporate web sites), these sources include potentially useful people, such as friends, family members, members of professional and social organizations, and people with contacts or who know people with contacts.

People who work in the company of interest can be particularly helpful. It is recommended that job candidates conduct information interviews with such people, that is, interviews that are designed to obtain useful information, not necessarily to obtain a job.[55] Moreover, candidates should enter these interviews with questions that are relevant to their preferred work environment. A relatively clear understanding of desired tasks, rewards, and opportunities should enable a candidate to identify many of the relevant features of an organization and its jobs.

The second dimension, effective interpersonal communication skills, reflects social skills and articulation. Although there is no guaranteed way to become articulate and socially adept, candidates can work toward reducing their anxiety so that their positive qualities can emerge during the interview.

Employment interviews are anxiety-provoking situations for most people. They are somewhat unpredictable and can play a major role in one's career. However, the literature suggests a number of ways to reduce anxiety to appropriate and manageable levels:

- Know yourself. People who know what they want can be more relaxed during an interview and can respond more naturally and effectively to questions about career goals and expected contributions to the organization.
- Research the company thoroughly and prepare salient questions to be asked.
- Participate in programs designed to enhance interview skills, job search focus, and assertiveness. Many such programs are available through college placement offices or organizationally sponsored training activities.

In short, adequate planning and preparation for interviews can make a candidate more relaxed and effective in recruitment situations.

· TABLE 7-3

TYPES OF INFORMATION FOR ORGANIZATIONAL ASSESSMENT AND INTERVIEW PREPARATION

1. Line(s) of business conducted by the organization
2. Size of the organization
3. Structure of the organization
4. Outlook of the industry(ies) in which the organization does business
5. Financial health of the organization
6. Organization's business plans for the future
7. Location of the organization's headquarters and major facilities
8. Availability of training and development opportunities
9. Promotion and advancement policies (e.g., promotion from within)

SOURCE: J. H. Greenhaus, "Career Management: A Guide for Planning Your Future," In Study Guide, *Management*, 2nd ed., ed. S. R. Hiatt (Fort Worth, TX: The Dryden Press, 1991), 535–634.

ASSESSING ORGANIZATIONS

To make a realistic job choice, a candidate needs to assess organizations carefully and systematically. A useful organizational assessment requires the collection and analysis of data from varied sources. Table 7.3 lists several different types of information that would be helpful in organizational assessment and interview preparation.

It may be difficult to obtain such data for two reasons. First, the candidates may be so preoccupied with making a positive impression and obtaining a job offer that they do not seek information or pay attention to information that is provided.[56] Second, organizations may be unable or unwilling to provide some important pieces of information.

Job candidates can overcome these potential obstacles in several ways. **First,** they should be conscious of their own motives and goals during recruitment. They must recognize that their desire to impress a company may possibly distract them from their task of collecting critical information. Candidates must understand that it is possible to impress and assess simultaneously. Indeed, companies may not even be impressed with candidates who fail to ask significant and perceptive questions.

Second, candidates must see the connection between their preferred work environment and the assessment of an organization. Otherwise, the questions they ask may turn out to be irrelevant or trivial. Candidates should review their preferred work environment summary before each interview and identify the specific information they will need to assess the compatibility of the organization with their values, interests, talents, and desired life-style.

Third, candidates should understand the most appropriate data collection techniques. Observing prospective supervisors and colleagues in their work environment can give some clues about their competence, cooperativeness, and attitudes toward the organization and each other. Even if one's observations

· TABLE 7-4

SAMPLE QUESTIONS ASKED
BY INTERVIEWEE

Target Job: Financial Analyst with Johnson Manufacturing Company

Sample Interview Questions

1. What is the role of financial analysis in Johnson Manufacturing?
2. What kind of training opportunities are available?
3. Do financial analysts work on a variety of projects at one time?
4. How much responsibility and independence do financial analysts have in their work?
5. What computer support is available?
6. What long-term career opportunities are available for financial analysts?
7. How are salary increases and promotions determined?
8. How much travel is involved?

SOURCE: J. H. Greenhaus, "Career Management: A Guide for Planning Your Future," In Study Guide, *Management*, 2nd ed., ed., S. R. Hiatt (Fort Worth, TX: The Dryden Press, 1991), 535–634.

cannot provide conclusive evidence, they can suggest areas to be pursued with direct questioning. In other words, take advantage of the site visit to understand the people, the organization, and the facilities.

In addition, it is important to understand that the way in which a question is asked can affect the impression you make and the likelihood that you will obtain useful information. Members of the organization are human beings who can become defensive if they believe the questions are personally threatening or embarrassing.

Therefore, questions should be asked in a sensitive, nonthreatening manner. To take an extreme example, if rapid promotion opportunities are important to you, and your prospective boss appears to be in his or her mid-50s, you would not want to ask whether his or her age is typical for people in that position. A more neutral question about past and current promotion rates and practices may give you the desired information without threatening and alienating a potential supervisor. The people you meet have their own needs and frustrations. This should not inhibit you from asking important questions but should sensitize you to the form of questioning. Table 7.4 gives a set of example questions that might be used during the interview process by a job candidate for a financial analyst position.

A **fourth** obstacle to overcome for a job candidate is an overload of information at the completion of an interview or a visit to an organization. To prevent information loss, candidates should complete a brief log immediately after a recruitment interview that records their reactions to the interview as well as objective data such as the time and place of the interview and the interviewer's name.[57] Items on the log should be tied to the important elements of one's preferred work environment (e.g., "Will the job take advantage of my talents?" "Is there likely to be sufficient autonomy on the job?" "Are there training opportunities?"). Not only would this practice help one assess alternative organizations, it also would permit one to identify issues for which further information is needed.

CHOOSING ORGANIZATIONS

Like the choice of an occupation, the selection of a job should not be a mechanical "by-the-numbers" decision. Nor should it be speculative or unsystematic. On the basis of one's preferred work environment, one should identify a set of desirable and undesirable outcomes and then estimate the compatibility of each alternative job with each outcome. Some job offers (or potential job offers) may be discarded quickly, whereas others may require more information and a more thorough analysis of the data.

The evaluation of alternative jobs on the basis of expected outcomes and other criteria should stimulate one to think about values and aspirations and the likelihood that competing jobs will meet preferences. Lists of advantages and disadvantages of each job can also help a candidate to visualize the relative attractiveness of each alternative. There is a subjective, emotional element in job choice that should not be suppressed. Although this book has emphasized the systematic collection and analysis of information, the decision to accept one job over another also has to "feel" right. It is encouraging to note that employed adults making a job choice or a career change tend to move in a direction of greater congruence or "matching" between their self-characteristics/abilities and the jobs/careers they choose.[58]

One should not rely too heavily on other people's views of one's needs and values. Although it is important to obtain input from a wide variety of people, it is a candidate's needs and values that must be met, not other people's visions of what one should want from work.

SUMMARY

Organizational entry is the process by which job candidates move from outside to inside an organization. Its objective is to attain a match between individual talents and needs and a job's demands and rewards. Two models, expectancy theory and unprogrammed decision making, have been used to explain how candidates choose jobs in organizations.

Candidates develop expectations that guide their selection of jobs and organizations. Often, however, these expectations prove to be unrealistically inflated. The development of unrealistic job expectations can be due to a radical career transition (e.g., moving from school to work), the recruitment process itself, stereotypes that candidates hold about particular organizations, the nature of candidates' prior educational and work experiences, and candidates' natural tendency to see things as they would like them to be, not necessarily as they are. New employees can become disillusioned and dissatisfied if they see that the reality of the job does not live up to their lofty expectations.

Organizations should develop recruitment techniques that attract candidates effectively. At the same time, organizations should consider developing realistic recruitment procedures in which candidates are given a balanced picture of the job—both the positive and negative features. Under certain conditions, realistic recruitment can reduce dissatisfaction and turnover among new employees.

Individuals also need to manage the organizational entry process. In particular, candidates should understand their own preferred work environment, develop networks to identify prospective employers, develop or refine job interview skills, conduct accurate assessments of organizations, and make job choices based on sound information and self-knowledge.

ASSIGNMENT

Think about an organization into which you were hired. List the characteristics of the organization that you evaluated before you made the choice. In making the choice did you consider one or two important characteristics of the company (as with unprogrammed decision making), or did you evaluate more thoroughly a longer list of salient characteristics (as with expectancy theory)? In retrospect, were you satisfied with the organizational choice you made? Do you think your approach to decision making influenced your subsequent satisfaction with the organizational choice you made? Explain why or why not.

DISCUSSION QUESTIONS

1. To what extent have your educational and/or prior work experiences given you a realistic picture of what it would be like to enter a new organization? How could colleges and universities help individuals develop more realistic job expectations?

2. What are the advantages that accrue to organizations that practice realistic recruitment? Are there any risks involved? In your prior attempts to seek employment, did organizations provide you with a balanced, realistic picture of the job and the organization? What were your reactions to the recruitment procedure?

3. Why is an understanding of one's preferred work environment so critical to effective job search and organizational entry? What does a job candidate risk if he or she lacks self-insight in this area?

4. What can you learn about a job or an organization by visiting its facilities? How can you prepare for a visit to maximize the amount of useful information you receive? How can you assess whether a prospective employer will fit with your preferred work environment (PWE)?

5. What can you do to develop realistic expectations about a job in which you are interested? Identify as many sources of information as possible.

6. What is the role of emotion or "instinct" in deciding whether to accept a job offer? What weights should be given to a formal, rational analysis of a job and to a more subjective, emotional appraisal?

ENDNOTES

1. J. P. Wanous, *Organizational Entry: Recruitment, Selection, Orientation and Socialization of Newcomers* (Reading, MA: Addison-Wesley, 1992).

2. Ibid.

3. Ibid.

4. P. O. Soelberg, "Unprogrammed Decision Making," *Industrial Management Review* 8 (1967): 19–29.

5. R. D. Gatewood, M. A. Gowan, and G. J. Lautenschlager, "Corporate Image, Recruitment Image, and Initial Job Choice Decisions," *Academy of Management Journal* 36 (1993): 414–427.

6. D. D. Baker, R. Ravichandran, and D. M. Randall, "Exploring Contrasting Formulations of Expectancy Theory," *Decision Sciences* 20 (1989): 1–13; J. P. Wanous, T. L. Keon, and J. C. Latack, "Expectancy Theory and Occupational/Organizational Choices: A Review and Test," *Organizational Behavior and Human Performance* 32 (1983): 66–86.

7. D. P. Osborn, "A Reexamination of the Organizational Choice Process," *Journal of Vocational Behavior* 36 (1990): 45–60.

8. W. F. Glueck, "Decision Making: Organizational Choice," *Personnel Psychology* 27 (1974): 77–93.

9. Ibid.

10. J. P. Wanous, "Organizational Entry: From Naive Expectations to Realistic Beliefs," *Journal of Applied Psychology* 61 (1976): 22–29.

11. A. Howard and D. W. Bray, *Managerial Lives in Transition* (New York: Guilford Press, 1988).

12. Wanous, *Organizational Entry*.

13. J. H. Greenhaus, C. Seidel, and M. Marinis, "The Impact of Expectations and Values on Job Attitudes," *Organizational Behavior and Human Performance* 31 (1983): 394–417; E. A. Locke, "The Nature and Causes of Job Satisfaction," in *Handbook of Industrial and Organizational Psychology*, ed. M. D. Dunnette (New York: Wiley, 1983), 1297–1349.

14. A. G. Athos, "From Campus . . . to Company . . . to Company," *Journal of College Placement* 24 (1963): 22–23, 112, 114, 116.

15. E. H. Schein, *Career Dynamics: Matching Individual and Organizational Needs* (Reading, MA: Addison-Wesley, 1978).

16. S. L. Rynes and J. W. Boudreau, "College Recruiting in Large Organizations: Practice, Evaluation, and Research Implications," *Personnel Psychology* 39 (1986): 729–757.

17. Ibid.

18. Ibid.

19. J. H. Greenhaus, T. Sugalski, and G. Crispin, "Relationships between Perceptions of Organizational Size and the Organizational Choice Process," *Journal of Vocational Behavior* 13 (1978): 113–125.

20. Gatewood et al., "Corporate Image, Recruitment Image, and Initial Job Choice Decisions."

21. D. Lang, "Preconditions of Three Types of Alienation in Young Managers and Professionals," *Journal of Occupational Behaviour* 6 (1985): 171–182; M. R. Louis, "Socialization and Recruitment in Organizations: A Clash Between Homeostatic and Adaptive Systems," Working Paper 80.4, Department of Administrative Sciences, Naval Postgraduate School, Monterey, CA, 1980.

22. Glueck, "Decision Making."

23. D. W. Bray, R. J. Campbell, and D. L. Grant, *Formative Years in Business: A Long-Term AT&T Study of Managerial Lives* (New York: Wiley, 1974).

24. V. H. Vroom, "Organizational Choice: A Study of Pre- and Post-decision Processes," *Organizational Behavior and Human Performance* 1 (1966): 212–225.

25. D. B. Turban, J. E. Campion, and A. R. Eyring, "Factors Related to Job Acceptance Decisions of College Recruits," *Journal of Vocational Behavior* 47 (1995): 193–213.

26. C. P. Alderfer and C. G. McCord, "Personal and Situational Factors in the Recruitment Interview," *Journal of Applied Psychology* 54 (1972): 377–385; N. Schmitt and B. W. Coyle, "Applicant Decisions in the Employment Interview," *Journal of Applied Psychology* 61 (1976): 184–192; M. S. Taylor and J. A. Sniezek, "The College Recruitment Interview: Topical Content and Applicant Reactions," *Journal of Occupational Psychology* 57 (1984): 157–168.

27. Rynes and Boudreau, "College Recruiting in Large Organizations Practice, Evaluation, and Research Implications."

28. Turban et al., "Factors Related to Job Acceptance Decisions of College Recruits."

29. Alderfer and McCord, "Personal and Situational Factors in the Recruitment Interview"; Taylor and Sniezek, "The College Recruitment Interview."

30. J. P. Wanous and A. Colella, "Organizational Entry Research: Current Status and Future Directions," *Research in Personnel and Human Resource Management* 7 (1989): 59–120.

31. B. Z. Posner, "Comparing Recruiter, Student, and Faculty Perceptions of Important Applicant and Job Characteristics," *Personnel Psychology* 34 (1981): 329–339.

32. T. Bergmann and M. S. Taylor, "College Recruitment: What Attracts Students to Organizations?" *Personnel* 61 (1984): 34–46.

33. Turban et al., "Factors Related to Job Acceptance Decisions of College Recruits."

34. Bergmann and Taylor, "College Recruitment: What Attracts Students to Organizations?"

35. Wanous, *Organizational Entry*.

36. Ibid.

37. J. P. Wanous, "Tell It Like It Is at Realistic Job Previews," *Personnel* 52 (1975): 50–60.

38. Ibid.

39. G. M. McEvoy and W. F. Cascio, "Strategies for Reducing Employee Turnover: A Meta-Analysis," *Journal of Applied Psychology* 70 (1985): 342–353; S. L. Premack and J. P. Wanous, "A Meta-Analysis of Realistic Job Preview Experiments," *Journal of Applied Psychology* 70 (1985): 706–719; Wanous and Colella, "Organizational Entry Research."

40. R. R. Reilly, B. Brown, M. R. Blood, and C. Z. Malatesta, "The Effects of Realistic Job Previews: A Study and Discussion of the Literature," *Personnel Psychology* 34 (1981): 823–834.

41. A. M. Saks, W. H. Wiesner, and R. J. Summers, "Effects of Job Previews on Self-Selection and Job Choice," *Journal of Vocational Behavior* 44 (1994): 297–316.

42. A. M. Saks, W. H. Wiesner, and R. J. Summers, "Effects of Job Previews and Compensation Policy on Applicant Attraction and Job Choice," *Journal of Vocational Behavior* 49 (1996): 68–85.

43. J. A. Breaugh, "Realistic Job Previews: A Critical Appraisal and Future Research Directions," *Academy of Management Review* 8 (1983): 612–619.

44. S. M. Colarelli, "Methods of Communication and Mediating Processes in Realistic Job Previews," *Journal of Applied Psychology* 69 (1984): 633–642; P. Popovich and J. P. Wanous, "The Realistic Job Preview as a Persuasive Communication," *Academy of Management Review* 7 (1982): 570–578.

45. R. D. Gatewood and H. S. Feild, *Human Resource Selection* (Hinsdale, IL: Dryden Press, 1994); B. Schneider and N. Schmitt, *Staffing Organizations* (Glenview, IL: Scott Foresman, 1986).

46. R. D. Bretz, S. L. Rynes, and B. Gerhart, "Recruiter Perceptions of Applicant Fit: Implications for Individual Career Preparation and Job Search Behavior," *Journal of Vocational Behavior* 43 (1993): 310–327.

47. D. E. Bowen, G. E. Ledford, and B. R. Nathan, "Hiring for the Organization, not the Job," *Academy of Management Executive* 5 (1991): 35–51; Wanous, *Organizational Entry.*

48. O. Behling, "Employee Selection: Will Intelligence and Conscientiousness Do the Job?" *Academy of Management Executive* 12 (1998): 77–86.

49. Ibid.

50. Bowen et al., "Hiring for the Organization, not the Job."

51. B. Dumaine, "The New Art of Hiring Smart," *Fortune,* August 17, 1987, pp. 78–81; S. L. Martin and K. B. Slora, "Employee Selection by Testing," *HR Magazine* June (1991): 68–70; T. Moore, "Personality Tests Are Back," *Fortune,* March 30, 1987, pp. 74–82.

52. J. G. Clawson, J. P. Kotter, V. A. Faux, and C. C. McArthur, *Self-Assessment and Career Development,* 3rd ed. (Englewood Cliffs, NJ: Prentice-Hall, 1992).

53. M. Granovetter, *Getting a Job: A Study of Contacts and Careers* (Cambridge, MA: Harvard University Press, 1974).

54. Clawson et al., *Self-Assessment and Career Development.*

55. M. London and S. A. Stumpf, *Managing Careers* (Reading, MA: Addison-Wesley, 1982).

56. L. W. Porter, E. E. Lawler, and J. R. Hackman, *Behavior in Organizations* (New York: McGraw-Hill, 1975).

57. Clawson et al., *Self-Assessment and Career Development.*

58. M. K. Moss and I. H. Frieze, "Job Preferences in the Anticipatory Socialization Phase: A Comparison of Two Matching Models," *Journal of Vocational Behavior* 42 (1993): 282–297; S. L. Wilk, L. B. Desmarais, and P. R. Sackett, "Gravitation to Jobs Commensurate with Ability: Longitudinal and Cross-Sectional Tests," *Journal of Applied Psychology* 80 (1995): 79–85; D. Oleski and L. M. Subich, "Congruence and Career Change in Employed Adults," *Journal of Vocational Behavior* 49 (1996): 221–229.

8

Early Career:
Establishment and Achievement

In previous chapters, we discussed the process of selecting career goals and choosing a job and an organization. This chapter examines the two dominant themes of the early career, the tasks of career establishment and achievement, and offers guidelines to improve career management at this stage.

In any new job, the first task is literally to become established. There is much to learn in this phase. One must become accustomed to the day-to-day routine and must demonstrate mastery of new assignments. Acceptance by one's colleagues and supervisors is another important consideration. In short, the hope is that one can become competent, productive, and satisfied in a new occupation and organization. Of course, it may take several years to determine whether competence, productivity, and satisfaction are attained. Once the establishment phase has passed, the next stage is achievement.

Specifically, having gained a measure of self-confidence and acceptance, the next major task of the early career is to increase one's level of achievement and to contribute to one's employer (or employers). Several questions can arise at this point. Should an employee move from his or her current functional area to another department? Should one make preparations to assume a managerial role? Are there sufficient opportunities at one's company to pursue a number of different options? This second phase of the early career typically reflects a concern for, if not a preoccupation with, achievement and accomplishment. Of course, the pursuit of career achievement and accomplishment has become more complicated over the past several years as companies have taken a more "transactional" approach to hiring and upward mobility. The personal disruptions brought on by the rapid expansion in corporate mergers and downsizings make it difficult for individuals to follow a standard path toward achievement of career goals.

Table 8.1 identifies changes that tend to occur during the course of the early career. Managers early in their tenure with an organization tend to rely on the organization for guidance and also exhibit a need for security. However, as they gain more experience, they become more confident, aggressive, dominant, independent, and achievement-oriented and less concerned with approval from others. In addition, their self-actualization needs become more prominent.[1]

CHANGES DURING THE EARLY CAREER

Establishment Themes	Achievement Themes
Fitting In	Moving Up
Dependence	Independencce
Learning	Contributing
Testing Competence	Increasing Competence
Insecurity	Self-Confidence
Seeking Approval	Seeking Authority

Although it is impossible to pinpoint the timing of the transition from establishment to achievement, such a shift is likely to occur. This fact does not suggest that first-year employees care little about achievement. Nor are veteran employees unconcerned about learning and gaining acceptance and security. Rather, it is the relative emphasis given these two themes that changes during the course of the early career.

ESTABLISHMENT PERIOD

A person beginning—or redirecting—his or her career is traveling in foreign territory. An unproven commodity at this point, the new employee needs to answer a number of questions.[2] Will the job give me an opportunity to test myself? Will I be considered worthwhile? Will I be able to maintain my individuality and integrity? Will I be able to lead a balanced life? Will I learn and grow? Will I find the work environment stimulating and enjoyable? The employee at this point is a newcomer to the organization but has not yet "fit into" the organization psychologically. Therefore, there is a strong need to become accepted as a competent, contributing member of the firm, while exhibiting positive work habits and attitudes and effective relationships with co-workers.[3]

At the same time, the organization must ensure that the new person learns how to perform the job and how to fit into the company. Fitting in requires more than a mastery of task skills. It also requires learning how the organization operates, what actions are rewarded or punished, and for what the organization stands. New hires and others in the establishment phase generally are the most receptive to information about the company and the ways they can make a contribution to it.[4] Acceptance of the organization's philosophies by newcomers should be a goal for all firms. To this end, the organization has to properly socialize recruits into their new work environment.

Just as a person growing up learns about society's values and norms (e.g., thrift, honesty, cooperation), so too must the newcomer learn how to function in the organization. Organizational socialization has been defined as "the process by which an individual comes to appreciate the values, abilities, expected behaviors, and social knowledge essential for assuming an organizational role, and for participating as an organizational member."[5]

In essence, socialization is a learning process wherein the individual moves or changes from an old role (perhaps that of a college student) into the new role of employee. Well-designed socialization and induction processes can positively influence individual motivation, job satisfaction, and organizational commitment.[6] Consequences of improvements in these variables include enhanced individual and organizational performance and lower levels of employee turnover.

From the new employee's perspective, successful socialization is critical because it is difficult, if not impossible, to be competent and accepted without learning about and adjusting to the organization. Socialization is also essential to organizations. After all, organizations have histories and procedures that have been tested by time and tradition and ongoing work groups with established norms and priorities. Somehow, the newcomer must learn how to operate within an organization's established cultural system to become successful.

An organization's culture can be defined as "a pattern of basic assumptions invented, discovered or developed by a given group as it learns to cope with its problems of external adaptation and internal integration that has worked well enough to be considered valid and, therefore is to be taught to new members as the correct way to perceive, think, and feel in relation to those problems."[7] Socialization of new organizational members is the primary mechanism by which an organization can ensure the stability and perpetuation of its culture. Thus, proper socialization has an influential role in the longer-term survival of the firm because it serves to ensure continued adherence to the norms, values, and essential mission of the enterprise.

CONTENT AREAS OF SOCIALIZATION

Based on a review of the socialization literature and research, Georgia T. Chao and her colleagues identified six content areas of socialization.[8] The six areas, as adapted from Chao et al. and presented below, represent the outcomes an organization would expect to result from the socialization process.

Performance Proficiency—the extent to which the individual has learned the tasks involved on the job.

People—the extent to which the individual has established successful work relationships with organizational members.

Politics—the extent to which the individual has been successful in gaining information regarding formal and informal work relationships and power structures within the organization.

Language—the extent to which the individual has learned the profession's technical language as well as the acronyms, slang, and jargon that are unique to the organization.

Organizational Goals and Values—the extent to which the individual has learned specific organizational goals and values, including informal goals and the values espoused by organizational members in powerful or controlling positions.

History—the extent to which the individual understands and appreciates the organization's traditions, customs, myths, and rituals, as well as the personal backgrounds and work histories of important or influential organizational members.

Well-designed socialization programs attempt to address most if not all of the six content areas as listed above. Nonetheless, a substantial amount of socialization takes place informally as individuals observe and monitor the behavior of others in the organization and as they are exposed to actual inner workings and lore of their employer.

STAGES OF ORGANIZATIONAL SOCIALIZATION

Several researchers have proposed that socialization follows a sequence of stages.[9] This approach is used to examine the process of organizational socialization in more detail.

STAGE 1: ANTICIPATORY SOCIALIZATION. The socialization process begins even before the employee joins the organization. Job candidates enter the recruitment process with a more or less stable set of talents, work values, and interests. Also, they develop specific expectations during recruitment about life in the organization. As discussed in Chapter 7, the major concern at this stage is that the expectations are realistic, so that individuals have a reasonable chance of meeting their important values and using their talents.

STAGE 2: ENCOUNTER. The recruit begins employment and encounters a new environment. In fact, the environment is not only new but may depart radically from the newcomer's expectations in many ways. Edgar Schein identified a set of values that are important to college graduates in choosing a first job (Table 8.2).[10]

The organization's view of a new recruit (see Table 8.2) is somewhat less flattering. This stereotype has important implications for how these newcomers are treated. The individual wants challenge and responsibility; the organization thinks the recruit is too inexperienced, theoretical, and naive to handle much responsibility. The individual wants to be creative and innovative; the organization has its own ways of doing things that could hardly be appreciated by a newcomer. The individual needs to test and apply his or her special talents; the organization thinks the recruit has a lot to learn before the talents can be used. It is no wonder that many employees have difficulties adjusting to their new work environment. In addition, new employees, especially younger ones who have never experienced a "relational" psychological contract with an employer, show a greater willingness to exit from an organization if talents are underused or if personal needs are not met. Indeed, it has recently been noted how "Generation X" employees, or the 45 million people born in the United States between 1965 and 1977, are far more self-reliant and willing to take job risks than their 78 million predecessors of the "baby boom" generation.[11]

· TABLE 8-2

COLLEGE GRADUATES' VALUES AND ORGANIZATIONS' PERCEPTIONS*

What College Graduates Consider Important in Choosing First Job	How Organizations View New College Graduates
Opportunity for advancement	Overly ambitious and unrealistic in expectations regarding advancement and increased responsibility
Doing something important	
Responsibility	Too theoretical, idealistic, and naïve to be given important initial assignment
Opportunity to use special aptitudes and educational background	Too immature and inexperienced to be given much responsibilty
Challenge and adventure	Too security-conscious and unwilling to take risks
Opportunity to be creative and original	Unwilling to work hard to get ideas across, unable to "sell" ideas
High salary	Potentially useful and innovative but must be "broken in" before this resource becomes available to the organization

*Based on material presented in E. H. Schein, "How to Break in the College Graduate," *Harvard Business Review* 42 (1964): 68–76.

There is also the matter of enormous learning requirements for the recruit. There are new tasks to learn, new relationships to cultivate, new work groups to enter, and new policies and procedures to grasp. In short, one needs to "learn the ropes." Organizational newcomers recognize this need to take an active role in learning the work processes and culture of their new company.[12]

Organizations realize that newcomers have a great deal to learn. Often, this recognition is couched in terms of "breaking in" the new recruit. Although it is debatable whether the treatment of people deserves the same term as applied to a new pair of shoes, it cannot be denied that substantial learning must take place during this early period of employment. But how do newcomers learn the ropes? Either consciously or unwittingly, organizations attempt to socialize newcomers in a variety of ways. Socialization tactics used by organizations can be broken down into two types: institutionalized and individualized.[13] Institutionalized socialization consists of common programs and learning experiences that are formally presented to all (or nearly all) new organizational members. However, individualized socialization consists of unique activities and learning experiences that are specifically targeted to one person. Listed below are some of the common organizationally sponsored socialization techniques:

1. **Recruitment** can be used to select candidates whose talents and values seem most compatible with the organization's requirements. In addition,

realistic recruitment can be used to set candidates' expectations at more appropriate levels, thereby reducing the degree of reality shock experienced.

2. **Training** activities are designed to provide instruction on job-related tasks and to orient the newcomer to the organization's goals and practices. Edgar Schein usefully distinguished three approaches to training.[14] "Training while working" involves an apprenticeship relationship in which the recruit is given assignments in a regular department under the tutelage of a more senior employee. In "working while training," the recruit is assigned to a formal training program and either is given small but challenging projects or is rotated among a number of departments or projects. Training activities are then either interspersed between assignments or held at specified periods on a regular basis. In "full-time training," recruits are assigned to the training department, which oversees their rotations through different assignments. They then either observe others at work or are given "special" projects. Unfortunately, as Schein pointed out, these assignments are often perceived as meaningless "make work" because they involve little continuity and provide no real responsibility for the accomplishment of significant tasks.

3. **Debasement experiences** are also used to socialize the newcomer.[15] In one version, sink or swim, the employee is given a difficult assignment with no guidance or support. Organizations may also provide an "upending experience" by assigning tasks that are trivial or insoluble, thereby making it clear to the new employee that the organization is in control. Milder forms of debasement might include hazing and "scutwork" designed to put newcomers in their place right from the start. Most people have played (or will play) the "gofer" role (go for coffee, etc.) that often befalls the lowest and newest person in the hierarchy. Regardless of their specific form, debasement strategies are intended to shake the newcomer's confidence so that the organization can influence or reshape his or her behavior.[16]

4. **Reward and control systems** also provide socialization experiences to the newcomer. New employees learn what an organization values by observing what activities or outcomes are rewarded. Objective market and financial indicators are used to monitor employees' accomplishments in such areas as increasing sales, improving profits, and serving as an agent for change. Performance appraisals and promotions normally are related to progress along pre-established dimensions.

STAGE 3: CHANGE AND ACQUISITION. We have seen how newcomers encounter the reality of a work environment and are subject to pressures to adapt to these realities. In what ways do they change as a result of encountering this new environment? Put another way, how do they know if the socialization process has been successful? Change and acquisition can take a number of forms:[17]

1. Has the employee learned the job? It is essential that task demands be sufficiently mastered so that the newcomer performs successfully and dependably and feels successful in the job role.

2. Has the employee been integrated into the work group? Successful integration requires an appropriate level of mutual trust and acceptance so the group can operate effectively. The recruit must typically adjust to the group's established practices, norms, and values. For example, a group that emphasizes cooperation and good-natured kidding is likely to put pressure on a new member to adopt these behaviors.

3. Has the employee achieved an acceptable level of role clarity? Can he or she handle the ambiguities and conflicts inherent in an organization? Conflicts may arise between work and outside life (family or leisure activities) and between the demands of the work group and other groups in the organization. The successful resolution of these conflicts is an important learning task for newcomers.

4. Has the employee learned how to work within the system? Working within the system means dealing with the supervisor and peers, overcoming resistance to new ideas, accepting initially low levels of responsibility, and understanding the reward system.

5. Does the employee understand and accept the organization's values? Is the recruit, for example, beginning to act, think, and feel like an integral part of the company? In other words, is the newcomer's self-concept changing to be more in line with the organization's values? Have the culture and norms of the organization been successfully transmitted? This is, in fact, the heart of the socialization process.

Edgar Schein distinguished pivotal or essential values (e.g., belief in free enterprise, acceptance of organizational hierarchy) from relevant values that are desirable but not absolutely essential for employee acceptance (e.g., dress codes).[18] One sign of unsuccessful socialization is a new employee's rejection of all values and norms, both pivotal and relevant. Newcomers who react with such "rebellion" are unlikely to survive in the organization, unless their talent level is so high as to make their "rebellious" behavior tolerable.

Schein also suggests that the blind acceptance of all values—pivotal, relevant, or peripheral—produces a level of conformity and sterility that can be disastrous for the individual and the organization. For example, newcomers who accept all values of an organization may become so tied to the system that they are incapable of making needed changes in the organization when they develop more influence later in their career. In line with this view, several researchers have found that the type and intensity of a newcomer's organizational socialization experience can detract from individual innovation.[19]

A third type of response, what Schein calls creative individualism, is the most desirable outcome of the socialization process. In this case, pivotal values and norms are accepted, but the less essential ones may be rejected. By retaining portions of their own identity, such creative individualists should be able to make the most innovative contributions to the organization over time. While accepting the core goals and values of the organization, creative individualists are able to question some of the organization's less useful qualities and can affect changes in these qualities as they acquire more influence in the system.

Mutual Acceptance and the Psychological Contract

Successful socialization is signified by a sense of mutual acceptance. The individual accepts the organization by sustaining high levels of involvement, motivation, and commitment and by deciding to remain with the organization for the present time.

Simultaneously, the organization accepts the newcomer as a trusted and valued member. Having survived the initial trials and obstacles, the individual has, to a certain extent, proved him- or herself in the eyes of the organization. Organizations signify their acceptance of the employee in a number of ways: by providing a positive performance appraisal or a more challenging assignment, by granting a promotion, by offering a significant salary increase, or by sharing secrets about the organization that would only be entrusted to a valued colleague.[20]

Mutual acceptance also shows an initial approval of the psychological contract between the individual and the organization. Psychological contracts serve to specify the contributions an employee believes are owed to the organization, as well as the inducements the employee believes are owed in return from the organization.[21] As we noted in Chapter 1, there exist two forms of psychological contracts: relational and transactional.[22]

The "traditional" view of careers assumes a relational contract between employer and employee. **Relational contracts** are normally longer term and typically involve a high degree of commitment based on a promise of job security by the employer in exchange for loyalty on the part of the employee.[23] By contrast, a **transactional contract** is more short term in nature and is predicated on performance-based pay, involves lower levels of commitment by both parties, and allows for easy exit from the agreement.

Historically, the relational psychological contract provided security to the organization and to the individual worker through the formation of an unwritten social bond between the employer and employee. From this historical perspective, adherence to the relational psychological contract made life simple and predictable for the employing organization and the individual. More precisely, the relational psychological contract promised security and the possibility of advancement in exchange for the employee's singular commitment to the organization.[24] For example, on entering an organization, an individual may have expected that in exchange for hard work, good performance, and loyalty, the organization would provide increasingly interesting and challenging work, substantial salary increases, and rapid advancement. Thus, the organization expected the employee to make many personal and family sacrifices for the good of the company.

Substantial evidence accumulated over the past two decades shows that the standard organizational career of the 1950s, 1960s, and 1970s, as based on the relational psychological contract, has ended. Both parties to the presumed relational psychological contract, employees and employers alike, now acknowledge its demise. Large-scale, high-profile organizations demand workers with task-relevant skills at specific points in time, sort of a "just-in-time" application of human capital. However, employees have come to understand, albeit slowly, what has been referred to as the dangers in presumed organizational benevolence.[25] The new reality is that employees no longer see loyalty to a specific company as meaningful or beneficial. Instead, the attitude is that one must at all times look out for one's best career interests, regardless of the consequences for a particular firm.

Even with the demise of the relational psychological contract, the employee and the organization still must go through the process of testing one another. This testing puts each party in a better position to evaluate the viability of its expectations. The individual has a better sense of the organization's responses to his or her efforts, and the organization has a better idea of what it can expect from the employee. Mutual acceptance, then, represents a tentative approval of continued employment, or a ratification of the psychological contract. Presented below is an example of mutual acceptance.

> Sarah started work in the budget department of a large department store chain a little more than 1 year ago. She was impressed with the company right from the start—everyone inside and outside of her department made her feel welcome. After 2 months with the company, Sarah's career got a boost, although she did not see it that way at the time. Specifically, the senior budget analyst who was in charge of tracking the company's capital expenditures and assessing future spending plans resigned suddenly. With no one else available to fill the void, Sarah stepped in and assumed the role. As a junior analyst with limited work experience, Sarah found the job of simultaneously learning the capital budgeting system and dealing with day-to-day expenditures to be extremely stressful. Her prior personal computer experience helped, and Sarah was determined to succeed in this work. Sarah performed so well that the company promoted her to budget analyst after only 6 months and she received a 10 percent raise. Time and again, her company's management has commented on her outstanding work. She has been identified as someone who can advance rapidly, and she has been given added responsibilities. Sarah enjoys her work and socializes frequently with the other people in her department. After 1 year, she is really committed to the company, and from all indications, the company is committed to her.

This case does not imply that mutual acceptance is an inevitable outcome of socialization. There are many situations in which a bad match is recognized by the individual and/or the organization—a violation, in a sense, of the initial psychological bond. Perhaps the individual did not live up to the organization's expectations or the organization did not provide the kind of work setting the individual expected. In such situations, employees may become less productive and less satisfied and may ultimately choose to leave the organization.

CONTINUING TASKS

Mutual acceptance does not really terminate the establishment period. Rather, it provides some concrete feedback to the individual and the organization. Schein identified four other general issues that must be addressed during this phase.[26]

First, the employee must continue to improve on the job. If a new assignment or promotion is granted, the employee needs to demonstrate continued capability at higher levels of complexity and responsibility.

Second, the employee normally develops competence in a specialization area (e.g., marketing, engineering, information systems) that will serve as a foundation for the future career. American businesses generally expect their managers to be specialists in their early career, regardless of whether they ultimately want to move into a more general management position.

Third, the employee must continue to learn how to work effectively as a less experienced member of the organization. The employee is still relatively new and may not receive all the autonomy he or she would like. In essence, employees must appreciate their status and must continue to learn how to work effectively within the constraints of the organization.

Fourth, employees should reassess their talents, values, and interests in the light of their recent work experiences. There should be sufficient insight at this point to reevaluate the appropriateness of the chosen occupation and the opportunities within the organization. Decisions to remain or leave the career field and the organization need to be made.

FLOUNDERING: LEARNING THROUGH EXPERIENCE

The establishment period can evolve within one occupational field and one organization. However, there may also be considerable floundering and trial before a person finds a suitable line of work and a compatible organization in which to pursue the chosen work. Therefore, many people may try to establish themselves a number of times before they find a satisfying connection to the work world.

Consider the situation of Bob, an MBA student, whose route to graduate school at age 30 demonstrates the tortuous path many people follow to establish a suitable career direction.

> Bob was an undergraduate management major who had given little thought to the kind of career he ultimately wanted. Because of limited job prospects, he accepted a position as a claims adjuster in a large insurance company as an opportunity to learn about himself and the world of work. In time, he acquired the technical and interpersonal skills that made him a successful adjuster—so successful that after 3 years, he was offered a promotion to claims supervisor. This promotion opportunity forced Bob to consider whether he really wanted a career in claims. Realizing that he wanted more autonomy and financial rewards than his current career path could offer, he declined the promotion and left the company shortly thereafter.
>
> Bob next accepted a sales position with a national manufacturer of office copiers. He quickly knew he had made the correct decision. He enjoyed sales immensely and became one of the top producers. However, a number of disturbing policy and personnel changes (including the promotion of a less-qualified peer) convinced him that this was not the kind of company in which he could grow and develop.
>
> Bob changed employers so he could pursue what was crystallizing as a natural career goal—to become a sales manager at a progressive company. He accepted a district sales manager position for a distributor of copiers. Although he performed well in this position, he thought the company's management style was too oppressive and authoritarian.
>
> At age 26, Bob wondered if he could ever find the kind of company that would suit his values and career goals. He quit his position and went to work for a former boss,

who was now regional manager at an office products firm. Although he started out as a sales representative, Bob was promised the position of branch manager at the end of 6 months, when the current branch manager was to leave. Unfortunately, the job went to someone else, another old friend of Bob's boss.

Disillusioned and bitter, Bob quit the office products firm and, along with four other aspiring entrepreneurs, founded an Internet-based marketing organization. He looked forward to testing his skills in marketing and selling an innovative service. After 6 months, though, clients were few and expenses drained the company's cash flow. Hope was rapidly vanishing.

In the midst of his risky business venture, Bob began to establish a serious romantic relationship and was now considering marriage. He became more concerned with stability in his career and his life. After 1 year of slow growth and an uncertain future, Bob cut his ties from the company he had helped to form.

Seeking a more stable career direction, Bob accepted a sales position with an audiovisual production company. He performed well in this position and, for the first time in his career, worked closely with marketing people. After 6 consecutive months of reaching his sales quota, however, Bob was fired in a cost-cutting move.

Bob was plagued with self-doubt. Was he unlucky or was he a failure? Was he unrealistic in his career goals or did he just have a series of bad breaks? Two months short of his 30th birthday and 9 months before his wedding, Bob was desperate. He called up friends to get a better handle on different career opportunities. He scanned newspapers for employment openings. Disillusioned with his experiences in sales, he listened with interest and excitement when his fiancée suggested he consider a career in marketing. Having spoken to a number of people, he was optimistic that marketing would satisfy his career interests. But he also learned that entry-level positions in marketing often required either prior marketing experience or an MBA degree.

With some trepidation, Bob returned to graduate school to pursue an MBA on a full-time basis. He joined the MBA Society, a student-run group and attended a "mentoring" session in which alumni spoke to students about career opportunities in different fields. Conversations with an alumnus eventually led to a summer internship in the marketing department of a large, prestigious consumer products company. Having just successfully completed the internship, Bob finally feels directed in his career. At the age of 30, his establishment as a marketing professional is just beginning.

This case illustrates the difficulties some people have in establishing their career. Finding a fit does not always come easily. Chronic career indecision, unrealistic expectations, personal shortcomings, lack of self-insight, organizational turmoil, and economic fluctuations can introduce considerable uncertainty and frustration into careers and lives.

On the positive side, however, people can learn from their experiences. Researchers at the Center for Creative Leadership in Greensboro, North Carolina, have examined the lives and work experiences of executives as they develop through their careers.[27] Their studies have documented the important role that career difficulties, hardships, and traumas can have in promoting individual development. These hardships can include business failures and mistakes, career setbacks (e.g., demotions, missed promotions, dissatisfying jobs), subordinate personal or performance problems, breaking out of a career rut, and personal difficulties (e.g., divorce, work-family conflict, illness or death of a loved one or co-worker). Successful responses to these career challenges were manifest in a number of ways, including a greater degree of sensitivity to others, recognition of one's personal limits, awareness of the need for balance between work and family life, acceptance of the need to take charge of one's career, and the development of coping strategies.[28]

No experience is really wasted, although it may appear so at the time. What Bob had going for him was a considerable degree of self-insight, a determination to make his career work, a willingness to leave situations that no longer seemed tenable, and a strong belief that he could influence the course of his career.

ORGANIZATIONAL ACTIONS DURING ESTABLISHMENT

EFFECTIVE RECRUITMENT

Discrepancies between job expectations and the realities of the organization can inhibit a new employee's adjustment to the organization. Realistic recruitment procedures, therefore, can play a significant role in helping newcomers establish themselves in their career and forge a healthy, candid relationship with the firm.

In addition, there is a tendency to select overqualified candidates for some positions because it is easier to choose the most qualified individuals than the best qualified. It is also easier to examine credentials than real job qualifications. Thus, college graduates may be sought to fill positions demanding a high school diploma, and MBAs are recruited for positions that require a bachelor's degree. In some instances, these high qualifications are justified because they are required for future jobs to which the employee might ultimately be promoted. In the meantime, however, many of these highly qualified newcomers may believe that their talents and training are underused in their first job and may leave (or become alienated) before they have had a chance to establish themselves. To avoid underuse in these situations, organizations should provide the newcomer with sufficiently challenging, responsible tasks to maintain high levels of motivation and involvement.

EFFECTIVE ORIENTATION PROGRAMS

The first few days or weeks in an organization can be particularly critical in orienting the newcomer to the work environment. Effective orientation programs can help new employees become part of the organization and inform them about the organization's policies, benefits, and services. Research has identified the following functions of new employee orientation programs:[29]

- Introduction to the company.
- Review of important policies and practices, including benefits and services.
- Benefit plan enrollment.
- Completion of employment forms.

- Review of employer expectations and development of accurate employee expectations.
- Introduction to peers and facilities.
- Introduction to the new job.

Research has also distinguished "in-advance" and "in-response" socialization practices.[30] In-advance practices provide information that the organization has decided (in advance) is important for the newcomer. Such information might include a review of company policies, practices, and benefits. In-response procedures provide information that is responsive to newcomers' specific questions and needs, such as information on particular career paths. A balance of these two approaches should provide the most comprehensive, useful information to a new employee. Therefore, some portion of an orientation program should involve small-group discussions and one-on-one sessions, in which more attention can be devoted to individual concerns. In addition, orientation programs can go beyond general matters to confront specific problems faced by new employees. For example, orientation programs can work to combat high levels of anxiety that new employees can experience with certain jobs or departments. The key is recognizing newcomers' needs and concerns so that proper orientation systems can be developed.

EARLY JOB CHALLENGE

Many employees desire and expect high levels of challenge and responsibility on a new job, but many organizations are hesitant to provide early challenge and instead exercise tight supervision and control until newcomers are more experienced, skilled, and trusted.

However, when early job challenge is provided to new employees, the results can be beneficial and long-lasting. Research has found that management trainees who were given demanding first jobs generally performed more effectively than their counterparts who were not given as much challenge.[31] In addition, the degree of initial job challenge can quicken promotion to higher-level management positions and can stimulate interest in further educational development.

Providing early challenge enables a new employee to internalize high work standards. A recruit who is exposed to substantial challenge learns that the organization is demanding, that it expects people to assume responsibility for decisions, and that it holds people accountable for results. As newcomers come to appreciate this emphasis on challenge, responsibility, and achievement, they will accept these standards as their own and will act in ways consistent with these standards. The job involvement of early-career employees often hinges on the degree to which their work provides autonomy and freedom.[32]

It is also well documented that other people's expectations affect our behavior. When supervisors expect their subordinates to handle additional challenge, they build more challenge into the job, offer help, encouragement, and support, and find that their optimistic predictions are confirmed by their subordinates' accomplishments—a self-fulfilling prophecy in action. Described below is an example of how a company can provide early job challenge.[33]

> The employee development program at PepsiCo Inc. uses early job challenge as the key activity in grooming managerial and executive talent. First, the company works to hire the brightest and most promising individuals available, and then they are each given an equal chance to show their mettle. In line with PepsiCo's decentralized decision-making approach, individuals are given significant autonomy, in which entrepreneurial behavior and risk taking are rewarded. In the earliest years of their career, individuals usually stay with one division but are rotated through a multitude of varying assignments. The recruits are presented with significant work demands right from the start and are expected to perform to exacting standards. Progress and performance of the junior managers are tracked closely. They receive feedback from both superiors and subordinates, and strengths and weaknesses are evaluated thoroughly. Under this type of aggressive system, turnover can be high. People tend to get weeded out early in their careers rather than later, when it is much harder to find another job. Although for many the PepsiCo program may be harsh and demanding, for those who survive the rewards are exceptional. In addition to rapid advancement and high compensation, PepsiCo's top managers receive such perks as first-class air travel, luxury hotels on the road, a company car every 2 years, and an annual bonus of 25 to 30 percent of salary. Certainly, the PepsiCo approach is not for everyone. Some individuals may be slower starters or may need a higher degree of nurturance. Nonetheless, the PepsiCo program supports the view that early job challenge and demanding assignments can be pivotal in career development and advancement.

Douglas Hall proposed that employees who accomplish sufficiently challenging tasks experience a sense of psychological success (an internal feeling of being successful) that raises their self-esteem and sense of competence, increases their career involvement, and spurs them on to want even more challenge.[34] Hall's psychological success model explains how "success breeds success"—by giving employees a real opportunity to develop a positive self-image.

Providing new employees with meaningful, challenging work right from the start may require the organization to reexamine its assumptions about recruits as well as its established traditions. Organizations also may have to reevaluate the most effective way to train recruits, perhaps moving in the direction of Schein's apprentice-like "training while working" strategy.[35] Indeed, evidence suggests that the use of apprenticeships has grown substantially in recent years. According to one review, more than 300,000 apprentices are being trained in the United States, covering more than 800 different occupations.[36]

Not all newcomers will be able to handle the same amount of challenge and responsibility. Nonetheless, organizations should not permit their stereotypes to interfere with early career growth. There is some evidence, for example, that women may be assigned to less challenging tasks than men, especially when the organization has had little experience working with competent women, or when the person making the assignment is male.[37] The message should be clear. If women or other stereotyped groups are initially given less challenging assignments, their early career growth may be unfairly stunted.

FREQUENT AND CONSTRUCTIVE FEEDBACK

Although performance appraisal and feedback are important at all stages of career development, they are particularly crucial during the establishment years because of the newcomer's need to become competent and accepted. It is not enough to assign challenging tasks. Newcomers have to know how well (or poorly) they are performing on these tasks. Feedback must be frequent enough so that employees can make changes in their behavior on an ongoing basis to maximize learning. Moreover, if the feedback is positive, it can serve as a powerful source of praise and reinforcement. Also, performance feedback sessions provide an opportunity for supervisors and subordinates to discuss their assumptions and expectations about each other—to clarify the psychological contract.

But feedback must be administered in a constructive, supportive manner if it is to be effective. Employees tend to hold two simultaneous yet conflicting needs.[38] On one hand, they want honest feedback; they want to hear the truth. On the other hand, they also want to hear only good news to protect their sense of self-esteem and to receive extrinsic rewards.

Sometimes, feedback is so negative and devastating that an adversarial and defensive relationship is created between supervisor and subordinate. In other cases, supervisors are so concerned about being "kind" that they provide no useful feedback to the subordinate. Perhaps most frequently, supervisors are so uncomfortable with performance appraisal that they simply avoid the process altogether.

In recent years, many organizations have attempted to improve the appraisal and feedback process. Such efforts involve developing more useful performance appraisal forms, encouraging subordinates to engage in self-appraisal, extending the appraisers to include peers and others in the organization, training supervisors in providing feedback, and separating discussions of performance feedback from discussions of salary and promotion decisions.

THE FIRST SUPERVISOR: A CRITICAL RESOURCE

A newcomer striving for competence and acceptance requires what Douglas Hall called "supportive autonomy"—sufficient challenge and autonomy to develop a sense of psychological success and a supportive environment in which to make mistakes, learn, and grow.[39] The newcomer's supervisor can play a major role in providing supportive autonomy.

Research has identified a number of task and personal needs that subordinates require from their supervisor at different career stages. Table 8.3 identifies the needs associated with the establishment period. It takes a certain type of supervisor to play the roles of coach, feedback provider, trainer, role model, and protector in an accepting, esteem-building manner. Supervisors must be personally

• **TABLE 8-3**

SUBORDINATE NEEDS DURING THE ESTABLISHMENT PERIOD*

Task Needs	Personal Needs
Objectives	Coaching
Plans for accomplishing objectives	Performance feedback
Performance feedback	On-the-job training
	Role modeling
	Acceptance and confirmation
	Protection in high-risk situations

*Based on material presented in L. Baird and K. E. Kram, "Career Dynamics: Managing the Superior/Subordinate Relationship," *Organizational Dynamics* 11 (1983): 46–64.

secure and unthreatened by subordinates' training, ambition, and values. In effect, supervisors should be viewed as the career developers of their subordinates and should be trained and rewarded for fulfilling this role.

ENCOURAGEMENT OF MENTOR RELATIONSHIPS AND OTHER SUPPORTIVE ALLIANCES

Mentoring can be defined as relationships between junior and senior colleagues, or between peers, that provide a variety of developmental functions.[40] The establishment of a relationship with a mentor is thought to be one of the critical events of early adulthood, and finding a mentor or sponsor is seen as a major developmental task of the early career.[41]

The term *mentor* can be traced to Greek mythology in which Odysseus, absent from home because of the Trojan Wars, charged his servant Mentor with the task of educating and guiding his son Telemachus. In fulfilling this obligation, Mentor acted variously as teacher, coach, taskmaster, confidant, counselor, and friend.[42] In this historical sense, the mentor-protégé relationship was comprehensive (it involved educational, occupational, physical, and spiritual development) and was based on a high degree of mutual affection and trust. In a similar vein, mentors fulfill both career and psychosocial functions (Table 8.4).

A survey of executives revealed that about two-thirds of the respondents reported having had at least one mentoring relationship during their career.[43] Most of these relationships were established when the protégé was in his or her early career, and only half of the relationships involved the protégé's immediate supervisor. It was also found that executives who had experienced a mentor relationship were earning more money at an earlier age, were better educated, and were more likely to follow a career plan than those who had not established a relationship with a mentor. In fact, research has consistently indicated that mentoring is related to a variety of positive work outcomes, including higher degrees of career and organizational commitment, recognition, satisfaction, career mobility, and compensation.[44] In addition, research has found that the positive

TABLE 8-4

MENTORING FUNCTIONS[a]

Career Functions[b]	Psychosocial Functions[c]
Sponsorship	Role Modeling
Exposure and Visibility	Acceptance and Confirmation
Coaching	Counseling
Protection	Friendship
Challenging Assignments	

[a]Taken from K. E. Kram, "Phases of the Mentor Relationship," *Academy of Management Journal* 26 (1983): 614, Reprinted with permission.

[b]Career functions are those aspects of the relationship that primarily enhance career advancement.

[c]Psychosocial functions are those aspects of the relationship that primarily enhance sense of competence, clarity of identity, and effectiveness in the managerial role.

outcomes of having a mentor are independent of gender or level in the organization. Thus, mentoring is "egalitarian" in its positive effect on individuals' job/career outcomes.[45]

Most people would readily agree that employees striving to establish their career would benefit from coaching, support, exposure to senior executives, sponsorship, and identification with a successful role model. The question is whether they need one mentor to fulfill all of these roles. James G. Clawson said that in contemporary society, employees do not need a single individual for learning purposes, but rather "may have relationships with one individual who will take an interest in teaching technical skills, another person who will outline the political realities of an organization, another who will push senior management for promotion, another who is willing to discuss world affairs, and yet another who is willing to listen and give advice on personal matters."[46] None of these aides is a mentor in the traditional sense, yet all may play a significant role in an employee's early career.

Other researchers have also rejected the notion that all employees need or can find an intense role model relationship.[47] Instead, a "patron" system has been proposed that reflects a wide spectrum of advise/support relationships, ranging from the traditional mentor through sponsors (strong patrons but less powerful than mentors), guides (who can explain the organization and help point out obstacles), and peer pals (who can share information and serve as sounding boards).

In short, although mentoring functions can be vital to the establishment of a career, it is not clear that a single individual must play all these roles in the traditional sense. As recommended by David Thomas and Kathy Kram, "individuals should be encouraged to develop and nurture a constellation of relationships that reflects their career and psychosocial needs at successive career stages."[48] It has already been indicated that the first supervisor is a critical career developer of the new employee as a coach, trainer, and feedback provider. Others in the constellation could include subordinates and peers, who may also provide job-related feedback, career strategy information, and emotional support.[49]

New employees can therefore obtain valuable information and support from a variety of sources. Organizations can stimulate such diverse relationships by making it easier for newcomers to interact with these multiple benefactors. Discussion groups, seminars, and social gatherings are among the vehicles that can be used. Further, organizations can promote equal access to other types of career management and assessment mechanisms to achieve understanding and growth among newer staff members who may not have access to a mentor.[50] These mechanisms, which could serve either as a supplement to or as a substitute for a formal mentoring program, could include career counseling and coaching, 360-degree feedback, and other forms of assessment.

Much has been written on the perceived and actual difficulties of women and minorities in finding and maintaining a mentor during the early career years.[51] With the upper echelons of corporate America still dominated by white males, minority and women employees may be excluded from the mentor network for at least part of their careers. For many women and minority employees, locating an older executive who will coach them and look out for their interests can be a difficult task. Nonetheless, one study found that although women perceived greater barriers to finding a mentor than their male counterparts, they were just as likely to actually obtain a mentor.[52] Other recent research found no differences between men and women in perceived barriers to mentoring.[53] In addition, research has shown that executive and mid-level minority employees experience mentorship in the majority of cases.[54] One of the possible hindrances to the development of mentor relationships by women and minority employees is an overall lack of informal contact with potential mentors.[55] Indeed, either by design or by default, women and minorities are often times excluded from the informal, but no less important, gatherings and networks where lasting bonds and mentor-protege relationships can be formed.

For many organizations, the answer to these barriers is the formal assignment of mentors to promising young employees, regardless of their race or gender. In this sense, the organization forces mentor alliances that likely would not occur on their own. Formal mentoring programs have several benefits, including: improved access to mentors, legitimization of developmental activities, ongoing monitoring of the quality of career-enhancing relationships, and increasing competence and motivation among those who participate in the relationships.[56] However, the "engineering" of relationships goes against the spontaneous and mutual attraction that normally characterizes mentoring alliances, and formal programs can cause anxiety and discomfort among participants, can create pessimism about career prospects for those not chosen to participate, and can overemphasize a single supportive relationship when in reality a constellation of developmental alliances is more enriching.[57]

Women and minorities in mentor relationships also face the potential difficulties that may arise from cross-gender and cross-race alliances. For cross-gender mentoring, these pitfalls might include marital disruption, sexual attraction, and gossip, all of which can impair the effectiveness of the relationship.[58] Because of these issues of intimacy and sexual attraction, male-female relationships often involve tension and anxiety. In addition, because of difficulties in finding a comfortable degree of intimacy, cross-gender relationships are often superficial and their developmental potential is unfulfilled.[59] In the case of cross-race mentor relationships, the parties may find difficulty making positive identifications and developing a significant level of trust and openness.[60] Again, the discomfort caused by cross-race mentoring could damage the overall effectiveness of the relationship. Organizations should recognize the substantial influence they have in fostering an environment that encourages the development of supportive alliances for women and minorities. Through formal mentoring programs, training and education, and organizational development approaches, organizations can increase the level and improve the quality of developmental relationships for all employees, regardless of gender, race, or other background factors.[61]

INDIVIDUAL ACTIONS DURING ESTABLISHMENT

Although the organization can take certain actions to facilitate the employee's career establishment, it is, as always, the individual who has the ultimate responsibility to manage his or her career effectively. Following are some steps individuals can take.

CAREER EXPLORATION AND GOAL SETTING

During the establishment years, it is essential that new employees understand their developmental needs. Similarly, newcomers should understand that this period is a time of mutual testing. Both the individual and the organization are assessing the presence or absence of a match. Without a conscious awareness of these issues, it is unlikely that useful information will be acquired and appropriate decisions made. It is, therefore, crucial for new employees to use their assignments, performance reviews, day-to-day observations, and informal relationships to learn more about themselves and the organization. With this knowledge and information, individuals should be willing and able to adjust career goals as necessary. Career management is a dynamic process, and one's goals can change as new insights are gained and organizational realities become clear.

CAREER STRATEGIES — INFLUENCING THE ENVIRONMENT

Although the establishment period often requires the individual to adjust to the demands of the new environment, the newcomer is not a passive victim at the complete mercy of the organization. In fact, newcomers can play an active role in the ultimate success of the socialization process. Newcomers with a strong sense of self-competence can adopt active strategies and coping responses to understand the organization's culture and influence the environment.[62]

Because information and help do not always come when they are most needed, an assertive strategy is often required. Such a strategy might include the following activities:

- Initiate discussions with your supervisor on ways to increase the level of challenge, responsibility, and variety in your job.
- Initiate discussions with your supervisor regarding your recent performance. If the feedback is not sufficiently specific or critical, politely but firmly seek greater detail.
- Analyze your supervisor's career needs and discuss ways in which you can help your supervisor become more effective in his or her job.
- Seek information from peers who are in a position to observe your performance.
- Participate in formal programs to learn as much about the organization as possible.
- Read literature on the organization and seek answers to your questions.
- Develop informal contacts in the organization who can provide you with information, insights, and accumulated wisdom about the organization.
- Be prepared to share your perceptions and opinions with others. Mutual information sharing is more likely to sustain relationships than one-sided communications.
- Try to learn where the organization is heading and what skills it will require in the future.
- Reexamine the compatibility between your values, interests, and talents and the values, requirements, and opportunities in the organization.

One of the ways these strategies can be implemented is through employee networks. Networks are groups of employees organized (either formally or informally) to provide individual members with information about the company and offer them advice on career management activities. One company that has sponsored formal employee networks is Avon Products, Inc. A summary is provided below.[63]

Avon formally supports three different employee networks: the Avon Asian Network, the Avon Hispanic Network, and the Black Professional Association. Each network holds quarterly meetings with a focused agenda, has an operating budget, and a mission statement. Each network also has as a member a senior official of the Avon organization who attends the meetings, keeping the other participants apprised on the future direction of the company. As part of a dual role, the senior official also keeps his or her senior management colleagues informed on the network's reactions to company policies and any other concerns. With Avon's support, the networks also hold regular workshops that provide a forum for the sharing of information on a variety of topics, such as career development and advancement.

ACHIEVEMENT PERIOD

At some point during the early career, the concern with acceptance and "fitting in" subsides and striving for achievement and authority takes precedence. The shift from establishment to achievement is neither fixed in time nor abrupt, although it seems that a certain degree of security and acceptance may trigger achievement striving. It is also significant to recall that a large portion of the achievement period coincides with the "BOOM" period, when the need to accomplish achievement-oriented goals becomes particularly strong.[64]

The achievement period has been referred to as an "advancement" stage by several researchers presumably because the desire for vertical mobility (i.e., promotions) is so strong. The term *achievement* rather than *advancement* is used here because it is a broader concept that can encompass many different forms of accomplishment. Achievement can mean different things to different people.

For example, as we noted in Chapter 3, Schein's concept of the career anchor recognizes different forms of orientation toward work.[65] It is important to recognize that a career anchor does not imply limited career growth or change.[66] In a similar vein, as we noted in Chapter 1, Michael Driver and his colleagues identified four career concepts that characterize the structure of individual careers.[67] Each career concept is based on a set of underlying motives and styles. The achievement-oriented **linear** career emphasizes upward mobility through promotions and job changes. The **expert** career reflects an early, lifelong commitment to an occupational field or specialty (e.g., medicine), with little likelihood of change and little emphasis on vertical mobility. Instead, the individual focuses on continued development and refinement of knowledge within the chosen specialty. The **transitory** career is characterized by frequent changes from job to job with little apparent pattern of growth or development. The **spiral** career involves cyclical changes in occupational fields every 5 to 7 years, in which growth and variety are sought.

The research of Schein and Driver reinforces the importance of understanding variations in career aspirations and patterns. The meaning of achievement, accomplishment, and success rests on the individual's particular career orientation. Further, compatibility between career orientation and job setting produces higher levels of job satisfaction, career satisfaction, and organizational commitment and a lower intention to leave an organization.[68] Conversely, incompatibility can result in higher degrees of dissatisfaction and a corresponding desire to leave the particular work setting. Consider the following example.

As Arun has discovered, there is a fine line between being in a satisfying work environment and a dissatisfying one. For the past 4 years, Arun has worked in a department where the officer-in-charge encouraged his people to be independent-minded. The officer wanted his staff to be able to complete their assignments from start to finish based on their own knowledge and judgment, with the freedom to suggest and implement changes when they thought them necessary. Arun thrived in this kind of setting. He loved the independence and autonomy. It made him feel like a real contributor to the department's success. Unfortunately for Arun, a new officer took over the department 5 weeks ago. Since that time, Arun has seen a 180-degree turn in the way his work group is managed. New rules and procedures have been put in place that require daily monitoring of activities and accomplishments. On several occasions, Arun has had to justify his routine decisions and has even been criticized for not seeking approval from the different layers of management. Arun has found the meddling from above and the strict approval process to be disconcerting. If a turnaround does not happen soon, Arun is certain he will have to look for another job.

We propose a number of general issues that concern many employees during the achievement period:

1. To demonstrate continued, increasing competence in one's work assignments.
2. To acquire additional levels of responsibility and authority in work assignments.
3. To determine the most appropriate type of contribution one can make to oneself, the occupation, and the organization, such as whether to remain in a specialized function or to move into general management.
4. To assess opportunities inside and outside the organization.
5. To develop long- and short-range career goals consistent with one's career aspirations.
6. To develop and implement strategies to attain one's career goals.
7. To remain flexible and adaptive to changing circumstances.

ORGANIZATIONAL ACTIONS DURING ACHIEVEMENT

PROVIDE SUFFICIENT CHALLENGE AND RESPONSIBILITY

During the establishment period, early job challenge enables newcomers to test their abilities and begin to make a real contribution to the organization. In the achievement period, employees have a greater urgency to enlarge their area of responsibility, to become more autonomous and independent, and to "call the shots." Having spent a number of years learning and launching their career, employees are ready to acquire more responsibility.

Although additional responsibility can come through promotions and other forms of job mobility, the current job also can be used to this end. Jobs can be "enriched" to provide high levels of responsibility and autonomy and to permit the employee to keep learning, growing, and stretching. The organization, especially the immediate supervisor, must consider ways to provide additional challenge and responsibility and must know its employees well enough to judge how much challenge they can handle. Participative goal setting, schedule and budget control, additional discretion on how jobs get accomplished, and participation in special assignments are all ways to enhance the level of challenge and responsibility. In addition, job rotation, especially among early-career employees,

· TABLE 8-5

DEVELOPMENTAL COMPONENTS FROM STUDIES OF ON-THE-JOB LEARNING*

Development Task	Component
Job transitions	Line to staff
	Increases in job scope
	Radical job moves
	Changes in employers, status, or function
Creating change	Start-up operation
	Fix-it assignment
Assuming higher levels of responsibility	Organizational level
	Large-scale operations
Nonauthority relationship	Serving on task forces
	Making deals and coordinating among departments
Overcoming obstacles	Difficult boss
	Hardships
	Negative experiences
	Experience with crises and diversity

*Adapted from C. D. McCauley, M. N. Ruderman, D. J. Ohlott, and J. E. Morrow, "Assessing the Developmental Components of Managerial Jobs," *Journal of Applied Psychology* 79 (1994): 544–560.

has a positive influence on such career outcomes as promotability, salary progression, and overall job performance.[69]

Employees who aspire to higher-level management positions will need additional challenge and responsibility on their current job to groom themselves and test their capabilities for future positions. Moreover, added challenge and responsibility enable employees who wish to stay in their functional area or even on their current job to remain competent, motivated, and involved.

A study of Japanese management development practices found that carefully managed on-the-job assignments, especially early in the career, were key factors in allowing optimum individual development and growth.[70] For the Japanese companies, the key developmental tool is an individual plan that takes into account the assignments that managers should be capable of handling at various levels from first-year trainee to senior executive; the types of on-the-job assignments that are appropriate at each stage; and the mechanisms for assessing development and delivering the appropriate assignments. The Japanese approach represents a formal way to ensure that stage-appropriate job challenge is provided and that the progress of the individual is monitored.

Using the results from a number of studies on the developmental experiences of managers and executives, researchers from the Center for Creative Leadership identified 14 different components of managerial jobs that have important developmental consequences.[71] The 14 components of managerial jobs are shown in Table 8.5. The components are grouped according to whether they represent a job transition (a change in work role, job content, status, or location), the need to create change (e.g., starting an operation from scratch or engineering a turnaround), assuming higher levels of responsibility (moving to a job characterized by increased visibility and scope), exercising influence in nonauthority relationships (participating in projects or serving on a team in which negotiation skills and coordination are required), and overcoming obstacles (dealing with difficult situations or adverse business conditions).[72] All these "assignments" serve to increase the level of job challenge and stimulation afforded the individual employee.

PERFORMANCE APPRAISAL AND FEEDBACK

The need to appraise performance never really ceases. Organizations must make a number of decisions about individual employees during their early career, decisions about promotability, training and development needs, and salary increases. These decisions are important not only for the so-called fast track manager, but for other managers and nonmanagers as well. In addition, employees continue to need ongoing performance feedback, especially as it relates to their career goals.

CONSTRUCTION OF REALISTIC AND FLEXIBLE CAREER PATHS

In a traditional sense, a career path is a sequence of job positions, usually related in work content, through which employees move during the course of their careers. A standard career path for someone in marketing might involve the following positions: marketing representative, branch manager, a staff position at corporate headquarters, district marketing manager, regional marketing manager, and vice president of marketing. The identification of career paths can be helpful to organizations in planning their staffing needs, and it can provide a structure to employees in planning their personal careers. Nonetheless, it is important to recognize that this traditional, standard view of career paths has been altered radically over the past two decades. The combined effects of mergers, downsizings, new technology, job restructurings, and new organizational designs either have eliminated (or mangled) career paths in many organizations or have made it difficult to formulate individual career plans that are based on a consistent path of jobs. As we have noted previously, these changes in the work environment dictate that individuals be more proactive or "self-centered" in the ways they attempt to manage their movements along a career path that has the potential to shift (or be eliminated) at any given time.

The traditional approach to career path identification has been to examine the paths that employees have historically traveled in the organization. Like the marketing example just cited, these traditional paths tend to be oriented along functional or departmental lines and emphasize vertical mobility. Although historically derived career paths may be useful, they tend to be overly narrow and constraining and are based on what has happened, not what might or should happen.

Instead of relying on history and tradition, an alternative approach develops paths based on similarity in required job behaviors and knowledge and skill requirements. The development of such career paths involves thorough analysis of job content, grouping of similar jobs into "job families," and identification of logically possible paths of progression among these job families.

This form of career path development is realistic in that various paths are defined by actual job behavior requirements, rather than by job title or tradition. This method provides an individual with flexibility in career mobility because one can more easily move across functional lines. Initially limited career mobility opportunities can be greatly expanded when career paths are analyzed according to their behavioral, knowledge, and skill requirements.

STIMULATE CAREER EXPLORATION

Many organizations sponsor workshops, seminars, discussion groups, and counseling to aid the self-assessment process. Moreover, because much self-insight can be gained through ongoing job experiences, timely, constructive performance feedback and coaching sessions with a supervisor or other significant person are useful ingredients in any self-assessment effort.

Organizations also can help employees gather information on alternative job opportunities. Effective job exploration requires up-to-date job descriptions that provide accurate information on job duties and behaviors, knowledge and skill requirements, demands, and rewards. However, information on jobs or career paths will not be useful unless it gets to the people who need it. Ideally, line managers should be provided with sufficiently detailed information on jobs and career paths to aid their subordinates' career-planning efforts. Job-posting programs and career days are other vehicles for disseminating job-related information. An example of a job-posting program is provided below.

> The Johnson and Johnson organization headquartered in New Brunswick, New Jersey, uses a company-wide job-posting program called the Growth Opportunities (GO) Network. Under this system, all open nonexempt and exempt positions up to the level of director are listed in a weekly publication available to all the employees at the Johnson and Johnson world headquarters and at their many subsidiaries. The GO network publication lists a variety of information on the open positions, including: title, company and location, date the job was posted, whether relocation assistance is available, whether internal candidates will be considered, and whether an external candidate search is being conducted simultaneously with the posting. Individuals wishing to use the GO network must meet eligibility requirements, must submit the proper paperwork including an experience summary to the hiring company, and must keep their present management informed on the status of their bid.

Exploration designed to understand the organization—its goals and strategies, future human resource needs, mobility opportunities, reward systems, and the like—can be encouraged and aided in a number of ways. Although much of this type of learning takes place informally through mentor or sponsor relationships, organizations can provide information on their business and human resource plans. Organizations should provide realistic information on mobility patterns, a sort of realistic career preview, so that employees' expectations are in line with the reality of the organization's environment.[73]

INDIVIDUAL ACTIONS DURING ACHIEVEMENT

A great deal of advice has been offered to employees who aspire to high positions in organizations. Nevertheless, many of the prescriptions are applicable to employees with a variety of achievement-oriented aspirations. Common to all these guidelines is individual initiative and self-determination—an active approach to career management. Several potentially useful actions recommended in the literature are discussed below.

SET REALISTIC GOALS

Goal-setting procedures were examined extensively in Chapter 4. At this time, it is important to remember that if the employee does not establish goals, the goals will likely be established (or assumed) by the organization to fit its own needs. Therefore, it is in the employee's best interest to periodically reconsider established career goals (conceptual and operational), set new goals when necessary, and communicate these aspirations to the organization.

One issue discussed earlier is the decision whether to remain in a specialized function within the organization or prepare to seek a general management position. The decisions to contribute as a specialist versus a generalist should be based on many factors, not the least important of which is the availability of positions in the current organization and other organizations.

Perhaps most critical is sufficient self-insight to understand one's interests, motives, and talents. Individuals who hold certain career orientations, such as a technical/functional career anchor, may wish to make their contribution as a specialist. Individuals who hold other orientations, the managerial competence anchor, for example, may see more challenge and rewards in a general management position. The achievement period of the early career can be a critical time to examine these kinds of alternatives. An analysis of one's cumulative work experiences, discussions with one's supervisor, and participation in career-planning programs can help employees assess their dominant career orientation.

Another issue to consider is that traditional advancement prospects, at least in a hierarchical sense, are comparatively far more limited in the current business environment. Intense competition, mergers and acquisitions, and the need to stay "lean and mean" are combining with the sheer number of people born in the baby-boom generation to effectively restrict upward mobility opportunities. As Douglas Hall and Judith Richter have pointed out, "The number of ways to achieve promotional success is finite (and shrinking), we believe that the number of ways of achieving psychological success is infinite."[74] Recognizing this fact is key to setting realistic, achievable career goals. Indeed, as recommended by Hall and Richter, individuals should be less concerned with upward advancement and instead show more diversity in career paths. This diversity may involve planning and setting goals that include lateral moves, downward moves, and attaining higher degrees of specialization in a given function. The premise is that one's sense of accomplishment, satisfaction, and achievement can be gained in diverse ways, not always through promotional success. We discuss this concept further in Chapter 9 when we cover possible reactions to career plateauing and obsolescence.

PERFORMANCE AND RESPONSIBILITY ON THE CURRENT JOB

It is often observed that mobile managers have learned to become a crucial subordinate to a mobile boss. Being crucial means demonstrating technical competence, of course, but it also means developing skills that complement the boss' skills and make the boss look good.

This strategy requires that subordinates understand their superiors' skills, needs, and aspirations. It has been observed that boss' needs depend on their own career stage.[75] For example, a boss in the establishment period needs technical and psychological support from the subordinate, whereas one in the achievement period requires loyal followership that enhances the performance and reputation of the boss. Subordinates should understand their needs, their boss' needs, and the constraints under which the boss operates and establish a feedback and evaluation system for assessing the relationship between themselves and their bosses.

Individuals also must recognize that the types of job experiences and the length of tenure in high-responsibility jobs can play a critical role in determining career performance and progress. As discussed in Chapter 4, career strategies should take into account not only those assignments that are important for future advancement, but also recognize that there are certain jobs that can cause untoward disruptions in career progress and thus should be avoided if possible. Awareness of dead-end jobs and "derailment" type assignments is a critical factor in successfully managing one's career.[76] Derailment, or the movement off an established track of upward mobility, normally represents a mismatch between the demands of the job/work situation and one's personal skills. Individual and contextual factors that can lead to derailment include one or more of the following: problems with interpersonal relationships, a failure to meet business objectives, an inability to build and lead a team, and an inability to develop or adapt to a new work situation or demands.[77]

It is also important not to be trapped by narrow job descriptions. Employees can attempt to expand their jobs by volunteering to take on new assignments and responsibilities. Again, this demands an active stance on the individual's part. If further expansion is not possible and further learning is unlikely, it may be time to leave the position.

MOBILITY PATHS

Employees with upward mobility aspirations should be willing to nominate themselves for future positions. But not all job changes are equally useful. Highly mobile managers are "route bright" in that they understand the most promising paths (and the related career strategies) that will allow them to achieve their goals.[78] In addition, they apply the "protean" concept of career management in that the career strategies they pursue for upward mobility are kept flexible enough to accommodate the inevitable twists and turns that are faced throughout their work lives.

Research has identified two types of upward mobility tracks: the apparent fast-track, and the real fast-track.[79] The apparent fast-track includes rapid promotions and salary increases that may reflect an individual's "hard-charging" personality, but in reality, hinder the development of skills and relationships that will be needed over the longer term and at the higher levels. Apparent fast-track managers are strongly rewarded in the early career phases for their independence and assertiveness, "but are often puzzled and then angry when they find, a few years later, that their independence is regarded as an unwillingness to be a team player and their assertiveness is viewed as pushiness and self-glorification."[80] Later in their careers, the apparent fast-track can be derailed or plateaued because of an inability to cope with the interdependence and diversity that arise at later points in the career. By contrast, the real fast-track manager experiences slower upward mobility in the early career years, spending a comparatively longer time in building key competencies and establishing lasting relationships. Thus, although real fast-track employees may experience less frequent promotions and lower salary increases in the early career, the skills they learn position them to better avoid derailment in the later career.

Route-bright managers recognize that the path toward the top includes both lateral and vertical moves, as long as the lateral moves offer opportunity to achieve competence. A greater number of lateral moves and a slower promotional track are now commonplace.[81] Route-bright employees now accept that lateral transfers are an inevitable part of the upward movement process in today's business environment and that frequent lateral moves can have a positive influence on salary increases.[82] They also understand the mobility patterns in the organization, avoid dead-end paths, and understand that it is time to leave a job when additional learning is thwarted. Moreover, highly mobile managers are willing to change organizations and consistently strive for jobs with high visibility and exposure. Although some of these suggestions are more relevant to the aspiring general manager, all employees with mobility aspirations need to learn about the viability of different career paths. Research has found that line experience and job mobility were, in general, important predictors of career success for both male and female MBA graduates.[83] Individuals can "signal" their readiness and willingness for promotion to their superiors through their actions and various background factors. Specifically, research has found that one's past positions, functional background, and the number of different jobs held all served to alert decision makers on promotional readiness.[84] For example, the number of different positions held likely increases a candidate's visibility and/or increases one's breadth of knowledge about the company, both of which could "signal" potential for upward mobility.

Although pursuing appropriate career strategies is critical to attaining upward mobility, it is also important to recognize the role of individual personality in career mobility. Specifically, an individual's personality can influence the "impressions" that are made on superiors. For example, one study examined the role that "self-monitoring" plays in career advancement.[85] Self-monitoring theory distinguishes between "high self-monitors," who are keenly aware of social expectations and cues and can modify their behaviors accordingly, and "low self-monitors," who tend to be themselves despite social expectations and cues.[86] High self-monitors were found to be more mobile across a range of outcomes related to managerial careers, including their promotability. The adaptability of high self-monitors to varying social and political demands allowed them to more skillfully manage the impressions they made on their superiors, which in turn allowed higher degrees of upward mobility.[87]

ATTAINING SPONSORSHIP

Support and sponsorship from superiors and mentors are often crucial to goal attainment. Although high visibility and exposure are necessary to attain sponsorship, they are not sufficient. The sponsored manager should also be a high performer and be loyal and trustworthy to superiors. That is, the manager helps the supervisor look good, "rescues" the supervisor from potentially embarrassing outcomes, and is predictable. In short, such an employee is a crucial subordinate. Developmental relationships and support are especially critical during the achievement phase of one's career. As discussed earlier, individual development can be supported by a constellation of individuals, including mentors, superiors, peers, subordinates, and family and friends.[88]

Nonetheless, it is generally accepted that the sponsorship and coaching as provided by a mentor who is a more senior work associate can influence a variety of favorable outcomes including a more rapid promotion rate and higher total compensation.[89] As such, mentors should be sought as a means to facilitate further advancement and career success.[90]

WORD OF CAUTION

Many of the strategies discussed above have a "chess-like" quality in that they involve constant strategizing and frequent movement. Each move is made as a stepping stone to the next position. There is nothing wrong with this strategy as long as the jobs comprising this route to success are themselves satisfying and compatible with the person's needs and values. One must also determine whether career goals and strategies are consistent with the desired balance of work, family, and leisure activities. Extensive work involvement, intense competition, and frequent relocations may provide career success but at the expense of personal failure.[91] Excessive levels of organizational and career commitment can have adverse consequences for the individual, including stress and tension in social and family relationships and limited time for family and leisure activities.[92] The impact of work experiences on stress and quality of life is examined in Chapters 10 and 11.

THE EARLY CAREER: A QUESTION OF TIMING

We have seen how the early career is initiated by a period of establishment followed by a dominant concern with achievement and accomplishment. We also positioned the early career within early adulthood (ages 25 to 40). It is in the era of early adulthood that socialization to work, launching a career, and settling down to pursue one's dream normally take place.

However, one must recognize that the establishment-achievement syndrome can be triggered by a career transition any number of times during adulthood. Any job change requires resocialization to a somewhat unfamiliar task and interpersonal environment.[93] Such resocialization is probably prerequisite to subsequent achievement and innovation. Changing employers or career fields would undoubtedly require more intense forms of resocialization and reestablishment because the new environments would be even more unfamiliar.[94]

Moreover, establishment and achievement concerns can be reactivated during middle or late adulthood. Individuals in their 40s, 50s, and 60s who change jobs, employers, or occupations are faced with similar pressures to establish themselves in a new environment. One can only speculate whether the establishment and achievement pressures of these people are as severe, given their more extensive work and life experiences.

Recall our example of Sharon from Chapter 7. She had spent 23 years with one company, rising to the level of vice president for planning and development. At the age of 46, she was cut loose by her employer and eventually found a new job (albeit with lower prestige and responsibility) as business planning manager for a small automotive products retailer. In beginning this new position, Sharon had to endure the demands of socialization, establishment, and achievement as described earlier in this chapter, even though chronologically she was in midlife. She had new people to meet, new rules and procedures to follow, and a new culture to comprehend. She had to accept early job challenge and "hit the ground running" to prove her worth.

Thus, as this example indicates, the dominant themes of the early career, establishment and achievement, are not strictly limited to people in their 20s and 30s. It follows that the organizational and individual actions recommended in this chapter may also be applied to a wider group of people than those in their early career. Ultimately, it behooves individuals to understand their own developmental needs (whatever their age) and organizations to recognize the implications of these needs for the individual's career growth and the organization's effectiveness.

SUMMARY

The early career poses two major tasks for an employee, establishment and achievement. The initial task of the early career is to establish oneself in a career field, that is, to gain competence in the job, to learn the ropes in an organization, and ultimately, to gain acceptance as a valued contributor. An organization attempts to socialize new employees by providing job-related training, rewarding desirable behavior and punishing undesirable behavior, and communicating and reinforcing its dominant values and norms. The new employee who has undergone successful socialization is competent on the job, is integrated into the work group, achieves a satisfactory level of role clarity, learns to work within the system, and internalizes the key values and norms of the organization.

Organizations can help new employees establish their careers by developing effective recruitment and orientation practices, offering important early job challenge, providing constructive performance feedback, and helping employees develop supportive relationships with their supervisor and other important members of the organization. At the same time, individual employees can engage in career exploration to understand themselves and their new environment and can develop strategies to help them influence their work situation.

When a new employee becomes relatively secure and established in his or her career, the concern with fitting into the organization subsides, and the desire for increasing levels of achievement, authority, and responsibility takes over. During this period, the individual needs to maintain effective performance on the job, develop more insight into career orientation, set realistic career goals, understand the influence of different career paths on goal accomplishment, and attain sponsorship from key members of the organization. To help individuals with these tasks, organizations can encourage career exploration, provide challenge and responsibility on the job, construct realistic and flexible career paths, provide constructive performance appraisals, and help employees formulate career management plans.

ASSIGNMENT

If you are employed presently, take a few minutes and consider the programs your company offers to help employees become established during the early part of their careers. What programs, if any, are being used? How would you rate the effectiveness of these efforts in assisting employees with the tasks of establishment? If you are not employed currently, think back to one of your prior employers or interview a close associate or relative about the programs at his or her organization. Then answer the assignment questions as given above.

DISCUSSION QUESTIONS

1. Why do organizations attempt to break in employees when they first join? Describe the major socialization practices used by organizations and relate them to experiences you have had as a newcomer. Identify the signs of a successful and an unsuccessful socialization experience.

2. Describe the meaning and significance of the psychological contract. What are the differences between a relational and a transactional psychological contract? How is the psychological contract formed, revised, and approved during the early career? What are the advantages (and disadvantages) of making the psychological contract more explicit?

3. Reexamine the case of Bob, the 30-year-old MBA student. How effectively has he managed his early career? What, if anything, could he have done differently to shorten his period of floundering?

4. What are the advantages of providing a new employee with a challenging initial job assignment that provides considerable responsibility and autonomy? Why do many organizations have reservations about providing this type of assignment? What can organizations do to provide challenging, meaningful work to newcomers and, at the same time, address the reservations they hold?

5. Describe the significance of the mentor-protege relationship. What functions does the mentor provide and how can they contribute to the development and growth of the protege's early career? Do you agree with the proposition that mentoring functions can be provided by a number of individuals? Why or why not?

6. Look at the eight career anchors proposed by Schein that are shown in Chapter 3. How would you characterize yourself in terms of these career orientations? How can employees gain greater insight into their career orientation? How would such insight contribute to more effective career management?

7. What is a route-bright employee and how can an employee become one? Why is a balanced concern with conceptual and operational career goals and an appreciation of instrumental and expressive components of a goal as discussed in Chapter 4 so critical to the mobility-minded employee?

ENDNOTES

1. D. W. Bray, R. J. Campbell, and D. L. Grant, *Formative Years in Business: A Long-Term AT&T Study of Managerial Lives* (New York: Wiley, 1974); D. T. Hall and K. Nougaim, "An Examination of Maslow's Need Hierarchy in an Organizational Setting," *Organizational Behavior and Human Performance* 3 (1968): 12–35.

2. E. H. Schein, *Career Dynamics: Matching Individual and Organizational Needs* (Reading, MA: Addison-Wesley, 1978).

3. J. E. Dix and M. L. Savickas, "Establishing a Career: Developmental Tasks and Coping Responses," *Journal of Vocational Behavior* 47 (1995): 93–107.

4. M. M. Graddick, "Corporate Philosophies of Employee Development," in *Career Growth and Human Resource Strategies,* ed. M. London and E. M. Mone (New York: Quorum Books, 1988), 99–109.

5. M. R. Louis, "Surprise and Sense Making: What Newcomers Experience in Entering Unfamiliar Organizational Settings," *Administrative Science Quarterly* 25 (1980): 226–251; quote is on pp. 229–230.

6. N. J. Allen and J. P. Meyer, "Organizational Socialization Tactics: A Longitudinal Analysis of Links to Newcomers' Commitment and Role Orientation," *Academy of Management Journal* 33 (1990): 847–858; G. T. Chao, "The Socialization Process: Building Newcomer Commitment," in *Career Growth and Human Resource Strategies,* ed. M. London and E. M. Mone, 31–47; J. Zahrly

and H. Tosi, "The Differential Effect of Organizational Process on Early Work Role Adjustment," *Journal of Organizational Behavior* 10 (1989): 59–74.

7. E. H. Schein, "Organizational Culture," *American Psychologist* 2 (1990): 109–119; quote is on p. 111.

8. G. T. Chao, A. M. O'Leary-Kelly, S. Wolf, H. J. Klein, and P. D. Gardner, "Organizational Socialization: Its Content and Consequences," *Journal of Applied Psychology* 79 (1994): 730–743.

9. D. C. Feldman, "The Multiple Socialization of Organization Members," *Academy of Management Review* 6 (1981): 309–318; L. W. Porter, E. E. Lawler, and J. R. Hackman, *Behavior in Organizations* (New York: McGraw Hill, 1975); J. P. Wanous, *Recruitment, Selection, Orientation and Socialization of Newcomers* (Reading, MA: Addison-Wesley, 1992).

10. E. H. Schein, "How to Break in the College Graduate," *Harvard Business Review* 42 (1964): 68–76.

11. N. Munk, "The New Organization Man," *Fortune,* March 16, 1998, 63–74.

12. E. W. Morrison, "Newcomer Information Seeking: Exploring Types, Modes, Sources, and Outcomes," *Academy of Management Journal* 36 (1993): 557–589.

13. Allen and Meyer, "Organizational Socialization Tactics."

14. Schein, "How to Break in the College Graduate."

15. Schein, *Career Dynamics.*

16. Wanous, *Recruitment, Selection, Orientation and Socialization of Newcomers.*

17. D. C. Feldman, "A Contingency Theory of Socialization," *Administrative Science Quarterly* 21 (1976): 433–452; Feldman, "The Multiple Socialization of Organization Members"; Schein, "How to Break in the College Graduate"; Schein, *Career Dynamics*; Wanous, *Recruitment, Selection, Orientation and Socialization of Newcomers.*

18. Schein, *Career Dynamics.*

19. Allen and Meyer, "Organizational Socialization Tactics"; G. R. Jones, "Socialization Tactics, Self-Efficacy, and Newcomers' Adjustments to Organizations," *Academy of Management Journal* 29 (1986): 262–279.

20. Schein, *Career Dynamics.*

21. S. L. Robinson, M. S. Kraatz, and D. M. Rousseau, "Changing Obligations and the Psychological Contract: A Longitudinal Study," *Academy of Management Journal* 37 (1994): 137–152.

22. I. R. MacNeill, "Relational Contracts: What We Do and Do Not Know," *Wisconsin Law Review,* Vol. 3 (1985): 483–525.

23. Robinson et al., "Changing Obligations and the Psychological Contract"; D. M. Rousseau and K. A. Wade-Benzoni, "Changing Individual-Organization Attachments: A Two-Way Street," in *The Changing Nature of Work,* ed. A. Howard (San Francisco, CA: Jossey-Bass, 1995), pp. 290–322.

24. N. Nicholson, "Career Systems in Crisis: Change and Opportunity in the Information Age," *Academy of Management Executive* 10 (1996): 40–51.

25. M. B. Arthur, "The Boundaryless Career: A New Perspective for Organizational Inquiry," *Journal of Organizational Behavior* 15 (1994): 295–306.

26. Schein, *Career Dynamics.*

27. E. H. Lindsey, V. Homes, and M. W. McCall, *Key Events in Executives' Lives* (Greensboro, NC: Center for Creative Leadership, 1987); M. W. McCall, "Developing Executives through Work

Experiences," *Human Resource Planning* 11 (1988): 1–11; M. W. McCall, M. M. Lombardo, and A. M. Morrison, *The Lessons of Experience: How Successful Executives Develop on the Job* (Lexington, MA: Lexington Books, 1988); C. D. McCauley, M. N. Ruderman, P. J. Ohlott, and J. E. Morrow, "Assessing the Developmental Components of Managerial Jobs," *Journal of Applied Psychology* 79 (1994): 544–560.

28. McCall et al., *The Lessons of Experience.*

29. R. E. Smith, "Employee Orientation: 10 Steps to Success," *Personnel Journal* 63 (1984): 46–48.

30. M. R. Louis, "Surprise and Sense Making: What Newcomers Experience in Entering Unfamiliar Organizational Settings," *Administrative Science Quarterly* 25 (1980): 226–251.

31. D. E. Berlew and D. T. Hall, "The Socialization of Managers: Effects of Expectations on Performance," *Administrative Science Quarterly* 11 (1966): 207–223.

32. S. Rabinowitz and D. T. Hall, "Changing Correlates of Job Involvement in Three Career Stages," *Journal of Vocational Behavior* 18 (1981): 138–144.

33. B. Dumaine, "Those Highflying PepsiCo Managers," *Fortune,* April 10, 1989, 78–86; T. J. Murray, "PepsiCo's Fast Track," *Business Month* June (1987): 50–52.

34. D. T. Hall, *Careers in Organizations* (Glenview, IL: Scott Foresman, 1976).

35. Schein, "How to Break in the College Graduate."

36. S. L. Berry, "Apprenticeships: A Medieval Idea Wins a 20th Century Edge," *Management Review* August (1991): 41–44.

37. R. R. Mai-Dalton and J. J. Sullivan, "The Effects of Manager's Sex on the Assignment to a Challenging or Dull Task and Reasons for the Choice," *Academy of Management Journal* 24 (1981): 603–612; M. S. Taylor and D. R. Ilgen, "Sex Discrimination against Women in Initial Placement Decisions: A Laboratory Investigation," *Academy of Management Journal* 24 (1981): 859–865.

38. Porter et al., *Behavior in Organizations.*

39. Hall, *Careers in Organizations.*

40. K. E. Kram, *Mentoring at Work: Developmental Relationships in Organizational Life* (Lanham, MD: University Press of America, 1988).

41. Schein, *Career Dynamics.*

42. J. G. Clawson, "Mentoring in Managerial Careers," in *Work, Family, and the Career,* ed. C. B. Derr (New York: Praeger, 1980), 144–165.

43. G. R. Roche, "Much Ado about Mentors," *Harvard Business Review* 57 (1979): 14–28.

44. S. G. Baugh, M. J. Lankau, and T. A. Scandura, "An Investigation of the Effects of Protege Gender on Responses to Mentoring," *Journal of Vocational Behavior* 49 (1996): 309–323; S. M. Colarelli and R. C. Bishop, "Career Commitment: Functions, Correlates, and Management," *Group & Organization Studies* 15 (1990): 158–176; E. A. Fagenson, "The Mentor Advantage: Perceived Career/Job Experiences of Proteges Versus Non-Proteges," *Journal of Organizational Behavior* 10 (1989): 309–320; T. A. Scandura, "Mentorship and Career Mobility: An Empirical Investigation," *Journal of Organizational Behavior* 13 (1992): 169–174; D. B. Turban and T. W. Dougherty, "Role of Protege Personality in Receipt of Mentoring and Career Success," *Academy of Management Journal* 37 (1994): 688–702; W. Whitely, T. W. Dougherty, and G. F. Dreher, "Relationship of Career Mentoring and Socioeconomic Origin to Managers' and Professionals' Early Career Progress," *Academy of Management Journal* 34 (1991): 331–351.

45. Fagenson, "The Mentor Advantage."

46. Clawson, "Mentoring in Managerial Careers"; quote is on p. 147.

47. E. C. Shapiro, F. B. Haseltine, and M. P. Rowe, "Moving Up: Role Models, Mentors, and the 'Patron System,'" *Sloan Management Review* 19 (1978): 51–58.

48. D. A. Thomas and K. E. Kram, "Promoting Career-Enhancing Relationships in Organizations: The Role of the Human Resource Professional," in *Career Growth and Human Resource Strategies,* ed. M. London and E. M. Mone, 49–66; quote is on p. 65.

49. K. E. Kram and L. A. Isabella, "Mentoring Alternatives: The Role of Peer Relationships in Career Development," *Academy of Management Journal* 28 (1985): 110–132.

50. G. F. Dreher and T. W. Dougherty, "Substitutes for Career Mentoring: Promoting Equal Opportunity through Career Management and Assessment Systems," *Journal of Vocational Behavior* 51 (1997): 110–124.

51. S. Feinstein, "Women and Minority Workers in Business Find a Mentor Can Be a Rare Commodity," *The Wall Street Journal,* November 10, 1987; Kram, *Mentoring at Work;* B. R. Ragins and J. L. Cotton, "Easier Said than Done: Gender Differences in Perceived Barriers to Gaining a Mentor," *Academy of Management Journal* 34 (1991): 939–951; D. A. Thomas and C. P. Alderfer, "The Influence of Race on Career Dynamics: Theory and Research on Minority Career Experiences," in *Handbook of Career Theory,* ed. M. B. Arthur, D. T. Hall, and B. S. Lawrence (Cambridge, UK: Cambridge University Press, 1989), 133–158; Thomas and Kram, "Promoting Career-Enhancing Relationships in Organizations."

52. Ragins and Cotton, "Easier Said than Done."

53. T. D. Allen, M. L. Poteet, J. E. Russell, and G. H. Dobbins, "A Field Study of Factors Related to Supervisors' Willingness to Mentor Others," *Journal of Vocational Behavior* 50 (1997): 1–22.

54. Thomas and Alderfer, "The Influence of Race on Career Dynamics."

55. Feinstein, "Women and Minority Workers in Business Find a Mentor Can Be a Rare Commodity."

56. Thomas and Kram, "Promoting Career-Enhancing Relationships in Organizations."

57. Ibid.

58. J. G. Clawson and K. E. Kram, "Managing Cross-Gender Mentoring," *Business Horizons* 27 (1984): 22–32.

59. D. T. Hall, "Careers and Socialization," *Journal of Management* 13 (1987): 301–321; G. J. Craig, *Human Development* (Englewood Cliffs, NJ: Prentice-Hall, 1976).

60. E. A. Ensher and S. E. Murphy, "Effects of Race, Gender, Perceived Similarity, and Contact on Mentor Relationships," *Journal of Vocational Behavior* 50 (1997): 460–481; Thomas and Kram, "Promoting Career-Enhancing Relationships in Organizations."

61. Ibid.

62. Dix and Savickas, "Establishing a Career"; G. R. Jones, "Psychological Orientation and the Process of Organizational Socialization," *Academy of Management Review* 8 (1983): 464–474.

63. C. M. Solomon, "Networks Empower Employees," *Personnel Journal* (October 1991): 51–54.

64. D. J. Levinson, C. N. Darrow, E. B. Klein, M. H. Levinson, and B. McKee, *Seasons of a Man's Life* (New York: Knopf, 1978).

65. E. H. Schein, *Career Anchors: Discovering Your Real Values* (San Diego, CA: University Associates, 1985).

66. D. C. Feldman, *Managing Careers in Organizations* (Glenview, IL: Scott Foresman, 1988).

67. K. R. Brousseau, M. J. Driver, K. Eneroth, and R. Larsson, "Career Pandemonium: Realigning Organizations and Individuals," *Academy of Management Executive* 4 (1996): 52–66; M. J. Driver, "Career Concepts and Organizational Change," in *Work, Family, and the Career,* ed. C. B.

Derr (New York: Praeger, 1980), 5–17; M. J. Driver, "Career Concepts: A New Approach to Career Research," in *Career Issues in Human Resource Management*, ed. R. Katz (Englewood Cliffs, NJ: Prentice-Hall, 1982).

68. M. Igbaria, J. H. Greenhaus, and S. Parasuraman, "Career Orientations of MIS Employees: An Empirical Analysis," *MIS Quarterly* June (1991): 151–169.

69. M. A. Campion, L. Cheraskin, and M. J. Stevens, "Career-Related Antecedents and Outcomes of Job Rotation," *Academy of Management Journal* 37 (1994): 1518–1542.

70. M. Wakabayaski, G. Graen, and M. Graen, "Japanese Management Progress: Mobility into Middle Management," *Journal of Applied Psychology* 73 (1988): 217–227.

71. C. D. McCauley, M. N. Ruderman, P. J. Ohlott, and J. E. Morrow, "Assessing the Developmental Components of Managerial Jobs," *Journal of Applied Psychology* 79 (1994): 544–560.

72. Ibid.

73. Y. Vardi, "Organizational Career Mobility: An Integrative Model," *Academy of Management Review* 5 (1980): 341–355.

74. D. T. Hall and J. Richter, "Career Gridlock: Baby Boomers Hit the Wall," *Academy of Management Executive* 4 (1990): 7–22; quote is on p. 7.

75. L. Baird and K. E. Kram, "Career Dynamics: Managing the Superior/Subordinate Relationship," *Organizational Dynamics* 11 (1983): 46–64.

76. B. E. Kovach, "The Derailment of Fast-Track Managers," *Organizational Dynamics* 15 (1986): 41–48.

77. E. Van Velsor and J. B. Leslie, "Why Executives Derail: Perspectives across Time and Cultures," *Academy of Management Executive* 9 (1995): 62–72.

78. E. E. Jennings, *Routes to the Executive Suite* (New York: Macmillan, 1971).

79. Kovach, "The Derailment of Fast-Track Managers."

80. Ibid.; quote is on p. 45.

81. D. Kirkpatrick, "Is Your Career on Track," *Fortune*, July 2, 1990, 38–48.

82. A. J. Murrell, I. H. Frieze, and J. E. Olson, "Mobility Strategies and Career Outcomes: A Longitudinal Study of MBAs," *Journal of Vocational Behavior* 49 (1996): 324–335.

83. T. H. Cox and C. V. Harquail, "Career Paths and Career Success in the Early Career Stages of Male and Female MBAs," *Journal of Vocational Behavior* 39 (1991): 54–75.

84. J. B. Forbes, "Early Intraorganizational Mobility: Patterns and Influences," *Academy of Management Journal* 30 (1987): 110–125.

85. M. Kilduff and D. V. Day, "Do Chameleons Get Ahead: The Effect of Self-Monitoring on Managerial Careers," *Academy of Management Journal* 37 (1994): 1047–1060.

86. Ibid.

87. Ibid.

88. Kram, *Mentoring at Work.*

89. Whitely et al., "Relationship of Career Mentoring and Socioeconomic Origin to Managers' and Professionals' Early Career Progress."

90. Turban and Dougherty, "Role of Protege Personality in Receipt of Mentoring and Career Success."

91. A. K. Korman, "Career Success and Personal Failure: Mid- to Late-Career Feelings and Events," in *Career Growth and Human Resource Strategies*, ed. M. London and E. M. Mone, 81–94.

92. D. M. Randall, "Commitment and the Organization: The Organization Man Revisited," *Academy of Management Review* 12 (1987): 460–471.

93. R. Katz, "Managing Careers: The Influence of Job and Group Longevities," in *Career Issues in Human Resource Management,* ed. R. Katz (Englewood Cliffs, NJ: Prentice-Hall, 1982), 154–181.

94. M. R. Louis, "Career Transitions: Varieties and Commonalities," *Academy of Management Review* 5 (1980): 329–340.

9

MIDDLE AND LATE CAREER ISSUES

As was discussed in Chapter 5, the midcareer years roughly span a 15-year period between the ages of 40 and 55. It is fortunate that a good deal has been learned about midcareer issues in recent years. The graying of America is no myth. According to information from the U.S. Census Bureau, the median age of the U.S. population has increased dramatically from about 24 years in 1910 to 36 years at the close of the 20th century. It is further estimated that nearly half of the U.S. work force in the year 2000 will be middle aged, as the 80 million people born in the post–World War II baby boom grow older. The implication is clear. Individuals and organizations must become more attuned to the needs and experiences of midcareer employees.

Also to be considered is the dramatic increase in the number of older adults in American society. The percentage of the U.S. population 55 years or older has more than doubled, from 10 percent of the population in 1910 to a projected 21 percent of the population in the year 2000. It is unclear how many of these people will choose to remain in the work force. Recent trends have pointed to a greater incidence of early retirement. In 1950, more than 40 percent of the nation's men and women older than the age of 65 were still working. Nearly 50 years later, that figure stands at 12 percent. However, it is possible that these trends may reverse themselves as demands for skilled labor prevent organizations from offering early retirement options, and as financial pressures coupled with longer life expectancies force people to delay retirement. In any event, older employees will have to make a number of significant decisions about the timing of retirement and the ways in which they would like to live their pre-retirement and retirement years.

In this chapter, we examine the middle and late stages of career development. We consider the tasks and challenges posed by each of these two career stages, examine some typical concerns experienced by employees in these stages, and offer career management guidelines to organizations and individuals.

MIDDLE CAREER YEARS

The midcareer years pose two major career/life tasks. *Confronting the midlife transition* involves reappraising one's accomplishments relative to ambitions and dreams and reexamining the importance of work in one's life.[1] Moreover, many midcareer employees may have to learn to cope with the stresses produced by the midlife transition. *Remaining productive* during midcareer may require employees to update and integrate their skills, exercise sufficient autonomy to express these skills, and develop new skills such as mentoring younger colleagues.

CONFRONTING THE MIDLIFE TRANSITION

Chapter 5 described how the midlife transition can be triggered by a number of experiences: fear of lost youth and missed opportunities, awareness of aging and mortality, failure to accomplish significant dreams, the inability to achieve an acceptable balance between work and family commitments, and the need to shed youthful illusions that propelled the earlier portion of one's career and life. In essence, the individual at midlife is increasingly forced to recognize that he or she has stopped growing up and has begun growing old.[2]

The midcareer employee may also experience rivalries with more energetic, ambitious, and highly educated younger colleagues and may feel defensive and guilty about these hostile feelings. Technical or managerial obsolescence, common among midcareer employees, can add to these frustrations. The recognition that one may not advance further in the organization—that one has reached a career plateau—can undoubtedly intensify feelings of failure and cast a gloom over one's future career. In addition, many highly successful and mobile employees experience feelings of personal failure at midlife, reflecting the guilt and regret over having sacrificed family relationships and other affiliations in the ambitious pursuit of career success.[3] It is no surprise, then, that many midcareer employees become restless. Although some people may make drastic occupational changes or pursue alternate life-styles, many more are psychologically conflicted. Some may exhibit a burst of ambition to fulfill long-standing goals, whereas others may reduce their involvement in work and turn their attention and energies toward their families and themselves.[4]

We have painted a somewhat negative picture of the midlife transition. Indeed, as we noted in Chapter 5, Daniel Levinson and his colleagues concluded that 80 percent of the men and 85 percent of the women in their research experienced a crisis during this period.[5] However, other researchers have questioned whether the midlife crisis is universally experienced, arguing that feelings of frustration, mortality, and stress may occur at different times for different people, depending on their particular pattern of life experiences and the culture and point in history in which they live. Thus, midlife is not universally seen as a period of trauma, crisis, and change.[6]

What can be concluded about the midlife transition? First, the notion that people need to reappraise their lives as they enter middle adulthood is compelling. Early adulthood and all that it entails—youth, feelings of immortality, dreams, and hopes—can never be relived. Coming to grips with that fact and making adjustments for the next era of life seem essential. Whether these issues arise between the ages of 40 and 45, as Daniel Levinson and his colleagues proposed,[7] or whether they can appear at different times for different people is unclear, but it seems reasonable that these issues should surface in the "early" part of middle adulthood.

Second, it is unclear whether the feelings that accompany midlife appraisal are so intense as to constitute a crisis. Perhaps it is sufficient to state that the entrance into middle adulthood raises certain issues that may produce crisis reactions in some people, although they may not be able to recognize the reasons behind their feelings until later. Moreover, these issues need to be acknowledged and confronted whether they reach crisis proportions or not. Although individuals may not truly experience a crisis during their 40s, their reappraisal of accomplishments and life goals enables them to find constructive ways to remain productive and fulfilled during their midcareer years. Ways in which individuals and organizations can address the midlife transition are examined later in the chapter.

REMAINING PRODUCTIVE: GROWTH, MAINTENANCE, OR STAGNATION?

The second major task of midcareer is to remain productive. For many, the middle career years are characterized by maintenance of the status quo, when individuals experience little compulsion to start in new directions. Nonetheless, some people do continue to grow and develop during midcareer, whereas others enter a period of maintenance or begin to stagnate and decline. Two midcareer experiences, plateauing and obsolescence, can affect midcareer productivity and trigger feelings of stress.

CAREER PLATEAU

Virtually everyone plateaus at one time or another. A plateau is "the point in a career where the likelihood of additional hierarchical promotion is very low."[8] Although plateauing can occur at any stage of a career, it is particularly relevant to employees older than 40. For that reason, the career plateau is considered a central issue in midcareer.

Why is plateauing such a universal experience?

1. At the most basic level, the pyramidal structure of most organizations provides fewer and fewer positions at higher levels of the hierarchy. The higher one rises in the organizational structure, the smaller the number of positions that are available for further advancement.

2. There is increasing competition for these few positions because of the glut of baby boomers reaching lower or middle levels of management, the

greater numbers of women and minorities entering management positions in recent years, and the downsizing of the corporate structures that has taken place over the past several years.

3. This problem is exacerbated in organizations that are growing slowly, not growing at all, or contracting their operations and work force. Furthermore, a company's business strategy can affect the number and type of growth opportunities and hence the incidence of plateauing in certain career paths.

4. The virtual elimination of mandatory retirement can clog career paths and prevent younger employees from progressing in the hierarchy.

5. Changes in technology may close certain career paths or open new paths for which employees are not prepared.

6. Particular employees may be more likely to plateau because they are thought to be too valuable in their present position, lack technical or managerial skills to advance farther, or lack career management skills required to develop a mobility-oriented strategy.

7. As was stated in Chapter 8, a variety of factors can cause executives and others to become "derailed" off the fast track and end up plateaued. These factors include problems with interpersonal relationships, a failure to meet business objectives, a failure to build and lead a team, and an inability to change or adapt during a transition.[9]

8. Reflecting the desire for a more balanced life-style, an increasing number of employees make the organization aware that they do not wish to be considered for further advancement because of the potential conflicts with family or leisure commitments.

In summary, these issues point to three reasons why one may be career plateaued. An employee may be plateaued for external reasons, or for reasons outside the employee's control. Points 1 through 5 noted above identify organizational constraints which may cause an employee to become plateaued. Points 6 through 7 speak to management's negative assessment of the individual, and hence for this reason the employee becomes plateaued. Finally, there may be internal reasons, as mentioned in point 8, why an individual might choose to become plateaued.[10]

What are the consequences of plateauing? There is evidence that many plateaued men feel like failures because they equate career success with masculinity.[11] For some men, the sense of failure is tinged with guilt over the little time they have spent with their families during their pursuit of career success. Some women may feel betrayed if they have foregone marriage and family to concentrate on a career that now seems to be going nowhere.

For an organization, the consequences of plateauing can represent a difficult management challenge. In a study based on the questionnaire responses of 600 human resource managers, Benson Rosen and Thomas Jerdee found five organizational consequences of plateauing.[12] The five, in order of prevalence, are clogged promotion channels, lower morale among co-workers and subordinates, lower overall productivity of the department or unit, hurt relationships with customers or clients, and increased absenteeism.

The overall implication is that plateaued employees may become angry, frustrated, bored, stagnant, and less involved and motivated in their work. Ultimately, they may exhibit deteriorated performance and cause a decline in the performance of their department and/or organization. After all, one of the most powerful incentives that has motivated performance to this point, the promise of further advancement, is no longer a feasible reward for effective performance. In recent studies, it was found that individuals who perceived themselves as career plateaued exhibited lower levels of job satisfaction, company identification, and career planning activities compared with nonplateaued individuals.[13]

Are such factors as resentment, apathy, lower job satisfaction, and poor performance inevitably linked to career plateauing? In an extensive study of AT&T managers, researchers concluded that the absence of further promotional opportunities is not necessarily seen as a personal tragedy.[14] It was observed that many managers might not strongly desire further advancement because of possible geographic relocation and potential pressure and politics. Researchers have also concluded that the career plateau can be functional for individuals, both in a professional and a personal sense.[15] Indeed, a leveling-off period (as represented by a career plateau) can have a positive influence on individual development and personal growth. Because a career plateau can represent a time of relative stability, the individual can master new work skills, pursue a more predictable family/personal life, and can replenish psychic energy. Research has found that while plateaued individuals may show significantly reduced identification with, and commitment to, their organizations, it is often replaced with a more humanistic identification with co-workers and customers.[16]

Consistent with these conclusions on the potentially positive aspects of career plateaus, researchers have observed that most managers adapt to their career plateau without too much trouble.[17] Such adaptations might involve developing off-the-job interests or emphasizing the negative aspects of a promotion. Whether due to a real change of values or simply a rationalization of their current situation, the job performance of these adaptable employees may not suffer greatly. Consider the following example:

> Jan emerged from her annual performance review feeling numb. For the third year in a row, she had received only a "good" rating—another indication that her promotion prospects were close to nil. It was not always like this for Jan. Earlier in her career she received "excellent" or "outstanding" evaluations, and she was promoted every 2 or 3 years. She was not necessarily on the fast track, but she continued to advance at a steady pace.
>
> In the course of her 25-year career, Jan could point to many accomplishments, both in her work and in her personal life. She had overseen the installation of a new automated system, had taken over an operation with poor performance and turned it around, and had made cost-saving recommendations to senior management that resulted in significantly reduced expenses. Moreover, Jan had obtained her MBA going part-time, had gotten married, raised two children, and gone through a divorce.
>
> All in all, she was pleased with her professional and personal development. But with her latest evaluation, Jan is uncertain what to do next. She realizes she will not be receiving more promotions, and she is feeling the heat from younger staff members

MODEL OF MANAGERIAL CAREERS

Current Performance	Likelihood of Future Promotion		
	Low		**High**
High	Solid Citizens (Effective Plateauees)		Stars
	Organizationally Plateaued	Personally Plateaued	
Low	Deadwood (Ineffective Plateauees)		Learners (Comers)

SOURCE: T. P. Ference, J. A. F. Stoner, and E. K. Warren, "Managing the Career Plateau," *Academy of Management Review* 2 (1977): 603. Reprinted with permission.

and colleagues who are eager to move up the ladder. Being on a career plateau has been a stressful experience for Jan. She could look for another job, but she has no idea of her prospects. Besides, she has asked herself why she would want to trade her current job, with good pay and benefits, for another job in which she would be an unknown commodity and would have to prove herself all over again.

After a period of time, Jan began to accept her plateaued state. She realized that not having to compete for higher-level positions had benefits. She now had more time for her children and was able to pursue other outside interests. She even had time to begin using the company's exercise facilities. At work, Jan refused to let her situation have a negative effect on her performance. She decided to do the best job she possibly could. Also, Jan looked for ways to expand her knowledge of personal computers and related applications, thinking this would increase her value to the firm. Eventually, Jan spoke with her boss about the prospects for a lateral move to another department in the company. She stressed that she wanted to go into an area in which she could gain new experiences. Jan's boss welcomed the idea and said she would see what she could do, but she also encouraged Jan to keep her eye on the posting board for opportunities.

Four months after their meeting, Jan posted out of the department—she is looking forward to putting her newly acquired personal computer skills to good use.

Unlike Jan, some plateaued employees are more prone to deteriorated attitudes and performance. A model that addresses this issue is shown in Table 9.1. Employees are classified along two dimensions: likelihood of future promotions and performance on the current job. Note that there are two kinds of plateaued employees: the "solid citizens," who are still performing effectively in their current job, and the "deadwood," whose job performance is substandard. Although the solid citizens perform the bulk of the organization's work, managerial attention and concern are frequently directed toward encouraging and rewarding the fast-track stars and punishing, shelving, or firing the deadwood. One major challenge for management, therefore, is to prevent solid citizens from becoming deadwood. Management actions relevant to this challenge are considered later in this chapter.

Obsolescence

Like plateauing, obsolescence is not a uniquely midcareer issue, but it may be more pronounced and more devastating in midcareer than in earlier years.[18] Obsolescence has been defined as "the degree to which organizational professionals lack the up-to-date knowledge or skills necessary to maintain effective performance in either their current or future work roles."[19]

Obsolescence has its root in change. Research has identified two types of change that can lead to obsolescence: job changes and personal changes.[20] Job changes can include alterations in technology (especially the information explosion), occupational requirements, and managerial methods, all of which produce demands on technical professionals and managers to keep up to date. Those who cannot incorporate new developments in their fields into their work processes are highly susceptible to obsolescence. However, personal changes that result from the midlife transition and other experiences could cause a reduced level of achievement orientation and a lower level of interest in work, which in turn, may adversely influence the desire to stay current in the job.

Although change is the underlying source of obsolescence, not all employees become obsolescent, at least not at the same rate. The organization's work environment and personal factors determine the impact of change on the development of obsolescence.[21] For example, the length of time that has elapsed since the completion of one's professional education can influence the rate of obsolescence. The concept of a "half-life" refers to the time it takes professionals to become half as technically up-to-date as they were when they completed their education. In today's environment, with rapid advances in research and technology, obsolescence of one's professional and technical training can occur more quickly.

This observation does not imply that all professionals are at their peak of competence at the completion of their formal education or that the passage of time inevitably erodes their effectiveness. Many managers and professionals integrate prior classroom learning with work experience, thereby widening their breadth of knowledge and increasing their effectiveness over time. However, it seems safe to say that "half-lives" will be short—and the potential for rapid obsolescence great—in fields that are changing rapidly and in which such changes find their way slowly into professional curricula.

Other personal factors affect a manager/professional's susceptibility to obsolescence. Some employees are more able than others to acquire the new knowledge required to keep up to date. Also, some are more highly motivated to keep current because of their needs, career goals, energy levels, or personal adaptability to change. Indeed, research has found that keeping current with new developments is a significant career concern of adults in midlife.[22]

The organization's work environment also plays a critical role in averting obsolescence. Obsolescence is less likely to manifest itself when jobs are challenging, when job reassignments are made periodically to maintain stimulation and avoid overspecialization, when people are given sufficient responsibility and authority on their job, when colleagues interact freely, and when organizations reward employees for keeping up to date by providing challenging work, promotions, and salary increases.[23] In fact, opportunities for continued learning and development on the job are probably the greatest deterrent to obsolescence. Suggestions for combating obsolescence are examined in more detail in a later section of this chapter.

MIDCAREER CHANGE

The popular press, TV shows, and movies would have people believe that middle-age restlessness almost inevitably leads to major career changes. Vivid examples of urban business executives who open general stores in a rural community, engineers who become artists, or accountants who leave their firms to pursue excitement and glamour elsewhere merely reinforce this view. Although many people in midcareer do shift career direction, career change is neither an inevitable product of the midlife transition nor is it limited to the midcareer years.

Career change has been viewed as movement into a different occupation that is not part of a typical career path.[24] It is obvious that more and more people are willing to consider different career fields during their lives. Moreover, although some career changes involve minimal movement in job demands and life-style, others represent major transitions. Douglas Hall states that career change is triggered when one's career "routine" is broken or busted.[25] A career routine is a cycle of common, ongoing behavior that develops through earlier experiences of psychological success.

What are the compelling reasons for people to make career changes? Although the number of reasons may seem endless, they can be grouped into general categories. First, there are several individual factors that can influence a career change. A personal dissatisfaction with one's current occupation or life-style can be a powerful stimulant to change. One source of this dissatisfaction is a lack of fit between current opportunities and significant needs, desires, or goals.[26] This dissatisfaction can increase as the gap between expectations and reality widens.[27] Also, dissatisfaction with one's life in general can have a significant influence on job satisfaction and the desire for career change.[28] Another individual factor is an underlying need for greater achievement and contribution beyond what the individual has done up to the point of the change. Other individual factors can include one's age, health, interests, values, and/or alterations in family relationships.

There are also a number of environmental factors that can induce career changes. Certainly the loss of one's job, or even the threat of loss, can be a direct reason to change one's path, but there are many others. These additional environmental factors might include a technological change, economic forces, corporate restructuring/downsizing, changes in the reward system, increased job demands, and other issues.

In addition to these individual and environmental factors, there must also be an *attractive alternative* to one's current situation for a career change to take place. The alternative is thought to provide a better fit with one's needs, values, or abilities than the current occupation. For example, career changers frequently mention the opportunity for more personally meaningful work and a greater fit with personal values as important reasons for their changes.[29] Other factors associated with successful career change include *confidence* that the change can

· EXHIBIT 9-1

DETERMINANTS OF CAREER CHANGE

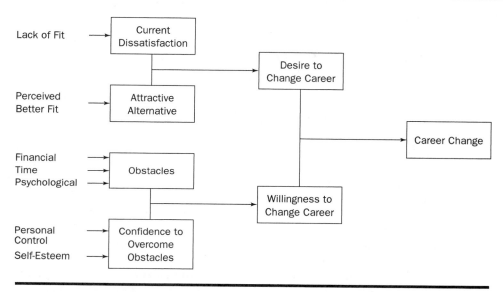

NOTE: The impact of dissatisfaction, alternative, obstacles, and confidence on career change is discussed in J. Neapolitan, "Occupational Change in Midcareer: An Exploratory Investigation," *Journal of Vocational Behavioral,* 16 (1980): 212–225.

actually be made, *believing* that one is in control of one's fate during the change, and the *presence of support* from one's social network.[30] Exhibit 9.1 summarizes the determinants of career change.

The factors described above can help explain why people in general decide to change careers. But what about midcareer employees in particular? Harry Levinson identified a number of "healthy" reasons for changing careers during the middle years:[31]

- Reaching a career plateau.
- Becoming obsolescent.
- Becoming bored.
- Feeling underused.
- Being in a position for which one is underqualified.
- Recognizing that the original occupational choice was inappropriate.

All these reasons relate in one way or another to a lack of fit in one's current career status and are likely to increase one's dissatisfaction with the current career role. Such feelings of dissatisfaction may intensify during midcareer, when more general issues of aging, mortality, and lost opportunities are also surfacing.

However, Levinson warns that midcareer change can also take place for the "wrong" reasons:

- Dissatisfaction with oneself as a person.
- Depression.
- Anxiety over feelings of mortality.
- Overvaluation of one's own competence and worth.
- Intense competition for status with friends and acquaintances.

Levinson has convincingly argued that before embarking on a midcareer change, people must understand their motives, their ideal image of themselves, and the nature of the changes they will have to undergo if they decide to shift career direction. Often, the career risks of jumping to a new job and company outweigh the stature and credits one has built with his or her current company.[32] Indeed, researchers have identified a number of obstacles to career change.[33] These obstacles may be financial (a salary cut, loss of income in a new business venture), time-related (the time required to train for a different occupation), or psychological (the uncertainty and insecurity about becoming competent in a different field). The next sections consider more specific actions that organizations and individuals can take to resolve some of the midcareer issues discussed to this point.

ORGANIZATIONAL ACTIONS DURING MIDCAREER

We have reviewed the major developmental tasks of midcareer as well as the potential for plateauing, obsolescence, and career change. Next, we examine the actions that organizations can take to help employees manage their careers during this period of development.

HELP EMPLOYEES UNDERSTAND MIDCAREER EXPERIENCES

Before any meaningful actions can be taken, organizations, through their top officials, must first appreciate the issues facing midcareer employees. In this way, they can avoid overreacting to employees who are having trouble adjusting to middle age and can begin to develop useful programs. Moreover, educating managers on these issues can help improve the supervisor-subordinate relationship when one or the other party is in midcareer.[34] The organization must also recognize that there are likely to be considerable differences in how individual employees react to midcareer. Seminars and workshops among upper-level managers can educate organizational members on midcareer dynamics.

Moreover, employees can cope more effectively with midlife transitions, plateauing, obsolescence, and restlessness when they understand that they are experiencing natural, normal reactions to a different career status.[35] People need to work through these feelings to enter middle adulthood stronger and healthier. The failure to confront these feelings, doubts, and frustrations may produce even greater problems somewhere down the line.

Seminars, workshops, and support groups can provide an opportunity for people to talk about their feelings and realize that they are not alone. Professional counseling might also be appropriate for some employees.

PROVIDE EXPANDED AND FLEXIBLE MOBILITY OPPORTUNITIES

Because promotional opportunities may be limited during midcareer, job rotation and lateral moves can be used to keep plateaued employees stimulated, challenged, and motivated. Lateral mobility may be particularly appealing to midcareer plateauees, especially when the moves do not involve geographic relocation. The judicious use of periodic rotation and lateral mobility may prevent solid citizens from becoming deadwood and may deter obsolescence.[36] Lateral rotations not only stretch and stimulate employees, but also provide a different perspective on solving an organization's problems.

Because some midcareer employees may be unable or unwilling to handle the pressures of their current job, downward transfers (demotions) can be used to stimulate development and motivation. However, downward transfers must be presented as a new learning experience to the employee and must be handled with sensitivity.[37] Downward moves are most effective when the new, lower position demands some skill or talent that the employee currently does not possess.[38]

Lateral and even downward transfers are useful to the extent to which they bring additional challenge, skill utilization, and stimulation. Because extended time in one job can produce negative attitudes or stagnation, perhaps mobility in any direction, if handled properly, can promote positive attitudes and motivation.

However, not all midcareer employees will experience a plateau. Many will hold realistic mobility aspirations and will need the organization's help in achieving these goals. Therefore, several of the organizational actions relevant to the achievement period of the early career—stimulation of career exploration, career pathing, and development planning to mention a few—are also appropriate for the mobile middle manager.

UTILIZATION OF THE CURRENT JOB

Although many midcareer employees may no longer expect advancement, their needs for achievement and autonomy can remain strong. An alternative or supplement to lateral mobility during midcareer is the improvement of the current job by building in more variety, challenge, and responsibility.[39] Participation in task forces, project teams, and temporary "trouble-shooting" assignments can provide stimulation and recognition and should be welcomed by many in midcareer if the responsibilities do not cut too deeply into their personal and family lives. Providing sufficient challenge and responsibility throughout the midcareer years can be a primary deterrent to development of "deadwood" attitudes and behaviors.[40]

One factor that improves the work experience of solid citizens is the presence of clear job duties and agreed-on performance objectives. Moreover, clear and accurate performance feedback is critical to maintain the high performance of plateaued employees, even though the absence of promotional opportunities may make these performance discussions unpleasant for the supervisor. Accurate performance appraisal is also essential to detect the presence or potential for obsolescence.[41]

ENCOURAGE AND TEACH MENTORING SKILLS

It was noted in Chapter 5 that generativity needs are particularly strong during middle adulthood. Moreover, the long-term service and broad experience of many midcareer employees may make them particularly suitable to mentor younger colleagues. However, before midcareer employees can help others, they must understand their own feelings about their career and lives. Special lectures or group discussions on midcareer issues can be developed to accomplish this. It is also likely that many midcareer employees will require some training on how to coach, counsel, and provide feedback.[42]

TRAINING AND CONTINUING EDUCATION

The use of training or retraining for plateaued or obsolescent employees has been suggested frequently in the literature,[43] although some management scholars have offered a rather critical evaluation of continuing education as a deterrent to obsolescence.[44] First, although organizations may formally support and endorse continuing education, participation in such activities is often discouraged and unrewarded by individual supervisors.

Second, it is not clear that participation in continuing education, in and of itself, can really help avert obsolescence. Instead, continual job challenge and periodic job rotation can be viewed as the most effective deterrents to obsolescence. Well-planned, demanding, and innovative continuing education programs can help if employees are counseled to enter the right program at the right time to meet their own needs and goals and if continuing education supplements rather than replaces stimulating, challenging job assignments.

One significant function of continuing education is preparing midcareer employees who wish to engage in a career change. Continuing education can serve as a catalyst that can encourage employees to consider the possibility of a different career field in a different organization at some point in their future. In this sense, educational benefits provided by the organization are used to help interested managers prepare themselves for a career shift. Organizations can then creatively encourage their "surplus" managers to take early retirement to pursue the alternative career field or perhaps become an entrepreneur.[45]

BROADEN THE REWARD SYSTEM

Many of the specific suggestions outlined here involve reexamination and expansion of the organization's reward system. Instead of focusing exclusively or primarily on promotions and compensation as the incentive for effective performance, alternative rewards should be considered.[46] Interesting and challenging jobs, stimulating reassignments, recognition, praise, and financial rewards can all be used to maintain the effectiveness of employees experiencing midcareer plateaus. These steps can help prevent solid citizens from becoming deadwood.

Rewarding employees for lifelong learning and development, success in challenging jobs, and participation in appropriate continuing education programs are the most effective means for forestalling technical or managerial obsolescence. Such an approach explicitly recognizes the importance of long-term career performance, not simply vertical mobility through the hierarchy or one's potential performance and mobility.[47]

INDIVIDUAL ACTIONS DURING MIDCAREER

Self-assessment is critical in midcareer. In addition to exploring one's values, interests, and talents, it is essential to understand one's real feelings about middle age and any shifts in the priority of work, family, and self-development. Specifically, individuals should conduct periodic self-assessments and reappraisals to determine whether their interests, values, and skills are in line with their established goals and plans. This awareness should empower individuals to better recognize and use opportunities as they arise and can allow a more proactive response to changes in the work environment. If the organization does not provide a mechanism to stimulate this reappraisal, then the employee must take the initiative through participation in formal career development programs or discussions with peers, friends, family members, or counselors.

An examination of alternatives involves exploration of work and family environments. In the work domain, one's current job needs to be examined for possible improvement, and the possibility of nonpromotional mobility opportunities should be explored if relevant. Exploration of different occupations and organizations, as discussed in Chapters 6 and 7, also may be appropriate. Moreover, relationships with one's spouse and/or children may need to be examined and new priorities set.

Midcareer employees considering a career change not only need to understand their own motives and interests, but also must anticipate and examine the consequences of career redirection. Employees contemplating a midcareer change should consider (1) the impact of the change on their family, (2) the risk of severing relationships with friends and colleagues in the current organization, (3) the possibility of reduced status in the community as a result of the career shift, (4) the time it might take to build a reputation in the new field, and (5) the possibility of experiencing psychological depression for some time, perhaps up to 1 year.[48] Potential midcareer changers should discuss these kinds of issues extensively with family members, friends, and colleagues prior to making a commitment to a career change.

The goal-setting process during midcareer is not fundamentally different than in other stages, although the goal itself may be less likely to involve hierarchical advancement. Of particular importance is the establishment of a conceptual goal that is not tied to a particular position. Success in managing one's career during midcareer is based on the ability to understand conceptual goals and see the possibilities of satisfying that goal in one's current position.

Career strategies or action plans, as always, must be tied to goals and tested for feasibility. The development of active, realistic strategies of any type requires an awareness of goals, a willingness to communicate those goals to others, and a talent in observation, listening, and analysis. Participation in special skill-building sessions for those in midcareer might help promote a more active, realistic strategy for dealing with the issues raised in this chapter. Most important, perhaps, is the conviction that one can influence, to a considerable extent, the course of one's career at any period of development.

However, corporate realities suggest that career planning is likely to be seen as meaningless and bureaucratic busywork to the majority of middle-aged managers.[49] If the focus of career planning is the achievement of hierarchical promotion, then this concern has great merit. However, if career management is defined more broadly than "making it to the top" and is seen as a process designed to improve the fit between the individual and his or her work life, then career management during midcareer is vital to the salvation of individual careers and the effective utilization of an organization's human resources.

DEALING WITH JOB LOSS

Loss of one's job can be a traumatic experience at any point in the life cycle, but it may be especially difficult and damaging for persons in the midlife phase.[50] First, individuals in midlife may be vulnerable to periods of self-doubt and a questioning of competence and worth; job loss can only add to the magnitude (and trauma) of the questioning process. Secondly, individuals in midlife are most susceptible to financial strains, with a peak in such demands as household expenses, acquisition of material goods, the planning for (or making) the payment of children's college tuition, and attempting to save for one's retirement. Again, the loss of one's job can only exacerbate the financial stress. Further, job loss can put strain on a marriage that may already be on shaky ground due to the pressures of midlife.

There are a number of well-documented reasons (or combination of reasons) why individuals are terminated by their employers. The most common causes include poor performance of the individual, a corporate-wide downsizing, unfavorable financial or economic conditions faced by the company, or a violation of company policy or some unethical behavior.[51] It is important to understand that poor performance may not necessarily indicate employee incompetence. Rather, it may reflect such factors as differences of opinion on priorities and strategies, personality clashes, and organizational politics.[52]

Individual reactions to job loss can be varied, depending on such factors as financial resources, social contacts and status, the meaningfulness of the work in the individual's life, and one's level of confidence and self-esteem.[53] In essence, job loss can disrupt the established equilibrium in various facets of one's life, including economic, psychological, physiologic, and social.[54] Reflecting the disrupted life equilibrium, common outcomes of job loss include reduced happiness, increased depression, mental and physical illness, increased anxiety, and disengagement. Other possible consequences of involuntary termination include higher death rates, suicide, reduced self-esteem, and family dysfunctions.[55] Conversely, for some people, job loss can be a growth experience. Even though it may not be viewed as a worthwhile occurrence at the time of dismissal, job loss could be a "blessing in disguise" because it could force people to reassess their interests and desires and look for new avenues for personal fulfillment. Regardless of one's initial financial and emotional state, researchers have found that the subsequent process of coping with job loss and landing a new job follow a predictable series of stages.[56]

In the **first stage,** individuals experience an initial response to the loss of a job. Researchers have identified four different types of initial response.[57] First, the individual may feel a sense of shock and disbelief, even when warning signs were in place to signal the impending termination. People often assume that job loss "won't happen to them." A second type of initial reaction is anger at the company and its management for allowing the termination to occur. A third response is a sense of relief, as the uncertainty and stress of potential termination is finally lifted. Lastly, individuals may show signs of escapism by displaying little or no emotion and attempting to totally divorce themselves from the difficult situation.

After the initial reaction subsides, individuals move into the **second stage,** in which they confront the tasks of becoming reemployed. The campaign to secure a new position involves a multitude of activities. In a personal account of his efforts in finding a new job, Gerald Parkhouse discusses a number of these activities—working with an outplacement firm, preparing an up-to-date resume, identifying former work associates who can serve as job contacts and leads, drafting cover memos and letters of introduction, and practicing proper interview performance.[58]

For the majority of people, coping with job loss ends after the second stage, when a new work position is found. However, if the job search continues for an extended period, individuals may enter a **third stage** in which the frustration of not finding work results in vacillation about one's career, lingering self-doubt about one's abilities, and anger that can involve displaced aggression toward others.[59] The **fourth stage** occurs when individuals experience such dismay over not finding a new job that they resign themselves to being unemployed and begin withdrawing from activities, including those aimed at finding work.[60]

From the above descriptions, it is clear that the second stage following job loss is the critical period in finding a new position. It is during this phase that one is likely to undertake a concerted job search effort. For this reason, it is important that the job-seeking individual apply the career management concepts discussed throughout this book. More precisely, individuals should first conduct a thorough appraisal of interests, talents, and life-style preferences. Second, the individual should assess the work environment, gathering information on alternative jobs, companies, and industries. Coincident with the self- and work-exploration processes, individuals should set tentative goals on the types of position (or positions) toward which they would like to target their reemployment efforts. Strategies would then be set on how to go about landing a preferred job.

Of course, no set of actions, regardless of how practical they are, guarantees that one will find a job in a timely fashion. Nevertheless, it is important that the model and the individual steps be followed to at least ensure that the individual is doing everything possible to locate a new job that is consistent with his or her interests and preferences.

There are a variety of actions that organizations can take to assist their employees in coping with job terminations. Basic programs include advance notification, severance pay and extended benefits, retraining, outplacement assistance, and counseling.[61] Further, in the case of an across-the-board downsizing, it is recommended that the organization attempt to dispel the inevitable self-blame that individuals place on themselves so as to minimize the loss of self-esteem and confidence that is likely to occur.[62] Also, it is important that organization-sponsored interventions to assist laid-off workers attempt to enhance confidence and self-efficacy about finding another job. Clearly, individual confidence can have a positive influence on subsequent job search behaviors.[63]

In addition to these basic efforts, employers must be sensitive to the individual's needs and fears during and immediately after the dismissal. Janina Latack and Harold Kaufman offer a number of suggestions on how to properly conduct a dismissal and, in turn, minimize the potential negative consequences for the employee and the organization. Some of their suggestions include:[64]

- Treat the employee with dignity and respect and protect individual integrity at all times.
- Choose a private place for dismissal, where visibility to other employees will be minimized.
- Time the dismissal to maximize the degree of emotional support the employee can receive from family and friends.
- Do not end the dismissal session prematurely. Give the individual time to react to the job loss.

In Chapter 15 we provide further discussion on the approaches companies use in handling employee dismissals and layoffs.

LATE CAREER

Businesses cannot afford to cast-off or take–for granted their older workers. For one thing, there are more older Americans now than ever before, and this trend will continue as the baby boom generation ages. Second, legislation including the

Age Discrimination in Employment Act (ADEA) protects workers 40 or older from discriminatory employment practices. Finally, it makes good business sense for companies to use all their human resources. The projected shortage of workers in the future attributed to worldwide economic growth and a declining birthrate places a greater value on the older worker who can provide stability and continuity to an organization's work force. Ironically, even in the face of a growing labor shortage, takeovers, restructurings, and other corporate actions have led many large organizations to "ease out" senior employees through early retirement programs.[65] Overall, the treatment of the older worker will be a major management issue facing employers for at least the next 30 years or more as the last of the baby boom generation reaches retirement age.

From the individual employee's perspective, three developmental needs stand out during the late career. First, a handful of late-career employees must prepare themselves for senior leadership roles in their respective organizations. However, for the vast majority, the primary tasks of the late career are to remain productive and to prepare for effective retirement.[66]

PRODUCTIVITY

Remaining competent and productive is important to the late-career employee. Few people wish to be "carried" as excess baggage, but there are several obstacles to remaining productive during the late career. For one thing, rapid changes in technology and organizations pose a threat of obsolescence, especially to older workers with limited education and skills.[67] Unless midcareer obsolescence is prevented or reduced, the situation can only get worse during the late career. This becomes even more devastating when changes in an organization's mission, structure, or technology eliminate jobs, career paths, or even whole functions.

Second, the plateauing process discussed earlier can have negative effects on the performance of late-career employees. Although it is likely that a plateau will initially be reached during midcareer, a midcareer solid citizen who is bored, unrewarded, and/or unmotivated may well become late-career deadwood. In other words, obsolescence and plateauing are often midcareer issues that can eventually produce increasing deterioration during the late career.

Maintaining effective performance during the late career also can be jeopardized by society's stereotypes and biases against older people, in general, and older workers, in particular. Older workers have typically (and erroneously) been viewed as deficient in several areas: productivity, efficiency, capability of working under pressure, ambitiousness, receptivity to new ideas, adaptability, versatility, and capability of developing new skills.[68]

Despite the inaccuracy of these stereotypes,[69] such biases can have a significant effect on how organizations treat and manage the older worker. A number of management actions, as listed below, can be traced to the negative stereotypes and myths concerning older workers.[70]

- If older workers are seen as rigid and resistant to change, then organizations will be less likely to help them improve their performance.

- If older employees are perceived as less motivated to keep up to date with changes, then organizations will be less willing to invest time and money in skill development programs for them.
- If older employees are seen as less creative or innovative, then organizations will be less willing to move them into a position requiring these qualities.

These management decisions can produce a self-fulfilling prophecy in which older workers, deprived of developmental experiences and mobility opportunities, never have an opportunity to disconfirm the original stereotypes. These inaccurate stereotypes can produce a negative attitude toward older workers, which, in turn, can produce bias in such areas as personnel selection, performance appraisal, and training availability.[71]

Organizations need to overcome these inherent biases and recognize the value of their older workers. Not only are older workers equal in productivity with their younger counterparts,[72] but evidence suggests that they have lower absenteeism, turnover, and accident rates, higher job satisfaction, and generally more positive work attitudes.[73] Thus, older workers can be dedicated, productive, and enthusiastic employees but must be treated with dignity and respect and must be recognized for their value to the firm.

PREPARATION FOR RETIREMENT

Retirement is a major career transition for most people because it can signify an end to nearly 40 or 50 years of continual employment. Daniel Feldman defines **retirement** as the exit from an organizational position or career path of considerable duration, taken by individuals after middle age, and taken with the intention of reduced psychological commitment to work thereafter.[74] Although this definition seems straightforward enough, the recent proliferation of available part-time positions and changes in attitudes toward working longer can sometimes make it difficult to determine when someone is actually retired. In general, retirees can be differentiated from non-retirees based on the following: retirees tend to be older, usually over the age of at least 50 years; they tend to spend less of their time working for pay; they are more likely to receive some income that is specially designated for retirees; and they tend to think of themselves as retired.[75]

Preparing for retirement involves deciding when to retire and planning for a satisfying, fulfilling life on retirement. However, the decision to retire has been complicated in recent years by government and corporate actions. On the one hand, the ADEA has virtually eliminated any mandatory retirement age. Essentially, the decision on when to retire is now a voluntary one for nearly all American workers. Changes in the Social Security system also can encourage employees to delay retirement. These actions provide older workers with greater latitude in the timing of retirement.

Attitudes toward retirement are likely to be rooted in one's attitude toward work. Work fulfills so many human functions and can be such an important part of one's identity that to leave the work role may be akin to leaving behind a part of oneself.[76] Work provides a niche in society and a feeling of usefulness and

· EXHIBIT 9-2

MODEL OF THE INDIVIDUAL
RETIREMENT DECISION PROCESS

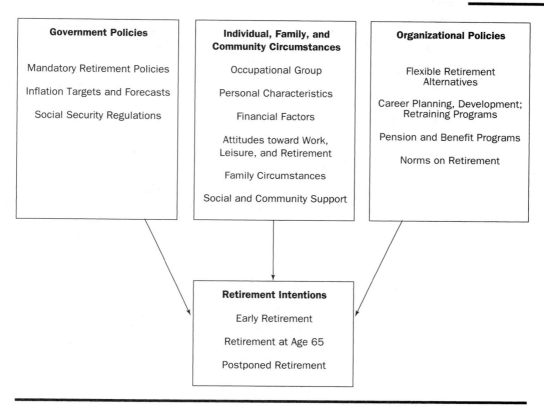

Government Policies	Individual, Family, and Community Circumstances	Organizational Policies
Mandatory Retirement Policies	Occupational Group	Flexible Retirement Alternatives
Inflation Targets and Forecasts	Personal Characteristics	Career Planning, Development; Retraining Programs
Social Security Regulations	Financial Factors	Pension and Benefit Programs
	Attitudes toward Work, Leisure, and Retirement	Norms on Retirement
	Family Circumstances	
	Social and Community Support	

Retirement Intentions

Early Retirement

Retirement at Age 65

Postponed Retirement

SOURCE: B. Rosen and T. Jerdee, *Older Employees: New Roles for Valued Resources*, © 1985, p. 143. Reprinted with permission of Dow Jones-Irwin, Homewood, Illinois.

purpose, and it allows people the opportunity to fulfill their basic needs for affiliation, achievement, power, and prestige. Work also provides financial rewards and a structure that helps people organize their daily lives. For many people, these tangible and intangible benefits are not easy to give up. Indeed, many employees who find retirement unfulfilling often embark on a "post-career career."[77] On the other hand, many employees relish the thought of retirement and look forward to days without the pressures of deadlines, supervisors, and long hours.

In an introspective look at his own retirement, Thomas Fitzgerald discusses the mental and emotional reactions one experiences in the voluntary withdrawal from work.[78] Fitzgerald calls retirement a potentially disabling time, where one can experience freedom, but perhaps without content. He concludes that because work plays such a central role, removing oneself from the work world can lead to a trying and difficult phase of life.

For these reasons, preferences toward or against retirement are likely to vary from person to person depending on a number of health, work, and personal factors. A model of individual retirement decisions is shown in Exhibit 9.2. Governmental and organizational policies, employee background, attitudes, and social circumstances all affect the decision to retire.[79] Research highlights the significance of the following factors:[80]

- Health concerns can quicken the decision to retire, especially when jobs are physically demanding.
- Employees who anticipate comfortable retirement incomes are more favorably disposed toward retirement.
- Employees who hold high-status jobs are less inclined to retire than those who hold low-status jobs.
- Employees who work on highly motivating jobs, are strongly committed to work, or are highly satisfied with their work role are less inclined to retire.
- Social pressure from family members can spur retirement decisions. One source of family pressure can be an unemployed spouse who can provide companionship to the retiree.

It is also important to understand why some people seem to adjust more favorably to retirement than others. Satisfaction in retirement has been linked with a variety of factors, including the extent to which the person had engaged in retirement planning while still employed, anticipated pursuit of hobbies or travel, a good pension, the presence of good health, absence of an overly emotional involvement with one's job, and high levels of self-esteem.[81]

ORGANIZATIONAL ACTIONS DURING LATE CAREER

Reasonable attempts to manage older workers require sensitivity to late career issues on the part of the organization's top management and supervisory staff. This necessitates a clear understanding of the differences between the myths and realities of aging and a recognition of the value differences among generations of workers.

PERFORMANCE STANDARDS AND FEEDBACK

Clear standards of effective performance should be developed and communicated to the older worker. When confronting low productivity among older workers, performance problems should be stated in clear behavioral terms, the consequences of continued ineffective performance should be identified, and options to improve performance should be explored.[82] Accurate, unbiased performance appraisals are essential to maintain effective performance and to document reasons for terminating an older worker if necessary.[83]

EDUCATION AND JOB RESTRUCTURING

Many of the suggestions made to prevent or ameliorate midcareer obsolescence and to manage the midcareer plateaued employee are also relevant to the employee in late career. Ongoing learning opportunities, through the integration of stimulating, responsible job assignments and continuing education, can play a major role in the revitalization of the late-career work force.

A model program for combating the obsolescence of older workers involves (1) a thorough assessment of employees' training and development needs, (2) the design of developmental experiences such as training for upgrading technical, managerial, and/or administrative skills, (3) a review and evaluation of the program's effectiveness, and (4) long-range planning to identify future retraining needs.[84]

DEVELOPMENT AND ENFORCEMENT OF NONDISCRIMINATION POLICIES

The ADEA forbids age discrimination in such areas as hiring and placement, compensation, advancement, and termination. Nondiscrimination makes good business sense and protects organizations from costly litigation.

DEVELOPMENT OF RETIREMENT PLANNING PROGRAMS

Retirement planning programs can smooth the transition between work and retirement.[85] Typically, retirement planning programs cover such topics as the challenge of retirement, health and safety, housing, time management, legal issues, and financial planning. Some conclusions on successful retirement planning programs are given below:

1. Retirement planning programs should focus on both the extrinsic and intrinsic aspects of retirement. Extrinsic elements include financial security, housing alternatives, and legal issues. Intrinsic factors associated with retirement include the various psychological issues related to disengagement from work. Some researchers have suggested instituting "realistic retirement previews" that provide a balanced, accurate picture of retirement.

2. Programs should be run in small groups that encourage two-way communication and provide opportunities for counseling. In this way, the social and psychological consequences of retirement can be discussed in a more candid fashion.

3. Ideally, participation in retirement planning programs should begin at least 5 years prior to anticipated retirement to allow adequate time to address all issues. Counseling activities should also continue for a specified period of time after retirement.[86]

4. Previously retired persons can be used as information resources and role models during retirement planning sessions.

5. Spouse participation in retirement planning programs can be beneficial and should be encouraged. In a survey of service firms, it was found that 81 percent extended invitations to spouses to attend their retirement planning programs.[87]

6. Special retirement planning programs should be offered for those employees who have an especially strong commitment to work. These employees may have a particularly difficult time dealing with the prospect of retirement.[88]

7. Retirement planning programs should be designed to help maintain positive attitudes and performance among pre-retirees, allow the organization to retain desirable older employees, and encourage others to take early retirement. However, programs must be carefully evaluated to determine whether they are meeting the needs of the employees and the organization.

ESTABLISHMENT OF FLEXIBLE WORK PATTERNS

Undoubtedly, many organizations prefer that the more competent, adaptable late-career employees continue working beyond "normal" retirement age and that others take early retirement. A system of flexible work patterns may enable both of these aims to be met.

Competent employees nearing retirement age could be induced to continue employment if they had more options than simply remaining a full-time member of the organization in their current position. These options can include part-time or seasonal employment, special consulting assignments, job sharing or job rotation, flexible or compressed working hours, and job restructuring. Such programs could help organizations retain the services of highly valued older employees while unclogging career paths for younger workers.

The flip side of the retirement issue is the encouragement of less talented or adaptable workers to take early retirement. Here, too, innovative programs may serve the needs of the employee and the organization. These innovations can include supplementing the reduced Social Security benefits for employees who retire before full benefits are given, cash bonuses, maintenance of fringe benefits until age 65, cost-of-living adjustments to pension benefits, and full pension benefits for early retirement.[89]

Organizations' responses to late-career issues, in general, and to retirement, in particular, take on a symbolic meaning that can have far-reaching effects on the work force. How a company treats its retirees is visible to every employee. Few events reflect the company's commitment to people more than the way the transition to retirement is handled.[90]

INDIVIDUAL ACTIONS DURING LATE CAREER

Active career management is no less significant during the late career than during earlier periods of development. The suggestions made to midcareer employees earlier in this chapter are equally applicable to those in late career. Moreover, given the presence of age stereotypes, there may be a number of obstacles to acquiring more challenging and responsible assignments or lateral mobility opportunities. Therefore, an awareness of one's current career needs and an assertive career strategy are necessary to ensure an individual-organizational fit during the late career.

Like many other career issues, retirement planning should be conducted by the individual employee, whether or not the employer offers a formal program. In addition, we recommend that the approaches the individual uses toward retirement planning resemble the active approaches to career management as outlined throughout this book. Pre-retirees are encouraged to gather relevant information about their financial assets and expenses, preferred life-style, and social and psychological needs. The development of financial, social, and personal objectives and the identification of action steps round out this planning process. Various types of software and Internet web sites can also help individuals set plans for retirement.[91] Overall, planning for retirement should involve as much concern and attention as for earlier events in a career.

Individuals making preparations for retirement should ask themselves a number of fundamental questions,[92] such as: How might I live in retirement? What do I really care about? What is of value and worth? By probing interests and values in this fashion, pre-retirement employees can gain a clearer picture of what they wish to accomplish and the life they would like to have in their retirement years.

Summary

The middle career years present employees with two major tasks—to confront the midlife transition and to remain productive in their work. The midlife transition serves as a bridge between early and middle adulthood. Triggered by an awareness of aging and a fear of lost youth, many employees need to reconcile their accomplishments in life with their youthful aspirations. Although midcareer employees may not necessarily experience a crisis during this period, some form of reappraisal of accomplishments and goals may be necessary to move into middle adulthood in a constructive, productive manner.

Productivity during midcareer can be hampered if employees realize that they have reached a career plateau in which future advancement opportunities are unlikely. Although some midcareer employees react to the plateauing experience with frustration, guilt, and stagnation, others adapt by substituting other goals for vertical mobility. Midcareer employees may also fall prey to technological or managerial obsolescence and ultimately job loss if they lack sufficient up-to-date knowledge and skills to maintain effective performance on their job.

Organizations can promote effective career management during midcareer by (1) helping employees understand their midcareer experiences; (2) providing a variety of mobility opportunities, including lateral and downward transfers; (3) providing sufficient challenge and responsibility on the current job to maintain involvement and productivity; (4) providing training or retraining as a supplement to challenging job assignments; and (5) encouraging some midcareer employees to serve as mentors to their junior colleagues. Individuals need to develop insight into their values and motives, reassess their current career prospects, and establish a conceptual career goal that can be achieved in a variety of jobs.

The late career also poses some potential threats to employee motivation and performance. Not only might older employees have to deal with the aftermath of midcareer obsolescence or plateauing, but they may also have to contend with negative age biases that obstruct continued growth and development on the job. Moreover, the late-career employee must begin to consider a number of issues regarding retirement.

Organizations can help late-career employees by (1) understanding their unique problems, (2) developing clear performance standards and offering concrete feedback, (3) providing job challenge and continual training to maintain motivation, (4) developing and implementing nondiscriminatory policies regarding older workers, (5) developing effective pre-retirement programs, and (6) establishing flexible work patterns for employees nearing retirement age. Individuals should maintain an active vigilance during the late-career years and should plan their retirement with care and attention.

ASSIGNMENT

If you are 40 years of age or older, take a few introspective minutes and consider your career and life history. Do you believe that you have gone through (or are going through) a midlife transition? If the answer is yes, what kinds of issues did you deal with (or you are dealing with) during the transition period? Describe the changes that you have undergone (in work, family, or personal life) as a result of the midlife transition. Did you (or do you) view this period of time as a "crisis"? Why or why not? If you do not believe that you have experienced a midlife transition, why not? How would you reconcile that with Levinson's theory as discussed in Chapter 5 and this chapter?

If you are younger than 40 years old, interview a friend, relative, or colleague who is in his or her mid- to late 40s. Determine whether the person has gone through a midlife transition. If the answer is yes, what kinds of issues did the person deal with during the transition period? Describe the changes that the person has undergone (in work, family, or personal life) as a result of the midlife transition. Did the person view this period of time as a "crisis"? Why or why not? If the person does not seem to have experienced the midlife transition, why not? How would you reconcile that with Levinson's theory as discussed in Chapter 5 and this chapter?

DISCUSSION QUESTIONS

1. Defend or attack the following statement: "Reaching a plateau in the organization drastically reduces the productivity and satisfaction of employees." Describe the reasoning behind your position.

2. What characteristics distinguish a solid citizen from a deadwood plateaued employee in an organization? What can organizations do to prevent solid citizens from becoming deadwood? What forces may prevent organizations from taking these actions?

3. What triggers a desire to make a midcareer change, and what factors inhibit people from actually making such a change? When is a midcareer change an adaptive behavior and when is it used to shield workers from their real problems?

4. What are some common stereotypes of the older employee? Do you think these stereotypes are generally accurate or inaccurate? How do stereotypes of aging affect the ways in which organizations manage their older employees?

5. Why do some older workers relish the thought of retirement whereas others dread the prospect of leaving their work life behind? What kind of planning should be conducted to prepare oneself for retirement? Why should retirement planning begin considerably before the anticipated retirement date?

ENDNOTES

1. D. J. Levinson, C. N. Darrow, E. B. Klein, M. H. Levinson, and B. McKee, *Seasons of a Man's Life* (New York: Knopf, 1978); E. H. Schein, *Career Dynamics: Matching Individual and Organizational Needs* (Reading, MA: Addison-Wesley, 1978).

2. E. Jaques, "Death and the Mid-Life Crisis," *International Journal of Psychoanalysis* 46 (1965): 502–514.

3. A. K. Korman, "Career Success and Personal Failure: Mid- to Late-Career Feelings and Events," in *Career Growth and Human Resource Strategies,* ed. M. London and E. M. Mone (New York: Quorum Books, 1988), 81–94.

4. J. R. Gordan and K. S. Whelan, "Successful Professional Women in Midlife: How Organizations Can More Effectively Understand and Respond to the Challenges," *Academy of Management Executive* 12 (1998): 8–24.

5. Levinson et al., *Seasons of a Man's Life;* D. J. Levinson and J. D. Levinson, *Seasons of a Woman's Life* (New York: Knopf, 1996).

6. S. J. Gill, L. C. Coppard, and M. A. Lowther, "Mid-Life Career Development Theory and Research: Implications for Work and Education," *Aging and Work* 6 (1983): 15–29; B. S. Lawrence, "The Myth of the Midlife Crisis," *Sloan Management Review* 21 (1980): 35–49.

7. Levinson et al., *Seasons of a Man's Life.*

8. T. P. Ference, J. A. F. Stoner, and E. K. Warren, "Managing the Career Plateau," *Academy of Management Review* 2 (1977): 602–612; quote is on p. 602.

9. E. Van Velsor and J. B. Leslie, "Why Executives Derail: Perspectives across Time and Cultures," *Academy of Management Executive* 9 (1995): 62–72.

10. A recent study observed that employees may plateau in their careers for three types of reasons: (1) no higher-level positions are available (organizational constraints); (2) the organization makes the determination that the employee lacks the skill set or motivation to be considered for promotion (organizational assessment); or (3) the employee does not wish to

acquire a higher-level position (personal choice). See V. M. Godshalk, "The Effects of Career Plateauing on Work and Non-Work Outcomes," unpublished doctoral dissertation, Drexel University, Philadelphia, PA, 1997.

11. J. M. Bardwick, *The Plateauing Trap* (Toronto, Canada: Bantam Books, 1986).

12. B. Rosen and T. H. Jerdee, "Middle and Late Career Problems: Causes, Consequences, and Research Needs," *Human Resource Planning* 13 (1990): 59–70.

13. G. T. Chao, "The Socialization Process: Building Newcomer Commitment," in *Career Growth and Human Resource Strategies,* ed. London and Mone, 31–47; D. K. Zaremba, "The Managerial Plateau: What Helps in Developing Careers?" *The International Journal of Career Management* 6 (1994): 5–11.

14. A. Howard and D. W. Bray, *Managerial Lives in Transition* (New York: Guilford Press, 1988).

15. D. C. Feldman and B. A. Weitz, "Career Plateaus Reconsidered," *Journal of Management* 14 (1988): 69–80.

16. S. K. Stout, J. W. Slocum, and W. L. Cron, "Dynamics of the Career Plateauing Process," *Journal of Vocational Behavior* 32 (1988): 74–91.

17. J. P. Near, "Reactions to the Career Plateau," *Business Horizons* 27 (1984): 75–79.

18. J. A. Fossum, R. D. Arvey, C. A. Paradise, and N. E. Robbins, "Modeling the Skills Obsolescence Process: A Psychological/Economic Integration," *Academy of Management Review* 11 (1986): 362–374.

19. H. G. Kaufman, *Obsolescence and Professional Career Development* (New York: AMACOM, 1974); quote is on p. 23.

20. Fossum et al., "Modeling the Skills Obsolescence Process: A Psychological/Economic Integration."

21. Kaufman, *Obsolescence and Professional Career Development.*

22. C. P. Williams and M. L. Savickas, "Developmental Tasks of Career Maintenance," *Journal of Vocational Behavior* 36 (1990): 166–175.

23. Kaufman, *Obsolescence and Professional Career Development.*

24. S. R. Rhodes and M. Doering, "An Integrated Model of Career Change," *Academy of Management Review* 8 (1983): 631–639.

25. D. T. Hall, "Career Development Theory in Organizations," in *Career Choice and Development,* ed. D. Brown, L. Brooks, et al. (San Francisco, CA: Jossey-Bass, 1990), 422–454.

26. Rhodes and Doering, "An Integrated Model of Career Change."

27. M. J. Driver, "Careers: A Review of Personal and Organizational Research," *International Review of Industrial and Organizational Psychology* (1988): 245–277.

28. T. A. Judge, J. W. Boudreau, and R. D. Bretz, Jr., "Job and Life Attitudes of Male Executives," *Journal of Applied Psychology* 79 (1993): 767–782; T. A. Judge and S. Watanabe, "Another Look at the Job Satisfaction-Life Satisfaction Relationship," *Journal of Applied Psychology* 78 (1993): 939–948.

29. L. E. Thomas, "A Typology of Mid-Life Career Changers," *Journal of Vocational Behavior* 16 (1980): 173–182.

30. M. J. Heppner, K. D. Multon, and J. A. Johnston, "Assessing Psychological Resources during Career Change: Development of the Career Transitions Inventory," *Journal of Vocational Behavior* 44 (1994): 55–74.

31. H. Levinson, "A Second Career: The Possible Dream," *Harvard Business Review* 61 (1983): 122–128.

32. W. Kiechel, "High Up and Nowhere to Go," *Fortune,* August 1, 1988, 229–236.

33. J. Neapolitan, "Occupational Change in Midcareer: An Exploratory Investigation," *Journal of Vocational Behavior* 16 (1980): 212–225.

34. L. Baird and K. E. Kram, "Career Dynamics: Managing the Superior/Subordinate Relationship," *Organizational Dynamics* 11 (1983): 46–64.

35. J. M. Bardwick, "Plateauing and Productivity," *Sloan Management Review* 24 (1983): 67–73; P. I. Morgan, J. Patton, and H. K. Baker, "The Organization's Role in Managing Midlife Crisis," *Training and Development Journal* 39 (1985): 56–59; J. W. Slocum, W. L. Cron, and L. C. Yows, "Whose Career Is Likely to Plateau," *Business Horizons* 30 (1987): 31–38.

36. D. T. Hall, "Breaking Career Routines: Midcareer Choice and Identity Development," in *Career Development in Organizations,* ed. Hall et al., 120–159; D. T. Hall and S. Rabinowitz, "Maintaining Employee Involvement in a Plateaued Career," in *Career Growth and Human Resource Strategies,* ed. London and Mone, 67–80; Kaufman, *Obsolescence and Professional Career Development;* Near, "Reactions to the Career Plateau."

37. D. T. Hall and L. A. Isabella, "Downward Movement and Career Development," *Organizational Dynamics* 14 (1985): 5–23.

38. Hall and Rabinowitz, "Maintaining Employee Involvement in a Plateaued Career."

39. Ibid.; D. T. Hall and J. Richter, "Career Gridlock: Baby Boomers Hit the Wall," *Academy of Management Executive* 4 (1990): 7–22; Morgan et al., "The Organization's Role in Managing Midlife Crisis"; Near, "Reactions to the Career Plateau."

40. D. R. Ettington, "Successful Career Plateauing," *Journal of Vocational Behavior* 52 (1998): 72–88.

41. Rosen and Jerdee, "Middle and Late Career Problems: Causes, Consequences, and Research Needs."

42. C. D. Orth, H. E. Wilkinson, and R. C. Benfari, "The Manager's Role as Coach and Mentor," *Organizational Dynamics* 9 (1987): 66–74.

43. Bardwick, "Plateauing and Productivity"; Morgan et al., "The Organization's Role in Managing Midlife Crisis"; Rosen and Jerdee, "Middle and Late Career Problems."

44. Kaufman, *Obsolescence and Professional Career Development.*

45. Hall and Richter, "Career Gridlock: Baby Boomers Hit the Wall."

46. Slocum et al., "Whose Career Is Likely to Plateau."

47. Hall and Richter, "Career Gridlock: Baby Boomers Hit the Wall."

48. Levinson, "A Second Career."

49. A. Howard and D. W. Bray, "Career Motivation in Midlife Managers," *paper prepared for Symposium, New Perspectives in Career Planning and Development,* annual meeting of the American Psychological Association, Montreal, 1980.

50. J. C. Latack and J. B. Dozier, "After the Ax Falls: Job Loss as a Career Transition," *Academy of Management Review* 11 (1986): 375–392; G. Wolf, M. London, J. Casey, and J. Pufahl, "Career Experience and Motivation as Predictors of Training Behaviors and Outcomes for Displaced Engineers," *Journal of Vocational Behavior* 47 (1995): 316–331.

51. J. C. Latack and H. G. Kaufman, "Termination and Outplacement Strategies," in *Career Growth and Human Resource Strategies,* ed. London and Mone, 289–313.

52. Ibid.

53. J. A. Schneer, "Involuntary Turnover and Its Psychological Consequences: A Theoretical Model," *Human Resource Management Review* 3 (1993): 29–47.

54. J. C. Latack, A. J. Kinicki, and G. E. Prussia, "An Integrative Model of Coping with Job Loss," *Academy of Management Review* 20 (1995): 311–342.

55. M. J. Driver, "Careers: A Review of Personal and Organizational Research," *International Review of Industrial and Organizational Psychology* (1988): 245–277; G. E. Prussia, A. J. Kinicki, and J. S. Bracker, "Psychological and Behavioral Consequences of Job Loss: A Covariance Structure Analysis Using Weiner's Attribution Model," *Journal of Applied Psychology* 78 (1993): 382–394; Schneer, "Involuntary Turnover and Its Psychological Consequences."

56. Latack and Kaufman, "Termination and Outplacement Strategies"; G. C. Parkhouse, "Inside-Outplacement—My Search for a Job," *Harvard Business Review* January–February (1988): 67–73.

57. Latack and Kaufman, "Termination and Outplacement Strategies."

58. Parkhouse, "Inside Outplacement—My Search for a Job."

59. Latack and Kaufman, "Termination and Outplacement Strategies."

60. Ibid.

61. Latack and Kaufman, "Termination and Outplacement Strategies"; C. R. Leana and D. C. Feldman, "When Mergers Force Layoffs: Some Lessons about Managing the Human Resource Problems," *Human Resource Planning* 12 (1989): 31–34.

62. Schneer, "Involuntary Turnover and Its Psychological Consequences."

63. D. Eden and A. Aviram, "Self-Efficacy Training to Speed Reemployment: Helping People to Help Themselves," *Journal of Applied Psychology* 78 (1993): 352–360; Prussia et al., "Psychological and Behavioral Consequences of Job Loss."

64. Latack and Kaufman, "Termination and Outplacement Strategies."

65. R. J. Paul and J. B. Townsend, "Managing the Older Worker—Don't Just Rinse Away the Gray," *Academy of Management Executive* 7 (1993): 67–74; S. Shellenbarger and C. Hymowitz, "Over the Hill? As Population Ages, Older Workers Clash with Younger Bosses," *The Wall Street Journal,* June 13, 1994, A-1.

66. E. H. Schein, *Career Dynamics: Matching Individual and Organizational Needs* (Reading, MA: Addison-Wesley, 1978); Williams and Savickas, "Developmental Tasks of Career Maintenance."

67. B. Rosen and T. H. Jerdee, *Older Employees: New Roles for Valued Resources* (Homewood, IL: Dow Jones-Irwin, 1985).

68. D. Goleman, "Studies Suggest Older Minds Are Stronger than Expected," *The New York Times,* February 26, 1996, A-1; Paul and Townsend, "Managing the Older Worker—Don't Just Rinse Away the Gray"; Rosen and Jerdee, *Older Employees;* H. L. Sterns and S. M. Miklos, "The Aging Worker in a Changing Environment: Organizational and Individual Issues," *Journal of Vocational Behavior* 47 (1995): 248–268.

69. C. P. Bird and T. D. Fisher, "Thirty Years Later: Attitudes toward the Employment of Older Workers," *Journal of Applied Psychology* 71 (1986): 515–517; Goleman, "Studies Suggest Older Minds Are Stronger than Expected"; G. M. McEvoy and W. F. Cascio, "Strategies for Reducing Employee Turnover: A Meta-Analysis," *Journal of Applied Psychology* 70 (1985): 342–353; Paul and Townsend, "Managing the Older Worker—Don't Just Rinse Away the Gray"; Rosen and Jerdee, Older Employees; Sterns and Miklos, "The Aging Worker in a Changing Environment"; D. A. Waldman and B. J. Avolio, "A Meta-Analysis of Age Differences in Job Performance," *Journal of Applied Psychology* 71 (1986): 33–38.

70. Paul and Townsend, "Managing the Older Worker—Don't Just Rinse Away the Gray"; Rosen and Jerdee, *Older Employees.*

71. Sterns and Miklos, "The Aging Worker in a Changing Environment."

72. McEvoy and Cascio, "Strategies for Reducing Employee Turnover."

73. Paul and Townsend, "Managing the Older Worker—Don't Just Rinse Away the Gray"; S. R. Rhodes, "Age Related Differences in Work Attitudes and Behavior: A Review and Conceptual Analysis," *Psychological Bulletin* 26 (1983): 328–367; Sterns and Miklos, "The Aging Worker in a Changing Environment."

74. D. C. Feldman, "The Decision to Retire Early: A Review and Conceptualization," *Academy of Management Review* 19 (1994): 285–311; quote is on p. 287.

75. J. A. Talaga and T. A. Beehr, "Are There Gender Differences in Predicting Retirement Decisions?" *Journal of Applied Psychology* 80 (1995): 16–28.

76. D. T. Hall, *Careers in Organizations* (Glenview, IL: Scott Foresman, 1976).

77. H. Lancaster, "Why Retire at All? Here's How to Launch a Postcareer Career," *The Wall Street Journal,* August 5, 1997, B-1.

78. T. H. Fitzgerald, "The Loss of Work: Notes from Retirement," *Harvard Business Review* March–April (1988): 99–103.

79. K. A. Hanisch, "Reasons People Retire and Their Relations to Attitudinal and Behavioral Correlates in Retirement," *Journal of Vocational Behavior* 45 (1994): 1–16; K. A. Hanisch and C. L. Hulin, "General Attitudes and Organizational Withdrawal: An Evaluation of a Causal Model," *Journal of Vocational Behavior* 39 (1991): 110–128; Talaga and Beehr, "Are There Gender Differences in Prediting Retirement Decisions?"

80. C. Dobson and P. C. Morrow, "Effects of Career Orientation on Retirement Attitudes and Retirement Planning," *Journal of Vocational Behavior* 24 (1984): 73–83; Hanisch, "Reasons People Retire and Their Relations to Attitudinal and Behavioral Correlates in Retirement"; Hanisch and Hulin, "General Attitudes and Organizational Withdrawal"; Rosen and Jerdee, *Older Employees;* N. Schmitt and J. T. McCune, "The Relationship between Job Attitudes and the Decision to Retire," *Academy of Management Journal* 24 (1981): 795–802.

81. R. L. Fuller and D. L. Redfering, "Effects of Preretirement Planning on the Retirement Adjustment of Military Personnel," *Sociology of Work and Occupations* 3 (1976): 479–487; Hanisch, "Reasons People Retire and Their Relations to Attitudinal and Behavioral Correlates in Retirement"; N. Schmitt, J. K. White, B. W. Coyle, and J. Rauschenberger, "Retirement and Life Satisfaction," *Academy of Management Journal* 22 (1979): 282–291.

82. Rosen and Jerdee, *Older Employees.*

83. N. J. Beutell, "Managing the Older Worker," *Personnel Administrator* 28 (1983): 31–38, 64; J. Sonnenfeld, "Dealing with the Aging Workforce," *Harvard Business Review* 56 (1978): 81–92.

84. Rosen and Jerdee, *Older Employees.*

85. S. R. Siegel, "Preretirement Programs in Service Firms," *Compensation and Benefits Review* (1989): 47–58.

86. Ibid.

87. Ibid.

88. Dobson and Morrow, "Effects of Career Orientation on Retirement Attitudes and Retirement Planning."

89. Rosen and Jerdee, *Older Employees.*

90. S. B. Wehrenberg, "Preparing to Retire: Educational Programs That Help Employees," *Personnel Journal* 63 (1984): 41–42.

91. D. Foust, "For the Good Life, Hit Enter," *Business Week,* July 21, 1997, 88–91.

92. Fitzgerald, "The Loss of Work."

2

NATALIE THE RETAIL MANAGER

Five years ago, Natalie graduated from a large state university in Pennsylvania with two important possessions—a combined marketing and management degree and high aspirations. She believed that her education, abilities, and ambition would lead to a rewarding career in management. As she interviewed with several companies for her first postgraduate job, it seemed that retail organizations offered the best opportunity for a quick rise to the management ranks. Also, retail firms seemed to give her a good chance to apply her dual majors. The "fast-track" program offered by Enigma,[1] a chain of upscale department stores, was especially intriguing to Natalie. The program included an intensive training course for aspiring managers combined with challenging on-the-job assignments. The recruiter told Natalie that those selected for this program could expect an unencumbered rise to upper management. Natalie was also impressed by what she had seen in the literature the recruiter had used to describe Enigma's proactive development programs and corporate culture. Natalie was so pleased with her choice of Enigma as her first employer that in all the excitement she did not get much of a chance to talk to her parents or friends about it. Also, the preparations for graduation and the end-of-year parties did not leave much time for her to check into Enigma as an employer. In Natalie's view, the recruiter gave her a fairly balanced overview of the company. One month after graduation, Natalie began the 3-month course that blended textbook learning with real life, store-based training at the company's Dallas headquarters.

Natalie found the training course to be demanding. Substantial emphasis was placed on individual initiative and accomplishments, often pitting trainees against one another in business simulations. Natalie thought the emphasis on individual action to be somewhat strange because the recruiter had stressed that Enigma's success was based on teamwork and esprit de corps. Although she was in a class with 40 other trainees, Natalie found it difficult to make friends with her cohorts. The rigors of the training and the emphasis on individual competitiveness left little time or inclination for personal bonds to be established. Near the end of the training period, Natalie received her first performance evaluation. The instructors saw her intelligence and technical skills as strong points but also noted that she needed to be more decisive, become more sensitive to customer needs, and develop a "killer instinct" when dealing with employee behavior difficulties. Even though the training was not exactly what she had expected, Natalie still believed that she was well prepared for a regular store assignment.

After completion of the training course, Natalie was filled with confidence as she began her career as an assistant manager at one of Enigma's busiest and most profitable stores in suburban New Jersey. Although the competitiveness of the training course was a surprise, she looked forward to the assignment in New Jersey because it was close to her parent's home in eastern Pennsylvania and it was within easy driving distance to New York and Philadelphia. As an assistant manager, Natalie was given significant responsibility for the Housewares department. She was told that her duties covered all aspects of the department, including inventory control, customer service, staff scheduling and hiring, and merchandise presentation. It was explained to Natalie that her "normal" work week would be Tuesday through Saturday, from 9:30 AM to 6:30 PM but that Enigma's culture dictated that the managers see their responsibility to their stores as being 24 hours a day, seven days a week.

ONE YEAR LATER

Natalie has really begun to dread these visits to the physician's office. The regular migraine headaches she developed from the very beginning of her time at Enigma were bad enough, but now the heartburn and stomach distress are almost unbearable. While she sat in the physician's office, Natalie began to reflect on the past year at Enigma. The first 6 months had been really overwhelming. It took her a while to comprehend Enigma's use of a Darwinian "survival of the fittest" approach to employee development and retention. She had been thrown into the Housewares department with virtually no advance preview on the workings of the operation or the personnel. When she did meet with her boss in the afternoon of her second day, Natalie was told, for the first of many times, that this is a "sink or swim assignment, so you better dive in and start swimming."

The staff in Housewares included a mixture of full- and part-time employees. Generally, the full-time staff were assigned to Housewares on a permanent basis, whereas part-timers could be assigned to any department in the store, depending on such factors as absenteeism or promotional campaigns. From the start of her assignment, Natalie felt a sense of hostility toward her from three full-time staff members, each of whom had been with Enigma for more than 5 years. Natalie believes that the hostility, which had subsided somewhat just in the past few weeks, resulted from two factors. First, the longer-tenured staff resented her being given the job of assistant manager without having paid any "dues" on the front lines of the department. Second, nearly all the staff at the Enigma store had a negative view of management, primarily because of what were seen at Enigma's abusive demands and "factory-like" approaches toward the supervision of its employees.

Natalie could accept the first factor because it was true that she was only out of college for less than 6 months and she was supervising people who had been with the store for many years. Natalie was dismayed over the second factor but saw its validity. During her recruitment, Enigma portrayed itself as a progressive and caring organization that was concerned about the quality of life of its employees. Yet the 3-month training program and her work experiences clearly pointed to a different organization, one that saw its employees as nothing more than human capital that could be used up and then replaced. Horror stories (and turnover) were commonplace. Employees were regularly called on to work ridiculous hours or abandon personal plans at the last minute because they were needed at the store. Also, the managerial culture dictated that employee difficulties were dealt with in an aggressive and dispassionate way. The abusive attitude toward the staff and the culture were troubling to Natalie because they went against the grain of her personality. She had always viewed herself as a friendly and caring person, but the store demanded that she think and act differently or risk being seen as not a team player.

Natalie's relationships with her boss and her fellow assistant managers were strained, to say the least. The competitiveness that was fostered in the training program carried over into operations of the stores. Natalie's boss, a single woman in her mid-30s, was overtly ambitious, and she had no qualms about telling everyone who would listen that her goal was to be a vice president and regional manager by the time she was 40. The boss appreciated the contributions of the people who worked for her, but only to the extent that they could be instrumental in taking her to the next level. Natalie believed that if she showed too much ambition or in any way tried to question the established procedures or culture, she would be seen as a threat and labeled a maverick and not supportive of the management team or Enigma's mission. So, Natalie learned to implement changes and improvements in her department in a quiet fashion. Also, she tried to create a new culture within Housewares that encouraged teamwork as a way to improve performance. Through her efforts, Housewares had shown steady performance gains, and by the end of Natalie's first year, it was one of the top two departments in the store.

When it came to her relationships with her contemporaries, Natalie continued to find it difficult to create any sort of personal or emotional ties with the 11 other assistant managers. The encouragement of individualistic behavior, brought on by the store's penchant for interdepartmental performance comparisons, created a working environment in which everyone was most concerned with his or her own performance, not the performance of the store in total. This environment also led to a variety of political behaviors being used, from backstabbing to outright sabotage. Although it took a little while, Natalie caught on to the self-serving games and had learned how to act when confronted with political behaviors.

In her personal life, it was tough for Natalie to engage in any social activities, let alone find an intimate relationship. She had been putting in 70-hour work weeks throughout her first year with Enigma, and the grueling schedule left little time for leisure or exercise. She realized that her health problems were partly attributable to a lack of outside interests that could have served to reduce stress. Just within the past 2 months, Natalie has vowed to spend more time in activities outside of work. She joined a health club and started socializing more with family and friends.

Despite all the tribulations of the past year, Natalie believed that she had grown in the managerial position at Enigma. The work culture was not real positive, and she still felt some residual hostility from her subordinates, but she had learned to cope and had actually been successful in putting her own imprint on the workings of her department and the store. After 6 months on the job she had wanted to quit, but now, even with the migraines, the heartburn, and the advice of her physician to find a less stressful job, she thought she would stick it out for a while longer.

FIVE YEARS LATER

Natalie's career at Enigma is now at a crossroads. She is confronted with some rough decisions concerning both her professional and her personal lives. Enigma has recently offered her the chance to become the manager of its Seattle store. She would be given complete responsibility for the store operations, would receive a 40 percent salary increase, and could garner a sizable performance bonus after 1 year. Although flattered by the opportunity, Natalie has other factors to consider. She is engaged to be married, and the wedding date is just 8 months away. Her husband-to-be has made it clear that he is not in favor of a move to the West Coast. Besides, they had talked about starting a family in the next 2 years and a move to Seattle would take them far away from their parents and other relatives who would willingly satisfy any child care needs that might arise if they did have children.

Natalie needed some time to ponder her choices. The past 4 years at Enigma had been an emotional roller coaster. She had thought about leaving Enigma on several occasions but had never "tested the waters." She always believed that the pros of staying with the company outweighed the cons. The extensive demands of the job had kept her busy, and the corporate culture still served to create unnecessary animosity and obstacles. But Enigma showed that they believed in her ability by promoting her a year ago to deputy store manager and by paying for her to attend a number of executive development programs. Most of her friends from college were still trying to move into an initial management position. They were amazed at the experiences Natalie had already encountered. Natalie had likened her situation to being in quicksand, the deeper she had gotten into Enigma, the harder it was to get out. In the back of her mind, she often wondered whether other employers or another type of career would be a better fit for her and her aspirations. In fact, she often dreamed of becoming an entrepreneur by opening up a high-end housewares store. Five years of her life had been devoted to Enigma, 5 years of headaches, stress, and various political battles. But the 5 years of rewards had been there, too, nice salary increases, bonuses, and a major promotion.

The West Coast regional manager wanted an answer in 2 days. If Natalie did not take the promotion, it would please her fiancé and her family, but she knew it would be difficult to get another opportunity to be a store manager anytime soon. If she did take the promotion, she was looking at escalating demands, with even more stress and headaches. Natalie believed that if she really pressured her fiancé he would, reluctantly, agree to move to Seattle. And she rationalized that they could always find some sort of child care arrangement out there when they did have kids. But she still had not ruled out the possibility of starting her own business. One way or another, this was the toughest decision she had ever faced in her life.

CASE ANALYSIS QUESTIONS

1. Critique the process Natalie went through in her selection of Enigma as an employer. Do you think the selection of Enigma was right for her? What could she have done differently in her job search?

2. Do think Enigma was right in the approaches it used to recruit Natalie? Should an employer have a moral obligation to always use realistic recruitment?

3. Do you believe that the "survival of the fittest" approach that Enigma used in developing its managers was an appropriate strategy? Do you think Natalie should have been more forceful in trying to correct managerial and cultural wrongs that she observed?

4. Do you agree with Natalie's decision to "stick it out for a while longer" with Enigma after she had been on the job for a year? Should Natalie have been more proactive in considering other employment options at this point in her career?

5. If you were in Natalie's shoes after 5 years with Enigma, what career and life choices would you be prepared to make? What are the key factors that you would consider in making your choices?

6. If you were to write a continuation to this case, what would you predict for Natalie for the future, say, 10 or 15 years after her college graduation? Would it be a happy or an unhappy future?

ENDNOTES

1. Enigma is a fictitious name and should not be confused with any real company.

3

GEORGE THE BANKER

George did not know what to think. The walk to the train, the train ride, and the drive home involved no effort at consciousness. His world was in turmoil, and he did not know whether to feel anger or relief, exhaustion or despair.

George had what most would consider a "good job," vice president in the accounting department of Obelisk Bank.[1] Obelisk was a medium-sized regional bank with just more than $2 billion in deposits. At 54 years of age, George had believed he would retire comfortably from Obelisk on his own terms and when he decided it was time. George had begun working at Obelisk nearly 23 years ago. After high school, he had spent 4 years in the marines and then used the GI bill to get his bachelors degree in accounting. After spending 6 years in public accounting, during which time he gained his CPA, George joined Obelisk as an assistant controller. His early career at the bank had progressed nicely, but he had held his current position for the past 8 years. George was generally pleased with his work and his record of achievements, although since his mid-40s a vague sense of unfulfillment and even disenchantment had taken hold. He knew that the lack of an MBA prevented him from advancing, and he recognized that he had been passed over for promotion, in deference to much younger colleagues, twice within the past 4 years. He even half-heartedly entertained the notion of returning to school for his MBA, but age and a lack of real desire, he believed, precluded this.

George's oldest daughter was graduating from college this year, and she was planning to attend graduate school in the fall. His youngest daughter was entering college as well. George was proud to tell his co-workers how he was putting his two daughters through college. George's wife returned to work 5 years ago, managing a gift shop. Her salary was a nice addition to the family income, but it really did not go very far in paying the bills. College tuitions were a real financial strain, and there were still 9 more years to go on the mortgage. As was the case with his father before him, George saw his primary life role as breadwinner of the family. For financial, emotional, and psychological reasons, George was nowhere near ready for retirement.

George had gone to work that morning as always. For the past 3 months, Obelisk had been abuzz with rumors that it was the object of a takeover by a large bank from another state. The bank's senior management had even written an open letter to the employees, telling them, in no uncertain terms, that the bank was not for sale and that the management would resist any and all takeover bids.

George felt encouraged by the letter to the employees. He personally believed that the bank's senior management would take whatever steps were necessary to keep the bank from being acquired.

George began to reflect back on one of the many maxims his high school football coach had told his players—"the worst hit in football is when you're blind sided, because you never see it coming and you really can't prepare for it." George now had a better appreciation than ever for his old coach's words of wisdom. In the late afternoon that day, he had gotten a call from one of the secretaries in Human Resources that the head of HR needed to see him immediately. The message from the senior vice president of Human Resources was delivered bluntly. Obelisk was cutting costs as a means to stave off the takeover, and several officers were being targeted for dismissal. George was given two options. The bank either would "credit" him with an additional 3 years of service so he could take early retirement and earn a full pension when he turned 59.5 years of age, or it would give him a severance package of 1 year's salary, 6 months of medical coverage, and 3 months of outplacement services. George was given until the next day to make a decision, but with either option, his last day at Obelisk would be on Friday, just 3 days away.

When George got home, the house was empty. His two daughters were out, and his wife was working until 10 that night. George rarely had a drink after work, but tonight was different. He eased back in his chair, sipped his drink, and thought. About 20 years ago his college roommate had prodded him to join his firm. The salary was about the same, but they would pay for his MBA degree. Also, the chances to move beyond accounting and into more general management were strong. Twelve years ago, George's cousin had encouraged him to join her at her fledgling CPA firm. He could have come in as her partner, but the income was less certain and the benefits were nowhere near as good as they were at Obelisk. George networked extensively when he was younger, which had led to other solid job opportunities over the past several years. But each time he had a chance to move, he would remember what he would be giving up by leaving Obelisk. The bank was like a rock. And he knew two things—the bank offered security, and they would never let him go because he was too valuable. George became depressed as he grasped the reality that he had opted for security over opportunity every time.

George started feeling bitter. He had given his life to Obelisk, willingly working nights and weekends when necessary. He recalled the times he missed his daughters' school functions because he was so dedicated to the bank. He had never even taken more than 1 week of vacation at a time because he believed he was needed too much at the office to spare more than a week. George tried to figure out all the questions he needed to answer in the next few hours. They came to him quickly and in no logical order. How much is college tuition going to cost me over the next 4 years? How many more years am I going to live? Will my wife and I be able to travel the world like we had planned? What company would be willing to hire a 54-year-old accountant with a limited range of work experiences? What severance package makes the most sense? Should I think about opening my own business? Should I hire a lawyer and hit Obelisk with an age discrimination lawsuit? Will my family think I am a failure? Should we sell the house and move to something smaller?

George poured himself another drink. He heard the garage door closing and the familiar words "Hi honey, how was your day?"

CASE ANALYSIS QUESTIONS

1. How would you rate Obelisk's approach to the dismissal of George? What could/should they have done differently?

2. Why do you think George was blind-sided by his dismissal? Do you think there was any way he could have seen the dismissal coming?

3. Why do you think George "opted for security over opportunity every time?"

4. Do you think George has a right to be bitter at Obelisk?

5. What do you see as the key issues for George as he decides what to do with his career in the short run and over the longer term? What actions should he take in seeking reemployment?

6. If you were to make a prediction, what do you think George's career and life will look like 5 years into the future?

ENDNOTES

1. Obelisk Bank is a fictitious name and should not be confused with any real company.

CONTEMPORARY ISSUES IN CAREER MANAGEMENT

10

Job Stress

Remember Richard's story from Chapter 1. Richard had been out of a job for the first time in his adult life, and had recently found a high level position in the information systems group of a brokerage firm. The firm was undergoing a major reorganization, and Richard was uncertain about his future. Today, Richard's life is even more complex than it had been.

Richard is now a 43-year-old father of two college students. He has worked hard all his life to enable his children to go to the colleges they chose—and now he is paying two substantial tuition bills with no financial assistance. Alicia, Richard's wife, has started her own decorative painting business and has been successful providing services for her customers. She is considering opening a retail store to provide wallpaper and other interior decorating items to complement her decorative painting services. Alicia is excited about this new opportunity and is deeply involved in making her business a success. She will need a sizable amount of capital to finance the retail store. Alicia and Richard have spoken about getting a bank loan to provide capital for her start-up business.

Richard had received a promotion about 1 year ago to vice president of information systems. Although the company continues to have major reorganizations and personnel reshufflings, Richard perseveres in his role, yet is troubled by many events. Richard has often had to meet his budgetary constraints, which included minimizing contract employees. Also, he does not believe that he will experience any growth in his current job, and with all the organizational turbulence, he does not foresee getting any other new job opportunities within his company in the future. He goes through the motions at work in an attempt to stay out of the "line of fire." Richard's drive to succeed in his business goals seems to be overshadowed by the daily worries of downsizings. Although he is happy for Alicia and her success, he is concerned about additional debt and their ability to repay her business loan, the kids' tuitions, and the mortgage.

Richard often feels like he has lost control of everything. Job and life stress have drained Richard of his enthusiasm and zest for work and life. He has difficulty communicating with his family and co-workers and oftentimes does not feel as close to people as he had been. Richard sometimes has anxiety attacks but does not think he needs to see a physician for help. Perhaps most significantly, although Richard is uncomfortable with his personal and professional situations, he does not know where to turn for support. Although from a distance Richard's career is an unqualified success, the quality of his life—his happiness and sense of well-being—leaves a great deal to be desired.

The presence of job stress in the workplace is a major concern both for employees and organizational managers. Stress has taken an immense toll on the physical and emotional health of individuals, as well as the bottom lines of organizations. Indeed, stress can lead to such negative consequences as depression, burnout, and psychosomatic illnesses, as well as low job satisfaction.[1] Further, it has been estimated that stress causes upwards of $200 billion in additional cost to American business due to increased absenteeism and turnover, lower productivity, and higher medical costs. Studies found that 72 percent of workers often experience stress-related illness, 34 percent have thought about quitting because of stress, and 27 percent say their job is the single greatest cause of stress in their lives. Although pressures emanate from several sources—long work hours and poor communication at work, greater job demands, and little control over one's work, as well as personal financial worries—the most frequently cited cause of stress was balancing work and family lives.[2] Richard's worries are more common than he may think.

The incidence and magnitude of stress experienced in today's business environment continue to escalate. Fierce international competition, mergers and acquisitions, and economic conditions have forced companies to cut costs and stay "lean and mean" to survive. These actions have placed additional work pressures and demands on nearly every employee, and the consequence is more stress. Further, individuals respond differently to high levels of stress. One study found that work-related stress caused many employees to act unethically, and in some cases illegally, on the job. Cutting corners on quality and covering up mistakes were the two most prevalent actions employees attributed to high stress levels.[3] Clearly, the effects of unmanaged stress may be devastating for the employee and for the organization.

In this chapter, we examine the implications of job stress. First, we define stress and identify its sources and consequences. Then, we examine three particular sources of job stress that have been subject to much scrutiny—Type A behavior, career transitions, and bias in the workplace. In addition, we discuss job burnout, which has been described extensively in the popular press. We conclude this chapter by offering ways in which individuals and organizations can better manage stress.

Individuals must become more aware of the role of stress in their lives. Extreme levels of stress can seriously impair an employee's physical and psychological functioning and an organization's effectiveness. Moreover, job stress will not go away by itself. One needs to understand the nature of job stress before it can be controlled. Finally, one needs to understand the support mechanisms that are available for coping with job stress.

JOB STRESS: AN OVERVIEW

Stress is produced by an interaction between a person and the environment that is perceived to be so trying or burdensome that it exceeds one's coping resources.[4] In a more basic sense, stress is aroused when a person is confronted with an opportunity, a constraint, or a demand.[5] An opportunity is a situation in which a person stands to gain additional gratification of his or her significant values or desires, as in a new work assignment or promotion. A constraint, however, threatens to block additional gratification, a limitation as, for example, when a job promotion is denied. A demand threatens to remove a person from a currently gratifying situation, as when one is fired from a job.

A particular situation can simultaneously represent an opportunity, a constraint, and a demand. A new, challenging work assignment, for instance, may represent an opportunity to develop skills and acquire needed exposure, but it can also constrain one from spending more time with family and can become a demand if it overloads one to the point that work effectiveness and satisfaction suffer. A situation—be it an opportunity, constraint, or demand—is stressful when it exceeds or threatens to exceed the individual's capacity to handle it.

For stress to be aroused, the outcome of the situation must be uncertain, yet important to the individual.[6] Uncertainty, unpredictability, and fear of the unknown breed stress. If one knows for sure that a new job will be satisfying and stable, it will not be nearly so stressful as if the outcome is in doubt. In addition, if people are indifferent to their reputation in the organization or if they are not terribly concerned about future advancement, then neither a new work assignment nor a new job will produce much stress. People have to care about situations for them to be stressful. Consider the case of Mary, a recent MBA, who

> spent a sleepless night contemplating her first presentation before the executive committee of her new employer. She had spent much of the past 6 months preparing the report for her presentation and viewed it as the first real test of her managerial potential. Mary's presentation lasted 5 minutes and was followed by about 10 minutes of questions from committee members. Mary was thanked for making a fine presentation and was then dismissed from the meeting by the firm's president. She quickly went to the nearest women's lounge and in a release of tension shook uncontrollably.[7]

Mary's presentation represented a potential opportunity to test herself and impress her boss, but it also posed a threat to her self-esteem and still-unformed reputation in the company. Although she did not know how well the presentation would go, she cared deeply about the outcome because it was important to her career. Under these circumstances, it is understandable why Mary experienced such stress.

SOURCES AND CONSEQUENCES OF STRESS

Exhibit 10.1 presents an overview of the job stress process. Based on research from many sources, this approach distinguishes environmental stressors from the perception of stress, from strain symptoms, and from the outcomes of stress.[8] Table 10.1 identifies a number of potential environmental stressors. Many of them are familiar and require little elaboration. Stress can be produced by work

· EXHIBIT 10-1

JOB STRESS PROCESS

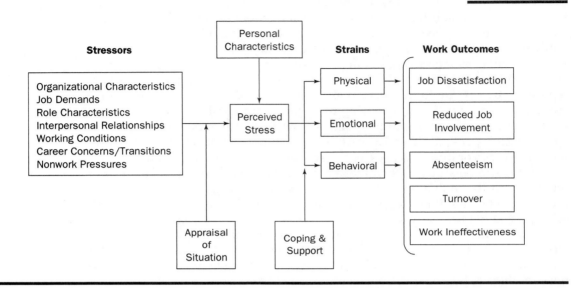

situations that are ambiguous, that overload (or underload) one's capacities, that require extraordinary time commitments, or that put one in the middle of two conflicting people or groups.[9]

Stress can have its roots in organizational policies or practices, in the demands of the job itself, and in the nature of the physical and social context of work. Moreover, different major occupational groupings can produce varying degrees of stress. Stress can be produced by work and nonwork pressures and by such career concerns as obsolescence, employment discrimination, and threatened job loss.[10]

The presence of an environmental stressor does not inevitably produce stress. It depends on how the situation is interpreted or appraised. Some people may not see a situation as particularly important, thereby reducing the level of perceived stress. For example, if Mary's career were not so important to her, the prospective presentation would not have produced much stress. Or one may be so confident about one's ability to handle a situation that it is not viewed as threatening or uncertain. Therefore, what is perceived as stressful by one person may not be seen as stressful by another.

It has also been argued that even though certain job conditions may inherently have an adverse influence on employees' emotional reactions, they may not have a negative effect on overall subjective well-being because of the economic necessity of the given job.[11] More precisely, individuals may accept the stress of

· **TABLE 10-1**

ILLUSTRATIONS OF
ENVIRONMENTAL STRESSORS

Organizational Characteristics

Centralization, low participation in
    decision making
Poor communication
Pay inequities

Job Demands

Time pressure and deadlines
Responsibility for people
Repetitive work

Role Characteristics

Role conflict: caught between conflicting
    expectations
Role ambiguity: lack of clarity about
    expectations or performance
Role overload/underload: too much or too
    little work

Interpersonal Relationships

Conflict within and between groups
Competition
Inconsiderate or inequitable supervision

Working Conditions

Crowding
Noise
Excessive heat or cold

Career Concerns/Transitions

Change of job, employer, location
Obsolescence
Career plateau
Bias in the workplace
Loss of employment
Retirement

Nonwork Pressures

Family conflicts
Life changes, for example, divorce, illness
or death of loved one, birth of child

Adapted from a longer list developed by Brief, Schuler, and Van Sell (1981). A. P. Brief, R. S. Schuler, and M. Van Sell. *Managing Job Stress.* Boston, MA: Little, Brown and Company, 1981.

an undesirable job because of the financial rewards and status that the job generates. In short, economic dependency can breed attachment to a job that one otherwise despises.

Certain personal characteristics can produce stress over and above the effects of particular environmental pressures. For example, highly anxious employees tend to experience high levels of stress, regardless of the environmental conditions.[12] Other personal qualities, such as Type A characteristics, inflexibility, intolerance of ambiguity, and neuroticism can also heighten feelings of stress.[13] In addition, some individuals may simply have a personal disposition toward stress, wherein a person experiences stress regardless of the work situation.[14] The important point is that stress can be produced by a particular situation that is interpreted as threatening, as well as by a general personal tendency to perceive life circumstances as stressful.

Perceived stress can produce a number of different strain symptoms. These strains may become manifest in a variety of physical, emotional, and behavioral

· TABLE 10-2

ILLUSTRATIONS OF STRAIN SYMPTOMS

Physical

Short-term: heart rate, galvanic skin response, respiration
Long-term: ulcer, blood pressure, heart attack
Nonspecific: adrenaline, gastric acid production

Behavioral

Sudden change in use of alcohol
Sudden change in smoking habits
Sudden, noticeable weight loss or gain
Difficult breathing

Emotional

Apathy, boredom
Inattentiveness, loss of ability to concentrate
Irritability
Negativism

Taken from a longer list developed by Schuler (1980)., R. S. Schuler, "Definition and Conceptualization of Stress in Organizations." *Organizational Behavior and Human Performance* 24(1980):115–130.

changes (Table 10.2). The impact of work stress on physical and psychological health is well documented. In fact, stress has been linked with cardiovascular disease, gastrointestinal disorders, susceptibility to viruses, overeating, drug and alcohol abuse, and other related health problems.[15]

Of course, not everyone who experiences stress will develop these strain symptoms. Some people have a naturally high capacity for stress. In addition, effective coping skills can help protect people from the ravaging effects of extreme stress. Further, the availability of support from others can help keep stress within manageable bounds so that people do not experience such negative reactions to stressful situations.

Extensive strain can reduce job involvement and productivity and increase job dissatisfaction, absenteeism, and turnover. In short, extensive work stress may not only prove dangerous to one's physical and emotional well-being but may also produce dysfunctional consequences for the organization. Exposure to stress over a long period of time can be so debilitating that it has a significant impact on both health and productivity.[16] Moreover, research has found that excessive stress is strongly related to workplace harassment and violence. Millions of Americans have been found to be victims of a physical assault on the job, physically threatened, or harassed.[17]

It is important to recognize that stress is not necessarily harmful per se. In fact, many researchers have concluded that a moderate level of stress enhances performance and health. As Exhibit 10.2 indicates, extreme levels of stress (low or high) can be distressful because they serve either to understimulate or overstimulate. Optimal levels of stress can be challenging and produce eustress (positive feelings and high involvement) rather than distress. Therefore, stress must be managed so that a proper balance is created which allows for optimum functioning for individuals and organizations.[18]

· EXHIBIT 10-2

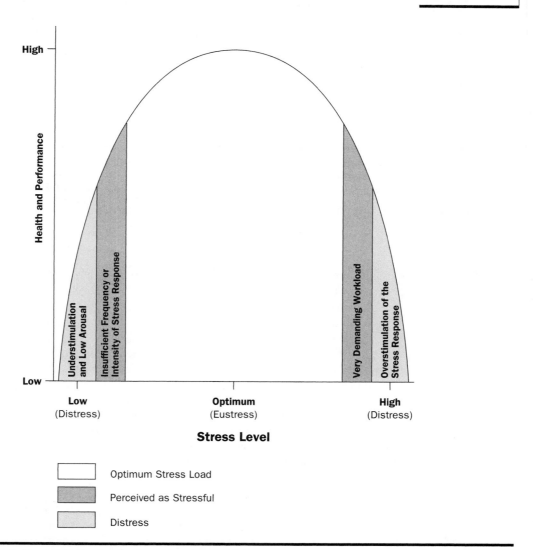

SOURCE: Quick, J. C., and J. D. Quick. *Preventive Stress Management in Organizations.* Washington, DC: American Psychological Association, 1997. Copyright © 1997 by the American Psychological Association. Reprinted with permission.

TYPE A BEHAVIOR AS A SOURCE OF STRESS

As noted earlier, personal needs, motives, and behavior patterns can produce stress. One such behavior pattern, known as Type A, is characterized by a hard-

· TABLE 10-3

**SALES TYPE A
PERSONALITY SCALE**

1. I hate giving up before I'm absolutely sure that I'm licked.

2. Sometimes I feel that I shouldn't be working so hard, but something drives me on.

3. I thrive on challenging situations. The more challenges I have, the better.

4. In comparison to most people I know, I'm very involved in my work.

5. It seems as if I need 30 hours a day to finish all the things I'm faced with.

6. In general, I approach my work more seriously than most people I know.

7. I guess there are some people who can be nonchalant about their work, but I'm not one.

8. My achievements are considered to be significantly higher than those of most people I know.

Type A Personality Scale developed by S. M. Sales and reported in Caplan, Cobb, French, Harrison, and Pinneau (1975). Each item is answered on a seven-point scale from 1 (very true of you) to 7 (not at all true of you). The lower the score, the stronger the indication of Type A personality. R. D. Caplan, S. Cobb, J. R. P. French, R. V. Harrison, and S. R. Pinneau. *Job Demands and Worker Health: Main Effects and Occupational Differences.* Washington, DC: Department of Health, Education, and Welfare Publication No. (NIOSH) 75–160, 1975.

driving competitiveness, a sense of extreme impatience and time urgency, a fast paced life-style, a preference for performing many activities simultaneously, and a constant striving for achievement and perfection.[19] In an extensive study of the Type A personality among employed adults, researchers found Type A individuals to be extraverted, job-involved, power-oriented, and achievement-oriented.[20] They were also tolerant of ambiguous situations, demonstrated characteristically male behaviors, and showed a comparatively high level of self-esteem. By contrast, the Type B pattern has been characterized as having low or moderate levels of competitiveness, a higher degree of patience, and a less intense need for accomplishment and perfection. A scale designed to assess Type A behavior is shown in Table 10.3.

It is believed that the Type A pattern is produced by certain beliefs and fears that people hold about themselves and the world. For example, Type A individuals tend to base their sense of self-worth on their attainment of material success. They often believe that there are no universal moral principles to guide behavior and that one has to take "revenge" on the world to get what is wanted.[21] It is no wonder that such individuals are constantly striving to accomplish and compete!

On the positive side, Type A employees tend to be involved in their jobs and hold high levels of occupational self-esteem.[22] Moreover, they can be more productive than their Type B colleagues, largely because of their internal belief of self-competence, ability to juggle multiple projects, and tendency to develop high performance goals.[23]

However, the Type A behavior pattern is not without its costs. These individuals are more likely to show aggressiveness, anger, hostility, and time urgency, factors that are predictive of coronary heart disease.[24] Indeed, Type As are more than twice as likely as Type Bs to die prematurely from coronary heart disease, are more likely to have a severe heart attack, and are more likely to have a second heart attack if they survive their first.[25] Furthermore, Type As tend to take on heavy work loads and complex work projects, work long hours, travel extensively, and develop workaholic tendencies and a high fear of failure. They are likely to feel alienated from others and dissatisfied with interpersonal relationships, feel depressed, and develop marital problems.[26]

Programs have been developed to help Type As alter their behavior. Many of these programs involve self-appraisal, a reorientation of one's philosophy of life, behavior therapy, and/or psychotherapy.[27] Might the reduction of Type A behavior, however, render the employee less productive on the job? Some researchers think not. A study observed that only one aspect of Type A behavior—work involvement—was related to productivity, whereas competitive drive and impatience were not.[28] Another study found that individuals with "personal power" (one's perception of control over time and resources) were more likely to stay healthy in work situations with high amounts of pressure.[29] The implications are that employees who successfully reduce their competitiveness and impatience, and who increase their "personal power," can reduce the likelihood of poor health under stressful situations without impairing their level of job performance.

CAREER TRANSITIONS AS A SOURCE OF STRESS

As noted in Chapter 7, interrole transitions involve changes in objective role characteristics, as when a person takes a first job, gets promoted, or changes employers. Intrarole transitions involve an adjustment in orientation to a role currently held, as illustrated by alterations in attitudes toward a job due to changes in job duties or colleagues. All career transitions involve changes and contrasts between old and new settings. There may also be surprises (positive or negative) when expectations do not match reality.[30]

For example, a recently transferred and relocated employee has many adjustments to make: a new job, a new boss, a new group of colleagues, a new office, maybe even new work norms and expectations. There also is a different home in a different community, new neighbors, and if there are children, new schools to enter and new friendships to form.

Granted, career transitions often require adjustments to new tasks, relationships, and expectations. But do they really produce extensive stress? As was discussed in Chapter 9, one form of transition, job loss, has been linked to such strain symptoms as poor health, depression, insomnia, irritability, low self-esteem, and a feeling of helplessness. Yet the research reveals no generally applicable relationship between career transitions and resultant stress. Janina Latack found virtually no association between job changes (primarily promotions) and stress.[31] In addition, there seem to be few differences in well-being between recently relocated managers and their less mobile colleagues.[32] In some cases, even recently terminated employees have been shown to adapt satisfactorily and emerge with a greater sense of control over their lives.[33]

When do career transitions produce high levels of stress?

1. Undesirable career transitions are more likely to be stressful than desirable transitions. Most employees probably desire promotions, and a promotion and salary increase generally accompany relocation. Job loss and uneployment, however, can be devastating to one's financial security and sense of self-worth. Evidence shows that life transitions that have negative connotations produce more psychological distress. In fact, several researchers have discussed how individuals who see being career plateaued as a "career failure" will experience job-related stress over time. Also, the reasons why employees plateau can affect the amount of stress they experience. For example, individuals who choose not to pursue a promotion experience less stress than those who believe that they have plateaued because the organization did not see them as worthy of a promotion.[34]

2. Career transitions that involve extensive changes, such as changing organizations or occupations, may produce more stress and a greater need to cope than transitions that involve fewer or smaller changes.[35]

3. Sudden, unexpected transitions may produce more shock and stress than gradual transitions. Also, uncertainty and fear over the effect of the transition can produce stress.[36] Expected changes with more certain consequences allow the individual to prepare for the transition and develop more constructive coping responses.

4. Career transitions accompanied by other life transitions (e.g., marriage, birth of a child, serious illness in the family) are likely to be more stressful than career transitions unencumbered by other major life alterations.[37] For example, Janina Latack found that employees undergoing a career transition and other substantial life transitions were more likely to cope by merely trying to reduce their stress symptoms, rather than by using problem-solving techniques to deal with the stressors themselves.[38]

5. Transitions that are forced on an individual may be more stressful than those under the individual's control.[39] A forced transition is probably less desirable than a self-initiated one, and the timing of such a change may be beyond the control of the individual. Transitions can be more stressful when the individual cannot control the onset or duration of the stress-producing situation.[40]

6. Some individuals are more resistant to transition-induced stress by virtue of their high level of self-esteem, feelings of personal control and tolerance for ambiguity, and an active, competent approach to life, qualities that have been refer to as "psychological resources" or "personal power."[41]

7. Support from family members, organizations, or friends can help reduce the harmful effects of transitions.

8. Individual coping strategies can help people deal with the changes and adjustments associated with transitions. For example, active problem

solving can turn a difficult transition into a positive learning experience.[42] A later section of this chapter reviews the characteristics of effective coping behavior.

In sum, transition-induced stress is likely to vary with specific characteristics of the transition, simultaneous life stresses, and the support, coping, and psychological resources available to the individual. Consider the following example:

> Debbie was feeling overwhelmed and desperate for help. Three months ago, she was unexpectedly promoted to quality assurance manager of her company. Although the promotion was flattering, the time demands have been extraordinary. She has been putting in 70-hour work weeks, and there is no relief in sight. Compounding matters, Debbie's home and family life are in a state of flux. As the divorced mother of a 3-year-old son, Debbie had relied on her mother to provide care for her child while she was at work. This child care arrangement was ideal for Debbie because it gave her flexibility to work as many hours as she needed without worry or guilt over the adequacy of supervision for her child. Unfortunately, 2 weeks ago Debbie received a call at work from the local hospital—her mother had a fall and had broken her hip. All at once, the stress in Debbie's life tripled—she had the demanding job, she lost the ideal child care arrangement for her son, and she had to find a way to care for her ailing mother. She feels like her head is about to explode, and she just does not know where to turn. She has no other immediate family members in the area, and her friends are just as busy with their lives as she is with hers. She knows her new boss would be unsympathetic, and she is unaware of any programs at her company to help her deal with the crisis situation.

This example highlights the multifaceted nature of transition-induced stress. The promotion to the new job, with the excessive time demands on Debbie, represents, in and of itself, a stress-provoking career transition. On top of that, other events in Debbie's life are producing added stress and strain. At the moment, Debbie does not see a way out of her plight (i.e., coping resources and support are not readily available to her). As we discuss later in this chapter, more innovative organizations are attuned to the needs of their employees who, like Debbie, are undergoing significant career transitions with related stress. Several programs are now offered by employers to assist their employees with transition-related conflicts, and researchers have discussed how organizations can help employees who are undergoing stressful transitions.[43] As an example, career transition workshops provide employees with support from others who are experiencing or have experienced the same transition, information about the transition and alternative options, and an opportunity to assess themselves and develop action plans. These workshop formats seem applicable to a wide variety of career transitions.

EMPLOYMENT BIAS AS A SOURCE OF STRESS

A wide range of factors, organizational and personal, can produce job stress. It is also possible that certain employees, especially women and people of color, can experience stress if they face bias and discrimination in their organization. Although it is not clear whether women and minorities experience more stress than other employees, it does seem likely that certain organizational and societal conditions can be particularly stressful for these groups.[44]

Debra Nelson and James Quick observed that women in male-dominated fields, especially professional women, are exposed to four unique stressors over and above the more general ones men experience: employment discrimination, sex role stereotyping, social isolation, and work-family conflicts.[45] In addition, many minority employees are subject to race stereotyping, restricted advancement opportunities, and social isolation.[46]

An employee exposed to bias, discrimination, and stereotyping becomes vulnerable to stress because of the lack of fit between talents/aspirations and organizational opportunities. An employee who occupies a token position is likely to feel alienated from the mainstream organization. And any "first"—for example, the first minority or female senior vice president in an organization—is likely to experience intense pressure and stress. These stressors include not just being the "first" through the glass ceiling but also having to deal with the biases of one's new organizational peers. Maintaining high levels of performance can create additional stress as women and people of color are usually watched closely to see if they are deserving of their new position. Stress can be experienced because the individual has become a role model for more junior minority group members in the organization.[47] Although being the "first" through the glass ceiling may be especially stressful, women and people of color at various positions throughout the organization may face extensive bias.

Again, not all minorities face bias and isolation, and not all organizations stereotype and discriminate against their employees who are female or people of color. Rather, the research suggests the potential for these stressors and indicates the need for individuals and organizations to understand and modify these stressors when present. Undoubtedly, there is a need for additional research that focuses on the stress experienced by minorities and women and its individual and organizational outcomes.[48] Employment bias is discussed more thoroughly in Chapter 12.

BURNOUT

Dick Vermeil, currently the coach of the St. Louis Rams in the National Football League, made headlines in the early 1980s when he cited burnout as the reason for leaving the coaching ranks. Since then, expressions of burnout have been voiced by many other corporate, government, and sports figures, who felt that the pressures of professional life were wearing them down. For example, Brenda Barnes, former PepsiCo executive, U.S. Representative Bill Paxon, and Diane Baker, The New York Times Company's former chief financial officer, have quit their jobs in an attempt to avoid burnout and better manage their family lives.[49]

Burnout is a psychological stress reaction most characteristic of people whose jobs involve a high degree of emotionally charged contact with other people.[50] Although initially it was thought that burnout was only associated with jobs concentrated in the human services sector of the economy, burnout is more widespread and appears in many professions.[51] Burnout has been likened to job depression and has been considered a motivational problem. Burned-out individuals become unable to do their jobs, mostly because of the powerlessness they experience when they get "in a rut."[52] Like depression, burnout is a complex phenomenon that may occur for a multitude of reasons and may become manifest in a variety of ways.

As Table 10.4 shows, burnout consists of three interrelated components or psychological reactions. First, continual contact with (and responsibility for) the problems of other people eventually produce a feeling of **emotional exhaustion.** To deal with the enervating features of their work, burned-out workers become cynical and callous toward others and begin to **depersonalize** relationships with the people they serve, treating them more like objects and less like people. Increasingly, the burned-out worker experiences a feeling of **low personal accomplishment** at work.[53]

Many of the causes of burnout are stressors encountered in the work environment: lack of rewards, control, clarity, and support. What enables these stressors to produce burnout are two personal characteristics mentioned in Table 10.4: idealistic expectations, and feelings of personal responsibility for failure.[54] For example, an idealistic technology consultant who enthusiastically expects to help his or her clients receive adequate resources from their organization to implement a new information system may feel frustrated and burned out when the resources are not forthcoming. The consultant may also begin to believe that his or her personal shortcomings are somehow responsible for the organization's unwillingness to provide these resources.

The other personal condition noted in Table 10.4 is an individual's predisposition to see the world in a positive or negative way. These tendencies to perceive events as either positive or negative may influence one's perception of stress.[55] Individuals with negative predispositions have been found to experience high role stress and high emotional exhaustion and depersonalization and to report low social support. Those with positive predispositions were found to report low burnout, high levels of personal achievement, high levels of organizational commitment and job satisfaction, and lower absenteeism and occupational injury.[56] Thus, the manner by which one views life events may increase (or decrease) chances for burnout.

Table 10.4 also identifies the consequences of employee burnout. Some common signs of burnout have been identified as,[57]

- Negative emotions. Although we all experience negative emotions, burned-out individuals experience negative emotions more often, usually until they become chronic and become emotionally fatigued.

- Interpersonal friction and withdrawal. When emotionally drained, burned-out individuals have less empathy for those with whom they work and live. Communications with these individuals becomes strained, and burnout victims are apt to withdraw to cope.

- Health suffers. As emotional reserves become depleted, so does physical resilience. Burnout victims often experience colds, headaches, insomnia, and backaches.

· **TABLE 10-4**

CAUSES AND CONSEQUENCES
OF EMPLOYEE BURNOUT

Causes	Psychological Reactions	Consequences
Organizational Conditions	Emotional Exhaustion	Negative Emotions
■ Lack of Rewards	Depersonalization	Interpersonal Friction
■ Lack of Control	Low Personal Achievement	Withdrawal
■ Lack of Clarity		Poor Health
■ Lack of Support		Declining Job Performance
		Substance Abuse
Personal Conditions		Feelings of Meaninglessness
■ Idealistic Expectations		
■ Personal Responsibility		
■ Predisposition to Stress		

SOURCE: Adapted from "Preventing Employee Burnout" by Susan E. Jackson and Randall S. Schuler, *Personnel*, March-April, 1983, p. 60. Copyright © 1983. Reprinted by permission of American Management Association International. The table has been amended to include findings from subsequent studies.

- Declining performance. As burnout progresses, individuals become bored and find it difficult to be enthusiastic and productive in their work.

- Substance abuse. To cope with stress, burnout victims may find themselves drinking more alcohol or coffee, using more drugs (prescription or otherwise), eating more (or less), and smoking more often.

- Feelings of meaninglessness. Burnout victims tend to become apathetic — thinking "so what" or "why bother?" Enthusiasm is replaced by cynicism.

The effects of burnout are not limited to the work domain. Burned-out police officers, for example, tend to be moody and anxious at home, spend off-hours away from family, have trouble sleeping at night, remain uninvolved in family matters, and become relatively dissatisfied with their marriages. It was also found that burnout, notably emotional exhaustion, influenced individuals' subsequent thoughts about leaving their jobs, as well as actual employee turnover.[58] Higher levels of burnout have also been related to increased violence in the workplace. Workers who describe themselves as highly stressed or burned out experienced twice the number of incidents of physical or emotional harassment than those who were less burned out.[59] Burnout, therefore, can have harmful effects on organizations, employees, and their families.

Organizations concerned about this problem can attempt to change the environment that is responsible for the burnout. Researchers recommended job previews that foster accurate expectations, participative decision making to increase the employee's control over the work environment, and positive performance feedback to enhance feelings of recognition.[60] Further, research has shown that supervisors' behavior and actions can play a major role in affecting the incidence of burnout.[61] Supervisors need to monitor the job demands that employees receive. Job demands that exceed one's capabilities create employee burnout. Employees in jobs with a high proclivity for burnout who receive supportive and considerate supervision show a lower incidence of burnout. Also, employees who are reassured of their worth and value show reduced degrees of burnout and increased organizational commitment.[62] In the light of these findings, organizations, especially those with jobs that have high susceptibility to burnout, should ensure that supervisors and others in leadership positions be supportive of their personnel and regularly acknowledge their value and worth. Organizational actions such as these can help prevent burnout from occurring.

Alternatively, organizations can help employees cope with the burnout they already experience. Counseling programs can be designed to help employees become aware of burnout symptoms, share their feelings with others, and examine changes they can make to alleviate the situation.[63] Employers are also offering on- or off-site wellness/fitness centers, karate and yoga classes, massages, and outdoor volleyball and basketball courts to allow employees to "burn off steam."[64] Obviously, these two approaches are not mutually exclusive. Organizations should try to change their environment to reduce the likelihood of burnout and, at the same time, provide counseling and support to employees who experience burnout symptoms.

COPING, SOCIAL SUPPORT, AND STRESS

None of us can, or should, go through life free of stress. All people experience career transitions, some of them traumatic. Jobs may be pressure-packed or routine and repetitive. Family circumstances, midlife reappraisal, job loss, and threats to health can all be stressful events. People who have survived life's trials are resourceful and have learned how to cope.

Coping behaviors enable individuals to avoid the harmful effects of stressful situations. Effective coping does not eliminate stress from our lives but reduces it to manageable levels and prevents it from producing severe emotional or physical strain. Research has identified three broad categories of coping responses.[65] First, one can attempt to change the situation that produces the stress; in other words, reduce or modify the actual stressors. Table 10.5 presents illustrations of this problem-focused coping strategy. Seeking clarification of job standards, reducing work load, taking on more varied assignments, or changing jobs are all examples of coping responses designed to alter the environment or the person's role in it.

A second type of coping response changes the meaning of the stressful environment without necessarily changing the stressors themselves. People can make a situation less threatening by cognitively reappraising it, making a comparison (favorable, of course) with others' conditions, looking for the positive and ignoring the negative features of the situation, or changing work or life priorities to be more consistent with the situation in which they find themselves.[66] The plateaued manager who places a greater emphasis on community service than on further vertical mobility illustrates this technique.

· TABLE 10-5

ILLUSTRATIONS OF COPING BEHAVIORS DESIGNED
TO CHANGE A STRESSFUL WORK ENVIRONMENT

1. Attempt to eliminate burdensome parts of job

2. Attempt to add or better use staff to relieve pressures

3. Attempt to build more challenge or responsibility into job

4. Seek clarification of job duties

5. Seek clarification of career prospects

6. Seek feedback on job performance

7. Seek more flexible work schedule

8. Seek job transfer

9. Seek different organization or career field

10. Seek others' advice

11. Attempt to upgrade job skills through education and/or experience

12. Attempt to resolve conflicts with supervisor, peers, and/or subordinates

13. Participate in career-planning program

A third form of coping attempts to manage the strain symptoms themselves. Relaxation techniques such as meditation or biofeedback, yoga, physical exercise, and recreation can effectively reduce such physical strains as elevated pulse rate and blood pressure.[67]

The first type of coping, in which one actively changes the source of the stress itself, seems to be the most useful strategy, especially in the long run. Yet it can be difficult to implement because it requires people to identify the source of the stress accurately and know how to modify the stressful situation. It is likely that changing the situation ought to be tried first because it attacks the root cause of the problem. If these efforts are either infeasible or unsuccessful, attempts can be made to change the meaning of the stressful environment. If neither of these strategies is appropriate or possible, employees can attempt to manage the strain symptoms directly. A combination of problem solving, cognitive reappraisal, and physical exercise/relaxation may be particularly useful in reducing some physical strains.[68]

Research has not yet indicated a specific type of coping response that is universally effective.[69] Like the implementation of specific career strategies discussed in Chapter 4, the effectiveness of specific coping activities undoubtedly depends on many factors: the severity of stress, the psychological and social resources of the individual, and the particular circumstances of the stressful situation. In effect, this is a contingency approach to coping, wherein a large repertoire of coping skills and positive attitudes toward oneself seems to be the most crucial factors in managing stress.

Edgar Schein developed a four-step approach that is consistent with this contingency approach to coping.[70] Step 1 involves diagnosing the situation and correctly identifying the real source of the problem. In this step, one needs to understand whether the stress comes from work, family, personal concerns, or some combination of these sources. Step 2 involves self-assessment. It is essential to take (and make) the time to reflect on feelings and motives and to be familiar with "blind spots" or other defenses that shield people from an insightful understanding of themselves.

In step 3, a coping response is selected. By talking with peers, family members, friends, neighbors, and community resources about problems and stresses and by establishing supportive relationships with others, one can choose an appropriate coping response. It is important to identify either an external coping resource (e.g., a confidant) or an internal resource (e.g., personal characteristic such as hardiness) so that the appropriate coping response is selected. Coping resources aid the person in choosing a healthy response.[71] The chosen response may involve changing an aspect of the stressful environment, shifting one's priorities and the meaning of the environment, or managing the strain symptoms themselves. Finally, step 4 involves understanding the effect (if any) of the coping response and making adjustments when necessary. Consider the following example:

Gene was scared. Over the past 3 months his health and physical well-being had gotten progressively worse. It started with recurring headaches and a nagging tightness in his back and shoulders. Over time, he experienced stomach distress, a shortness of breath, and chest pains. On top of it all, Gene had trouble sleeping, spending many nights just staring at the ceiling. The culmination of Gene's physical problems occurred one night while he was driving home from work, when he suddenly experienced an episode of tachycardia (a rapid heartbeat). He pulled off to the side of the road thinking his life was about to end. Eventually his heartbeat returned to normal, but the incident left him deeply concerned.

Gene called in sick the next day and saw his physician. He also began contemplating why these health problems were occurring. He concluded that his problems were the outcome of the stress he was experiencing in his life. He was recently transferred to another division of his company that, although not causing him to move his family, did double his commuting time. His commute now took 1.5 hours each way. In addition to the demands of the new job, Gene has had to deal with turmoil at home. His 16-year-old son was having problems in school—skipping classes and being disruptive when he did attend. The principal of the school had threatened suspension unless his son's behavior changed. Gene was afraid his son's current difficulties might eventually lead to something far more serious.

After diagnosing the sources of his stress, Gene began thinking about what was really important in his life. His job allowed him and his family to live comfortably and gave them financial security, but the commuting and work demands left little time for leisure and family activities. In short, he concluded that the excessive time he gave to his job had a negative effect on his and his family's well-being. His introspection and the conclusions he reached left Gene feeling a bit more at ease. He decided to talk to his wife and his brother about his thoughts. They both confirmed what he already knew—his job was causing physical and emotional harm.

Gene began discussing his options with his wife. They agreed that a new job, especially one closer to home, might give Gene the opportunity to spend more time with his family. He also knew that he needed to pay more attention to his diet and to begin an exercise program. With the support of his family, Gene started looking for a new job and he began playing tennis on a regular basis. Until he found a new position,

Gene resolved to devote as much time as he could to his son. By being there to listen to what his son had to say, Gene hoped to help his son through the emotional turmoil of being a teenager.

Overall, Gene recognized that he likely would be sacrificing financial rewards by taking a new job, but the anticipated reduction in stress and increased time for family and leisure activities would be well worth it.

This example highlights the effective use of the contingency approach to coping with stress. The physical manifestations of Gene's stress forced him to take time and evaluate his situation. This set the stage for Gene to go through a period of self-assessment, examining his values and goals. He then selected coping responses—finding a new work position, improving his diet and getting more exercise, and vowing to allow more time for his family. Finally, Gene sought to understand the effect of his intended actions—a trade-off between financial rewards and a lower level of stress.

Edgar Schein's approach emphasizes the importance of other people as sources of information and support. Social support has long been recognized as an invaluable aid to individuals undergoing conflict and stress, and its utilization is itself a form of coping.[72] Support from others can help people alter the stressful environment and "buffer" or protect them from the harmful effects of stress. In fact, individuals who reported high strain symptoms and high levels of social support reported lower health care costs than individuals who reported low strain symptoms. This finding suggests that individuals with social support systems may be better at coping and may interpret strains as eustress rather than distress.[73]

Support to help deal with stress can come from many sources, both informal (family, friends, co-workers) and formal (self-help groups, mental health or other professionals, and child care or other service providers). James House identified four classes of supportive behaviors: emotional, instrumental, informational, and appraisal.[74] Definitions and illustrations of these four types of support are provided in Table 10.6.

Again, no magic formula exists to identify the sources and types of social support that are most applicable to a specific situation. Understanding oneself, as well as the sources of stress and available resources, is a necessary preliminary step, but it is important to recognize that supportive relationships are not a one-way street. Especially with informal sources of support such as family or friends, one has to be willing to give support to receive it.

ORGANIZATIONAL ACTIONS

Organizations have begun to develop programs to reduce the level of employee stress. Using the distinction among the three types of coping responses, organizations can either alter the stressful environment, work with employees to change their interpretation of the environment, or help them manage their strain symptoms.

Illustrations of these approaches are shown in Table 10.7. Any particular program is likely to incorporate two or more of the coping strategies. For example, a program designed to build supportive work groups may simultane-

· TABLE 10-6

Type of Support	Meaning	Illustrations
Emotional	Empathy, caring, trust, love	Boss praises your effective performance
Instrumental	Behavior that directly helps person in need	Subordinate's improving performance relieves you of pressure
Informational	Information to be used by person to cope with problem	Co-worker gives you advice on how to discipline a subordinate
Appraisal	Information that provides feedback to person	Boss gives you constructive feedback on your most recent assignment
		Close friend gives you her opinion of your interpersonal style

Types and meanings of social support based on House (1981). J. S. House, *Work Stress and Social Support*. Reading, MA: Addision-Wesley, 1981.

ously try to change the stressful environment (by fostering constructive communication between individuals) as well as the meaning of the environment (e.g., understanding when competition is healthy and when cooperation is necessary).

Before any program is initiated, organizations must properly diagnose the extent and roots of employee stress. Such diagnoses may be organization-wide or may be applied to select groups of employees based on level (e.g., senior executives), job category (e.g., air traffic controllers), location (e.g., employees at a nuclear generating plant), or other relevant criteria (e.g., single parents). Organizational diagnoses can focus on the assessment of organizational stressors, the degree of employee strain, or employee characteristics that modify the strain symptoms. Organizations also need to be aware that each employee may react differently based on his or her affective response to the stressor (i.e., techniques that work for one employee may not work for all employees).[75] Examples of each type of diagnostic activity are shown below:

ASSESSMENT OF ORGANIZATIONAL STRESSORS

- Objective indicators of stress (e.g., turnover, absenteeism, accidents)
- Standardized questionnaires that measure organizational conditions (e.g., Stress Diagnostic Survey, Quality of Employment Survey)

ASSESSMENT OF EMPLOYEE STRAINS

- Physiological measures (e.g., pulse rate, blood pressure)
- Medical checklists
- Burnout or anxiety inventories

• TABLE 10-7

Reducing Stressors

Eliminate racial/gender stereotypes, biases, and discrimination
Redesign jobs to be more in line with employees' capabilities and interests
Clarify employee expectations through goal-setting program
Provide constructive performance feedback
Build supportive work groups
Train supervisors in interpersonal skills
Eliminate noxious elements of physical working conditions
Help employees with problem-solving/coping skills
Develop flexible work schedules
Develop programs for transitioned (e.g., relocated) employees

Changing the Meaning of Stressful Situations

Offer counseling services to employees
Run programs to ameliorate Type A behavior, burnout
Run programs on time management
Run social support groups for employees

Managing Strain Symptoms

Provide relaxation programs (e.g., meditation)
Provide facilities for physical exercise
Provide counseling and medical treatment
Provide comprehensive "wellness" programs

ASSESSMENT OF EMPLOYEE MODIFIERS OF STRAIN

- Coping mechanisms
- Social support
- Type A behavior pattern

Are organizations obligated to remove stressors from the work environment, or should they simply teach employees to adjust to the stressful environment more effectively? James Quick and Jonathan Quick offered this observation:

It is unreasonable to expect individuals to manage unnecessary and unreasonably harsh organizational demands. Some organizations wrongly expect individuals to adjust to inhumane working environments. However, individuals should expect organizational life to be demanding, and they must learn to manage reasonable requirements effectively. Therefore, the preventive management of organizational stress involves changing demands and practices within organizations as well as teaching individual methods for managing these stressors and their own responses to them.

Integration of individual and organizational approaches to preventive management is essential for optimal use of available human and material resources. Individuals should learn how to minimize the distress caused by inevitable and unchangeable stressors. At the same time, individual interventions should not be used to pacify employees in the face of unnecessarily distressful organizational practices. Organizational and individual health will be promoted by a balanced program of preventive management.[76]

Organizations must be attuned to the physical and emotional toll that stress can take on employees and the effect it can have on increased operating costs and reduced profit. As this chapter has discussed, stress can be minimized or managed through a number of actions, both individual and organizational. Organizations should ensure that basic steps are taken to reduce stress to the extent possible and that programs are offered to help individuals manage stress when its occurrence is inevitable.

The following are examples of organization-sponsored programs that help employees cope with stress, burnout, and other types of conflicts.

In 1979, Johnson & Johnson (J&J) headquartered in New Brunswick, New Jersey, began to take a proactive approach in dealing with employee stress. First, J&J attempts to minimize the amount of stress that is experienced. The provision of on-site child care facilities (six are located in New Jersey and Pennsylvania), the offering of elder care assistance, the allowance of up to 1 year of family care leave, and the training of supervisors and managers to be supportive of their employees, are all examples of programs intended to restrict the amount of stress produced. J&J also helps employees manage and cope with the stress they incur. The company's Health & Wellness® program represents a series of employee wellness initiatives designed to assist employees in stress management and physical well–being. Specific activities include a medical health assessment, weight control sessions, off-site confidential family and marital counseling, nutrition seminars, and state–o f–the–art physical fitness facilities. The Health & Wellness® program and the physical fitness centers at the various J&J facilities are managed by another J&J subsidiary, known as J&J–Health Care Systems Inc. (HCS). This subsidiary also manages similar wellness programs for other organizations. With total corporate sales rising from about $8 billion in 1987 to nearly $23 billion in 1997, J&J recognizes that rapid growth carries with it the danger of ever greater stress levels. To its credit, J&J has taken steps to limit the amount of stress generated and has put in place programs that help its employees manage stress when its occurrence is inevitable.[77]

Employees at Foster & Gallagher, Inc., in Peoria, Illinois, receive "Stress Buster" training. At these training sessions, employees learn what may cause stress in the workplace and how they might reduce stress. Ways to reduce stress include exercises that can be done right at the employee's desk, as well as "cool-down breaks." Employees may leave their work desks and go outside for walks or listen to music in their cars.[78]

Many companies, including Ameritech, offer employee assistance programs (EAPs). These programs were originally designed to treat employee alcohol and drug abuse problems but now include many benefits—from help with child/elder care services, to professional mental health assistance, to marital, legal, and financial help. EAPs attempt to aid employees with personal concerns so that they can be more focused and productive in the workplace.[79] One study found when organizations offered both EAPs and work/family programs, the level of employee stress was reduced, as was the incidence of tardiness, absenteeism, and turnover.[80]

Finally, many organizations, including IBM, Chase Manhattan Bank, and the U.S. Army, offer outplacement programs to assist employees as they transition from one career to another or from one employer to another. By offering these services, organizations help to relieve the employee's stress and ease the employee into a new position. Also, outplacement programs improve the organization's corporate image among both former and remaining employees, particularly after downsizings. A typical outplacement program involves three phases: the initial shock phase, when the program attempts to provide psychological and emotional support; the job search phase, when the program provides assistance in searching for new employment; and the phase-out period, when the program prepares clients to continue job searches independently.[81]

SUMMARY

Stress is aroused when an individual faces an opportunity, a constraint, or a demand. A situation is likely to be most stressful when the outcome is uncertain but is important to the individual. Stress can be produced by a number of conditions in the work environment—organizational characteristics, job demands, the quality of interpersonal relationships, working conditions, and career concerns—as well as pressures arising outside of work. Because individuals have different needs, competencies, and perspectives, a situation that is stressful to one person may not be stressful to another. A high level of stress can manifest itself in physiologic, emotional, and behavioral changes. It can ultimately lead to a decrease in job satisfaction, involvement, and performance and an increase in absenteeism and turnover.

This chapter examined three particular sources of stress. The Type A behavior pattern, characterized by a hard-driving competitiveness and sense of time urgency, can be physically and emotionally destructive. In addition, career transitions (e.g., promotions, relocations, or terminations) can be stressful under certain conditions: when they require extensive, unwanted adjustments, when they are accompanied by changes in other parts one's life, when they are unexpected and forced on an individual, and when the individual's coping and social support mechanisms are absent or ineffective. It was also suggested that stress is likely to be experienced by women and minorities who are exposed to bias and discrimination in their work environment.

Also examined was the concept of burnout, a stress reaction in which an individual in a highly charged work setting experiences emotional exhaustion, depersonalizes relationships with others, and begins to hold lower feelings of personal accomplishment. Burnout is most likely to be experienced by employees who initially held idealistic expectations about their job and who ultimately come to believe they are personally responsible for organizational failures.

People who survive stressful conditions have likely learned effective coping skills and/or have used supportive relationships with others. Because no single coping behavior is likely to be effective in all situations, individuals must learn to assess the situation and select appropriate responses. These coping responses may be directed toward changing the stressful environment, reappraising the environment, or reducing the resultant strain symptoms through such activities as relaxation and physical exercise. In a similar manner, organizations can help alleviate employee stress through a series of programs designed to change the stressful conditions, help employees adjust to the conditions, and/or reduce the negative strain symptoms.

ASSIGNMENT

Think about the types of work and nonwork stressors you may be experiencing. What types of symptoms have you encountered? How have you attempted to cope with these stressors? What types of positive or negative work outcomes have you experienced?

DISCUSSION QUESTIONS

1. Using House's four types of social support, provide examples of emotional, instrumental, informational, and appraisal support that you have received.
2. Characterize your levels of distress and eustress. What levels of stress can you tolerate? What levels of stress are harmful to you? What levels of stress are beneficial?
3. Using Schein's four-step coping model, describe a stressful situation that you currently experience and develop a plan for coping with the stress.

ENDNOTES

1. J. C. Latack, "Work, Stress, and Careers: A Preventive Approach to Maintaining Organizational Health," in *Handbook of Career Theory*, ed. M. B. Arthur, D. T. Hall, and B. S. Lawrence (Cambridge, UK: Cambridge University Press, 1989), 252–274.

2. P. Froiland, "What Cures Job Stress?" *Training* 30 (1993): 32–35; S. McKee, "Take It Easy! Companies Offer New Ways for Employees to Beat Job Stress," *Peoria Journal Star*, September 5, 1995. C1; L. Schiff, "Downsizing Workplace Stress," *Business and Health* 15 (1997): 45–46.

3. Schiff, "Downsizing Workplace Stress."

4. Latack, "Work, Stress, and Careers"; R. S. Lazarus and S. Folkman, *Stress, Appraisal and Coping* (New York: Behavioral Science Books, 1984).

5. R. S. Schuler, "Definition and Conceptualization of Stress in Organizations," *Organizational Behavior and Human Performance* 24 (1980): 115–130.

6. T. A. Beehr and R. S. Bhagat, *Human Stress and Cognition in Organizations: An Integrated Perspective* (New York: Wiley, 1985); Schuler, "Definition and Conceptualization of Stress in Organizations."

7. A. P. Brief, R. S. Schuler, and M. Van Sell, *Managing Job Stress* (Boston, MA: Little, Brown and Company, 1981); quote is on p. 7.

8. J. R. Eulberg, J. A. Weekley, and R. S. Bhagat, "Models of Stress in Organizational Research: A Metatheoretical Perspective," *Human Relations* 41 (1988): 331–350; S. Parasuraman and J. A. Alutto, "Sources and Outcomes of Stress in Organizational Settings: Toward the Development of a Structural Model," *Academy of Management Journal* 27 (1984): 330–350.

9. J. Schaubroeck and D. C. Ganster, "Chronic Demands and Responsivity to Challenge," *Journal of Applied Psychology* 78 (1993): 73–85; J. L. Xie and G. Johns, "Job Scope and Stress: Can Job Scope Be Too High?" *Academy of Management Journal* 38, no. 5 (1995): 1288–1309.

10. A. Keenan and T. J. Newton, "Work Difficulties and Stress in Young Professional Engineers," *Journal of Occupational Psychology* 60 (1987): 133–145; J. H. Greenhaus and S. Parasuraman, "A Work-Nonwork Interactive Perspective of Stress and Its Consequences," *Journal of Organizational Behavior Management* 8 (1986): 37–60.

11. A. P. Brief and J. M. Atieh, "Studying Job Stress: Are We Making Mountains out of Molehills?" *Journal of Occupational Behaviour* 8 (1987): 115–126.

12. Ibid.

13. M. J. Burke, A. P. Brief, and J. M. George, "The Role of Negative Affectivity in Understanding Relationships between Self-Reports of Stressors and Strains: A Comment on the Applied Psychological Literature," *Journal of Applied Psychology* 78, no. 3 (1993): 402–412; K. Fortj-Cozens, "Why Me? A Case Study of the Process of Perceived Occupational Stress," *Human Relations* 45 (1992): 131–141; Latack, "Work, Stress, and Careers."

14. D. L. Nelson and C. Sutton, "Chronic Work Stress and Coping: A Longitudinal Study and Suggested New Directions," *Academy of Management Journal* 33 (1990): 859–869; B. M. Staw, N. E. Bell, and J. A. Clausen, "The Dispositional Approach to Job Attitudes: A Lifetime Longitudinal Test," *Administrative Science Quarterly* 31 (1986): 56–77.

15. D. R. Frew, "How Stress Affects Productivity in Material Management," *Hospital Material Management Quarterly* 7 (1985): 30–36; J. Schaubroeck, D. C. Ganster, and B. E. Kemmerer, "Job Complexity, 'Type A' Behavior, and Cardiovascular Disorder: A Prospective Study," *Academy of Management Journal* 37, no. 2 (1994): 426–439.

16. Ibid.

17. Froiland, "What Cures Job Stress?"

18. J. C. Quick and J. D. Quick, *Organizational Stress and Preventive Management* (New York: McGraw-Hill, 1984).

19. Brief, Schuler, and Van Sell, *Managing Job Stress*; R. J. Burke and E. Deszca, "Career Success and Personal Failure Experiences and Type A Behaviour," *Journal of Occupational Behaviour* 3 (1982): 161–170.

20. D. C. Ganster, J. Schaubroeck, W. E. Sime, and B. T. Mayes, "The Nomological Validity of the Type A Personality among Employed Adults," *Journal of Applied Psychology* 76 (1991): 143–168.

21. R. J. Burke and E. Deszca, "What Makes Sammy Run—So Fast and So Aggressively? Beliefs and Fears Underlying Type A Behaviour," *Journal of Occupational Behaviour* 5 (1984): 219–227.

22. R. J. Burke and T. Weir, "The Type A Experience: Occupational and Life Demands, Satisfaction and Well-Being," *Journal of Human Stress* 6 (1980): 28–38.

23. J. M. Ivancevich and M. T. Matteson, "Type A Behavior and the Healthy Individual," *British Journal of Medical Psychology* 61 (1988): 37–56; C. Lee, S. J. Ashford, and P. Bobko, "Interactive Effects of Type A Behavior and Perceived Control on Worker Performance, Job Satisfaction, and Somatic Complaints," *Academy of Management Journal* 33 (1990): 870–881; M. S. Taylor, E. A. Locke, C. Lee, and M. E. Gist, "Type A Behavior and Faculty Research Productivity: What Are the Mechanisms?" *Organizational Behavior and Human Performance* 34 (1984): 402–418.

24. A. A. Booth-Kewley and H. S. Friedman, "Psychological Predictors of Heart Disease: A Quantitative Review," *Psychological Bulletin* 101 (1987): 343–362; C. Lee, S. J. Ashford, and P. Bobko, "Interactive Effects of Type A Behavior and Perceived Control on Worker Performance, Job Satisfaction, and Somatic Complaints," *Academy of Management Journal* 33 (1990): 870–881.

25. Burke and Deszca, "What Makes Sammy Run—So Fast and So Aggressively?"

26. A. P. Brief, D. E. Rude, and S. Rabinowitz, "The Impact of Type A Behavior Pattern on Subjective Workload and Depression," *Journal of Occupational Behaviour* 4 (1983): 157–164; Brief, Schuler, and Van Sell, *Managing Job Stress*; Burke and Deszca, "Career Success and Personal Failure Experiences and Type A Behaviour"; R. J. Burke and T. Weir, "The Type A Experience: Occupational and Life Demands, Satisfaction and Well-Being," *Journal of Human Stress* 6 (1980): 28–38; R. J. Burke, T. Weir, and R. E. DuWors, "Type A Behaviour of Administrators and Wives' Reports of Marital Satisfaction and Well-Being," *Journal of Applied Psychology* 64 (1979): 57–65; J. H. Howard, D. A. Cunningham, and P. A. Rechnitzer, "Work

Patterns Associated with Type A Behavior: A Managerial Population," *Human Relations* 30 (1977): 825–836; Schaubroeck, Ganster, and Kemmerer, "Job Complexity, 'Type A' Behavior, and Cardiovascular Disorder."

27. Quick and Quick, *Organizational Stress and Preventive Management*.

28. Taylor, Locke, Lee, and Gist, "Type A Behavior and Faculty Research Productivity."

29. Froiland, "What Cures Job Stress?"

30. M. R. Louis, "Career Transitions: Varieties and Commonalities," *Academy of Management Review* 5 (1980): 329–340.

31. J. C. Latack, "Career Transitions within Organizations: An Exploratory Study of Work, Nonwork, and Coping Strategies," *Organizational Behavior and Human Performance* 34 (1984): 296–322.

32. J. M. Brett, "Job Transfer and Well-Being," *Journal of Applied Psychology* 67 (1982): 450–463.

33. N. K. Schlossberg and Z. Leibowitz, "Organizational Support Systems as Buffers to Job Loss," *Journal of Vocational Behavior* 17 (1980): 204–217.

34. R. S. Bhagat, S. J. McQuaid, H. Lindholm, and J. Segovis, "Total Life Stress: A Multimethod Validation of the Construct and Its Effects on Organizationally Valued Outcomes and Withdrawal Behavior," *Journal of Applied Psychology* 70 (1985): 202–214; P. M. Elsass and D. A. Ralston, "Individual Responses to the Stress of Career Plateauing," *Journal of Management* 15 (1989): 35–47; V. M. Godshalk, "The Effects of Career Plateauing on Work and Non-work Outcomes," unpublished doctoral dissertation, Drexel University, 1997; J. Joseph, "Plateauism and Its Effect on Strain as Moderated by Career Motivation and Personal Resources," unpublished doctoral dissertation, University of Iowa, 1992.

35. Louis, "Career Transitions."

36. S. Ashford, "Individual Strategies for Coping with Stress during Organizational Transitions," *Journal of Applied Behavioral Science* 24 (1988): 19–36; Schlossberg and Leibowitz, "Organizational Support Systems as Buffers to Job Loss."

37. Schlossberg and Leibowitz, "Organizational Support Systems as Buffers to Job Loss."

38. Latack, "Career Transitions within Organizations."

39. Latack, "Work, Stress, and Careers."

40. R. I. Sutton and R. L. Kahn, "Prediction, Understanding and Control as Antidotes to Organizational Stress," in *Handbook of Organizational Behavior*, ed. J. Lorsch (Englewood Cliffs, NJ: Prentice-Hall, 1987), 272–285.

41. S. Ashford, "Individual Strategies for Coping with Stress during Organizational Transitions," *Journal of Applied Behavioral Science* 24 (1988): 19–36; S. Fineman, "A Psychosocial Model of Stress and Its Application to Managerial Unemployment," *Human Relations* 32 (1979): 323–345; Froiland, "What Cures Job Stress?"; Schlossberg and Leibowitz, "Organizational Support Systems as Buffers to Job Loss.

42. J. C. Latack and S. J. Havlovic, "Coping with Job Stress: A Conceptual Evaluation Framework for Coping Measures," *Journal of Organizational Behavior* 13 (1992): 479–508.

43. P. Herlihy, "Employee Assistance Programs and Work/Family Programs: Obstacles and Opportunities for Organizational Integration," *Compensation and Benefits Management Spring* (1997): 22–30; Latack and Havlovic, "Coping with Job Stress"; Z. B. Leibowitz and N. K. Schlossberg, "Critical Career Transitions: A Model for Designing Career Services," *Training and Development Journal* 36, no. 2 (1982): 12–18.

44. G. K. Baruch, L. Biener, and R. C. Barnett, "Women and Gender in Research on Work and Family Stress," *American Psychologist* 42 (1987): 130–136; G. Hackett and A. M. Byers, "Social

Cognitive Theory and the Career Development of African American Women," *The Career Development Quarterly* 44 (1996): 322–340; L. T. Zappert and H. M. Weinstein, "Sex Differences in the Impact of Work on Physical and Psychological Health," *American Journal of Psychiatry* 142 (1985): 1174–1178.

45. D. L. Nelson and J. C. Quick, "Professional Women: Are Distress and Disease Inevitable?" *Academy of Management Review* 10 (1985): 206–218.

46. D. L. Ford, "Job-Related Stress of the Minority Professional: An Exploratory Analysis and Suggestions for Future Research," in *Human Stress and Cognition in Organizations*, ed. T. A. Beehr and R. S. Bhagat (New York: Wiley, 1985), 287–324; J. H. Greenhaus and S. Parasuraman, "Job Performance Attributions and Career Advancement Prospects: An Examination of Gender and Race Effects," *Organizational Behavior and Human Decision Processes* 55, no. 2 (1993): 273–297; J. H. Greenhaus, S. Parasuraman, and W. M. Wormley, "Effects of Race on Organizational Experiences, Job Performance Evaluations, and Career Outcomes," *Academy of Management Journal* 33 (1990): 64–86; R. Nixon, *Black Managers in Corporate America: Alienation or Integration?* (Washington, DC: Research Department, National Urban League, 1985); R. Nixon, *Climbing the Corporate Ladder: Some Perceptions among Black Managers* (Washington, DC: Research Department, National Urban League, 1985).

47. D. Brown, C. W. Minor, and D. A. Jepson, "The Opinions of Minorities about Preparing for Work: Report of the Second NCDA National Survey," *Career Development Quarterly* 40 (1991): 5–19; K. M. Evans and E. L. Herr, "The Influence of Racism and Sexism in the Career Development of African American Women," *Journal of Multicultural Counseling and Development* 19 (1991): 130–135; Hackett and Byers, "Social Cognitive Theory and the Career Development of African American Women."

48. Latack, "Work, Stress, and Careers."

49. S. Shellenbarger, "More Executives Cite Need for Family Time as Reason for Quitting," *Wall Street Journal*, March 11, 1998, B1.

50. A. J. Kinicki, F. M. McKee, and K. J. Wade, "Annual Review, 1991–1995: Occupational Health," *Journal of Vocational Behavior* 49 (1996): 190–220; B. Perlman and E. A. Hartman, "Burnout: Summary and Future Research," *Human Relations* 35 (1982): 283–305.

51. S. E. Jackson, R. L. Schwab, and R. S. Schuler, "Toward an Understanding of the Burnout Phenomenon," *Journal of Applied Psychology* 71 (1986): 630–640.

52. B. A. Potter, *Overcoming Job Burnout: How to Renew Enthusiasm for Work* (Berkeley, CA: Ronin Publishing, 1998).

53. C. L. Cordes and T. W. Dougherty, "A Review and Integration of Research on Job Burnout," *Academy of Management Review* 4 (1993): 621–656; R. T.Lee and B. E. Ashforth, "Work-Unit Structure and Processes and Job-related Stressors and Predictors of Managerial Burnout," *Journal of Applied Social Psychology* 21 (1991): 1831–1847; K. I. Miller, E. G. Zook, and B. H. Ellis, "Occupational Differences in the Influence of Communication on Stress and Burnout in the Workplace," *Management Communication Quarterly* 3 (1989): 166–190.

54. S. E. Jackson and R. S. Schuler, "Preventing Employee Burnout," *Personnel* 60 (1983): 58–68.

55. Burke, Brief, and George, "The Role of Negative Affectivity in Understanding Relations between Self-Reports of Stressors and Strains"; T. A. Judge, "Does Affective Disposition Moderate the Relationship between Job Satisfaction and Voluntary Turnover?" *Journal of Applied Psychology* 78 (1993): 395–401.

56. R. Cropanzo, K. James, and M. A. Konovsky, "Dispositional Affectivity as a Predictor of Work Attitudes and Job Performance," *Journal of Organizational Behavior* 14 (1993): 595–606; R. D. Iverson and P. J. Erwin, "Predictors of Occupational Injury: The Role of Affectivity," *Journal of Occupational and Organizational Psychology* 70 (1997): 113–128; R. D. Iverson, M. Olekalns, and P. J. Erwin, "Affectivity, Organizational Stressors, and Absenteeism: A Causal Model of

Burnout and Its Consequences." *Journal of Vocational Behavior* 52 (1998): 1–23; J. C. Latack, A. Kinicki, and G. E. Prussia, "Response to 'Negative Affectivity and Coping with Job Loss,'" *Academy of Management Review* 21, no. 2 (1996): 331–332.

57. Potter. "Overcoming Job B"; Jackson and Schuler, "Preventing Employee Burnout."

58. Jackson and Maslach, "After-Effects of Job-Related Stress"; Jackson, Schwab, and Schuler, "Toward an Understanding of the Burnout Phenomenon."

59. Froiland, "What Cures Job Stress?"

60. Ibid.; Jackson and Schuler, "Preventing Employee Burnout."

61. S. L. Kirmeyer and T. W. Dougherty, "Workload, Tension and Coping: Moderating Effects of Supervisor Support," *Personnel Psychology* 41 (1988): 125–140; D. N. Russell, E. Altmaier, and D. Van Velzen, "Job-Related Stress, Social Support, and Burnout among Classroom Teachers," *Journal of Applied Psychology* 72 (1987): 269–274; J. Seltzer and R. E. Numerof, "Supervisory Leadership and Subordinate Burnout," *Academy of Management Journal* 31 (1988): 439–446.

62. R. Eisenberger, P. Fasolo, and V. Davis-LaMastro, "Perceived Organizational Support and Employee Diligence, Commitment, and Innovation," *Journal of Applied Psychology* 75, no. 1 (1990): 51–59; Russell, Altmaier, and Van Velzen, "Job-Related Stress, Social Support, and Burnout among Classroom Teachers"; Seltzer and Numerof, "Supervisory Leadership and Subordinate Burnout."

63. M. D. Glicken, "A Counseling Approach to Employee Burnout," *Personnel Journal* 62, no. 3 (1983): 222–228; Froiland, "What Cures Job Stress?"

64. S. McKee, "Take It Easy!"

65. Latack, "Work, Stress, and Careers"; Latack and Havlovic, "Coping with Job Stress"; L. I. Pearlin and C. Schooler, "The Structure of Coping," *Journal of Health and Social Behavior* 19 (1978): 2–21.

66. Ibid.

67. N. S. Bruning and D. R. Frew, "The Impact of Various Stress Management Training Strategies: A Longitudinal Field Experiment," unpublished paper, 1985; McKee, "Take It Easy!"

68. Ibid.

69. Latack, "Work, Stress, and Careers"; Latack and Havlovic, "Coping with Job Stress."

70. E. H. Schein, *Career Dynamics: Matching Individual and Organizational Needs* (Reading, MA: Addison-Wesley, 1978).

71. J. C. Latack, A. J. Kinicki, and G. E. Prussia, "An Integrative Process Model of Coping with Job Loss," *Academy of Management Review* 20, no. 2 (1995): 311–342.

72. R. D. Caplan, A. D. Vinokur, R. H. Price, and M. van Ryn, "Job Seeking, Reemployment, and Mental Health: A Randomized Field Experiment in Coping with Job Loss," *Journal of Applied Psychology* 74 (1989): 759–769; J. F. Constable and D. W. Russell, "The Effect of Social Support and the Work Environment upon Burnout among Nurses," *Journal of Human Stress* 12 (1986): 20–26; M. R. Fusilier, D.C. Ganster, and B. T. Mayes, "The Social Support and Health Relationship: Is There a Gender Difference?" *Journal of Occupational Psychology* 59 (1986): 145–153; J. H. Greenhaus and S. Parasuraman, "Work Family Conflict, Social Support, and Well-being," in *Women in Management: Current Research Issues*, ed. M. J. Davidson and R.J. Burke (London: Paul Chapman, 1994), 213–229; D. N. Russell, E. Altmaier, and D. Van Velzen, "Job-Related Stress, Social Support, and Burnout among Classroom Teachers," *Journal of Applied Psychology* 72 (1987): 269–274.

73. Latack, Kinicki, and Prussia, "An Integrative Process Model of Coping with Job Loss"; M. R.

Manning, C. N. Jackson, and M. R. Fusilier, "Occupational Stress, Social Support, and the Costs of Health Care," *Academy of Management Journal* 39, no. 3 (1996): 738–750.

74. J. S. House, *Work Stress and Social Support* (Reading, MA: Addison-Wesley, 1981).

75. Iverson, Olekalns, and Erwin, "Affectivity, Organizational Stressors, and Absenteeism"; Quick and Quick, *Organizational Stress and Preventive Management.*

76. Quick and Quick, *Organizational Stress and Preventive Management*; quote is on p. 312.

77. Interview with Deborah Davis, Health & Wellness® program administrator, Johnson & Johnson, August 1998.

78. McKee, "Take It Easy!"

79. Ibid.

80. Herlihy, "Employee Assistance Programs and Work/Family Programs."

81. Anonymous, "Developing an Effective Outplacement Program," *Business Forum* 16 (1991): 14–17; Anonymous, "Dealing with Downsizing," *Incentive* 10 (1993): 58–60: S. Garmhausen, "Career Tracks: Chase Illustrates Kinder, Gentler Approach to Layoffs," *American Banker* 163 (1998): 1–3; S. J. Harvey, "How Effective Are Large-Scale Outplacement Programs?" *The Human Resources Professional* 8 (1995): 11–15.

11

INTERSECTION OF WORK AND FAMILY ROLES: IMPLICATIONS FOR CAREER MANAGEMENT

Work and family lives touch each other in so many ways.[1] Think of how your family responsibilities can affect your career: how much time and energy are you willing to devote to work, how many weekends are you willing to spend in the office, and how many relocations are you willing to accept? Think also how a good (or bad!) day at work affects your mood at home or the times you missed a child's music recital or ball game because of a work commitment.

It is no wonder that work-family balance has become a hot topic on the nation's social agenda, especially when organizational downsizings have left many of us with more work to do and fewer resources with which to do it. Articles on flextime, parental leave legislation, "mommy tracks," and child care arrangements filled the pages of the popular press and the professional journals in the 1980s and have continued with even greater frequency in the 1990s. With the movement into the new millennium, individuals and families are increasingly concerned with finding ways to "juggle" their work and family responsibilities.

Why has the need to balance work and family lives become more intense in recent years? First, more individuals than ever are simultaneously pursuing a career and are committed to a family relationship. This is largely attributable to the increasing participation of women in the work force. Consider the following statistics:[2]

- Sixty-one percent of all married women aged 16 and older were in the work force in 1996, compared with just 30 percent in 1960.
- Nearly 63 percent of all married women with children younger than 6 were in the work force in 1996, compared with only 19 percent in 1960; the employment rate for married women with children aged 6 to 17 was 76.7 percent in 1996 compared with 39 percent in 1960.

- In 1996, nearly 70 percent of all divorced, separated, and widowed women with children younger than 6 were in the work force, and this figure jumped to more than 80 percent for those with children aged 6 to 17.

- By the year 2000, approximately two-thirds of the new entrants into the work force will be women, and 75 percent of them will become parents during their work lives.

- Approximately 81 percent of women MBAs from a prestigious business school intended to work their entire adult lives; more than half were already mothers, many with two or more children.

In addition, men are increasingly required to juggle their work and family lives. With their wives employed outside the home in greater frequency, more re-sponsibility for home chores and child care fall on husbands, who then need to balance these responsibilities with their work demands. Moreover, a small but significant number of divorced men assume custody of their children and feel the crunch of extensive family and career commitments.

The combination of heavy work commitments and extensive family responsi-bilities has put pressure on individuals and families to cope effectively with the stresses of this demanding life-style. It has also posed a challenge to employers to develop "family responsive" policies and practices, or risk losing their edge in attracting and retaining talented women and men.[3] This chapter examines the relationship between work and family lives.

We discuss the factors that produce work-family conflict and the consequences of conflict for individuals, families, and employers. We also consider the ways in which work and family lives can strengthen and enrich one another. Next, we discuss potential stresses in a two-career relationship and the ways individuals and couples can manage this stress. We also identify actions that organizations can take to help their employees resolve their work-family challenges. The chap-ter discusses the "career success/personal failure" syndrome and presents career management guidelines that take work and nonwork lives into account.

MODEL OF WORK-FAMILY CONFLICT

There are many times when our work and family lives are in conflict with one another. Work-family conflict exists when pressures from work and family roles are mutually incompatible, such that participation in one role is made more difficult by virtue of participation in another role.[4] Exhibit 11.1 identifies three forms of work-family conflict: time-based conflict, strain-based conflict, and behavior-based conflict.

Time-based conflict is a common type of work-family conflict. Life roles compete for a precious commodity—time. The time spent in one role generally cannot be devoted to another role. Out-of-town business meetings or late evenings at the office can conflict with family dinners and children's parent-teacher conferences.

· EXHIBIT 11-1

WORK-FAMILY ROLE
PRESSURE INCOMPATIBILITY

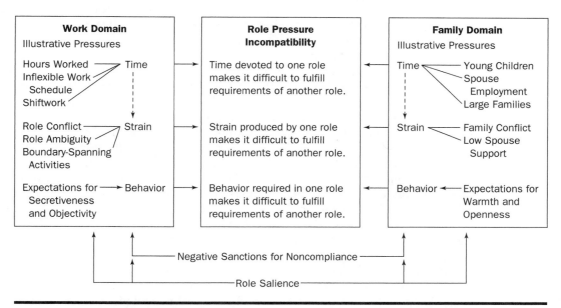

SOURCE: J. H. Greenhaus and N. J. Beutell, "Sources of Conflict between Work and Family Roles," *Academy of Management Review,* 1985, vol 10, p. 78. Reprinted with permission.

It is simply impossible to be in two places at once. Time-based conflict is likely to be most prevalent for employees who work long hours, travel extensively, frequently work overtime, and have inflexible work schedules. All these work characteristics increase or fix the time at work that cannot be spent on family role activities.

Time pressures that arise from the family domain can also produce work-family conflict. Employees who experience the most extensive work-family conflict tend to be married, have young children, have large families, and have spouses or partners who hold responsible jobs. All these family characteristics increase the amount of time required to fulfill family role requirements, which can interfere with work-related activities.

Strain-based conflict exists when the strain produced within one role affects experiences in another role. Work stressors can produce such strain symptoms as tension, irritability, fatigue, depression, and apathy. It is difficult to be an attentive partner or a loving parent when one is depressed or irritable. Strain-based conflict is likely to be most intense for employees who experience conflict or ambiguity within the work role, who are exposed to extensive physical, emotional, or mental work demands, whose work environment is constantly changing, and who work on repetitive, boring tasks. All these stressful conditions can produce a "negative emotional spillover" from work to nonwork.[5]

Of course, many sources of strain can arise from the family role as well. Individuals who experience difficulties with partners or children or receive little support and aid from their families may find that their family stress intrudes into their work life. It is difficult to give oneself fully to work when preoccupied with a stressful family situation.

Sometimes, behavior that is effective in one role is simply inappropriate in another role. It has been suggested, for example, that managers are expected to be self-reliant, aggressive, detached, and objective.[6] Family members, however, may expect you to be warm, nurturing, emotional, and human in your relationships with them. If people cannot shift gears when they enter different roles, they are likely to experience *behavior-based conflict* between the roles. Behavioral styles that employees exhibit at work (logic, objectivity, power, and authority) may be incompatible with the behaviors desired by their partners and children on the home front.[7] Partners and children do not appreciate being treated like subordinates!

Therefore, a variety of role pressures can produce work-family conflict. Some of these pressures demand excessive time commitments, others produce extensive stress, and many produce both. Where do these pressures come from? Some come from role senders, persons with whom we interact in our work and family lives. Bosses, colleagues, partners, and children are all role senders who place demands on us to finish projects, attend weekend meetings, wash the dishes, and paint the house. People tend to experience more conflict when there are strong penalties for failing to comply with these demands from work and family roles. If a boss insists that we attend a Saturday work meeting, and a partner refuses to change vacation plans by one day, we are caught between the proverbial rock and a hard place. If either the boss or the partner permits latitude to deviate from expectations, there is room to maneuver.

However, many pressures to participate or excel at work or in family activities come not from other people, but from the expectations we place on ourselves—we become our own role senders. For example, Type A employees, as we discussed in Chapter 10, place tremendous pressure on themselves to work long hours and be highly successful. Not surprisingly, they experience more job tension and work-family conflict than Type Bs.[8] In the family realm, the desire to be the "perfect" partner or parent can place pressure on us that goes far beyond any pressure that children or partners can muster.

The pressures people put on themselves depend on the importance or salience of the role to their self-concept. If work is important, people will be more demanding on themselves to participate fully and competently in that role, thereby exacerbating the degree of conflict. Those who are highly involved in both work and family are likely to experience the most conflict.[9] They want to be highly productive in their careers and be an attentive parent and partner, and they feel guilty if they cannot do both all the time. Consider the following three scenarios.

Bill is a hard-working attorney in his early 30s, married with two children. He is preoccupied with his career, working long hours, traveling extensively, and bringing work home most evenings and weekends. Despite his heavy work pressures and a young family, Bill does not feel intense work-family conflict. He is so concerned about his career that he hardly notices the family pressures that surround him. Because he often convinces his wife to make only minor demands on his time and emotion, he does not even see the impact of his work on his family life, or if he does see it, it does not bother him deeply. It is not so much that his family is unimportant, but rather that it takes a back seat to his career.

Malik, also married with two children, has a demanding, time-consuming career as an executive. Unlike Bill, however, Malik is concerned about spending time with his family and sharing experiences with his wife and young children. His career is important but so is his family. Despite his best efforts to juggle work and family activities, Malik experiences chronic, intense work-family conflict. He cares so much about both roles that the tug on his time and emotion is inevitable.

Rajan's situation is slightly different. He works as an accountant for a state government agency. Although he likes his job, Rajan's career is not a crucial part of his life. He works primarily to earn enough money to support his wife and two young children. He puts in a 35-hour week, actively avoids business travel, and almost never brings work home. His passions are his family, his home, and his hobbies. Rajan does not experience intense work-family conflict. His job leaves him sufficient time to pursue his real interests, and it does not drain him of his energy.

In these three scenarios, the husband's work-family conflict depends on the relative importance he attaches to his work and family roles. Who is most typical—Bill, Malik, or Rajan? Twenty years ago, Fernando Bartolome and Paul Evans observed that most young male managers were obsessed with their careers, enmeshed in their career success, and driven by a need to achieve that seemed to overshadow family life.[10] Family was important to these men, but they tended to take it for granted. Although men, in general, may not be as obsessed with their careers now as they were two decades ago, there will still be individual differences in the importance of work based on employees' underlying life values and the nature of their career fields.

It is not a question of who is right and who is wrong. All three situations require trade-offs between work and family pursuits. Bill's career progress has been rapid and successful but not without costs—his family relationships. Malik gets a great deal of satisfaction both from work and family roles. However, his heavy involvement in both roles can leave him frustrated and wondering what kind of father/husband (or executive) he could have been if he had centered his life even more on his family (or work). Rajan's satisfaction with his family and home life also came at a price—lack of extensive career accomplishments—although he may be willing to pay that price. To understand the consequences of a trade-off, people must know what values are most important to them and must understand the risks they assume to pursue these values.

We intentionally described the experiences of three men to illustrate that males are not immune to work-family conflict and guilt. However, it is generally believed that employed women are more likely to experience work-family

• TABLE 11-1

INVENTORY OF WORK-
FAMILY CONFLICT

Below are 14 statements about the relationship between your work life and your family and home life. Indicate your agreement or disagreement by placing the appropriate number in front of each statement:

1 = Strongly Disagree
2 = Disagree
3 = Uncertain
4 = Agree
5 = Strongly Agree

___ 1. My family takes up time I would like to spend working
___ 2. My personal interests take too much time away from my work
___ 3. The demands of my family life make it difficult to concentrate at work
___ 4. At times, my personal problems make me irritable at work
___ 5. My work schedule often conflicts with my family life
___ 6. After work, I come home too tired to do some of the things I'd like to do
___ 7. On the job, I have so much work to do that it takes away from my personal interests
___ 8. My family dislikes how often I am preoccupied with my work when I am at home
___ 9. Because my work is demanding, at times I am irritable at home
___ 10. The demands of my job make it difficult to be relaxed all the time at home
___ 11. My work takes up time that I'd like to spend with my family
___ 12. My job makes it difficult to be the kind of spouse or parent I'd like to be
___ 13. I am not able to act the same way at home as I do at work
___ 14. When I am assertive at home, it is not appreciated by my family

Modification of a scale initially developed by R. E. Kopelman, J. H. Greenhaus, and T. F. Connolly, "A Model of Work, Family, and Interrole Conflict: A Construct Validation Study," *Organizational Behavior and Human Performance* 32 (1983): 198–215.

conflict than men, because women have far greater responsibilities for home chores and child care than do men.[11] However, anyone who encounters both work and family pressures can experience work-family conflict, especially if he or she cares deeply about performing well in both spheres of life.

Table 11.1 presents a scale that measures work-family conflict. Strong agreement with an item reflects a relatively high level of work-family conflict. Therefore, the higher the score, the more extensive the work-family conflict. Extensive work-family conflict can produce high levels of stress and can detract from marital or family satisfaction, job satisfaction, and overall life satisfaction.[12] This does not mean that everyone who experiences work-family conflict will experience dissatisfaction with their families, jobs, and lives. A certain level of conflict is inevitable in a society in which women and men are required to juggle work and family responsibilities. Dissatisfaction is probably most pronounced when the level of work-family conflict is so intense that it exceeds individuals' capacities to cope with the conflict. We discuss coping skills in a later part of the chapter.

WORK-FAMILY INTEGRATION

Although many of us experience work-family conflict—sometimes rather intensely—we should not conclude that work and family are always at odds with one another. In many ways, our work can enrich our family lives, just as our family experiences can improve our work lives. We refer to these beneficial effects of work and family on one another as work-family integration.[13]

Let's look first at the ways in which work enriches the quality of our family lives. Work can provide many resources that benefit our families. The most obvious resource derived from work is income, which may provide a satisfying standard of living, and can purchase such essentials as quality child care, education, and medical care for the entire family. Work schedule flexibility—in the form of flextime, job sharing, or telecommuting—can enable us to spend more time with our families and can help us reduce the number of scheduling conflicts between our work and family responsibilities.

In addition to these rather concrete resources, we may receive information and advice from our managers, co-workers, and human resource professionals that give us better ideas about how to improve our family lives. For example, discussions with a colleague at work may provide us with useful suggestions on parenting, resolving conflicts with our partners, or finding suitable care for our elderly parents. In addition, positive growth experiences at work—such as working on challenging assignments and possessing a great deal of autonomy on our jobs—can boost our self-esteem, giving us the confidence to solve problems at home more effectively. In sum, work experiences can be a boon to our family lives, especially if the work environment provides substantial flexibility, supportive colleagues, and challenging assignments.

So, too, can our family improve the quality of our work lives. A supportive partner provides many resources that we can apply to our careers. We saw in Chapter 10 that support may be (1) *instrumental*, that is, direct help on a task; (2) *informational*, in which a person gives us information or advice to help us solve a problem; (3) *emotional*, in which a person displays affection, love, concern, trust, and empathy toward us; or (4) *appraisal*, in which a person provides feedback to us regarding our behavior or performance. Family members—especially partners—can provide all four types of support that can help us considerably in our careers.

For example, a partner's instrumental support can come in the form of assistance with household chores and child care. When a partner devotes time to home and children, it not only gives us the flexibility to devote more of our time to work but also enables us to be less distracted by family matters while at work. A partner who provides emotional support listens to our concerns and makes us feel accepted for who we are—a big boost to our self-esteem. A partner who provides appraisal and informational support furnishes useful feedback, information, and suggestions when requested. Not surprisingly, then, men and women who receive a great deal of support from their partners tend to pursue their careers effectively and derive a great deal of satisfaction from their work.[14]

In summary, when our work and family lives jostle for our time and attention, we experience conflict and stress. However, when work and family strengthen each other, we experience integration in our lives. Nowhere is the opportunity for conflict—or integration—more apparent than in the daily lives of two-career families, who are constantly juggling their work and family responsibilities. We examine this increasingly popular life-style next.

TWO-CAREER FAMILY

The "traditional" household—husband employed, at-home wife, two or more children—currently represents only a small percentage of American families. Instead, there are a greater variety of life-styles, including single-parent house-holds, childless couples, "house-husbands" tending to the domestic front, and of course, two-career families. We define a two-career couple as two people who share a life-style that includes an ongoing love relationship, cohabitation, and a work role for each partner.[15] Consistent with the definition of a career offered in Chapter 1, each partner in a two-career couple need not necessarily hold a professional or managerial job or a job that is emotionally absorbing. Moreover, the couple need not be married or of opposite gender.

Why has the two-career life-style become so prominent? Certainly, one attractive feature is the financial security derived from two incomes. Many couples believe they need two incomes to acquire and maintain a desired standard of living.

However, money does not tell the whole story. Each partner's quality of life can be enriched as well. From a woman's perspective, employment can satisfy a whole range of needs—achievement, challenge, variety, and power—that may not be fully satisfied in a homemaker role. A woman's employment can enhance her self-esteem and emotional well-being, especially if her job provides opportunities for challenging, interesting work.[16] A rewarding, satisfying job can contribute to the richness of a woman's life. Moreover, the pursuit of a career can promote an independence and self-sufficiency that is healthy in its own right and critical if the marriage ends through divorce or death of the partner.

From a man's perspective, participation in a two-career relationship often involves additional responsibility at home. A more extensive involvement in child-rearing can provide a closer bond with the children and expand the meaning and enjoyment in a man's life. Because the husband in a two-career relationship is not solely responsible for the financial well-being of the family, he may feel less pressure to "succeed" and have more freedom to leave a dissatisfying job.

The two-career life-style can also benefit the quality of the relationship between the two partners. A two-career relationship often has a greater balance of power and decision making than a single-earner relationship, in which one partner (usually the man) is solely responsible for the family income.[17] The employment of both partners can increase their mutual respect as equals, bring them closer together, and make for a more interesting, compatible couple.[18]

SOURCES OF STRESS IN THE TWO-CAREER RELATIONSHIP

The preceding section does not imply that two-career relationships are stress-free. Although two-career couples seem to be at least as happy with their marriages as single-earner couples,[19] there are a number of significant issues that need to be faced in such relationships. This section examines these issues, recognizing that they are not equally relevant to all two-career couples. But first, consider the following situation.

> Rob and Helen are business executives in their mid-30s with two young daughters. Although they love their jobs and are deeply committed to their family, Rob and Helen feel frazzled much of the time. Juggling business meetings, birthday parties, and trips to the pediatrician leave them physically and mentally exhausted. They are also concerned with the quality of the family day-care center their daughters attend.
>
> Rob and Helen feel occasional pangs of guilt. At times, Helen wonders whether she is as good a mother to her daughters as her own homemaker mother was to her. And although Rob is proud of Helen's accomplishments at the public relations firm where she works, he secretly wonders how long it will be before her salary outstrips his own. Rob and Helen feel guilty when they are not devoting enough time to their work and feel guilty when they cannot spend as much time with their children as they would like. Rob and Helen both wonder whether their careers will suffer as a result of their extensive family responsibilities, and they realize that their employers have done little to help them balance work and family.

This example highlights the many forms of stress that can be experienced in a two-career family. We now discuss the specific sources of stress in more detail.

WORK-FAMILY CONFLICT

We have shown that extensive work and family demands can produce work-family conflict. Many men find that their work demands conflict with the responsibilities they are expected to assume at home. Challenging jobs, extensive travel, and long work hours can easily conflict with pressures and desires to participate in family activities.

Nevertheless, women still bear the brunt of the responsibility for homemaking and child care. Although women have added another role to their lives—the work role—they have not typically relinquished the home and child care roles to any substantial degree. Two-career husbands overwhelmingly report that their wives take major responsibility for most household chores as well as raising the children.[20] Moreover, even when husbands do increase their participation in these domestic roles, they are often seen as "helping out" rather than assuming real responsibility for the activities.

In effect, two-career wives often work a "second shift" of home and family chores, with their "work day" only half over when they return home from their paid employment.[21] One recent study revealed that mothers averaged about 52 hours a week on combined home and child care activities compared with the 23 hours spent by fathers on these activities.[22] Even more imbalance on the home front was observed in a survey of corporate men who revealed that their wives spent four times as many hours a week on home chores and child care than they did.[23] Even marriages that start out with an equitable sharing of home responsibilities often revert back to a gender-based division of labor after the birth of a child.[24]

The overload and stress experienced by two-career partners can threaten the relationship in several ways. First, many parents experience guilt over not spending enough time with their children. Second, the couple may simply not have the time to nurture their own relationship. Work demands and children's needs leave partners with little time for each other. The absence of shared time can pose a threat to the romantic and emotional relationship and can estrange partners from one another. Third, family and work responsibilities frequently leave little time for individuals themselves. Time to relax, reflect, or pursue leisure activities does not come easily, if at all.

In short, partners in two-career relationships often lead hectic, frenetic lives, especially if there are children in the family. There are work pressures, carpools, overnight business trips, children's dance lessons, demanding bosses, housework—the list seems endless. The two-career life-style can be rewarding, but it is not easy.

RESTRICTED CAREER ACHIEVEMENTS

The two-career life-style may restrict or slow down an individual's career accomplishments. This is especially likely to occur for women. Many mothers reduce their career involvement in an attempt to alleviate the conflict they experience between work and family. Two-career mothers often cut back on the number of hours they work, turn down career development opportunities that would conflict with their family responsibilities, refuse promotions that require relocation, or put their career "on hold" by leaving the work force for a period of time. In this respect, two-career mothers may incur a "family penalty" because their extensive family responsibilities limit their career progress.[25] This penalty is partly self-imposed because two-career mothers often "voluntarily" cut back on their career involvement to meet their family responsibilities. However, employers may also discriminate against mothers by restricting their investment in them—for example, by providing limited opportunities for mentoring and challenging job assignments—because of their belief that mothers are more committed to their families than to their careers.[26]

Whereas many mothers experience a family penalty that impedes their career success, men often experience a "family bonus" that actually helps their career. One recent study found that fathers earned more money, reached higher levels in their organization, and were more satisfied with their careers than men without children.[27] Why? Because fathers experienced more autonomy on their jobs than did men without children. Although it is possible that the fathers in this study sought additional autonomy, employers may also have granted fathers more autonomy because they perceive them to be more responsible and stable than men without children.

Of course, not all fathers experience a family bonus. Men who are highly involved in their family lives—who believe that their family is a critical part of their lives—cut back on their involvement in work, just as many two-career mothers do.[28] Such men may switch careers, limit travel, and turn down promotions or relocations for family reasons.[29] In addition, two-career husbands may have to do without some of the career support traditionally provided by homemakers in the so-called two-person career—party hostess, organizer of the home, and willing partner in geographic moves.[30]

The extent to which career achievements are restricted in two-career families may depend, in part, on the time commitments required in a particular career field. A man or woman may not experience obstacles to career progress in a field that has reasonable, predictable, and flexible hours. However, job performance and career progress may suffer in a field requiring extensive work hours and travel. In addition, career achievements may depend on the relative importance of each partner's career, each partner's commitment to the family, the availability of outside help for housework and child care, the support received from the partner, and the employer's flexibility in addressing work-family concerns.[31]

Two-career couples often must decide whose career has priority at any particular point in time. Who stays home with a sick child? Who takes a few hours off to attend an afternoon parent-teacher conference? For whose job will the family relocate? The partner whose career takes priority will make fewer career accommodations and will pursue his or her career more intensely than the other partner. Traditionally, a man's career took precedence over his family responsibilities, whereas a woman's family responsibilities were expected to take precedence over her work. Generally, the rationale was that the husband's job was more important, more demanding, and provided a larger portion of the family's income. These assumptions may no longer be accurate.

Couples can handle the issue of career priorities in different ways. Some couples insist that both careers have equal priority and that the partners share family-related tasks and make relocation decisions based on the needs of both careers. Other couples attach priority to one partner's career and the family makes accommodations for the needs of that career. In other cases, the relative priority of each career shifts, depending on the needs and stages of each career. What is most important is not the eventual solution that is reached, but rather the process the couple uses to reach the solution. This process should involve openness, flexibility, and concern for the partner. At the very least, both partners must agree on the relative priority of each other's career or risk extensive strain in the marriage.[32]

Therefore, the pressures and constraints of a two-career relationship may impede the career progress of one or both partners, especially if career progress is defined as rapid mobility up the organizational ladder. However, researchers have found that two-career professional women ultimately made significant career contributions, although at a somewhat later stage in their lives than their single or childless counterparts.[33] It would not be surprising if the same trend holds true for men. In the long term, then, career accomplishments may not be seriously hampered, at least not in occupations and organizations that permit flexibility in the pace of career growth. We discuss this issue further when we examine organizations' responsiveness to employees' work-family concerns later in this chapter.

COMPETITION AND JEALOUSY

The division of labor in the so-called traditional family makes for a neat, non-competitive world. The man achieves competence in the work world, the woman masters the domestic demands, and comparisons of relative success in their respective ventures are unlikely. When both parties are employed, however, it is likely that one partner will ultimately become more "successful" than the other.[34] A husband may be threatened if his wife's career success outstrips his own. Indeed, one study found that the better a women performs on her job, the lower her level of marital satisfaction, suggesting that her success at work might produce resentment by her husband.[35] Jealousies on the part of the man or the woman, if left unattended, can threaten the stability of the relationship.

Does the potential for competition increase when both partners are in the same career field? On one hand, two partners working in the same or similar field can intensify competition. It is far easier for two accountants or two attorneys to compare their relative success (consciously or unconsciously) than it would be for a business executive and a college professor. Researchers have observed that women in two-career relationships were less inclined to provide emotional support to their partners when both were in the same career field.[36] On the other hand, it has been suggested that two partners in the same field can understand and appreciate each other's pressures and, therefore, can provide each other with greater empathy and support.[37]

Both positions make a great deal of sense. The effect of a partner's career success on feelings of competition and jealousy probably depends on the orientations of the two partners. Perhaps the most intense feelings of competition and jealousy are experienced by individuals who place substantial importance on their own career success, yet are insecure about their sense of worth. Under these conditions, a partner's career accomplishments can be particularly threatening. We must add, however, that in extensive discussions with undergraduate and graduate business students, we have found few men or women who believed that a partner's career success would provoke intense feelings of competition or jealousy.

IDENTITY PROBLEMS

Partners in a two-career relationship can experience ambivalence and stress if they believe that their current life-style is not consistent with their earlier sex-role socialization.[38] Women who were taught that "good wives" stay home, raise children, and do not compete with men may feel guilty about their life-style and question their femininity. Men who equate masculinity with career success and being the sole provider may feel ambivalent about the roles they and their partners have adopted. Because the two-career life-style can still run counter to social norms, many partners may get little understanding or help from parents, other relatives, friends, and work organizations. However, because society's attitudes toward women's employment are becoming more positive, identity problems may be less extensive in the future.

IMPACT OF TWO-CAREER STATUS ON CHILDREN

According to a *Fortune* survey of working parents, a majority of men (55 percent) and women (58 percent) believe that "children of working parents suffer by not being given enough time and attention."[39] However, most of these same parents also believe that children benefit by having working parents as role models. Perhaps these findings reflect the ambivalence experienced by many two-career parents.

On the positive side, children in two-career families appear to be more resourceful and independent than those in more traditional family structures.[40] In addition, children reared in two-career homes tend to hold egalitarian sex-role attitudes.[41] On the other hand, it has been observed that children who have both a working mother and a working father are often neglected by their parents.[42] The popular press has often portrayed a negative picture of the so-called latchkey children, fending for themselves and falling victim to drugs and educational failure.

However, the research suggests that a mother's employment (which for married couples usually translates into both parents' employment) has no consistent positive or negative effect on children's development.[43] Ultimately, the impact of a two-career life-style on children's adjustment depends on such factors as the quality of the parent-child relationship, the quality of child care, and the personal satisfaction of the parents.

QUALITY OF LIFE IN TWO-CAREER FAMILIES

Some of the potential advantages and risks associated with a two-career relationship have already been presented. How can families maximize the advantages and minimize the risks? Three closely related factors are particularly significant: social support, effective coping, and flexibility.

SOCIAL SUPPORT

We talked earlier about support as a resource that can help people improve the quality of their lives. Support can enable husbands and wives to solve work and family problems effectively and is strongly associated with partners' well-being.[44] Two-career couples can benefit from a wide variety of supportive relationships.

Emotional support, especially from family members, is particularly important because the partners are involved in a life-style that requires compromises and can produce identity problems, jealousies, and guilt. Robert and Rhona Rapoport spoke of the "facilitating husband," who is understanding and caring, as a major contributor to the success of a two-career relationship.[45] Men, too, need the support of an understanding partner. Indeed, support must be mutual, in that each partner must provide as well as receive support. Partners react negatively when they consistently provide more extensive support than they themselves receive.[46]

Because most two-career couples frequently experience novel situations, partners will benefit from information and advice on work- and family-related problems so that marital difficulties do not become too intense. Men need to contribute substantially in terms of action—home maintenance and child care being the primary areas—if there is to be balance and sharing in the relationship. Although hired help, another form of instrumental support, can substantially reduce conflict and overload, it cannot fully replace a mutually agreed-on and balanced sharing of responsibilities.

Finally, support can provide each partner with useful feedback. Partners may find it difficult to assess how well they are balancing work and family roles, whether the children are handling the situation satisfactorily, and how the relationship between the two partners is faring. Accurate, constructive feedback can serve as a confirmation of each partner's efforts and as a way to improve the functioning of the family unit.

Although support can and should come from a variety of sources, the support received from one's partner plays a special role because it reflects a commitment to the relationship. The relative emphasis placed on work and family by each partner may determine the degree of support each is willing to extend. Families in which at least one partner is strongly family oriented may be most able to balance work and family roles with minimal stress. A family orientation among husbands, for example, has been strongly associated with marital happiness, especially when the woman places a great deal of importance on her career.[47] Presumably, family-oriented husbands, who are willing to accommodate their careers to their family role, are less competitive and more supportive than their career-driven counterparts.[48]

Perhaps the most stressful and least supportive relationship is one in which both partners are highly involved in their careers and minimally involved in the family, yet both partners value a satisfying home and family life. Such relationships, described by Francine and Douglas Hall as "adversaries," may be threatened by constant conflicts over career priorities and division of labor in home and family tasks. As they state, neither partner "may be willing or able to make career sacrifices to facilitate the career of the other or to fulfill home and family roles."[49]

COPING WITH TWO-CAREER ISSUES

Douglas Hall identified three strategies for coping with work-family conflict.[50] Using *structural role redefinition*, we reduce work-family conflict by changing role senders' expectations of our responsibilities. A partner who arranges with the boss to leave work early on certain days or to limit the amount of work-related travel is altering other people's expectations. The woman who negotiates with her husband and children to do more work around the house or who hires outside help is reducing some of her domestic pressures. Structural role redefinition is an active, problem-solving approach to changing a part of the environment that is producing conflict and stress.

With *personal role reorientation,* we change expectations not by directly confronting role senders, but by changing our own conception of requirements. The woman who decides that standards for housekeeping can be relaxed or the man who gradually reduces his involvement at work is reorienting the priority of certain tasks or roles to reduce conflict.

With *reactive role behavior,* we try to meet all expectations more efficiently. Getting up earlier, going to bed later, and managing one's time more efficiently are all attempts to "do it all." This strategy, so characteristic of the "supermother,"[51] is mentally and physically taxing, fails to address the underlying conflicts, and is not generally successful.[52]

These three coping strategies are individual responses to stressful situations. Couples need to develop joint coping strategies to solve the problems of the family unit as a whole, moving from a "me" orientation to a "we" orientation.[53] In effect, self-interest, coercion, and suppression of conflict are replaced by mutual goals, encouragement, a healthy expression of differences, and a willingness to compromise.

Hall and Hall offered many useful suggestions in such areas as housework, parenting, and time management. But what works for one couple may not work for another; there can be no cookbook formula for success. However, what is applicable from one situation to another is the need to establish a climate of communication and problem solving. Hall and Hall suggested the following strategy to establish such a climate: talk about problems regularly, listen to your partner and express your own feelings, discuss goals and explore expectations, practice problem solving, and practice negotiating compromises.

These actions take time, skill, and practice, but they are essential if real problems and stressors are to be identified and managed. Problem solving and compromise are necessary to prevent sex-role stereotypes or old behavior patterns from disrupting a couple's attempt to find fresh solutions to novel problems.

FLEXIBILITY

Satisfactory coping requires a great deal of flexibility on the part of all members of a two-career family. The ability to see problems from another person's perspective and to change behavior or attitudes that are outmoded are hallmarks of effective coping. Rigid patterns of behavior, by definition, are not conducive to the resolution of stressful situations.

In Chapter 1, we discussed the notion of protean careers to illustrate the importance of flexibility. A protean career involves greater control over one's work life in which career success is judged by internal standards (satisfaction, achievement, a balanced life) rather than the traditional external standards of salary and rank in an organizational structure. People pursuing protean careers are likely to be found in high-autonomy settings such as universities or self-owned businesses, although it is possible, to some extent, to march to the beat of a different drummer in a large organization.

In a protean relationship, the main focus is on the growth and development of the partners, relatively unstifled by society's norms and expectations. The protean family is willing to adjust its relationship to meet the needs of family members, whether that involves remaining childless, living apart a portion of the time, or reversing the traditional sex roles within the relationship.[54]

The ability of two-career couples to adopt a more flexible life-style is often dependent on the policies and practices of their employers. Until recently, organizations did not see a need to help their employees balance their work and family roles. Fortunately, this attitude of neglect is changing. An organization's role in addressing work-family issues is examined in the following section.

ORGANIZATIONAL RESPONSES TO WORK-FAMILY ISSUES

Many organizations now realize that it is in their best interest to help their employees balance their work and family lives. What used to be considered a "woman's issue" is increasingly recognized as a business necessity. What accounts for this shift in attitudes among the nation's largest employers?

First, more employees are struggling to balance their work and family responsibilities than in prior years. As discussed earlier, the emergence of the two-career life-style requires parents to coordinate their work demands with their family responsibilities. Although women face the most extensive pressures to juggle work and family demands, men are increasingly involved in home and child care activities, either by choice or necessity. In addition, the rising divorce rate has resulted in an increasing number of single-parent households. Because the vast majority of single parents are employed women, they are confronted with a steady stream of work and family pressures, with no partner to share the responsibilities.

Moreover, employees are increasingly called on to care for elder parents or other adult relatives. One survey revealed that 22 percent of the managers and professionals in their sample expected to have elder care responsibility in the upcoming 5-year period.[55]

In addition, employees' values are shifting to place a greater emphasis on quality of life. Indeed, employees are demanding opportunities to attain balance between their work and family, and a sizeable number are willing to make sacrifices in their careers to achieve a higher quality of life.[56] More and more job seekers are raising the issue of work-life balance in their employment interviews.[57] And substantial numbers of men and women are refusing promotions, relocations, and jobs with extensive pressure or travel, because of the strains these positions would put on their family lives.

These changes in family and employment patterns, as well as shifts in employee values, are playing havoc with organizations' ability to staff themselves effectively, especially in the light of the nation's shrinking talent pool. For one thing, organizations are losing the services of many talented young women managers and professionals who leave their jobs following the birth of a child. Many of these "career-and-family"—oriented women want to continue their career but not with 50- to 60-hour weeks and extensive travel requirements.[58] Because employers have not typically provided an alternative work schedule for parents of young children, the employees often leave. This represents a substantial blow to employers who have invested time and money and now face extensive recruiting and training costs to replace these valued employees.

The talent pool is not only shrinking, but it is increasingly female. It is projected that by the year 2000, 63 percent of all women will be employed, and 47 percent of the work force will be women. In addition, with increasing numbers of women receiving bachelors, masters, legal, and medical degrees, employers find that many of their best and brightest job candidates are women. Extensive turnover among this group results in high costs and low productivity.[59]

In addition, mothers and fathers who remain in the work force are often preoccupied with the difficulties of balancing work and family responsibilities. One study found that 59 percent of women and 38 percent of men missed at least 1 work day in a 3-month period because of family responsibilities.[60] Excessive work-family conflict can produce high levels of absenteeism and extensive stress, both of which can detract from an organization's productivity. Not surprisingly, a family-supportive work environment can improve employees' commitment to their organizations.[61]

Despite the demographic changes outlined in this chapter, employers usually run their operations on the assumption that the vast majority of managerial and professional employees will be willing to devote as many hours as necessary to complete a project, including evenings and weekends; will travel at the drop of a hat; and will relocate whenever it is to the advantage of the organization and the employee's career progress. Of course, this approach assumed that the managerial and professional work force would be male, married to a homemaker, and therefore able to devote full time and attention to work.

Nobody likes to change assumptions, attitudes, and behaviors, especially if they have been working well for a long time. Employers are no exception. Organizations have been slow to address work-family issues for a variety of reasons: they do not know how to solve the problem, they are threatened by the demand for work-family balance that violates their "upward mobility ethic," they see it as a "woman's issue," and they do not see the payoff to the organization for addressing these issues.[62] However, this resistance to change is weakening as more companies experience difficulties attracting and retaining valued employees. We now turn our attention to actions that organizations can take to help their employees balance their work and family lives.

Table 11.2 summarizes a variety of policies and practices that have been adopted by organizations in response to the work-family issues discussed in this chapter. The table also shows the percentage of large companies offering each program, as reported recently by Dana Friedman and Arlene Johnson.[63] We classify these organizational actions into three broad categories: dependent care, flexible work arrangements, and changing the organization's work-family culture.

DEPENDENT CARE

Concerns about the welfare of their children are keenly felt by working parents. In response to these concerns, employers have supported a wide range of child

· TABLE 11-2

FAMILY-RESPONSIVE POLICIES AND PRACTICES

Dependent Care	Percentage of Large Companies Offering
Child care resource and referral	54.5
Elder care consultation and referral	21.1
Child care centers	13.0
Discounts or vouchers for child care	5.9
Sick child care	4.3
Community involvement	—
Flexible Work Arrangements	
Part-time schedules	87.8
Personal days	77.4
Flexible work schedules	77.1
Personal leaves of absence	70.4
Job sharing	47.9
Telecommuting (flexplace)	35.1
Family, child care leaves	28.0
Family illness days	4.8
Flexible career paths and assignments	—
Changing Work-Family Culture	
Spouse employment assistance	51.9
Work-family seminars	25.7
Work-family management training	9.6
Work-family support groups	5.3
Redesign work processes	—
Include work-family in mission statement	—

NOTE: When available, percentages of large companies offering a practice are based on D. E. Friedman and A. A. Johnson, "Moving from Programs to Culture Change: The Next Stage for the Corporate Work-Family Agenda," in *Integrating Work and Family: Challenges and Choices for a Changing World*, ed. S. Parasuraman and J. H. Greenhaus (Westport, CT: Quorum, 1997), 192–208.

care programs. Although only 13 percent of the companies surveyed by Friedman and Johnson provide on-site or near-site child care centers for their employees' children, other forms of direct support for children include subsidies (discounts and vouchers) for private child care facilities and emergency assistance for sick children. Another widespread form of support is the administration of flexible spending accounts in which pretax dollars can be used to pay for child care services.[64]

The most popular—and probably least expensive—initiative is a resource and referral system that provides useful information and assistance to employees with a variety of child care needs. IBM created the first nationwide network of referral services that has been used by many other corporations.[65] Referral programs may also be supplemented by seminars, support groups, libraries, and newsletters.

In addition, employers are working with community groups to expand and improve a variety of child care services. For example, some companies have funded after-school programs in schools or community agencies, others have supported "sick child care centers" in private child care centers, and still others have provided money to family day-care associations to increase the number of child care providers in family homes.[66] One insurance company in Florida has worked with a local school system that operates kindergarten through second-grade classes in a facility built by the company.[67] On a larger scale, 137 employers across the country invested $25 million in their 1992 launch of the American Business Collaborative. This joint venture has sought to improve the dependent care programs in the communities in which their employees live.[68]

There is considerable diversity among employees in terms of the type of child care assistance they find most useful. To accommodate this diversity, employers should attempt to offer packages of child care assistance that are reexamined periodically to ensure compatibility with employees' preferences.[69]

Although dependent care is often equated with child care, a growing area of concern is the care of elder relatives, most notably parents. With ever-increasing life spans, senior citizens are expected to make up 20 percent of the population by the year 2030.[70] In previous generations, nonemployed daughters and daughters-in-law often looked after their elders. Increasingly, these demands are being felt by employees who may not have the time, knowledge, or resources to help care for their loved ones.

As a result of these pressures, organizations are beginning to provide elder care support to their employees. This support can take the form of the flexible use of time to care for elders' needs, information about available services and policies, and support groups through employee assistance programs.[71] Some companies provide employees with subsidies to defray the costs of elder care and provide social workers to visit employees' elderly relatives.[72]

FLEXIBLE WORK ARRANGEMENTS

FLEXIBLE WORK SCHEDULES. As important as child care assistance can be to working parents, additional flexibility in the workplace remains a major priority for many employees. One of the early efforts in this regard was the establishment of flexible work schedules, which is now offered by more than 77 percent of the companies in the Friedman-Johnson survey. Flextime usually involves a core set of hours in which all employees must work (e.g., 10 AM to 3 PM), with a band of several hours around the core to provide flexible starting and leaving times.

Because flexible work schedules offer employees some degree of control over their time, they can help employees balance their work and family responsibilities and can reduce absenteeism and turnover.[73] Although the results have not been uniformly positive and the characteristics of the program must match the specific needs of the employees, flexible work schedules remain a central component of an organization's comprehensive approach to work-family issues.

FAMILY LEAVES. Another form of workplace flexibility is the opportunity to take a leave to care for children or other family members. As Arlene Johnson observed, many countries have maternity-leave legislation based on three principles: entitlement to a specific leave period (typically 14 weeks) before and after childbirth; partial or full pay during the leave period; and a guaranteed job on return from the leave.[74] Some countries have adopted supplementary parental leave (unpaid or partially paid) for parents to spend additional time with their infants. In 1993, the United States passed the Family and Medical Leave Act that provides employees with up to 12 weeks of unpaid, job-protected leave to care for a newborn or newly adopted child or a sick child, parent, or partner. This act applies to employees who work for organizations with 50 or more workers and who have been employed in the organization for at least 1 year, having worked a minimum of 1,250 hours within the prior 12-month period. In addition to the federal statute, many states have passed parental and family leave legislation.

Moreover, some action regarding family leaves has been taken in the private sector. A Conference Board survey found that 90 percent of the large companies polled provide disability leave for childbirth and 60 percent provide additional leave for new mothers (usually unpaid), averaging 11 weeks beyond disability. Parental leaves for fathers were reported by 44 percent of the firms, the vast majority unpaid. Friedman and Johnson report that 28 percent of the companies in their survey provided family or child care leaves for mothers, 22.3 percent for fathers, and 23.4 percent for adoptive parents.

It appears that family leave programs can improve recruitment and retention, although there has not been substantial research conducted. It is interesting that men have not generally taken advantage of parental leaves in great numbers, in part because they believe that it would hurt their careers.[75] Alan Deutschman reported that only 2 percent of men have used unpaid parental leave, although they may informally combine vacation time and sick leave to spend time with their newborn child.[76]

PART-TIME EMPLOYMENT. In the early 1990s, Felice Schwartz created a storm in corporate, feminist, and academic circles when she advocated part-time employment options for women managers and professionals with young children.[77] Schwartz observed that many career-and-family–oriented mothers were serious about their careers but also wanted to spend substantial time with their young children. When faced with the option of full-time employment or no employment, many of these women quit their jobs altogether.

Schwartz urged employers to provide part-time employment in managerial and professional positions until the woman was ready to return to her full-time job. This part-time arrangement could be in effect from several months to several years. Schwartz further recommended a job-sharing program in which pairs of part-timers could be jointly responsible for a full-time assignment. Dubbed the "mommy track" by journalists, part-time and job-shared positions have been hailed by some as a viable option for young mothers (and fathers) and have been criticized by others as a form of second-class citizenship for women. It has often been observed that men have informally negotiated lower levels of work involvement during periods of heavy family responsibility without the stigma attached to part-time employment. In fact, relatively few men have opted for part-time employment so far.[78]

Is part-time employment a reasonable alternative for working parents? Schwartz's view is that companies will continue to experience high turnover among women professionals and managers until part-time options are provided. Moreover, productivity can be higher for part-time employees than full-timers and may not necessarily stall career progress.[79]

However, it is feared that part-time employment, even for a brief period of time, signals to the organization a lack of serious commitment on the part of the woman. Perhaps it does have this connotation in organizations that lack insight on and experience with work-family issues. But Schwartz asks us to consider the "worst-case scenario" in which a woman pursues part-time employment for as many as 5 years following childbirth or adoption. Even in this situation, Schwartz argues, the "typical" woman would pursue a full-time career for 38 years (ages 22 to 31 and ages 36 to 65) compared with a typical man's continuous employment of 43 years.[80]

Should 5 years of part-time work (out of a career span of 43 years) severely curtail the career of a high-performing employee? The answer to this question depends on the organization's attitudes and behavior. If the employer or its managers stigmatize women who work part-time temporarily, interpret part-time employment as a lack of career interest, fail to provide challenging and important work to the women, hold to a rigid timetable for career success, and do not see a significant future for working mothers in the organization, then a self-fulfilling prophecy can be set in motion, and the woman's career is likely to derail.

However, if the organization or its managers understand the work-family dilemmas experienced by many women, perceive the woman's desire for part-time employment as temporary, provide challenging work during this period, and enable the woman to reenter the full-time work force in a supportive manner, then the long-term careers of women who opt for temporary part-time employment may not be seriously impaired. We would add that part-time employment opportunities should also be provided for men who are highly involved with their families. It is likely that the stigmas associated with part-time employment would be as strong, if not stronger, for men than women. Therefore, employers must prevent stereotypes and self-fulfilling prophecies from limiting the contributions that women and men can make to the organization.

FLEXIBLE CAREER PATHS. Beyond the establishment of part-time employment opportunities for parents of young children, organizations need to recognize that an employee's career path can have significant implications for his or her family life. Many men and women, aware of the trade-offs involved, wish to avoid a "fast-track" linear career path. Other career models that do not involve immense time commitments, extensive travel, or frequent relocation must be seen by the organization as viable and significant as long as the employee is performing effectively and contributing to the organization. Organizations, in other words, should legitimize and reward alternative career directions for employees.

Moreover, employees need to understand the effect of a particular career path on their family and personal lives. Just as a realistic job preview can present an accurate picture of entry-level positions in organizations, realistic information about jobs in alternative career options can help partners in two-career relationships make informed career decisions that are consistent with work, family, and personal values.[81] Consider the following two illustrations of companies providing more flexible careers paths:

> PricewaterhouseCoopers is a worldwide professional services firm of more than 50,000 partners and staff members, practicing in 118 countries, including 90 offices in the United States. During the early part of the 1990s, management recognized the need for greater flexibility in its career progression system. The old system in existence up to that point was somewhat rigid, and employee career goals were based on attaining the designation of partner within a set number of years. This career model required employees to work very long hours and travel extensively. Those not making partner in the specified time frame were expected to leave.
>
> Unfortunately, this rigid model of career success produced a high rate of undesirable turnover. It became apparent that PricewaterhouseCoopers would need to provide alternative career tracks if it wished to achieve better retention of professionals with specialized expertise, better service to clients, and more varied ways for employees to succeed.
>
> In essence, the new program emphasized a competency-based approach to career progression in which employees can develop the abilities needed to perform in more demanding roles at a rate that is more compatible with their life-style. With the new system, employees have the opportunity to develop expertise in multiple areas or choose to build an in-depth focus in a single function. They are not required to achieve partner status in a specified number of years to remain with the firm and can contribute to the firm in significant ways even if they do not aspire (or have not developed the skills) to become a partner.[82]
>
> Employees in one division of a large high-technology company began to resist vertical mobility along the dominant, marketing-oriented career path. Some employees resisted because they did not want to relocate for family reasons. Others were pleased with their current job assignment and were not interested in further promotion. Still others wanted to remain in the company but were getting bored with their present career field. Most of these people were productive employees the organization did not want to lose.
>
> The organization responded by conducting job analyses and identifying a wide range of alternative career paths. The information was used to prepare a handbook describing career opportunities within the division and specifying the key features of each job. The line managers were then trained to use the handbook to counsel their subordinates on career-related decisions.

Even employees on a fast track can be developed in ways that are less disruptive to their family lives. For example, companies can place a variety of facilities at a central location, so employees can acquire a breadth of experience without the need to relocate. Companies can also use membership on task forces and special project assignments as an alternative to relocation, and employers that require overseas assignments can shorten these assignments to a matter of months rather than years. When relocation is essential, it is often critical that the organization support the career-oriented partner of the relocated employee. Such support could include career guidance, help in skill assessment and resume preparation, and the waiver of policies prohibiting husbands and wives from simultaneously working for the same organization.[83]

Telecommuting, often called *flexplace*, permits work to be performed at a satellite office or more typically from home.[84] Work-at-home programs, made more feasible with advanced computer technology, can give employees more discretion over their use of time to balance work and family demands. Telecommuting does not eliminate work-family conflict and, in fact, may exacerbate stress at times because of the parents' physical presence at home and the feelings of social isolation.[85] Nor does it eliminate the need for additional child care assistance.[86] Nevertheless, telecommuting can still be a viable option for parents whose ability to juggle work and family is enhanced through their physical presence at home and/or the substantial reduction in commuting times.

CHANGING THE ORGANIZATION'S WORK-FAMILY CULTURE

Organizations that are responsive to employees' work-family concerns have revised their cultures to achieve compatibility with the needs of the contemporary work force. Some cultural assumptions that need to be revised include the following:[87]

- "Keep your personal problems at home."
- "Give them (employees) an inch and they will take a mile."
- "Put in long hours regardless of family responsibilities."
- "Travel when and where the organization dictates."
- "Relocate without concern for family needs."
- "Presence (at the workplace) equals performance."
- "Hours (worked) equal output."

The family-responsive organization must replace these assumptions with a more supportive culture. Central components of this culture are the recognition of the legitimacy of family issues to all employees as well as the significance of work-family issues to the organization itself. Such a culture will stimulate an awareness of the potential for work-family conflict and will encourage discussion of the impact of the conflict on the employee and the organization. The organization will understand that many employees value both career and family, and it will develop policies and programs to mesh employees' values with the organization's need to be effective and competitive.

A family-responsive organization should establish an explicit corporate policy regarding work and family and communicate this policy throughout the organization. Some companies such as DuPont have incorporated work-family issues into their mission statements to reflect and reinforce their commitment in this area:

> DuPont believes it will be beneficial to the company, the communities in which it operates, and future generations if the company's increasingly diverse work force is enabled to lead full and productive lives, both at work and at home.
>
> The company is committed to making changes in the workplace and fostering changes in the community that are sensitive to the changing family unit and the increasingly diverse work force.

Companies have also formed work-family groups or departments within the organizational structure whose primary function is to develop and administer the kinds of work-family programs discussed in this chapter.[88] Communication regarding work-family issues is strengthened through seminars, support groups, and newsletters.[89]

Because the supervisor is a critical link in administering policy, responsive employers have sponsored training to help supervisors react with flexibility to work scheduling and career planning. Organizations that have successfully changed their work-family culture also focus on measuring performance results rather than the number of hours or weekends spent at the office or other symbols of organizational commitment. Perhaps most important, the responsive organization realizes that its actions can benefit its employees and give itself a competitive edge in the marketplace.

One of the most powerful ways to affect culture change is to reexamine the basic ways in which work is conducted. Lotte Bailyn describes efforts toward achieving work-family integration at three work sites in the Xerox Corporation: an engineering group, a customer administration center, and a sales and service district.[90]

At each work site, Bailyn and her colleagues sought to identify and reduce the cultural barriers to work-family integration; barriers such as the belief that time spent at work reflects an employee's commitment and productivity, and that managers must closely monitor employees' work activities to achieve control. Working with managers and groups of employees, work-family issues were openly discussed. Often, teams of employees were given the responsibility for restructuring their work in ways that met their work goals *and* enabled them to meet their family and personal needs. Bailyn presents positive results in all three of the work sites, although she cautions that not all the problems have been solved.

Finally, a supportive organization avoids relying on patchwork solutions to problems and instead develops a comprehensive program that addresses a variety of work-family issues. A description of DuPont's comprehensive corporate programs regarding work-family issues is summarized below:[91]

SURVEY RESEARCH

- Employee surveys regarding work-family issues were conducted in 1985, 1988, 1990, 1991, and 1995. The results of the surveys produced many recommendations to assist DuPont employees and their families with work-family concerns and resulted in the formation of a work/life division within the human resource function.
- The most recent survey results indicate a direct correlation between a supportive work environment and employee productivity. Employees who knew of or who had used work/life programs felt more productive and more loyal to the company.

FAMILY LEAVE

- A 6-month family leave is offered to all full-service employees for maternity, paternity, adoption, or serious illness of a parent, partner, or child. This unpaid leave is in addition to paid time off for disability and vacation.
- During this period, benefits continue at the same level as before the leave, there is an option of part-time work, and there is a commitment to return the employee to the same or similar job of comparable pay and status.

FLEXIBLE WORK SCHEDULES

- Flexible work practices are designed to help employees manage their complex lives effectively.
- Specific flexible work practices include flextime, part-time work, job-sharing/job-splitting, a compressed work week, work-at-home, and leaves.

SPOUSE RELOCATION PROGRAM

- All attempts are made to place a spouse of a relocated employee within a DuPont site.
- Up to $500 is provided to a spouse of a relocated employee for fees related to career counseling and résumé preparation.
- In the case of a dual-career couple, both of whom are employed by DuPont, a 6-month leave of absence is granted to the spouse of the relocated employee to conduct a job search.

BENEFITS

- Employees are reimbursed for child care expenses caused by overnight business travel.
- A national dependent-care resource and referral service was established for DuPont employees in 1990 to provide consultation and referrals to

caregivers and community services for child care and elder care, education, and adoption.

■ Flexible spending accounts are available for before-tax savings on medical and dependent-care expenses.

■ An adoption assistance program provides up to $3,000 for the adoption of a child.

INVOLVEMENT IN CHILD CARE ACTIVITIES WITHIN THE COMMUNITY

■ DuPont donated $2 million and 5 acres of land to build a child care center at their Chestnut Run site that will be open to the public.

■ DuPont provided seed money for a referral service in Delaware and funded child care centers near DuPont facilities.

COMMUNICATIONS

■ DuPont provides a variety of communications programs for its employees, including a lending library of books and videos for working families; corporate guidelines on flexible work practices to help managers respond to employee and business needs; and publications and videos on work-family benefits and programs.

■ Supervisor awareness training is conducted to assist managers and supervisors to use flexibility as a business management tool.

■ The work/life group conducts site presentations on work-family issues on request.

■ A network of work/life committees has been formed throughout the United States to disseminate information and share ideas.

CAREER MANAGEMENT AND THE QUALITY OF LIFE

As shown throughout this chapter, work experiences can affect physical, emotional, and family lives. Although many societies throughout the world seem to assume that career success paves the way for a life of happiness and satisfaction, many "successful" managers and professionals exhibit considerable self-doubt, frustration, and alienation. Abraham Korman believes that certain features of organizational and family life can produce a sense of alienation, regardless of the level of career success. Research indicates that[92]

■ Highly successful male executives in midlife often doubt themselves, their career, and the meaning of success.

■ Successful young executives often experience high levels of stress and feelings of meaninglessness in life.

- A number of successful managers report difficulties relating to others and feeling their own emotions.
- Many middle-aged professionals and managers go through periods of intense frustration, from which some never recover.

Personal alienation involves separation or estrangement from oneself to the point that a person does not act in ways that meet his or her personal needs. Social alienation involves separation from others and an inability to care about and relate to other people. Why should people who have accomplished so much feel so alienated?

For one thing, life's realities can contradict some of people's most cherished expectations: that work will be interesting and meaningful, that family and personal lives will be satisfying, and that life will be fair. When one experiences the drudgery of work, the imperfection of personal and family lives, and the unfairness in the world, frustration and anger may result.

Second, work puts people in many conflicting situations in which they are unable to satisfy everyone's demands, including the tug between work and family. No matter how hard people try to resolve these conflicts, they are likely to experience stress and guilt.

Third, many people begin to feel powerless as they realize how many things they do (e.g., pursuing promotions) or buy (e.g., bigger homes and more expensive cars) because they are expected to, not because they really want to. Feelings of powerlessness remind people that their behavior frequently does not reflect who they really are.

Fourth, the pursuit of career success can make it difficult to satisfy the need for close relationships with other people. The world of achievement and competition pays little attention to people's emotional and affiliative needs. How can people become close to colleagues with whom they are constantly competing for promotions and other scarce resources? Why should people develop deep relationships with neighbors when an imminent relocation will take them away from these newly found friends?

Disconfirmed expectations, conflicting demands, a feeling of powerlessness, and lack of affiliative satisfaction may all begin to hit home near the midlife transition when an awareness of mortality triggers a reappraisal of life's accomplishments and meaning. Although it is not yet clear how widespread this career success/personal failure syndrome is, the message seems to be clear: Career success does not guarantee personal satisfaction.

However, we believe that it is not career success itself that produces family and personal problems, but rather some of the things people do to pursue success. For example, a recent study of business professionals found that preoccupation with work—not career success—interfered with a satisfying family life.[93] Moreover, career success is most likely to produce alienation and feelings of failure for people who ignore their family's emotional needs, disregard their own needs to be close to other people, perform tasks at work that are neither satisfying nor meaningful, and emphasize material success to the exclusion of emotional, social, and spiritual gratification.

However, deteriorated personal lives cannot be blamed entirely on work experiences. Although job stress and extensive career commitment can lead one to overlook his or her private life, managers may also use work as an alibi to explain an unhappy marriage. Instead, the real culprit may be one's own fears and ineptitudes in the family domain. In particular, Fernando Bartolome observed a number of disturbing tendencies among otherwise successful, competent managers.[94] The first is the widespread assumption that it is easy to be a good spouse or a good parent, such that one does not have to work at it and does not have to learn how to relate to a family. Some managers believe that if they concentrate on work, their family life will take care of itself. Second, Bartolome observed a pervasive fear of confronting conflicts in marriages. Because many people do not know how to argue and confront differences constructively, they avoid honest discussions and difficult decisions. Of course, unresolved marital conflicts usually get worse if left unattended.

Third, candid discussions of marital problems are often preempted by time-consuming jobs and child-rearing responsibilities. "Work and children are dangerous distractions from dealing with marital issues. They are dangerous because they are such legitimate, right, and perfect excuses."[95] These three obstacles to effectiveness in the family role inevitably lead to the fourth—procrastination. As Bartolome observes, people believe that they can take care of their private lives "tomorrow."

Joan Kofodimos has examined the imbalance that many executives experience between their work and their family lives.[96] Based on interviews of male executives, Kofodimos describes how the intense time and energy that go into establishing a career produce a vicious cycle. Intense work involvement brings career rewards and success but also leaves little time to establish and nourish family relationships. These family relationships begin to disintegrate over time and contrast sharply in the executive's mind with the satisfaction and success derived from work. As the executive's family life becomes less and less satisfying, more and more time is devoted to the satisfying and rewarding career. Due to this escape to the world of work, family relationships deteriorate even further.

These analyses by Korman, Bartolome, and Kofodimos point to the importance of integrating work and nonwork lives. People need to think in terms of how their career affects their entire life. Career management, as an active problem-solving process, is entirely suitable to this task. Each component of the career management model presents a number of specific suggestions relevant to the integration of work and nonwork lives. These include:

EXPLORATION

- Assess the importance of work, family, and leisure roles. Discuss these lifestyle preferences with family members.
- Learn how to interact constructively with family members.
- Understand your family's values and resources.

- Understand the effect of work experiences on your physical and psychological health.
- Be aware of the implications of different career fields and career paths on your family and personal life.
- Seek professional help to understand these issues if necessary.

GOAL SETTING

- Emphasize the expressive component of your career goal.
- Appreciate the satisfactions that can be derived from today's work.
- Recognize that your conceptual career goal can be achieved in a variety of different jobs.
- Pursue goals that have real meaning to you, not those that require you to live up to other people's expectations.
- Understand your family's view of your career goal.
- Understand how the achievement of your career goal affects your family and personal life, and how your family situation affects the likelihood of achieving your career goal.

CAREER STRATEGIES

- Recognize the implications of specific career strategies (e.g., extended work involvement, rapid mobility) on your family and personal life.
- Discuss career strategies with significant people in your life before and during their implementation.
- Always consider the personal acceptability of a strategy as well as its instrumental value. Avoid strategies that violate ethical or moral beliefs.

CAREER APPRAISAL

- Seek feedback regarding different parts of your life. Be open to feedback from work and nonwork sources.
- Discuss changes in personal and career values with family members.
- Examine the effects of career strategies on your work and nonwork lives on an ongoing basis.
- Be willing to admit mistakes and redirect career or family life if necessary.

In sum, active career management—specifically, career management that incorporates work and nonwork issues—is vital to enhancing one's quality of life. A common element that cuts across all components of career management is communication. People need to enlarge their scope of thinking—about work, family, and personal values—and discuss these issues with supportive people on a regular basis, not just when a crisis appears.

SUMMARY

Work and family lives affect each other in a variety of ways. Although the two roles are mutually supportive in many respects, there are times when they conflict. Three forms of work-family conflict were identified: time-based conflict, in which the time spent in one role interferes with the requirements of the other role; strain-based conflict, in which stress in one role affects experiences in the other role; and behavior-based conflict, in which behavior that is appropriate in one role is dysfunctional in the other role.

Also examined was the nature of two-career relationships in contemporary society. Despite its many rewards, a two-career relationship faces a number of potentially stressful conditions: extensive work-family conflict, gender identity problems, competition and jealousy between partners, negotiation of career priorities, and the possibility of somewhat limited or slow career progress. To manage these potential stressors, two-career couples need to learn effective coping behavior, use supportive relationships with other people, and remain flexible in their careers or family arrangements.

Organizations can respond to work-family issues by providing their employees with various forms of dependent-care assistance. Employers can also provide more flexible work arrangements, including flexible work schedules, family leave, part-time employment, and opportunities for job sharing. They should also legitimize alternative career paths so that employees can contribute to the organization in a way that is consistent with their family values. Employers' actions will be most effective if they develop a culture that understands and supports employees' attempts to balance their work and family responsibilities.

Employees need to manage their careers in the context of their overall quality of life. They must realize that career success does not guarantee personal happiness. Some people who are successful in society's eyes are frustrated and alienated. In addition, many people have great difficulty facing family problems and avoid confronting issues, thereby risking even greater problems in the future. The career management process can be used to address these kinds of issues. Exploration, goal setting, strategies, and appraisal all require communication about work and nonwork issues on an ongoing basis.

ASSIGNMENT

If you are currently employed, examine your responses to the items in Table 11.1 and assess your level of work-family conflict. Why is your level of conflict high or low? Do you think your level of conflict will change or remain the same in the near future? Why? If your conflict is high, how can you cope with the conflict more effectively?

If you are not currently employed, what level of work-family conflict do you anticipate in the next 2 years? Five to 10 years? Why do you feel that way?

If you are married or in a significant relationship, ask your partner to answer the items in Table 11.1. What do your partner's score and your score tell you about work-family issues in your relationship?

DISCUSSION QUESTIONS

1. Develop a profile of the type of person most likely to experience extensive work-family conflict. Identify work pressures, family pressures, and personal characteristics most likely to produce work-family conflict.

2. You are likely to become a partner in a two-career relationship at some point in your life. Perhaps you are already. What might be the major sources of stress in the relationship? Do the stresses outweigh the potential advantages of a two-career relationship? Why or why not?

3. Some people contend that children are the victims of a two-career relationship. Defend or attack that contention, giving the reasoning behind your position.

4. Two-career couples cope most effectively when they collaborate to solve problems. Explain how a couple could work collaboratively in the following situation:

   Your partner has just received an exciting job offer that would require relocation to a small town in another part of the country. The job is an excellent career opportunity for your partner, a private accountant, but you think you would have difficulty finding a job in your field (public relations) in a small town. Besides, you and the 14-year-old twins are extremely happy in your community.

5. Defend or attack the following statement: "Career success inevitably produces alienation and feelings of personal failure." Provide the reasoning behind your position.

ENDNOTES

1. J. Barling and D. Sorensen, "Work and Family: In Search of a Relevant Research Agenda," in *Creating Tomorrow's Organizations,* ed. C. L. Cooper and S. E. Jackson (New York: Wiley, 1997), 157–169; J. H. Greenhaus and S. Parasuraman, "Research on Work, Family, and Gender: Current Status and Future Directions," in *Handbook of Gender and Work,* ed. G. N. Powell (Newbury Park, CA: Sage, 1999); S. A. Lobel, "Allocation of Investment in Work and Family Roles: Alternative Theories and Implications for Research," *Academy of Management Review* 16 (1991): 507–521; S. Parasuraman and J. H. Greenhaus, "Personal Portrait: The Life-Style of the Woman Manager," in *Women in Management: Trends, Issues, and Challenges in Managerial Diversity,* vol. 4, ed. E. A. Fagenson (Newbury Park, CA: Sage, 1993), 186–211; S. Zedeck, "Introduction: Exploring the Domain of Work and Family Concerns," in *Work, Families and Organization,* ed. S. Zedeck (San Francisco, CA: Jossey-Bass, 1992), 1–32.

2. U. S. Bureau of the Census, *Statistical Abstract of the United States: 1997* (117th ed.). (Washington, DC: U.S. Bureau of the Census, 1997),; L. Genasci, "Firms Pledge Millions for Dependent Care," *Philadelphia Inquirer,* July 17, 1992, C10, C16; K. A. Samon, "Great Expectations: An Update on the Wharton Women of '80," *Working Women* July (1991): 66–69, 92.

3. D. E. Friedman and A. A. Johnson, "Moving from Programs to Culture Change: The Next Stage for the Corporate Work-Family Agenda," in *Integrating Work and Family: Challenges and Choices for a Changing World,* ed. S. Parasuraman and J. H. Greenhaus (Westport, CT: Quorum, 1997), 192–208.

4. J. H. Greenhaus and N. J. Beutell, "Sources of Conflict between Work and Family Roles," *Academy of Management Review* 10 (1985): 76–88.

5. P. Evans and F. Bartolome, *Must Success Cost So Much?* (New York: Basic Books, 1980); Greenhaus and Parasuraman, "Research on Work, Family, and Gender."

6. V. E. Schein, "The Relationship between Sex Role Stereotypes and Requisite Management Characteristics," *Journal of Applied Psychology* 57 (1973): 95–100.

7. R. J. Burke and P. Bradshaw, "Occupational and Life Stress and the Family," *Small Group Behavior* 12 (1981): 329–375.

8. R. J. Burke, T. Weir, and R. E. DuWors, "Type A Behaviour of Administrators and Wives' Reports of Marital Satisfaction and Well-Being," *Journal of Applied Psychology* 64 (1979): 57–65; K. E. Kelly and B. K. Houston, "Type A Behavior in Employed Women: Relation to Work, Marital, and Leisure Variables, Social Support, Stress, Tension, and Health," *Journal of Personality and Social Psychology* 48 (1985): 1067–1079.

9. M. R. Frone and R. W. Rice, "Work-Family Conflict: The Effect of Job and Family Involvement," *Journal of Occupational Behaviour* 8 (1987): 45–53.

10. F. Bartolome and P. Evans, "Professional Lives versus Private Lives: Shifting Patterns of Managerial Commitment," *Organizational Dynamics* 7, no. 4 (1979): 3–29.

11. Although some studies have found greater conflict among women than men, other studies report no sex difference in work-family conflict or even greater conflict among men than women. See Greenhaus and Parasuraman, "Research on Work, Family, and Gender."

12. Ibid.; E. E. Kossek and C. Ozeki, "Work-Family Conflict, Policies and the Job-Life Satisfaction Relationship: A Review and Directions for Organizational Behavior-Human Resources Research," *Journal of Applied Psychology* 83 (1998): 139–149.

13. Much of the discussion of work-family integration is based on the work of S. D. Friedman and J. H. Greenhaus, *Allies or Enemies? How Choices about Work and Family Affect the Quality of Men's and Women's Lives* (New York: Oxford, in press).

14. Ibid.

15. F. S. Hall and D. T. Hall, *The Two-Career Couple* (Reading, MA: Addison-Wesley, 1979).

16. G. K. Baruch and R. C. Barnett, "Role Quality, Multiple Role Involvement and Psychological Well-Being in Midlife Women," *Journal of Personality and Social Psychology* 5 (1986): 578–585; G. Spitze, "Women's Employment and Family Relations: A Review," *Journal of Marriage and the Family* 50 (1988): 595–618; R. A. Valdez and B. A. Gutek, "Family Roles: A Help or Hindrance for Working Women?" in *Women's Career Development,* ed. B. A. Gutek and L. Larwood (Newbury Park, CA: Sage, 1987), 157–169.

17. Spitze, "Women's Employment and Family Relations."

18. Parasuraman and Greenhaus, "Personal Portrait."

19. N. Gupta and G. D. Jenkins, "Dual-Career Couples: Stress, Stressors, Strains, and Strategies," in *Human Stress and Cognition in Organizations: An Integrated Perspective,* ed. T. A. Beehr and R. S. Bhagat (New York: Wiley Interscience, 1985), 141–175; Friedman and Greenhaus, "Allies or Enemies?"

20. E. Galinsky, J. T. Bond, and D. E. Friedman, *The Changing Workforce* (New York: Families and Work Institute, 1993).

21. A. Hochschild, *The Second Shift* (New York: Viking, 1989).

22. Friedman and Greenhaus, "Allies or Enemies?"

23. S. D. Nollen, "The Work-Family Dilemma: How HR Managers Can Help," *Personnel* May (1989): 25–30.

24. B. M. Campbell, *Successful Women, Angry Men* (New York: Random House, 1986).

25. Friedman and Greenhaus, "Allies or Enemies?"

26. Ibid.

27. Ibid.

28. Ibid.

29. J. M. Brett and A. H. Reilly, "On the Road Again: Predicting the Job Transfer Decision," *Journal of Applied Psychology* 73 (1988): 614–620; C. Hymowitz, "Stepping Off the Fast Track," *The Wall Street Journal,* June 13, 1989, B1; D. T. Hall, "Promoting Work/Family Balance: An Organization–Change Approach," *Organizational Dynamics* Winter (1990): 5–18.

30. H. Papanek, "Men, Women and Work: Reflections on the Two-Person Career," *American Journal of Sociology* 78 (1973): 852–872.

31. A. S. Baron, "Working Partners: Career-Committed Mothers and Their Husbands," *Business Horizons* September–October (1987): 45–50; B. A. Gutek, R. L., Repetti, and D. L. Silver, "Nonwork Roles and Stress at Work," in *Causes, Coping, and Consequences of Stress at Work,* ed. C. L. Cooper and R. Payne (New York: John Wiley & Sons, 1988), 141–174; F. N. Schwartz, *Breaking with Tradition* (New York: Warner Books, 1992); C. R. Stoner and R. I. Hartman, "Family Responsibilities and Career Progress: The Good, the Bad, and the Ugly," *Business Horizons* May–June (1990): 7–14.

32. J. H. Greenhaus, S. Parasuraman, C. S. Granrose, S. Rabinowitz, and N. J. Beutell, "Sources of Work-Family Conflict among Two-Career Couples," *Journal of Vocational Behavior* 34 (1989): 133–153.

33. M. M. Poloma, B. F. Pendleton, and T. N. Garland, "Reconsidering the Dual-Career Marriage: A Longitudinal Approach," in *Two Paychecks: Life in Dual-Earner Families,* ed. J. Aldous (Beverly Hills, CA: Sage, 1982), 173–192.

34. Hall and Hall, "The Two-Career Couple."

35. J. H. Greenhaus, A. G. Bedeian, and K. W. Mossholder, "Work Experiences, Job Performance, and Feelings of Personal and Family Well-Being," *Journal of Vocational Behavior* 31 (1987): 200–215.

36. S. Parasuraman and J. H. Greenhaus, "An Exchange Perspective on Support Provided by Partners in Two-Career Relationships," *paper presented at the 1992 Annual Meeting of the Academy of Management,* Las Vegas, Nevada, 1992.

37. Hall and Hall, "The Two-Career Couple."

38. D. A. Skinner, "Dual-Career Family Stress and Coping: A Literature Review," *Family Relations* 29 (1980): 473–480.

39. F. S. Chapman, "Executive Guilt: Who's Taking Care of the Children?" *Fortune,* February 16, 1987, 30–37.

40. P. K. Knaub, "Growing Up in a Dual-Career Family: The Children's Perceptions," *Human Relations* 35 (1986): 431–437.

41. C. W. Stephan and J. Corder, "The Effects of Dual-Career Families on Adolescents' Sex-Role Attitudes, Work and Family Plans, and Choices of Important Others," *Journal of Marriage and the Family* 47 (1985): 921–929.

42. K. Labich, "Can Your Career Hurt Your Kids?" *Fortune,* May 20, 1991, 38, 40, 44, 48, 52, 56.

43. Spitze, "Women's Employment and Family Relation."

44. Friedman and Greenhaus, "Allies or Enemies?"

45. R. Rapoport and R. N. Rapoport, "Further Considerations on the Dual Career Family," *Human Relations* 24 (1971): 519–533.

46. Parasuraman and Greenhaus, "Personal Portrait."

47. L. Bailyn, "Career and Family Orientations of Husbands and Wives in Relation to Marital Happiness," *Human Relations* 23 (1970): 97–113.

48. Parasuraman and Greenhaus, "Personal Portrait."

49. Hall and Hall, "The Two-Career Couple"; quote on p. 24.

50. D. T. Hall, "A Model of Coping with Role Conflict: The Role Behavior of College-Educated Women," *Administrative Science Quarterly* 17 (1972): 471–489.

51. B. Friedan, " Takes a New Turn," *New York Times Magazine,* November 18, 1979, pp. 40, 92, 94, 96, 98, 100, 102, 106.

52. N. J. Beutell and J. H. Greenhaus, "Integration of Home and Nonhome Roles: Women's Conflict and Coping Behavior," *Journal of Applied Psychology* 68 (1983): 43–48.

53. Hall and Hall, "The Two-Career Couple."

54. Ibid.

55. Galinsky, Bond, and Friedman, "The Changing Workforce."

56. Ibid.; S. Shellenbarger, "More Job Seekers Put Family Needs First," *The Wall Street Journal,* November 15, 1991, B1, B12.

57. S. Shellenbarger, "New Job Hunters Ask Recruiters 'Is There a Life after Work.'" *The Wall Street Journal,* January 29, 1997, B1.

58. F. N. Schwartz, "Management Women and the Facts of Life," *Harvard Business Review* January–February (1989): 65–76; Schwartz, "Breaking with Tradition."

59. Schwartz, "Breaking with Tradition."

60. See Chapman, "Executive Guilt"; a more recent study reported by Galinsky, Bond, and Friedman, "The Changing Workforce," found that women with children younger than the age of 13 missed about 1 day of work for child-related reasons in a 3-month period. A recent survey by David J. Maume of the University of Cincinnati's Kunz Center for the Study of Work and Family reported that only 20 percent of Ohio's working parents lost time from work in the winter of 1998 because of a problem with their child care arrangement.

61. Friedman and Greenhaus, "Allies or Enemies?"; Galinsky, Bond, and Friedman, "The Changing Workforce."

62. D. T. Hall and J. Richter, "Balancing Work Life and Home Life: What Can Organizations Do To Help? *Academy of Management Executive* 2 (1988): 213–223.

63. Friedman and Johnson, "Moving from Programs to Culture Change."

64. D. E. Friedman, "Work and Family: The New Strategic Plan," *Human Resource Planning* 13, no. 2 (1990): 79–89.

65. Ibid.

66. Ibid.

67. F. S. Rodgers and C. Rodgers, "Business and the Facts of Family Life," *Harvard Business Review* November–December (1989): 121–129.

68. Friedman and Johnson, "Moving from Programs to Culture Change."

69. E. E. Kossek, "Diversity in Child Care Assistance Needs: Employee Problems, Preferences, and Work-Related Outcomes," *Personnel Psychology* 43 (1990): 769–791.

70. Friedman, "Work and Family: The New Strategic Plan."

71. Ibid.

72. S. Shellenbarger, "Employers Put Money behind Elder Care," *The Wall Street Journal,* May 6, 1992, B1.

73. Rodgers and Rodgers, "Business and the Facts of Family Life."

74. A. A. Johnson, "Parental Leave—Is It the Business of Business?" *Human Resource Planning* 13, no. 2 (1990): 119–131.

75. G. N. Powell, "The Sex Difference in Employee Inclinations Regarding Work-Family Programs: Why Does It Exist, Should We Care, and What Should Be Done about It (If Anything)?" in *Integrating Work and Family: Challenges and Choices for a Changing World,* ed. S. Parasuraman and J. H. Greenhaus (Westport, CT: Quorum, 1997), 167–174.

76. A. Deutschman, "Pioneers of the New Balance," *Fortune,* May 20, 1991, 60–62, 64, 68.

77. Schwartz, "Management Women and the Facts of Life."

78. Powell, "The Sex Difference in Employee Inclinations."

79. Rodgers and Rodgers, "Business and the Facts of Family Life"; Deutschman, "Pioneers of the New Balance."

80. Schwartz, "Management Women and the Facts of Life."

81. N. J. Beutell and J. H. Greenhaus, "Balancing Acts: Work-Family Conflict and the Dual-Career Couple," in *Not as Far as You Think: The Realities of Working Women,* ed. L. L. Moore (Lexington, MA: Lexington Books, 1986), 149–162; R. Y. Magid, "When Mothers and Fathers Work: How Employers Can Help," *Personnel* December (1986): 56.

82. The discussion of Price Waterhouse is based on M. Connor, K. Hooks, and T. McGuire, "Gaining legitimacy for Work Arrangements and Career Paths: The Business Case for Public Accounting and Professional Services Firms," in *Integrating Work and Family: Challenges and Choices for a Changing World,* ed. S. Parasuraman and J. H. Greenhaus (Westport, CT: Quorum, 1997), 154–166, as well as G. A. Callanan and J. H. Greenhaus, "Personal and Career Development," in *Changing Concepts and Practices for Human Resources Management,* ed. A. I. Kraut and A. K. Korman (San Francisco, CA: Jossey-Bass, 1999, 146–171).

83. Rodgers and Rodgers, "Business and the Facts of Family Life"; S. Shellenbarger, "Allowing Fast Trackers to Stay in One Place," *The Wall Street Journal,* January 7, 1992, B1; C. H. Driessnack, "Spouse Relocation: A Moving Experience," *Personnel Administrator* August (1987): 94–102.

84. F. Riley and D. W. McCloskey, "Telecommuting as a Response to Helping People Balance Work and Family," in *Integrating Work and Family: Challenges and Choices for a Changing World,* ed. S. Parasuraman and J. H. Greenhaus (Westport, CT: Quorum, 1997), 133–142.

85. B. Shamir and I. Salomon, "Work-at-Home and the Quality of Working Life," *Academy of Management Review* 10 (1985): 455–464.

86. Riley and McCloskey, "Telecommuting as a Response."

87. Friedman, "Work and Family: The New Strategic Plan," 87; Magid, "When Mothers and Fathers Work," 50.

88. Many companies refer to such organizational units and practices as "work-life" rather than "work-family" to be more inclusive of employees who may not have partners or children but do have a personal life.

89. Magid, "When Mothers and Fathers Work"; C. M. Solomon, "Marriott's Family Matters," *Personnel Journal* October (1991): 40–42.

90. L. Bailyn, "The Impact of Corporate Culture on Work-Family Integration," in *Integrating Work and Family: Challenges and Choices for a Changing World*, ed. S. Parasuraman and J. H. Greenhaus (Westport, CT: Quorum, 1997), 209–219.

91. We thank Richard Vintigni of DuPont's work/life group for his description of these programs.

92. A. K. Korman, "Career Success and Personal Failure: Mid- to Late-Career Feelings and Events," in *Career Growth and Human Resource Strategies*, ed. M. London and E. M. Mone (New York: Quorum Books, 1988), 81–94; K. Labich, "Can Your Career Hurt Your Kids?" *Fortune*, May 20, 1991, 38, 40, 44, 48, 52, 56; A. K. Korman, U. Wittig-Berman, and D. Lang, "Career Success and Personal Failure: Alienation in Professionals and Managers," *Academy of Management Journal* 24 (1981): 342–360.

93. Friedman and Greenhaus, "Allies or Enemies?"

94. F. Bartolome, "The Work Alibi: When It's Harder to Go Home," *Harvard Business Review* 61, no. 2 (1983): 67–74.

95. Ibid.; quote is on p. 70.

96. J. R. Kofodimos, "Why Executives Lose Their Balance," *Organizational Dynamics* 19, no. 1 (1990): 58–73.

12

Managing Diversity

According to projections reported in Workforce 2000, the U.S. work force is becoming increasingly diverse.[1] Of course, as the work force becomes more diverse, employers will also become substantially more diverse. Organizations that can manage their diversity effectively are likely to be more productive and competitive.[2] The significance of work force diversity can best be conveyed by considering the following statistics and demographic forecasts:[3]

- By the year 2050, one-half of the U.S. population will consist of African-Americans, Asians, Hispanics, and Native Americans.
- By the year 2000, African-Americans will comprise 12 percent of the U.S. work force, Asians 4 percent, Hispanics 10 percent, and women 48 percent.
- Between 1983 and 1996, the percentage of women managers increased from 32 to 44, black managers from 4.7 to nearly 7, and Hispanic managers from 2.8 to 4.8.
- In 1996, nearly 63 percent of married women with children younger than 6 were in the work force, and that percentage is likely to increase in the future.
- Worldwide competition requires organizations to be staffed with the most talented employees available.
- Large companies increasingly cross national boundaries in their operations, and the consumer behavior of women and minorities is critical to the competitiveness of many organizations.

The increasing diversity of the population and the work force requires organizations to recognize their dependency on a more varied employee base. There is justifiable concern about organizations' ability to manage employees who are not only different from the traditionally dominant white male managerial base but are also different from one another in many respects. In part, this concern is due to the career difficulties experienced by many women and minorities. As Anne Morrison and Mary Ann Von Glinow have noted, although the number of women, blacks, and Hispanics in management has risen dramatically, the upward career mobility of these groups has been stymied. They observed the presence of a glass ceiling or "a barrier so subtle that it is transparent, yet so strong that it prevents women and minorities from moving up in the management hierarchy."[4] The glass ceiling effect has also been observed in an analysis conducted by the U.S. Department of Labor.[5]

Taylor Cox and Stacy Blake have provided six arguments for why an organization can improve its competitive advantage through the effective management of its cultural diversity.[6] A brief summary of these six arguments is presented below:

- Cost Argument—Organizations have not been as successful in managing women and minorities as in managing white males. Therefore, organizations that are unable to manage an increasingly dominant part of the work force will incur considerable additional costs that will detract from their productivity.

- Resource-Acquisition Argument—Organizations that have the most favorable reputation for managing a culturally diverse work force will attract the most talented women and minorities into their ranks.

- Marketing Argument—Organizations that serve multinational or domestically multicultural consumers will benefit from a diverse work force that brings a blend of insights and cultural sensitivities to the organizations' marketing efforts.

- Creativity Argument—The representation of varying perspectives in a culturally diverse work force should enhance the level of creativity in the organization.

- Problem-Solving Argument—Varying perspectives in a culturally diverse work force should enable problem-solving groups to produce high-quality solutions and decisions.

- System Flexibility Argument—Organizations that manage diversity effectively become more fluid and flexible, which enables them to respond to environmental changes more quickly and efficiently.

Later in this chapter, we present our opinions on the strength of these arguments. But first, we examine barriers to fairness in organizations, identify programs and policies that organizations can provide to manage diversity effectively, and propose actions that individuals can take to manage their careers in a culturally diverse organization.

FAIRNESS IN ORGANIZATIONS

As noted earlier, one reason for the concern about organizations' ability to manage diversity is the suspicion that women and minorities are not growing in their careers to a degree commensurate with their talents. For example, although about 44 percent of all managers are women, only 3 to 5 percent of senior managers are women. The percentage of minority senior managers is also extremely small.[7] If women and minorities have faced substantial obstacles in reaching the upper echelons of their organizations in the past, how can organizations be expected to manage an increasingly diverse group of employees in the future?

An organization is acting fairly when its employment decisions (regarding such issues as hiring, pay, and advancement) are based on job-related criteria rather than an individual's membership in a population subgroup (e.g., sex, race, and age). Conversely, discrimination occurs when organizational practices have a negative effect on the employment of subgroup members that is not based on job-related factors. Two types of discrimination have been distinguished: access discrimination and treatment discrimination.

In cases of *access discrimination,* subgroup members are less likely to be hired for a particular job than members of the dominant group despite the fact that they could have performed the job as effectively as members of the dominant group. For example, if bias in employment interviews disproportionately rejects talented women for a construction management position in favor of equally (or less) talented men, women (as a group) will have limited access to that particular job. Discrimination in hiring was the target of the early fair employment movement during the 1960s and 1970s.

Treatment discrimination occurs when the treatment of employees already in an organization is based on their status as a member of a subgroup rather than on their merits or achievements; that is, when such employees receive fewer opportunities than they legitimately deserve on the basis of job-related criteria. For example, minorities or women systematically excluded from key committee assignments or sponsorship opportunities experience treatment discrimination within their organization.

Although access discrimination has certainly not been eliminated, women and minorities have been entering managerial and professional positions in increasing numbers. Therefore, a key question is how fairly women and minorities are treated once they are in an organization. For this reason, Chapter 12 focuses on understanding treatment discrimination in organizational settings.

Much of the concern regarding fairness is based on the more restricted career advancement historically experienced by minorities and women as compared with white men. Therefore, we begin our discussion with career advancement and then move to an examination of those factors that may explain differences in career advancement between women and men as well as between minority and nonminority employees.

CAREER ADVANCEMENT

In his insightful analysis reported in the *Harvard Business Review,* Edward Jones observed the frustration and disillusionment experienced by many black managers who find their careers stalled at levels far below their aspirations.[8] The relatively slow progress of minorities up the corporate ladder has been documented frequently, and it has been suggested that minorities have to outperform whites to get ahead in the organization.[9]

One could argue that the sparse representation of minorities in senior management is due to the fact that they entered the managerial pipeline later than nonminorities. Although this may explain a portion of minorities' restricted career advancement, it is unlikely that it is the sole explanation. Research has found that black managers are more likely to plateau in their career—and are less likely to be seen by their bosses as promotable—than whites of *comparable* age, experience, and job function.[10] Thus, factors other than years of experience and "paying one's dues" are necessary to explain the apparent glass ceiling.

This is not to say that minorities are always at a disadvantage in their quest for upward mobility; some employers are as likely to promote people of color to senior positions as whites.[11] Nor can we say that a hostile environment necessarily stifles the aspirations of each and every minority manager in the same way. But, as a group, minorities have experienced more restricted advancement opportunities than whites.

The career advancement of women presents a similar picture. The small proportion of women at senior management levels suggests that their careers are stalled or slowed down at lower and middle levels of management.[12] Moreover, a recent study by Belle Rose Ragins, Bickley Townsend, and Mary Mattis suggests that many CEOs may not fully appreciate the barriers to advancement that women experience.[13] In addition, the possession of an advanced degree such as an MBA does not eliminate these hurdles. Women MBAs often have to prove themselves more than men, yet can experience fewer managerial promotions and slower salary progression than men.[14]

JOB PERFORMANCE ASSESSMENTS

Why have minorities and women experienced restricted career advancement? One possible explanation is that they perform less effectively in their current job assignments than white men. The research bearing on this issue presents a somewhat different picture for minorities than for women. Most of this research has examined differences in supervisory ratings of job performance as a function of the employee's sex or race. In general, women have been perceived to perform at least as effectively on the job as men, and in some situations more effectively.[15] Therefore, it is unlikely that women's restricted advancement is due to the belief that they are ineffective on their current jobs.

Most of the research on race differences in job performance and career advancement has examined white and black employees. A review of 74 studies observed a small but statistically significant tendency for black employees to receive lower job performance ratings than white employees.[16] Similar findings were observed in military and managerial samples, although the race differences in job performance ratings were again very slight.[17] In general, then, the research reveals a tendency for black employees to receive somewhat lower job performance ratings than white employees.

Are supervisory ratings of job performance biased against minority employees? There is no simple answer to this question, although several streams of research suggest the potential for bias. For example, one major study found that white raters rated whites higher than they rated blacks, whereas black raters rated blacks higher than they rated whites.[18] The tendency to give higher performance ratings to same-race subordinates can harm minorities, because the vast majority of supervisors (and hence performance evaluators) in organizations are white. This study also found that race differences in job performance ratings were more substantial in organizations in which blacks comprised a very small proportion of the work force. One explanation is that blacks in small numbers are "put under the microscope" in the assessment of their job performance. It is also possible that different or additional criteria are used to assess the job performance of blacks than whites. For example, Taylor Cox and Stella Nkomo found that interpersonal behavior on the job had a more powerful effect on assessments of job performance for blacks than for whites, and they speculated that black employees may have an additional obstacle to face compared with white employees in the assessment of their performance.[19]

Bias in the evaluation of job performance can take another form as well. One study found that black managers who performed successfully on their jobs were not given as much "credit" for their success as the white managers.[20] When white managers succeeded, their bosses were likely to attribute this success to the managers' ability. However, when black managers succeeded, their bosses were less likely to attribute this success to the managers' ability and were more likely to attribute it to the help and assistance the managers received from other people. The bosses, in effect, discounted black managers' success by attributing it to forces outside the manager. This form of bias can have a detrimental effect on the careers of blacks, because most organizations would prefer to promote individuals who succeed by virtue of their talents.[21]

In summary, there is some evidence that the job performance of black employees is rated somewhat less favorably than the job performance of white employees. It is impossible to determine how much of this difference reflects true differences in job peformance and how much represents bias in the evaluation process. Nevertheless, we believe that the potential for bias has been sufficiently demonstrated to require a careful scrutiny of organizations' performance evaluation systems.

LOST OPPORTUNITIES

What factors other than job performance evaluations restrict career advancement? It has been suggested that women and minorities receive fewer opportunities to exert authority on their jobs, develop supportive relationships within the organization, and become part of the informal network of friendship, power, and influence. Systematically withholding these resources represents "lost opportunities" for women and minorities to develop job-related skills and establish important career contacts.[22] These lost opportunities, which may be reflected in the absence of an influential mentor or the assignment to mundane tasks, can reduce the work effectiveness of women and minorities over time and can diminish their opportunities for further growth, development, and advancement.

AUTHORITY. There is some indication that women and minorities report less authority and power in their jobs than white men.[23] It has been suggested that women and minorities are often assigned to jobs that permit less authority and discretion and are underrepresented in functional line career paths.[24] However, race and sex differences in power and authority persist even when women and minorities are in comparable jobs as white men.[25] If women and minorities possess limited authority in their job, their opportunity to develop new skills and exercise political clout is likely to be diminished.

EXCLUSION FROM INFORMAL NETWORKS. It is often observed that some of the most critical decisions affecting employees' career accomplishments are made over lunch, during the cocktail hour, or at the golf club. Unfortunately, women and minorities tend to be excluded from these informal activities and feel less accepted by their organization than do white men.[26] Isolation from informal networks of information and power can restrict the career opportunities of women and minorities.

ESTABLISHMENT OF MENTOR RELATIONSHIPS. The importance of mentoring and other developmental relationships to an individual's career was established in Chapter 8. Although it has been asserted that women and minorities have a difficult time finding a mentor or sponsor, much of the research seems to indicate that white men are no more likely to have had a mentor than minorities or women.[27] Perhaps it is not so much a question of the establishment of a mentor relationship but rather the nature and quality of the relationship.

Because of the sheer numbers of white men in most organizational hierarchies, many minorities develop cross-race mentor relationships and many women have cross-sex mentor relationships. For example, David Thomas observed that only 48 percent of the black managers in his study had a developmental relationship with a black mentor, whereas 70 percent of the black managers had cross-race mentors.[28] Moreover, although cross-race relationships provided career support to the protégés, they were less likely to provide psychosocial support and were of shorter duration than same-race relationships. Cross-race relationships may add certain complications that inhibit the development of minority employees.

In a similar vein, cross-sex developmental relationships seem to provide the protégé with less psychosocial support and role modeling opportunities than same-sex relationships, although the evidence regarding the provision of career support is mixed.[29] Again, it would appear that cross-sex developmental relationships are more complicated and perhaps more inhibiting than same-sex relationships. Moreover, because of the potential misinterpretation of a relationship as sexual, many men may either avoid mentoring women or restrict the intensity of the relationship.

TOKENISM. A token is a member of a particular subgroup that constitutes a very small percentage (perhaps 15 percent or less) of a population in an organization.[30] The impact of token status on women and minorities can be substantial. Tokens are highly visible because they are perceived to be different from members of the dominant group. This heightened visibility and attention can produce performance pressures because the token's performance is scrutinized more carefully than the performance of nontokens.[31] Under these conditions, every performance problem experienced by a token may be magnified in the eyes of the organization's management. In addition, women and minorities may feel substantial stress because their accomplishments not only affect their own careers but may also influence management's attitude toward other women and minorities in the organization.

Token status can isolate women and minorities from the mainstream organization as differences between tokens and nontokens become exaggerated. This isolation can exclude tokens from informal social networks and make it difficult for them to attract a mentor or sponsor.[32] Moreover, the isolation of tokens from informal groups and their representation in such small numbers can reinforce existing stereotypes held by the dominant group, because there are not enough direct experiences with tokens to counteract the stereotypes.

MODEL OF ORGANIZATIONAL FAIRNESS

We have seen that the career advancement of women and minorities has often lagged behind that of white men. In some instances, restricted career advancement is due to the belief that the job performance of women and minorities is lower than that of the white men with whom they compete for promotion. In addition, women and minorities are often excluded from informal relationships within the organization, experience less authority and power in their jobs, and have difficulties establishing fully effective developmental relationships. Occupying token status may exacerbate these problems.

It is important to reemphasize that the restricted career opportunities discussed in this chapter are not experienced by all women and minorities, and they are not experienced to the same degree in all organizations. In this section, we explore the reasons behind unfairness in organizational settings.

Exhibit 12.1 presents a model of organizational fairness that explains the reasons why women and people of color may experience restricted career advancement opportunities. The model indicates that cultural dissimilarities between groups in organizations produce stereotypes, feelings of psychological distance, and cultural misunderstandings. These beliefs and feelings, in turn, can result in differential treatment for women and minorities compared with white men. Differential treatment represents lost opportunities for women and minorities to develop job-related talents, which can detract from job performance and eventually dampen career advancement prospects.

**MODEL OF ORGANIZATIONAL FAIRNESS
IN CAREER ADVANCEMENT OPPORTUNITIES**

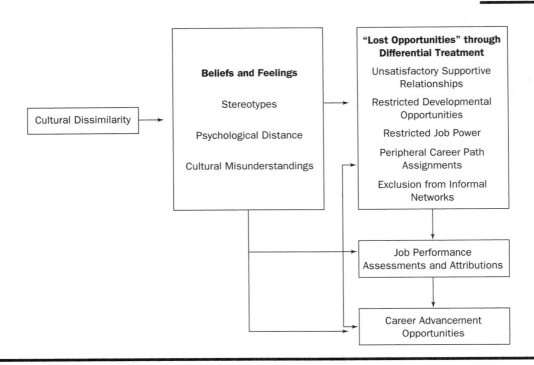

STEREOTYPES

A stereotype is a preconceived perception or image one has of another person based on that person's membership in a particular social group or category. We may believe that Mary, an accountant, is logical and organized because we believe that accountants in general are logical and organized. We may perceive John, a social worker, to be compassionate and fair-minded because we perceive social workers to possess these characteristics. Of course, not all stereotypes are so flattering. For example, we may believe that investment broker Susan is unethical and engineer Brad is narrow-minded because we perceive brokers and engineers to be unethical and narrow-minded, respectively.

Moreover, the actions we take in response to our stereotype can ultimately confirm the stereotype. For example, because of our belief that members of a particular group are lazy, we may not provide an individual from that group with attention or encouragement or with a great deal of challenge and responsibility on the job. The individual might respond to this lack of support by not appearing to care about the organization and by not expending much effort on the job. This reaction might well reinforce our original perception of the individual as lazy. Although neither party's actions necessarily operate at a conscious level, their consequences are real. Stereotypes can easily become self-fulfilling prophecies.

Unfortunately, negative attitudes and stereotypes based on an individual's race have not disappeared in contemporary society.[33] Edward Jones believes that social stereotypes have been a significant obstacle to the careers of black managers.[34] Moreover, the most difficult stereotypes to combat are those that malign a minority employee's ability and qualifications.[35]

Sex-characteristic stereotypes also persist in contemporary society. Women are thought to possess several qualities that are seen as incompatible with success in many managerial and professional positions. Whereas men are often perceived as aggressive, rational, confident, and tough, women are likely to be perceived as emotional, sensitive, and gentle.[36] As a result of these stereotypes, women are often expected to perform more poorly than men on tasks that are thought to be "masculine" in nature.[37]

As we observed in Chapter 11, women are also subject to stereotypes regarding their ability to balance their career and family responsibilities. Many men (and some women) believe that women should be primarily responsible for home and child care activities. Moreover, because of their extensive family responsibilities, women are often stereotyped as less committed than men to their work and the organization.[38] Indeed, a significant portion of the gender gap in compensation can be traced to women's extensive responsibilities for home and family.[39]

PSYCHOLOGICAL DISTANCE

Cultural similarity produces feelings of psychological closeness between people in a relationship, whereas dissimilarity in cultural background and experiences may produce a feeling of psychological distance.[40] It is possible that white men feel more psychologically distant from women and minorities than they do from other white men.

Psychological distance can provoke mistrust and even fear because of the belief that people who are different from us are more difficult to understand and therefore more difficult to predict.[41] For example, if we feel different and distant from a person, we may not understand what motivates the person or how to influence the person. In organizational settings, supervisors often form an "in-group" of trusted and favored subordinates and relegate subordinates who are mistrusted to "out-group" status.[42] It is possible that the placement of an individual into an out-group is attributable in part to the psychological distance a supervisor feels toward that individual.[43]

Note that stereotypes can create psychological distance and psychological distance can reinforce existing stereotypes. If we stereotype a subordinate as lazy or ineffective, we may accentuate the differences between that individual and ourselves, ascribe the individual out-group status, and provide few opportunities for the individual to demonstrate his or her strengths. The individual may assume (accurately) that he or she is not valued and therefore show little initiative or interest in improving job performance. This understandable reaction is likely to be interpreted as a lack of interest in work, which will reinforce our initial stereotype and increase our feeling of psychological distance.

CULTURAL MISUNDERSTANDINGS

As a result of cultural differences, stereotypes, and psychological distance, there are many opportunities for people to misunderstand each other. For example, a man may perceive a woman's willingness to cooperate with a stubborn colleague as a sign of weakness and accommodation rather than the strength and resolve it may actually represent. A supervisor unfamiliar with Asian culture might misinterpret the modesty and deference of an Asian as a lack of confidence or even as a lack of talent, rather than as a sign of respect for another person based on cultural norms.

Cultural misunderstandings can be exacerbated by language difficulties and conflicts. John Fernandez found that many employees (especially whites and Native Americans) are bothered by hearing different languages in the workplace.[44] Several quotes from Fernandez's respondents illustrate the problem. A white man said, "This is an English-speaking country. If a person wants to advance in an English-speaking country, he should learn the language and learn it well." An Asian man reported, "People of color with foreign accents are often treated as less intelligent. It takes too long to prove yourself . . . among peers."

Perhaps the most serious consequence of stereotypes, psychological distance, and cultural misunderstandings is the tendency to discount the present or future contributions of persons who come from different backgrounds. If one believes that members of a particular group are unqualified, that women are not sufficiently aggressive, that an employee's language or cultural differences pose insurmountable obstacles, or that mothers of young children are not committed to their careers, one will be unwilling to invest the time and the organization's resources to develop these individuals and groom them for additional responsibility.

An organization's unwillingness to invest time and resources in particular groups of employees can take several forms—assignment to less significant career paths, exclusion from informal networks within the organization, reluctance to encourage the exercise of power and authority on the job, assignment to fewer tasks or projects designed to build skills or visibility, and provision of less extensive sponsorship or mentorship opportunities. As noted earlier, these actions (or inactions) represent lost opportunities for women and minorities to gain valuable experience and exposure. An accumulation of lost opportunities over time can diminish the employee's talents and dampen motivation, both of which can reduce job performance.

Even when lost opportunities do not lessen job performance, stereotyping can produce bias in the organization's evaluation of the individual's job performance. Performance that exceeds stereotyped expectations is "explained away" by attributing the performance to forces outside the individual.[45] Recall that the highly successful performance of female and black managers was less likely to be attributed to their talents than the comparable performance of white men.[46] The tendency of supervisors to discount the performance of their employees was especially pronounced in the case of black male subordinates, whose successful performance was most likely to be attributed to the supervisor's belief that their subordinate was lucky or had an easy job.

Psychological distance between supervisor and subordinate can also affect the performance evaluation process. The tendency of supervisors to give lower job performance ratings to subordinates of a different race might be explained by the psychological distance experienced by subordinates and supervisors of different races. Moreover, the observation that performance evaluation biases lessen as supervisors gain more experience working with a subordinate suggests that work experience can reduce feelings of psychological distance.[47]

We have been emphasizing the stereotyping, psychological distancing, and misunderstanding by white men because they generally possess the most power in organizations. However, it is also possible for women and people of color to stereotype white men, misunderstand their intentions, and experience psychological distance from them. We return to this issue when we discuss organizational and individual actions that can be taken to manage diversity.

In summary, cultural differences within an organization can produce stereotyping, feelings of psychological distance, and misunderstandings. These beliefs and feelings may result in lost opportunities for women and minorities to cultivate developmental relationships and acquire needed skills and experiences. Not only may lost opportunities erode job performance over time, but stereotyping, distancing, and misunderstandings can bias the assessment of the job performance of women and minorities. Perceptions of ineffective performance and low potential, real or imagined, can curtail the career advancement of women and minorities.

Although diversity is most closely associated with race and sex, other dimensions of diversity are significant in contemporary organizations. For example, organizational diversity may be viewed in terms of age, religion, sexual orientation, and physical disability, and significant diversity issues can also revolve around line-staff interactions and functional differentiation, such as engineering versus marketing or production versus sales.[48] Although the specific concerns will vary depending on the dimension of diversity being considered, there are common elements as well—different backgrounds and perspectives, stereotyping, distancing, and misunderstandings.

IS DIVERSITY INHERENTLY VALUABLE?

There are two schools of thought regarding why organizations should be concerned about managing diversity. According to one approach, the world and the workplace are becoming increasingly diverse. Because this trend is inevitable, it behooves the organization to cope with this new demographic reality. Therefore, organizations must hire and develop the most talented individuals from all backgrounds in an effective and fair manner. It is not a question of whether diversity is inherently desirable or undesirable, but rather it is a fact of life. This approach is most consistent with the cost and the resource acquisition arguments presented earlier in the chapter.

The second approach, which goes beyond the demographic necessity of becoming more diverse, asserts that organizational diversity is healthy and beneficial in its own right. This approach, which is most consistent with the marketing, creativity, and problem-solving arguments, assumes that employees from different cultural groups bring different strengths and perspectives to the organization that can enhance its effectiveness. For example, it is suggested that because of their unique socialization experiences, women view problems differently than men. Because women are more attuned to social relationships, they are more likely than men to involve colleagues and subordinates in a collaborative manner, share power and information, and include others in decision making.[49] The implication is that women possess special qualities and skills (e.g., communication, cooperation, emotionality, intimacy) that will provide different perspectives to the management of organizations.[50] In a similar vein, it has been suggested that because racial and ethnic minorities have experienced the world differently than the dominant cultural group, they can bring different views, approaches, perspectives, and understandings to the solution of organizational problems.[51]

Are women and people of color substantially different from white men in how they view work-related tasks, approach problems, and relate to other people? The research provides few firm answers to this question. Studies comparing men and women in managerial and professional careers have generally revealed considerable similarity in personality, work-related values, and behaviors. After a comprehensive review of the research on this issue, Gary Powell answered the question "Do female and male managers differ?" as follows: "They differ in some ways and at some times, but, for the most part, they do not differ."[52]

This does not mean that men and women react identically in all situations. However, the research does call into question the assumption that women in managerial roles *necessarily* bring different strengths and perspectives to the organization than men bring. In fact, it is likely that there is considerable variation in talent and perspective within each sex group. What is apparent, however, is that there are many women who bring special strengths and perspectives to an organization not necessarily—or only—because of their sex but rather because of their intelligence, education, training, and unique work and life experiences.

Similarly, it is not clear that people of color *necessarily* have different perspectives on work-related issues by virtue of their race. Although there is some evidence that members of black, Hispanic, and Asian cultures hold a more collectivist (group-oriented) orientation than Anglos, other studies suggest that blacks value independence more and congenial colleagues less than whites.[53] Moreover, although some race differences have been observed in managers' life-style, personality, and expectations, there are also considerable similarities across race groups as well.[54]

Even if there are not consistent and substantial race differences in managers' perspectives or behaviors, it is clear that there are many minority employees who bring special strengths and perspectives to an organization not necessarily—or only—because of their race but rather because of their intelligence, education, training, and unique work and life experiences.

The "different perspective" approach has been viewed critically by Stephen Carter, who states,

> *Viewpoint, outlook, perspective*—whatever word is used, the significance is the same. We have come to a point in the evolution of our ways of talking about race when it is not only respectable but actually encouraged for public and private institutions alike to make policy based on stereotypes about the different ways in which people who are white and people who are black supposedly think.[55]

Carter suggests that this view can put pressure on minorities (and we would add women) to represent the "minority perspective" (female perspective) and see things the way minorities (women) see things. This approach, in our view, runs the risk of replacing old race and gender stereotypes with new and different "perspective" stereotypes.

CONCLUSION

We do not claim that women and racial minorities are the same as white men in how they define issues and problems, see the world, or interact with other persons. However, the research does not convince us at the present time that there are substantial and consistent differences in "perspective" between women and men or between different cultural groups within a country. Moreover, although several studies illustrate the potential advantages of sexually and racially diverse work groups,[56] the research is too limited for us to draw firm conclusions. Along these lines, Roosevelt Thomas observed,

> Many individuals believe that there is a richness in diversity that you can't get from a homogeneous workforce. This may be true, but it's not necessary to support managing diversity. Whether there is a richness or not, managers will have employees with significant differences and similarities. The compelling case for managing diversity lies in the fact that diversity is a reality—or soon will be. By focusing on the richness, you risk suggesting that the manager has a choice.[57]

Our skepticism regarding group differences in "perspective" does not detract at all from what we see as an organizational imperative to manage diversity effectively. Organizations desperately require talent, and talent is distributed amply across different groups. Organizations simply cannot afford to ignore the talents and contributions of employees because of their sex, race, religion, age, physical disability, or sexual orientation. It is in the best interest of the employee, the organization, and society for all talent to be identified, developed, and rewarded.

Moreover, it is also apparent that there are sufficient cultural differences in language, customs, and experiences that can lead us into the trap of stereotyping and misunderstanding other people. Biases, conscious or not, run deep, and what is unfamiliar is often denigrated. We need to understand different groups and cultures to acknowledge our similarities and to appreciate our differences. We also need to understand our stereotypes and their effects on our behavior as well as on the behavior of others with whom we interact.

Whether there is inherent value in diversity, there is value in mutual understanding and respect, and there is certainly value in ensuring that all employees have the opportunity to demonstrate their talents and be rewarded for their accomplishments. With these thoughts in mind, let us consider ways in which organizations can manage diversity.

ORGANIZATIONAL ACTIONS

CHARACTERISTICS OF THE MULTICULTURAL ORGANIZATION

Before we examine specific programs and policies that organizations can implement to manage diversity, we describe the characteristics of an "ideal" organization that is capable of managing diversity effectively. Taylor Cox referred to such an organization as "multicultural" and identified its distinguishing characteristics.[58] Table 12.1, which identifies the key elements of a multicultural organization, is adapted from the work of Cox. Let us examine each element of a multicultural organization.

ELIMINATION OF ACCESS DISCRIMINATION

As noted earlier in this chapter, access discrimination occurs when members of a particular subgroup are disproportionately excluded from joining an organization by virtue of their subgroup membership rather than job-related factors. Applicant qualifications must determine hiring decisions, not race, sex, religion, national origin, sexual orientation, age, physical disability status, or any other nonperformance-related factors. An organization cannot even begin to fully

---

· TABLE 12-1

ELEMENTS OF A
MULTICULTURAL ORGANIZATION

   I. Elimination of Access Discrimination
  II. Mutual Accommodation
 III. Elimination of Treatment Discrimination
 IV. Structural Integration
  V. Minimal Intergroup Conflicts
 VI. Responsiveness to Work-Family Issues

NOTE: These elements are based extensively on T. H. Cox, "The Multicultural Organization," *Academy of Management Executive* 5, no. 2 (1991): 34–47, with some modifications and additions.

use its human resources if it hires (or fails to hire) people on the basis of irrelevant factors.

MUTUAL ACCOMMODATION

We observed in Chapter 8 that the socialization process encourages new employees to learn and accept the organization's assumptions, norms, values, and expectations—in short, to assimilate into the organization's dominant culture. We stressed that organizations possess established ways of accomplishing tasks—what should be done, how it should be done, and by whom it should be done—and that employees must adapt to these expectations to become accepted and successful.

Socialization has generally been viewed as a one-way street in which employees adapt and assimilate into the organization's culture. However, a multicultural organization realizes that members of cultural groups in today's society may not be willing to assimilate fully into the organization's culture.

Moreover, it may not be in the best interest of the organization to demand full assimilation. If members of different groups do possess different views and perspectives (an assertion we consider an important proposition rather than an established fact), then organizations should encourage members of different groups to retain their uniqueness. Total accommodation to an organization's culture could reduce the contributions that members of different groups can make to the organization.

Of course, employees from diverse cultural backgrounds must assimilate and accommodate to some degree. They must accept the mission of the organization and many of its most cherished norms and values. But the organization needs to accommodate the social and cultural norms of its employees. As Roosevelt Thomas has observed, "All companies will and should require some individual adaptation. The challenge is to ensure that the prescriptions are essential to the integrity of the organization and not unnecessarily restrictive."[59]

ELIMINATION OF TREATMENT DISCRIMINATION

As we discussed earlier, an organization can intentionally or unwittingly discriminate against members of subgroups. Employees who are excluded from informal networks, and those who experience restricted developmental opportunities, limited power, and peripheral career path assignments may prematurely plateau in their careers. These experiences diminish the opportunities for learning, skill development, and career contacts and can dampen job performance and career advancement prospects.

The multicultural organization understands the potential for treatment discrimination. It recognizes that discrimination not only impedes the progress of individual employees, but also prevents them from maximizing their contributions to the organization. Therefore, multicultural organizations develop mechanisms that aim to eliminate bias and discriminatory treatment, including "reverse discrimination."

STRUCTURAL INTEGRATION

Structural integration refers to the representation of cultural groups at all levels and functions within the organization.[60] In many instances, members of some cultural groups are clustered at the lower levels of the organization, often reflecting the effect of the glass ceiling. In some instances, women may be disproportionately represented in human resource departments, blacks or Hispanics in community relations, Asians in technical positions, and so on. Of course, there is nothing wrong with pursuing careers in human resources, community relations, or technical fields if these areas are consistent with employees' career goals. However, when there is a systematic overrepresentation of subgroup members at different levels or functions, it is essential to determine the factors that are responsible for these patterns of career achievements.

The multicultural organization strives to ensure that members of all groups are at levels and in jobs that are commensurate with their talents and consistent with their aspirations. Artificial obstacles to full representation in different parts of the organization—stereotypes, bias, or indifference—must be removed.

MINIMAL INTERGROUP CONFLICTS

As Taylor Cox has noted, "Conflict becomes destructive when it is excessive, not well managed, or rooted in struggles for power rather than the differentiation of ideas."[61] Culturally diverse organizations are susceptible to potential conflicts between different cultural groups. Language difficulties, stereotyping, mutual misunderstanding, and resentments of perceived preferential treatment can also exacerbate intergroup conflict.

The multicultural organization recognizes the difference between healthy conflict (clash over ideas) and unhealthy conflict (clash over life-styles or cultures). Moreover, the multicultural organization takes steps to ensure that unhealthy intergroup conflicts are minimized and that those conflicts that occur are dealt with quickly and effectively so they do not fester into more extensive and damaging conflicts.

RESPONSIVE TO WORK-FAMILY ISSUES

As we discussed in Chapter 11, a significant source of diversity in contemporary organizations is the substantial representation in the work force of women (and increasingly men) who are concerned with balancing their career involvement with family activities and responsibilities. This concern is reflected in excessive turnover, a refusal to accept assignments or promotions, as well as extensive feelings of conflict and stress. The multicultural organization acknowledges the connections and conflicts between work and family and seeks to create a culture that legitimizes work-family issues and helps employees balance their involvements in different life roles.

ORGANIZATIONAL APPROACHES TO THE CHALLENGES OF DIVERSITY

We have presented a portrait of the multicultural organization in its idealized form. Very few organizations, if any, have achieved this ideal level of multiculturalism. Nevertheless, some progress has been made, and employers can learn from the experiences of other organizations that have begun this effort. Before we discuss specific programs and policies, it would be helpful to describe three general approaches to the challenge of diversity: affirmative action, valuing differences, and managing diversity.[62]

AFFIRMATIVE ACTION

Roosevelt Thomas believes that affirmative action, born during the civil rights movement of the 1960s, was based on five assumptions:[63]

1. Adult, white men make up the U.S. business mainstream.
2. The U.S. economy is solid and unchanging.
3. Women, minorities, and immigrants should be allowed to join organizations for reasons of common decency.
4. Extensive prejudice keeps women, minorities, and immigrants out of organizations.
5. Legal and social pressure is required to bring women, minorities, and immigrants into organizations.

According to Thomas, these five assumptions may no longer be valid. First, because of the demographic shifts we have discussed, the "mainstream" is already diverse. Second, the economy is anything but stable, and it has forced organizations to become more competitive and to seek talent from all segments of society. Third, the major problem is no longer getting women and minorities into organizations but rather using their capabilities fully throughout the organization. Fourth, blatant prejudice on the basis of color and sex has been replaced by concerns about education and perceived qualifications. Finally, coercion is less likely to play a dominant role today. Beliefs in high productivity and competitiveness are the motivating forces to the challenge of diversity.

Although affirmative action has been successful in many respects, it is unlikely to solve the long-term needs of organizations and employees in and of itself.[64] Moreover, it is increasingly under legal attack as witnessed by the recent dismantling of affirmative action programs in Texas and California.[65] As organizations change their focus toward ensuring the full contributions of all members of a diverse organization, other approaches are required.

VALUING DIFFERENCES

This approach goes beyond "meeting the numbers" of affirmative action by attempting "to encourage awareness and respect for diversity within the workplace."[66] Through various types of educational and training activities, the valuing-differences approach attempts to improve interpersonal relationships in a diverse organization by achieving one or more of the following objectives:[67]

- An understanding of differences among people
- An understanding of one's own feelings toward people who are different in some respect
- An understanding of how differences among people can be an advantage to an organization
- Improved working relationships between people who are different from one another

Thomas points out that valuing-differences activities can help improve the quality of relationships between employees and can reduce blatant forms of prejudice and discrimination. However, because an understanding and acceptance of diversity are not sufficient in and of themselves to maximize the contributions of all employees, a third approach—managing diversity—is called for.

MANAGING DIVERSITY

In Thomas's view, "Managing diversity is a holistic approach to creating a corporate environment that allows all kinds of people to reach their full potential in pursuit of corporate objectives."[68] He believes that the need to manage diversity is derived from the following questions:

> Given the competitive environment we face and the diverse work force we have, are we getting the highest productivity possible? Does our system work as smoothly as it could? Is morale as high as we would wish? And are those things as strong as they would be if all the people who worked here were the same sex and race and nationality and had the same lifestyle and value system and way of working? [69]

ORGANIZATIONAL PROGRAMS AND POLICIES

We now turn to a discussion of programs and policies that organizations can use to manage diversity. Some of these programs are derived from affirmative action, because the need to ensure equitable access to organizations has not yet disappeared. Other programs involve valuing differences because special efforts are often required for employees to understand their feelings about people who are different. But taken together, the programs represent a set of actions designed to manage diversity as Thomas has used the term: a comprehensive attempt to change the culture of an organization so that all employees can contribute to the

· TABLE 12-2

COMPONENTS OF A COMPREHENSIVE
DIVERSITY MANAGEMENT PROGRAM

I. Communication Regarding the Meaning and
Importance of Diversity
Expanded Meaning of Diversity
Mission Statement
Orientation

II. Unbiased Hiring Systems

III. Identification of Critical Diversity Issues
Assessment of Organizational Culture
Ongoing Research
Diversity Task Forces

IV. Diversity Training: Valuing Differences

V. Language Policy and Programs

VI. Sexual Harassment Policy

VII. Full Utilization of Career Systems
Career Planning
Mentoring and Other Supportive Relationships
Developmental Experiences
Proactive Promotion Planning
Ongoing Monitoring of All Systems

VIII. Family-Responsive Programs and Policies
Dependent Care
Flexible Work Arrangements
Legitimize Work-Family Issues

IX. Leadership and Accountability

productivity and profitability of the organization. Table 12.2 identifies key components of a comprehensive process to manage diversity.

COMMUNICATION REGARDING THE MEANING AND IMPORTANCE OF DIVERSITY

To manage diversity effectively, an organization must understand what constitutes diversity in its world and must signify the importance of managing diversity to the internal and external environment. Central to Thomas's views is the recognition that diversity goes beyond race and gender. Diversity includes all significant differences in the experiences, perspectives, and backgrounds of different groups within an organization's work force. Many organizations experience difficulties establishing cooperative relationships between the line and staff functions, or between manufacturing and sales, or between older and younger employees. These difficulties may impede certain segments of the work force from making contributions that they can and should make. Organizations should determine the relevant dimensions of diversity that need to be managed successfully.

Having established the meaning of diversity for its purposes, an organization must signify to all its stakeholders—for example, employees, board of directors, stockholders, suppliers, and customers—that it is committed to managing diversity. As we saw in Chapter 11, some companies have included statements regarding work-family balance in their mission statements. In the same spirit, the incorporation of a statement regarding diversity in its mission statement would communicate an organization's serious commitment in this area.

Orientation programs represent an important vehicle for an organization to communicate significant elements of its culture to newcomers in the workplace.

Orientation sessions can be used to inform new employees about the meaning and significance of diversity in the organization and can begin to lay the foundation for positive attitudes toward diversity.

UNBIASED HIRING SYSTEMS

Organizations must constantly guard against discriminatory hiring practices. Not only is it illegal to discriminate against members of "protected" groups, but it is also unwise from a business perspective. As noted many times, an organization cannot afford to exclude effective employees from its work force, and talent, motivation, and commitment are found in all groups within society, irrespective of race, sex, religious, national origin, age, sexual orientation, and physical disability status.

For these reasons, organizations must engage in aggressive recruiting practices to locate the most talented applicants from all groups within society. Then they must scrutinize each part of the hiring process—application blanks, interviews, psychological tests—to ensure that they are valid and nondiscriminatory. An excellent treatment of hiring systems can be found elsewhere.[70]

IDENTIFICATION OF CRITICAL DIVERSITY ISSUES

It is recommended that organizations seeking to manage diversity conduct an assessment of their culture.[71] An organization's culture includes its assumptions about people, its norms and values, and its expectations regarding what people should do and how they should do it. For example, the following assumptions and beliefs may not be conducive to the effective management of diversity:

■ "It's production that counts around here—not people."
■ "There's only one way to do things—our way."
■ "To be successful, you have to show how you're better than your colleagues."
■ "Employees' family problems are not our concern."
■ "Loyalty to the organization means doing what you're told to do without question."

Companies can assess their culture by administering surveys, conducting interviews, and observing what goes on in the organization. A culture assessment can help to identify sources of bias and can determine what elements of the culture might have to be changed to create opportunities for all employees to develop in their careers and contribute effectively to the organization.

In addition to a culture assessment, ongoing research into management practices and employee attitudes can help organizations identify problems associated with a diverse work force. Employee surveys can cover a wide range of topics relevant to diversity: perceptions of advancement opportunities, usefulness of human resource practices (e.g., performance appraisal, mentoring), supervisor-subordinate relationships, and organizational reward systems. Focus groups can also be conducted in which small groups of targeted employees (e.g., women, older employees) can share their perceptions regarding the organization and the practices that have helped and hindered their career growth.

Useful information can also be obtained from diversity task forces or committees. For example, at BankAmerica, "diversity business councils" meet monthly to discuss programs and practices that can help *all* employees experience growth in their careers. At Tenneco, a Women's Advisory Council has worked with the human resources function and management to identify and solve problems regarding the career development of women.[72]

DIVERSITY TRAINING

Diversity training programs—which can be useful components of the diversity management process—frequently include presentations, role-playing activities, team-building experiences, and videos. Consider the program on "valuing differences" developed by Digital Equipment Corporation (DEC).[73]

Many managers at DEC initially believed that candid discussions about race and sex were taboo. Therefore, small groups of top managers were formed to discuss these and other topics regarding diversity. As these groups evolved and spread throughout the company, they focused on uncovering the racial and gender stereotypes they held.

However, as groups gained experience, they began to broaden their conception of diversity to a variety of "differences," including differences between manufacturing and engineering and between U.S. and European operations. Groups also discovered four steps that are required to address diversity of any type: (1) eliminating stereotypes; (2) identifying underlying assumptions about people and groups; (3) building relationships with others who are different from oneself; and (4) increasing one's feeling of personal empowerment.

LANGUAGE POLICIES AND PROGRAMS

Companies can experience difficulties that arise from multiple languages spoken in the workplace. Employees who do not speak English may misunderstand a supervisor's directive and may resent the fact that others in the organization have not taken the trouble to learn their native language. English-speaking employees, however, may resent the difficulties and inconveniences imposed by employees who do not communicate well (if at all) in English.

Organizations need to understand the difficulties stemming from language differences and must be willing to provide flexible solutions. As one example, Roosevelt Thomas recommends that an organization that employs predominantly Hispanics ask, "Is there is compelling business reason for these workers to speak English? Does the nature of their work require it? Is it too much to ask me to speak English and Spanish?"[74] In fact, some companies that are staffed primarily by Hispanics have printed their publications in English and Spanish, conducted meetings in both languages, and administered employment tests in Spanish.[75]

SEXUAL HARASSMENT POLICY

Sexual harassment is a form of sex discrimination in violation of Title VII of the Civil Rights Act of 1964. The Equal Employment Opportunity Commission has adopted the following definition of sexual harassment:

> Unwelcome sexual advances, requests for sexual favors, or other verbal or physical conduct of a sexual nature constitute sexual harassment when
>
> ■ submitting to or rejecting such conduct is an explicit or implicit term or condition of employment;
>
> ■ submitting to or rejecting the conduct is a basis for employment decisions affecting the individual; or
>
> ■ the conduct unreasonably interferes with an individual's work performance or creates an intimidating, hostile, or offensive working environment.[76]

The allegation of sexual harassment by Anita Hill against then Supreme Court nominee and now Associate Justice Clarence Thomas in 1991 heightened the awareness of sexual harassment, and allegations against President Bill Clinton in the late 1990s kept the issue in the forefront of the public's attention. In the year following the televised Hill-Thomas hearings, Congress passed legislation making it easier for victims to prove their complaint and making it possible for them to collect monetary damages. In one recent year alone, the number of sexual harassment complaints reached 15,000, with monetary compensation of more than $24 million.[77]

Clearly, sexual harassment is a serious situation for all parties involved in the action. Not only does the victim (usually but not necessarily a woman) suffer a personal indignity, but the victim's job satisfaction and health may deteriorate as well.[78] The harasser is subject to severe disciplinary action including termination, and the employer may be liable for the actions of its employees.

It is likely that the most effective deterrent to sexual harassment is the knowledge that it will not be tolerated in the workplace. A strong sexual harassment policy statement that defines sexual harassment, indicates its seriousness, and specifies the consequences for the harasser is necessary. However, the credibility of the policy will be sustained only if the employer investigates complaints swiftly and seriously and enforces the disciplinary action warranted.

Although perhaps not as well known as sexual harassment, age harassment is a violation of the Age Discrimination in Employment Act of 1967 and the Civil Rights Act of 1964. Harassment on the basis of race, religion, or national origin is also a violation of the Civil Rights Act of 1964. Clearly, any form of harassment is inconsistent with an appreciation of diversity and can perpetuate a culture of disrespect and mistrust.

FULL USE OF CAREER SYSTEMS

We have seen throughout this book that career growth is enhanced when employees actively manage their careers and when organizations provide support in the form of performance appraisal and feedback systems, mentoring, training and development programs, job design, developmental assignments, and promotion planning. By managing diversity, organizations attempt to create a culture in which all employees can benefit from such support and grow in their careers and in which individuals are not disadvantaged because of their cultural background. As Roosevelt Thomas has observed, "Managing diversity is a comprehensive managerial process for developing an environment that works for all employees."[79]

Why do special attempts have to be made to ensure that some individuals are not disadvantaged in their pursuit of career growth? We have discussed the difficulties that women and minorities may experience in acquiring an effective relationship with a mentor. We observed a potential for bias in the evaluation of job performance. And we have seen how negative stereotypes may prevent a manager from providing critical opportunities for learning and development to subordinates. Whether the organization has intentionally favored one group over another, these lost opportunities can hamper the careers of affected individuals.

Therefore, organizations should take steps to ensure that support and career opportunities are available to all employees. For example, Pacific Enterprises, a southern California utility holding company, developed its "readiness for management" program to prepare employees for managerial positions. To avoid the pitfalls of the "old boy network," Pacific Enterprises encourages employees to nominate themselves for the program. Employees accepted into this development program take self-assessment instruments to help them understand their strengths and weaknesses and pursue formal (training) and informal (job assignments) developmental activities. In this way, the company places the primary responsibility of career management on the employee, supports the employee's career management efforts, and reduces the likelihood that potential management candidates will be overlooked.[80]

The following program illustrates another multifaceted approach to managing diversity through the effective use of career systems.[81]

A major defense laboratory conducted research to identify the reasons behind complaints voiced by minority employees. Interviews were conducted with five groups of managers: blacks, Hispanics, white women, Asians, and white men. Although many positive attitudes were reported, several problem areas emerged from the interviews.

- Although white men experienced relatively few barriers to career advancement, white women believed that management was uncomfortable with women. They reported that they received inadequate feedback and were excluded from informal networks.
- Hispanics perceived negative stereotyping in the organization.
- Asians perceived that they were subject to discrimination because of their culture and were stereotyped as "technologists."
- Blacks perceived that negative racial attitudes were their primary obstacle, and they were disturbed by the informal and ambiguous route to upward mobility.

- Members of some groups had difficulties learning and adjusting to the organization's culture.
- The informal mentoring system worked better for some groups than for others, with particular difficulties experienced by blacks.
- Members of all groups reported a need for greater commitment to people in the organization.

In response to these and other concerns, management:

- Tracked the progress of women and minorities by setting goals, assessing managers' potential, and conducting meetings of senior managers to discuss the experiences and career advancement of women and minorities.
- Developed a structured career development program for black managers, which was supplemented with a cultural awareness program for the supervisors of these managers.
- Established a special program for black Ph.D.s to improve their opportunities for advancement within the technical hierarchy.

Effective diversity initiatives seem to have several qualities in common. First, top management is committed to diversity and is actively involved in the process. Second, the companies are systematically tracking women and minorities to ensure that they are provided with useful developmental opportunities and to assess their progress in the organization. Indeed, one primary aim of such efforts is to make sure that talented candidates for promotion are not overlooked in the decision-making process.

FAMILY-RESPONSIVE PROGRAMS AND POLICIES

In Chapter 11, we discussed the need for organizations to help their employees balance their work and family lives, and we proposed three types of programs that organizations can provide (see Table 11.2):

- Dependent care (e.g., on-site child care, elder care).
- Flexible work arrangements (e.g., part-time employment, job sharing).
- Culture change to legitimize work-family issues.

The reader may wish to review the material on work-family interaction discussed in Chapter 11 in the broader context of managing diversity.

LEADERSHIP AND ACCOUNTABILITY

A lack of commitment and responsibility on the part of an organization can be a major impediment to the successful management of organizational diversity.[82] Taylor Cox and Stacy Blake provide the following assessment of the role of organizational leadership in managing diversity.[83]

Top management support and genuine commitment to cultural diversity is crucial. Champions for diversity are needed—people who will take strong personal stands on the need for change, role model the behaviors required for change, and assist with the work of moving the organization forward. Commitment must go beyond sloganism. For example, are human, financial, and technical resources being provided? Is this item prominently featured in the corporate strategy and consistently made a part of senior-level staff meetings? Is there a willingness to change human resource management systems such as performance appraisal and executive bonuses? Is there a willingness to keep mental energy and financial support focused on this for a period of years, not months or weeks? If the answer to all these questions is yes, the organization has genuine commitment. If not, then a potential problem with leadership is indicated.

Effective leadership must be found in lower and middle management levels as well as in senior management. Leadership at all levels requires:

- An understanding of the importance of managing diversity to the productivity of the organization and an appreciation of the similarities and differences between members of different cultural groups.

- An ability to manage a diverse group of subordinates. Interpersonal skills are crucial in most leadership roles. Effective leaders have to understand human behavior, communicate accurately, listen carefully, provide feedback constructively, and build commitment among followers. These skills are even more crucial when subordinates come from diverse backgrounds. Training programs designed to improve interpersonal skills should be a significant component of a program to manage diversity.

- An accountability for results. Managers throughout the organization will take their responsibility for diversity seriously when their performance in this area is appraised and rewarded. At BankAmerica, for example, managers are evaluated on a "balanced scoreboard" that includes their support for diversity initiatives. And Advantica—the parent company of Denny's restaurant chain— includes "valuing diversity" as one of the 10 competencies in their managers' performance appraisal and assesses their ability to work with racially diverse teams.[84] Managerial accountability has also been emphasized by DEC, Unisys, and Hughes Aircraft among other firms.[85]

MANAGING DIVERSITY: OPPORTUNITIES AND COMPETENCE

This section examines two additional questions regarding the diversity management process: (1) Should there be "special programs" for targeted groups within the organization?; (b) should organizations practice "preferential treatment"? Each question is complex, controversial, and politically sensitive, and neither question has an easy answer.

We have indicated throughout this chapter that the aim of the diversity management process is to enable all employees to contribute to the organization and reap the benefits from their accomplishments. Recall Roosevelt Thomas's observation that managing diversity helps an organization's management systems work for everyone. In an attempt to accomplish this aim, many organizations have developed programs for targeted groups, for example, a mentoring program for black managers or a career-planning program for women professionals. There is increasing discussion about "backlash" among white men, some of whom perceive these special programs as unfair because they provide "special considerations" for other groups. In addition, special programs can feed existing stereotypes by making it appear that certain individuals or groups would not have succeeded without this special help. Are programs targeted for select groups consistent or inconsistent with a philosophy of managing diversity?

On the one hand, it can be argued that if mentoring is so important, all employees (e.g. not just black managers) should be provided with an opportunity to participate in a mentoring program. Similarly, if career-planning activities are vital to success, all employees (e.g., not just women professionals) should be provided with career planning opportunities. To do otherwise, it is suggested, would be unfair to one group—white men—and would put this group at a disadvantage.

On the other hand, it is asserted that special programs are needed because the existing systems that have worked for white men—performance appraisal, developmental assignments, promotion planning, sponsorship—are not as available or are not as effective for other groups in the organization. It is suggested that bias, stereotyping, and neglect have historically excluded many women and minorities from the formal and informal systems that have served white men so well for so many years. According to this view, targeted programs are designed to level the playing field, not to give any group an unfair advantage.

In a sense, the argument boils down to whether the current practices and systems within organizations do work for women and minorities. One can point to the emergence of women and minorities throughout an organization and conclude that special programs are no longer needed and, in fact, are more divisive (pitting "us" against "them") than they are helpful. However, one can also point to the frustration and alienation experienced by many women and minorities who believe that the organization is not providing sufficient opportunities for them to grow in their careers. The restricted opportunities may not be intentionally planned but can be very real in their consequences: the informal contacts made at a restricted golf club, the meetings to which one is uninvited, the early morning "power breakfasts" that are unattended by women who get their children off to school.

It is our belief that organizations must determine whether their practices and systems are currently effective for diverse groups. A combination of survey research, focus group interviews, observation, and deep soul searching should provide insight into this issue. If it is concluded that current systems are effective for all groups, perhaps no special programs are needed. However, if it is concluded that certain groups are disadvantaged by the current practices, then the organization has two options. One option is to provide programs or practices to all employees within a given job category (e.g., all middle managers) and to ensure that no one is excluded from the program or practice by virtue of his or her membership in a subgroup. The second option is to provide programs especially targeted for selected groups. It is our opinion that the first option is the preferable long-term goal. However, targeted programs may be useful initially, especially if the group has special needs, or if the organization is concerned that the needs and the contributions of the group will simply not be recognized in a general program.

A second and related issue concerns the perceived preferential treatment in career development and advancement accorded to women and minorities. We emphasize "perceived" because it is difficult to determine objectively whether preferential treatment (often referred to as "reverse discrimination") is practiced.

Companies committed to affirmative action often set goals for the hiring or promotion of women and minorities. Given the powerful effect of goal setting on task performance, the establishment of affirmative action goals is not unreasonable in and of itself—goals motivate action and often produce success. However, many observers believe that goals quickly become "quotas" and ultimately lower standards of job qualifications and job performance. We do not want to enter this fray, in part because "standards" are not always easily measured and because biases and stereotypes themselves can interfere with the objective assessment of standards.

However, it is important to reemphasize that most diversity advocates (and apparently a large segment of the public) firmly believe that decisions about hiring, training, development, and promotions must be made on the basis of competence rather than race, sex, or other social groupings. Managing diversity is entirely consistent with the ideology of meritocracy. However, Roosevelt Thomas has persuasively suggested that merit has three components: task merit (capability to perform a task); cultural merit (capability to conform to the organization's culture); and political merit (capability to receive the endorsement of a powerful sponsor). He believes that people who are "different" from the organization's power base often possess task merit but are not perceived to possess cultural merit or political merit. Moreover, all individuals, including (or especially) white men, have benefited from political assistance in their careers. "Managing diversity simply calls for the manager to ensure that cultural and political realities do not advantage or disadvantage anyone because of irrelevant considerations."[86]

Therefore, competence is and should be the major criterion for decisions affecting the careers of all employees. A key challenge in managing diversity is to provide sufficient support to all individuals so that competence can be developed and to provide sufficient attention to all individuals so that competence can be recognized and rewarded.

INDIVIDUAL ACTIONS

Several writers have recommended strategies that minorities or women can follow to achieve success in diverse work organizations. John Fernandez recommended the following strategies for minority group members:[87]

- Understand racism and develop a positive self-concept.
- Understand that dual performance standards exist, obtain the best education and experience possible, take creative risks, and be assertive in seeking an equitable performance appraisal.
- Seek and exercise power on the job.
- Make contacts and become part of the informal work group.
- Develop oral and written communication skills.
- Network with other minorities.
- Engage in "reality testing" before concluding that a negative experience is due to racism.

Also recommended in the literature are the following "lessons for success" to women:[88]

- Learn the ropes—understand the organizational culture.
- Be assertive in taking control over your career.
- Develop self-confidence.
- Learn to rely on others, and seek a broad network of supporters.
- Become "results oriented" without compromising your values; go for the "bottom line."
- Integrate life and work, and develop a clear sense of priorities.

The career management approach emphasized throughout this book has several specific implications for all employees pursuing careers in culturally diverse organizations.

AWARENESS OF SELF AND ENVIRONMENT

- Understand the stereotypes you hold about members of other cultural groups. Be willing to admit that you (like all people) may hold preconceived biases against people who are different from you.
- Understand other people, including those from different cultural backgrounds than yours. Understand similarities and differences among cultures.
- Recognize that there is considerable variation in ability, interests, values, and personality within each cultural group.
- Understand situations from other people's (and other groups') perspectives.
- Understand your current organization's culture and its view of diversity. When seeking a new job in a different organization, assess its culture and view of diversity.

CAREER GOAL SETTING

- Set career goals that are personally meaningful to you.
- Avoid setting career goals based on race or gender stereotypes unless they also are compatible with your talents, values, and interests. Pursue your vision of success and do not be constrained by what women (or men, or whites, or people of color) are supposed to want.

CAREER STRATEGIES

- Do not compromise personal values in pursuing career goals.
- Do not give up your uniqueness or cultural identity in trying to achieve success.

CAREER APPRAISAL

- Be willing to modify your attitude toward other people or groups as a result of your ongoing experiences with them.
- Be willing to change your own behavior toward people who are "different" from you.

SUMMARY

The work force of the future will become increasingly diverse. It will include more women, minorities, and immigrants. Because of these demographic changes and the need for increased global competitiveness, it is extremely important for organizations to manage diversity effectively. Organizations need to understand the reasons why members of different subgroups may experience restricted career opportunities. Stereotypes, feelings of psychological distance from people who are "different," and cultural misunderstandings can have subtle but important consequences for career achievement. Employees subjected to stereotyped attitudes may have difficulties establishing or maintaining supportive relationships, may not be provided with sufficient opportunities to develop or demonstrate their competence, may experience limited power on their jobs, and may be excluded from important informal networks of contacts and support. These "lost opportunities" can have negative effects on employees' job performance and on their prospects for career advancement.

An organization seeking to manage diversity effectively should develop a vision of multiculturalism that is central to the organization's mission and communicate that vision to all the organization's constituencies; eliminate discrimination in hiring; identify the most salient issues that interfere with effectiveness in the diverse work environment; provide opportunities for employees to understand and appreciate differences among people; address significant language conflicts; develop and implement an effective sexual harassment policy; ensure that its career policies and systems do not give unfair advantage or disadvantage to members of different cultural groups; develop family-responsive programs and policies; and exercise consistent leadership and accountability for diversity throughout the organization.

ASSIGNMENT

Interview an individual (e.g., a friend, classmate, or co-worker) who is not of the same sex or race as you are. Ask the individual about his or her career values (perhaps through the rankings provided in Learning Exercise IV), career goals, and strengths and weaknesses. Then have the individual interview you on the same topics. Discuss the extent to which the individual's career experiences/career plans and your career experiences/career plans have been influenced by your respective cultural backgrounds.

DISCUSSION QUESTIONS

1. Examine Cox and Blake's six arguments regarding why the effective management of diversity can improve an organization's competitive advantage. Which arguments do you find most convincing and least convincing? Why?

2. To what extent do you believe that women and minorities experience the "lost opportunities" indicated in Exhibit 12.1: unsatisfactory supportive relationships, restricted developmental opportunities, restricted job power, peripheral career path assignments, exclusion from informal networks? Do you think the experiences of women differ from the experiences of members of racial/ethnic minority groups? Why or why not?

3. What stereotypes, if any, do you hold regarding members of the opposite sex? What stereotypes, if any, do you hold regarding individuals from different racial or ethnic groups? How accurate are these stereotypes and how do you think they were formed? What stereotypes do you think others hold of members of your sex and race/ethnic group? How accurate are these stereotypes?

4. Do you believe that a work group or organization that is culturally diverse (in terms of the sex and racial/ethnic composition) is more effective than a culturally homogeneous group or organization? Why or why not?

5. Can discrimination be eliminated from the workplace? Why or why not? What should employers do to eliminate or reduce workplace discrimination? How much progress has been made in eliminating workplace discrimination in recent years? What do you predict for the next 5 to 10 years?

ENDNOTES

1. W. B. Johnston and A. H. Packer, *Workforce 2000: Work and Workers for the 21st Century* (Indianapolis, IN: Hudson Institute, 1987).

2. T. H. Cox and S. Blake, "Managing Cultural Diversity: Implications for Organizational Competitiveness," *Academy of Management Executive* 5, no. 3 (1991): 45–56.; F. J. Milliken and L. L. Martins, "Searching for Common Threads: Understanding the Multiple Effects of Diversity in Organizational Groups," *Academy of Management Review* 21 (1997): 402–433; G. Robinson and K. Dechant, "Building a Business Case for Diversity," *Academy of Management Executive* 11, no. 3 (1997): 21–31; R. R. Thomas, Jr. *Beyond Race and Gender* (New York: AMACOM, 1991).

3. J. P. Fernandez, *Managing a Diverse Work Force* (Lexington, MA: Lexington Books, 1991); A. T. Segal and W. Zellner, "Corporate Women," *Business Week,* June 8, 1992, 74–78; D. W. Sue, "A Model for Cultural Diversity Training," *Journal of Counseling and Development* September/ October (1991): 99–105; Thomas, *Beyond Race and Gender;* U.S. Bureau of the Census, *Statistical Abstract of the United States: 1997* (117th ed.) Washington, DC, 1997, 404, 410.

4. A. M. Morrison and M. A. Von Glinow, "Women and Minorities in Management," *American Psychologist* 45 (1990): 200–222; quote is on p. 200.

5. L. Martin, *A Report on the Glass Ceiling* (Washington, DC: U.S. Department of Labor, 1991). See also a more recent report of the Glass Ceiling Commission, *A Solid Investment: Making Full Use of the Nation's Human Capital* (Washington, DC: Federal Glass Ceiling Commission, 1995).

6. Cox and Blake, "Managing Cultural Diversity."

7. Federal Glass Ceiling Commission, *A Solid Investment;* K. S. Lyness and D. E. Thompson, "Above the Glass Ceiling? A Comparison of Matched Samples of Female and Male Executives," *Journal of Applied Psychology* 82 (1997): 359–375.

8. E. Jones, "Black Managers: The Dream Deferred," *Harvard Business Review* 64, no. 3 (1986): 84–93.

9. Fernandez, *Managing A Diverse Work Force.*

10. J. H. Greenhaus, S. Parasuraman, and W. M. Wormley, "Effects of Race on Organizational Experiences, Job Performance Evaluations, and Career Outcomes," *Academy of Management Journal* 33 (1990): 64–86.

11. G. N. Powell and D. A. Butterfield, "Effect of Race on Promotions to Top Management in a Federal Department," *Academy of Management Journal* 40 (1997): 112–128.

12. A. M. Morrison, R. P., White, and E. Van Velsor, *Breaking the Glass Ceiling: Can Women Reach the Top of America's Largest Corporations?* (Reading, MA: Addison-Wesley, 1987). For a study that found no sex difference in promotions to senior management, see G. N. Powell and D. A. Butterfield, "Investigating the 'Glass Ceiling' Phenomenon: An Empirical Study of Actual Promotions to Top Management," *Academy of Management Journal* 37 (1994): 68–86.

13. B. R. Ragins, B. Townsend, and M. Mattis, "Gender Gap in the Executive Suite: CEOs and Female Executives Report on Breaking the Glass Ceiling," *Academy of Management Executive* 12, no. 1 (1998): 28–42.

14. T. H. Cox and C. V. Harquail, "Career Paths and Career Success in the Early Career Stages of Male and Female MBAs," *Journal of Vocational Behavior* 39 (1991): 54–75; A. Harlan and C. L. Weiss, "Sex Differences in Factors Affecting Managerial Career Advancement," in *Women in the Workplace,* ed. P. A. Wallace (Boston, MA: Auburn House Publishing Company, 1982), 59–100.

15. Greenhaus, Parasuraman, and Wormley, "Effects of Race on Organizational Experiences, Job Performance Evaluations, and Career Outcomes"; G. N. Powell, *Women and Men in Management* (2nd ed.). (Newbury Park, CA: Sage, 1993).

16. K. Kraiger and J. K. Ford, "A Meta-Analysis of Ratee Race Effects in Performance Ratings," *Journal of Applied Psychology* 70 (1985): 56–65.

17. Greenhaus, Parasuraman, and Wormley, "Effects of Race on Organizational Experiences, Job Performance Evaluations, and Career Outcomes"; E. D. Pulakos, L. A. White, S. H. Oppler, and W. C. Borman, "Examination of Race and Sex Effects on Performance Ratings," *Journal of Applied Psychology* 74 (1989): 770–780.

18. Kraiger and Ford, "A Meta-Analysis of Ratee Race Effects in Performance Ratings."

19. T. H. Cox and S. M. Nkomo, "Differential Performance Appraisal Criteria," *Group and Organization Studies* 11 (1986): 101–119.

20. J. H. Greenhaus and S. Parasuraman, "Job Performance Attributions and Career Advancement Prospects: An Examination of Gender and Race Effects," *Organizational Behavior and Human Decision Processes* 55 (1993): 273–297.

21. M. E. Heilman and R. A. Guzzo, "The Perceived Cause of Work Success as a Mediator of Sex Discrimination in Organizations," *Organizational Behavior and Human Performance* 21 (1978): 346–357.

22. D. R. Ilgen and M. A. Youtz, "Factors Affecting the Evaluation and Development of Minorities in Organizations," in *Research in Personnel and Human Resource Management: A Research Annual,* ed. K. Rowland and G. Ferris (Greenwich, CT: JAI Press, 1986), 307–337; R. M. Kanter, "Differential Access to Opportunity and Power," in *Discrimination in Organizations,* ed. R. Alvarez (San Francisco, CA: Jossey-Bass, 1989), 52–68.

23. Greenhaus, Parasuraman, and Wormley, "Effects of Race on Organizational Experiences, Job Performance Evaluations, and Career Outcomes"; Lyness and Thompson, "Above the Glass Ceiling?"

24. Kanter, "Differential Access to Opportunity and Power"; Martin, *A Report on the Glass Ceiling.*

25. Greenhaus, Parasuraman, and Wormley, "Effects of Race on Organizational Experiences, Job Performance Evaluations, and Career Outcomes."

26. J. P. Fernandez, "Human Resources and the Extraordinary Problems Minorities Face," in *Career Growth and Human Resource Strategies,* ed. M. London and E. M. Mone (New York: Quorum Books, 1988), 227–239; Greenhaus, Parasuraman, and Wormley, "Effects of Race on Organizational Experiences, Job Performance Evaluations, and Career Outcomes"; Kanter, "Differential Access to Opportunity and Power"; H. Ibarra, "Race, Opportunity, and Diversity of Social Circles in Managerial Networks," *Academy of Management Journal* 38 (1995): 673–703.

27. B. R. Ragins, "Diversified Mentoring Relationships in Organizations: A Power Perspective," *Academy of Management Review* 22 (1997): 482–521; G. F. Dreher and T. H. Cox, "Race, Gender, and Opportunity: A Study of Compensation Attainment and the Establishment of Mentoring Relationships," *Journal of Applied Psychology* 81 (1996): 297–308.

28. D. A. Thomas, "The Impact of Race on Managers' Experiences of Developmental Relationships (Mentoring and Sponsorship): An Intra-Organizational Study," *Journal of Organizational Behavior* 11 (1990): 479–492.

29. Ragins, "Diversified Mentoring Relationships in Organizations"; B. R. Ragins and D. B. McFarlin, "Perceptions of Mentor Roles in Cross-Gender Mentor Relationships," *Journal of Vocational Behavior* 37 (1990): 321–339; Thomas, "The Impact of Race on Managers' Experiences of Developmental Relationships."

30. R. M. Kanter, *Men and Women of the Corporation* (New York: Basic Books, 1977).

31. Ilgen and Youtz, "Factors Affecting the Evaluation and Development of Minorities in Organizations"; Kanter, *Men and Women of the Corporation.*

32. Ilgen and Youtz, "Factors Affecting the Evaluation and Development of Minorities in Organizations."

33. J. F. Dovidio, J. C. Brigham, B. T. Johnson, and S. L. Gaertner, "Stereotyping, Prejudice, and Discrimination: Another Look," in *Stereotypes and Stereotyping*, ed. C. N. Macrae, C. Stangor, and M. Hewstone (New York: Guilford, 1996), 276–319.

34. Jones, "Black Managers."

35. Fernandez, *Managing a Diverse Work Force*.

36. R. L. Dipboye, "Problems and Progress of Women in Management," in *Working Women: Past, Present, and Future,* ed. K. S. Koziara, M. S. Moskow, and L. D. Tanner (Washington, DC: BNA Books, 1987), 118–153; Lyness and Thompson, "Above the Glass Ceiling?"

37. M. E. Heilman, "Sex Bias in Work Settings: The Lack of Fit Model," in *Research in Organizational Behavior* (vol. 5), ed. L. L. Cummings and B. M. Staw (Greenwich, CT: JAI Press, 1983), 269–298.

38. S. Parasuraman and J. H. Greenhaus, "Personal Portrait: The Life-Style of the Woman Manager," in *Women in Management: Trends, Issues, and Challenges in Managerial Diversity,* vol. 4, ed. E. A. Fagenson (Newbury Park, CA: Sage, 1993), 186–211.

39. K. Cannings, "An Interdisciplinary Approach to Analyzing the Managerial Gender Gap," *Human Relations* 44 (1991): 679–695.

40. S. G. Green and T. R. Mitchell, "Attributional Processes of Leaders in Leader-Member Interactions," *Organizational Behavior and Human Performance* 23 (1979): 429–458; for research on the impact of ethnic differences on a supervisor's liking of a subordinate, see A. S. Tsui and C. A. O'Reilly III, "Beyond Simple Demographic Effects: The Importance of Relational Demography in Superior-Subordinate Dyads," *Academy of Management Journal* 32 (1989): 402–423.

41. A. K. Korman, *The Outsiders: Jews and Corporate America* (Lexington, MA: Lexington Books, 1988).

42. R. L. Heneman, D. B. Greenberger, and C. Anonyuo, "Attributions and Exchanges: The Effects of Interpersonal Factors on the Diagnosis of Employee Performance," *Academy of Management Journal* 32 (1989): 466–476.

43. Ilgen and Youtz, "Factors Affecting the Evaluation and Development of Minorities in Organizations."

44. Fernandez, *Managing a Diverse Work Force*.

45. Heilman, "Sex Bias in Work Settings."

46. Greenhaus and Parasuraman, "Job Performance Attributions and Career Advancement Prospects."

47. Ibid.

48. J. R. W. Joplin and C. S. Daus, "Challenges of Leading a Diverse Workforce." *Academy of Management Executive* 11, no. 3 (1997): 32–47; Robinson and Dechant, "Building a Case for Diversity."

49. J. B. Rosener, "Ways Women Lead," *Harvard Business Review* November–December (1990): 119–125.

50. J. Grant, "Women as Managers: What They Can Offer to Organizations," *Organizational Dynamics* Winter (1988): 56–63.

51. Cox and Blake, "Managing Cultural Diversity."

52. Powell, *Women and Men in Management;* quote is on p. 175.

53. O. C. Brenner, O. C., A. P. Blazini, and J. H. Greenhaus, "An Examination of Race and Sex Differences in Managerial Work Values," *Journal of Vocational Behavior* 32 (1988): 336–344; O. C. Brenner and J. Tomkiewicz, "Job Orientation of Black and White College Graduates in

Business," *Personnel Psychology* 35 (1982): 89–101; T. H. Cox, S. A. Lobel, and P. L. McLeod, "Effects of Ethnic Group Cultural Differences on Cooperative and Competitive Behavior on a Group Task," *Academy of Management Journal* 34 (1991): 827–847.

54. A. Howard and D. W. Bray, *Managerial Lives in Transition* (New York: Guilford Press, 1988).

55. S. L. Carter, *Reflections of an Affirmative Action Baby* (New York: Basic Books, 1991); quote is on p. 32.

56. For a review of this literature, see Milliken and Martins, "Searching for Common Threads."

57. Thomas, *Beyond Race and Gender;* quote is on pp. 171–172.

58. T. H. Cox, "The Multicultural Organization," *Academy of Management Executive* 5, no. 2 (1991): 34–47; also see T. H. Cox, *Cultural Diversity in Organizations: Theory, Research & Practice.* (San Francisco, CA: Berrett-Koehler, 1993).

59. Thomas, *Beyond Race and Gender;* quote is on p. 174.

60. Cox, "The Multicultural Organization."

61. Ibid.; quote is on p. 46.

62. R. R. Thomas, Jr., "From Affirmative Action to Affirming Diversity," *Harvard Business Review* March–April (1990): 107–117; Thomas, *Beyond Race and Gender.*

63. R. R. Thomas, Jr., "From Affirmative Action to Affirming Diversity"; quote is on p. 107.

64. Thomas, *Beyond Race and Gender.*

65. A. M. Konrad and F. Linnehan, "Affirmative Action: History, Effects and Attitudes," in *Handbook of Gender and Work,* ed. G. N. Powell (Newbury Park, CA: Sage, 1999).

66. Ibid.; quote is on p. 24.

67. Ibid.

68. Ibid.; quote is on p. 167.

69. Ibid.; quote is on p. 26.

70. R. D. Gatewood and H. S. Feild, *Human Resource Selection* (3rd ed.) (Fort Worth, TX: The Dryden Press, 1994).

71. Cox and Blake, "Managing Cultural Diversity"; Thomas, *Beyond Race and Gender.*

72. The discussion of BankAmerica is based on R. S. Johnson, "The 50 Best Companies for Asians, Blacks & Hispanics," *Fortune,* August 3, 1998, 94–96, 98, 100–104, 106; the discussion of Tenneco is based on M. N. Martinez, "The High Potential Woman," *HR Magazine* June (1991): 46–51.

73. This discussion is based on a longer description by B. Hanson and B. Walker, "Valuing Differences at Digital Equipment Corporation," paper presented at the Careers Division Pre-Conference Workshop at the Annual Meeting of the Academy of Management, August 7, 1988, Anaheim, CA.

74. Thomas, *Beyond Race and Gender;* quote is on p. 174.

75. See the description of Pace Foods, Inc., San Antonio, Texas, site in S. Nelton, "Meet Your New Work Force," *Nation's Business* July (1988): 14–21.

76. C. D. Fisher, L. F. Schoenfeldt, and J. B. Shaw, *Human Resource Management* (Boston, MA: Houghton Mifflin, 1990); quote is on p. 134.

77. The year was 1995; see Robinson and Dechant, "Building a Case for Diversity."

78. L. F. Fitzgerald, F. Drasgow, C. L., Hulin, M. J. Gelfand, and V. J. Magley, "Antecedents and Consequences of Sexual Harassment in Organizations: A Test of an Integrated Model," *Journal of Applied Psychology* 82 (1997) 578–589.

79. Thomas, *Beyond Race and Gender;* quote is on p. 10.

80 The discussion of Pacific Enterprises is based on R. S. Johnson, "The 50 Best Companies for Asians, Blacks & Hispanics," *Fortune,* August 3, 1998, 94–96, 98, 100–104, 106.

81. Thomas, *Beyond Race and Gender*

82. Martin, *A Report on the Glass Ceiling.*

83. Cox and Blake, "Managing Cultural Diversity"; quote is on pp. 52–53.

84. BankAmerica's evaluation system is discussed in Johnson, "The 50 Best Companies for Asians, Blacks & Hispanics"; Advantica's system is discussed in A. Faircloth, "Guess Who's Coming to Denny's?" *Fortune,* August 3, 1998, 108–110.

85. S. Overman , "Managing the Diverse Work Force," *HR Magazine* April (1991): 32–36.

86. Thomas, *Beyond Race and Gender;* quote is on p. 180.

87. Fernandez, *Managing a Diverse Work Force.*

88. Morrison, White, and Van Velsor, *Breaking the Glass Ceiling.*

13

ENTREPRENEURIAL CAREERS

Just about everyone has, at one time or another, fantasized about owning his or her own business. A great many people actually make the fantasy a reality by becoming an entrepreneur. Indeed, the past two decades have seen an explosion in the pursuit of entrepreneurial careers. In 1980, there were 533,520 new business incorporations in the United States. By 1986 that number had grown to 702,100. Although the recession of the early 1990s caused a decline in the formation of new businesses (629,901 in 1991), the number of incorporations continue to increase. In fact, in 1995 more than 740,000 new businesses were incorporated. This may be a conservative estimate, because many new businesses do not incorporate during their early stages of development. It has been estimated that the number of new businesses may be as high as 23 million in 1998, generating two-thirds of all new jobs.[1]

Entrepreneurs are agents of change. They play an important role in the overall welfare of society by spurring economic growth, creating new jobs, and serving as role models for future generations of entrepreneurs. For example, from 1979 to 1995, the payrolls of Fortune 500 companies declined by more than 4 million jobs. Yet, within that period, more than 24 million jobs were created within entrepreneurial organizations. These small but growing organizations have fueled the American economy and have made many entrepreneurs wealthy in the process. In 1984, 40 percent of the Forbes 400 Richest People in America were entirely self-made; by 1994, 80 percent of the Forbes 400 list were self-made.[2]

Why the burgeoning interest in entrepreneurial careers? Answering this question is not an easy task—the reasons are almost as varied as the number of entrepreneurs. They can range from seeking freedom from the corporate rat race to inheriting a business from a long-lost relative or from having a passion for a certain product or activity to taking advantage of favorable economic conditions. Whatever the factors involved, the decision to become an entrepreneur represents an appealing career choice to many people, and the interest in entrepreneurship continues to grow. In this chapter, we present an in-depth examination of the unique aspects of the entrepreneurial career. First, we define entrepreneurship and consider the various factors that lead individuals to seek entrepreneurial careers. Next, we review the social and educational support available to current and aspiring entrepreneurs. We then review the career experiences and the challenges faced by women and minority entrepreneurs. We conclude the chapter with suggestions for managing the entrepreneurial career that are linked with the career management model presented in this book.

———————— ■ ————————

ENTREPRENEURSHIP: AN OVERVIEW

There exist in the literature a variety of definitions for the terms *entrepreneur* and *entrepreneurship*, each reflecting a distinct perspective on the topic.[3] The 19th-century economist John Stuart Mill identified "risk bearing," or the ability to accept and take risks, as the characteristic that distinguishes an entrepreneur from an organizational manager.[4] Another economist, Joseph Schumpeter, saw entrepreneurship as simply the "creative activity of an innovator."[5] In this case, innovation is the distinguishing characteristic. Some researchers apply the term *entrepreneur* only to those individuals who are the founders of a new business (i.e., a person who started a new firm where one had not existed before).[6] This view is limited because it excludes those individuals who inherit or acquire an enterprise.

In their attempt to define entrepreneurship, researchers have identified five relevant schools of thought, each taking a somewhat different perspective on the term:

1. The "Great Person" school views entrepreneurs as having inborn, intuitive abilities to successfully run an enterprise.
2. The "Psychological Characteristics" school views entrepreneurs as having unique values, attitudes, and needs that drive them to be in charge of a firm.
3. The "Classical" school views entrepreneurs simply as innovators.
4. The "Management" school views entrepreneurs as organizers and managers of an economic venture.
5. The "Leadership" school views entrepreneurs as leaders of people.[7]

Several additional views of entrepreneurship are given below.

6. It involves the identification and exploitation of an opportunity.
7. It involves uncertainty and risk, complementary managerial competence, and creative opportunism.
8. It requires a wide range of skills capable of enhancement, to add value to a targeted niche of human activity.

9. It covers a wide range of activities such as creating, founding, adapting, and managing a venture.

10. It is the process of creating something different with value by devoting the necessary time and effort, assuming the accompanying financial, psychic, and social risks, and receiving the resulting rewards of monetary and personal satisfaction.

11. It necessitates risk taking and innovation from the individuals who establish and manage a business for purposes of profit and growth.[8]

The consistent themes in these views are creativity, innovation, and risk-taking propensity. Taking all these prior ideas into account, *we define entrepreneurship as managing a business of one's own that requires personal sacrifice, innovation, and risk taking to create something of value.* This definition combines the relevant aspects of prior definitions covering ownership, management, innovation, risk taking, and creativity — themes that the literature consistently applies to the term *entrepreneurship.*

CHOOSING AN ENTREPRENEURIAL CAREER

Several factors make an entrepreneurial career distinct from the more traditional career in which one is employed by an organization. First, entrepreneurial careers are marked by a substantially higher degree of personal commitment to the success of the firm because the career and the business are intertwined. In this sense, the career is the business and the business is the career. Success or failure in one domain is directly tied to success or failure in the other. Thus, as we have indicated, the entrepreneurial career involves a substantially higher degree of risk — of personal failure, monetary loss, and career turbulence. Indeed, although new business incorporations continue to rise, the failure rates on new U.S. business ventures are significant. From 1994 through 1996, business failures averaged around 71,500 failures per year. In 1997, business failures were up to 83,384.[9] Yet although these figures seem high, the failure rate was close to 1 percent per annum in 1993, with only 33 percent of new businesses failing within a few years of inception.[10] Although these statistics suggest that entrepreneurial efforts may be risky, the savvy entrepreneur does have a fairly good chance of having his or her business survive.

Another factor that makes the entrepreneurial career unique is the lower degree of structure, predictability, and support as compared with what the standard organization would provide. Of course, for some, structure and predictability are the exact reasons to avoid an organizational career. But for others who are unprepared, the lack of corporate infrastructure and support systems can be discomfiting.[11]

A third distinguishing factor is that those in entrepreneurial careers must possess a greater tendency toward action and innovation. Specifically, the nature of smaller firms is that decisive actions are required to respond to changing market conditions. By extension, the entrepreneur, as the person in charge, must show the ability to respond quickly to environmental change. By contrast, life in an organizational career is slower paced. The entrenched bureaucracy with risk-averse layers of management normally does not allow, nor does it necessarily reward, quick and innovative decision making.

A fourth distinctive element of the entrepreneurial career is that the entrepreneur simultaneously performs a number of functional roles. More precisely, the entrepreneur can be involved with operations, marketing, accounting, human resources, and planning functions all at the same time. Conversely, those in an organizational career typically play one functional role at a time. The chance for organizational managers to have multifunctional influence is limited.

With the comparatively higher risk for personal and financial failure, the more extensive demands, and the lack of structure and support, one could ask why so many individuals would throw caution to the wind and embark on an entrepreneurial career. Research points to several general factors that can influence the choice of an entrepreneurial career.[12] These factors include seeking autonomy and independence, personality characteristics and psychological conditions that predispose one to an entrepreneurial career, environmental conditions, passion for a specific product or activity, and the presence of role models. We explore each of these factors in depth.

AUTONOMY AND INDEPENDENCE

In their study of the values expressed by the members of the baby boom generation, Douglas T. Hall and Judith Richter found the "need for autonomy" and a "questioning of authority" to be prominent.[13] One could argue that all employees, regardless of their ages, value a certain degree of autonomy and independence in their work. Autonomy and independence imply that the individual experiences a substantial amount of freedom in his or her job—freedom of choice in decision making, freedom of expression in work, freedom from close supervision, and freedom from the bureaucratic process. With autonomy, the individual can implement his or her self-concept and live out important values.[14] Pursuing an entrepreneurial career is one of the primary ways that individuals can find an outlet for their autonomy and independence needs. Indeed, the need for freedom, the lack of patience with formal corporate structure, and a high degree of cynicism toward the meaningfulness of corporate work can drive people out of corporations and into their own business.[15]

Early research on entrepreneurs indicated that they often have trouble responding to authority figures, in that entrepreneurs may be unwilling to submit to authority, feel uncomfortable working under it, and consequently need to escape from it.[16] One study found the goals of autonomy and independence to be the primary motivators among those who started or purchased a business. Looking at the motives for why people become business proprietors, another study found that "autonomy" had the highest frequency of response for both male and female entrepreneurs.[17] According to Kenneth Labich, many entrepreneurs who drop out from traditional corporate jobs "complain of the bureaucratic rigidities of corporate life. They moan that top bosses denied them the freedom to tackle a project on their own, without incessant reports and a lot of meddling from above."[18]

From the prior discussion, it is clear that the desire for autonomy, independence, and freedom are significant motivators for many entrepreneurs. Being one's own man or woman by owning and managing a business is an alluring proposition, one that more and more members of our society are acknowledging.

PERSONAL CHARACTERISTICS

Several researchers have proposed that entrepreneurs possess certain personality and psychological characteristics, traits, and attitudes that predispose them to the undertaking of, and success in, business ventures of their own. In this sense, it is believed that current and future entrepreneurs have common personalities and background factors that allow them to embark more easily on an entrepreneurial career.

NEED FOR ACHIEVEMENT.   Writing in the 1960s, David McClelland proposed that need for achievement is an important psychological characteristic of entrepreneurs. According to McClelland, those high in need for achievement exhibit three main behavioral traits: they take personal responsibility for finding solutions to problems; they set moderate performance goals and take moderate, calculated risks; and they desire specific feedback concerning performance.[19] Despite extensive research, the linkage between need for achievement and entrepreneurship has been tenuous. On one hand, the work of McClelland and other researchers indicates a discernible link between achievement motivation and entrepreneurship.[20] On the other hand, in a review of published articles on the subject, Robert Brockhaus and Paul Horwitz concluded that a "causal link between ownership of a small business and a high need for achievement has not been proven."[21] Further, it has been noted that high need for achievement is characteristic of many successful people, not just entrepreneurs.[22] Even with the somewhat conflicted research findings, there is enough evidence to suggest that a high need for achievement may influence an individual's decision to become an entrepreneur.

INTERNAL LOCUS OF CONTROL.   Individuals with an internal locus of control believe they can largely control their environment and their fate through their own actions and behaviors. In theory, those who believe they alone can control their destiny may be more likely to become, and be successful as, entrepreneurs than those who do not. As with need for achievement, locus of control has shown an inconsistent relationship with entrepreneurial behavior.[23] Donald Bowen and Robert Hisrich have concluded that a comparatively higher internal locus of control "differentiates entrepreneurs from the larger population but not from other (organizational) managers."[24] It does appear that there is a strong relationship between internal locus of control and success as an entrepreneur.[25] Similar to need for achievement, an internal locus of control is generally associated with successful people, not just entrepreneurs. Nonetheless, an internal locus of control may serve as another underlying factor that influences the undertaking of and success in an entrepreneurial career.

TOLERANCE FOR AMBIGUITY. The ability to accept and deal with conflicting and uncertain situations and to handle multiple, ambiguous assignments does appear to distinguish the entrepreneurial personality from nonentrepreneurs.[26] Studies support the view that entrepreneurs have a greater capacity to tolerate ambiguity in their lives than do organizational managers.[27] As mentioned in Chapter 10, a high tolerance for ambiguity in one's life is also associated with Type A behavior, so it is not surprising that many entrepreneurs are also classified as Type As.

RISK-TAKING PROPENSITY. In discussing prior definitions of entrepreneurship, we noted that a willingness to take risks was a common element in describing the entrepreneur. As with other personality variables, prior research has shown mixed results regarding risk-taking propensity as a personality trait of entrepreneurs. Some studies have indicated that entrepreneurs can be differentiated with respect to risk taking, whereas others have failed to show a linkage.[28] Researchers have speculated that entrepreneurs themselves may not have a higher willingness to take risks but instead are blind to the degree of risks involved in their ventures. It has been suggested that entrepreneurs have such a strong belief in their ability to influence business goal outcomes that the perceived possibility of failure is perceived as relatively low. Therefore, given similar situations, the entrepreneur is likely to perceive lower levels of risk than the nonentrepreneur.[29] Overall, researchers state that little can be concluded about risk-taking propensity as a personality trait of entrepreneurs. It may be more insightful to view entrepreneurs as capable risk managers whose abilities tend to defuse what nonentrepreneurs might view as high-risk situations.[30]

ENTREPRENEURIAL SELF-CONCEPT. As we discussed earlier in the book, individuals can have certain orientations toward work that reflect their personal motives, values, and talents. This orientation, known as a career anchor, is the manifestation of the individual's self-concept or image in his or her career choice.[31] Recall from Chapter 3 that one of the career anchors described by Edgar Schein is entrepreneurship, in which Schein suggested that the individual's "primary concern is to create something new, involving the motivation to overcome obstacles, the willingness to run risks and the desire for personal prominence in whatever is accomplished."[32] The entrepreneurship anchor also reflects a desire to have freedom and autonomy to build the organization and create the business into the entrepreneur's own self-image. In effect, the entrepreneurship career anchor takes into account the prior personality traits discussed thus far—need for achievement, an internal locus of control, a tolerance for ambiguity, the willingness to bear risks, and desire for autonomy and control.

DEMOGRAPHIC AND BACKGROUND FACTORS. Several studies have been conducted to see if entrepreneurs could be differentiated from nonentrepreneurs based on a variety of demographic characteristics. These factors include parents' occupation, parents' socioeconomic status, birth order of the entrepreneur, and several others. As with virtually any career choice, one's parents can play an important role in influencing the decision. But with the selection of an entrepreneurial career, influence from one's parents can be especially salient. The father or mother may play a very powerful role in establishing the desirability and credibility of an entrepreneurial career for the off-spring.[33] Another background factor that appears related to the selection of an entrepreneurial career is being the first-born child in the family. As researchers have noted, the first-born is most likely to receive special attention as well as opportunities for the development of self-confidence.[34] Increased self-confidence and self-esteem may allow the child to view entrepreneurship as a viable career alternative.

In an extensive study of entrepreneurs, Arnold Cooper and William Dunkelberg found that entrepreneurs tend to be better educated than the general population and come from families in which parents owned a business.[35] In addition, several researchers have pointed out the positive influence that prior business experience can have on the success of entrepreneurial firms, and how a lack of experience can lead to business hardship and failure. However, Cooper and Dunkelberg also noted a high degree of diversity in the backgrounds of the entrepreneurs they studied. In fact, they concluded that diversity appeared to be a central characteristic of their sample.[36] Other researchers have stated that entrepreneurs are innovative and idiosyncratic and tend to be so unique that they cannot easily be categorized.[37]

As this section has shown, trying to gain a handle on what constitutes a typical entrepreneur in terms of personality traits and background characteristics is a difficult, if not impossible, task. Researchers have suggested that any attempt to identify characteristics of the "typical" entrepreneur is inherently futile.[38] Nonetheless, research has given us insights into what makes the entrepreneur tick, at least in a general sense. Indeed, we can conclude that entrepreneurs generally show a need for autonomy and independence, have a high achievement motivation, view themselves as being personally able to determine their own destiny, have the ability to effectively handle multiple assignments and ambiguous situations, are willing to take risks, and may have been favorably influenced by their parents and others in their social network. Although these same characteristics are commonplace among many successful people, entrepreneurs and nonentrepreneurs alike, it is apparent that entrepreneurs as a group consistently possess this combination of traits. As Edgar Schein indicates, the entrepreneurial self-concept, which includes innovation, need for autonomy and independence, risk-bearing ability, and creativity, seems to predispose certain individuals to embark on an entrepreneurial career.[39] It may be that any one of these aspects of the entrepreneurial self-concept, in conjunction with the right environmental conditions, predisposes an individual to become an entrepreneur.

ENVIRONMENTAL CONDITIONS

Becoming an entrepreneur can also be influenced by a number of environmental conditions and experiences. We consider three prominent environmental factors: job loss, work dissatisfaction, and favorable business conditions.

JOB LOSS. During the 1980s, average job loss was 2.3 million people annually. This trend has accelerated throughout the 1990s, with average job losses totaling 3.2 million employees annually being downsized through 1995. However, in the period from 1995 to 1997, 8 million people were involuntarily pushed out of their jobs. Although this latest period suggests a slowdown in the number of jobs lost, job loss has been more prevalent in the 1990s than in any prior decade to date.[40] For many of these displaced employees, starting (or acquiring) their own firm represented a worthwhile career option. Studies have shown that as many as 15 to 20 percent of the managers who lose their jobs choose to become entrepreneurs.[41] It should not be surprising that employees who are the unwitting victims of downsizings and restructurings and who still have unique competencies and a motivation to achieve start their own firms. Being discharged from an organization may provide the final impetus for aspiring entrepreneurs. Also, individuals who are terminated may vow never again to become a pawn in a large organization's chess game. Of course, deciding to become an entrepreneur after being discharged from an organization should only be done after a thorough analysis of all available options. Given the uncertainties, the sacrifices, and the risks involved, the entrepreneurial career is not for everyone. Entering into a business venture without proper planning and insight can only compound the personal toll that was started with the loss of one's job.

WORK DISSATISFACTION. In addition to job loss, another form of "negative displacement" that can influence the undertaking of an entrepreneurial career is job dissatisfaction.[42] Research has shown that dissatisfaction with their most recent previous job is a major reason for entrepreneurs to begin their own firms. Indeed, extreme dissatisfaction can push aspiring entrepreneurs from their previous place of employment and can also serve to convince them that no other place of employment represents an acceptable alternative.[43] Assuming the individual's perception to be true, the only viable solution would be to own your own firm (i.e., be your own boss).

As was the case with job loss, using work dissatisfaction as the primary (or sole) reason for becoming an entrepreneur may lead to difficulties. As we discuss in more detail later in this chapter, aspiring entrepreneurs need to explore their interests, values, and life-style preferences and then examine whether having one's own business will satisfy these personal needs. If the decision to become an entrepreneur is not based on a thorough self-evaluation but instead represents a knee-jerk reaction to an onerous work situation, then the individual is likely destined for personal unhappiness and further disappointment. Work dissatisfaction may contribute to the choice of an entrepreneurial career, but it should never be the sole deciding factor.

FAVORABLE BUSINESS CONDITIONS. Media pundits and commentators referred to the 1980s as the "greed" decade and the 1990s as the "just do it" decade. These references tap into the changing national view on the desirability of being an entrepreneur. As Roger Kaplan observed, the last quarter of the 20th century was a "boom time for free enterprise, and the hero of the boom is the self-made man, the intrepid capitalist, the person who gets rich—and makes everyone a little richer—gambling on a new product or an innovative service."[44] Responding to this trend, a number of magazines, Internet web sites, and how-to books were published to help existing entrepreneurs sustain their business and aspiring entrepreneurs to start their own. The national support for entrepreneurship has been well documented. America has cheered for its entrepreneurs, has raised them to the status of heroes, and has made entrepreneurship a national mission.[45]

Another key business condition that has spurred (and continues to spur) entrepreneurship is new technology. This includes personal computers and printers, software that can do everything from balancing your accounting books to keeping track of your potential clients, fax machines, high-speed copiers, voice mail, cell phones, beepers, and other related types of equipment. Today's reality is that the capabilities afforded by personal computers and other office technology products give the entrepreneur working at home the power of a big business.[46] In fact, the Internet has changed the way many companies, and especially entrepreneurial companies, conduct business. Those firms that are not knowledgeable about nor doing business on the Internet may not survive in the long run.[47]

It is apparent that several environmental, economic, and technological factors have combined to provide fertile ground for the undertaking of a business of one's own. Nonetheless, it is still important to recognize that the decision to become an entrepreneur should be the product of thorough analysis, covering personal desires, as well as conditions in the business environment.

Passion for a Product or Service

Some people embark on an entrepreneurial career because of a personal zeal for a specific type of product or activity. Thus, someone with a passion for cooking may decide to open a restaurant or perhaps start a catering business. Michael Selz provides examples of people who turned the loves of plants, animals, and fishing into a small commercial nursery, a pet sitting service, and a bass fishing enterprise, respectively.[48] The allure of a certain activity can be a strong motivator for entrepreneurs. Often, the product or service represents an extension of the individual's self-concept, wherein the individual identifies so closely with the product or service that the provision of such becomes a natural career choice. Further, entrepreneurs are often able to associate two seemingly unrelated things and create a marketplace phenomenon. The following examples describe this ability, also known as "bisociation":

- Michael Dell, who combined computers and mail order to launch Dell Computer Corporation.
- Fred Smith, who related mail and overnight delivery to start Federal Express.
- Debbie Fields, who linked cookies and information technology to build Mrs. Fields Cookies.[49]

Consider the following example:

> When Al was employed in corporate finance he would often find himself daydreaming about woodworking—he could almost smell the scent of freshly sawed oak in his office. On other occasions, Al would be penciling sketches of a new dresser he could make, or maybe a coffee table. On nights and weekends you could always find Al working away in his woodworking shop (which doubled as his garage), turning out carefully crafted wood products. He never made a profit on his creations, charging his friends and family only the cost of the raw materials he used. Al loved woodworking so much that the creation itself, and the admiration of his customers, was satisfaction enough.
>
> Al liked working for the corporation. He had majored in accounting as an undergraduate and had gotten his MBA in finance. Solving complex financial questions and preparing business plans were stimulating to him. But woodworking continued to be his first love—it was in his blood. His father was a carpenter, and he passed on to Al a passion for creativity with wood. Al had never seen woodworking as a vocation, only as a hobby to relieve the stress of the corporate world.
>
> After 10 years in corporate finance, Al began seeing woodworking in a new light. The demand for his creations was more than he could fulfill. Comparable wood products at commercial establishments were selling for double and triple what Al charged. Also, Al's corporation was the subject of takeover rumors—the grapevine said that Al's department would be one of the first to go if a merger did take place. Al began talking seriously to his wife about starting his own woodworking business. They concluded that her job as head of corporate research for an investment banking firm would cover them financially while the business was getting started. They spent time looking for commercial real estate properties to rent to set up the shop. Once they found the proper location, they spent $20,000 on equipment and tools. The merger finally occurred at Al's company, and he was happy to resign, take his severance package, and become a full-fledged entrepreneur. Al and his wife took out advertisements in upscale magazines, and they used their friends and families to spread the word of their nascent business to other potential customers. They took orders by mail and by phone. After 3 months in business, the demand for Al's wood products was exceeding his capacity and he was now thinking about hiring an assistant. Personally, Al is happier than he has ever been. The time pressure and demands are intense, but he is doing what he loves. He is wondering why he did not start the business sooner.

Al's example is hypothetical, yet identifies the process many fledgling entrepreneurs go through as they begin their new ventures. The following two examples are real stories about entrepreneurs who have become successful following their passion for a product or service. These examples were published on the *Entrepreneur* magazine's Web site:[50]

> John Paul Beltran and Richard Hirsh have shown both entrepreneurial and fashion flair with John Paul Richard Inc., their Chatsworth, California, women's apparel company—so much flair, in fact, that they landed the No. 1 spot in *Entrepreneur's* Hot 100 ranking with revenues of $46.5 million in 1997, their first full year in business.
>
> The founders joined forces after working together at Melrose, a women's apparel manufacturing company Hirsh had founded in 1974. Hirsh sold the company in 1986 and, after spending 10 years working for the new owner, he and Beltran found the corporate life less than fulfilling. "We decided we'd had enough of the corporate environment," recalls Hirsh. "We wanted to get out and start our own business."

Their experience in the apparel industry proved to be their key to success. With $1 million in start-up capital culled from personal savings, they secured $1.6 million in loans and created a relationship with Heller Financial Inc., a Chicago-based international commercial finance company. This helped them garner $25 million in factor loans (loans backed by outstanding invoices and current orders) last year to purchase raw materials and keep the company above water while it grew. "[Heller] was the financial engine behind our colossal growth," says Hirsh. "It was critical in making [funding] available." "Heller took a big chance on us because of our extensive industry experience," says Beltran. With these resources, the partners had no problem gathering an experienced staff from industry contacts. They were also able to land accounts with such national retailers as Macy's, Mervyn's, and Sears almost immediately.

"Giving a start-up company like John Paul Richard financing for its stores was not so far-fetched because these were people we'd had tremendous experience with over the years," Hirsh explains. But most important, the partners' familiarity with the market and potential customers helped them discover an unfilled niche: fashionable misses' clothes. "We fill a gap in the department store business," explains Beltran, 44. "The misses' department is filled with traditional merchandise. We bring in merchandise that is more fashionable and still very reasonably priced." "We understand our market and each individual player we deal with," adds Hirsh, 45. "And we have a keen understanding of what will sell at what price point."

Not content to stop with just one clothing line, Beltran and Hirsh are ready to conquer other departments with their fashions. "I think the next [thing to do] is to seek more accounts," says Beltran. "In the future, we'll go after the petite-sized and large-sized customers [markets] we have barely touched on so far." With plans to double its astounding first-year revenues this year, John Paul Richard's success shouldn't wear out any time soon.

Comedians often target the South as redneck heaven, but Deborah R. and Jim Ford, Jr., owners of *Entrepreneur's* Hot 100 No. 35-ranked Grits Inc. in Birmingham, Alabama, make it their business to create a positive image of the place they call home. Their affection for Southern traditions has blossomed into success worth millions.

The husband-and-wife team found its niche in the gift and apparel industries by putting phrases that exemplify Southern traditions and upbringing (e.g., "Southern Girls Don't Sweat—They Glisten") on mugs, wine glasses, pillows, apparel, and more. Their story dates back to August 1995, when native Alabaman Deborah, now 45, screen-printed a phrase she has heard most of her life, "Grits: Girls Raised in the South," onto her volleyball players' T-shirts at the junior high school where she taught and coached. A few months later, she met Jim, now 47, who saw dollar signs in the catch phrase. With an extensive background in sales and marketing, he told his soon-to-be-wife that he thought she was sitting on a gold mine. Deborah then applied to trademark the "Grits" phrase and thought up 25 more Southern sayings, such as "PMS: Precious Moody Southerners" and "Southern Girls Know That Friends Are Forevah."

When they sold $65,000 worth of embroidered goods, such as T-shirts, sweatshirts, and hats, at the Atlanta Apparel Mart's July Gift Show in 1996, the now-married couple decided to quit their jobs and take on Grits full time. "At the next show, we did more than $100,000, and at the next show, we did more than $150,000," says Jim. The days of relying only on trade shows for visibility are long gone. No strangers to the word *expansion*, the Fords have increased their warehouse space three times, and for good reason: They now have 1,620 active accounts, including Lebanon, Tennessee-based restaurant chain Cracker Barrel and 500 Hallmark stores. And this year's Atlanta Gift Mart will see the premiere of a voice chip-enhanced book and stuffed animal series geared toward youngsters.

Success did not come without some hurdles, however. The Fords encountered theft early on—$50,000 worth of merchandise was stolen from one of their warehouses—and their $4 million-plus sales figures for 1997 could have been close to $5 million if they had not suffered an $800,000 loss in revenue due to vendor shipping delays. But a booming business makes it easier to recover. Jim attributes their overwhelming success to their distribution network, the strength of their trademark, their devoted staff, and recent CFO addition Doug Johnson.

With Deborah's flair for color, style, and catchy sayings and Jim's knack for running a business, these dynamos are making millions embracing—and marketing—the South. The Fords project sales of $8 million for 1998 and hope to expand nationwide.

Both of these examples point out that without the passion for a particular product or service, which may help entrepreneurs through good and bad times, these entrepreneurs may not have followed their dream and may not have experienced the successes they each have.

PRESENCE OF ROLE MODELS

In Chapter 6 we discussed the influence of social forces on the selection of an occupation. Specifically, we advanced the view that parents, other family members, and friends can serve as important role models and mentors in making career decisions. The influence of the social environment on entrepreneurship has emerged as an interesting area of research.[51] The key question is this—Does having an entrepreneurial role model encourage the selection of an entrepreneurial career? In reviewing the findings from prior studies, Robert Brockhaus and Paul Horwitz have found support for the idea that "seeing someone else succeed encourages prospective entrepreneurs to take the risk. In summary, the existence of a successful role model encourages entrepreneurial efforts."[52]

Perhaps the most important role models for budding entrepreneurs are parents. Several studies have found that either the father or mother, working in an entrepreneurial venture, help to establish the entrepreneurial career as a desirable and credible career alternative for their children.[53]

A special case of parental influence on the undertaking of the entrepreneurial career concerns the encouragement of the children of entrepreneurs to enter the family business. Often, entrepreneurial parents see their children as the future standard-bearers of the company, the ones who can carry the company on for future generations. In fact, recent studies found the majority of owners of family-owned firms wished to transfer ownership and control to their children.[54] For many children of entrepreneurs, the decision to enter the family company is uneventful and free of stress, due to a desire to carry on the family legacy and build on the efforts of one's parents. In this case, the children feel unthreatened, free to choose the career goals they desire. But for others, the decision to join and help run the family business can be a stressful experience, as the need to assert independence from the family unit clashes with parental pressure to enter the family enterprise. The pressure to be employed by the family firm would likely be highest when the individual is emerging from the school years when one's formal education is complete. But at this time, the individual is in the process of entering the adult world, confronting the psychological conflict that results from the need to be one's own person versus the pull of the safety and security of the family.

The issue of succession, that is who will run the family-owned business after the owner steps down, is often a point of contention. Research reveals that the owner's sons are groomed to succeed the owner. Daughters of owners are often considered "invisible successors," with their major responsibility being the passing of family traditions and history onto the next generation.[55] However, as attitudes change toward women's roles (in families and in the workplace), many more daughters will be taking over family businesses. Named to the 1998 *Forbes* 400 Richest People in America, Maggie Hardy Magerko followed her father Joseph Hardy, as owner of the 84 Lumber stores. Abigail Johnson, heir to the largest mutual fund family, Fidelity Investments, is currently a senior vice president and is following in her father's (Ned Johnson III) footsteps. Christie Hefner, Hugh Hefner's daughter, and CEO of Playboy Enterprises, may be the most celebrated example of a daughter taking over her father's business.[56]

Regardless of the level of pressure one feels from family, the process of considering whether to enter the family business should follow the career management model presented earlier. The individual should thoroughly assess personal values, interests, talents, and life-style preferences and assess the work environment (both within and outside the family firm) to have sufficient knowledge to determine the most appropriate career goals. One's decision to enter the family firm should only be made if it is consistent with personal desires and fits with conditions in the internal and external work environments.

In contrast to the positive influence that family members can have on the undertaking of an entrepreneurial career, some research has found that individuals who had a mentor in the development of their businesses tended to be less successful than those entrepreneurs who did not have an identifiable mentoring relationship.[57] It may well be that the independent and risk-taking nature of the entrepreneur is unduly inhibited by the presence of a mentor or similar advice giver. In other words, the presence of a mentor may be dysfunctional to the extent that he or she adversely restricts the innovation, independence, risk taking, and business judgment of the entrepreneur.

In summary, the relative importance of role models and mentors in the undertaking and success of entrepreneurial ventures is somewhat uncertain. It does appear that parents can play an influential role in encouraging their children to pursue entrepreneurial careers. Once one becomes an entrepreneur, the role of parents, mentors, and other alliances may diminish considerably. The nature of the entrepreneurial career is such that decisive individual action is paramount. Advice and intrusion from the social network may only inhibit the entrepreneur from taking required actions.

SUPPORT FOR THE ENTREPRENEURIAL CAREER

Coincident with the national surge in entrepreneurial activity is the emergence of a variety of support mechanisms. These mechanisms include social networks and alliances, training and education programs, publications, and web sites. This whole infrastructure of support for the entrepreneur has grown up corresponding with the rapid increase in entrepreneurial activity. Let us briefly consider each type of support.

SOCIAL NETWORKS AND ALLIANCES. Entrepreneurs can be helped by a number of different social groups and mutual benefit organizations. Social networks operate at two different levels. Informal alliances include business support from friends and relatives. Formal assistance can come from such larger organizations as community groups, governmental agencies, ethnic institutions, religious associations, fraternal organizations, and other small business associations. Other supportive alliances, such as cooperative housing and buying arrangements, trade groups, joint capital-raising activities, and community professional advice, provide help for potential entrepreneurs.[58] Alliances increase the entrepreneur's likelihood of making contact with other entrepreneurs and, most important, with potential venture capital providers.[59] Small business owners help each other through clubs and roundtables that meet regularly across the country. There are approximately 120 such venture clubs throughout the United States.[60] One such club is the Connecticut Venture Group, which started with six members back in 1974 and is now the model for more than 100 organizations around the world.[61]

A city's chamber of commerce can also help entrepreneurs and their businesses. Since 1980, the Greater Philadelphia Chamber of Commerce has annually organized entrepreneurial business fairs.[62] The Greater Philadelphia Venture Group (GPVG), a council of the Greater Philadelphia Chamber of Commerce was founded in 1984 and is the umbrella organization for this region's venture capital community. The GPVG's primary goal is to facilitate communication among venture capitalists and professional service providers to foster the creation and growth of entrepreneurial companies. As an example of activities provided by GPVG in 1998, a 2-day fair featured the region's most promising expansion-stage companies that are technology and service providers in the telecommunications, computer hardware and software, information technology, health care, and life science industries. Forty-eight companies made presentations and 50 companies were exhibitors.[63]

TRAINING AND EDUCATION PROGRAMS. During the 1980s, colleges and universities began to recognize the importance of, and student demand for, educational programs in entrepreneurship.[64] The provision of entrepreneurship education programs has grown from a half-dozen universities offering programs in 1967 to approximately 370 in 1998. And the trend in the number of programs continues on an upward track, with only a few examples of schools scaling back or eliminating programs once they are started.[65] There exist at least 89 endowed positions in entrepreneurship in U.S. educational institutions, and it is hard to find a major college or university without a center for entrepreneurial studies.[66] Courses in entrepreneurship are extremely popular among students. At Babson College, a school known for its entrepreneurial studies, 30 percent of 1,600 undergraduates majored in entrepreneurship, making it the school's most popular major.[67] On average, approximately 25 percent of MBA students graduating each year in the United States have probably had at least one entrepreneurship course. At some graduate schools, such as the Harvard Business School and MIT's Sloan School of Management, upward of 90 percent of the graduating students have taken at least one entrepreneurship course. The largest fraction of these students, based on course surveys, take the courses with a goal of becoming self-employed following graduation. In the Harvard Business School Class of 1997, 22 percent of graduates took jobs with small companies.[68]

The growing demand for entrepreneurial education programs reflects the increasing level of perceived desirability of the entrepreneurial career. Business college graduates perceive business ownership in a positive light, and being an independent entrepreneur is a long-term goal for a significant number of business school students.[69]

Courses and programs in entrepreneurship at the university level are designed to meet career and training needs of essentially two groups: traditional undergraduate and graduate students interested in an entrepreneurial career and nontraditional students such as practicing and potential entrepreneurs not involved in an academic program.[70] Content of the courses and programs can vary somewhat from school to school, but in general they cover traditional business subjects (e.g., marketing, finance, accounting, management), combined with practical "hands-on" instruction and simulations and related case analyses. Often, educational and assistance programs for current entrepreneurs are handled through centers or institutes established by universities expressly for that purpose. These centers tend to deal with entrepreneurs in the local geographic region by providing a program focused on their issues.[71] Universities and colleges can also pool their efforts to achieve a degree of synergy in serving the needs of entrepreneurs. An example of a cooperative effort is given below:

> The National Consortium of Entrepreneurial Centers is an alliance of 10 organizations dedicated to entrepreneurship education. The consortium is sponsored by The Ewing Marion Kauffman Foundation and is supported through the Center for Entrepreneurial Leadership (CEL) Clearinghouse on Entrepreneurship Education (CEE). The purpose of the consortium is to share information and aid in the growth of entrepreneurs in each of the communities these organizations serve.

The founding members are:

- Babson College's Center for Entrepreneurial Studies (Wellesley, MA)
- Baylor University's John F. Baugh Center for Entrepreneurship (Waco, TX)
- Carnegie Mellon University's Donald H. Jones Center (Pittsburgh, PA)
- The Council for Entrepreneurial Development (Raleigh, NC)
- The Midwest Entrepreneurial Education Center (Indianapolis, IN)

- Rensselaer Polytechnic Institute's Center for Entrepreneurship of New Technological Ventures (Troy, NY)
- The UCLA Harold Price Center for Entrepreneurial Studies (Los Angeles, CA)
- The Wharton School of Business' Sol C. Snider Entrepreneurial Center at the University of Pennsylvania (Philadelphia, PA)
- The University of St. Thomas (Minneapolis, MN)
- The University of Texas' IC2 (Austin, TX)[72]

Entrepreneurial interest is now so high that education programs are being offered at the high school level. A recent survey found that 70 percent of high school students wanted to start a business.[73] Experienced-based readiness programs are available for children in the fourth through 12th grades, as evidenced by the following programs: YESS! (Youth Empowerment and Self-Sufficiency) Mini-Society, An Income of Her Own, EntrePrep, and New Youth Entrepreneur.[74]

PUBLICATIONS. Recognizing the heightened interest in entrepreneurial careers and the trend in new business formations, the publishing industry has moved forcefully to supply related literature. Indeed, there now exists a variety of periodicals, journals, magazines, and books that covers such topics as owning your own firm and being successful once you become an entrepreneur. These publications play an important role in advancing the understanding of entrepreneurship by providing advice on starting and/or managing a business venture and giving realistic previews of what one will encounter in an entrepreneurial career. Both male and female entrepreneurs have been found to use magazines, journals, and books as the primary impersonal sources of information regarding the operation of their businesses.[75]

Even large businesses are helping smaller business to be successful. The general idea is that helping small companies to grow is good business and may lead to more business for the large company. An example is Sprint Business, a telecommunications company, which has published a list of 25 helpful phone numbers, from government agencies to nonprofit organizations and corporations, to aid the nascent entrepreneurial business get up and running.[76]

CHARACTERISTICS AND EXPERIENCES OF FEMALE AND MINORITY ENTREPRENEURS

In earlier sections of this chapter, we discussed two different views of entrepreneurial career selection—as a product of certain personality and psychological characteristics and as a function of environmental influences. Much has been written over the past 10 years concerning whether female and minority entrepreneurs possess the typical entrepreneurial personality profile (i.e., need for autonomy and independence, high need for achievement, risk-taking propensity, internal locus of control, tolerance for ambiguity) and/or display similar background and social learning experiences (i.e., entrepreneurial parents, encouragement, and support) as men and nonminorities. The following sections discuss our knowledge of the entrepreneurial experiences of women and people of color.

FEMALE ENTREPRENEURS

Although the overall growth in new business formations during the past decade has been exceptional, the growth in female-owned businesses has been especially impressive. Indeed, the number of sole proprietorships owned by women has recently been growing 50 percent faster than the total. Between 1987 and 1996, the number of women-owned firms increased 78 percent. In 1998, there were more than 8 million women-owned firms with 18.5 million employees, and these firms employed 80 percent more people than the Fortune 500 combined.[77] Paralleling the rise in female-owned firms, many research studies have investigated female entrepreneurs. Several questions emerge from a review of this literature.

- Are women entrepreneurs characteristically different from either their male counterparts or female managers in organizations?

In general, research has found few, if any, differences between female entrepreneurs and either their male counterparts or female organizational managers in terms of risk-taking propensity, need for achievement, desire for autonomy, level of education, level of prior work experience, borrowing and financing routes, and the degree of planning conducted.[78] Therefore, motivations of female entrepreneurs are similar to those of men—to be financially independent, to be autonomous and achieve, and to use their unique skills and talents.[79] In their extensive review of the literature on female entrepreneurs, Donald Bowen and Robert Hisrich found that "female entrepreneurs are (a) relatively well-educated in general, but perhaps not in management skills; (b) high in internal locus of control; (c) more masculine or instrumental than other women in their values; (d) likely to have had entrepreneurial fathers; (e) likely to have been first born or an only child; (f) unlikely to start a business in traditionally male-dominated industries; (g) more likely than not to be married; (h) seldom owners of a large business; and (i) experiencing a need for additional managerial training."[80] Of course, these identified characteristics and experiences are generally representative of all entrepreneurs, not just women.[81]

- What are the underlying reasons why women enter an entrepreneurial career?

As we just discussed, female entrepreneurs do not appear to display any major differences in personality compared with either their male counterparts or female organizational managers. One could therefore question whether there are other special factors or circumstances that underlie the entrepreneurial career selection of women. In Jeremy Main's view, "Entrepreneurship seems to suit women particularly, partly as an antidote to discrimination they encounter in corporations. Creating their own businesses offers an escape."[82] It has been found that for women younger than 30 years of age, career dissatisfaction was a predominant reason to seek entrepreneurial careers. Because these working women are dissatisfied with their current employers and frustrated with their slow advancement, entrepreneurship is perceived as a viable mechanism to establish oneself.[83] Although dissatisfaction with one's career is also a significant reason for men to select an entrepreneurial career, the real and perceived presence of the "glass ceiling" can intensify the frustration and dissatisfaction of women. In 1998, women comprised close to 50 percent of the U.S. work force, yet represented less than 10 percent of Fortune 500 corporate officer positions.[84] Recognizing the slow progress to the top, it is no wonder that many achievement-oriented women opt out of corporations to run their own firms, in which success is more a matter of one's own abilities and hard work.

Another factor that can influence women in the choice of an entrepreneurial career is the desire to combine career aspirations and the role of mother. In this sense, the less restrictive entrepreneurial career offers a greater opportunity for flexibility in scheduling work hours, thus allowing more time for family demands. Women entrepreneurs with young families find that their entrepreneurial efforts create an opportunity for flexibility in terms of hours and work location. This flexibility also allows women entrepreneurs to attend to the needs of their children.[85] In fact, three of four home-based women business owners are college educated, are in their 30s and 40s, are married with kids, and have work experience.[86]

Not surprisingly, women entrepreneurs are comparatively more likely than men to choose to work part-time because they want to accommodate their work and child-rearing roles simultaneously. Of course, combining entrepreneurship with extensive family time can have a downside in that work-family conflict and time demands may diminish the success of the enterprise. Research has noted the need to resolve the time-related conflicts brought on by family demands for female-owned firms to be successful. It has been cautioned that work-family conflict, a real concern for the women entrepreneur, can be particularly troublesome in the lean initial years in the life of the firm.[87]

Thus, it appears that the relationship between entrepreneurship and family obligations is paradoxical. On the one hand, the generally greater personal freedom offered by entrepreneurship can allow individuals flexibility in allotting time to family commitments. But on the other hand, entrepreneurial success usually carries with it escalating demands that can diminish the amount of time the entrepreneur can spend with his or her family. Yet, some evidence suggests that women entrepreneurs are more satisfied with their careers than are men.[88] It may be that those woman entrepreneurs who resolve work-family conflict make choices on the relative importance of the different spheres of one's life and are satisfied with those choices.

■ Are there limiting factors in the career choices of female entrepreneurs?

As we discussed in Chapter 6, women generally tend to make career choices and select occupations from a narrower range of alternatives than do men. Consistent with this view, it has been found that women tend to have a lower overall preference for entrepreneurship than men and that women entrepreneurs tend to be concentrated in mainly retail and service firms.[89] Statistics from a 1992 U.S. Census Bureau report indicate that for female-owned businesses with fewer than 100 employees, approximately 40 percent are service organizations, whereas another 31 percent are in retail trade. However, women-owned businesses in "nontraditional" business sectors have grown dramatically (more than 50 percent since 1987), with about 12 percent in construction and 22 percent in mining and manufacturing.[90]

The reasons for lower entrepreneurial preference among women are varied. It has been suggested that cultural conditioning, social learning, a lack of encouragement and role models, and low self-confidence can channel women away from an entrepreneurial career.[91] Moreover, it has been found that women tend not to enter certain fields because of a lack of business or technical skills and/or a lack of confidence in financial, marketing, and purchasing abilities.[92] Among female entrepreneurs, the most consistently noted difficulties include access to credit/credit discrimination, inability to delegate responsibility and authority to subordinates, and conflicts between work and family/personal lives.[93]

Regardless of the potentially limiting factors that they face, there are a number of positive qualities generally possessed by female entrepreneurs. These qualities include high energy levels, skill in influencing others and gaining consensus, and a high degree of pragmatism in their business decisions.[94] As this chapter has discussed, all current and aspiring entrepreneurs face a variety of challenges, limitations, and difficulties in launching and operating their businesses. However, it appears that female entrepreneurs must confront a unique set of hurdles primarily because of societal influence and cultural conditioning. Fortunately, as more and more women become successful entrepreneurs, it is expected that the identified limitations and barriers will diminish.

MINORITY ENTREPRENEURS

Even with the burgeoning interest in entrepreneurial activity overall, only a limited amount of research attention has been given to the characteristics and experiences of minority entrepreneurs. This may be because few small businesses are owned by people of color. In 1998, only 3 percent were owned by African-Americans, less than 2 percent were owned by Hispanics, and 10 percent were owned by Koreans.[95] Despite these small percentages of minority-owned firms, the personality characteristics and motivations of minority entrepreneurs are similar to those of nonminorities. Robert Hisrich and Candida Brush found need for achievement to be the primary motivator in starting one's own firm among minority owners.[96] Other related factors such as independence were also rated as important motivators among minority business owners.

In terms of background and environmental factors, minority role models and family role models are influential for people of color while starting a business and gaining access to key markets.[97] For many minority entrepreneurs, extensive support can come from mutual-benefit associations that are centered around racial or ethnic ties. Strong ethnic networks can provide aid in the form of venture capital, lines of credit, market and/or product information, training opportunities, and the regulation of competition.[98] Many groups have followed this model of strong ethnic solidarity and assistance to achieve entrepreneurial success.

As with female entrepreneurs, one of the most important factors that lead people of color into entrepreneurial careers is treatment discrimination and bias in the corporate business environment. Indeed, real and perceived closure of upper-level management positions to minority employees can cause frustration and a reduced level of commitment to the corporation. Thus, the lack of access in the corporate world can be a motivator in the undertaking of an entrepreneurial career. Consider the following example:

> Roberta has been a top real estate executive at a large fast-food franchiser for the past 15 years. Starting at the lowest levels of the managerial hierarchy after college, she rose to her current status through much hard work and effort. In fact, Roberta has been so involved in her job that she has had little to no personal life—choosing not to marry or have children.
>
> Roberta's personnel evaluations are always excellent, and she has been told that the next high-level job to open up will be hers. However, Roberta realizes that she has been in her current job for the past 2 years, and recently one of her white male counterparts received the promotion to chief operating officer that she was expecting to receive. When she inquired as to why she was not even offered an interview for the job, Roberta was told that her counterpart had more experience and had a better working relationship with the CEO. Roberta was miffed by these comments. She had been the one to put this fast-food chain literally "on the map" by expanding the operation on the East Coast over the past 10 years. And while she was rewarded financially for her efforts, she wanted to receive the position for which she had worked so hard.
>
> Roberta began to think that her talents might be better suited if she ran her own company. There are many discount drug chains, food stores, and other retail outlets that need to negotiate real estate deals throughout the East Coast. Roberta knew the territory and had contacts in every state. She had been the contract negotiator many times and enjoyed the thrill those negotiations entailed. Roberta began considering a career as a "free-lance" real estate negotiator and looking for the opportunity to pursue such a career.

Also similar to female entrepreneurs, minority-owned firms tend to be concentrated in service and retail trade businesses. According to 1992 data from the U.S. Census Bureau and the Department of Commerce, 11 percent of the 17.3 million small businesses surveyed were owned by minorities, with approximately 48 percent in service firms and 16 percent in retail trade firms. Like female entrepreneurs, satisfying financing needs and gaining business experience in key areas such as marketing and finance are significant concerns of minority entrepreneurs.[99]

In total, it appears that minority entrepreneurs possess personality characteristics and face demands and concerns that are similar to those of entrepreneurs in general. Unfortunately, minority entrepreneurs also face additional challenges that must be overcome, including built-in racism and bias, a generally less affluent customer base, possibly lower degrees of business experience, and other barriers to business establishment and success. As with female entrepreneurs, the elimination of these barriers can be accelerated through greater self-determination among current and future minority entrepreneurs, combined with increased social and educational support for minority enterprises.[100] It must be recognized that minority entrepreneurs not only play an increasingly important role in the economic vitality of the country as a whole but also are crucial to the economic development of many communities across the nation.

SELECTING AND MANAGING THE ENTREPRENEURIAL CAREER

Throughout this book, we have underscored the need for a systematic and informed approach to career management. Selection of an entrepreneurial career, although admittedly somewhat different from the choice of an organizational career, should still be based on a thorough analysis of personal desires and characteristics as well as a detailed review of conditions and expectations in the work environment. In addition, the setting of entrepreneurial career goals and the establishment of related career strategies should be a function of the information gained from the assessment of personal desires and environmental conditions. Throughout one's entrepreneurial career, regular reappraisal should occur regarding whether key expectations and goals are being fulfilled. Let us consider each of these steps in more detail.

SELF-ASSESSMENT. In Chapter 3, we discussed the view that self-awareness is critical in choosing career goals that are compatible with one's interests, values, and life-style preferences. Previously discussed assessment instruments such as the Strong Interest Inventory and the Career Anchors Inventory,[101] have separate categories that indicate whether an entrepreneurial self-concept or theme is present. For example, the Strong Interest Inventory has as one of its six occupational themes an "enterprising" type. Sandra K. Hirsch and Thomas Vessey characterized entrepreneurs as "energetic, ambitious, fast-paced individuals who enjoy power, status, and wealth. They are willing to make a decision and act on it. They move quickly to action, enjoying the challenges, risk, and adventure. They enjoy competition."[102] This description closely parallels the typology of the entrepreneur that we advanced previously in the chapter. In a similar fashion, Edgar Schein's entrepreneurial career anchor can give an indication that one's self-concept fits in with the life-style and activities of an entrepreneur.[103]

In addition to gaining insight into the more personal issues of one's self-concept and psychological characteristics, aspiring entrepreneurs also need to ask themselves more fundamental questions concerning business success. The following lists a number of these questions:[104]

- Is my business idea good enough?
- Do I have the management skills needed to succeed?
- How important is money to me?

- Can I live with the risk of owning my own business?
- What will be my family's reaction to my becoming an entrepreneur?

The interlocking nature of the entrepreneur's career and the business itself dictates that the individual's assessment of interests, needs, and chances for success becomes an assessment of the business's interests, needs, and chances for success.

ASSESSMENT OF THE WORK ENVIRONMENT.   As with the gathering of self-information, the accumulation of knowledge on the work environment takes on a broader meaning for the aspiring entrepreneur. Thus, a personal analysis of conditions in the business environment becomes a wider assessment of expected conditions that one's hypothetical company would face. In this sense, the individual's assessment of the work environment can represent an environmental analysis for the company, covering expectations on economic conditions, changes in demographics, market preferences, legal and regulatory issues, technologic advancements, and a host of other factors. The choice of an entrepreneurial career, and the selection of the type of business to own, should take into account the knowledge gained through this environmental review.

SETTING CAREER GOALS.   Individuals who see themselves in an entrepreneurial career should set career goals that reflect this aspiration. Instrumental and operational goals for an entrepreneurial career would likely indicate expectations for personal success and achievement of the firm. In this way, personal career goals and business objectives intersect. But entrepreneurial career goals can also be conceptual and expressive, reflecting one's significant values and the intrinsic enjoyment gained from the entrepreneurial experience.

Many times, entrepreneurs take a circuitous route to business ownership. As with any career selection, it may take a relatively long period of time to fully understand one's likes and dislikes, interests, special talents, and aspirations. Also, the realities of the business environment may change rapidly or may become apparent only after several years of experience. An example of this type of "trial and error" approach to entrepreneurial career selection is provided below.

> As chairman of the $165 million (in revenues) John Paul Mitchell Systems company, John Paul Jones DeJoria is by all accounts a successful entrepreneur. But his route to the chairmanship of the Beverly Hills–based maker of hair care products and beauty aids was anything but routine. From 1964, when he got out of the Navy, to 1980, when he cofounded the John Paul Mitchell Systems company, DeJoria held (and then was fired from or quit) a long list of sales jobs. He began his career working for such large corporations as Savin and Time but did not last in either job because he did not see eye-to-eye with either company's management. Indeed, he quit Savin because he disliked wearing neckties on his sales calls. After his time with the large corporations, DeJoria became a door-to-door salesman, selling such products as life insurance, encyclopedias, and medical linens. In 1971, DeJoria landed a job with Redken Laboratories selling shampoo through hair salons but left after a short period. He held additional jobs in the beauty business but did not last in any of them. At one organization, his commission schedule had him making more money than the person who owned the company.

Finally in 1980, DeJoria came to the conclusion that the only boss for whom he could work was himself. That year he teamed with a Scottish hairdresser named Paul Mitchell to found the John Paul Mitchell Systems company. Working in a more free-wheeling environment of self-determination, DeJoria flourished. His company experienced many consecutive years of double-digit sales increases, and pretax profit margins have exceeded 30 percent. In 1996, John Paul Mitchell Systems marketed more than 35 different hair care products in 29 countries. DeJoria revels in his celebrity status and enjoys the life-style that successful entrepreneurship allows. After years of struggle and floundering, John Paul Jones DeJoria was able to achieve success and satisfaction in an entrepreneurial career.[105]

DEVELOPMENT OF CAREER STRATEGIES. Some of the career strategies that we covered in Chapter 4 do not necessarily have direct relevance to the entrepreneurial career. For example, such strategies as image building and organizational politics would most likely be unnecessary for the entrepreneur. More appropriately, the entrepreneur's career strategies would reflect the strategies of the company, such as expansion of the product line or perhaps a move into another geographic market. Other strategies that we discussed are appropriate for the entrepreneur. Competency in one's job (in this case as a business owner), extended work involvement, skill development, and opportunity development would all be relevant career strategies for the entrepreneur. Additional strategies that could have instrumental value include the development of business relationships with other firms, locating access to capital and financing sources, utilization of social networks and support groups, and other related activities.

CAREER APPRAISAL. Once an entrepreneurial career is undertaken, regular reappraisal should occur. Assessing one's career accomplishments in the light of established goals and strategies could lead to the conclusion that no changes are necessary, or that some fine-tuning is required, or that wholesale alterations in career goals and strategies are mandatory. For the entrepreneur, feedback on career progress can be immediate and crystal clear, because progress in the business venture should track closely with the success of the entrepreneur's career. Often, but not always, failure of the business portends a lack of achievement in meeting the entrepreneur's career goals, especially if the career goals are focused on the success and accomplishment of the enterprise. Of course, if one's career goals or strategies are centered around gaining hands-on business experience or learning about financing options, then the time in the entrepreneurial career is well spent, regardless of the success of the firm. Further, the entrepreneur should assess the effect that business ownership has (either positively or negatively) on family responsibilities. In any case, the entrepreneur should occasionally reappraise his or her career to see if important needs are being met. If they are not, then changes may be warranted—perhaps even leaving the world of entrepreneurship!

It is interesting to note that current research shows only limited differences between entrepreneurs and salaried organizational members in terms of job attitudes and career outcomes. For example, a study found essentially no differences between entrepreneurs and salaried organizational members for such outcomes as life satisfaction, satisfaction with free time, degree of comfort at work, satisfaction with financial rewards, satisfaction with co-workers, and the number of psychosomatic complaints.[106] Self-employed individuals did report higher levels of satisfaction with job challenge, supporting the view that entrepreneurs may experience greater degrees of stimulation and vibrancy in their lives brought on by the constant demands of the company.

In summary, we believe that the process of managing the entrepreneurial career is essentially the same as that for an organizational career. The aspiring (and current) entrepreneur needs to attain a thorough understanding of self and the work environment, set realistic and informed career goals, develop career strategies to fulfill these goals, and regularly reappraise progress and personal fulfillment.

SUMMARY

The past 15 years have seen a worldwide explosion of interest in entrepreneurial careers. Political changes, economic turbulence, corporate restructuring and downsizing, employee discontent with life in the corporation, and a host of other factors are all influencing the expansion of entrepreneurship.

This chapter explored several topics relevant to the entrepreneurial career. Prior definitions of entrepreneurship have focused on the themes of creativity, innovation, and risk-taking propensity. Taking these themes into account, we defined entrepreneurship as managing a business of one's own that requires personal sacrifice, innovation, and risk taking to create something of value.

Becoming an entrepreneur means experiencing a career that is different from the traditional organization-based notion. The entrepreneurial career is marked by extensive personal commitment to the success of the firm, acceptance of lower degrees of structure and predictability, an orientation toward action and decisiveness, the simultaneous performance of multiple roles, and a willingness to accept risk. Because of these distinctive features, entrepreneurs find substantial challenge and stimulation in their work but also must confront the precarious nature of business ownership.

Past research has questioned whether the selection of an entrepreneurial career is more a function of personal traits and characteristics or a product of environmental influence, or perhaps a combination of both. Such personal factors as the need for autonomy and independence, the need for achievement, an internal locus of control, a tolerance for ambiguity, a risk-taking propensity, an entrepreneurial self-concept, and various demographic/background factors have been found to have a positive influence on the choice of an entrepreneurial career. Of course, these same characteristics are present among many successful people, entrepreneurs and nonentrepreneurs alike. But they do give a fairly distinct picture of the common traits that constitute a "typical" profile of the entrepreneur.

In addition to personality characteristics, a number of environmental conditions can work to direct people toward an entrepreneurial career. In this chapter, we concentrated on three such factors—job loss, work dissatisfaction, and favorable business conditions. We discussed how a passion for a particular product or service can be a strong motivator in the undertaking of business ownership. We also reviewed how the presence of role models and/or mentors has been shown to affect positively the pursuit of entrepreneurship. Having a successful entrepreneurial role model, whether it be parents, relatives, or friends, can often encourage entrepreneurial effort.

The national and worldwide surge in entrepreneurial activity has brought with it the establishment of social networks and alliances, training and education programs, and publications that are all designed to assist the aspiring and existing entrepreneur in dealing with the challenges of business ownership and provide a realistic preview of what can be expected from the entrepreneurial career.

In line with the general trend, entrepreneurial activity among women and minorities has grown considerably during the past two decades. Although the personal motivations and background factors of female and minority entrepreneurs are consistent with entrepreneurs in total, they must confront and overcome a variety of unique challenges. These include built-in discrimination and bias, social learning and cultural conditioning that may discourage entrepreneurial activity, lower self-efficacy regarding entrepreneurship, and in the case of women, additional role demands regarding family commitments.

As with any career choice, the decision to become an entrepreneur should follow the career management model as outlined in this book. Specifically, entrepreneurial career goals should be based on a thorough understanding of individual interests, talents, values, and preferences, as well as information on the work environment. The entrepreneur should then set career strategies that will help achieve the established career goals. Finally, career reappraisal should be conducted regularly to ensure that relevant needs and expectations are being met.

ASSIGNMENT

Interview someone who owns his or her own business. Determine the factors that led this person into an entrepreneurial career. How successful is the person's enterprise? To what factors does he or she attribute this level of success? What are the rewards and stresses the person experiences in his or her entrepreneurial career?

DISCUSSION QUESTIONS

1. Do you think you would be successful and happy as an entrepreneur? Why or why not?

2. Do you believe that there is a "typical" entrepreneurial personality? Why or why not?

3. How does the entrepreneurial career differ from an organizational one? How do these differences influence the setting of career strategies among entrepreneurs?

4. How can social learning and cultural conditioning influence the choice of an entrepreneurial career? What role do one's parents play in the choice?

5. What special career challenges do women and minority entrepreneurs face in launching and operating their businesses? What actions can women and people of color take to overcome these challenges?

6. What types of social support are available to current and aspiring entrepreneurs? How do colleges and universities contribute to the level of entrepreneurship across the country?

ENDNOTES

1. J. G. Burch, "Profiling the Entrepreneur," *Business Horizons* September–October (1986): 13–16; K. G. Salwen, "Editors Note," *Wall Street Journal,* March 30, 1998, R4; D. L. Sexton and R. W. Smilor, eds. *Entrepreneurship 2000* (Chicago, IL: Upstart Publishing Company, 1997); U.S. Bureau of the Census, *Statistical Abstracts of the United States:* 1997 (117th ed.) (Washington, DC, 1997).

2. J. Freear, J. E. Sohl, and W. E. Wetzel, "The Informal Venture Capital Market: Milestones Passed and the Road Ahead," in *Entrepreneurship 2000,* ed. D. L. Sexton and R. W. Smilor (Chicago, IL: Upstart Publishing Company, 1997), 47–69.

3. D. D. Bowen and R. D. Hisrich, "The Female Entrepreneur: A Career Development Perspective," *Academy of Management Review* 11 (1986): 393–407; A. Shapero and L. Sokol, "The Social Dimensions of Entrepreneurship," in *Encyclopedia of Entrepreneurship,* ed. C. A. Kent, D. L. Sexton, and K. H. Vesper (Englewood Cliffs, NJ: Prentice-Hall, 1982), 72–90.

4. J. S. Mill, *Principles of Political Economy with Some Applications to Social Philosophy* (London: John W. Parker, 1848).

5. J. A. Schumpeter, *The Theory of Economic Development* (Cambridge, MA: Harvard University Press, 1934).

6. W. B. Gartner, "Who Is an Entrepreneur? Is the Wrong Question," *American Journal of Small Business* Spring (1988): 11–31.

7. J. B. Cunningham and J. Lischerson, "Defining Entrepreneurship," *Journal of Small Business Management* January (1991): 45–61.

8. Cunningham and Lischerson, "Defining Entrepreneurship"; G. Gunderson, "Thinking about Entrepreneurs: Models, Assumptions, and Evidence," in *Entrepreneurship Education: Current Developments, Future Directions,* ed. C. A. Kent (New York: Quorum Books, 1990), 41–52; R. D. Hisrich and C. G. Brush, *The Woman Entrepreneur: Characteristics and Prescriptions for Success* (Lexington, MA: Lexington Book, 1985); W. Long, "The Meaning of Entrepreneurship," *American Journal of Small Business* 8 (1983): 47–56; P. D. Olson, "Entrepreneurship and Management," *Journal of Small Business Management* July (1987):7–13; R. Peterson, "Raising Risktakers," *Metropolitan Toronto Business Journal* 75 (1985): 30–34.

9. Anonymous, "Number of Businesses That Failed Remained Unchanged Last Year," *Wall Street Journal,* February 12, 1997, C19; Anonymous, "Business Failures Rose by 16% during 1997 as Start-ups Fell 2%," *Wall Street Journal,* March 3, 1998, A12; U.S. Bureau of the Census, *Statistical Abstracts of the United States:* 1997.

10. J. W. Duncan, "The True Failure Rate of Start-ups," *D&B Reports* 43 (1994): 6.

11. K. Labich, "Breaking Away to Go on Your Own," *Fortune,* December 17 (1990): 40–56.

12. Cromie, "Motivations of Aspiring Male and Female Entrepreneurs."

13. D. T. Hall and J. Richter, "Career Gridlock: Baby Boomers Hit the Wall," *Academy of Management Executive* 4 (1990): 7–22.

14. Ibid.

15. J. Main, "A Golden Age for Entrepreneurs," *Fortune,* February 12, 1990, 120–125.

16. O. F. Collins and D. G. Moor, *The Enterprising Man* (East Lansing, MI: Michigan State University Press, 1964).

17. A. C. Cooper and W. C. Dunkelberg, "Entrepreneurship and Paths to Business Ownership," *Strategic Management Journal* 7 (1986): 53–68; Cromie, "Motivations of Aspiring Male and Female Entrepreneurs."

18. Labich, "Breaking Away to Go on Your Own"; quote is on p. 48.

19. D. C. McClelland, *The Achieving Society* (New York: The Free Press, 1967).

20. J. DeCarlo and P. R. Lyons, "A Comparison of Selected Personal Characteristics of Minority and Non-Minority Entrepreneurs," *Journal of Small Business Management* December (1979): 22–29; B. R. Johnson, "Toward a Multidimensional Model of Entrepreneurship: The Case of Achievement Motivation and the Entrepreneur," *Entrepreneurship Theory and Practice* Spring (1990): 39–54; McClelland, *The Achieving Society;* J. B. Miner, N. R. Smith, and J. S. Bracker, "Role of Entrepreneurial Task Motivation in the Growth of Technologically Innovative Firms," *Journal of Applied Psychology* 74 (1989): 554–560.

21. R. H. Brockhaus and P. S. Horwitz, "The Psychology of the Entrepreneur," in *The Art and Science of Entrepreneurship,* ed. D. L. Sexton and R. W. Smilor (Cambridge, MA: Ballinger, 1986), 25–48; quote is on p. 27.

22. M. B. Low and I. C. MacMillan, "Entrepreneurship: Past Research and Future Challenges," *Journal of Management* 14 (1988): 139–161.

23. D. E. Jennings and C. P. Zeithaml, "Locus of Control: A Review and Directions for Entrepreneurial Research," *Proceedings of the 43rd Annual Meeting of the Academy of Management* (1983): 417–421.

24. Bowen and Hisrich, "The Female Entrepreneur: A Career Development Perspective"; quote is on p. 398.

25. Brockhaus and Horwitz, "The Psychology of the Entrepreneur"; R. H. Brockhaus and W. R. Nord, "An Exploration of Factors Affecting the Entrepreneurial Decisions: Personal Characteristics vs. Environmental Conditions," *Proceedings of the 39th Annual Meeting of the Academy of Management* (1979): 364–368.

26. Low and MacMillan, "Entrepreneurship."

27. J. Schere, "Tolerance of Ambiguity as a Discriminating Variable between Entrepreneurs and Managers," *Proceedings of the Annual Meeting of the Academy of Management* (1982): 404–408; D. L. Sexton and N. Bowman, "The Entrepreneur: A Capable Executive and More," *Journal of Business Venturing* 1 (1985): 129–140.

28. Brockhaus and Nord, "An Exploration of Factors Affecting the Entrepreneurial Decisions: Personal Characteristics vs. Environmental Conditions"; D. L. Hull, J. T. Bosely, and G. G. Udell, "Renewing the Hunt for the Heffalump: Identifying Potential Entrepreneurs by Personality Characteristics," *Journal of Small Business* 18 (1980): 1–18; D. L. Sexton and N. Bowman, "The Effects of Preexisting Psychological Characteristics on New Venture Initiations," paper presented at the Annual Meeting of the Academy of Management, 1984.

29. Brockhaus and Horwitz, "The Psychology of the Entrepreneur."

30. Bowen and Hisrich, "The Female Entrepreneur"; Low and MacMillan, "Entrepreneurship."

31. E. H. Schein, *Career Anchors: Discovering Your Real Values* (San Diego, CA: University Associates, 1985).

32. Ibid.; quote is on p. 30.

33. A. Shapero and L. Sokol, "The Social Dimensions of Entrepreneurship," in *Encyclopedia of Entrepreneurship*, ed. C. A. Kent, D. L. Sexton, and K. H. Vesper (Englewood Cliffs, NJ: Prentice-Hall, 1982), 72–90.

34. M. Henning and A. Jardim, *The Managerial Woman* (Garden City, NY: Anchor Press/Doubleday, 1977).

35. A. C. Cooper and W. C. Dunkelberg, "Entrepreneurial Research: Old Questions, New Answers, and Methodological Issues," *American Journal of Small Business* 11 (1987): 1–20.

36. Ibid.

37. Low and MacMillan, "Entrepreneurship."

38. Ibid.

39. Schein, *Career Anchors.*

40. L. Uchitelle, "Survey Finds Layoffs Slowed in Last 3 Years," *The New York Times,* August 20, 1998, 1; L. Uchitelle, " Layoffs Are Out; Hiring Is Back," *The New York Times,* June 18, 1996, D1; L. Uchitelle and N. R. Kleinfield, "On the Battlefields of Business, Millions of Causalities," *The New York Times,* March 3, 1996, 1.

41. T. Beaudoin, "Pushed Out of the Nest and Flying," *Management Review* September (1988): 10; H. Page, "Executive Decision," *Entrepreneur* July (1996): 149–153.

42. Shapero and Sokol, "The Social Dimensions of Entrepreneurship."

43. Brockhaus and Horwitz, "The Psychology of the Entrepreneur"; Cromie, "Motivations of Aspiring Male and Female Entrepreneurs"; R. D. Hisrich and C. G. Brush, "The Woman Entrepreneur: Implications of Family, Educational, and Occupational Experience," in *Frontiers of Entrepreneurship Research,* ed. J. A. Hornaday, J. A. Timmons, and K. H. Vesper (Wellesley, MA: Babson College Center for Entrepreneurial Studies, 1983), 255–270.

44. R. Kaplan, "Entrepreneurship Reconsidered: The Antimanagement Bias," *Harvard Business Review* May–June (1987): 84–89; quote is on p. 84.

45. Main, "A Golden Age for Entrepreneurs."

46. Ibid.

47. R. McGarvey, "Brave New World," *Entrepreneur* August (1996): 134; D. Tapscott, *The Digital Economy: Promise and Peril in the Age of Networked Intelligence* (New York: McGraw-Hill, 1996).

48. M. Selz, "Follow Your Heart," *The Wall Street Journal,* November 22, 1991, R6.

49. Sexton and Smilor, *Entrepreneurship 2000.*

50. Tiffany, "Dressed for Success"; Goins, "Power Broker"; M. Prather, "Talk of the Town," [online]. *Entrepreneur Magazine,* available: http://www.entrepreneurmag.com/startup/hot100.html [September 12, 1998].

51. A. L. Carsrud, C. M. Gaglio, and K. W. Olm, "Entrepreneurs—Mentors, Networks, and Successful New Venture Development: An Exploratory Study," *American Journal of Small Business* Fall (1987): 13–18; G. W. Nelson, "Factors of Friendship: Relevance of Significant Others to Female Business Owners," *Entrepreneurship Theory and Practice* Summer (1989): 7–18; R. F. Scherer, J. S. Adams, S. S. Carley, and F. A. Wiebe, "Role Model Performance Ef-

fects on Development of Entrepreneurial Career Preference," *Entrepreneurship Theory and Practice* Spring (1989): 53–71.

52. Brockhaus and Horwitz, "The Psychology of the Entrepreneur"; quote is on p. 36.

53. Scherer, Adams, Carley, and Wiebe, "Role Model Performance Effects on Development of Entrepreneurial Career Preference"; Shapero and Sokol, "The Social Dimensions of Entrepreneurship."

54. MassMutual, *Family Business: 1995 Research Findings* (Springfield, MA: MassMutual, 1995); N. B. Upton and R. K. Z. Heck, "The Family Business Dimension of Entrepreneurship," in *Entrepreneurship 2000,* ed. D. L. Sexton and R. W. Smilor (Chicago, IL: Upstart Publishing Company, 1997), 243–266.

55. Upton and Heck, "The Family Business Dimension of Entrepreneurship."

56. Anonymous, "The Forbes 400 Richest People in America" [online] *Forbes* magazine, available: http://www.forbesasap.com [October 8, 1998]; P. Sellers, "The 50 Most Powerful Women in American Business," *Fortune,* October 12, 1998, 76–87; P. W. Stephens, "Christie Hefner Kept Re-engineering of Playboy All in the Family," *National Real Estate Investor* 37, no. 4 (1995): 58–59.

57. Carsrud, Gaglio, and Olm, "Entrepreneurs—Mentors, Networks, and Successful New Venture Development."

58. H. Aldrich and C. Zimmer, "Entrepreneurship through Social Networks," in *The Art and Science of Entrepreneurship,* ed. D. L. Sexton and R. W. Smilor (Cambridge, MA: Ballinger, 1986), 3–23.

59. Ibid.

60. Main, "Golden Age for Entrepreneurs."

61. Anonymous, "About CVG" [online] Connecticut Venture Group, available: http://www.ctventure.org/ [July 31, 1998].

62. A. R. Wood, "A Big Affair for Small Business," *Philadelphia Inquirer,* June 5, 1992, C9.

63. Anonymous, "1998 Mid-Atlantic Venture Fair" [online] Greater Philadelphia Chamber of Commerce, available: http://www.gpvg.com/main.html [October 8, 1998].

64. W. F. Kiesner, "Post-Secondary Education at the Collegiate Level: A Synopsis and Evaluation," in *Entrepreneurship Education: Current Developments, Future Directions,* ed. C. A. Kent (Westport, CT: Quorum Books, 1990), 89–110.

65. F. O. Ede, B. Panigrahi, and S. E. Calcich, "African American Students' Attitudes toward Entrepreneurship Education," *Journal of Education for Business* 73 (1998): 291–296; K. H. Vesper and W. E. McMullan, "Entrepreneurship: Today Courses, Tomorrow Degrees," *Entrepreneurship Theory and Practice* Fall (1988): 7–13.

66. Main, "A Golden Age for Entrepreneurs."

67. Ibid.; C. R. Schoenberger, "Understanding the Spirit of Entrepreneurship," *Boston Globe,* July 2, 1998, D1; Vesper and McMullan, "Entrepreneurship"; C. P. Zeithaml and G. H. Rice, "Entrepreneurship/Small Business Education in American Universities," *Journal of Small Business Management* January (1987): 44–50.

68. Schoenberger, "Understanding the Spirit of Entrepreneurship"; Vesper and McMullan, "Entrepreneurship."

69. O. C. Brenner, C. D. Pringle, and J. H. Greenhaus, "Perceived Fulfillment of Organizational Employment versus Entrepreneurship: Work Values and Career Intentions of Business College Graduates," *Journal of Small Business Management* July (1991): 62–74; K. Sandholtz, "M. B. A. Attitudes," *The College Edition of the National Business Employment Weekly* Spring (1990): 14–15.

70. C. A. Kent, "Entrepreneurship Education at the Collegiate Level: A Synopsis and Evaluation," in *Entrepreneurship Education: Current Developments, Future Directions,* ed. C. A. Kent (New York: Quorum Books, 1990), 111–122.

71. Zeithaml and Rice, "Entrepreneurship/Small Business Education in American Universities."

72. Anonymous, "National Consortium of Entrepreneurial Centers" [online] Babson College, Arthur M. Blank Center for Entrepreneurship, available: http://www.babson.edu/entrep [October 23, 1998].

73. M. L. Kourilsky and S. R. Carlson, "Entrepreneurship Education for Youth: A Curricular Perspective," in *Entrepreneurship 2000,* ed. D. L. Sexton and R. W. Smilor (Chicago, IL: Upstart Publishing Company, 1997), 193–214.

74. Ibid.

75. L. R. Smeltzer and G. L. Fann, "Gender Differences in External Networks of Small Business Owners/Managers," *Journal of Small Business Management* April (1989): 25–32.

76. Anonymous, "25 Helpful Phone Numbers for Small Businesses: Entrepreneurs Get by with a Little Help from Their Friends," *PR Newswire,* March 18, 1998, 1.

77. L. Kroll, "Entrepreneurial Moms," *Forbes,* May 18, 1998, 84–92; Main, "A Golden Age for Entrepreneurs"; Schoenberger, "Understanding the Spirit of Entrepreneurship."

78. Birley, Moss, and Saunders, "Do Women Entrepreneurs Require Different Training?"; C. G. Brush, "Research on Women Business Owners: Past Trends, A New Perspective and Future Directions," *Entrepreneurship Theory & Practice* Summer (1992): 5–30; Cromie, "Motivations of Aspiring Male and Female Entrepreneurs"; E. Kaplan, "Women Entrepreneurs: Constructing a Framework to Examine Venture Success and Failure," *Proceedings of the Babson Entrepreneurship Conference* (1988): 643–653; R. Masters and R. Meier, "Sex Differences and Risk-Taking Propensity of Entrepreneurs," *Journal of Small Business Management* January (1988): 31–35; L. Neider, "A Preliminary Investigation of Female Entrepreneurs in Florida," *Journal of Small Business Management* July (1987): 22–29; Smeltzer and Fann, "Gender Differences in External Networks of Small Business Owners/Managers."

79. Longstreth, Stafford, and Maudlin, "Self-Employed Women and Their Families."

80. Bowen and Hisrich, "The Female Entrepreneur"; quote is on p. 401.

81. Ibid.

82. Main, "A Golden Age for Entrepreneurs"; quote is on p. 121.

83. Kaplan, "Women Entrepreneurs."

84. M. Ewell, "Valley Women Are Pressed for Success: Rewards and Challenges Great for Female Execs," *San Jose Mercury News,* January 20, 1998, 1A; A. T. Segal and W. Zellner, "Corporate Women," *Business Week,* June 8, 1992, 74–78.

85. Kaplan, "Women Entrepreneurs."

86. Kroll, "Entrepreneurial Moms."

87. Longstreth, Stafford, and Maudlin, "Self-Employed Women and Their Families"; C. R. Stoner, R. I. Hartman, and R. Arora, "Work-Home Role Conflict in Female Owners of Small Businesses: An Exploratory Study," *Journal of Small Business Management* January (1990): 30–38.

88. A. C. Cooper and K. W. Artz, "Determinants of Satisfaction for Entrepreneurs," *Journal of Business Venturing* 10 (1995): 439–457.

89. N. E. Betz and L. F. Fitzgerald, *The Career Psychology of Women* (Orlando, FL: Academic Press, 1987); S. Birley, "Female Entrepreneurs: Are They Really Different?" *Journal of Small Business Management* January (1989): 32–37; Bowen and Hisrich, "The Female Entrepreneur"; S.

Hesse–Biber, "Male and Female Students' Perceptions of Their Academic Environment and Future Career Plans," *Human Relations* 38 (1985): 91–105; Kaplan, "Women Entrepreneurs"; L. Neider, "A Preliminary Investigation of Female Entrepreneurs in Florida," *Journal of Small Business Management* July (1987): 22–29.

90. U.S. Bureau of the Census, *Statistical Abstracts of the United States: 1997.*

91. Birley, "Female Entrepreneurs"; Cromie, "Motivations of Aspiring Male and Female Entrepreneurs"; Neider, "Preliminary Investigation of Female Entrepreneurs in Florida"; R. F. Scherer, J. D. Brodzinski, and F. A. Wiebe, "Entrepreneur Career Selection and Gender: A Socialization Approach," *Journal of Small Business Management* April (1990): 37–44.

92. Bowen and Hisrich, "The Female Entrepreneur"; R. D. Hisrich and C. G. Brush, "The Woman Entrepreneur: Implications of Family, Educational, and Occupational Experience," in *Frontiers of Entrepreneurship Research,* ed. J. A. Hornaday, J. A. Timmons, and K. H. Vesper (Wellesley, MA: Babson College Center for Entrepreneurial Studies, 1983), 255–270; Neider, "Preliminary Investigation of Female Entrepreneurs in Florida."

93. Cromie, "Motivations of Aspiring Male and Female Entrepreneurs"; R. Cuba, D. Decenzo, and A. Anish, "Management Practices of Successful Female Business Owners," *American Journal of Small Business* 8 (1983): 40–46; Kaplan, "Women Entrepreneurs"; Neider, "Preliminary Investigation of Female Entrepreneurs in Florida."

94. Neider, "Preliminary Investigation of Female Entrepreneurs in Florida"; G. W. Nelson, "Factors of Friendship: Relevance of Significant Others to Female Business Owners," *Entrepreneurship Theory and Practice* Summer (1989): 7–18.

95. Ede, Panigrahi, and Calcich, "African American Students' Attitudes toward Entrepreneurship Education."

96. R. D. Hisrich and C. G. Brush, "Characteristics of the Minority Entrepreneur," *Journal of Small Business Management* October (1986): 1–8.

97. K. Q. Dadzie and Y. Cho, "Determinants of Minority Business Formation and Survival: An Empirical Assessment," *Journal of Small Business Management* July (1989): 56–61.

98. Aldrich and Zimmer, "Entrepreneurship through Social Networks."

99. Dadzie and Cho, "Determinants of Minority Business Formation and Survival"; Hisrich and Brush, "Characteristics of the Minority Entrepreneur"; U.S. Bureau of the Census, *Statistical Abstracts of the United States: 1997.*

100. R. D. Dickson, "The Business of Equal Opportunity," *Harvard Business Review* January–February (1992): 46–53; S. Green and P. Pryde, *Black Entrepreneurship in America* (New Brunswick, NJ: Transaction Publishers, 1990); M. A. MacDowell, "Approaches to Education for the Economically Disadvantaged: Creating Tomorrow's Entrepreneurs and Those Who Will Work for Them," in *Entrepreneurship Education: Current Developments, Future Directions,* ed. C. A. Kent (Westport, CT: Quorum Books, 1990), 261–270.

101. J. C. Hansen and D. P. Campbell, *The Strong Manual* (Palo Alto, CA: Consulting Psychologists Press, 1985); Schein, *Career Anchors: Discovering Your Real Values,* 1985).

102. S. K. Hirsch and T. Vessey, *Introduction to the Strong in Organizational Settings* (Palo Alto, CA: Consulting Psychologists Press, 1987); quote is on p. 24.

103. Schein, *Career Anchors.*

104. J. Hyatt, "Should You Start a Business?" *INC.* February (1992): 48–58.

105. C. Palmeri, "Often Down but Never Out," *Forbes,* March 4, 1991, 138; anonymous, "Hoover's Company Profiles: John Paul Mitchell Systems" [online] Hoover's Inc., available: http://www.pathfinder.com/money/hoovers [September 12, 1998].

106. T. J. Naughton, "Quality of Working Life and the Self-Employed Manager," *American Journal of Small Business* Fall (1987): 33–40.

4

STRESSED SALESWOMAN

Sally, 29 years of age, has been selling industrial equipment to manufacturers since she graduated from college nearly 8 years ago. She is obviously good at her job. Not only has she consistently met or exceeded her sales quota, but her customers report that she is knowledgeable about her products and continually puts in long hours keeping tabs on their needs and providing valuable consulting to them. Sally's employer, GA Industries (fictitious name), recognizes her value to the organization and has rewarded her handsomely over the years.

The past few months have been rough on Sally. She seems to be tired all the time. She has had trouble shaking a month-long cold, and for the first time she can remember, she canceled an appointment with a customer because she just could not get herself out of her apartment that morning.

Sally has also been short-tempered of late. Although it has not affected her sales volume yet, she has had to catch herself a few times from snapping at some thick-headed customers. How many times does she have to explain the same things to these people? But that cannot be the entire problem.

She has found herself getting into a lot of petty arguments with Steve, her fiancé. She just seems to be preoccupied with her job wherever she is. The plans for Sally and Steve's wedding have taken a back seat to her work, and their wedding date has been put off a couple times, much to Steve's dismay. On top of this dilemma, Sally and Steve have had many discussions about where they will live and if and when they will have children. They have not been able to come to agreement on these issues.

"Why am I so irritable?" Sally keeps asking herself. She is doing well and still finds her job interesting and challenging. It is true that her boss, Marie, GA's industrial sales manager, keeps poking her nose into Sally's business and giving her unneeded advice about how to handle customers. Marie wants her to put more pressure on several customers to purchase certain pieces of equipment that they really do not need. Her customers would not tolerate a hard sell like that. But Sally will avoid that issue as long as she can. She hardly sees Marie nowadays, maybe once every other week, and she is usually too busy to talk to her. Sometimes Sally wonders what Marie really thinks of her. Fortunately, her customers tell her how good she is at her job.

Sally admits that she has been a little peeved at the company for expanding her territory 6 months ago. Not that she is uninterested in new business, but she cannot do a thorough job with such a large territory. And she's been finding herself out of town 4, sometimes 5, days a week. The larger territory has left Sally drowning in paperwork, and she is beginning to wonder how she can ever maintain a relationship with her fiancé when they hardly ever see each other anymore. And then there are the wedding plans . . .

But the job is so challenging. And GA is coming out with a new product line next week, microprocessor-based control panels. The whole sales force has been attending weekend meetings for about 4 weeks to learn more about these new products. It is exciting to introduce a new product on the cutting edge. Sally just wishes she understood the new product line better. She has not been able to focus at the training classes, has not really understood the lectures at the meetings, and has been unable to make much sense out of the manuals either. She probably should have taken a few more technical courses back in college. But that is water under the bridge.

Sally would like to talk to someone about her feelings. But who? Talking to her boss Marie is out of the question. She would think she was being ungrateful. Sally is convinced that her family and her fiancé just would not understand the situation. The other salespeople, she guesses, would be pretty uncaring. But she does need to talk to someone. And soon!

CASE ANALYSIS QUESTIONS

1. What evidence is there that Sally is experiencing job stress? What are the symptoms?

2. What conditions are producing Sally's stress?

3. How is Sally's job stress affecting her family and personal life? And are her family and personal life affecting her work? What type(s) of work-family conflict is Sally experiencing?

4. If you were Sally, what would you do? Identify as many alternative plans of action as possible and indicate the advantages and disadvantages of each. Which plan(s) of action would you choose? Why?

5. What types of social support would Sally find most helpful: appraisal, instrumental, emotional, or informational? From whom should she seek such support? Why?

6. If you were the president of GA Industries and just heard Sally's story, what, if anything, would you do? Why?

5

BUDDING ENTREPRENEUR

Dave began reflecting on the progress of his career over the past 15 years. He remembered how early on he received a great deal of support and assistance from the Xtel Corporation (fictitious name). In 1976, Xtel had instituted a program with two basic goals in mind: to help inner city minority youths have access to a college education, and to create a ready pool of minority college graduates to help Xtel satisfy affirmative action hiring goals. Under the program, Xtel would pay the college tuition of the minority students in exchange for a commitment to work summers for the corporation and to accept employment with the firm after graduation for a minimum of 2 years. Xtel would accept four new participants into the program each year, so that a maximum of 16 students would be active at any one time.

Dave had always shown outstanding ability in math, winning awards in grade school and high school for his proficiency. During his junior year in high school, Dave began looking at colleges in the area. He set his sights on the Ivy League school in the city. At the same time, Dave's high school guidance counselor told him about Xtel's assistance program. Dave applied immediately to the Xtel program, sending in a brief background statement, a sketch of his career interests, two letters of recommendation, and the newly arrived acceptance letter from the Ivy League school. After 2 months, Dave received a letter from Xtel stating that he had been accepted into their program.

At college, Dave majored in computer science and did exceptionally well. He joined the Black Student Union at the school and also worked for the college radio station. During his summer internships, Dave worked in a number of different departments at Xtel, mainly assisting in the development of computer processing applications in each function. Dave was impressed with the fact that even though Xtel was a Fortune 200 company, it was still caring for its employees—Dave had expected Xtel to be more impersonal in its treatment of employees.

In the middle of his senior year, Dave began discussing with Xtel's staffing manager where he would be working when he graduated. Dave was pleased that his first job would be in the audit department, working as an EDP auditor. After 2 months of full-time work at Xtel, Dave had gotten a call from one of his former professors who inquired on his progress. During their conversation, she encouraged Dave to begin thinking about graduate school. With his grades, the professor was certain that Dave would have no trouble being accepted into the Ivy League school's master of science program in computer science. Dave sent a letter to Xtel's head of human resources seeking company support of his pursuit of the master's degree—he was pleased that Xtel encouraged his attendance and also offered tuition reimbursement. Dave finished the degree in 2 years, again doing exceptionally well in his studies.

In his first 5 years at Xtel, Dave progressed rapidly, rising to the level of EDP audit manager at the age of 28. Over this period, he had received challenging assignments and had even made a presentation to a committee of the company's board of directors. With a wife and a young son, Dave was interested in continuing his advancement at Xtel mainly to provide a nice income and financial security for his family. He hoped to be an officer within 1 year. But Dave was getting a subtle message from Xtel's upper management that maybe he had advanced as far as he could at Xtel—he was not receiving the challenging assignments or support anymore, and his latest performance review cryptically indicated the need for broader-based experience. One particular example of the lack of support stood out. Dave had thought that attendance at one of the premier executive management programs would be beneficial as a career advancement strategy. But Xtel refused to support Dave in this endeavor, indicating that they had already identified those individuals who would be attending executive programs. Of course, Dave knew that Xtel had never sent a minority to any executive management program.

Dave had never believed that his race had any influence on his treatment or career progress at Xtel, but he was beginning to wonder. Dave had seen Xtel's newly published 5-year goals for affirmative action placement. He noted that the 5-year objective for minority representation at the junior officer level had already been achieved. All at once, Dave began to feel a little used. He questioned whether his progress at Xtel was truly a reflection of his ability and contributions, or was it more a function of helping to fulfill Xtel's affirmative action targets at successive levels in the hierarchy? He did find it interesting that the affirmative action targets were managed closely, with minority representation in a given grade usually hitting right on the target.

Dave thought about his situation for some time, contemplating his next step. His skills and educational background made him highly marketable. After a while, Dave decided to meet with Xtel's vice president of human resources to discuss career prospects. At the meeting, Dave stated his strong desire to move up to the officer level within 1 year; after all, some of his less qualified contemporaries had already reached that level. The lukewarm response Dave received from the vice president gave him a clear message—his career at Xtel was in a holding pattern. Dave concluded that it was time for a change.

While in graduate school, Dave had become friendly with a fellow student who was interested in developing and marketing software that could be used in helping control production operations. Dave had been intrigued with the prospects for the software especially since he saw its potential application at Xtel Corporation. Dave decided to give his friend a call to see what progress she had made. Dave also sought the advice of one of his neighbors who had experience in financing business start-ups. Working part-time on nights and weekends, Dave and his partners were able to finalize the software and put together a realistic business plan. They sought and received financing for their venture from a local commercial bank. Once they lined up their first client, Dave felt confident enough to resign from his position at Xtel Corporation. The resignation was tendered with mixed emotions. He felt a sense of gratitude and loyalty to Xtel for the financial support they had given him, but he was also disturbed by the treatment he received during the latter part of his career.

In any event, Dave was enthusiastic about his prospects as an entrepreneur. He was confident that he and his partners had tapped into a potentially lucrative market. He was strongly motivated to make the venture succeed and achieve financial security for his family.

CASE ANALYSIS QUESTIONS

1. If Dave had the opportunity, what questions—if any—should he have asked the president of the Xtel Corporation regarding his recent treatment?

2. Do you believe that the Xtel Corporation has discriminated against Dave on the basis of his race? Why or why not?

3. To whom—inside or outside Xtel—could Dave have gone for social support? What types of support would have been most helpful: appraisal, instrumental, emotional, or informational? Why?

4. What qualities does Dave have that will help him in his entrepreneurial venture? Does Dave have any shortcomings that might limit his success as an entrepreneur?

5. Once Dave embarked on his entrepreneurial career, to whom might he have gone for personal and professional support, advice, and assistance?

CAREER MANAGEMENT IN WORK ORGANIZATIONS

14

HUMAN RESOURCE SUPPORT SYSTEMS

The dynamic and competitive business environment faced by nearly all business firms demands organizational flexibility and innovation to ensure survival. The contingency view of organizational management states that a company's strategic direction, structure, internal systems, culture, and leadership approaches should be consistent with the requirements and challenges of the external environment and the expectations of stakeholders in the organization.[1] More organizations are opting to strategically deploy their human resources and align their human resource management practices in a way that supports the firm's chosen strategy. In fact, several studies have found that organizations that integrate their human resource systems with their strategic direction have lowered turnover, increased productivity, and increased corporate financial performance.[2]

Therefore, the human resource systems, such as recruitment and selection procedures, incentive compensation, performance management, career management programs, and training and development efforts, need to be consistent with the strategic plans of the firm. For example, a company with strong growth objectives requires a steady supply of qualified, motivated, and talented human resources to support the business expansion, and its human resource and career management systems should reflect this corporate strategy. In the case of a firm whose strategic direction includes downsizing and shedding of businesses, the human resource system and related career programs may be more concerned with outplacement, helping employees identify their interests and career goals, and assisting them with the process of finding a new job.

In addition to the need for a broad-based fit, the organization's internal systems must be mutually supportive. In particular, companies need to integrate human resource systems with career management approaches to enhance capabilities and effectiveness. In this sense, the human resource systems should support individual career management programs and vice versa. There are a number of ways companies can link their human resource strategies with individual career management activities.

In this chapter, we discuss a model of an integrated human resource system that depicts how individual and organizational actions can be matched or linked to improve overall effectiveness. We examine related actions at the organizational and individual levels, and we describe the ways that these seemingly diverse activities can be linked. We review how a firm's human resource systems can support its organizational plans as well as individual employee development. In Chapter 15, we provide examples of corporate programs that position their human resource systems to support individual career development. Chapter 16 concludes this section with some final thoughts on the individual's role in the management of his or her career and also discusses the future arena within which we will be managing our careers.

■

INTEGRATION OF CAREER MANAGEMENT WITH HUMAN RESOURCE SYSTEMS

To be most effective, career management programs need to be supported by appropriate personnel or human resource systems. Human resource systems represent the organization's mechanisms for forecasting its human resource needs and for recruiting, selecting, training, developing, appraising, promoting, and rewarding its people. Career management and human resource systems are linked or integrated to the extent to which they help each other to meet individual and organizational needs. We believe that Edgar Schein's model of a human resource planning and development system, shown in Exhibit 14.1, is the most comprehensive approach to the integration of these two components.[3]

On the left-hand side of the model, Schein indicates the necessary activities at the organizational level to achieve consistency between the firm's strategic direction and the level and type of human resources used. Specifically, the organization's human resource system should be intertwined with the organization's business plans (Boxes A and B). The firm then assesses the extent to which its human resources are capable of meeting or fulfilling organizational needs (Box E). From this assessment, the organization determines the actions necessary to ensure a proper level of resources with the talents needed to meet corporate plans. Recruitment, staffing, and development activities (Box F) are tools available to ensure the right mix of human resources.

Just as organizations have business growth and development objectives, individuals have personal growth and development needs. The right-hand side of Schein's model depicts individual activities that may occur simultaneously within this overall scheme. It indicates that individuals might conduct a self-assessment on where they have been (Box G) and what values and talents they hold (Box H). They then engage in career planning/goal setting (Box I) that must take place in the context of the organization's business plans (Box A) and human resource plans (Boxes B, E, and F). Individual goals, in other words, must be consistent with organizational needs if there is to be a match between the employee and the employer. For example, it is unrealistic to pursue a career path

· EXHIBIT 14-1

MODEL OF A HUMAN RESOURCE
PLANNING AND DEVELOPMENT SYSTEM

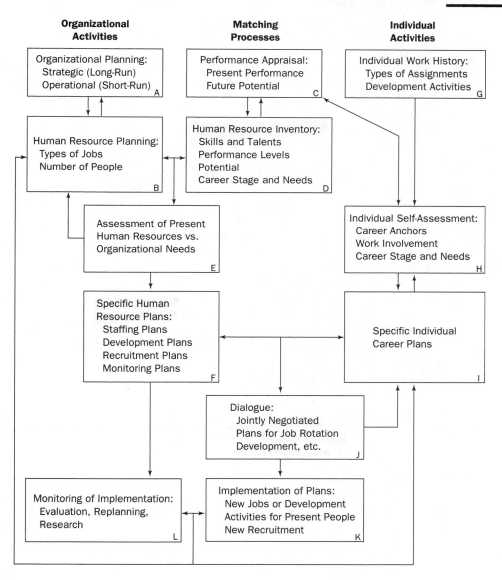

SOURCE: E. H. Schein, *Career Dynamics* (Figure 14.1, p. 191) © 1978 Addison Wesley Longman. Reprinted by permission of Addison Wesley Longman.

in a technical area that the organization is planning to abandon. Similarly, in estimating its future need for production supervisors, the organization must understand the career aspirations and plans of its current employees. Neither the individual nor the organization can afford to make plans in a vacuum.

Schein proposed a matching process to help synchronize individual and organizational needs and plans. More precisely, organizations must assess the performance and potential of their people (Box C) and store the data in an accessible human resource inventory (Box D) to be in a position to compare their present human resources with their projected needs (Box E). A human resource inventory should include assessments of employees' talents, performance, and potential, as well as assessments of the subjective elements of the career. An understanding of each employee's career needs and career stage-related tasks should help prevent the organization from making unwarranted assumptions about what is "best" for the employee. Human resource information systems (HRIS) can provide data warehouses of information regarding the organization's talent pool. Human resource information systems are more fully discussed later in this chapter.

Also, as we have indicated previously, performance appraisal serves as a powerful source of feedback and self-assessment to the individual (Box H). Mutually agreed-on development plans or career strategies (Boxes J and K) also serve to link the individual's aspirations (Box I) with the organization's human resource needs (Box F). Finally, as with any process, both the individual and the organization need to continually update and monitor progress toward goals (Box L). Only on careful reflection and evaluation of the current situation can goals be reformulated for future growth opportunities.

In total, Schein's model is useful because it demonstrates the fundamental interdependence between individuals' career plans and organizations' human resource plans. It is likely, however, that some human resource systems are more career-oriented than others. Career-oriented human resource systems have been found to have the following characteristics:[4]

- Components in the system use information from other parts of the system. For example, the human resource planning function must use information about the organization's long-range strategic plans if it is to develop useful human resource strategies.

- Components of the system are consistent with one another. For example, the selection and training efforts of an organization ought to be consistent with the organization's projected human resource needs. If the organization is going to need many technically oriented managers in the next 5 to 10 years, then recruiting plans should focus on technically trained candidates who have the interest and capacity to become managers. In addition, after a period of time on the job, these employees need to be exposed to formal training and on-the-job learning experiences to facilitate their transition from a primarily technical role to a managerial role.

- Human resource practices have sufficient diversity to accommodate the needs of different individuals and units within the organization. For example, employees at different career stages may need different types of information, skills, and support. A career-oriented human resource system can accommodate these differences and develop diversified programs for its various constituencies.

- The human resource system examines itself periodically and adapts to changing environments. These environmental changes may occur outside the organization (changing technologies, new legislation on fair employment) or within the organization (changing demographic characteristics of the work force, more vocal demands of employee rights).

- The human resource system is closely linked to the organization's business strategy.

- The human resource system stresses individual and organizational needs and takes into account individuals' nonwork lives. The whole concept of an individual-organizational fit requires the organization to understand employee needs and seek ways to integrate them with organizational goals. Moreover, because it is so important for employees to balance their work and nonwork lives, organizations' human resource practices (e.g., those described in Chapter 11) must continually address the interaction between work and nonwork roles.

- The human resource system applies knowledge derived from the behavioral sciences and balances objectivity and subjectivity in its approach to appraisal and control.

Let us consider the three main pieces of the model, the organizational-level activities, the individual-level activities, and the matching process, taking into account the essential characteristics outlined above.

ORGANIZATIONAL-LEVEL ACTIVITIES

The contingency view of organizational functioning states that there needs to be consistency between an organization's strategic direction and its human resource plans for full effectiveness to be realized.[5] As Stephen Colarelli and Terry Beehr state, "Because of the importance of human resources to productivity in the next century, effective organizations will routinely integrate human resource technologies and planning with corporate strategy."[6] Moreover, the following have been identified as significant factors influencing human resource policies: (1) demands from the customer or marketplace; (2) changes in the job mix; (3) new technology; and (4) competitor's actions.[7] To address these issues, human resource planners and corporate strategists should establish close, cooperative relationships to ensure alignment between organizational and human resource plans.[8]

Business plans, an organization's phase in its life cycle, and other competitive factors would ordinarily dictate the level and type of human resources that are used. For the goals outlined in the business strategy of the firm to be achieved, a human resource strategy must be developed such that the organization deploys its people to critical tasks.[9] In fact, David Ulrich has suggested that human resource executives refocus their attention from internal staff to external stake-holders.[10] This shift allows the focus to move from the firm's human resource plans being developed in a vacuum to the development of a human resource strategy that emphasizes customer criteria. Thus, customer needs, organizational plans, and unique competencies determine whom the firm employs and how they are developed. This overall process involves several steps, including human resource forecasting, staffing, training and development, promotions, redeployment, and outplacement. Let us briefly consider each one of these steps.

HUMAN RESOURCE FORECASTING. Once a firm's strategic direction is determined, it then must assess the level and type of human resources needed to fulfill strategic expectations. As Manuel London states, "Human resource planning requires analyzing employees' current skills, the skill levels needed by the business in the future, and the availability of those needed skills in the internal and external labor market."[11] Randall Schuler suggests a number of factors relevant to human resource forecasting, including number and types of jobs available, the skills required, the level of training needed, and the type of organizational structure and reporting relationships.[12] An organization that has plans for substantial growth (in sales or geographic expansion) or a firm in the early or growth phase of the organizational life cycle would likely need to add personnel with an orientation toward growth. By contrast, firms with limited growth expectations and/or in the later stages of the organizational life cycle may want to consolidate human resources and concentrate on maintaining a trained and dedicated core of personnel.

In determining the types of resources needed, organizations have a basic choice of selecting (or buying) their personnel from the external labor market or developing (or making) their personnel from the internal labor market. The "buy" or "make" decision is one that virtually all organizations face. The organizational decision as to whether selection or training is the appropriate strategy depends on the availability and accessibility of people with the right skills in the external labor market compared with the feasibility of training current employees.[13] Of course, organizations use a combination of the buy and make approaches, using the external labor market when appropriate and developing from within when possible.

Jeffrey Kerr and Ellen Jackofsky discuss how an organization's culture and context can influence the selection versus development choice.[14] They state that each process has distinct costs and benefits but that "selection is congruent with a mechanistic view of organizational functioning in which managerial traits and abilities are viewed as fixed," and "development is congruent with a fluid, organic view of organizations in which both managers' abilities and strategic demands are viewed as evolving over time."[15] These researchers believe that businesses have overemphasized the mechanistic view of organizations, which leads to an overreliance on selection (i.e., bringing people in from outside the organization) to achieve a match between human resources and strategic direction. They advocate that organizations take a more organic view by focusing on managerial development as a way to achieve the human resource/business strategy alignment. In any event, Kerr and Jackofsky posit, "The objective of both selection and development is to contribute to the organization's capacity to adapt to environmental and strategic change."[16] However, it must also be stressed that depending exclusively on either personnel source can create problems. Hiring solely from external labor markets reduces opportunities for existing employees and thus weakens their commitment to the organization, whereas exclusively hiring from within may limit the number of fresh ideas brought into the organization.[17] David Ulrich and Dale Lake found that an optimum level of innovation, performance, and flexibility is achieved when organizations use an 80/20 ratio in hiring, 80 percent promoting from within and 20 percent staffing from outside.[18]

ORGANIZATIONAL STAFFING. Once a firm has determined its human resource needs and has concluded that the internal system cannot fully supply the required talent, then selection from the external (or outside) labor market is necessary. It has been suggested that staffing is a critical management function because the quality of the people hired by the organization is the single greatest determinant of the firm's effectiveness. In effect, staffing allows a company to buy its needed competencies from outside the organization.[19]

In Chapter 7 we discussed organizational selection and staffing from the individual's perspective, covering such topics as interviewing, recruitment, and choice of job and organization. When organizations go through the staffing process, many of the steps are the same, albeit from a different perspective. As a first step, the organization determines, through the human resource forecasting process, the number and types of employees it needs to hire.

The number of required employees is dictated by expected expansion and related resource needs, as well as expected turnover among existing staff at all levels and in all functions within the company. The type of employee needed is related to the skill level, professional experience, and abilities required of the jobs to be filled. It is obvious that openings in entry-level positions would require a different set of skills and experiences than senior executive positions.

Once the number and type of resources are determined or as open positions arise through turnover and internal transfer, the organization then has several options in terms of the actual hiring approach used. College recruiting, unsolicited inquiries, advertisements, search firms, and personal recommendations or nominations are various ways for job candidates to become known to a hiring company.

After the candidates are known, the next step in the staffing process normally is the personal interview. Usually, the interviewee will first meet with a representative of the firm's human resource department who will conduct a general screening. Next, the candidate will be interviewed by one or more members of the hiring department. Once the interviewing phase is complete, the hiring area assesses all the candidates and then makes its offers. These basic steps are followed regardless of the level in the organization that is being filled.

David Ulrich and Dale Lake offer a number of key factors to consider in the external sourcing of job candidates.[20]

First, the organization needs to consider the degree of professional experience that is required. In particular, it must review the trade-off between hiring at the entry level, where candidates usually lack extensive experience but are more "malleable and amenable" in terms of new work ideas and approaches, versus hiring at a higher level, where candidates usually have more experience but are less flexible or adaptive in reaction to new methods.

Second, Ulrich and Lake suggest that companies expand the pool of talent that is considered.[21] Specifically, these authors suggest, "One way to meet the challenge of finding employees at all levels is to expand the pool of candidates. When the talent pool from which to draw employees is large, the probability of identifying better candidates increases."[22] Companies should pay particular attention to achieving diversity in their hiring to meet the challenge of the global marketplace. In this sense, effective recruitment may require "going beyond national boundaries" to hire individuals from overseas to help enter and service international markets.[23]

Related to the expansion in the candidate pool, Ulrich and Lake recommend the serious consideration of multiple candidates and the use of multiple interviews. They cite several historically successful companies, such as IBM and General Electric, in which hiring managers spend what seems like an inordinate amount of time finding the exactly right person for an open position.

Finally, in line with our discussion in Chapter 7, Ulrich and Lake recommend that organizations use realistic job previews. We have already spelled out the benefits to the individual and the company that can accrue from realistic job previews. In summary, these authors state that "realistic job previews ensure that future employees will have the capacity to build competitiveness, adapt to change, accomplish business strategies, and contribute to unity within the company."[24]

In addition to the influence of the firm's strategic plan, environmental trends and general business conditions also affect staffing from the external market. Factors such as the available labor force, population demographics, social trends, economic conditions, government regulations, and legislative actions may all influence the type and quality of potential employees who are available to the corporation.[25] Downsizing and reorganizations have also changed the available labor market, in most cases creating a greater employee pool. Yet at the same time, these laid-off workers may not have the necessary skills for new jobs made available by changing trends (e.g., technological innovations, delayerings, reorganizations). Hence, honest self-appraisal and "reskilling" may be necessary for these workers to find their way back into gainful employment.[26]

EMPLOYEE DEVELOPMENT.   In contrast to buying resources from the external labor market, organizations can support their business strategies by developing their resources to achieve greater levels of competence. In this sense, the existing staff is viewed as a critical resource, one that is necessary, willing, and able to sustain organizational growth.[27] Richard Campbell and Joseph Moses state that "the ability of organizations to shift and adapt their career development strategies will result in manpower pools that are sufficient to meet ongoing staffing needs. Large excesses or deficiencies in such pools may be a clear signal that career development practices are out of synch with marketplace, environmental, or social forces."[28]

Developmental activities can be grouped into two basic categories: education/training and on-the-job experiences. Education and training programs are generally formal activities that can take place either in the work setting or at an outside organization. The decline of the U.S. public educational system at the primary and secondary school levels has severely limited the pool of qualified employees from which corporations can hire. Many firms need to take on the job of U.S. schools by providing remedial education in math and reading. Motorola University is an example of these efforts and is discussed shortly.[29] In addition to in-house training, business organizations are also attempting to assist school districts directly in their educational programs through monetary support, the donation of equipment, and the loaning of staff. Between 1990 and 1995, Motorola spent some $30 million to support public school reform and Chevron spends $7.8 million a year to support education.[30] As Stephen Colarelli and Terry Beehr state, "A literate work force will be the most important economic resource in the twenty-first century. It will be in business's self-interest to take a leading role in improving public education in primary and secondary schools."[31]

Many of the largest organizations spend millions of dollars to offer a variety of in-house training classes—ranging from remedial education, to technical and general management courses, to leadership development programs.[32] These training classes can be conducted by in-house training staff or by external consultants. Some of the higher profile efforts are in place at General Electric, International Business Machines, and American Telephone & Telegraph. The following are examples of training and education initiatives at Motorola and the Whirlpool Corporation.[33]

Faced with the reality that most of its work force was illiterate, being unable to read and not knowing simple arithmetic, Motorola decided to go on the training offensive. A broad-based in-house training program was established that offered skill instruction from grade school basics through more complex topics covering new concepts of work, quality, and leadership.

The expanded training program was carried out by an established service division—the Motorola Training and Education Center (MTEC). In 1990, the budget for this effort totaled $120 million on an annual basis—$60 million in direct outlays and another $60 million in lost work time while the training is going on. Moreover, Motorola had at that time 1,200 employees involved in providing training.

In 1989, the company formally christened the "Motorola University," an in-house school that provides education and training at all levels of complexity. The educational curriculum at the university is relevant to the corporation, the job, and the individual. Although the university does not grant degrees, it does offer courses that accrediting boards would certify and that the universities that give degrees will count. Motorola University has 110 full-time and 300 part-time faculty. There is a functional curriculum, covering such areas as engineering, manufacturing, sales, and marketing. Within each area, specific courses cover relational skills, technical skills, and business skills. In addition to these courses, university classes are offered in remedial reading and math. The university also serves to properly socialize Motorola's employees, by imparting important cultural values and shared philosophies such as risk taking and teamwork.

Motorola University also has entered into course development and presentation partnerships with such established universities as Northwestern, the Illinois Institute of Technology, and Arizona State. Further, the Motorola University Press prints more than 1 million pages per month and plans to publish a series of books on design and quality written by one of the company's employees.

In addition to raising the skill and competence levels of its employees, Motorola sees its university as a recruiting tool, with one of its goals to have the best graduates of the best institutions wanting to work for Motorola. Overall, the Motorola program is an extensive, ambitious effort to raise the skill levels and the value of its employees. By 1996, Motorola gave all employees 40 hours of training a year (and plans to quadruple that number by the turn of the century). The investment may seem excessive, but in Motorola's view it is money well spent. Motorola's goal is a work force that is disciplined yet free-thinking.

Whirlpool Corporation conducted a needs analysis of its human resources to determine those factors most critical to future competitiveness and success. This assessment led to a significant investment in executive education. Instead of purchasing an off-the-shelf program, Whirlpool decided to customize its own program, focusing on such topics as managing change, becoming a global competitor, and becoming more competitive. External faculty hired by the company were asked to first learn about Whirlpool's unique business challenges and to tailor presentations to deal with those challenges. Faculty spent time with Whirlpool's CEO and other executives to obtain a perspective on how the educational material is related to the company's corporate goals. The results of the executive education initiative were favorable. Participants gained an understanding of where to focus attention and acquired specific skills to make change happen.

The outcomes of formal development programs traditionally focus on developing a better conceptual understanding of a given business-related issue or in building the skill level of the participants.[34] But for development programs to be a real force of change and increase organizational competence, participants need to learn how to apply the concepts to the business setting. A successful program is one in which participants acquire not only the concepts and skills needed to be competitive but also gain an appreciation of how these skills may be used within their organizational context.[35]

The second way that organizations can develop their employees is through on-the-job learning. Even with the heavy corporate investment in formal programs, most development and learning occurs through on-the-job experiences. Researchers suggest that if learning is going "to stick," training needs to be continuous and should provide opportunities for practice and reinforcement.[36] On-the-job learning experiences not only provide this type of learning environment but also are cost-efficient.[37]

To cite an old maxim, there is no substitute for experience. Individuals who have a relatively long tenure in a given job or function are often valuable employees because they normally have a full range of knowledge on various aspects of the job. These individuals might become "inside consultants" and be asked to share their knowledge with junior employees. Bristol Myers Squibb has set up a "management consulting and innovation group." This group undertakes issues ranging from logistics, marketing, organizational and strategic tasks, sometimes in association with external consulting firms.[38] It has also been argued that people in support functions—such as finance, human resources, information technology, and procurement—should strive to become internal consultants. They often possess technical expertise that might even preserve them in the next round of downsizing.[39] In this way, information sharing and organizational learning occur, and both parties, employees and their organization, benefit.

As we discussed in Chapter 8, on-the-job learning is a critical way for organizations to prepare their employees for the future. Through the use of different assignments and multifunctional experiences, companies can ensure a steady supply of trained staff who understand the business and the key strategic issues. Effective organizations integrate training programs into all business functions and work experiences and make on-the-job learning part of every manager's job.[40] There are many different projects, assignments, and other activities that can serve as on-the-job developmental experiences, paving the way for future advancement. Some of these activities are listed below: [41]

- Serve on a task force to address a business problem.
- Install a new system.
- Make speeches on behalf of the organization.
- Resolve conflict among warring subordinates.
- Conduct a problem prevention analysis.
- Become active in a professional organization.
- Work with a charitable organization.

Another method to support employee development is the performance appraisal process. If conducted properly, performance reviews and appraisals can focus employee attention on desired behaviors, can reinforce those actions that are most successful, and can pinpoint any weaknesses. The employee then uses this feedback to determine when changes are needed and when further learning is warranted. A company's reward system can also support individual development by reinforcing the development and/or maintenance of competencies.[42]

PROMOTIONS, REDEPLOYMENT, AND OUTPLACEMENT. A company's strategic plans often require the movement of personnel to achieve alignment between human resources and strategic needs. Promoting employees, either within the same function or across units, is one way to ensure that competent, knowledgeable people are placed in key positions within the organization. Several criteria are appropriate to determine usefulness of promotions.[43] First, promotions should be intended to build competitiveness and should be tied to future business needs. Second, promotions should be linked with performance and not related to internal politics or cliques. Succession planning at well-run companies requires that performance be the primary factor in determining promotions. Third, companies should track their high-potential candidates to ensure that these individuals receive the challenging assignments that will stretch their skills. The early job challenge used by PepsiCo, as we described in Chapter 8, is an example of how firms can cultivate high-potential employees. Last, the use of dual career ladders may be another means to ensure a properly functioning promotion system. Dual ladders allow all members of the organization to have access to hierarchical advancement and to remain productive members of the firm.

According to Manuel London, redeployment "refers to transferring employees from their current job functions where they are not needed to new job functions where they are needed."[44] Often, but not always, the new job requires the learning of new skills and knowledge and may also necessitate a change in geographic location. Redeployment is used for two basic reasons: to improve the skill levels and broaden the experiences of certain personnel, and as a strategic response to business conditions. In the former, the movement of employees is a planned developmental technique to gain more seasoned staff. For example, a company with extensive international interests may want its fast-track employees to take one or more tours of duty in its overseas operations so that they gain a multinational perspective. In the latter case, redeployment is used as a strategic response to a shift in business conditions resulting from internal or external factors. For example, the closing of a plant in one geographic location to take advantage of a better business climate in another geographic area is a strategic decision that may necessitate the redeployment (and relocation) of key staff. All organizations must recognize the disruptions of human life and the threat to self-esteem that redeployment and internal transfers can cause. To state the obvious, unnecessary or poorly planned transfers are not only inefficient but can lead to alienated, unproductive workers.

When business conditions call for drastic action, organizations may need to eliminate individual positions or whole units to improve competitiveness. In Chapter 9, we discussed outplacement from the individual's perspective. From the organization's view, eliminating staff is normally a difficult decision, one that some companies try to avoid at all cost. 3M has implemented outplacement services that identify employees who are in transition, automatically place these employees in career transition workshops, and provide individualized counseling for them.[45] In keeping with their traditions and founding values, IBM and Hewlett Packard have gone to great lengths to avoid staff layoffs. Both companies have tried to hold to that credo even during difficult times. Although both companies have faced business contractions, they have attempted to minimize layoffs by using such techniques as internal transfers, lateral and downward shifts, shortened work weeks, and early retirement.[46]

As was the case with redeployment, organizations should never treat layoffs as a routine business practice. Organizations must weigh the emotional and financial toll that layoffs can take on individual lives versus the strategic and financial benefits that can accrue from a reduced staff. The decision to cut staff should only be made when the benefits clearly outweigh the tangible and intangible costs to the individual employees.

INDIVIDUAL LEVEL ACTIVITIES

Earlier in this chapter, we briefly discussed the right-hand side of Edgar Schein's model (Exhibit 14.1), which shows the individual activities in an integrated human resource planning and development system. The individual steps in the model are consistent with the career management process outlined throughout this book. Specifically, the centerpiece of individual career management is awareness—of self and the internal work environment. In Chapter 3, we discussed how self-awareness is facilitated through knowledge of one's interests, talents, values, and life-style preferences. Individuals can gain this knowledge in several ways—some formal and organizationally sponsored, as we review in Chapter 15, and others less formal, such as discussions with family and friends.

Schein's model also shows that the individual should recognize possible career anchors (i.e., their occupational self-concept), the degree of work involvement that is acceptable and desired, and needs related to one's career stage. In addition, the model indicates that employees can improve self-awareness by taking into account their personal work histories, including types of assignments undertaken and developmental activities pursued. A review of experience can indicate the types of work activities one likes (and dislikes) and those that should be actively sought (and those that should be avoided). The results of one's performance appraisal can also serve as a source of information for self-awareness. Objective feedback from one's manager and co-workers could provide insight and revelations on an individual's personality and behavior by indicating how one is perceived by others. In this way, personal blind spots can be eliminated and possible new career directions conceived.

Once the individual has achieved a satisfactory level of self-awareness, specific individual career plans can be formulated, including career goals and related strategies. Of course, individual plans are not conceived in a vacuum but should reflect the human resource plans of the organization. Certain individual career goals may be rendered impossible to achieve if one's employer is moving in a direction counter to the goal. For example, an individual's goal to become director of economic research for an insurance company would be unachievable if the company were going to eliminate its in-house economic research department and instead contract out this function. Through dialogue, corporate communications, the grapevine, and other sources, individuals can keep abreast of changes in corporate direction and can rework their career plans accordingly.

Although we have stressed a systematic, rational approach to career management, the reality of most organizations is such that being systematic and rational in making plans is difficult, to say the least. Organizational uncertainty, quick shifts in direction, hostile takeovers, and a cloud of impermanence can remove any semblance of structure and assuredness in individual career plans. Karl Weick and Lisa Berlinger[47] pose two related questions: What does it mean to survive, grow, and advance in a firm that is always changing? and What does it mean to have a career amidst impermanence? The rhetorical nature of the two questions leaves an exact answer to either one impossible. Nonetheless, one can see how the uncertainty of organizational life makes a protean, self-directed approach to career management a necessity.

In this sense, although the organization can help employees in the process of mapping their careers, the ultimate responsibility for adapting career plans rests with the individual. Moreover, the meaning and measure of career success should be individually determined. Self-satisfaction and fulfillment, not the title or the trappings of an impermanent position, are the true barometers of success. Weick and Berlinger suggest, "If people pursue processes rather than outcomes, competencies rather than titles, fulfillment rather than advancement, and roles rather than positions, they will accomplish career growth and, in doing so, will also become indispensable resources for the self-designing organization."[48]

MATCHING PROCESSES

Edgar Schein's model clearly indicates how the convergence of organizational and individual plans can be achieved through a number of matching processes. By linking the two levels, the strategic needs of the organization can be met and the career growth needs of the individual fulfilled. Indeed, a match between individual and organizational career plans is a key determinant of such favorable outcomes as individual satisfaction with the organization and intention to remain with the firm.[49]

Essentially, the different matching processes facilitate the sharing of information between parties, such that the employees have knowledge of organizational plans and the organization is aware of individual desires. Several indicators of the linkage between organizational and individual plans include whether business plans and forecasts are publicized; whether people have easy access to job information; whether networks foster innovation, high performance, and exploration of career options; and whether employees and managers are mutually supportive.[50] To these indicators we can add whether the organization uses an information system to match corporate staffing and development plans with information that has been gathered on individual employees. Let us briefly consider each of these indicators.

PUBLICATION OF BUSINESS PLANS AND FORECASTS. We have already discussed the importance of awareness of the internal work environment in relation to individual career planning. Companies can facilitate this awareness by making known, at least in a general sense, their business plans and forecasts. This includes an articulation of the corporate and divisional mission and objectives, an overview of industry trends and developments, and insight into possible structural changes within the company. Written documents, in-house publications, business forecasts, Intranet sites (Internet web sites that are for internal company use only), and other formal communication mechanisms are all ways that organizations can publicize their plans.

ACCESS TO JOB INFORMATION. Individual career planning can also be supported by knowledge of jobs within the various functions of the company. Many organizations use job postings as a way to broadcast open positions. Normally, postings include the job title, a brief position description, the grade level, skill and educational requirements, and the salary range. Recall from Chapter 8 that we provided a description of Johnson & Johnson's job posting program that included these elements.

Job descriptions that are up-to-date and readily available can help employees understand the requirements of different positions and departments. Organizations should ensure that current descriptions are easily available to any employee who wishes to review them. Likewise, organizations can offer information on career paths and dual ladders that shows typical hierarchical advancement in the company.

Finally, organizations can foster a culture that allows and encourages the free flow of information on jobs and opportunities. Managers might describe job activities within their functional area, not only to their own staff but also to individuals from other departments. Intranets are a vehicle through which organizations make their job postings known to employees. For example, the Unisys Corporation has focused on keeping its employees' careers and skills up-to-date. Any Unisys worker can log onto the company's interactive Intranet-based Career Fitness Center to access a listing of potential mentors, direct links to skills training web sites, job postings, and career advice. Similarly, in 1998, US West's Intranet site received 6.5 million hits per month, and more than 28,000 employees visit the site. Although the Intranet site has internal job postings, it is truly used as a companywide communication tool, with more than 60 applications on the site and the ability to communicate internally (to employees) and externally (to business partners and customers).[51]

USE OF NETWORKS. Formal and informal employee networks are another technique for the sharing of information. As we discussed in Chapter 8, networks are groups of employees organized to provide individual members with information about the company and offer advice on career management activities. Networks also allow participating members to make their career desires known to more senior colleagues.

MUTUAL SUPPORT. Individual and organizational planning can be facilitated through the mutual support and sharing of information that takes place between managers and their employees. Among more formal techniques, performance appraisals give employees an opportunity to gain feedback about their current skills and competencies and also allow employees to test their self-perceptions against their manager's perception of reality.[52] In addition, coaching and regular feedback give employees information on their performance and indicate when changes in behaviors or attitudes are warranted. Coaching and feedback can be received from supervisors, peers, and subordinates. Implementers of 360-degree feedback programs note that employees receive support and direction from others in their circle of influence, and insights and points of view are offered that a supervisor may be unable to provide. Allied Signal, Tenneco, and Coca-Cola have successfully implemented 360-degree feedback programs and report employees who appreciate the assistance such programs offer.[53]

In the opposite direction, mutual support implies that managers can learn about individual career desires and goals, which may influence organizational staffing decisions. Employees might offer management excellent ideas for deployment of resources based on their own career interests. Good two-way communication can build trust between parties. As a result, trust allows employees to know where they stand with each other and minimizes time and energy wasted on worrying and wondering about their future career directions. Employees can funnel their energy into the attainment of goals and results that will, in the long run, advance their own goals as well as the organization's.[54]

HUMAN RESOURCE INFORMATION SYSTEMS.   In today's business environment, with advanced computer technology and widespread use of personal computers, the link between organizational needs and individual desires can be made more efficient through the use of automated information systems. For example, inventories can be maintained that store data on employees' skills, experience, training, education, publications, and special awards/recognition. More sophisticated systems might also include data on individual career interests and aspirations, relocation preferences, and full descriptions of work experiences. With this personnel data coded in automated form, the system can quickly match open jobs with individuals who have the required competencies and work experiences. Tellabs Inc., a leading-edge manufacturer of digital telecommunications equipment, has used a computer-based human resource information system.[55] The installed system included a skills bank that facilitated human resource planning, helped identify training needs, and supported selection based on skills possessed. 3M has a Job Information System that electronically posts job descriptions and job opportunities up to the director level. The system was also linked to the human resource review process and was tied to employee development. Thomas Gutteridge, Zandy Leibowitz, and Jane Shore stated that the objectives of the system "were to enable 3M's hiring managers to identify internal candidates and to help employees identify skills and qualifications needed to prepare for different job requirements."[56]

It should be clear that organizational effectiveness is maximized when organizational and individual planning activities are linked. Synchronization of plans requires broad-based programs that take into account the wide diversity of employer and employee needs. Certainly, a "stand-alone" career management practice, such as a career planning workshop or a retirement planning program, can serve the needs of particular people at a specific point in time. But development of a comprehensive career management system capable of meeting individual and organizational needs is aided by complementary human resource systems. This does not mean that an organization has to have all elements of the system in place at once, but rather that it should see the interrelationships between career management and human resource systems and make a systematic attempt to fill the voids it identifies.

As an initial step, an organization can examine how effectively it is managing its human resources. Such indicators might include its ability to recruit and retain capable people, its present level of productivity and creativity, its success in developing people to meet its present and future staffing needs, its success in managing its diversity, and the adaptability of its work force to changing organizational needs. Effectiveness in these areas can be assessed within certain units of the organization (e.g., a profit center or division) or for specific subsets of employees (e.g., fast-track managers, midcareer employees).

An identification of current or potential problems in these areas would enable the organization to select career management practices that are most appropriate to the particular circumstances. The organization also needs to consider the human resource practices required to support a career management program. Forecasting human resources, training managers to conduct career counseling and coaching, evaluating job performance, and identifying career paths may require attention prior to, or concurrent with, the introduction of major career management activities. Mechanisms for evaluating a career management program's effectiveness should also be put in place before the program is introduced.

Perhaps what is most important is a climate of openness and candor and a genuine concern for people. It is unlikely that individuals will be willing to reveal their weaknesses, fears, anxieties, and hopes in a cold, punitive, secretive climate. Effective career management requires collaboration between the individual and the organization, and collaboration requires mutual trust and respect.

ILLUSTRATIONS OF CAREER-ORIENTED HUMAN RESOURCE SYSTEMS

This section describes two examples of human resource systems that are integrated with corporate business plans. These systems support individual career management as one way to help ensure fulfillment of those plans.

A program implemented by Amoco Production Company, a wholly owned subsidiary of Amoco Corporation, as described by Thomas Gutteridge, Zandy Leibowitz, and Jane Shore,[57] illustrates many features of a career-oriented human resource system. Gutteridge, Leibowitz, and Shore described the objectives of the program as follows:

- To view career development as a business strategy for profitability and competitiveness
- To encourage employees to define and pursue their visions of career success
- To facilitate career discussions and individual development plans supported by complementary human resource practices

After a 4-year implementation phase, Amoco Production Company has seen significant results. The individual development plan is designed to take employees through a process that helps them identify their vision of career success, understand how that vision fits with company needs and expectations, produce a development plan, and gather feedback from their immediate supervisor and other levels of management as appropriate. The process is a system because its elements are integrated with each other and with other Amoco strategic and human resource initiatives and practices, in particular performance management and continuous improvement. Amoco's view of this process is that career and performance management systems, continuous improvement, and several other related processes are designed to promote competitive advantage, not simply individual advancement.

Corning, a supplier of specialty glass, ceramic materials, consumer housewares, laboratory sciences, and telecommunications, is another example of a company that integrates its career-planning program with its strategic resource needs. The key issues and program description below were taken from Gutteridge, Leibowitz, and Shore.[58]

- Career development and implementation are linked to specific business needs.
- Conditions of success are established.
- Work-team development is part of the planning process.
- Continuous improvement is achieved through measurement and evaluation processes.
- Accountability mechanisms are identified.
- Information systems are integrated throughout the process.

Corning's aim, articulated formally and informally to all employees, is to be one of the 10 most admired American companies in terms of performance, quality, and diversity. Acknowledging that versatility requires development, Corning's management has chosen to communicate a standard for everyone, without stipulating right or wrong ways to reach it. Each business division is mandated to meet or exceed the company's criteria. Significantly, divisional business strategies must incorporate plans for people development.

At Corning there are few preconceived notions about proper career paths; temporary assignment, job redesign, and other career options are all possible. This lack of structure can be difficult for employees who are less confident in their ability to manage their own development, which is where the company's training and career development programs come into play. The idea is to give people tools for diagnosing their own strengths and weaknesses and plenty of opportunities to explore how best to merge their needs with Corning's.

SUMMARY

An important consideration for all organizations is the implementation of career-oriented human resource support systems. Human resource support systems that have a focus on career development and are integrated with corporate business plans appear to provide a strong foundation for the organization in the achievement of its strategic goals. Edgar Schein provides a model and proposes a matching process that might occur between individuals and their career needs and organizations with their strategic needs. Organizational activities include strategic planning, human resource planning, assessment and monitoring of plans, as well as replanning and the reimplementation of new plans. Individual activities include self-assessment, identifying career goals, and identifying plans to meet these goals. Matching of individual and organizational plans occurs through joint dialogue. Organizations may manage human resource inventories so that they understand when and where certain skill sets are needed. Individuals at the same time may search through human resource inventories, some on-line, which detail the types of skills and experiences jobs throughout the company might require. Through conversations with supervisors and others, feedback may be offered to direct the employee toward appropriate job opportunities. Neither employees nor management should make strategic decisions (regarding careers or organizational plans) in a vacuum.

ASSIGNMENT

Choose an organization for which you have worked or one you can investigate. Identify the company's unique culture and describe the career management practices that it provides. Explain how the organization's culture has either helped or hindered the development of an effective career management system. Describe the type of culture that is ideally suited for an effective career management system.

DISCUSSION QUESTIONS

1. What techniques can organizations use to ensure that their strategic direction and business plans are reflected in their human resource systems and career development programs?

2. To what extent should organizations be committed to developing and promoting their resources from within? Are organizations better off just hiring their resources from the external labor market? Which situations might warrant the development approach and which might warrant the selection approach?

ENDNOTES

1. J. R. Galbraith and R. K. Kazanjian, *Strategy Implementation: Structure, Systems and Process* (St. Paul, MN: West Publishing, 1986); T. C. Powell, "Organizational Alignment as Competitive Advantage," *Strategic Management Journal* 13 (1992): 119–134.

2. J. B. Arthur, "Effects of Human Resource Systems on Manufacturing Performance and Turnover," *Academy of Management Journal* 37, no. 3 (1994): 670–687; M. A. Huselid, "The Impact of Human Resource Practices on Turnover, Productivity, and Corporate Financial Performance," *Academy of Management Journal* 38, no. 3 (1995): 635–672; P. M. Wright and G. C. McMahan, "Theoretical Perspectives for Strategic Human Resource Management," *Journal of Management* 18 (1992): 295–320.

3. E. H. Schein, *Career Dynamics: Matching Individual and Organizational Needs* (Reading, MA: Addison-Wesley, 1978).

4. M. A. Von Glinow, M. J. Driver, K. Brousseau, and J. B. Prince, "The Design of a Career Oriented Human Resource System," *Academy of Management Review* 8 (1983): 23–32.

5. Galbraith and Kazanjian, *Strategy Implementation;* J. L. Kerr and E. F. Jackofsky, "Aligning Managers with Strategies: Management Development versus Selection," *Strategic Management Journal* 10 (1989): 157–170; A. S. Thomas, R. J. Litschert, and K. Ramaswamy, "The Performance Impact of Strategy–Manager Coalignment: An Empirical Examination," *Strategic Management Journal* 12 (1991): 509–522.

6. S. M. Colarelli and T. A. Beehr, "Effective Organizations in the Twenty-First Century," in *Applying Psychology in Business*, ed. J. W. Jones, B. D. Steffy, and D. W. Bray (New York: Lexington Books, 1991), 58–67; quote is on p. 65.

7. P. H. Mirvis, "Human Resource Management: Leaders, Laggards, and Followers," *Academy of Management Executive* 11, no. 2 (1997): 43–56.

8. J. G. Goodale, "Strengthen HR Management: Transcend Its Reactionary Role," *Personnel Journal* November (1986): 14–20.

9. J. W. Slocum and W. L. Cron, "Business Strategy, Staffing, and Career Management Issues," in *Career Growth and Human Resource Strategies,* ed. M. London and E. M. Mone (New York: Quorum Books, 1988), 135–151.

10. D. Ulrich, *Human Resource Champions* (Boston, MA: Harvard Business School Press, 1997).

11. M. London, "Career Development and Business Strategy," in *Applying Psychology in Business,* ed. J. W. Jones, B. D. Steffy, and D. W. Bray (New York: Lexington Books, 1991), 430–437; quote is on p. 433.

12. R. S. Schuler, "Repositioning the Human Resource Function: Transformation or Demise," *Academy of Management Executive* 4 (1990): 49–60.

13. London, "Career Development and Business Strategy."

14. Kerr and Jackofsky, "Aligning Managers with Strategies: Management Development Versus Selection."

15. Ibid.; quote is on p. 167.

16. Ibid.; quote is on p. 167.

17. D. Ulrich and D. Lake, *Organizational Capability* (New York: John Wiley, 1990).

18. Ibid.

19. Ibid.

20. Ibid.

21. Ibid.

22. Ibid.; quote is on p. 103.

23. Ibid.

24. Ibid.; quote is on p. 106.

25. London, "Career Development and Business Strategy."

26. N. Nicholson, "Career Systems in Crisis: Change and Opportunity in the Information Age," *Academy of Management Executive* 10, no. 4 (1996): 40–51.

27. M. M. Graddick, "Corporate Philosophies of Employee Development," in *Career Growth and Human Resource Strategies,* ed. M. London and E. M. Mone (New York: Quorum Books, 1988), 99–109.

28. R. J. Campbell and J. L. Moses, "Careers from an Organizational Perspective," in *Career Development in Organizations,* ed. D. T. Hall et al. (San Francisco, CA: Jossey-Bass, 1986), 274–309; quote is on p. 305.

29. K. Kelly, "Motorola: Training for the Millennium," *Business Week,* March 28, 1994, 158–163; W. Wiggenhorn, "Motorola U: When Training Becomes Education," *Harvard Business Review* July–August (1990): 71–83.

30. B. Avishai, "Manager's Journal: Companies Can't Make Up for Failing Schools," *The Wall Street Journal,* July 29, 1996, A12; M. Messmer, "Steer Clear of the Skills Gap," *Personnel Journal* 75, no. 3 (1996): 44.

31. Colarelli and Beehr, "Effective Organizations in the Twenty-First Century"; quote is on p. 65.

32. Mirvis, "Human Resource Management."

33. Kelly, "Motorola"; Messmer, "Steer Clear of the Skills Gap"; Wiggenhorn, "Motorola U."

34. Ulrich and Lake, *Organizational Capability.*

35. Ibid.

36. T. G. Gutteridge, Z. B. Leibowitz, and J. E. Shore, *Organizational Career Development: Benchmarks for Building a World-Class Workforce* (San Francisco, CA: Jossey-Bass, 1993); quote is on p. 202.

37. Ibid.

38. Anonymous, "Where It's an Inside Job," *Management Today* October (1996): 13.

39. Ibid.

40. Colarelli and Beehr, "Effective Organizations in the Twenty-First Century."

41. Ulrich and Lake, *Organizational Capability.*

42. Ibid.

43. Ibid.

44. M. London, *Managing the Training Enterprise* (San Francisco, CA: Jossey-Bass, 1989); quote is on p. 236.

45. Gutteridge, Leibowitz, and Shore, *Organizational Career Development.*

46. T. Brown, "The '100 Best Companies': Do They Point the Way for All Business?" *Industry Week* 242, no. 8 (April 19, 1993): 12–20; M. W. Miller, "Hard Times Threaten IBM's Long Tradition of Eschewing Layoffs," *The Wall Street Journal,* July 31, 1992, A1.

47. K. E. Weick and L. R. Berlinger, "Career Improvisation in Self-Designing Organizations," in *Handbook of Career Theory,* ed. M. B. Arthur, D. T. Hall, and B. S. Lawrence (Cambridge, UK: Cambridge University Press, 1989), 313–328; quote is on p. 320.

48. Ibid.; quote is on p. 320.

49. C. S. Granrose and J. D. Portwood, "Matching Individual Career Plans and Organizational Career Management," *Academy of Management Journal* 30 (1987): 699–720.

50. Z. B. Leibowitz, C. Farren, and B. L. Kaye, *Designing Career Development Systems* (San Francisco, CA: Jossey-Bass, 1986).

51. G. Rosenberg, "Exercising Career Control," *Working Woman* 23, no. 6 (1998): 44; C. Sliwa, "How the Intranet Was Won: US West Pioneers Push Change," *Computerworld* 32, no. 11 (1998): 14.

52. Leibowitz, Farren, and Kaye, *Designing Career Development Systems.*

53. M. R. Edwards and A. J. Ewen, *360-Degree Feedback: The Powerful New Model for Employee Assessment & Performance Improvement* (New York: AMACOM, 1996).

54. Leibowitz, Farren, and Kaye, *Designing Career Development Systems.*

55. M. Michaels, "Computer–Based Human Resource Planning and Management," in *Applying Psychology in Business,* ed. J. W. Jones, B. D. Steffy, and D. W. Bray (New York: Lexington Books, 1991).

56. Gutteridge, Leibowitz, and Shore, *Organizational Career Development;* quote is on p. 161.

57. Ibid.

58. Ibid.

15

Organizational Career Management Systems

Throughout this book, we have examined individual and organizational actions relevant to career management. Although it is ultimately the employee's responsibility to manage his or her career, the organization can support the individual's attempts at career management in a variety of ways.

Effective career management can enable individuals at each stage of development to make informed career decisions that are consistent with their talents, aspirations, and values. Moreover, organizations can improve their effectiveness by supporting career management activities. Reflecting this dual purpose, organizations develop and offer career management programs to achieve a variety of objectives, including the development and promotion of employees from within, assistance to individuals in their career planning efforts, improvement in worker productivity through optimal utilization, enhancement of human resource planning, achievement of diversity commitments, reduction in high levels of turnover, attainment of a more positive recruiting image, and the achievement of strategic business goals.[1]

The concept of fit is relevant to individual and organizational applications of career management. Individuals want to achieve career and life outcomes that fit their significant values and talents. Organizations expect that supporting career management will provide a fit between the satisfaction of individual needs and the organization's requirements for productivity and effectiveness. This chapter discusses and illustrates the variety of career management activities that organizations can provide.

———————— ■ ————————

OVERVIEW OF CAREER MANAGEMENT PRACTICES IN ORGANIZATIONS

Career management is the process by which individuals develop insight into themselves and their environment, formulate career goals and strategies, and

· TABLE 15-1

TYPES OF CAREER MANAGEMENT
PRACTICES AND PROGRAMS

1. Anticipatory Socialization via Internships
   and Apprenticeships
2. Realistic Recruitment
3. Employee Orientation
4. Individual Learning and Development
5. Job Challenge and On-the-Job Experiences
6. Performance Feedback and Coaching

7. Mentoring and Supportive Alliances
8. Dual Promotion Ladders
9. Dealing with the Career Plateau
10. Late Career Activities
11. Redeployment and Outplacement Programs
12. Pre-retirement Programs

acquire feedback regarding career progress. A career management practice is an activity or set of activities designed to promote employee insight, goal and strategy development, and/or appropriate feedback.[2]

Table 15.1 identifies major management practices that organizations can sponsor to improve individual career management, development, and advancement throughout the various stages of the work life. As we discuss specific career management practices, we review the purpose of the practice and offer specific examples of related programs in action. Of course, the described programs are intended to illustrate what has been done in a particular area and are not necessarily endorsed as "model" programs.

ANTICIPATORY SOCIALIZATION VIA INTERNSHIPS AND APPRENTICESHIPS

Chapters 7 and 8 described the process by which individuals enter work organizations and become socialized into their new work roles. It was noted that anticipatory socialization begins even before the newcomer joins the organization on a full-time basis. During this stage, values and talents are clarified and expectations are formed. One of the major tasks of this stage is the development of accurate, realistic expectations about one's chosen career field and, more generally, about the world of work. In addition, anticipatory socialization practices can help companies gain a positive recruiting image and ensure an available pool of talented newcomers.

Several large companies, including Aetna Life & Casualty Co., Allstate Insurance Co., Boeing Co., Hewlett Packard, Kodak, Lucent Technologies, Nabisco, and Procter & Gamble, use internships to achieve more efficient recruitment and staffing. During the summer of 1997, Hewlett Packard employed more than 900 interns, which is double the number used previously. At Boeing, 500 college interns spent the summer of 1997 working with information technology and engineering mentors. Lucent Technologies invests significantly in interns, so much so that it winds up extending job offers to 65 percent of its interns. Nabisco also invests substantially in interns by offering signing bonuses to the "best and brightest" interns.[3]

Cooperative education is another vehicle that can be used to facilitate the transition from school to work. The following brief description of the cooperative education program at Drexel University is based on material supplied by Drexel's Cooperative Education and Career Services Center.[4]

> At Drexel University, cooperative education provides an opportunity for the student to integrate classroom theory and practical work experience. Drexel calls this unique learning experience the "ultimate internship." With the cooperation of more than 1,665 business firms, government agencies, and nonprofit organizations, Drexel's cooperative education program allows the student to sample the beginning of a career before graduation. The top five employers of Drexel interns include SmithKline Beecham, Lockheed Martin, Arco Chemical Co., PECO Energy Co., and E. I. DuPont de Nemours & Co., Inc. International internships are also available at such companies as Kawasaki Industries (Japan), Alcatel (France), BASF (Germany), and Dow Europe (The Netherlands). More than 44,000 Drexel students have participated in the cooperative education experience.
>
> Virtually all undergraduate students at Drexel, in a wide variety of majors, participate in cooperative education. Beginning in their sophomore year, students typically alternate 6 months of full-time paid employment with 6 months of on-campus study. During each 6-month internship, Drexel students are paid a competitive wage. At the end of the 5-year program, students have accumulated up to 18 months of professional work experience in their chosen career field.
>
> The cooperative education program is designed to help students develop a greater sense of responsibility, maturity, and self-confidence, as well as a better understanding of other people, a more serious appreciation of their academic studies, and a more practical, realistic orientation to the world of work. The experience gained through cooperative work assignments can either reinforce students' original occupational choices or convince them to consider other fields of study. Many students return to a former cooperative organization for full-time employment on graduation from Drexel. Each year, about one-third of Drexel graduates are hired full-time by a past employer.

Although internships help to socialize college graduates into their first work-related experience within organizations, apprenticeship programs provide similar functions for high school graduates. In Chapter 8, we discussed how organizations can use apprenticeships as a way to effectively train new recruits in a particular work position. Apprenticeships allow the potential employee to "learn while doing," producing workers who are being trained in a specific job while simultaneously contributing to the company.

Corporations and municipalities are using apprenticeship programs across the United States. And legislation promoting school-to-work apprenticeship activities is being introduced at the federal and state levels to ease the transition from high school to full-time employment and to ensure a supply of trained, competent workers.[5] In fact, the U.S. Department of Labor has a Bureau of Apprenticeship and Training (BAT) that registers apprenticeship programs in 23 states and the District of Columbia, Puerto Rico, and the Virgin Islands. BAT has field representatives who work with sponsor organizations to develop a set of apprenticeship training standards that include an on-the-job training outline, related classroom curriculum, and apprenticeship program operating procedures. When the organization's apprenticeship program meets federal requirements, it will be registered with BAT. BAT then funnels applicants who satisfy the sponsor organization's requirements for ability, aptitude, and education to the prospective employers.[6]

Companies stand to benefit from anticipatory socialization activities. Cooperative education, internships, and apprenticeships provide a ready supply of candidates to consider for full-time employment. These students have already been exposed to the company's culture, have familiarity with the firm's facilities and equipment, and have been trained in specific functional areas. Anticipatory socialization programs also benefit the neophyte. The soon-to-be or newly minted graduate is provided with an opportunity to learn about one's self, one's chosen career field, and working, in general. Specific skills, both technical (e.g., marketing research) and interpersonal (working as a member of a group), can be learned, practiced, and reinforced by internship and apprenticeship experiences. In all, anticipatory socialization programs such as these advance all parties toward their desired goals.

REALISTIC RECRUITMENT

Chapter 7 discussed the tendency of many employers to present themselves in an overly favorable light during the recruitment process. It was noted that job candidates who develop unrealistic expectations are likely to experience "reality shock" on entering the organization. This can contribute to employee dissatisfaction and turnover. Realistic recruitment, in which candidates receive a balanced, accurate view of the prospective job and organization, is designed to reduce levels of reality shock, dissatisfaction, and turnover. The following is a description of a program that attempts to create a realistic recruitment process both for the recruit and the organization.

> The Vanguard Group, one of the world's fastest growing and largest mutual fund companies, also faces a challenge of keeping the ranks staffed with employees who understand their job, the company and its culture, and the fast-paced market within which the company works. The company also understands that most good candidates are entertaining multiple job offers. Recruiters need to accurately portray the job opportunities. They also need to be quick and efficient regarding the entire process— from initial contact with the candidate to extending an offer.
>
> Vanguard's key to recruiting success is the development of interview teams that work with the manager making the hiring decision. The manager is ultimately responsible for the new hire and therefore is asked to customize an interview team based on the position for which the company is recruiting. The interview team is composed of employees with the most direct knowledge about the position and often can provide multiple perspectives regarding the job. The candidates are introduced to the interview team and can learn from the team much more about the job than can they from the hiring manager alone. The team can also learn a lot about the candidate and whether the recruit will fit the job description and, more broadly, Vanguard's culture.
> Vanguard's goal is to select recruits the team generally agrees will be a good fit for the company. The process also allows the recruit to learn about the job from the individuals with whom he or she will be working. This recruiting process permits the hiring

manager to make a quick offer, once the interview team has been consulted, thereby allowing Vanguard to hire the best people before the competition can.[7]

Some organizations allow job seekers to view internal resumes of employees currently holding the jobs. This realistic recruitment technique assumes that recruits are capable of analyzing and comparing their skills and abilities with those individuals who are already competent in the positions to be filled. Since the Cort versus Bristol-Myers lawsuit in 1982, the court ruled that personnel records, which may include resumes, are not confidential but are the property of the employer to be used at its discretion.

The benefits that resume viewing offers to job seekers are twofold. First, candidates are enabled to make decisions about their experiences and how these may fit the job for which they are interviewing. Candidates may actually self-select out of the running for jobs they think they are not competent to fill. Second, recruits (who believe they are fully competent for the job in question) are enabled to negotiate more knowledgeably about the job they are seeking. In both cases, the recruitment process is enhanced. The candidate has realistic information about the necessary skills and abilities for the job. The candidate and the organization can quickly come to an agreement about the terms for employment.[8]

Case interviews and behavioral event interviews are two methods that create a realistic situation in which the candidate needs to respond. The content, creativity, deductive reasoning, and common sense nature of the candidate's response may indicate to recruiters the candidate's ability to perform in the work environment. Companies such as J. P. Morgan and Microsoft have become famous for the "wacky" questions they ask recruits. Microsoft's two most famous questions are "How much water flows through the Mississippi each day?" and "How many tennis balls are there in the U.S.?" These questions may be interspersed with questions based on work-related scenarios that inquire about the recruit's behavior given the situation: "A client wants to do such and such . . . What do you do?"[9]

Interview techniques such as these may appear at first to provide the interviewer with more information than the interviewee. However, these techniques, particularly behavior event interviews, provide recruits with the opportunity to present their values and also give recruits the ability to learn more about the values and culture of the organization. The example given above would permit the recruit to ask questions about the type of customers the position would interface with, about how the company maintains customer satisfaction, and finally about the overlap between departments that serve a particular customer (e.g., customer service, accounting, credit). This information would clarify the relationships the company has with its clientele and would provide the candidate with a framework in which the candidate may be able to decide if this is the type of company for which he or she could work.

Finally, an effective way to provide a realistic view of the organization or the job for the recruit is to have employees refer friends, family, and acquaintances for upcoming job postings. Studies have found employee referrals to be the most successful ways to recruit new employees. Employees tell their friends about the company and what they know about the job, the department, and the work group. Certainly, individuals trust and understand what their friends/colleagues tell them about potential job opportunities. Companies also benefit because employee referrals seem to yield motivated and multiskilled workers who fit well in the work environment. The down side of using employee referrals exclusively is that these sources may present some diversity implications if they tend to reach few members of minority groups.[10]

These realistic recruitment programs were described because of the variety of techniques offered. As discussed in Chapter 7, the impact of realistic recruitment on turnover varies across different situations. The presentation of realistic information on jobs and careers to candidates and employees remains a positive approach to integrating individual and organizational needs.

EMPLOYEE ORIENTATION PROGRAMS

Even if an organization practices realistic recruitment, new employees still have to adjust to a new environment when they enter the organization. Orientation programs can not only help new employees become integrated into the work environment in a general sense but can also address some specific problems experienced by newcomers in the organization. Presented below is a description of the orientation program used by Walt Disney World in Orlando, Florida.[11]

> For a company such as Disney, with extensive contact between customers and employees, it is imperative that the staff be knowledgeable, courteous, and always willing to meet the needs of the guests. To ensure that new recruits are properly integrated into this culture, Disney uses a 3-day orientation program. The orientation program is known as "Traditions I." The first day of employment at Disney World involves attendance at a full-day session that describes the history of the organization. The session emphasizes the four key values of the Disney culture—safety, courtesy, show, and efficiency. All employees are taught that they have a role in serving the guests and that they should observe how employees perform this role during a tour of the facilities. On the second day of the orientation, the employees hear about the support systems, policies, and procedures within the company, with the primary focus on safety and benefits. The third day involves on-the-job buddy training. The recruit is assigned to an experienced co-worker who, during the next 2 days to 2 weeks, exposes the new employee to a series of experiences specific to his or her work role. These peer trainers are role models who work with supervisors to provide the coaching, feedback, and reinforcement needed to help the newcomer learn the job and acquire the Disney spirit.
>
> Once trainees begin working, they are eligible for cross-utilization training. One example is volunteering to teach "Traditions I." This gives employees the opportunity to practice presentation skills, work with groups, and become good candidates for other positions. Some 70 percent of the promotions at Walt Disney Attractions come from within. Disney attributes its ability to promote from within to the strong orientation program and its employees' affinity to the Disney culture. The strongest elements in the Disney culture are teamwork, leadership, and planning.

Even smaller entrepreneurial firms can benefit from well-designed orientation programs. Hal Rosenbluth, owner and CEO of Rosenbluth Travel, literally wrote the book on valuing the employee. The book, "The Customer Comes Second," describes his philosophy that employees best serve the customer—and the company—when they are happy themselves. Rosenbluth Travel has also been named one of the top companies for having fun on the job. Offbeat programs and zany, spirit-building activities are features of life at Rosenbluth. The following is a detailed description of the orientation process for new employees at Rosenbluth Travel, headquartered in Philadelphia, Pennsylvania.[12]

> Rosenbluth Travel offers an imaginative 2-day new employee orientation program. First, new recruits are introduced to the company theme of providing "elegant customer service"—attentiveness to the customer that is beyond the call of duty. Next, the recruits are told of the need for esprit de corps, wherein all the employees are expected to help and support one another. Hal Rosenbluth has made this comment about Rosenbluth Travel's orientation program: "We do this almost every week at our headquarters for entry-level and high-level executives. It isn't a gimmick; it's a way to capture the first couple of days, set expectations, and put priorities in place. During orientation, we do skits to show how to turn a bad customer service experience into an elegant one, and then we talk about the business philosophy and company values. At the end of orientation, I come in with other company leaders to serve 'high tea.' Why? One, we want people to feel comfortable among the officers of the company. Two, to let people know we appreciate them coming to work for us. Three, to discuss what's on their minds and make sure there's no generational gap between veterans and new employees."

The initial task in developing a successful orientation program is to identify the specific information, skills, and support required by new employees. The major strengths of the Disney and Rosenbluth programs were accurate identification of a corporate theme (outstanding customer service) as well as a determination of how best to get the message across. These orientation approaches demonstrate how a custom-made program can be used to improve trainees' understanding of the organization's core values and modes of operation.

INDIVIDUAL LEARNING AND DEVELOPMENT

Chapter 8 discussed how human development and career advancement can be facilitated through learning. Many have argued that career advancement is the responsibility of the employee, and advancement occurs when the employee enhances his or her knowledge base. Organizations can assist employees by becoming "knowledge creators" by developing "their human resources in ways that enhance the supply of information and knowledge available to the firm."[13] Employee learning can occur in a variety of ways: through on-the-job experience and challenge, through formal training and education, and through other more specialized activities such as business and behavioral simulations. Stephen Stumpf describes how simulations can stimulate learning and development.[14]

> Simulations are learning programs that attempt to replicate a company-like environment, with all the associated realities, in a controlled, training setting. Participants are expected to become fully involved in the "simulated" company to gain a full understanding of the demands of senior organizational management. A simulation is an intensive, interactive experience that differs dramatically from most other educational methods. The emphasis is on experiential learning through doing. The interactive,

experiential nature of business simulations can be used to facilitate the learning of new behaviors that the organization wants to reinforce. The two most common benefits of business simulations are that they help employees see their organizations from a senior management perspective and that they stimulate the learning of various cognitive and behavioral skills viewed as necessary to manage effectively and advance within the firm.

In summary, business simulations require managers to use a wide range of managerial competencies and skills. Unlike other forms of management development, business simulations allow managers to act on what they think should be done in particular situations. Individuals iterate between thought and action, and they get to see the financial and interpersonal results of their managerial style. Because of the experiential nature of business simulations, managers better understand the cause-and-effect relationships of their actions and gain a keen awareness of their individual strengths and weaknesses.

Stumpf suggests that the objective of business simulation programs is to allow individuals to learn by enhancing understanding of the relationship between managerial behavior and organizational performance; examining how individual actions promote or inhibit effective teamwork; and providing a basis for the diagnosis of managerial skills, skill development, and action planning for improved on-the-job performance. He likens learning about management to learning to dance by stating that an individual cannot learn to dance just by reading about dance. Similarly, a person cannot learn to be an effective manager only by reading books.[15]

Learning can also occur in an environment that promotes self-assessment. The Career Action Center, headquartered in Cupertino, California, provides such an environment. The center helps design and staff career management centers for such major corporations as Sun Microsystems, Hewlett Packard, IBM, AT&T, and Raychem. Although these corporations may have provided similar services in the past through human resource departments, now many companies outsource such activities to organizations such as the Career Action Center. A core feature of the Career Action Center program is the promotion of career resilience through lifelong learning. The Career Action Center works with employees of sponsoring companies to identify and address skill areas in need of updating.

> Specifically, the center's approach emphasizes continual learning and adjustment on the part of the employee to ensure that skill levels are consistent with organizational requirements. As opposed to traditional approaches, the program places less emphasis on vertical or hierarchical movement within the sponsoring organization, but greater emphasis on individual employability and value through lifelong learning. The Career Action Center maintains strict confidentiality in working with individual employees as a way to gain their trust and confidence.[16]

Individual learning and development can be fostered through a number of individual and organizational actions. Many organizations are investing in their employees' development by providing on-site training programs or "universities," such as the Ford Motor Company's Leadership Education and Development (LEAD) program and Motorola University.[17] The speed and degree of career advancement are often a direct outcome of how well and quickly the employee is able to comprehend the business realities and master new skills.

JOB CHALLENGE AND ON-THE-JOB EXPERIENCES

During the early career years, employees can benefit from job challenge and the opportunity to experience a number of different assignments. Through job challenge and rotational opportunities, employees build a base of experience and develop a wider range of competencies that can positively influence career success in later years. In Chapter 8, we reviewed how PepsiCo presents new employees with significant challenge to stimulate their personal and professional development. In a similar fashion, Air Products and Chemicals, Inc., uses an innovative approach to encourage rotational work assignments during the early years of employment.[18]

Since its inception, Air Products and Chemicals, Inc., has encouraged recent college graduates to take an active role in the planning and development of their careers. This philosophy was formalized in 1959 with the establishment of the Career Development Program (CDP) which allows individuals with finance, marketing, engineering, chemistry, or information technology undergraduate or graduate degrees to fulfill their immediate, individual career objectives while preparing for and defining the challenges and opportunities that lie ahead. The CDP is characterized by diversified movement and flexibility, while providing an environment where the individual has a real influence on the direction of his or her career from the very beginning. The long-term goal of the program is to help participants identify and begin to cultivate professional skills, interests, and potential to the best benefit of the individual and Air Products.

The CDP is not a structured training program. Instead, it challenges new employees with actual work experience and gives them a broad perspective on the company's operations and objectives. Positions are designed to give each person exposure to a variety of company activities and to provide a high degree of visibility among all levels of management.

Typically, within a period of 2–3 years, employees have the option of taking several assignments in areas in which their personal and professional interests lie. Individuals have flexibility in the choice of functional area, sequence, and to a degree, duration of assignments. Assignments can cover such areas as engineering, research, marketing, manufacturing, information technology, finance, auditing, and purchasing.

The initial assignment is generally in a function that is compatible with the employee's education and experience as well as the opportunities available within the company. After becoming acclimated to Air Products, new employees are encouraged to take the initiative and explore future assignments through discussion with the CDP supervisor, fellow program participants, supervisors, and co-workers. Individuals are expected to seek new challenges as interests develop, taking a proactive role in tailoring their own career paths. Employees typically complete up to three CDP assignments before moving into a regular position.

The number of employees active in the CDP at any one time can range from 120 to 180. Currently, there are approximately 900 alumni of the program working for Air Products out of a total worldwide work force of approximately 16,800 employees. Many of the top executives from Air Products are CDP alumni, including Chief Executive Officer Harold "Hap" Wagner, President John Paul Jones III, Corporate Executive

Vice President Joseph Kaminski, and Executive Vice President of Chemicals Robert Gadomski. The ultimate goal of the CDP is to establish an optimal match between an individual's longer-term plans and opportunities within the company.

The CDP supervisor plays an integral role in the new employee's career development experience at Air Products. The supervisor is available to provide meaningful direction, to facilitate assignment selection, and ultimately to help the employee realize long-term aspirations. The program supervisor serves as a strategic resource, meeting with program participants on a regular basis to help them further define their career interests and development needs.

The underlying tenet of the CDP is that the company's future depends on people who have the potential and ambition to grow and develop as individuals. Through the CDP, Air Products encourages a proactive, entrepreneurial approach to career planning.

Job challenge and rotational assignments that occur early in one's career can set the stage for later advancement. Organizations can benefit from employees who become more experienced and well rounded after their participation in such efforts. However, on-the-job learning experiences cannot stop within the early stages of one's career. Developmental job challenges need to continue throughout one's career. On-the-job experiences are crucial for managerial development, and managers learn the most when they approach these opportunities with a variety of learning tactics. For instance, tackling a new task, completing a start-to-finish mandate, and being responsible for end-result accountability are recommended learning experiences. These examples benefit the manager by requiring that he or she learn new perspectives while simultaneously relying on others to get the job done. As these developmental tasks are accomplished, it is important for managers to receive feedback and guidance on how effectively they completed the task and how they learned during the process.[19]

PERFORMANCE FEEDBACK AND COACHING

All employees need feedback so they can monitor and improve their job performance. Although this requirement is particularly critical during the early career, performance feedback is important throughout one's career. Multisource assessment systems, commonly known as 360-degree feedback, are growing in popularity. And there is good reason why 360-degree feedback systems are popular. 360-degree feedback "taps the collective wisdom of those who work most closely with the employee: supervisor, colleagues (peers), direct reports (subordinates), and possibly internal and external customers. The collective intelligence these people provide on critical competencies or specific behaviors and skills gives the employee a clear understanding of personal strengths and areas ripe for development."[20]

Companies such as Amoco, Allied Signal, and Ford are using 360-degree feedback systems to help achieve strategic goals and carry out organizational change efforts. The connection between performance feedback systems and change efforts to achieve a firm's goals is that the organization only changes when its people change. Multisource feedback supports this process in several ways. First, feedback helps the company identify the skills and competencies needed to meet business goals. Then, feedback received from those who work most closely with the employee allows an employee to articulate his or her strengths and weaknesses. Finally, training programs can be offered so the employee can develop the needed skills and can track his or her progress in applying the skills on the job.[21]

Coca-Cola provides an example in which performance review, feedback, and coaching are specifically used to facilitate a discussion of career issues. Coca-Cola has had much success implementing a 360-degree feedback system because the 360-degree process improves the quality of the performance measures. The employee learns much more about his or her performance with feedback from a knowledgeable network of co-workers, who have first-hand experience with the employee and who offer insight about work behaviors that a supervisor may not be able to observe. Coca-Cola's process is summarized as follows:[22]

> The Coca-Cola Company embraces a management philosophy of empowerment, in which decision making is pushed down to the lowest possible level in the organization where information to make decisions is available. Coca-Cola also has adopted a 360-degree feedback process and finds that behavioral feedback from multiple sources encourages every employee to take actions aligned with the new organizational culture.
>
> The four central objectives of Coca-Cola's career development program include to promote from within whenever possible, to develop talent in advance of staffing needs, to give managers the responsibility for evaluating and assisting in the development of their employees, and to expect individuals to take primary responsibility for their career development. The centerpiece of the career development system is an in-depth performance review process using multisource assessments. Each employee is evaluated on the attainment of specific objectives and desired work behaviors, as well as several performance factors. Data received from the 360-degree feedback sessions give employees information on developmental growth needed for building successful careers. This evaluation process provides an opportunity for managers and employees to meet (at least annually) to discuss job performance, but ongoing coaching and feedback are essential. These regular performance reviews often lead to a discussion of individual career issues. In addition, managers are encouraged to conduct career discussions separately from the performance reviews. A recent survey of Coca-Cola USA Fountain employees found that 3.9 percent of those surveyed thought that feedback should only come from the supervisor, whereas 94.8 percent thought that feedback should come from both the supervisor and co-workers. Multisource assessment appears to have become an integral part of the Coca-Cola culture.

It is impossible to develop realistic career goals in the absence of useful performance feedback on one's current job. Periodic coaching sessions that focus on specific job behaviors, in conjunction with more quantitative indices of accomplishment, are most likely to improve current performance and build a solid foundation for future career growth.

MENTORING AND SUPPORTIVE ALLIANCES

Although orientation, internship, and apprenticeship programs can help integrate newcomers into the organization, early-career employees can also benefit from the ongoing advice, support, and sponsorship of a more senior colleague.

Chapter 8 showed how having a mentor and/or experiencing other supportive alliances can satisfy the task and emotional needs of more junior members of the company. Many organizations have established formal programs to ensure that each junior employee develops a relationship with a mentor. The following description of a mentoring system at the E. I. DuPont de Nemours & Co. was excerpted from a lengthy article by Frank Jossi.[23]

> For the past 2 and a half years, Steve Croft and Janet Graham have met at least once a month for an hour to share problems, information, and advice on issues arising from their work at E. I. DuPont de Nemours & Co.'s corporate headquarters in Wilmington, Delaware. Although Croft serves in the role of mentor, he has on more than a few occasions asked for Graham's opinions about how corporate initiatives are playing out in her particular division, the Haskell Toxicology Laboratory. She has been a good source, providing reliable information about how management decisions affect front-line employees. He, in turn, has offered insight into the reasoning behind corporate programs and given her networking opportunities within the corporation.
>
> For Graham, the monthly meetings provide a chance to learn more about other departments, budgetary priorities, and networking from Steve Croft. "He's helped me look at other avenues or places where I could contribute to the organization," she says. "I've also asked for advice on things like presenting, which I hadn't done before. I've had a lot of growth and heard a lot of encouragement in the process."
>
> For Croft, mentoring offers a chance to share what he has learned in decades at DuPont and to discover how changes at the corporate level are received by the troops. When DuPont changed the Haskell Laboratory's budget source from a straight grant from the general fund to a fee-for-service arrangement, the lab was forced into a dramatic transformation; suddenly, it had to charge for its services and pay for its overhead. Finding out what employees really think about management decisions like that has been "one of the values of working with Janet," Croft says. "She gives me an idea of what people are understanding and how people are processing this."
>
> Graham and Croft are part of an ambitious mentoring program that creates relationships among 7,000 of DuPont's 60,000 U.S. employees. Managers and executives maintain formal arrangements with staff members outside their supervision to discuss work-related issues at least once a month. Protégés choose from a list of volunteer mentors whose skills and experience the protégés seek to tap in their quest to climb the corporate ladder.
>
> What comes around goes around. Graham herself now serves as mentor to a secretary at the lab, helping her with career decisions and other issues. In DuPont's formal program, many employees are both mentors and protégés, wearing the different hats of advisers and students.

Provided below is a summary of another planned mentoring program as described in an article by Michelle Martinez.[24]

> Knight-Ridder, Inc., a Fortune 500 communications company, creates diversity through its leadership ranks by providing mentoring experiences to high-potential employees. A handful of senior executives target a diverse list of employees for growth and create annual development plans. "We stay in contact with the individual assigned to us and ensure that we hold ourselves accountable for these people developing and growing in their careers," explains Mary Jean Connors, senior vice president of human resources. Juanita Cox Burton, a former executive with U.S. West, says her mentor offered many

developmental opportunities at Knight-Ridder. "He put me in situations where I was visible and had to take risks," she says, recalling a training project he assigned. Her task was to train high-level employees (directors and above) in selling methods that would take into account the market and the competition. "It was a scary thought for me to be training a group of men . . . [yet] I decided to take the task on because it was high exposure," Burton says. Burton attributes her confidence to the learning opportunity she received from her mentor.

Even though the mentoring programs at DuPont and Knight-Ridder seem successful, at least in the eyes of the companies' management, as we discussed in Chapter 8 there are a number of risks associated with formal mentoring programs. First, an assigned or forced association between mentor and protege may not evolve into a full, caring, developmental relationship. Second, there may be a mismatch between the assigned junior and senior colleagues; indeed, the two parties may not even like each other. In cross-gender dyads, insinuations about inappropriate sexual relationships may scare off both parties. Also, the mentor may feel pressure to participate in the program, despite a lack of enthusiasm or required skills.

David Thomas and Kathy Kram[25] believe that some of these risks could be reduced by making the program voluntary and by training mentors in the appropriate interpersonal skills. Texas Commerce Bank's formal program begins with a 2-day training session that teaches mentors and protégés what to expect from the relationship and how to get the most out of it. DuPont similarly holds a training program for both mentors and protégés stressing what their individual roles should be.[26] In this way, the positive aspects of "a formal program—easy access to mentors, legitimization of developmental activities, ongoing monitoring of the quality of career-enhancing relationships, and increasing competence and motivation among those who participate—outweigh the costs."[27] As an alternative to formal programs, Kram suggests creating opportunities for spontaneous mentor-protégé relationships to emerge.[28] Access to information, special assignments, and projects are additional ways in which junior employees can meet senior colleagues under less contrived circumstances.

DUAL PROMOTION LADDERS

Traditionally, career advancement in organizations has meant moving up the corporate ladder, when the individual is offered (and accepts) higher levels of managerial responsibility. But for many individuals, the emphasis placed on career attainment through managerial competence is at odds with their self-concept and their work interests. Indeed, the career anchor notion states that employees tend to identify with a specific career orientation that is a reflection of their self-concept.[29] Seeking a managerial career is just one of many possible anchors. The question then is how can someone with a career anchor other than managerial competence advance within the corporation? One answer is for organizations to offer dual or multiple promotion ladders that provide alternative career paths for advancement, where each ladder's rungs offer candidates similar status, power, and financial rewards. Examples of multiple promotion ladders

· EXHIBIT 15-1

DOW CORNING'S
MULTIPLE CAREER PATHS

Level	Managerial	Technical Leader*	Research	Technical Service and Development	Process Engineering	Product Development
	Vice-President					
	Director					
VIII	Department Manager	Team Leader**	Senior Research Scientist**	Senior Industry Scientist**	Senior Process Engineering Scientist**	Senior Development Scientist**
VII	Department Manager	Team Leader**	Research Scientist**	Industry Scientist**	Process Engineering Scientist**	Development Scientist**
VI	Program Manager	Team Leader**	Associate Research Scientist**	Associate Industry Scientist**	Associate Process Engineering Scientist**	Associate Development Scientist**
V		Project Leader	Senior Research Specialist	Senior Industry Specialist	Senior Process Engineering Specialist	Senior Development Specialist
IV		Project Leader	Research Specialist	Industry Specialist	Process Engineering Specialist	Development Specialist
III		Project Leader	Associate Research Specialist	Associate Industry Specialist	Associate Process Engineering Specialist	Associate Development Specialist
II			Senior Chemist	Senior Engineer	Senior Engineer	Senior Engineer
I			Chemist	Engineer	Engineer	Engineer
Entry			Associate Chemist	Associate Engineer	Associate Engineer	Associate Engineer

*Technical Leader positions carry both Team/Project Leader titles and professional titles (e.g., Associate Industry Scientist and Team Leader).

**These levels go through the Promotion Review Committee for approval.

within the Dow Corning Corporation are provided in Exhibit 15.1. Below are summaries of multiple and dual promotion ladder approaches taken by Dow Corning and Caterpillar, Inc.

The Dow Corning Corporation created multiple promotion paths that recognize, encourage, and reward employees regardless of the career path they choose. Dow Corning uses multiple-progression paths: (1) technical, (2) technical leader, and (3) managerial. These are available in each of the core Science and Technology departments of Research, Process Engineering, Technical Service and Development, and Product Development. An internal promotion review committee, composed of both technical and administrative staff, has the responsibility of ensuring equity among the departments and maintaining guidelines for promotability within the technical and technical leader positions. Employees in Science and Technology are rated on seven criteria: Science and Technology contribution, customer focus, professionalism (recognition through publications and peer acknowledgement), leadership, teamwork, business awareness, and continuous improvement. Dow Corning believes that the formal nature of their program, with multiple paths and established criteria for progression, fosters improved career planning by the employees and gives the company a mechanism for recognizing and rewarding the contributions of every staff member.[30]

Caterpillar, Inc., recognized the need to keep its information technology (IT) professionals. In 1997, Caterpillar implemented multiple career paths to give employees job alternatives. Besides a supervisory path, the company introduced an applications path that allows employees to focus on specific business applications and lets them make strategic contributions in that area. Caterpillar also created a technical path that allows IT professionals to become experts in operating systems, databases, or networking products. Although the company understands that it is difficult to measure the impact of multiple career paths on retention, it believes that information technology professionals are now less likely to leave because they have more opportunities for job growth and salary increases than they had previously had.[31]

DEALING WITH THE CAREER PLATEAU

In Chapter 9, we talked about how individuals in midcareer may face the possibility that the opportunity for further hierarchical advancement is limited or even nonexistent. Employees in this circumstance are said to be on a career plateau. They can react to the plateau in two basic ways—in a positive fashion by remaining "solid citizens," or in a negative fashion by becoming "deadwood." Although career plateauing has traditionally occurred among midcareer individuals, younger colleagues are no longer immune to experiencing a career plateau. This is due mainly to the changes in organizational structure as many companies reorganize but also because of the large numbers of baby boomers throughout the organization. In both cases, fewer managerial positions are available to younger employees, and hence these employees plateau at lower levels within the organization.

Of course, organizations play a role in helping their employees to remain stimulated and interested in their work, that is, helping them remain contributing members (solid citizens) in the organization. For example, companies can replace the traditional promotion culture with one that is based on the achievement of psychological success.[32] There are many more ways to achieve psychological success (by providing opportunities to learn and grow) than there are to achieve promotional success (strictly defined as hierarchical movement). An approach that has been used by a number of organizations to maintain the work interest of plateaued employees is lateral job rotation. The following are examples of job rotation programs at RJR Nabisco and American Greetings Corporation.

The Nabisco Foods Group of Parsippany, New Jersey, a unit of parent RJR Nabisco, has encouraged employees who have limited promotional opportunities to seek greater personal fulfillment in lateral transfers to other positions in the company. Specifically, individuals can work with their supervisors to either broaden their current job description or plan a sideways move to another work position. Employees are also enabled to self-nominate for other opportunities within the company. To support this program, Nabisco added new tiers to each salary range to increase the chances that a lateral move might allow a modest increase in pay. Participants in the Nabisco program first meet with consultants from an outplacement firm to review career interests. They then meet with representatives from their human resource department and their bosses to discuss career options and prospects for a lateral transfer. Nabisco is currently promoting opportunities for lateral job transfers on its company's Intranet.[33]

In 1992, American Greetings Corporation of Cleveland, Ohio, redesigned 400 work positions in its creative division. Subsequently, they asked their employees to reapply to the redesigned positions, in what amounted to a large-scale game of lateral "musical chairs." All individuals were guaranteed that they would have a job at the end of the process with no pay cut. Management of American Greetings believed that this approach was one way to motivate workers when promotions and pay raises are unlikely. Because employees found themselves in new positions, with somewhat different responsibilities and skill requirements, they were more stimulated and their creative output increased. Because American Greetings used this approach to lateral job transfer with much success, it expects to use this technique again in the future when there is a need to rebuild employees' careers.[34]

Employers can also provide some of the following strategic variations to improve senior employees' jobs:

■ Create generalists or in-house consultants. This allows senior colleagues' contributions to become well known and also allows organizational memory to be shared. Organizations benefit from a more fluid work force.

■ Pay people for performance and skill growth.

■ Base career paths on skill and mastery, rather than on pay-related promotions.

■ Recognize employees for experience and knowledge, rather than for years on the job.

■ Allow others to learn by using line people as instructors. This not only enriches the employee's job but also benefits the training offering by taking advantage of available experience and skills.

■ Provide project management opportunities for senior employees. These opportunities provide employees with a sense of novelty, an ability to use multiple skills, and an environment within which to exercise functional authority.[35]

As these examples show, employers can take a variety of steps to assist their employees who are on a career plateau. By being innovative, organizations can keep their valued employees interested in their jobs and their careers and ultimately ensure that their solid citizens avoid becoming corporate deadwood.

LATE-CAREER ACTIVITIES

Chapter 9 discussed several obstacles to productivity and career growth for late-career employees. Older workers are stereotyped as individuals with low levels of adaptability, decisiveness, activity, and satisfaction. However, many older employees are actually highly reliable and flexible. A study by Manuel London found that older workers are just as career motivated as their younger counterparts.[36] Several studies have found that older employees are highly reliable and productive as well.[37] With the prospect of an increasingly aging work force, organizations should encourage high performance levels from their older workers by enhancing productivity and career options among this group. The following are examples of late-career activities.

A 12-hour workshop was designed for supervisors in a large research and development laboratory. Using lectures, case analyses, and individual assessment activities, the workshop addressed the changing demographic characteristics of the national and laboratory work force, the stereotypes and realities of the aging process, and the differences in attitudes and values between younger and older workers. After these issues were aired, participants developed action plans to enhance the performance of their older (i.e., older than 50) workers. The following plans are illustrative of the steps proposed by supervisors who participated in these workshops:

- More attention will be paid to older workers by providing more feedback and recognition, clearer goals, and a greater use of rewards.

- Fuller use will be made of older workers' experience by assigning them to special projects such as recruiting, strategic planning, and mentoring junior colleagues.

- Increased training opportunities will be offered to older workers, including cross-training to broaden their skills and prepare them for different assignments.

- Age stereotypes in the work group will be examined to determine their pervasiveness, accuracy, and impact on the careers of older employees.[38]

Retiree-work programs are popping up at many companies and will probably increase in use for several reasons. First, baby boomers continue to age, and by the year 2016, the number of annual retirees will double to approximately 4 million. Also, many firms are continuing to downsize or are offering early retirement packages to shrink the employment ranks. These situations cause many 40-, 50-, and 60-year-olds to become prematurely retired. Many of these individuals prefer to continue working on a more limited time basis, and retiree-work programs seem to fit their needs. Companies such as Travelers Insurance have benefited by rehiring retirees. By using its own job bank of retirees to fill temporary work needs, Travelers saved more than $1 million in 1995. The company boasts 700 available workers whom it can call on, with 125 to 150 retirees on the job at any one time. Honeywell also hires back retirees on a part-time basis. These individuals are often used in positions for which they have expertise or skills gained through their tenure at Honeywell.[39]

There is a new model for the family-owned business. The children as business owners are now hiring their parents, grandparents, in-laws, and aunts and uncles as employees. The traditional family business is being flipped upside-down as graying parents are foregoing retirement and working for their children instead, many of whom have launched their own successful businesses. Like other employers in the tight labor market of the late 1990s, family businesses are searching for top-notch hires—and older relatives may bring more to the business than one might think. There are problems associated with the close relationships families have in difficult business situations. Parents may have trouble taking directives from children or may make decisions around the top executive (the child). Yet, when the arrangement does work, both parents and children say both the business and their personal relationships gain.[40]

REDEPLOYMENT AND OUTPLACEMENT PROGRAMS

Termination of employment is a career transition that can represent a threat to one's livelihood and self-esteem. In addition to individual performance criteria, large-scale termination may result from a sluggish economic climate; business contractions; changes in the mission, technology, or structure of the organization; and mergers or acquisitions. Although termination can occur at any time during a person's career, it is likely to be most traumatic during the middle or late career stages.

As noted in Chapter 10, career transitions such as job loss can be managed most effectively when the employee has adequate forewarning, develops satisfactory coping skills, and has sufficient support from organizational and nonorganizational sources. Organizations may offer outplacement programs, either internally or through a third party, to assist the "pink-slipped" employee in dealing with the career transition and in looking for employment elsewhere. Although many companies see outplacement as an expedient way to reduce staffing levels, other organizations look first to redeployment of employees whose present skills are inconsistent with business demands. Redeployment does require further investment in the employee to make skill levels consistent with current and future requirements.[41] Yet, many organizations believe the investment made in these employees is worth it. Current employees already understand the company, its culture, and customers, which may take new employees a while to learn. Below are descriptions of redeployment programs at Chevron and Intel and an outplacement program through the Talent Alliance.

During the late 1980s, the oil industry had been beleaguered. Chevron Corporation, in 1992, instituted a special "mix-and-match" program that rematched employees with jobs internally, instead of laying those employees off. "The process was based on the premise that these are highly skilled, bright people, and we should think of using those skills in other operating companies," says Sam Fortune, manager of human resources for the Gulf of Mexico business unit. To ensure use of the program, human resources set up a job bank. Organizations were first required to post their jobs in the database before they hired outside the company. Employees would identify and match the skills they have (with posted jobs) and train for those they lack. Although most operating companies were looking for specific technical skills, they found that they were swayed by the "softer" skills employees identified—ability to work in teams, problem solving, leading others. Employees who could not find another Chevron job are still offered opportunities to develop marketable skills for job hunting on the outside. This effort has protected hundreds of workers from the unemployment lines and saved Chevron millions of dollars in severance payments.[42]

Intel Corporation has attempted to reprogram its employees as fast as its chips. Craig Barrett, Intel's chief operating officer, speaks of the redeployment program as "a corporate responsibility but also something that is very much in our long-term self-interest." Although Intel offers retraining opportunities to workers in transition, it provides no guarantees. In the redeployment program, workers are given 4 months to shop for new jobs within the company. Anyone who cannot find a job has to leave to the company, although employees working on engineering, production, and manufacturing projects that only last a few months can extend the deadline. About 86 percent of those in the redeployment program have found jobs within Intel. "Our message to our employees is that they are responsible for gaining new skills so they can continue to be employable, either inside or outside the company," said Dorinda Kettmann in human resources. Intel fulfills its responsibility in helping the employee upgrade his or her competency level through the training Intel offers. Intel spends more than $120 million a year on training, or nearly $3,000 per employee, more than double the national average.[43]

A unique example of the use of outplacement is the Talent Alliance. Some of the largest companies, including AT&T, DuPont, and Johnson & Johnson, announced in early 1997 that they are collaborating to form an organization that provides career management and job matching services to employees of the member corporations. Other companies in the Talent Alliance include GTE, Lucent Technologies, TRW, Unisys, and UPS. The purpose of the alliance is to provide career management assistance to member organization employees—in the form of skill tests, counseling about career paths, appropriate educational offerings, and a job-matching system. These employees may have already faced, or will face, termination. The alliance also prepares employees for job change from both a personal and professional perspective. A Career Transition Center is available to help employees move from their job to another job opportunity in either their current company or another member company. The alliance also assists organizations by making it easy to post jobs on its web site—www.talentalliance.org. The alliance does not promise greater job security for employees but instead promises greater employability through this cooperative network.[44]

The redeployment and outplacement programs described above touch on many components of career management. Career exploration and goal setting were facilitated through self-assessment activities, and strategy development was aided by instruction in job search, resume preparation, and interview behavior. Although terminations are undoubtedly unpleasant and threatening experiences, an active career management approach can maximize learning and even improve personal and career growth opportunities.

PRE-RETIREMENT PROGRAMS

Chapter 9 showed how the prospect of retirement could evoke a range of emotions, from anticipation to gloom. Pre-retirement counseling is becoming a popular addition to an organization's repertoire of career management activities. In fact, a 1995 survey found 43 percent of public firms were inclined to provide ongoing pre-retirement counseling programs. Spouses were invited to 84 percent of the programs surveyed.[45] The following discussion of pre-retirement programs in organizations is based on articles by Donna Brown and Mary Ann C. Fusco.[46]

> Many human resource managers favor a two-pronged approach to pre-retirement planning. This approach involves getting employees to rigorously examine their own finances, taking a particularly hard look at the adequacy of their current retirement plans, and then providing as much information as possible about ways in which employees can improve their plans. Organizational steps for getting started on creating a pre-retirement program include (1) analyzing when current employees will be retiring; (2) forming a program budget; (3) developing criteria for service providers; and (4) distributing a benefits statement to each employee before the program begins.

Pre-retirement programs can be presented in four basic formats: seminar, lecture, lecture/workshop, and self-study. A fifth approach is one-to-one counseling. A variety of topics should be included in the program, such as sources of income, financial planning, investment strategies, work options, physical fitness, housing and life-style, attitude and role adjustments, meaningful use of time, legal affairs, and estate planning. Such programs may be offered to both the employee and his or her spouse.

As with the other career management practices we have discussed, pre-retirement planning programs must be based on an assessment of employee needs and concerns. What is most crucial for one employee may not be especially important for another. Retirement planning programs may not only ease the transition from work to retirement but may also influence the decisions of employees to either hasten or postpone retirement. One might also suspect that if such programs succeed in relieving the anxiety of employees nearing retirement, they might make the remaining years of employment more satisfying and productive. One study has found that human resource professionals in organizations that have adopted pre-retirement programs notice a halt in the productivity decline of workers as they near retirement. When these workers are confident in their preparation for their next stage of life, they devote their time on the job to work, not to worry.[47]

Summary

Organizations can offer an array of programs that help their employees manage their careers throughout the life cycle. Recognizing that individuals at different career stages have varying career needs and challenges, companies can tailor their career management assistance activities to meet the requirements of all their employees.

In the early career years, employees must deal with the demands of establishment and achievement. Such organizational programs as anticipatory socialization, internships and apprenticeships, realistic recruitment, orientation, and rotational assignments can help the new employee become established. To assist individuals during the achievement phase, organizations can offer a number of career-enhancing programs, including learning and development activities, mentoring, performance feedback, and coaching. These career management programs integrate a number of tools to assist employees in gaining a better understanding of themselves and their work environments, in setting career goals and strategies, and in reappraising career progress. With this information, individuals hopefully can be more successful in managing their careers.

Employees in midcareer generally confront a different set of demands. For many, the prospects for continued hierarchical advancement are diminished or nonexistent, and the individual finds him- or herself on a career plateau. Through the encouragement of lateral moves, the offering of dual promotion ladders, and a replacement of the standard promotional view of achievement with a culture based on psychological success, organizations can encourage all their employees to remain interested, stimulated, and contributing members of the firm. Late-career employees may also have special needs. Corporations can use various techniques such as workshops, redeployment and outplacement assistance, and pre-retirement activities to help late-career employees remain productive and/or deal with the coming transition to retirement. In all, these organizational practices provide the employee with a sense of career (and in some situations—personal) empowerment and allow the employee to focus on being productive in the workplace.

ASSIGNMENT

Ask a friend, relative, or colleague who has recently participated in some type of career management program to describe the experience. What were the aims of the program? What activities did the person participate in as part of the program? Was the program effective or ineffective? Why?

DISCUSSION QUESTIONS

1. Examine the career management programs presented in Table 15.1. For each type of activity, identify the benefits and risks for organizations that offer the program and for employees who participate in the program.
2. Why is it important for organizations to help their employees manage their careers over the entire life cycle? Do you believe that employers have a moral obligation to assist employees in managing their careers and dealing with related demands?

ENDNOTES

1. G. J. Gooding, "Career Moves—for the Employee, for the Organization," *Personnel* April (1988): 112–116; T. G. Gutteridge, Z. B. Leibowitz, and J. E. Shore, *Organizational Career Development: Benchmarks for Building a World-Class Workforce* (San Francisco, CA: Jossey-Bass, 1993).

2. J. E. Russell, "Career Development Interventions in Organizations," *Journal of Vocational Behavior* 38 (1991): 237–287.

3. D. Jones, "Internships Take on New Shape in Workplace," *USA Today*, March 23, 1998, 6B; K. C. Leong, "IT Internships Make the Grade," *Internetweek*, March 30, 1998, 31; M. E. Scott, "Internships Add Value to College Recruitment," *Personnel Journal* April (1992): 59–63.

4. Anonymous, "Drexel Co-op 'The Ultimate Internship'" [online]. Drexel University, available: http://www.drexel.edu/minisite/undergrad/pages/COOP/coop.html [December 2, 1998].

5. R. Wartzman, "Learning by Doing: Apprenticeship Plans Spring Up for Students Not Headed to College," *The Wall Street Journal*, May 19, 1992, A1.

6. Anonymous,. "ETA Individuals Apprenticeship" [online]. United States Department of Labor, Employment and Training Administration, available: http://www.doleta.gov/individ/apprent.htm [December 2, 1998].

7. Anonymous, "Case Study: At the Vanguard of Successful Recruiting," *HR Focus* May (1998): 9.

8. J. G. Pesek, "The Flip Side of Recruitment: Allowing Job Candidates to View Current Employees' Resumes," *Journal of Applied Business Research* 7, no. 3 (1991): 1–7.

9. M. Wheatley, "The Talent Spotters," *Management Today* June (1996): 62–66.

10. D. E. Terpstra, "The Search for Effective Methods," *HR Focus* 73, no. 5(1996): 16–19; C. Wiley, "Recruitment Research Revisited: Effective Recruiting Methods According to Employment Outcomes," *Journal of Applied Business Research* 8, no. 2 (1992): 74–79.

11. M. London, *Managing the Training Enterprise* (San Francisco, CA: Jossey-Bass, 1989); M. N. Martinez, "Disney Training Works Magic," *HRMagazine* 37, no. 5 (1992): 53–57.

12. Anonymous, "From Family Farm to Global Giant: Rosenbluth Leads the Way," *HR Focus* 75, no. 9 (1998): 9–10; quote is on p. 9; E. E. Spragins, "Training: First Impressions," *INC.* December (1991): 157.

13. A. Bird, "Careers as Repositories of Knowledge: A New Perspective on Boundaryless Careers," *Journal of Organizational Behavior* 15 (1994): 325–344; quote is on p. 328; P. H. Mirvis and D. T. Hall, "Psychological Success and the Boundaryless Career," *Journal of Organizational Behavior* 15 (1994): 365–380.

14. S. A. Stumpf, "Business Simulations for Skill Diagnosis and Development," in *Career Growth and Human Resource Strategies*, ed. M. London and E. M. Mone (New York: Quorum Books, 1988), 195–206.

15. S. A. Stumpf, "The Dynamics of Learning through Management Simulations: Let's Dance," *Journal of Management Development* 9, no. 2 (1990): 7–15.

16. G. A. Callanan and J. H. Greenhaus, "Personal and Career Development: The Best and Worst of Times," in *Evolving Practices in Human Resources Management: Responses to a Changing World of Work*, ed. A. K. Korman and A. I. Kraut (San Francisco, CA: Jossey–Bass, 1999), 146–171.

17. Gutteridge, Leibowitz, and Shore, *Organizational Career Development*; W. Wiggenhorn, "Motorola U: When Training Becomes Education," *Harvard Business Review*, July-August (1990): 71–83.

18. Anonymous, "The Career Development Program" [online]. Air Products and Chemicals, Inc., available: http://www.airproducts.com/employ/emplinfo.html [January 13, 1999]; J. Brockington, personal communication with the Director of University Relations, Air Products and Chemicals, Inc., January 25, 1999.

19. M. A. Dalton, *Becoming a More Versatile Learner* (Greensboro, NC: Center for Creative Leadership. 1998); M. M. Lombardo and R. W. Eichinger, *Eighty-eight Assignments for Development in Place: Enhancing the Developmental Challenge of Existing Jobs* (Greensboro, NC: Center for Creative Leadership. 1998); E. Van Velsor and M. W. Hughes-James, *Gender Differences in the Development of Managers: How Women Managers Learn from Experience* (Greensboro, NC: Center for Creative Leadership. 1990).

20. M. R. Edwards and A. J. Ewen, *360-Degree Feedback: The Powerful New Model for Employee Assessment & Performance Improvement* (New York: AMACOM, 1996); quote is on p. 4.

21. S. Gebelein, "Employee Development: Multi-Rater Feedback Goes Strategic," *HR Focus* 73, no. 1 (1996): 1–5.

22. Edwards and Ewen, *360-Degree Feedback*; L. Slavenski, "Career Development: A Systems Approach," *Training and Development Journal* February (1987): 56–60.

23. F. Jossi, "Mentoring in Changing Times," *Training* 34, no. 8 (1997): 50–54.

24. M. Martinez, "Prepared for the Future," *HRMagazine* April (1997): 80–88; quote is on p. 85.

25. D. A. Thomas and K. E. Kram, "Promoting Career-Enhancing Relationships in Organizations: The Role of the Human Resource Professional," in *Career Growth and Human Resource Strategies,* ed. M. London and E. M. Mone (New York: Quorum Books, 1988), 49–66.

26. Jossi, "Mentoring in Changing Times."

27. Thomas and Kram, "Promoting Career-Enhancing Relationships in Organizations"; quote is on p. 61.

28. K. E. Kram, *Mentoring at Work: Developmental Relationships in Organizational Life* (Lanham, MD: University Press of America, 1988).

29. E. H. Schein, *Career Anchors: Discovering Your Real Values* (San Diego, CA: University Associates, 1985).

30. C. W. Lentz, "Dual Ladders Become Multiple Ladders at Dow Corning," *Research-Technology Management* May/June (1990): 28–34; G. E. Mayville (personal communication with the Human Resource Development Manager, Science and Technology, Dow Corning Corp., January 20, 1999).

31. N. Engler, "Management? Phooey!" *Computerworld* 32, no. 22 (1998): 71–73.

32. D. T. Hall and J. Richter, "Career Gridlock: Baby Boomers Hit the Wall," *Academy of Management Executive* 4 (1990): 7–22.

33. M. Costello (personal communication with Consumer Relations, Nabisco Foods, January 11, 1999); J. E. Rigdon, "Sideways Moves Grow More Common," *The Wall Street Journal*, January 27, 1992, B1; J. E. Rigdon, "Using Lateral Moves to Spur Employees," *The Wall Street Journal*, May 26, 1992, B1.

34. S. Eams (personal communication with Public Relations, American Greetings, January 12, 1999); Rigdon, "Sideways Moves Grow More Common"; Rigdon, "Using Lateral Moves to Spur Employees."

35. D. T. Hall and M. R. Louis, "When Careers Plateau," *Research-Technology Management* March–April (1988): 41–45; Z. B. Leibowitz, B. L. Kaye, and C. Farren, "What To Do about Career Gridlock," *Training and Development Journal* April (1990): 28–35.

36. M. London, "Career Motivation of Full- and Part-time Workers in Mid and Late Career," *International Journal of Career Management* 5, no. 1 (1993): 21–29.

37. T. A. Glass, T. E. Seeman, A. R. Herzog, R. Kahn, and L. F. Berkman, "Change in Productive Activity in Late Adulthood: MacArthur Studies of Successful Aging," *Journal of Gerontology* 50, no. 2 (1995): 65–80; S. R. Kaufman, *The Ageless Self: Sources of Meaning in Late Life* (Madison, WI: The University of Wisconsin Press, 1986).

38. V. Kaminski-da Roza, "A Workshop That Optimizes the Older Worker's Productivity," *Personnel* 61, no. 2 (1984): 47–56.

39. D. Cyr, "Lost and Found-Retired Employees," *Personnel Journal* 75, no. 11 (1996): 40–47.

40. S. Armour, "More Kids Putting Parents on Payroll," *USA Today*, April 29, 1998, 1B.

41. Callanan and Greenhaus, "Personal and Career Development."

42. G. Flynn, "New Skills Equal New Opportunities," *Personnel Journal* 75, no. 6 (1996): 77–79.

43. D. E. Sanger and S. Lohr, "Intel Corp. Offers Model for Adjusting to Workplace Change," *The Oregonian,* March 23, 1996, A08; quotes on p. A08.

44. Anonymous, "The Talent Alliance" [online]. The Talent Alliance, available: http://www.talent-alliance.org [December 7, 1998]; H. Lancaster, "Managing Your Career: Companies Promise to Help Employees Plot Their Careers," *The Wall Street Journal*, March 11, 1997, B1.

45. S. LaRock, "Ongoing Preretirement Counseling Programs: Survey Reveals Prevalence, Characteristics," *Employee Benefit Plan Review* 50, no. 10 (1996): 22–24.

46. D. Brown, "Preretirement Planning and the Bottom Line," *Personnel* 68, no. 6 (1991): 3–5; M. A. C. Fusco, "Increasing Numbers of Employers Are Learning That Helping Employees with Preretirement Planning Makes Good Business Sense," *Employment Relations Today* 17, no. 2 (1990): 165–168.

47. J. L. Wiley, "Pre-retirement Education: Benefits Outweigh Liability," *HR Focus* 70, no. 8 (1993): 11.

16

CLOSING THOUGHTS ON CAREER MANAGEMENT

In this book, we have shown how individuals face constant change as they move through the course of their careers. These changes emanate from a host of sources—personal, environmental, and organizational. From the personal side, there are several factors that influence our careers. Just the process of aging alone produces changes in our perspectives on our careers. In most respects, for example, the concerns of a 25-year-old are vastly different from those of a 65-year-old. Beyond aging, behavioral scientists can point to several alterations in individual attitudes and behaviors that have occurred over the past two decades. Some of these changes reflect cultural shifts in beliefs, whereas others are reactions to social forces. Perhaps the most significant cultural change affecting individuals is the heightened challenge of managing commitments to both work and family. Many two-career couples face new dilemmas in juggling work and family obligations. By necessity, members of such relationships must learn to balance two careers as well as extensive family responsibilities.

Individual workers have also adapted to the new work environment that has evolved over the past 15 years. Significant changes have occurred both in the way people are employed and in the types of jobs they hold. Specifically, the use of contract staff and temporary workers has jumped markedly, as organizations have sought to become more efficient by using their human capital in a just-in-time fashion. For many individuals, working on a contingent basis has become a permanent way of life. In this new environment, standard jobs have been replaced by evolving work situations, which require flexibility and adaptability on the part of the worker. Under the old environment, jobs were tailored or structured to reflect the abilities of the workers. In the new work landscape, the individual must be increasingly adaptable to the work situation. Companies now have a Darwinian view ensuring that the fittest or most adaptable are the ones who survive in the organization.

These recent alterations in work organizations and in their approaches to staffing directly challenge the career competencies of affected workers.[1] The result has been that the playing field for the individual management of careers has changed, with a new set of individual behaviors and actions required. As Robert J. DeFillippi and Michael B. Arthur state, "Multiple changes in organizational career contexts reflect a new era of interfirm competition in both national and global markets. The changes reflect not only corporate restructuring and downsizing, but also a range of new organizing principles developed in response to the new era. These principles imply distinct changes in the kinds of career competencies to be encouraged."[2]

Although organizations have been shifting their levels of and approaches to staffing, the work force itself has seen dramatic changes over the past two decades. For example, the work force is becoming more culturally diverse. The increasing proportion of women, racial minorities, and immigrants has put pressure on organizations to manage this diversity effectively. Work force diversity also challenges employees to understand cultural similarities and differences and to work cooperatively with others who may have different values and perspectives. Career advancement could well depend on an employee's ability to thrive in a multicultural environment.

PREPARING FOR THE FUTURE

Regardless of the challenges and uncertainties, career management as a problem-solving process does not really change in fundamental form. Information, insight, goals, plans, and feedback are essential at all career stages. Reflecting this view, we offer below our thoughts on several career issues that transcend a particular time or place.

First, effective career management requires individual initiative—an active, probing approach toward life. It requires a certain inquisitiveness about oneself and the world and a willingness to take action and appropriate risks. Career management is based on the belief that people can exert control over significant portions of their lives. Although total control is impossible, the willingness to explore, set goals, and develop and implement plans can make a difference in the quality of one's career and one's life. In this sense, it is critically important that one establish a clear self-identity. The primary building block for career success and fulfillment is the need for one's work to be consistent with one's self-identity. This maxim is even more relevant in the current environment of job instability, when one's personal needs can easily get overlooked. Establishment of a clear self-identity normally involves a process of self-exploration in which individuals use standard assessment tools in conjunction with introspection and feedback from trusted others in the social network to understand better their interests, talents, and life-style preferences.

Second, people must appreciate the relationship between work and nonwork lives. Career management efforts should be based on an awareness of life goals, not just career goals. Career goals and achievements will affect (and be affected by) participation in the family, community, and leisure spheres of one's life. Even if people cannot "have it all," they can decide what they want and what trade-offs they are willing to make. Understanding the interplay between work and nonwork and discussing the impact of the delicate balance with other significant persons are essential ingredients of career and life management.

Third, people must avoid succumbing to other people's definition of success for their lives. Many individuals pursue a specific career path to satisfy other persons—parents, professors, friends, bosses, spouses, or perhaps some general notion of what one "should" do. Happiness and fulfillment, however, depend on satisfying one's own, not other people's, values and aspirations. Much of the recent popularity of entrepreneurial careers can be traced to individuals pursuing their own career interests (i.e., being one's own man or woman). Nonetheless, this book has not advocated a hedonistic "me" attitude toward career management. Sacrifices and compromises are necessary if people are to live in a larger world, share their lives with other persons, and become committed to a cause, a community, or an organization. Taking other people's or institutions' needs into account and trying to achieve mutually acceptable and beneficial solutions to career dilemmas are healthy actions. However, continually trying to please others at the expense of oneself can be destructive to one's sense of well-being.

Fourth, employees are responsible for ensuring that their portfolio of skills is transferable to other work situations and other employers.[3] Individuals should ensure that they have the competitive skills to improve their chances of finding a new position when it is needed.[4] In this sense, the individual would possess a set of what might be called portable competencies that could be applied in any number of organizations or work settings.

Related to the idea of a portable set of skills is the recommendation that individuals invest in lifelong learning to keep their skills relevant (and thereby transferable). Continuous learning can take many forms. One category would involve pursuing additional schooling; another category could include seeking out assignments that allow new competencies to be learned. A commitment to learning might also involve staying abreast of developments within one's current organization as well as other firms in the industry.

Finally, career management is not the exclusive domain of the elite. It does not belong only to the top executive, the upwardly mobile, the affluent, or the entrepreneur. Career management is for everyone who wants to enhance the quality of his or her life. Career management is not always easy, but to paraphrase an old phrase, nothing important ever is. Hopefully, this book has shown that effective career management is possible for individuals who are ready to take on the challenge.

At its core, career management is a personal process. Although organizational programs and practices can aid it immeasurably, only individuals can develop insight into themselves and their environment, become committed to career goals and strategies, and accurately appraise the course of their careers and make necessary adjustments. Nothing can ever replace the commitment of the individual to the active management of his or her own career.

Assignment

It is difficult to predict what the future holds for career management. We do know that organizations will continue to make changes in their structures and staffing approaches and that the global work environment will see further evolution. While recognizing the uncertainties, in this assignment you are asked to try and predict the future challenges that individuals will face as they go through the process of career management. Specifically, you are to write a scenario of the future that depicts your view of how the work world will look in a decade and describes the related implications for individual careers and organizational career management systems. Your narrative could address such issues as the new career competencies individuals will need to achieve career success in the future, the role of new technologies in helping people manage their careers, the techniques that might be available to achieve better integration of work and family lives, the effects on careers of continued international integration of work organizations and cultures, the career assistance strategies that organizations will use to help retain their human resources, and the degree to which individuals and organizations will see loyalty as playing a role in their career decisions. Try to be as creative as possible in making your predictions about the future.

DISCUSSION QUESTION

Do you think that the waves of staff layoffs that have occurred over the past several years indicate a general lack of loyalty toward their employees on the part of most organizations? Do you think that job security and lifetime employment are passe as organizational philosophies? What are the implications of your answers in terms of your career management?

ENDNOTES

1. R. J. DeFillippi and M. B. Arthur, "The Boundaryless Career: A Competency-based Perspective," *Journal of Organizational Behavior* 15 (1994): 307–324.

2. Ibid.; quote is on p. 311.

3. M. B. Arthur, "The Boundaryless Career: A New Perspective for Organizational Inquiry," *Journal of Organizational Behavior* 15 (1994): 295–306.

4. R. H. Waterman, J. A. Waterman, and B. A. Collard, "Toward a Career Resilient Workforce," *Harvard Business Review* July-August (1994): 87–95.

CASE OF THE STAR PERFORMER

Throughout Claudia's senior year in college, she was actively recruited by a number of firms. As one of the top business students in her graduating class, Claudia believed that she could be choosy in selecting an employer. One of her strongest selection criteria was whether the hiring firm would pay for her MBA. Claudia eventually settled on a research assistant position with a medium-sized commercial bank. The salary was competitive, and the bank would reimburse her for her graduate work.

Holding true to her goal, Claudia immediately began pursuing her MBA, attending one of the premier business schools in the country on a part-time basis. After 3 years and an investment of $45,000 by her company, Claudia received an MBA in finance with a minor in international business.

Unbeknown to her employer, Claudia had signed up for several of the on-campus interviews that were being held for graduating MBA students. She was especially interested in the large investment banking companies that were actively recruiting on campus. She was also interested in relocating to New York City. It was not that Claudia was displeased with the commercial bank; in fact, the opposite was true—the bank had treated her well, giving her challenging assignments and two promotions. Claudia just wanted to determine her market value and gain some leverage with the bank. Also, a job with one of the top investment banking firms would allow Claudia to pursue her lifelong dream of living in New York City and attending the theater frequently.

Claudia was pleasantly surprised when she received offers from two prestigious New York investment banks. Both offers represented a 50 percent increase over her present salary and would pay her relocation expenses. Claudia believed she had no choice but to ask the commercial bank if it would match the offers. Of course, she knew that the bank, with its rigid pay structure, would be loath to give her that kind of an increase. True to her expectation, the bank refused to match the offer but stated that she would receive a generous increase at her next performance review. Claudia, feeling as if the bank offered her little choice, resigned the next day.

Claudia felt only a little remorse on leaving the bank, rationalizing that the open labor market was the efficient, capitalistic way. Claudia also thought that this might be a one-time opportunity to pursue both personal and professional interests while living in New York City. The bank's management was bitter that it had lost one of its star performers and saw a significant investment go down the drain. But this was not the first time the bank lost a star performer to a competitor after the employee had received a graduate degree. Indeed, at the most recent meeting of its executive management committee, the bank was considering dropping all support for graduate school tuition reimbursement, reviewing instead whether hiring MBAs from the outside was a more prudent course of action.

CASE ANALYSIS QUESTIONS

1. Do you think that Claudia acted ethically in quickly accepting the job from the investment bank? What alternatives could Claudia have pursued?

2. What are the economic implications for the bank? If you were a member of the executive management committee, what path would you have recommended at the meeting?

3. Discuss the strategic decisions companies face when considering the human resource implications of "making versus buying" personnel.

CASE OF THE CORPORATE POLICY CHANGE

Located in the beautiful Adirondack Mountains of upstate New York, Be Our Guest Family Resort (BOGF—fictitious name) was recently sold to an East Coast hotel chain. Previously, BOGF had been a family-owned business, and the owners treated all employees like an extended family. BOGF is well known for its friendly, top-notch accommodations. In the summer and fall, BOGF offers families a variety of outdoor activities, including six tennis courts, an 18-hole golf course, a lake for boating and fishing, an indoor/outdoor pool, and horseback riding. During the winter and spring, downhill and cross-country skiing are the outdoor activities of choice at BOGF. Other activities available throughout the year include bowling and an on-site movie theater. BOGF also has four restaurants and a tavern.

Because BOGF provides many amenities, it has a large year-round staff, many of whom have worked for the company for up to 15 years. In fact, BOGF often hired members from multiple generations of the same family. BOGF has a focused mission that is made clear to all its employees—to provide a premium vacation experience to all who come to BOGF. This means that the customer comes first. Employees are asked to do all they can to keep customer satisfaction high. This focus encourages customers to schedule return visits to BOGF and also to tell their friends about their vacations at BOGF. BOGF employees know that their town relies almost exclusively on the tourism generated by the resort, because few other substantial businesses are located in the immediate area.

BOGF has a "home-grown" mentality regarding the advancement of its human resources. Many of the hotel and restaurant managers grew up working summers as valets, house cleaners, and wait staff. This human resource policy was initiated by the small town and privately held atmosphere of BOGF. The policy also allowed the employees to have a variety of experiences and to learn first-hand what customers expect from a top-of-the-line resort. Many children of BOGF employees attend a local university that has a hotel administration major. This education allowed the young adults to come back to their hometown and work. Yet, the acquisition of BOGF will cause its human resource policies to soon change.

The Mansion Corporation (fictitious name), a well-known hotel and restaurant conglomerate, has recently purchased BOGF. The Mansion's human resource strategies are dramatically different from those of the BOGF. The Mansion attracts "star" quality employees from other hotels and provides them with high-level administrative positions. These positions may be offered at any one of a number of the Mansion's resort holdings. The Mansion is very generous with offering relocation packages to lure potential employees away from their current employer.

The Mansion's policy regarding human resource selection is more of the "buy" rather than the "make" approach. The Mansion fills its skill gaps by hiring needed personnel from outside the company. In fact, the Mansion has recently hired a CFO and chief technologist from competitors. Both employees and their families moved from the Midwest to the Mansion's headquarters in Virginia. Many of the hotel's general managers are from either top hotel or restaurant chains. The general premise the Mansion operates under is that it is more cost-efficient to bring in the "best and the brightest." This allows the Mansion to hire the skills it needs when and where it may need those skills. The Mansion plans to make this policy known to BOGF's personnel as part of its *Introduction to the Mansion's Human Resources Policies* package. The policy becomes effective January 1. The Mansion does not intend to discuss the effect of this policy with BOGF employees unless asked.

CASE ANALYSIS QUESTIONS

1. What effect, if any, will this policy change have on BOGF's personnel?

2. What effect, if any, will this policy change have on BOGF's culture?

3. If asked, how might the Mansion communicate this policy change to BOGF employees? What type of career management systems are most compatible with the Mansion's human resource strategy?

4. If you were an employee of the BOGF community, what might you do given this human resource policy change?

LEARNING EXERCISES

Eight learning exercises, each involving a different aspect of career management, follow. As discussed in the beginning of Chapter 3, the learning exercises can also be found in the Web site **http://www.dryden.com/management/humresources/html.** We recommend that you download the learning exercises from the Web site and complete them using a personal computer. This approach will allow you a great deal of flexibility since it permits you to add more information to a previous exercise at a later point. If you choose to complete the learning exercises using a paper-and-pencil approach, we recommend that you use a separate notebook in which to write your responses to these exercises. A separate career management notebook should provide the same flexibility to add more information to an exercise at a later point.

By investing time in these exercises, you can develop and practice such critical career management skills as exploration, goal setting, and strategy development. It is recommended that you read the appropriate chapter before beginning each exercise. Although it may be possible to complete all exercises in one sitting, it is less tiring and more effective to allow some time for reflection in between them.

LEARNING EXERCISE I
SELF-EXPLORATION: DATA COLLECTION

Learning Exercise I contains a number of activities designed to provide self-assessment data. Be as thorough as possible in answering all questions. Remember that the more you write, the more self-assessment information will be available for you to interpret.

LEARNING EXERCISE IA: AN AUTOBIOGRAPHY. Here you are today—a college undergraduate or graduate student, an employee with substantial work experience under your belt, or someone ready to reenter the job market after an absence of several years. Think of all the yesterdays that made you what you are today.

Given all that you know about yourself, write an autobiographical story that traces your history up to now. Divide the story into chapters; each chapter should cover a five-year period, starting with birth to 5 years old, 5 to 10 years old, and so on. In each chapter, try to answer the following questions if they are relevant: Who were the important people in your life and why were they important? What was your family life like at the time? What were your school experiences like and how did you react to school? What were your work experiences like and how did you react to work? Did you develop hobbies and interests and what did you like about them? To what extent did your parents influence the activities you've pursued and the choices you've made? How have other family relationships shaped your experiences? What happened to you during this period that changed the course of your life?

Write as much as you can about each question. Don't worry about whether these chapters have anything to do with your career—you'll find that out later. If you are in doubt about whether or not to include something, include it. The more you write, the better.

LEARNING EXERCISE IB: FOCUS ON SCHOOL. Now identify your favorite and least favorite courses and subjects, those subjects in which you did best and worst, and significant extracurricular activities (e.g., sports, music, clubs) in which you participated.

Junior/Senior High School

FAVORITE COURSES   *LEAST FAVORITE COURSES*

_____   _____
_____   _____
_____   _____

COURSES IN WHICH YOU DID BEST   *COURSES IN WHICH YOU DID WORST*

_____   _____
_____   _____
_____   _____

EXTRACURRICULAR ACTIVITIES: _____
_____
_____

College

FAVORITE COURSES   *LEAST FAVORITE COURSES*

_____   _____
_____   _____
_____   _____

COURSES IN WHICH YOU DID BEST   *COURSES IN WHICH YOU DID WORST*

_____   _____
_____   _____
_____   _____

EXTRACURRICULAR ACTIVITIES: _____
_____

What do your responses tell you about your interests and particular strengths and weaknesses? _____
_____
_____

LEARNING EXERCISE IC: FOCUS ON WORK. Think about the BEST JOB you ever had. It could be your current job or a prior job, either part-time, full-time, or temporary.

What do (did) you like most about the job? Be specific in terms of tasks, people, and other aspects. _____

_____

_____

What do (did) you dislike about the job? Again, be specific. _____

_____

_____

On what specific tasks or projects did you accomplish something significant? Why were you able to accomplish it? _____

_____

_____

_____

On what specific tasks or projects did you not perform as well as you would have liked? What was the reason? _____

_____

_____

_____

Now think about the WORST JOB you ever had. It could be your current job or a prior job, either part-time, full-time, or temporary.

What do (did) you dislike most about the job? _____

_____

_____

_____

What do (did) you like about the job? _____

_____

_____

_____

On what specific tasks or projects did you accomplish something significant? Why? _____

_____

_____

On what specific tasks or projects did you not perform as well as you would have liked? What was the reason? _____

_____

_____

_____

Now describe your conception of an IDEAL JOB. What would it be like? Be specific in terms of the kinds of tasks, other people, rewards, and anything else that is important to you. _____

_____

_____

_____

Next rank the following ten factors in terms of how important each is to you for a career-related job. Enter a 1 next to the factor that is most important to you, a ten next to the least important factor, a 2 next to the second most important, a 9 next to the second least important, and so on until you have ranked all ten factors.

How important is it that your job . . .

___ Permits you to work on a wide variety of tasks?

___ Gives you the opportunity to help others?

___ Provides you with a great deal of independence in deciding how the work gets done?

___ Enables you to make a great deal of money?

___ Offers you a secure future?

___ Gives you the opportunity to develop friendships at work?

___ Has pleasant working conditions?

___ Enables you to work with a supervisor who is competent and supportive?

___ Provides you with power and influence over other people?

___ Gives you a feeling of accomplishment?

Indicate any other job factors not listed above that are important to you. _____

_____

_____

_____

_____

LEARNING EXERCISE ID: LIFE ROLES.   How important are different parts of your life? Rank the following five life roles from 1 (most important) to 5 (least important).

___   Your career

___   Your religious and spiritual life

___   Your family life

___   Your participation in community service activities

___   Your leisure and recreational pursuits

Explain why each of these life roles is important (or unimportant) to you:

Your career: _____

_____

_____

_____

_____

Your religious and spiritual life: _____

_____

_____

_____

_____

Your family life: _____

_____

_____

_____

_____

Your community service: _____

_____

_____

_____

_____

Your leisure and recreational pursuits: _____

_____

_____

_____

_____

LEARNING EXERCISE II
SELF-EXPLORATION: THEME IDENTIFICATION

Now that you have generated data about yourself in Learning Exercise I, and perhaps have gathered other self-assessment information, the next step is to derive a set of themes based on your data. Review the steps for identifying themes presented in Chapter 3 and reexamine Table 3.2 for illustrations of self-assessment themes and supporting evidence. You should be able to identify between five and ten themes from your data. Jot down your preliminary thoughts first, and then list your final set of themes along with supporting evidence.

Theme 1: _____

_____

Evidence: _____

_____

Theme 2: _____

_____

Evidence: _____

_____

Theme 3: _____

_____

Evidence: _____

_____

Theme 4: _____

_____

Evidence: _____

_____

Theme 5: _____

_____

Evidence: _____

_____

Theme 6: _____

_____

Evidence: _____

_____

Theme 7: _____

_____

Evidence: _____

_____

Theme 8: _____

_____

Evidence: _____

_____

Theme 9: _____

_____

Evidence: _____

_____

Theme 10: _____

_____

Evidence: _____

_____

LEARNING EXERCISE III
A SUMMARY OF PREFERRED WORK ENVIRONMENT

As indicated in Chapter 3, a preferred work environment (PWE) is a summary of the work experiences you find desirable, for example, the kinds of tasks you find interesting, the talents you wish to express, the importance of autonomy and freedom on the job, and so on. Reexamine your responses to Learning Exercises I and II and write down a comment for each component of the PWE listed below. For example, under tasks and activities, you might write, "I enjoy working on tasks that are technical in nature and that require a great deal of analysis."

Components of PWE   **Comments**

Tasks and activities most interesting to you _____

_____

Significant talents you want to express at work _____

_____

Importance of independence and autonomy on the job _____

_____

Work relationships (Work alone? With others? Supervise?) _____

_____

Physical work setting _____

_____

Importance of money _____

_____

Importance of job security _____

_____

Relationship between work and other parts of life _____

_____

Other components of preferred work environment _____

_____

LEARNING EXERCISE IV
ENVIRONMENTAL EXPLORATION

You can practice environmental exploration by completing either Learning Exercise IVA or IVB. If you are not currently employed, you should complete exercise IVA, which will give you an opportunity to explore an occupation. If you are employed, you might find exercise IVB (job exploration) more useful. Examine the exercises before you decide which one to pursue.

LEARNING EXERCISE IVA: OCCUPATIONAL EXPLORATION. Choose an occupation about which you would like to learn more. Maybe it is one you are considering pursuing. Or perhaps you are pretty sure you want to pursue a certain occupation and would like to examine it in more detail. If you are completely undecided about an occupation at this time, read Chapter 6 (especially "The Development of Accurate Occupational Information") to help you decide which occupation to explore in this exercise. Write down the name of the occupation you have chosen to explore.

Review the preferred work environment (PWE) statement you constructed in Learning Exercise III. Then look at the suggested sources of occupational information described in Chapter 6. Using as many sources as possible, collect information relevant to each component of your PWE in relation to the occupation you have chosen to explore. Summarize the information and the sources (so you can reexamine the raw data) in the format shown below. Remember to use many different sources of information—get out there and talk to people!

Name of Occupation: _____

Components of the PWE	Relevant Information about Occupation	Information Source
What tasks and activities are performed?		
What talents are required? Do you possess them or can you learn them?		
What type of working relationships with other people is likely?		
What is the physical work setting?		
How much money can be earned in the long term and short term?		
How much job security is likely?		

Components of the PWE	Relevant Information about Occupation	Information Source
Effect of pursuit of occupation on family, leisure, religion, community		
Other significant issues (e.g., job prospects, opportunities for mobility, etc.)		

LEARNING EXERCISE IVB: JOB EXPLORATION.   If you are employed, choose a job in your organization other than the one you currently hold. It could be a job you expect to enter next or a job you would like to learn more about.

Review the preferred work environment (PWE) summary you constructed in Learning Exercise III. Consider the following sources of information about a job: a written job description, occupational files and books in a library, your supervisor, employees who hold or previously held the job, members of the human resources department, and people who hold or held a similar job in a different organization. Using as many sources as possible, collect information relevant to each component of your PWE. Summarize the information and the sources (so you can reexamine the raw data) in the same format shown below. Remember to use many different sources of information—read and talk to people.

Job Title to Explore: _____

Components of the PWE	Relevant Information about Job	Information Source
What tasks and activities are performed?		
What talents are required? Do you possess them or can you learn them?		
How much freedom and autonomy can be obtained?		
What types of working relationships with other people are likely?		
What is the physical work setting?		
How much money can be earned in the long term and short term?		
How much job security is likely?		
Effect of pursuit of job on family, leisure, religion, community		
Other significant issues (e.g., prospects of being offered job, usefulness of job for desired career path, etc.)		

LEARNING EXERCISE V
GOAL SETTING

So far, you have developed a summary of your preferred work environment (PWE) (Learning Exercise III) and have begun to explore the relevant work environment (Learning Exercise IV). In Learning Exercise V, you will practice the development of career goals. Before you begin, reread the discussion of career goal setting in Chapter 4. Remember that your long-term goal need not be very precise at this time. Simply be as specific as you can.

The first step is to develop a long-term (7-10-year) conceptual goal. In formulating it, try to address all of the significant elements of your PWE. List the elements of your long-term conceptual goal below and consult Learning Exercise III to verify that all-important elements of your PWE are incorporated in the long-term conceptual goal.

Elements of the Long-Term Conceptual Goal

1. _____

_____

2. _____

_____

3. _____

_____

4. _____

_____

5. _____

_____

6. _____

_____

The next step is to convert the long-term conceptual goal listed above into long-term operational goals. (See Table 4.1 for an example.) First, list (from the preceding section) all of the elements of the long-term conceptual goal in the space below. Then choose two operational goals (occupations or specific job positions) in which you think you might be interested. Identify them in the space provided.

Significant Elements of Long-Term Conceptual Goal	Long-Term Operational Goals	
	A	B

Next, list all of the positives (advantages) and negatives (disadvantages) you can think of regarding the operational goals you have identified.

Long-Term Operational Goal A
Positives

1. _____

2. _____

3. _____

4. _____

5. _____

6. _____

Negatives

1. _____

2. _____

3. _____

4. _____

5. _____

6. _____

Long-Term Operational Goal B
Positives

1. _____

2. _____

3. _____

4. _____

5. _____

6. _____

Negatives

1. _____

2. _____

3. _____

4. _____

5. _____

6. _____

If you are still not sure which (or if either) operational goal is appropriate for you, do not be concerned. The important thing is that you are thinking about your long-term future and have identified several goals for further thought and action.

The next step is to identify a short-term (1 to 3-year) conceptual goal. Reexamine the summary of your PWE as well as your long-term conceptual and operational goal analyses. To formulate a short-term conceptual goal, answer the following question: What type of work, educational, and other experiences and responsibilities would help prepare you to attain the long-term conceptual and operational goals? List the elements of your short-term conceptual goal below.

Elements of the Short-Term Conceptual Goal

1. _____

2. _____

3. _____

4. _____

5. _____

6. _____

Now, convert your short-term conceptual goal into operational goals. As before, list all significant elements of your short-term conceptual goal, and choose two alternative short-term operational goals.

Short-Term Operational Goal A: _____

Positives

1. _____

2. _____

3. _____

4. _____

5. _____

6. _____

Negatives

1. _____

2. _____

3. _____

4. _____

5. _____

6. _____

Short-Term Operational Goal B: _____

Positives

1. _____

2. _____

3. _____

4. _____

5. _____

6. _____

Negatives

1. _____

2. _____

3. _____

4. _____

5. _____

6. _____

If you are still not sure which short-term operational goal is more appropriate for you, it may be necessary to examine one or both goals in more detail. That is, part of your career strategy would include plans for additional data gathering.

LEARNING EXERCISE VI
CAREER STRATEGY DEVELOPMENT

In this exercise, you will develop strategies to help you attain your stated career goals. Reread the guidelines for the development of career strategies in Chapter 4. Then, follow the five-step process described in Chapter 4 and enter the relevant information below.

Strategy to Achieve Long-Term Goal (Goal = _____)

Activity	Purpose	Time Frame

Strategy to Achieve Short-Term Goal (Goal = _____).

Activity	Purpose	Time Frame

Now, combine the lists of strategies for the short-term and long-term goals. Keep the final list manageable by ordering the strategic activities in a logical time sequence. What should evolve from this activity is an overall plan of action—what you will be doing, why, and when. Describe this plan below.

_____

_____

_____

_____

LEARNING EXERCISE VII
REEXAMINATION OF PREFERRED WORK ENVIRONMENT (PWE)

Reread your responses to Learning Exercise I, II, and III before completing Exercise VII.

Component of PWE	Is PWE Accurate?	Is PWE Complete?	Where Can You Get More Information?
What tasks do you find interesting?	Yes No	Yes No	_____
What talents do you want to use?	Yes No	Yes No	_____
How much freedom and independence do you want?	Yes No	Yes No	_____
What type of relationships with others do you want?	Yes No	Yes No	_____
What physical work setting do you prefer?	Yes No	Yes No	_____
How important is money?	Yes No	Yes No	_____
How important is security?	Yes No	Yes No	_____
How important is balance of work, family, and leisure?	Yes No	Yes No	_____

LEARNING EXERCISE VIII
FORMULATION OF CAREER STRATEGY
TO ENTER CHOSEN OCCUPATION

Activity	Purpose	Time Frame
_____	_____	_____
_____	_____	_____
_____	_____	_____
_____	_____	_____
_____	_____	_____
_____	_____	_____
_____	_____	_____
_____	_____	_____

Cropanzo, R., 273, 286n
Cuba, R., 379, 391n
Cunningham, D. A., 269, 284n
Cunningham, J. B., 362, 386n
Cyr, D., 439, 445n
Cytrynbaum, S., 107, 124n

Dadzie, K. Q., 380, 391n
Dalton, G. W., 121, 126n
Dalton, M., 32, 40n
Dalton, M. A., 432, 444n
Darrow, C. N., 46, 65n, 108, 124n, 201, 215n, 220,
    221, 243n
Daus, C. S., 335, 357n
Davis-LaMastro, V., 275, 287n
Day, D. V., 33, 40n, 209, 216n
Deaux, K., 14, 20n
DeCarlo, J., 365, 387n
Decenzo, D., 379, 391n
Dechant, K., 325, 355n
DeFillippi, R. J., 12, 20n, 85, 98n, 447, 450n
Desmaris, L. B., 54, 66n, 175, 180n
Deszca, E., 268, 284n
Deutschman, A., 308, 322n
Dickson, R. D., 381, 391n
Dipboye, R. L., 333, 357n
Dix, J. E., 182, 200, 212n, 215n
Dobbins, G. H., 198, 215n
Dobson, C., 238, 240, 247n
Doering, M., 226, 244n
Douce, L. A., 139, 151n
Dougherty, T. W., 196, 198, 209, 214n, 216n, 273,
    274, 286n, 287n
Dovidio, J. F., 333, 357n
Downes, M., 43, 64n
Dozier, J. B., 232, 245n
Drasgow, F., 346, 358n
Dreher, G. F., 196, 198, 209, 214n, 216n, 330, 356n
Dressler, C., 8, 19n
Driessnack, C. H., 311, 323n
Driver, M. J., 11, 15, 20n, 201, 215n, 216n, 226,
    233, 244n, 246n,
    404, 420n
Dubin, R., 24, 38n
Dumaine, B., 170, 180n, 194, 214n
Duncan, J. W., 363, 386n
Dunkelberg, W. C., 364, 367, 388n
Durrance, J. C., 57, 66n
DuWors, R. E., 269, 284n, 292, 320n

Eams, S., 438, 445n
Ede, F. O., 374, 389n
Eden, D., 234, 246n

Edwards, M. R., 415, 422n, 432, 444n
Eichinger, R. W., 432, 444n
Eisenberger, R., 275, 287n
Ellis, B. H., 273, 286n
Elsass, P. M., 270, 285n
Elton, C. F., 130, 149n
Eneroth, K., 11, 15, 20n, 201, 215n
Engler, N., 437, 445n
Ensher, E. A., 199, 215n
Epstein, G. F., 139, 151n
Erez, M., 31, 39n
Erikson, E. H., 107, 124n
Erwin, P. J., 273, 286n
Ettington, D. R., 230, 245n
Eulberg, J. R., 263, 283n
Evans, K. M., 143, 153n, 272, 286n
Evans, P., 46, 64n, 292, 293, 320n
Ewell, M., 378, 390n
Ewen, A. J., 415, 422n, 432, 444n
Eyring, A. R., 164, 179n

Fagenson, E. A., 196, 197, 214n
Faircloth, A., 349, 359n
Fann, G. L., 376, 390n
Farren, C., 414, 421n, 438, 445n
Fasolo, P., 275, 287n
Faux, V. A., 47, 65n, 171, 180n
Feild, H. S., 26, 38n, 169, 180n, 344, 358n
Feinstein, S., 198, 215n
Feldman, D. C., 86, 99n, 184, 186, 201, 213n,
    215n, 223, 236, 244n, 247n
Feldman, I. C., 16, 21n
Feldman, S., 138, 151n
Ference, T. P., 16, 21n, 221, 243n
Fernandez, J. P., 325, 330, 355n, 356n
Finegold, S. N., 5, 19n
Fineman, S., 270, 285n
Fiore, M., 139, 151n
Fisher, C. D., 92, 99n, 346, 358n
Fisher, T. D., 235, 241, 246n, 247n
Fitzgerald, L. F., 42, 64n, 113, 125n, 130, 136,
    138, 149n, 150n, 151n, 346, 358n, 379,
    390n
Fitzgerald, T. H., 236, 247n
Fitzpatrick, J. L., 141, 152n
Flynn, G., 440, 445n
Folkman, S., 263, 283n
Forbes, J. B., 208, 216n
Ford, D. L., 272, 286n
Ford, J. K., 328, 355n
Fortj-Cozens, K., 265, 284n
Fossum, J. A., 224, 225, 244n
Fouad, N., 131, 149n
Foust, D., 241, 247n